HISTORIC ARCHITECTURE SOURCEBOOK

HISTORIC ARCHITECTURE SOURCEBOOK

Edited by

CYRIL M. HARRIS, Ph.D.

Professor of Architecture, Columbia University

McGRAW-HILL BOOK COMPANY

New York St. Louis San Francisco Auckland Bogotá Düsseldorf
Johannesburg London Madrid Mexico Montreal
New Delhi Panama Paris São Paulo
Singapore Sydney Tokyo Toronto

Library of Congress Cataloging in Publication Data
Main entry under title:

Historic architecture sourcebook.

1. Architecture—Dictionaries. I. Harris, Cyril M.
NA31.H56 720′.3 76-39802
ISBN 0-07-026755-3

1234567890 VHVH 786543210987

The editors for this book were Harold B. Crawford, Patricia A. Allen, and Betty Gatewood, and the production supervisor was Teresa F. Leaden. It was set in Imperial by Lehigh/Rocappi.

Printed and bound by Von Hoffman Press, Inc.

PREFACE

Properly presented and illustrated, historic architecture is enjoyable in itself. There is much practical value in its study as well. Let me cite one personal example. In 1965, I joined three colleagues in designing a thousand-seat theatre for the U.S. Department of State under a Ford Foundation grant. We were under no constraints other than a single formidable one—the entire theatre had to be capable of being disassembled and fitted into two large cargo aircraft. Three years and 27 different schemes later, we had developed a theatre-in-the-round which met all design requirements. In plan it was essentially two ancient Roman theatres with their seating areas (see **cavea, 1**, page 100) joined to form a circle. After our final design was complete, out of curiosity (for ancient Greek and Roman theatres first stimulated my interest in historic architecture some years ago), I compared the slope of our seating with the average slope of the seating in a number of ancient Roman theatres. Our slope was within one degree of that average. Then I compared our aisle arrangement with that recommended for Roman theatres by Vitruvius in his *Ten Books on Architecture* written about the time of the birth of Christ. They were identical. In these respects I had the curious feeling that we had re-invented the wheel.

The *Historic Architecture Sourcebook* is a unique presentation of the history of architecture in the form of 5000 lucid definitions of terms illustrated by 2100 line drawings. The subject areas include the following architectural periods:

- Ancient
- Greek and Hellenistic
- Roman
- Early Christian
- Chinese
- Japanese
- Indian
- Islamic
- Mesoamerican
- Romanesque
- Gothic
- Renaissance
- Modern

These subjects cover a span of 5000 years, and each is treated in detail. They will be valuable to the layman, the student, and the specialist interested in history, architectural history, art history, or art appreciation. The definitions contain enough information to guide a reader toward appropriate reference books if he wishes to pursue any topic in greater depth. Both the definitions and the illustrations are complete enough to serve as important research tools, because emphasis has been placed on clarity and accuracy.

The line drawings have been chosen to stress the significant aspects of architectural styles as well as details. For many years, as a hobby, I collected very old books on historic architecture, and built a collection of over 12,000 line drawings which were alphabetized and individually mounted. To these I added several thousand photographs I had taken in many parts of the world, with a view of using them eventually in a book on historic architecture. Many of these were included in the *Dictionary of Architecture of Construction* (McGraw-Hill, 1975). The entire collection has formed the basis for the illustrations in the present volume. The decision to use line drawings rather than photographs (with a few exceptions) is based upon the particular usefulness of such drawings in emphasizing salient features of the term being illustrated. The illustrations include (1) drawings chosen from my complete collection, which were redrawn or otherwise modified to emphasize essential details, (2) entirely new drawings, prepared when suitable illustrations could not be found, and (3) drawings which have been reproduced by permission of the copyright owners.

Cyril M. Harris

ACKNOWLEDGMENTS

Many of my colleagues have been helpful in the preparation of the *Sourcebook* and I am grateful for their assistance. I am particularly indebted to Professor Adolf K. Placzek, Librarian of Avery Library of Columbia University for his valuable advice and contributions during its preparation.

In the initial editorial stages, Ross J. Kepler, my production editor at McGraw-Hill, offered many helpful suggestions. After his retirement, Betty Gatewood provided painstaking assistance in the production of the book. I also wish to thank Miye Schakne and others who provided skilled artwork for the illustrations.

The resources of Avery Library of Columbia University, the world's largest architectural library, were invaluable in checking and cross-checking information.

Acknowledgment is gratefully made to holders of copyrighted material who have granted permission for its reproduction. Particular thanks are due Abraham Ascher and the editors of the Newsweek Book

Division, *Newsweek*, for permission to reproduce the drawing of the Kremlin from *The Kremlin* (New York, 1972); to George Kubler and the Pelican History of Art Series for five illustrations of Mesoamerican architecture from *The Art and Architecture of Ancient America* (Penguin Books, Baltimore, 1962), and to *The Old-House Journal* (Brooklyn, New York) for several drawings.

CONTRIBUTORS

The definitions in the *Historic Architecture Sourcebook* were prepared by a staff of experts. Contributors in particular fields are listed below. There is much overlap between many of the special fields covered in this book, so this listing indicates the principal area of responsibility for each contributor.

ADOLF K. PLACZEK, S.A.H. *Avery Librarian; Adjunct Professor of Architecture, Columbia University* (ARCHITECTURAL STYLES)

EDGAR KAUFMANN JR., H.A.I.A. *Adjunct Professor of Art History and Architecture, Columbia University* (RENAISSANCE ARCHITECTURE, MODERN ARCHITECTURE)

EVERARD M. UPJOHN, M. ARCH. *Professor Emeritus of Art History, Columbia University* (CHURCH ARCHITECTURE, GOTHIC ARCHITECTURE)

CYRIL M. HARRIS, PH.D. *Professor of Architecture, Columbia University* (CLASSICAL ARCHITECTURE, GENERAL HISTORIC ARCHITECTURE)

JOSEPH M. SHELLEY, B. ARCH. *Retired Associate Professor of Architecture, City University of New York; formerly Commissioner, Landmarks Preservation Commission, New York* (CLASSICAL ARCHITECTURE)

TAKASHI HIRAYAMA *Professor Emeritus of Architecture, University of Tokyo* (JAPANESE ARCHITECTURE)

C. K. CHANG, A.I.A. *Architect, New York, N.Y.* (CHINESE ARCHITECTURE)

CURT MUSER *Research Associate, Museum of the American Indian (Heye Foundation), New York, N.Y.* (MESOAMERICAN ARCHITECTURE)

PAUL LAMPL, A.I.A. *Design Coordinator and Associate, The Eggers Partnership, New York, N.Y.* (MIDDLE EASTERN, ISLAMIC, AND INDIAN ARCHITECTURE)

MARVIN TRACHTENBERG, PH.D. *Associate Professor of Fine Arts, New York University* (MEDIEVAL ARCHITECTURE)

In addition to these fields, definitions in several more specialized areas which were originally prepared for the *Dictionary of Architecture and Construction* have been included in this volume. Contributors include:

JOSEPH SCHEIN, A.I.A. *Partner, Russo and Sonder, Architects, New York, N.Y.*

BRONSON BINGER, A.I.A. *Project Director, South Street Seaport Museum, New York, N.Y.*

ROY J. MASCOLINO, A.I.A. *Fletcher-Thompson, Inc., Architects-Engineers, Bridgeport, Connecticut*

JOHN BARRATT PATTON, PH.D. *Professor of Economic Geology, Indiana University, Bloomington, Indiana*

HISTORIC ARCHITECTURE SOURCEBOOK

Aaron's rod An ornament or molding consisting of a straight rod from which pointed leaves or scroll work emerge on each side, at regular intervals.

abaciscus **1.** A **tessera,** as used in mosaic work. Also called **abaculus.** **2.** A small **abacus,** 1.

abaculus See **abaciscus,** 1.

abacus **1.** The uppermost member of the capital of a column; often a plain square slab, but sometimes molded or otherwise enriched. **2.** In ancient construction, a square table, placed on the head of wood columns, to provide a broad flat surface for the superincumbent beam which supported the roof. **3.** A slab of marble used in finishing the walls of rooms in ancient Roman construction; occasionally the marble was simulated in paint.

left: **abacisci,** 1
below: **various styles of abaci,** 1

A, **abacus,**1

Decorated

Doric

Corinthian

Ionic

Early English

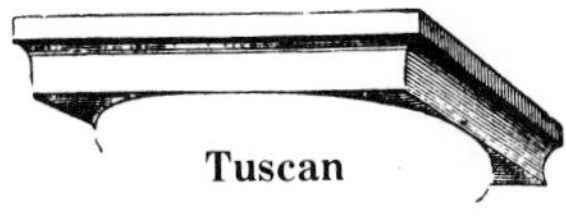

Tuscan

Composite

Norman

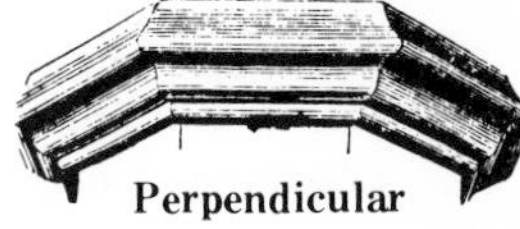

Perpendicular

abacus,2

abacus,3

abamurus A buttress, or a second wall added to strengthen another.

abated Cut away or beaten down so as to show a pattern or figure in low relief.

abat-jour Any beveled aperture, or a skylight, in a wall or in a roof to admit light from above.

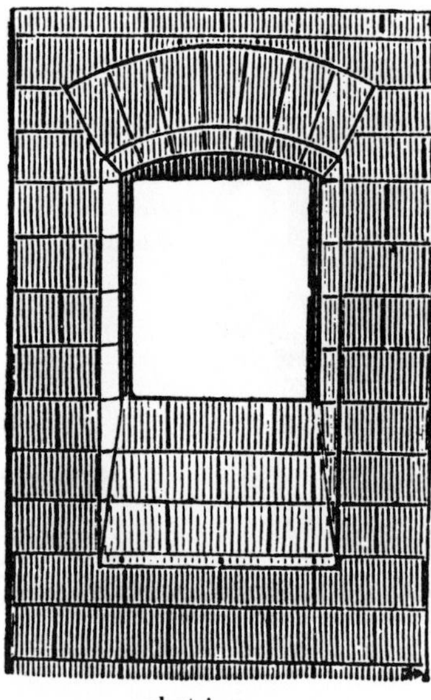

abat-jour

abaton A sanctuary not to be entered by the public; a holy of holies.

abat-vent Louvers which are placed in an exterior wall opening to permit light and air to enter but to break the wind.

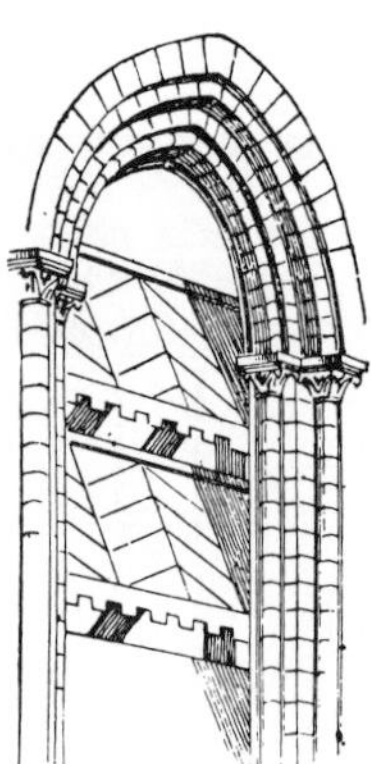

abat-vent

abat-voix In a church, a sound reflector behind and over a pulpit.

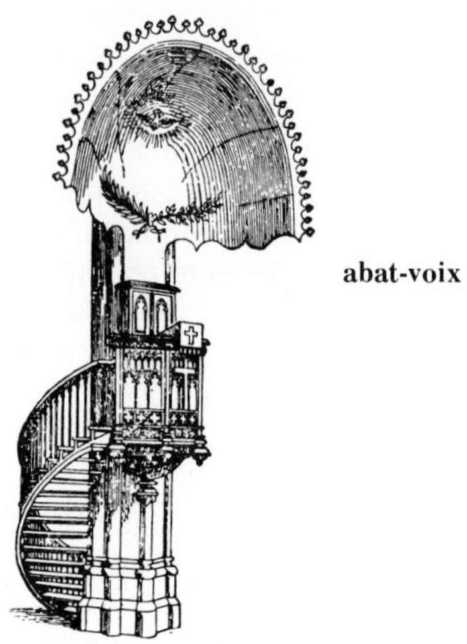

abat-voix

abbey A monastery or convent; particularly the church thereof.

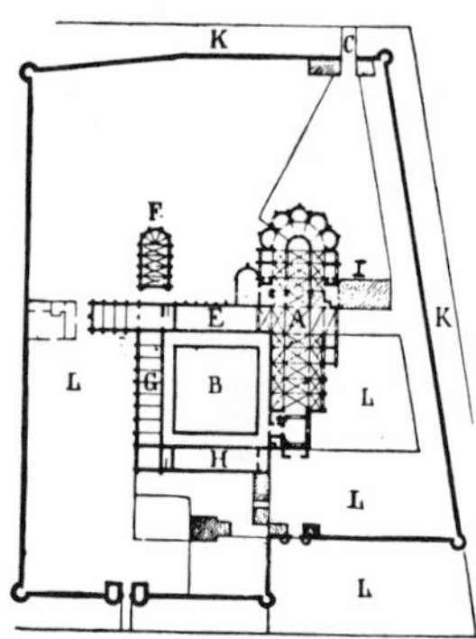

abbey: *A*, church; *B*, cloister; *C*, city gate; *E*, chapter house; *F*, chapel of the Virgin; *G*, refectory; *H*, cellars and presses; *I*, abbot's lodging; *K*, ditches; *L*, gardens

abbreuvoir Same as **abreuvoir.**

abreuvoir In masonry, a joint or interstice between stones, to be filled with mortar or cement.

absidiole Same as **apsidiole.**

absis Same as **apsis.**

abutment A masonry mass (or the like) which receives the thrust of an arch, vault, or strut.

A, abutment

acaina, akaina An ancient Greek measure of length, equal to 1215 in. (3,086 cm).

acanthus A common plant of the Mediterranean, whose leaves, stylized, form the characteristic decoration of capitals of Corinthian and Composite orders. In scroll form it appears on friezes, panels, etc.

acanthus

accolade An ornamental treatment, used over an arch, a door, or a window, composed of two ogee curves meeting in the middle; often a richly decorated molding.

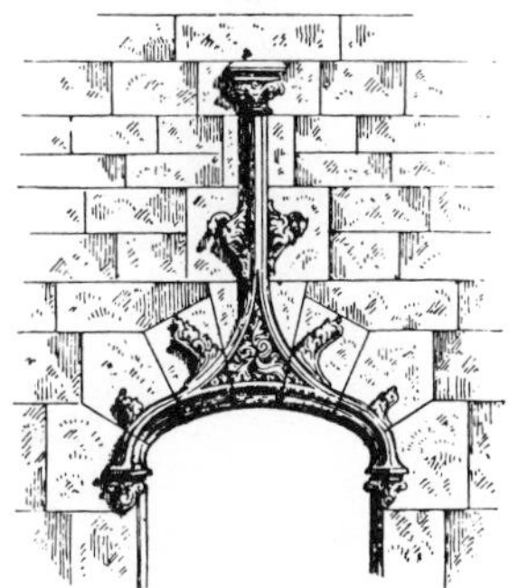

accolade

accouplement The placement of columns or pilasters close together, in pairs.

accouplement

Achaemenid architecture An architecture developed under the Achaemenid rulers of Persia (6th to 4th cent. B.C.) by a synthesis and eclectic adaptation of architectural elements which included those of surrounding countries. In the hypostyle hall it achieved a highly original new building type.

achchaday In Indian architecture, the outer stone facing of a **stupa.**

achelor, achiler, achlere Same as **ashlar.**

acorn A small turned ornament, conical or globular in shape, or in the form of an acorn; used as a finial, knob, or pendant.

acorn

acoustic resonators See **golosniki.**

acroaterion In ancient Greece, a hall or place where lectures were given.

acrobaticon In ancient Greek construction, scaffolding.

acrolith A statue or sculptured figure in which only the head, hands, and feet are of stone, the rest being usually of wood.

acropodium **1.** An elevated pedestal bearing a statue, particularly if raised from the substructure on supports. **2.** The plinth of a statue if resting on supports.

acropolis **1.** The elevated stronghold of a Greek city, usually with the temple of the patron divinity. **2.** *(cap.)* The Acropolis of Athens. **3.** Any elevated group of buildings serving as a civic symbol.

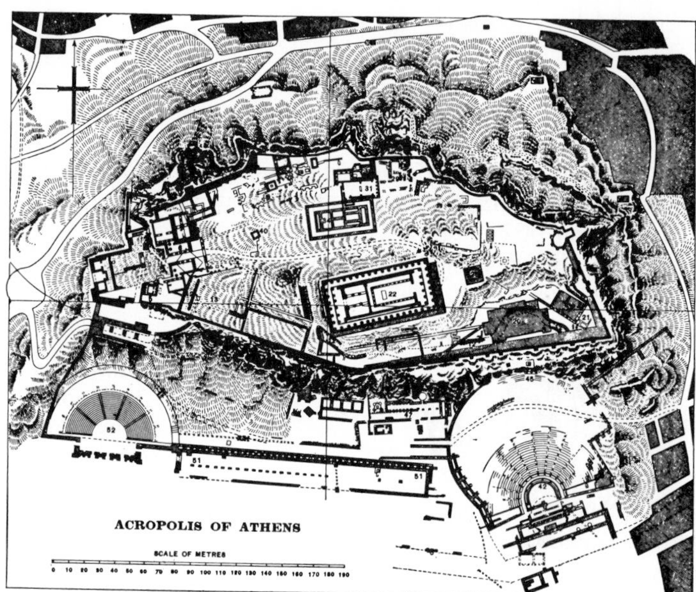

PLAN OF THE ACROPOLIS OF ATHENS.

5. Temple of Nike Apteros.
6. Propylæa.
12. Fortified wall of Pelasgic work.
13. Precinct of Artemis Brauronia.
20. 21. The two modern museums.
22. Parthenon.
26. Roman Temple (traces only).
31. Erechtheum.
34. Temple of Athena before the Persian invasion.
40. Place of colossal bronze statue of Athena Promachos.
42. Theatre of Dionysus.
45. Choragic Monument of Thrasyllus.
47. Sanctuary of Æsculapius.
51. Portico of Eumenes.
52. Odeum of Herodes Atticus.

acroterion, acroter, acroterium **1.** Strictly, a pedestal at the corners or peak of a roof to support an ornament. **2.** More usually, the ornament itself.

Temple at Aegina showing acroterion at peak and corners

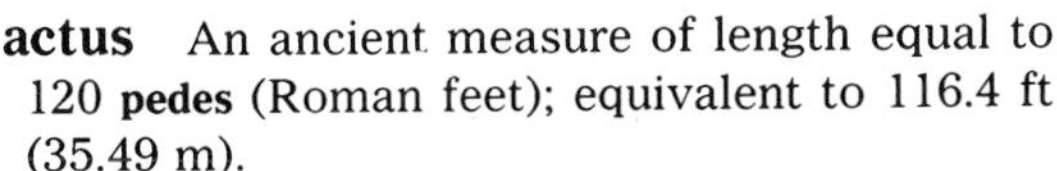

acroterion at peak of pediment, Temple at Aegina (490 B.C.)

acroterion on corner pediment, Temple at Aegina

a corner acroterion

actus An ancient measure of length equal to 120 **pedes** (Roman feet); equivalent to 116.4 ft (35.49 m).

acuminated Finished in a point, as a lofty Gothic roof.

acute arch, lancet arch A sharply pointed **two-centered arch** whose centers of curvature are farther apart than the width of the arch.

Adam style An architectural style based on the work of Robert Adam (1728–1792) and his brothers, predominant in England in the late 18th cent. and strongly influential in the U.S.A., Russia, and elsewhere. It is characterized by clarity of form, use of color, subtle detailing, and unified schemes of interior design. Basically Neoclassical, it also adapted Neo-Gothic, Egyptian, and Etruscan motifs.

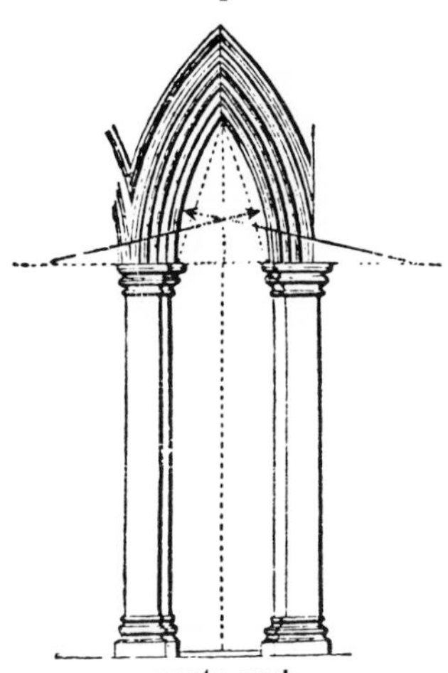

acute arch

Adam style

additus maximus In an ancient Roman amphitheatre, a main entrance.

addorsed, adorsed Said of animals or figures in decorative sculpture placed back to back.

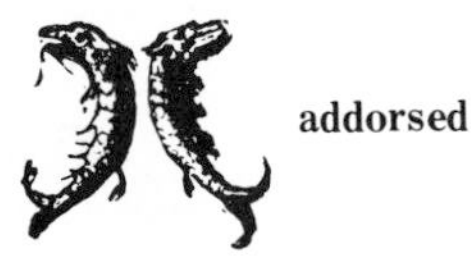
addorsed

adit An entrance or passage.

adobe brick Large, roughly molded, sun-dried clay brick of varying sizes.

adytum, adyton **1.** The inner shrine of a temple reserved for the priests. **2.** The most sacred part of a place of worship.

aedes **1.** In Roman antiquity, any edifice or a minor shrine, not formally consecrated. **2.** Now, any chapel or temple.

aedicula **1.** A canopied niche flanked by colonnettes intended as a shelter for a statue or as a shrine. **2.** A door or window framed by columns or pilasters and crowned with a pediment. **3.** *Dim.* of **aedes.** **4.** A small chapel.

aedis Same as **aedes.**

aegicranes Sculptured representations of the heads and skulls of goats or of rams, which were used as decorations on altars, friezes, etc.

aenum Same as **ahenum.**

aerarium In ancient Rome, the public treasury.

aes In ancient Rome or Greece: copper, tin, or any alloy of these metals.

aethousa **1.** The portico on the sunny side of the court of a Greek dwelling. **2.** The place in an ancient Greek dwelling where strangers slept.

aetoma A pediment, or the tympanum of a pediment.

aetos, aetoma A pediment.

affronted, affronté Said of animals or figures facing each other, as in pediments, overdoors, etc.

agalma In ancient Greece, any work of art dedicated to a god.

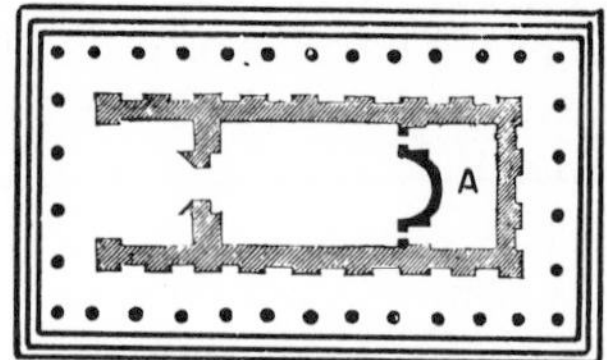

adytum

aedicula

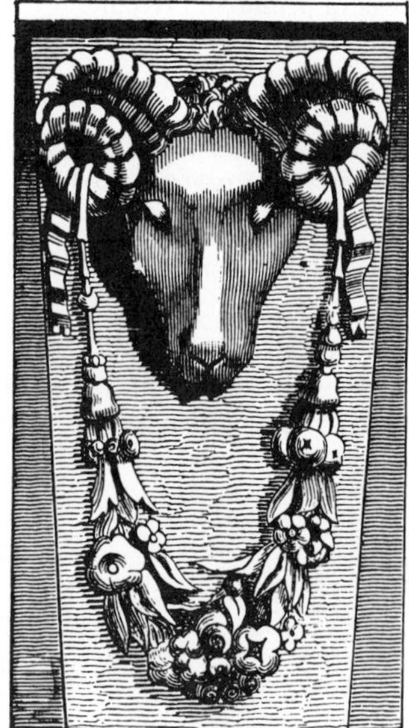
aegricranes

affronted

agger In ancient Rome, an earthwork; an artificial mound or rampart.

agger murorum An embankment upon which the walls and towers of an ancient fortified Roman city were built, and which served as a rampart upon which the garrison was stationed to defend it.

agger viae The central part of an ancient Roman highway which was paved with stones imbedded in cement laid upon several strata of broken rubble, and slightly raised in the center.

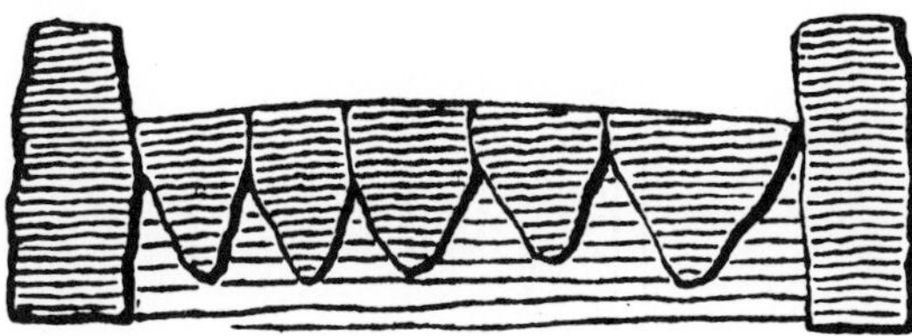

agger viae

agiasterium In the early church, that part of a basilica in which the altar was set up.

agnus dei Any image or representation of a lamb as emblematic of Christ, esp. such a representation with a halo and supporting the banner of the cross.

agora The chief meeting place or marketplace in an ancient Greek city.

agrafe, agraffe The voussoir or keystone of an arch, esp. when carved as a cartouche.

agrafe

aguilla An obelisk, or the spire of a church tower.

agyieus An altar or statue of Apollo, as guardian of the streets and public places; generally placed at the street door of Greek houses, and at the center door of the scena of Greek theatres.

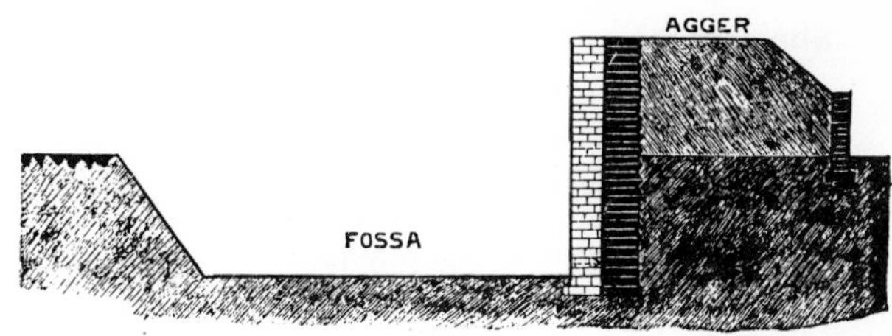

agger

agger murorum

agnus dei

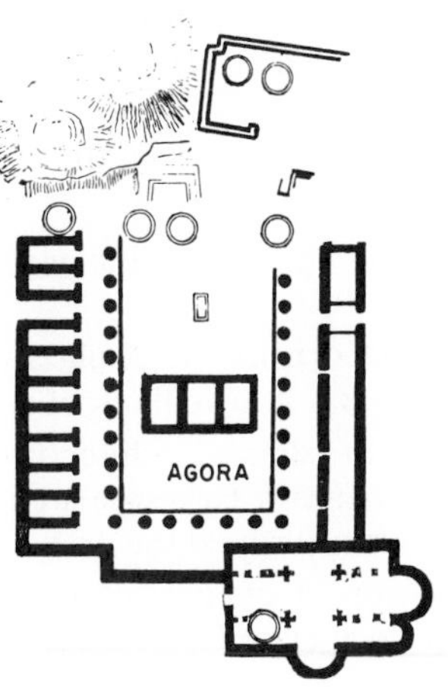

ahenum A boiler system for supplying hot water for ancient Roman baths; consisted of three copper vessels placed one above the other over the furnace to conserve fuel. The largest vessel was directly over the furnace; the smallest (coolest), at the top, received cold water directly from the cistern; hot water drawn from the lowest vessel was replaced by water from the middle one, which had already acquired a certain amount of heat.

aileron A half gable, such as that which closes the end of a penthouse roof or of the aisle of a church.

ailure Same as **alure.**

aisle **1.** A longitudinal passage between sections of seats in an auditorium or church. **2.** In a church, the space flanking and parallel to the nave; usually separated from it by columns, intended primarily for circulation but sometimes containing seats.

aiwan A reception hall in an ancient Parthian building.

ajaraca In southern Spain, an ornament in brick walls, formed of patterns, a half brick deep, more or less complicated.

ajimez In Islamic architecture, a twin window having arched lights which are separated by a column or mullion; characteristic of **Mozarabic architecture** and **Mudejar style** architecture of the Iberian peninsula.

a jour, ajouré Pierced, perforated, or cut out to form a decorative opening in wood, stone, metal, or other material.

akaina See **acaina.**

ala An alcove or small room opening off the atrium of an ancient Roman house.

alabaster Fine-grained, translucent variety of very pure gypsum, generally white or delicately shaded.

alameda A shaded public walk or promenade.

alatoria, alatorium **1.** A piazza, corridor, or covered walk. **2.** The flank of a building.

albanega In Islamic architecture, a spandrel formed between a **horseshoe arch** and the rectangular frame around the arch.

albani stone A pepper-colored stone used in buildings in ancient Rome before the introduction of marble.

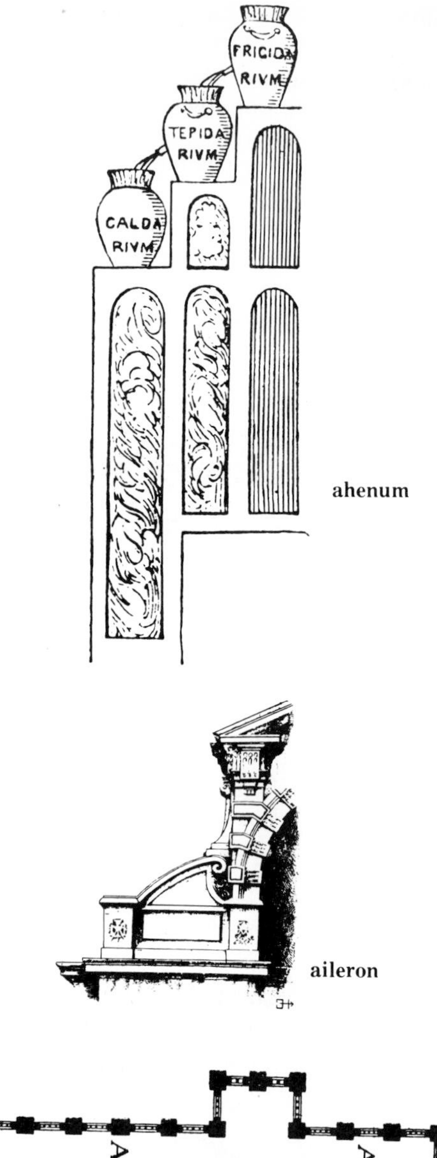

ahenum

aileron

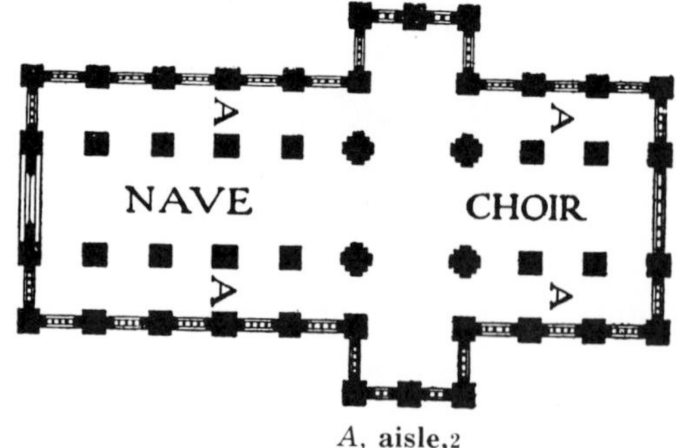

A, aisle,2

albarium A white lime used for stucco; made by burning marble.

albarium opus A setting coat of pure lime, finished as white as possible, and not intended to receive color.

albarius Same as **albarium opus.**

album In ancient Roman architecture, a space on the surface of a wall covered with white plaster, located in a public place, on which public announcements and records, etc., were written.

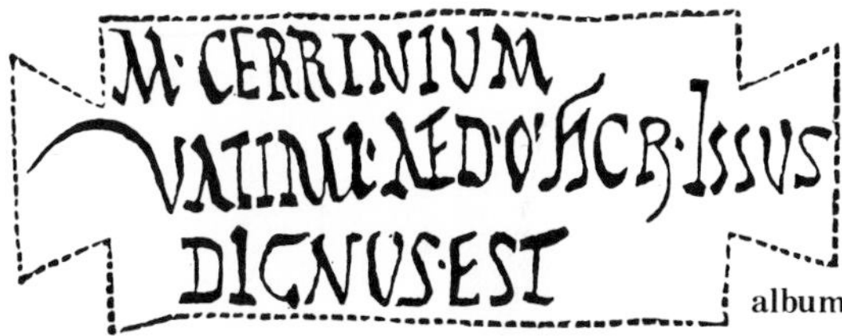

album

alcala A Moorish citadel.

alcazaba A Moorish fortress.

alcazar A Moorish or Spanish fortress or castle.

alcoran Same as **minaret.**

alcove A small recessed space, opening directly into a larger room.

aleaceria A castle, palace, or other large edifice.

aleatorium In ancient Roman architecture, a room in which dice games were played.

aleipterion Same as **alipterium.**

aleois The **loopholes** in castle walls through which arrows could be discharged.

alette **1.** A minor wing of a building. **2.** A door jamb. **3.** A rear pilaster, partially visible within a cluster of columnar elements. **4.** The wing of the pier on both sides of an engaged column.

Alexandrian work Same as **opus Alexandrinum.**

Alexandrinum opus Same as **opus Alexandrinum.**

alfarje In Islamic architecture, the timber framework which supports the roof; often decorated with moldings carved in geometrical patterns. Also see **laceria.**

alfiz A rectangular molding which frames a **horseshoe arch;** typical in Moorish architecture.

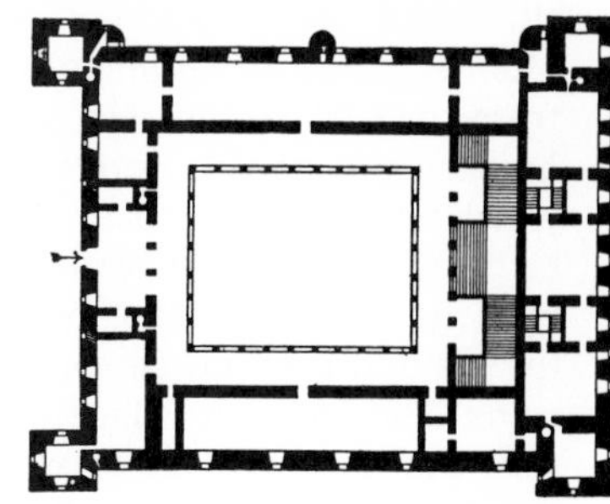

Alcazar, Toledo (1537–53): plan

Alcazar, Toledo: front view

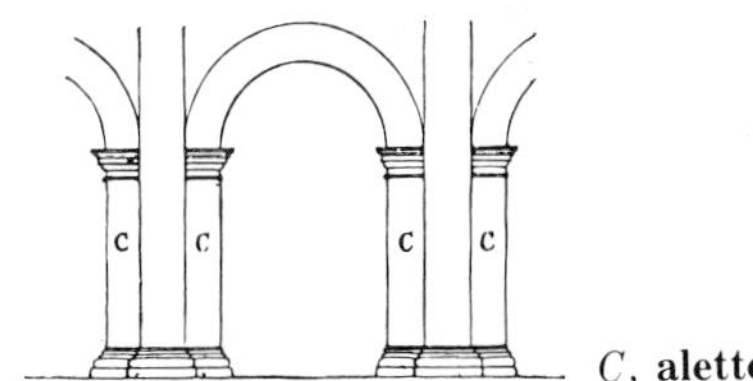

C, alette,4

alfiz

Alhambra A fortress and palace built by the Moorish kings of Granada in southern Spain from the 11th to the 15th cent. The name *Alhambra* probably is derived from the Arabic word for "red" because of the color of the brick used in its construction. The Citadel, with its massive walls, protected by strong towers and fortified gates, is today mostly in ruins. The Moorish Palace contains many patios, the most famous of which are the Lion Court and the Myrtle Court, around which are chambers of the officials; the courts are lavishly decorated with tiles of many shapes and colors and with polychrome stuccos carved in rich patterns; the vaults and domes are decorated with muqarnas; the wooden ceilings are carved and inlaid. Around the courts are arcades with unusually slender columns which support multicolored filagree stucco arches.

Lion Court, Alhambra (1338–90)

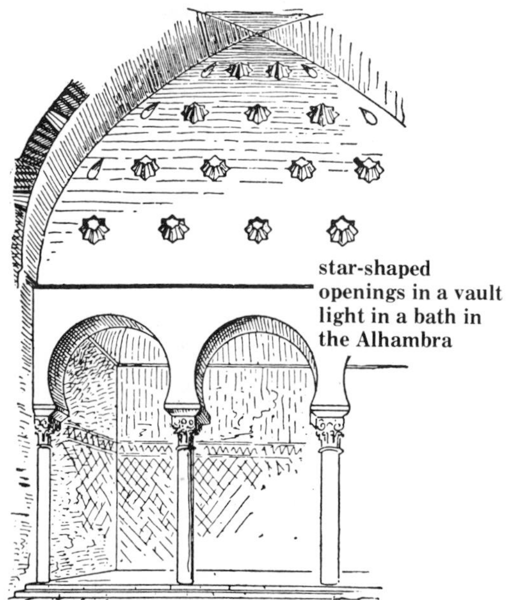

star-shaped openings in a vault light in a bath in the Alhambra

alicatado Tile work which is executed with **azulejos;** used to decorate pavements and walls, esp. in patios.

aliform Having a wing-like shape or extensions.

alignment The theoretical, definitive lines that establish the position of construction (such as a building) or the shape of an individual element (such as a curved or straight beam).

alinda In the architecture of India, a verandah.

alipterium, alipterion, aleipterion In ancient Roman architecture, a room used by bathers for anointing themselves.

alkoran Same as **minaret.**

allée A broad walk, planted with trees on each side, usually at least twice as high as the width of the walk.

allege A part of a wall which is thinner than the rest, esp. the spandrel under a window.

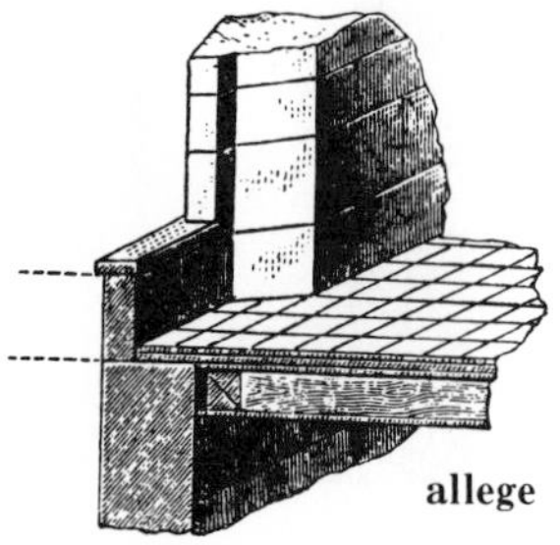

allege

Moorish wall decoration, Alhambra

allegory A figurative representation in which the meaning is conveyed symbolically.

allegory

alley A garden walk between rows of trees; an **allée.**

allieny Same as **alure.**

allover A pattern covering an entire surface; usually one which is repeated.

allure See **alure.**

almariol A storage place for ecclesiastical vestments; an **ambry.**

almary See **ambry.**

almehrabh In Arabian architecture, a niche in a mosque which marks the direction of Mecca.

almemar, almemor **1.** A **bema, 2.** **2.** In a synagogue, a desk on which the Torah is placed while being read to the congregation.

almena An indented trapezium serving as an embattled parapet.

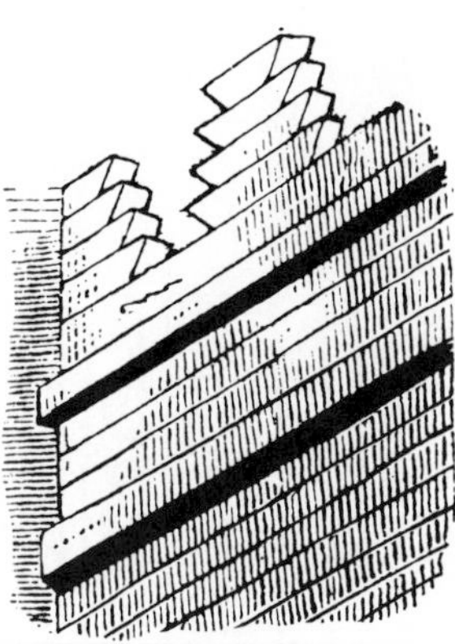
almena

almery See **ambry.**

almimbar Same as **minbar.**

almocarabe Same as **ajaraca.**

almonry A building or part thereof where alms are distributed.

almorie Same as **almariol.**

almorrefa In southern Spain, brickwork intermixed with **azulejos,** used as flooring.

almshouse **1.** A building where the indigent are cared for, usually privately supported in England. **2.** An **almonry.**

alorium Same as **alatoria.**

aloryng Same as **alure.**

alourde Same as **alure.**

altar **1.** An elevated table, slab, or structure, often of stone, rectangular or round, for religious rites, sacrifices, or offerings. **2.** The Communion table in certain churches.

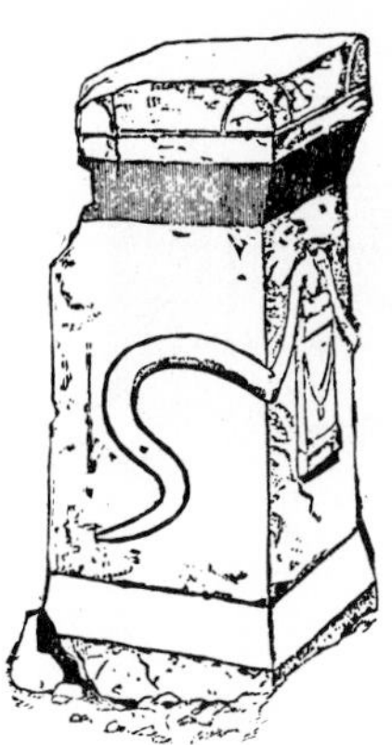
Greek altar

Roman altar

high altar, Notre Dame, Paris (13th cent.)

altar, England (c. 1420)

altar frontal An ornamental hanging or panel for the front of an altar.

altar of repose In a Roman Catholic church, a side altar, repository, or storage niche where the Host is kept from Maundy Thursday to Good Friday.

altarpiece A decorative screen, painting, or sculpture above the back of an altar.

altar rail A low rail or barrier in front of the altar, running transversely to the main axis of the church and separating the officiating clergy from the other worshipers.

altar screen A richly decorated partition of stone, wood, or metal, separating the altar from the space behind it.

altar slab, altar stone A flat stone or slab forming the top of an altar.

altar tomb A raised tomb, or monument covering a tomb, whose shape resembles an altar.

altar tomb

alto-rilievo, alto-relievo See **high relief.**

alure, allure, alur, alura, alourde, alury A gallery or passage, as along the parapets of a castle, around the roof of a church, or along a cloister.

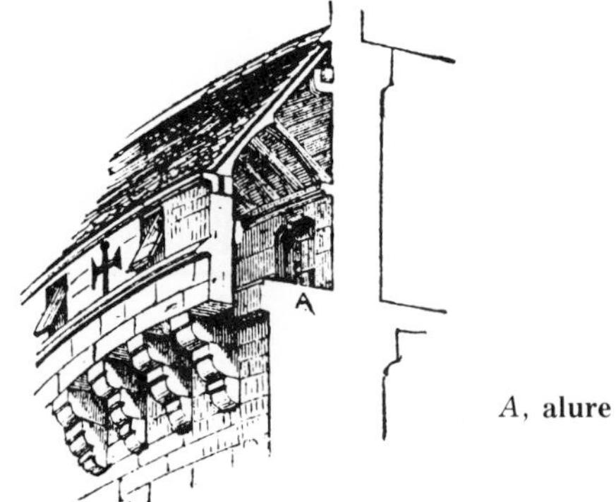

A, alure

alveus In ancient Rome, a bath constructed in the floor of a room, the upper part of it projecting above the floor, the lower part being sunk into the floor itself.

alvus In the caldarium of Roman baths, a space left vacant for a walk between the **schola** and each **alveus.**

amado 雨戸 In traditional Japanese architecture, a type of storm shutter made of sliding wooden panels which (when not in use) slide into a box-like storage cabinet attached to the exterior of the building at one side of the opening; usually set in place in the evening.

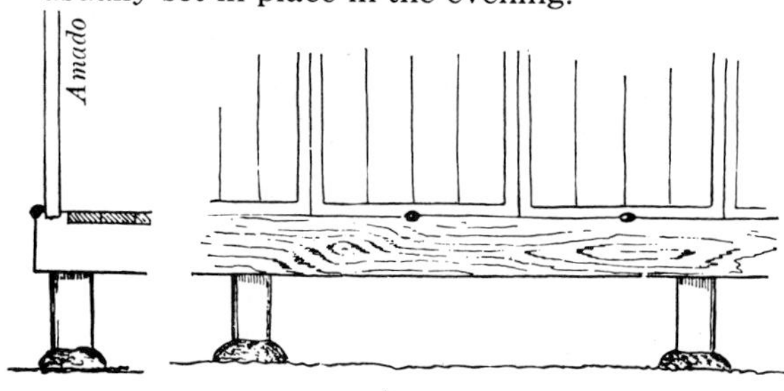

amado

amalaka, amalasari, amalasila In Indo-Aryan architecture, a flattened, fluted, melon-shaped massive stone member crowning the top of a **sikhara.**

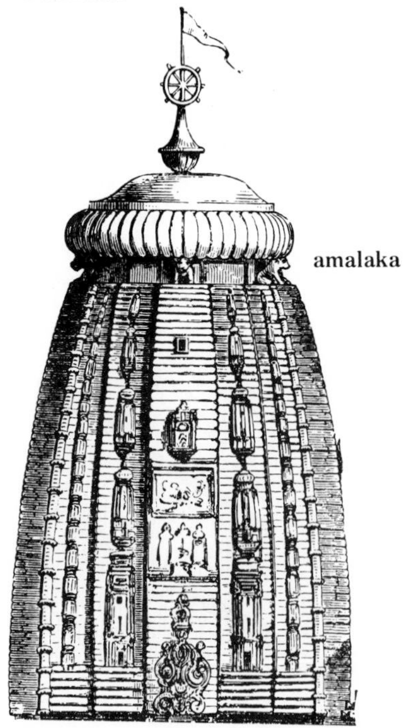

ambitus **1.** A small niche in underground Roman or Greek tombs, forming a receptacle for a cinerary urn. **2.** In the Middle Ages, such a niche, but enlarged to admit a coffin. **3.** In the Middle Ages, the consecrated ground surrounding a church.

ambivium An ancient Roman road or street that went around a site rather than through it.

ambo, ambon **1.** In early Christian churches, a pulpit for reading or chanting the Gospels or the Epistles. **2.** In contemporary Balkan or Greek churches, a large pulpit or reading desk.

ambo

ambre, ambrie Same as **ambry.**

ambrices In ancient Roman construction, the cross laths inserted between the rafter and tiles of a roof.

ambry, almary, almery, aumbry **1.** A cupboard or niche in a chancel wall for the utensils of the Eucharist; an **armarium.** **2.** A storage place, storeroom, closet, or pantry.

ambry, 1

ambulacrum Any promenade shaded by trees, but esp. for the **parvis** in front of basilica.

ambulatio A promenade, either open to the sky or covered.

ambulatory **1.** A passageway around the apse of a church, or for circumambulating a shrine. **2.** A covered walk of a cloister.

ambulatory, 2

ambulatory church A church having a domed center bay which is surrounded on three side by aisles.

amorini Same as **putti.**

amortizement The sloping top of a buttress or projecting pier.

amortizement

amphiprostyle Marked by columns in porticoes only at the front and back (of a classical temple), not on the sides.

amphistylar Said of a classical temple having columns across the length of both sides or across both ends.

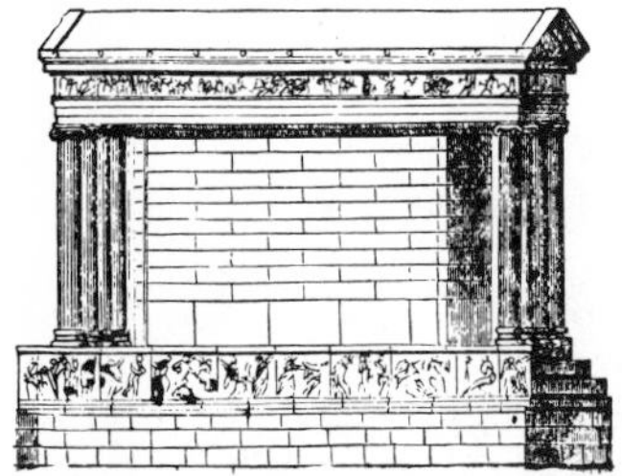

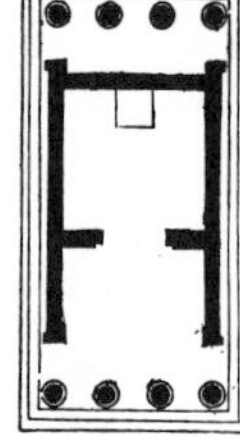

amphiprostylar temple

amphithalamos In an ancient Roman house, a chamber opposite the main bedchamber and separated from it by a passageway.

amphitheatre, amphitheater **1.** A circular, semicircular, or elliptical auditorium in which a central arena is surrounded by rising tiers of seats. **2.** A building erected by the Romans in circular or oval form, having an area in the center for the exhibition of combats between gladiators and wild beasts; the arena could be filled with water for naval spectacles. **3.** Any outdoor theatre, esp. of the Greek type.

amphi-antis A temple having columns between antae at both ends.

amussis A plane table of marble, used by the ancient Romans for testing the flatness of a surface.

amygdalatum opus A type of **opus reticulatum.**

an A Chinese nunnery.

anabathra In Classical antiquity, the steps to an elevated area, as in a theatre or circus, or leading to a pulpit.

anacampteria In ancient religious establishments, the apartments or lodgings of persons who sought the privilege of sanctuary.

anaglyph An embellishment carved or chased in low relief. Also see **bas-relief.**

anaimaktos Ancient Greek altars on which fruits or inanimate things were offered, without fire or blood.

above: section through amphitheatre
below: elevation and partical section

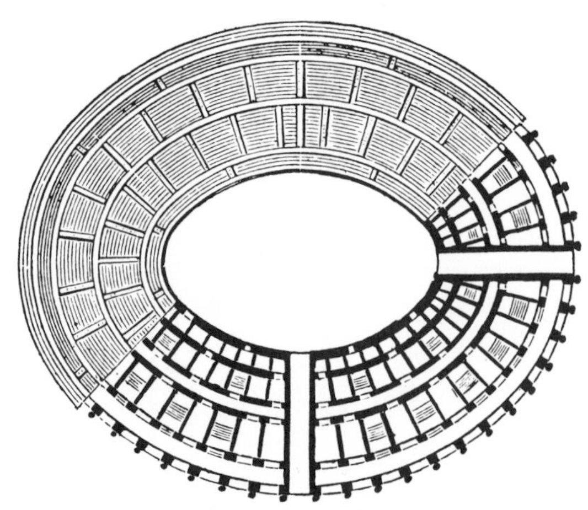

ground plan of amphitheatre

analemma 1. A retaining wall at the side of an ancient Greek or Roman theatre. 2. Any raised construction which serves as a support or rest, such as a buttress, pier, foundation, or one wall which supports another.

analogion, analogium 1. A reading desk, lectern, or ambo. 2. In the Eastern church, a stand on which choir books rest.

analoi A pulpit or lectern in the Russian Orthodox church.

anamorphosis A drawing which appears to be distorted unless viewed from a particular angle or with a special device.

anamorphosis

anatarium In ancient Rome, a house (and yard) for raising ducks.

anathyrosis A Greek method of fitting masonry without mortar by carefully dressing the contact edges of the blocks, leaving the center rough and slightly recessed.

anchor 1. The anchor-shaped dart in the egg-and-dart molding; also called **anchor dart.** 2. A metal clamp, often of fanciful design, fastened on the outside of a wall to the end of a tie rod or metal strap connecting it with an opposite wall to prevent bulging.

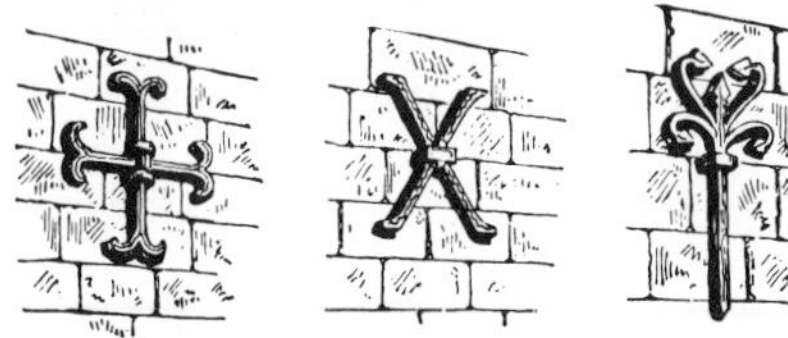

medieval anchors,2

anchorage Same as **anchoridge.**

anchor dart See **anchor.**

anchoridge The room over the vestry attached to the north side of the chancel; a common appendage to churches in northern England.

anchor iron Same as **beam anchor.**

ancillary One of a group of buildings having a secondary or dependent use, such as an annex.

ancon, ancone 1. A scrolled bracket or **console** which supports a cornice or entablature over a door or window. 2. A projecting boss on a column **drum** or wall block. 3. A cramp to fasten blocks of stone.

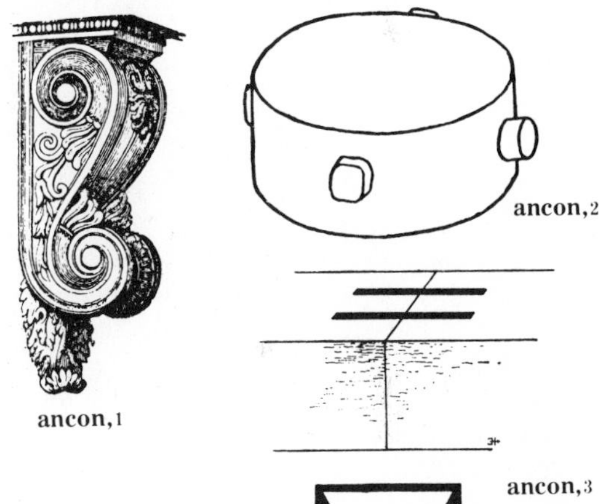

ancon,1

ancon,2

ancon,3

anda The hemispherical dome of an Indian **stupa.**

andron, andronitis 1. In ancient Greece, the part of a building used by men, esp. the banquet room. 2. A passage beside the tablinum in a Roman house.

ang In traditional Chinese construction, a **kung** (in the **tou kung** system of construction) which is raked at an angle; functions as a leverage arm to counterbalance the force applied by the purlins. After the Sung dynasty (10th to 13th cent.), served only as a decoration.

angel light A small triangular **light, 1** between subordinate arches of the tracery of a window, esp. in the English Perpendicular style.

angiportus In ancient Rome, a narrow road passing between two houses or a row of houses, or an alley leading to a single house.

Angkor Wat A temple complex in Cambodia erected by Suryavarman II from 1113 to 1150 A.D., intended as a funerary monument to him as god-king; located south of the capital city of Angkor Thom. Perhaps the world's largest religious structure, it was conceived as a "temple mountain," symbolizing **Meru.** Within an enormous enclosure surrounded by a wide moat, it is approached by a monumental causeway enclosed by balustrades, formed by giant *nagas* (mythical serpents), which leads to the entrance gate of the temple. The temple is built on a series of stepped terraces; each terrace is surrounded by a gallery with towers at each corner; the vaulted galleries receive light through an open colonnade, illuminating the continuous relief friezes which decorate the inner walls with mythological themes, covering a vast area. The central sanctuary of the temple is on top of a **step pyramid** above the terraces, culminating in a large central pagoda-like tower that is joined by passageways to towers at each of the four corners of the base.

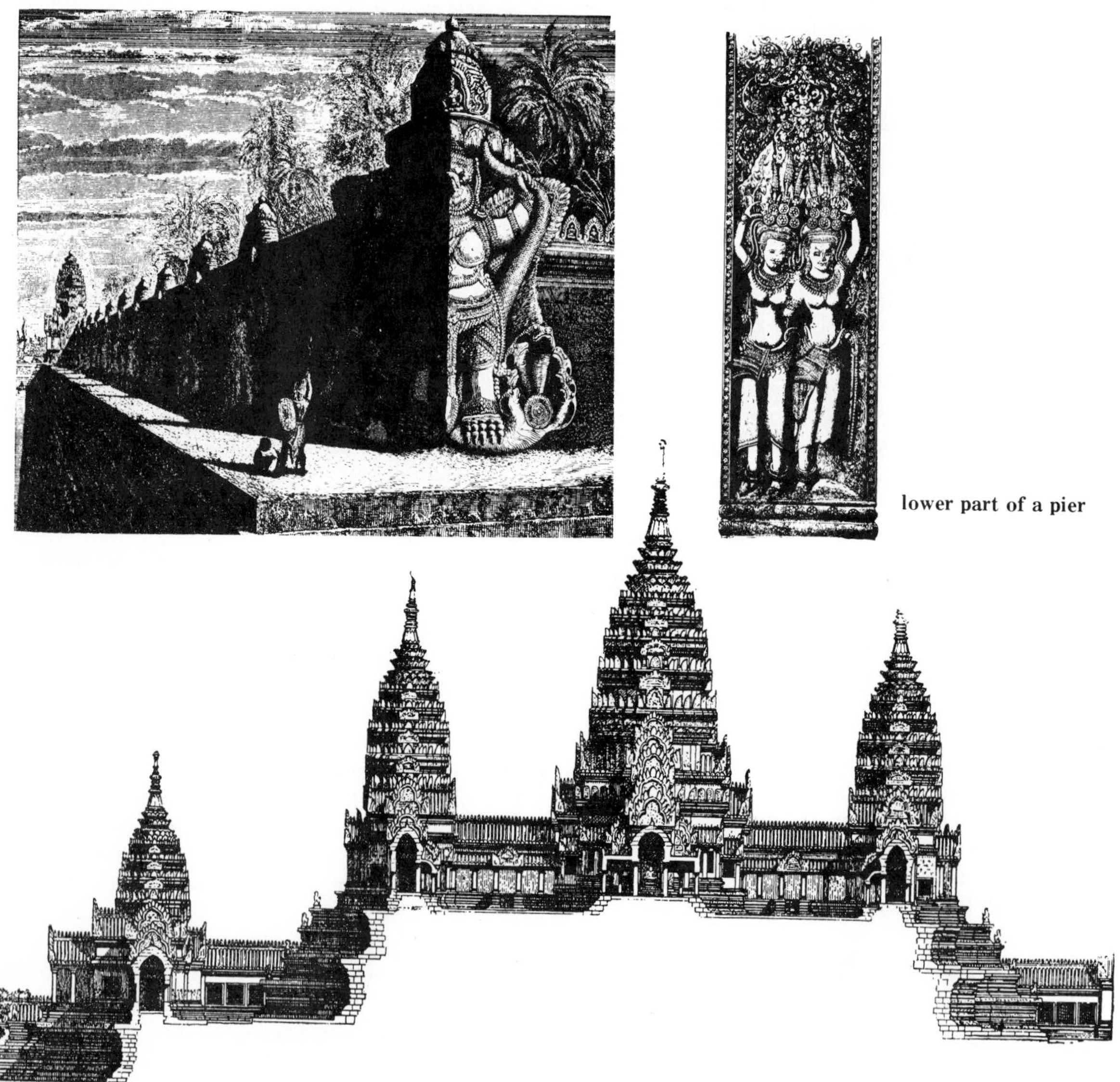

lower part of a pier

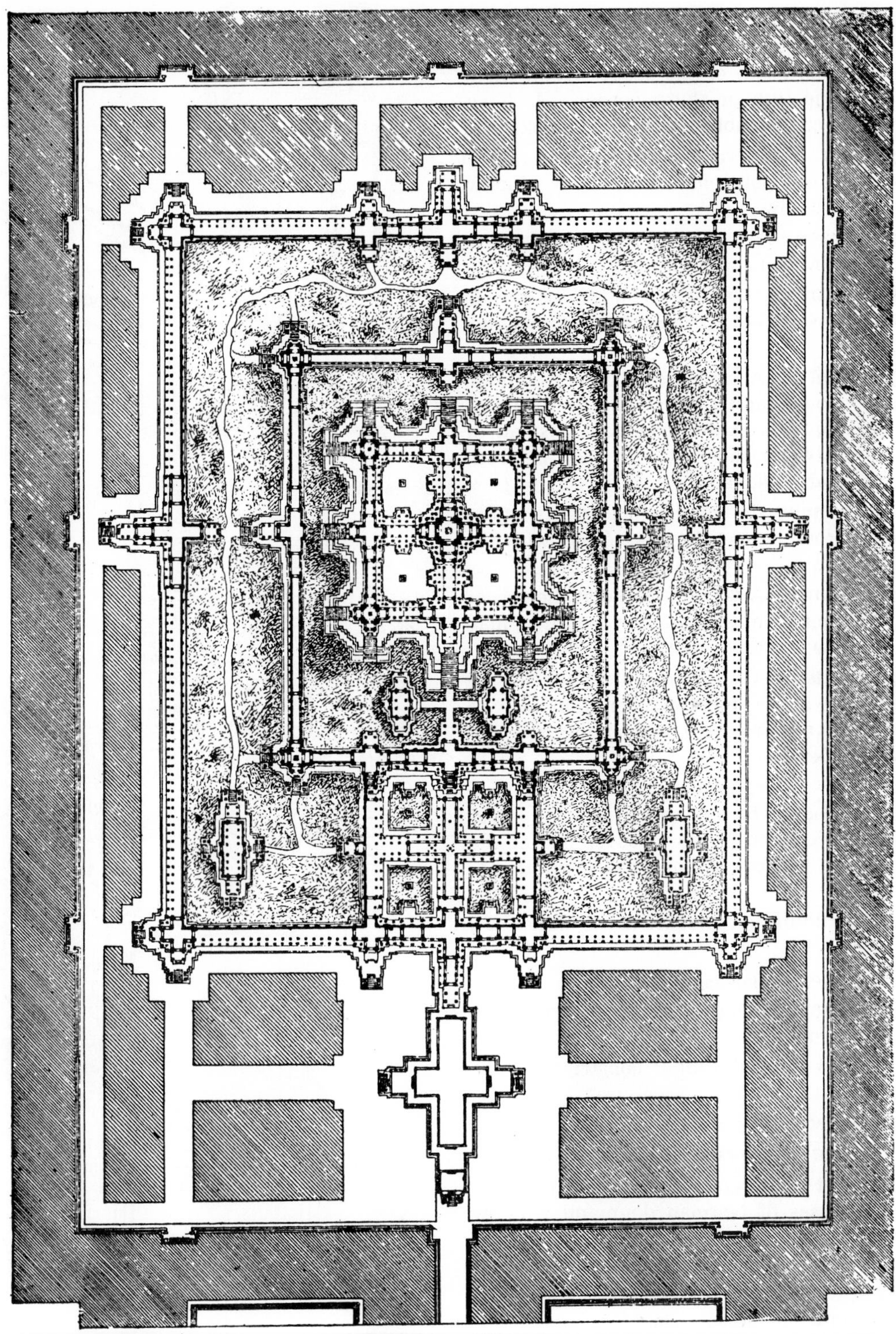

plan of Angkor Wat (restored)

angle **1.** The figure made by two lines that meet. **2.** The difference in direction of such intersecting lines, or the space within them. **3.** A projecting or sharp corner. **4.** A secluded area resembling a corner; a nook.

angle bar An upright bar at the meeting of two faces of a polygonal window, bay window, or bow window.

angle brace A bar or brace which is fixed across a frame to make it rigid.

angle buttress One of two buttresses at right angles to each other, forming the corner of a structure.

angle capital A capital at a corner column, esp. an Ionic capital where the four volutes project equally on the diagonals, instead of being in two parallel planes; used by both Greeks and Romans.

angle chimney A chimney placed so that the sides of the chimney form an angle with the side walls.

angle column A column placed at the corner of a building, as at the corner of a portico; may be freestanding or engaged.

angled stair A stair in which successive flights are at an angle of other than 180° to each other (often at 90°), with an intermediate platform between them.

angle leaf In medieval architecture, a carved claw or **spur, 1** which projects from the lower **torus** of a column, so as to cover one of the projecting corners of the square plinth beneath.

angle modillion A **modillion** at the corner of a cornice.

angle newel A **landing newel.**

angle niche A niche formed in the corner of a building; common in medieval architecture.

angle post In half-timber construction, the corner post.

angle rafter A **hip rafter.**

angle ridge A **hip rafter.**

angle shaft **1.** A column within the right-angled recesses of Norman door and window jambs. **2.** A decorative member, such as a colonnette or enriched corner bead, attached to an external angle of a building.

angle stone Same as **quoin.**

anglet A groove, usually containing an angle of 90°.

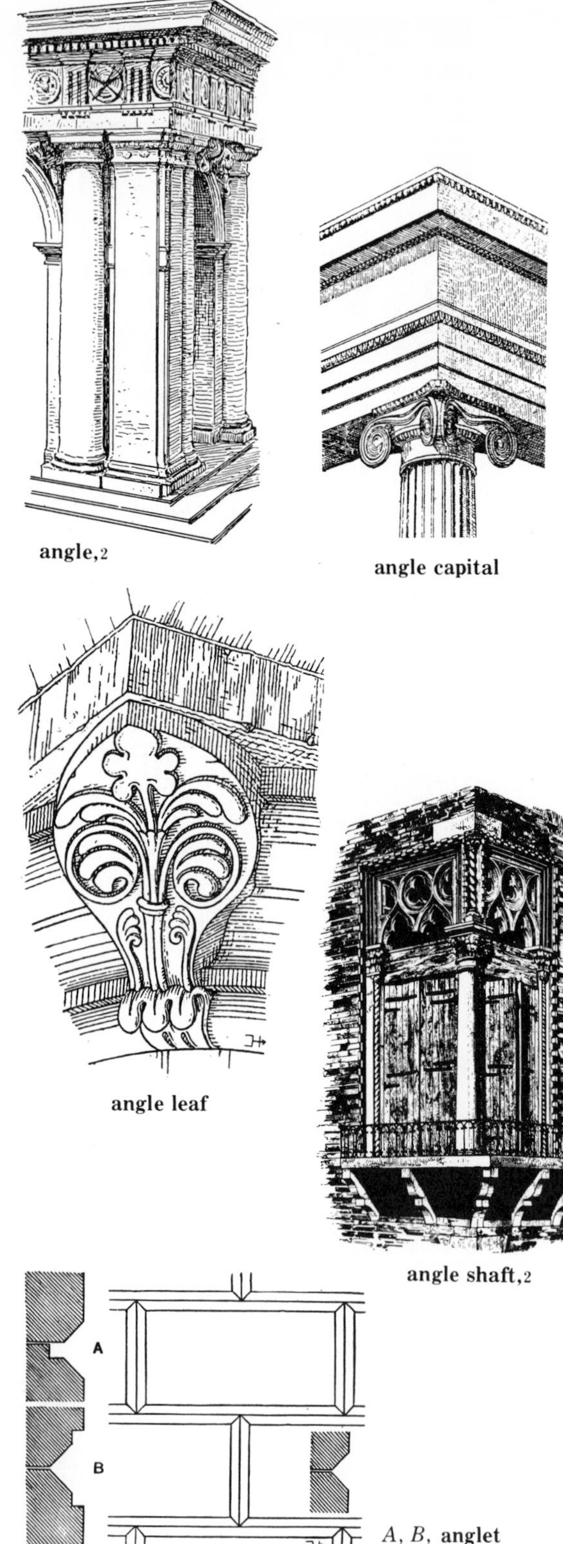

angle, 2

angle capital

angle leaf

angle shaft, 2

A, B, anglet

Anglo-Saxon architecture The pre-Romanesque architecture of England before the Norman Conquest (1066), which survived for a short time thereafter, characterized by massive walls and round arches.

double windows (c. 950 A.D.)

annex, annexe A subsidiary structure near or adjoining a larger principal building.

annular molding Any molding which is circular in plan, such as the **torus** of a base.

annular vault A **barrel vault** in the shape of a ring, instead of a straight line; covers a space of which the plan is formed by the area between two concentric circles, or any portion of such a space.

annular vault

annulated column A shaft or cluster of shafts fitted, at intervals, with rings.

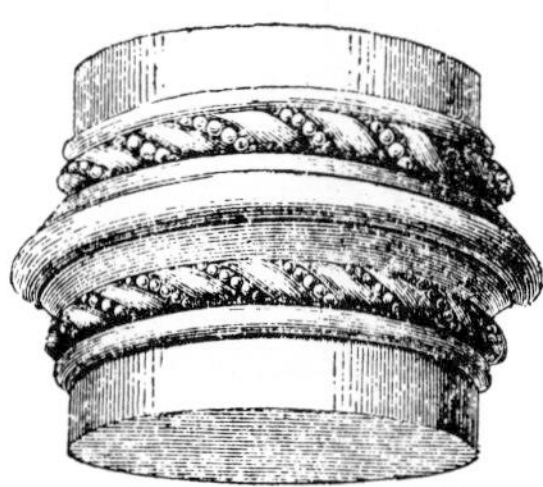

annulated column

annulet A small molding, usually circular in plan and square or angular in section; esp. one of the fillets encircling the lower part of the Doric capital above the necking.

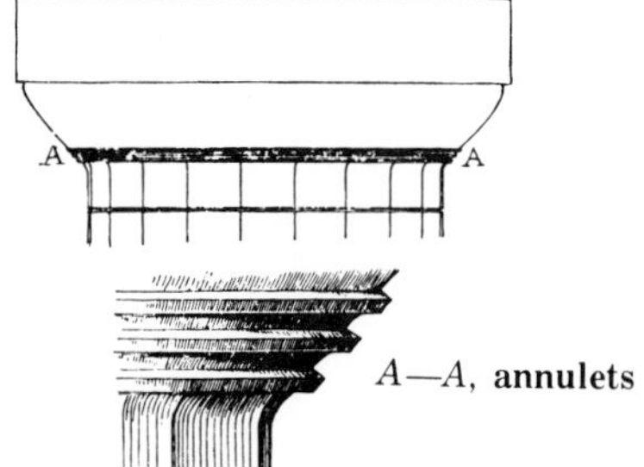

A—A, annulets

anse de panier A **basket-handle arch.**

anserarium In ancient Rome, a shelter for the raising of geese; consisted of a court surrounded by a high wall, with a portico inside.

anta A pier or pilaster formed by a thickening at the end of a wall; its capital and base differ from those of the columns forming part of the same order. Antae often occur in pairs beyond the faces of the end walls. The columns are said to be **in antis.**

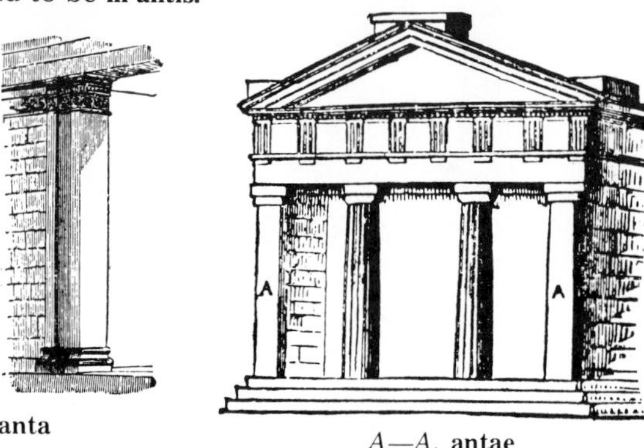

anta

A—A, antae

antecabinet A room, often spacious and elegant, leading to a private audience room or cabinet.

antechamber A room preceding a chamber.

antechapel A separate entrance space, as a porch or vestibule, in front of a chapel.

antechoir The space, more or less enclosed, between the inner and outer gates of the choir screen.

antechurch A deep narthex at the front of a church, usually with a nave and side aisles.

antecourt An entrance court or outer court which precedes the principal court, as at Versailles; a **forecourt.**

antefix **1.** A decorated upright slab used in classical architecture and derivatives to close or conceal the open end of a row of tiles which cover the joints of roof tiles. **2.** A similar ornament on the ridge of a roof.

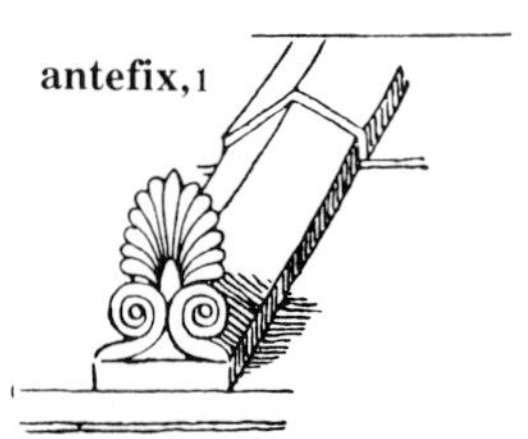

antefix,1

antefix,1

antemural The outerworks or wall surrounding and protecting a castle.

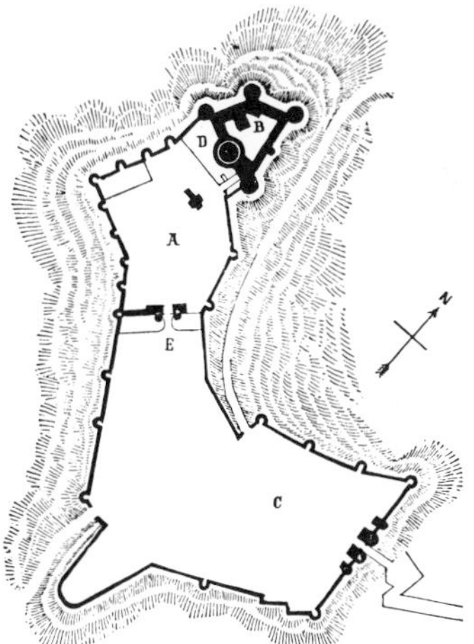

A, outer court; *B*, castle; *C*, town; *D*, castle moat; *E*, antemural

antenave A narthex or porch of any description leading into the nave of a church.

antepagment, antepagmentum **1.** The stone or stucco decorative dressings enriching the jambs and head of a doorway or window; an **architrave, 2.** **2.** In ancient Roman construction, a **doorjamb.**

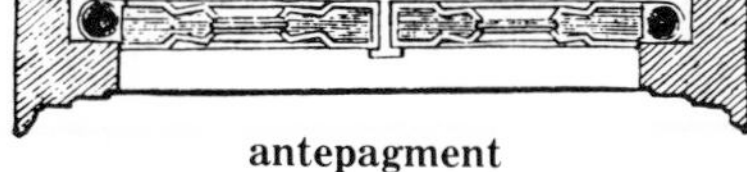

antepagment

antepagmentum superius The **lintel** over a door.

antependium A hanging which was suspended over and in front of the altar in medieval churches.

antepodium A seat behind the dais in a choir, reserved for the clergy.

anteport A preliminary portal; an outer gate or door.

anteportico An outer porch or a portico in front of the main portico in a classical temple.

anterides In ancient Greek and Roman architecture, a structure to strengthen another; a type of buttress placed against an outer wall, esp. in subterranean construction.

anterides

anteroom A room adjacent to a larger, more important one; frequently used as a waiting area.

antevanna In ancient Roman construction, a boarded roof projecting over a window or opening.

anthemion, honeysuckle ornament A common Greek ornament based upon the honeysuckle or palmette. Used singly on stela or antefixes, or as a running ornament on friezes, etc.

anthemion

antic, antic work A grotesque sculpture consisting of animal, human, and foliage forms incongruously run together and used to decorate molding terminations and many other parts of medieval architecture. Sometimes synonymous with **grotesque** or **arabesque.**

anticum **1.** The front of a classical building. **2.** Same as **janua, 2.**

antiparabema One of two chapels at the entrance end of a Byzantine church.

antiquarium The apartment of a Roman villa in which ancient vases, statues, and the like were kept.

antique crown, eastern crown A heraldic device consisting of a headband with an indefinite number of pointed rays projecting from it.

antiquing, broken-color work A technique of handling wet paint to expose parts of the undercoat, by combing, graining, or marbling.

antiquum opus Same as **opus incertum.**

antis, in See **in antis.**

antrum A temple of the early Christians, who were obliged to perform their devotions in caves (*antra*).

Anubis An Egyptian deity, represented with the head of a dog or jackel, and identified by the later Greeks and Romans with their Hermes or Mercury.

apadana The columnar audience hall in a Persian palace.

apex In architecture or construction, the highest point, peak, or tip of any structure.

apex stone, saddle stone The uppermost stone in a gable, pediment, vault, or dome; usually triangular, often highly decorated.

apiary A house or place where bees are kept; contains a number of beehives.

apodyterium A room in Greek or Roman baths, or in the **palaestra 1**, where the bathers or those taking part in gymnastic exercises undressed and dressed.

apogeum, apogoeum Same as **hypogeum.**

aponsa A **shed roof** having rafters that are let into or rest upon a wall.

apophyge **1.** That part of a column which is molded into a concave sweep where the shaft springs from the base or terminates in the capital. Also called **scape** or **congé.** **2.** The hollow or scotia beneath the **echinus** of some archaic Doric capitals.

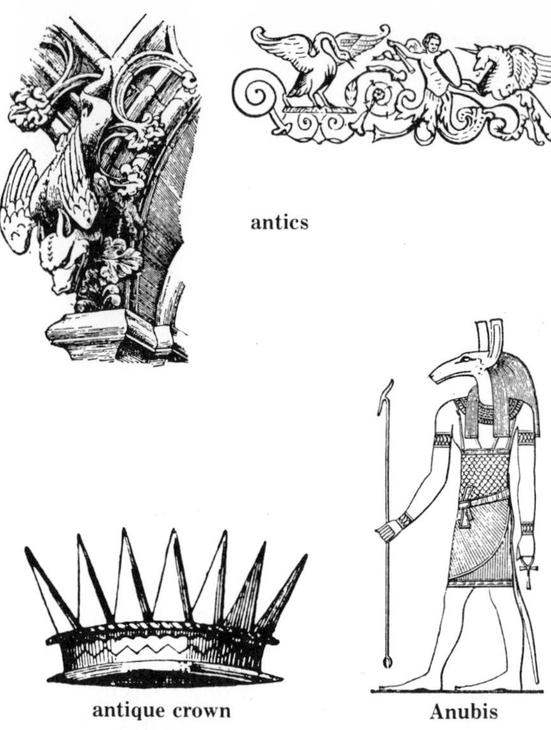

antics

antique crown

Anubis

apodyterium

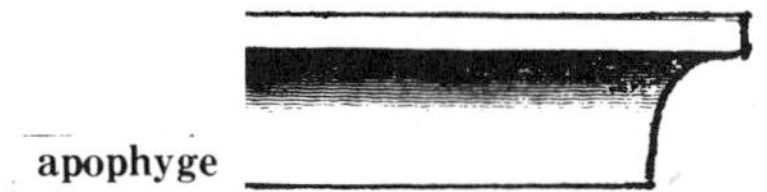

apophyge

apostolaeum, apostolium A church dedicated to an apostle and named after him.

apotheca In ancient Greece and Rome, a storeroom of any kind, but esp. one for storing wine.

apothesis Same as **apophyge.**

appareille The slope or ascent to the platform of a bastion.

appentice, pent, pentice A minor structure built against the side of a building, with a roof of single slope; a **penthouse, 2.**

Appian Way See **Via Appia.**

applied molding A **planted molding.**

applied trim Supplementary and separate decorative strips of wood or moldings applied to the face or sides of a frame, as on a doorframe.

appliqué **1.** An accessory decorative feature applied to an object or structure. **2.** In ornamental work, one material affixed to another.

apron piece, pitching piece A horizontal wood beam, fixed into a wall and projecting horizontally, which supports the ends of carriage pieces, roughstrings, and joists at the landings of a wooden staircase.

apsara A celestial nymph; appears as a figure in the sculptural repertory of a Hindu temple.

apse A semicircular (or nearly semicircular) or semipolygonal space, usually in a church, terminating an axis and intended to house an altar.

apse aisle An aisle or ambulatory extending around an apse or chevet.

apse chapel A chapel opening from an apse; such a radial chapel is a conspicuous feature of French Gothic architecture.

appentice

apse

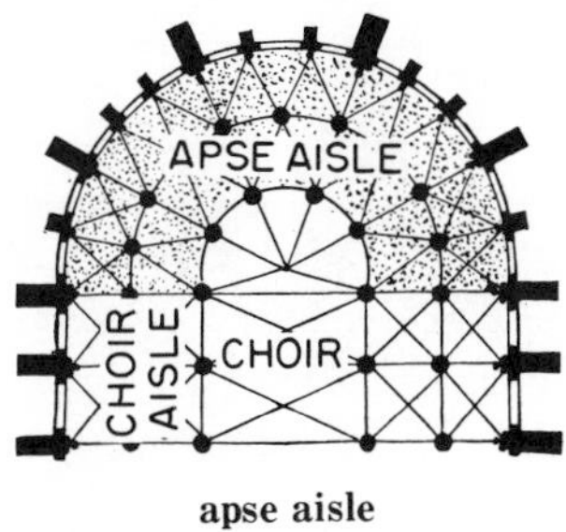

apse aisle

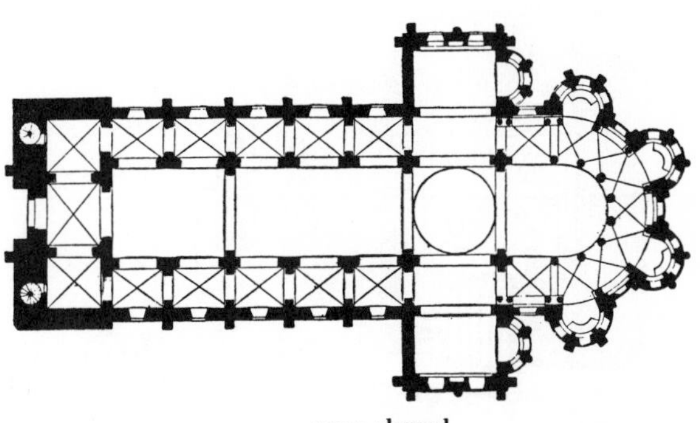

apse chapel

apsidal Pertaining to an apse or similar to one.

apsidiole A small apsidal chapel, esp. one projecting from an apse.

apsis The semicircular termination of any rectangular chamber, a form employed in courts of justice in ancient Rome to make a convenient place for the judges' seats or in temples to form a recess for the statue of the deity to whom the edifice was consecrated; an apse.

apsis gradata A bishop's seat or throne, in ancient churches; raised on steps above the ordinary stalls.

apteral Describing a classical temple or other building which has no columns along the sides but may have a portico at one or both ends.

apyroi Altars on which sacrifices were offered without fire.

aquaminarium Same as **bénitier.**

aqueduct A channel for supplying water; often underground, but treated architecturally on high arches when crossing valleys or low ground.

aquila A **tympanum** decorated with carvings; properly a Greek term, originating from their very early practice of carving an eagle in the pediment of a temple, esp. one dedicated to Zeus (Jupiter). In Etruscan or other edifices of araeostyle construction, the aquila was formed of wood to lighten the weight on the architrave.

ara **1.** A Roman altar. **2.** Any structure elevated above the ground and used to receive offerings to the gods.

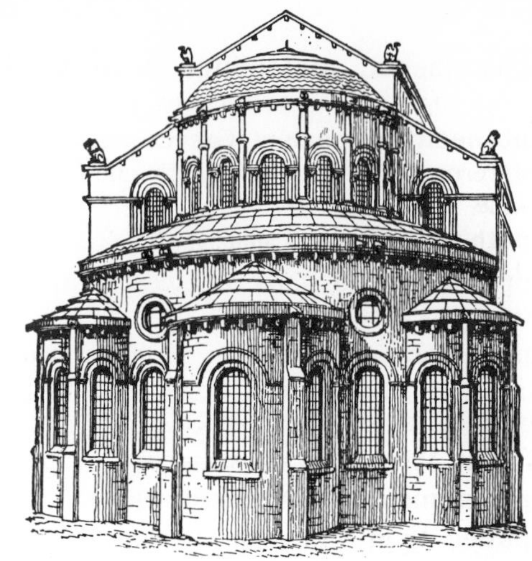

apsidioles

aqueduct of Tarragona, Segovia (c. 10 A.D.)

ara,1 in a street in Pompeii against a housewall

ara,1 along the edge of an impluvium

arabesque **1.** Intricate overall pattern of geometric forms or stylized plants used in Muhammadan countries. **2.** Overall decorative pattern of acanthus scrolls, swags, candelabrum shafts, animal or human forms, on panels or pilasters, in Roman and Renaissance architecture. **3.** A species of ornament of infinite variety used for enriching flat surfaces or moldings, either painted, inlaid, or carved in low relief.

arabesque, 1

arabesque, 1: details

Renaissance arabesque, 2

Arabic arch A **horseshoe arch.**

araeostyle See **intercolumniation, 2.**

araeosystyle: columns spaced 4 diameters apart

araeosystyle, areosystyle Alternately **systyle** and **araeostyle;** having an intercolumniation alternately of two and four diameters.

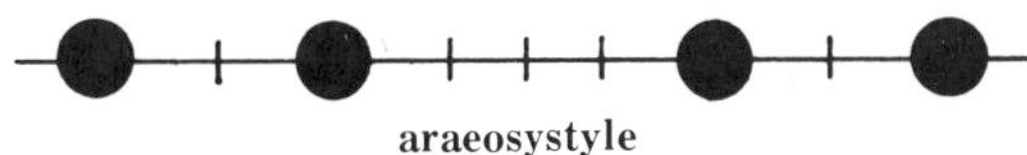

araeosystyle

arakabe The rough undercoat or first coat of plaster applied to the wall of a traditional Japanese-style building.

ara turicrema An altar on which frankincense was sprinkled and burnt.

arbalestina, arbalisteria Same as **balistraria, 2.**

arbor A light open structure of trees or shrubs closely planted, either twined together and self-supporting or supported on a light latticework frame.

lattice framework for a Renaissance arbor

arboretum An informally arranged garden, usually on a large scale, where trees are grown for display, educational, or scientific purposes.

arca custodiae In ancient Roman architecture, a type of cell for the confinement of prisoners.

arcade **1.** A line of counterthrusting arches raised on columns or piers. Also see **interlacing arcade, intersecting arcade.** **2.** A covered walk with a line of such arches along one or both long sides. **3.** A covered walk with shops and offices along one side, and a line of such arches on the other. Also see **stoa.** **4.** A covered walk, lit from the top, lined with shops or offices on one or more levels.

arcade, 1

arcading A line of arches, raised on columns, that are represented in relief as decoration of a solid wall; sometimes seats are incorporated in the composition.

Norman arcading

Transitional arcading

arcae In ancient Roman architecture, the gutters of the **cavaedium.**

arcature **1. Arcading.** **2.** An ornamental, miniature arcade.

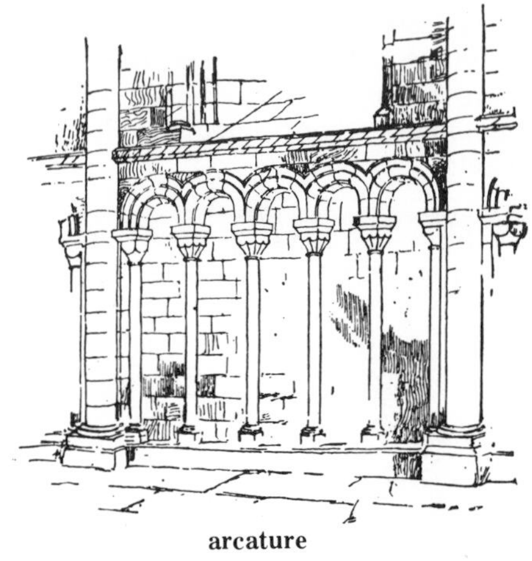

arcature

arc-boutant Same as **flying buttress.**

arc de triomphe Same as **triumphal arch.**

arc de triomphe: Arc de Triomphe de l'Etoile, Paris (1808–36)

arc doubleau An arch, usually very massive, carried across a wide space, to support a groined vault or to stiffen a barrel vault.

arcella A cheese room, in medieval architecture.

arceps Same as **archivium.**

arc formeret The wall arch or wall rib, or the corresponding rib coming next to the arcade between nave and aisle, or the like, as in Gothic vaulting.

arch A curved construction which spans an opening; usually consists of wedge-shaped blocks called **voussoirs**, or a curved or pointed structural member which is supported at the sides or ends. Arches vary in shape from the horizontal flat arch through semicircular and semielliptical arches to bluntly or acutely pointed arches.

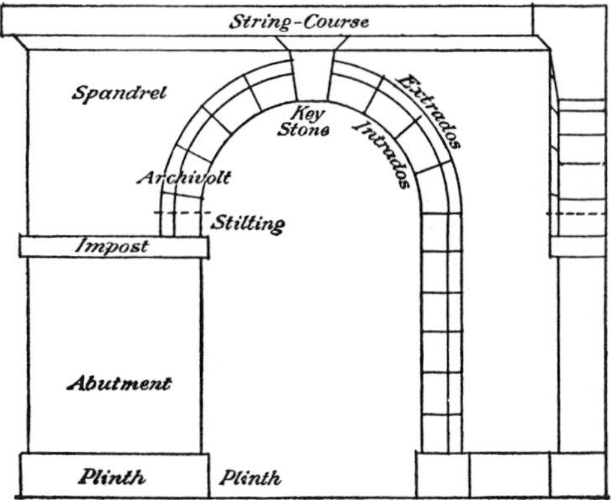

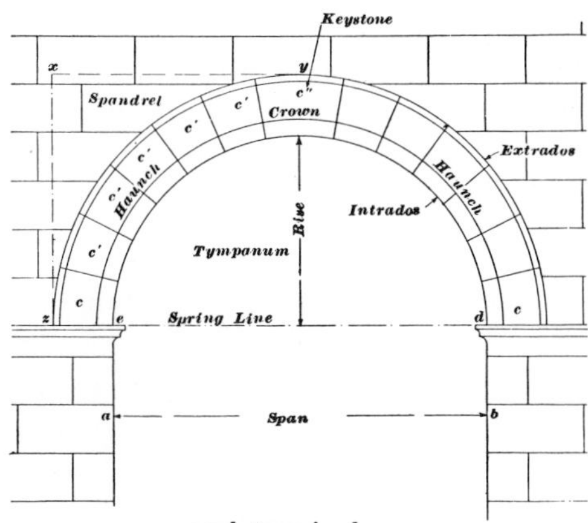

arch terminology

Anglo-Saxon

Norman

Transitional

Early English

Roman

horseshoe (Moorish)

Decorated

Perpendicular

archarium Same as **archivium.**

arch band Any narrow elongated surface forming part of, or connected with, an arch.

arch beam Same as **arched beam.**

arch brace A curved brace, usually used in pairs to support a roof frame and give the effect of an arch.

arch brick, compass brick, featheredge brick, radial brick, radiating brick, radius brick, voussoir brick A wedge-shaped brick used in arch or circular construction; has the two large faces inclined toward each other.

arch buttant Same as **flying buttress.**

arch buttress A **flying buttress** in the shape of an arch.

arch buttress

arch center Formwork to support the voussoirs of an arch during construction.

arch corner bead A corner bead which is cut on the job; used to form and reinforce the curved portion of arch openings.

arched barrel roof See **barrel vault.**

arched beam **1.** A beam whose upper surface is slightly curved. **2.** A **collar brace** which is supported by a **hammer beam** at its lower end.

arched butment Same as **flying buttress.**

arched buttress Same as **flying buttress.**

arched corbel table In Early Christian and Romanesque architecture and derivatives, a raised band (often at the top of a wall) composed of small arches resting on corbels, the arcading regularly punctuated by junctures with pilaster strips.

arched tomb A tomb in which a **tomb chest** lies within an arched niche in a wall.

archeion See **archivium.**

archeria In medieval fortifications, an aperture through which an archer or longbowman might discharge arrows.

archibus Same as **archivium.**

archiepiscopal cross A cross with two transverse arms, the longer one nearer the center.

arching **1.** A system of arches. **2.** The arched part of a structure.

architectonic Related or conforming to technical architectural principles.

architectural **1.** Pertaining to architecture, its features, characteristics, or details. **2.** Pertaining to materials used to build or ornament a structure, such as mosaic, bronze, etc.

architectural fountain A system of pipes and nozzles through which water is forced under pressure to produce ornamental jets, spouts, or showers.

architectural terra-cotta A hard-burnt, glazed or unglazed clay unit used in building construction; plain or ornamental; machine-extruded or hand-molded; usually larger in size than brick or facing tile.

Mesopotamian terra-cotta

Greek terra-cotta

architecture **1.** The art and science of designing and building structures, or large groups of structures, in keeping with aesthetic and functional criteria. **2.** Structures built in accordance with such principles.

architrave **1.** In the classical orders, the lowest member of the **entablature;** the beam that spans from column to column, resting directly upon their capitals. Also see **order.** **2.** The ornamental moldings around the faces of the jambs and lintel of a doorway or other opening; an **antepagment.**

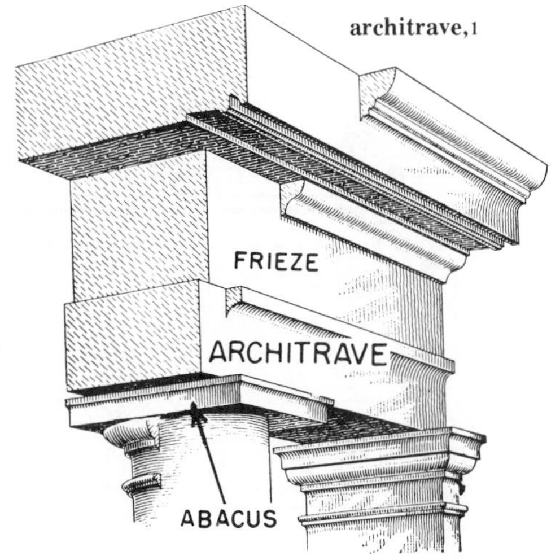

architrave, 1

architrave cornice An entablature in which the cornice rests directly on the architrave, the frieze being omitted.

archivium In ancient Greece and Rome, a building in which archives of a city or state were deposited; also called **archeion** or **tabularium.**

archivolt An **architrave, 2** modified by being carried around a curved opening instead of a rectangular one; an ornamental molding or band of moldings on the face of an arch following the contour of the extrados.

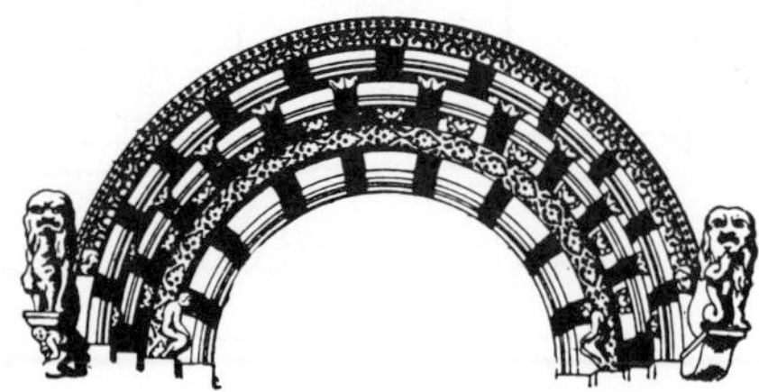
archivolt

archivoltum A medieval conduit or receptacle for waste materials, as a sewer or cesspool.

arch order **1.** In Roman architecture, arches enframed by engaged columns and entablatures. **2.** In medieval architecture, successive vertical planes of arches and colonettes set one within another.

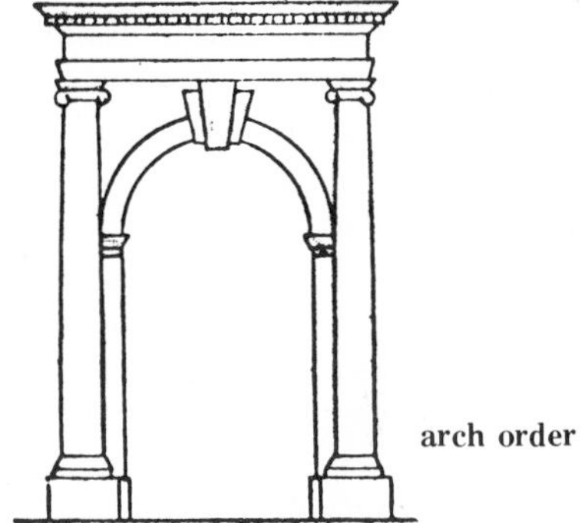
arch order

arch rib **1.** In Romanesque architecture, a transverse rib crossing the nave or aisle at right angles to its length. **2.** A principal load-bearing member of a ribbed arch.

arch ring In an arched structure, the curved member that sustains the principal load.

arch stone Same as **voussoir.**

arch truss A **truss** having an arched upper chord (concave downward) and a straight bottom chord; there are vertical hangers between the two chords.

archway A passage through or under an arch, esp. when long, as under a **barrel vault.**

arcibus, arcibum Same as **archivium.**

arcivum Same as **archivium.**

arcosolium An arched recess or sepulchral cell in a Roman subterranean burial place or catacomb.

arcosolium

arcs doubleaux Same as **arch band.**

arctuated lintel Same as **Syrian arch.**

arcuated Based on, or characterized by, arches or archlike curves or vaults. It is common to distinguish between trabeated (beamed) and arcuated buildings.

arcuatio In ancient Rome, a structure formed by means of arches or arcades and employed to support a construction of any kind, such as an aqueduct.

arcus **1.** In ancient Roman construction, an arch. **2.** A **triumphal arch.**

arcus ecclesiae In medieval architecture, the arch by which the nave of the church was divided from the choir or chancel.

arcus ferreus An ancient Roman method of plastering tiles laid on straight or curved iron bars.

arcus presbyterii In medieval architecture, the arch marking the upper boundary of the **tribune, 2.**

arcus toralis The lattice separating the choir from the nave in a basilica.

arcus triumphalis A **triumphal arch.**

area **1.** A large open space in an ancient Roman town, left free and unencumbered by buildings for the exercise and recreation of the townspeople; many were consecrated to some deity whose altar was erected in the center and under whose protection they were placed (as the area of Mercury). **2.** The open space of ground in front of a Roman house, temple, or other edifice, which forms the area of the vestibule. **3.** An open space in front of a cemetery, around which the sepulchers were placed and which served as an **ustrinum** where the funeral pyre was raised and the body was burnt.

arena **1.** An acting space of any shape surrounded by seats. **2.** A type of theatre not having a proscenium, the spectators' seats, rising in tiers, wholly surrounding the stage. **3.** The sanded central area in a Roman amphitheatre or circus, surrounded by the seats.

arenarium, arenaria In ancient Rome, an amphitheatre, cemetery, crypt, grave, sepulcher, or sandpit.

arena vomitory A **vomitory** through a section of seats which provides a special access, for actors, to an arena stage.

areola Diminutive of **area.**

area, 1: fragment of an ancient marble plan of Rome depicting the area of Apollo

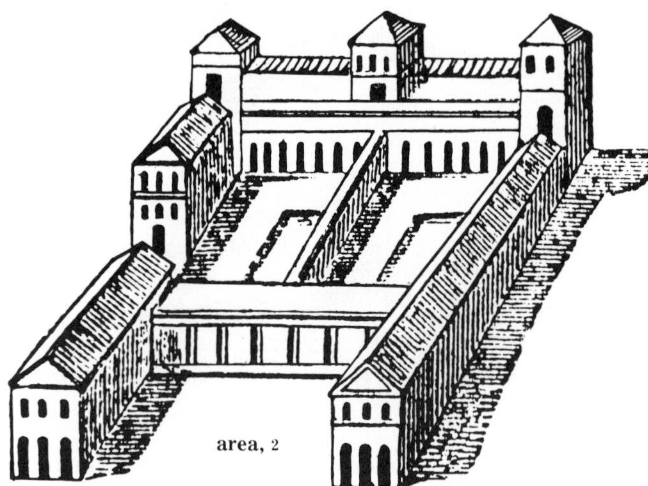

area, 2

area, 3

areostyle, araeostyle See **intercolumniation, 2.**

areosystyle See **araeosystyle.**

Argei Certain sites in the ancient city of Rome (probably between 24 and 27 in number) with small chapels attached to them, consecrated by Numa for the performance of religious rites.

argurokopeion In ancient Greece, a place where money was coined; a mint.

aris See **arris.**

ark An ornamental, enclosed repository in a synagogue for the scrolls of the Torah.

ark

armariolum A wardrobe in the treasury of cathedrals and monastic churches for keeping the eucharistic and other vestments; an **armarium, 2.**

armarium **1.** Same as **ambry.** **2.** Originally a place for keeping arms; later a cupboard, in which were kept, not only arms, but also clothes, books, money, ornaments, and other articles of value. **3.** A division in an ancient Roman library.

armature Structural ironwork in the form of framing or bars (commonly employed in medieval buildings) used to reinforce slender columns, or to consolidate canopies or hanging members such as bosses, and in tracery.

armory **1.** A building used for military training or storage of military equipment. **2.** A weapons-manufacturing plant.

armoury Same as **armory.**

aroura Same as **arura.**

arrectarium In ancient Roman construction, an upright pillar or post which is load-bearing.

arrière-voussure, rear arch **1.** A **rear vault, 2;** an arch or vault in a thick wall carrying the thickness of the wall, esp. one over a door or window frame. **2.** A relieving arch behind the face of a wall.

arriere-voussure

arris, aris **1.** An external angular intersection between two planar faces (an edge), or two curved faces, as in moldings or between two flutes on a Doric column or between a flute and the fillet on an Ionic or a Corinthian column. **2.** The sharp edge of a brick.

arris gutter A V-shaped wooden gutter fixed to the eaves of a building.

arris rail A rail of triangular section, usually formed by slitting diagonally a strip of square section; the broadest surface forms the base.

arris tile Any angularly shaped tile.

arrow loop, loophole A vertical slit for archers in medieval fortification walls, with jambs deeply splayed toward the interior.

arrow loop

arsenal 1. A repository or magazine for arms and military equipment. 2. An establishment where arms or military equipment is manufactured. 3. A repository for any type of equipment.

Art Deco A decorative style stimulated by the Paris Exposition Internationale des Arts Decoratifs et Industrieles Modernes of 1925, widely used in the architecture of the 1930s, including skyscraper designs such as the Chrysler Building in New York; characterized by sharp angular or zigzag surface forms and ornaments. Also referred to as **Style Moderne.**

artemision 1. A building or shrine dedicated to the worship of Artemis. 2. (*cap.*) The Temple of Artemis, Ionic octastyle, dipteral, built at Ephesus during the reign of Alexander the Great (336–323 B.C.). In many respects this was the most magnificent and celebrated of all Greek temples; the last temple built on the site ranked as one of the Seven Wonders of the World.

Art Nouveau A style of decoration in architecture and applied art developed principally in France and Belgium toward the end of the 19th cent.; characterized by organic and dynamic forms, curving design, and whiplash lines. The German version is called *Jugendstil,* the Austrian variant *Sezession;* in Italy one speaks of *Stile Liberty,* in Spain of *Modernismo.*

Arts and Crafts English movement in applied art and indirectly in architecture during the second half of the 19th cent., emphasizing the importance of craftsmanship and high standards of design for everyday objects.

arula Diminutive of **ara.**

arura An ancient Egyptian measure of area; equivalent to 2,740 sq. m.

arx The fortress or citadel of an ancient town; it contained the principal temples of the deities who presided over the city, which were placed within the enclosure for the sake of protection.

aryaka In Indian architecture, a line of five columns which symbolize the Five Dhiyana Buddhas.

asarotum A type of painted pavement used by the ancient Romans before their use of mosaic work.

ascendant See **chambranle.**

ashlar 1. Squared building stone. 2. **Ashlar masonry.** 3. A vertical stud between the floor beams and rafters of a garret.

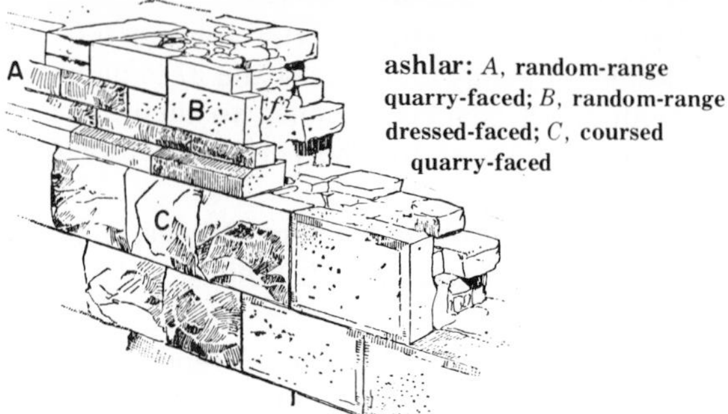

ashlar: *A*, random-range quarry-faced; *B*, random-range dressed-faced; *C*, coursed quarry-faced

ashlar brick, rock-faced brick A brick whose face has been hacked to resemble roughly hacked stone.

ashlaring 1. **Ashlars,** 1, collectively. 2. In garrets, the short wood upright pieces between the floor beams and rafters, to which wall lath is attached.

ashlar line A horizontal line at the exterior face of a masonry wall.

ashlar masonry Masonry composed of rectangular units of burnt clay or shale, or stone, generally larger in size than brick and properly bonded, having sawn, dressed, or squared beds and joints laid in mortar.

ashlar piece See **ashlar,** 3.

ashlering See **ashlaring.**

ashpan A metal receptacle beneath a grating for collection and removal of ashes.

ashpit A chamber located below the fireplace or firebox for the collection and removal of ashes.

ashpit door A cast-iron door providing access to an ashpit for ash removal.

Asiatic base A type of **Ionic base;** consists of a lower disk with horizontal fluting or scotias (there may be a plinth below the disk) and an upper torus decorated with horizontal fluting on relief; developed in Asia minor.

asidua Same as **assidua.**

aspasticum, aspaticum An apartment or place adjoining the ancient churches or basilicas in which the bishop or presbyters received visits of devotion, ceremony, or business.

aspaticum Same as **salutatorium.**

aspersorium A holy-water stoup or font.

asphaltum Natural asphalt.

asser In ancient carpentry: **1.** A rib or bracket of an arched ceiling. **2.** A purlin or a rafter of a roof. **3.** A beam or joist.

assidua That part of a church in which the altar is placed.

assis In ancient Roman construction, a flat board or plank.

assize **1.** A cylindrical block of stone forming one unit in a column. **2.** A course of stonework.

assommoir A gallery built over a door or passage of a fortified place, from which stones and heavy objects could be hurled down on the enemy.

assula In ancient Roman construction, a chip of any type of material.

Assur See **Assyrian architecture.**

Assyrian architecture Architecture of the Assyrian empire (centered between the Tigris and the Upper and Lower Zab rivers in southwest Asia) was expressive of its might, as conquerors of Mesopotamia and much of the adjacent countries between the 9th and 7th cent. B.C. Mud brick was used as the building material, although stone was available; stone was used only for carved revetments and monumental decorative sculptures. Vaulting played a much greater role than in southern Mesopotamia. Excavations have uncovered large palaces and temple complexes with their ziggurats in Assyrian cities such as Assur, Calah (Nimrud), Nineveh, and Dur Sharrukin (Khorsabad), as well as extensive fortifications.

astler Old English term for **ashlar.**

pavement slab at Nimrud (end of 9th cent. B.C.)

Assyrian decorative relief

city gateway at Khorsabad (722–705 B.C.)

colored tiling from Khorsabad

Assyrian head

astragal 1. A **bead,** usually half-round, with a fillet on one or both sides. It may be plain, but the term is more correctly used to describe the classical molding consisting of a small convex molding decorated with a string of beads or bead-and-reel shapes. 2. A plain **bead molding.** Also called **roundel, baguette,** or **chaplet.** 3. A member, or combination of members, fixed to one of a pair of doors or casement windows to cover the joint between the meeting stiles and to close the clearance gap.

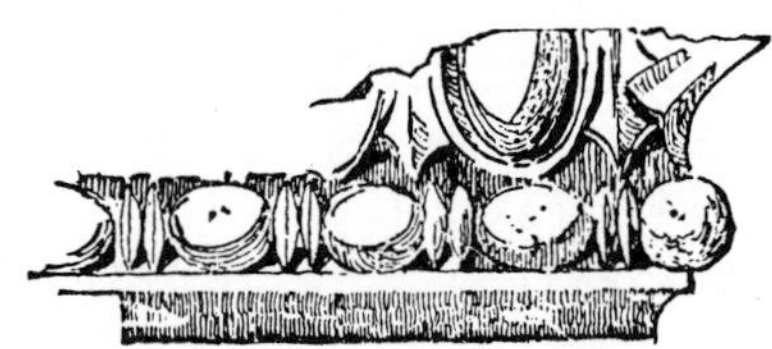

astragal,1 in Greek architecture

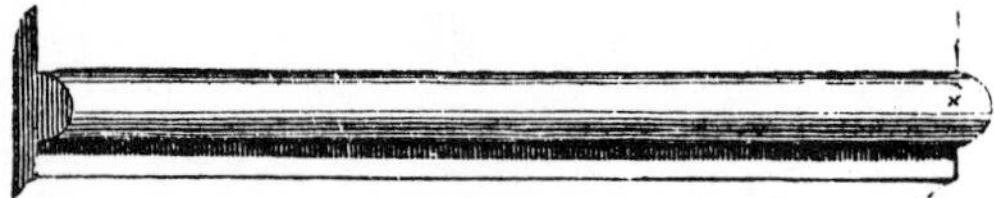

astragal,2: Theatre of Marcellus, Rome (23–13 B.C.)

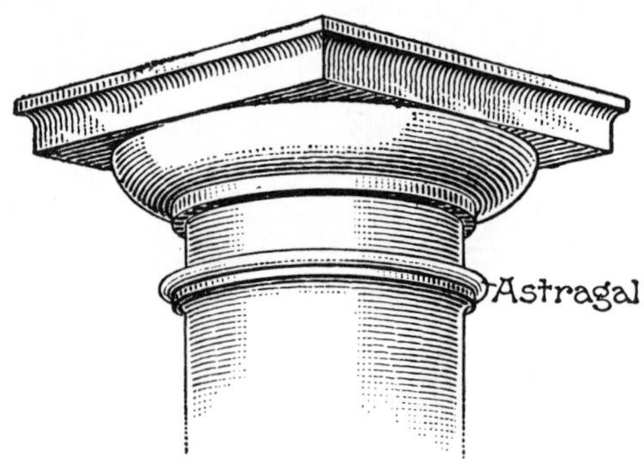

astragal,2

astragal joint A spigot-and-socket joint used on a lead **downspout** (or the like), where the socket incorporates ornamental moldings called astragals.

astreated Decorated with star-like ornaments.

astula Same as **assula.**

astylar Columnless; usually describing a façade without columns, pilasters, or the like.

asula Same as **assula.**

atadura In Maya architecture, a façade molding, above and below a continuous horizontal decorative frieze on the exterior of a building; characteristic of the **Puuc style.**

ataracea Inlaid woodwork of various colors.

ataurique Decorative leaf and flower plasterwork; esp. used in Moorish architecture.

'atebe A depressed paved area or court in front of the **ka'a** or salon in Muslim houses of the Near East.

atelier 1. An artist's workshop. 2. A place where artwork or handicrafts are produced by skilled workers. 3. A studio where the fine arts, including architecture, are taught.

Athenaeum A temple or place dedicated to Athene, or Minerva; specifically an institution founded at Rome by Hadrian for the promotion of literary and scientific studies, and imitated in the provinces.

atlantes See **atlas.**

atlas, *pl.* **atlantes** A figure (or figures) of a man used in place of a column to support an entablature; also called a **telamon.**

one of the atlantes at the Theatre of Dionysus (4th cent.)

atriolum 1. In ancient Rome, a small atrium. 2. In large ancient Roman mansions, a second or back atrium. 3. A small antechamber forming the entrance of a tomb.

atrium Corinthium

atrium **1.** The main inner hall of a Roman house with an aperture in the roof (compluvium) for rainwater and a rectangular basin (impluvium) to receive the water. Also called **cavaedium.** **2.** The forecourt of an early Christian basilica, with colonnades on all four sides, and usually a fountain for ablutions in the center.

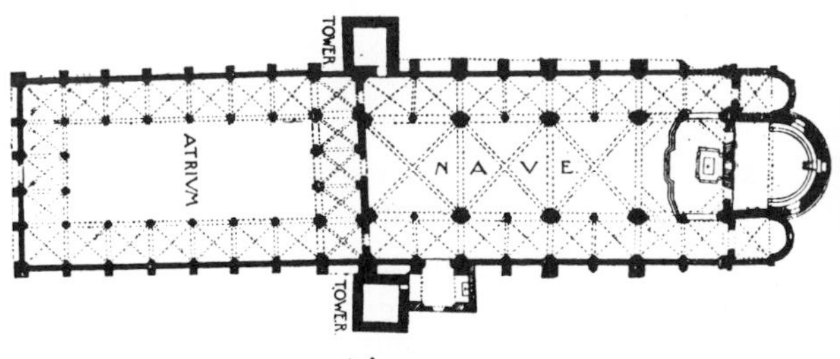

atrium,2

atrium tetrastylum

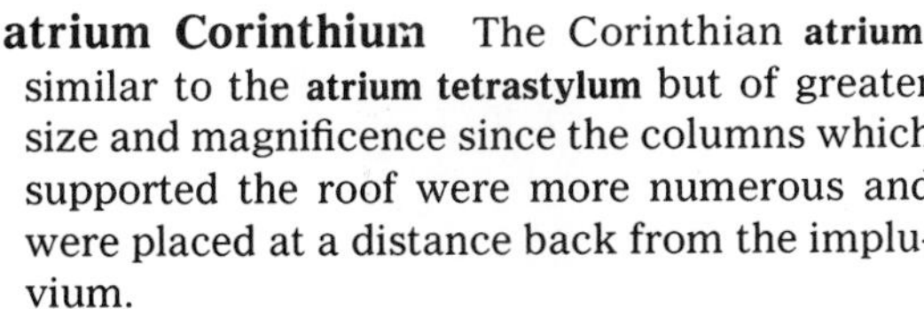

atrium Corinthium The Corinthian **atrium,** similar to the **atrium tetrastylum** but of greater size and magnificence since the columns which supported the roof were more numerous and were placed at a distance back from the impluvium.

atrium displuviatum An **atrium** with the roof sloping away from the **compluvium,** instead of toward it, so that the rainwater fell into gutters on the outside instead of into the **impluvium.**

atrium testudinatum The testudinated or covered **atrium,** which had no compluvium, the whole apartment being covered over by a roof of the **testudo** type.

atrium tetrastylum The tetrastyle **atrium,** supported by four columns, one at each corner of the impluvium.

atrium Tuscanicum

atrium Tuscanicum The Tuscan **atrium;** the simplest and probably the most ancient of all atria, adopted at Rome from the Etruscans. It could be employed only for an apartment of small dimensions; the roof structure was carried by two beams placed lengthwise from wall to wall, into which two shorter beams were mortised at equal distances from the wall, so as to form a square opening in the center between them.

attached column An **engaged column.**

attegia A Moorish hut made of reeds and thatch.

attic **1.** A **garret.** **2.** In classic building, a story built above the wall cornice. **3.** That part of the entablature above the cornice used to hide the roof of a structure or to make the structure more impressive. **4.** *(cap.)* Pertaining to the district of Attica in Greece.

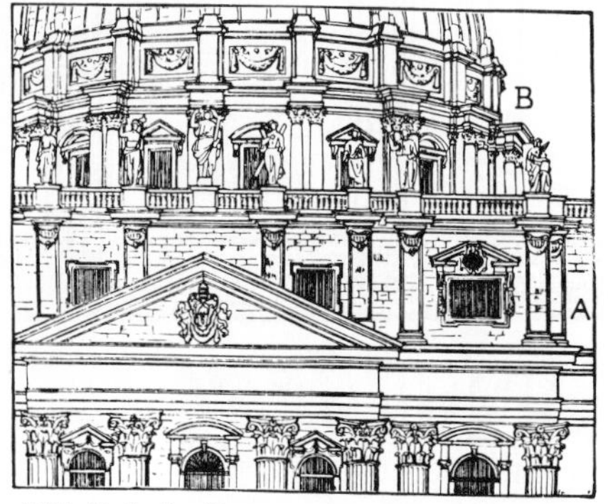

attic,2 of St. Peter's, Rome: *A*, **attic of main edifice;** *B*, **dome attic**

attic,3

Attic,4: tomb relief

Attic base An Ionic base consisting of a concave scotia between two tori; often also with a plinth.

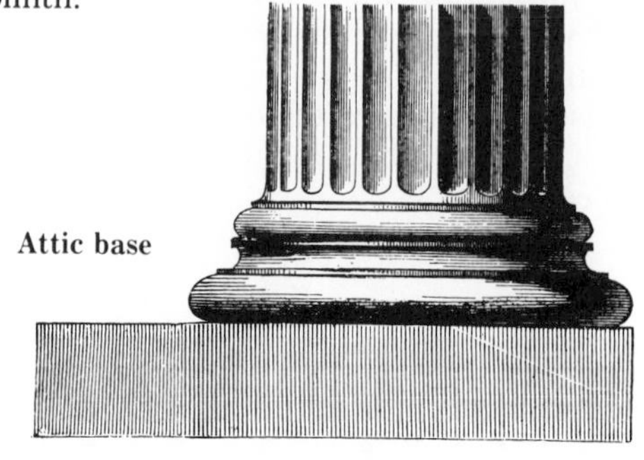

Attic base

attic order Small pillars or pilasters decorating the exterior of an **attic, 2.**

attic story See **attic, 2.**

Atticurge Said of a doorway having jambs which are inclined slightly inwards, so that the opening is wider at the threshold than at the top.

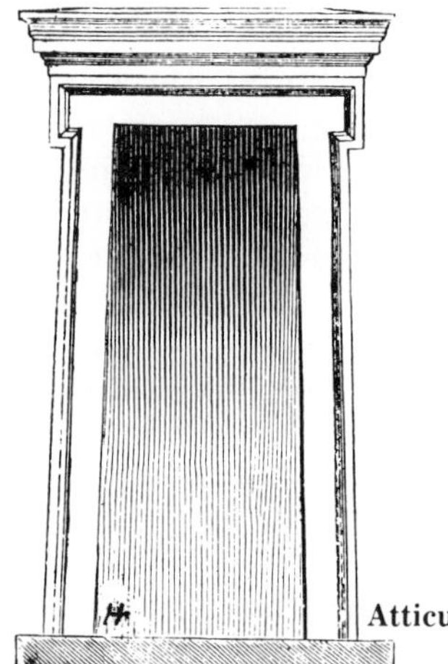

Atticurge doorway

auditorium **1.** That part of a theatre, school, or public building which is set aside for the audience for listening and viewing. **2.** In ancient Rome, a place where poets, orators, and critics presented their compositions.

auditory In ancient churches, that part of the church where the people usually stood to be instructed in the gospel; now called the **nave.**

Augusteum A building or temple dedicated to the deified Augustus.

aula In ancient architecture, a court or hall, esp. an open court attached to a house.

aulaeum **1.** On the ancient Roman stage, a curtain which portrayed a scene; it was lowered at the beginning of the play and raised when the play was over. **2.** A hanging used in a temple to veil the statue of a divinity. **3.** A hanging in a house, used as a tapestry, curtains, or (when hung from the ceiling) as a canopy. **4.** A hanging on the outside of a house to close an open gallery. **5.** A hanging stretched over colonnades to form a tent.

aula regia The central portion of the scene in the Greek and Roman theatres, esp. for tragic performances, representing a noble mansion.

auleolum A small church or chapel.

aumbry See **ambry.**

aureole A pointed oval frame or glory around the head or body of a sacred figure; the radiance surrounding it.

quatrefoil aureole

aureole

auvanna Same as **antevanna.**

avant-corps That part of a building which projects prominently from the main mass, e.g., a pavilion.

aventurine Glass (or glazes) containing colored spangles of nonglassy material.

avenue **1.** A wide street, usually planted with trees; generally straight. **2.** A way of approach or access.

awning pole See **malus.**

axed brick, rough-axed brick A brick, shaped with an ax, that has not been trimmed; when laid, the joints for such bricks are thicker than those for gauged brick.

axed work A hand-dressed stone surface showing toolmarks made by an ax, pick, or bushhammer.

axicia **1.** In ancient construction, the upright axis around which a door pivoted. **2.** Same as **assis.**

ayaka A type of pillar, such as one placed on a platform attached to a Buddhist **stupa.**

Aya Sophia Same as **Hagia Sophia.**

azekura An ancient Japanese building, used for storage, made of logs which have been carefully shaped so that they are triangular in section.

azotea, azothea In Spanish architecture, the terrace or platform on the roof of a house.

Aztec architecture An architecture emerging in the 14th cent. from the austere **Toltec architecture.** Aztec pyramids characteristically supported two temples, dedicated to their major gods; parallel stairways led to a common platform on which the temples were placed. The temple pyramids were surrounded by a **coatepantli.** At Malinalco, Mexico, the entrance to the temple is a serpent's mouth; its circular interior is hewn out of rock and carved with eagles and jaguars—symbols of the two Aztec warrior fraternities. Destruction of Aztec architecture by the Spanish left few remains; the Aztec capital of Tenochtitlán is entirely buried under modern Mexico City.

azulejo An earthenware tile of Spanish manufacture, painted and enameled in rich colors, esp. one having a metallic luster.

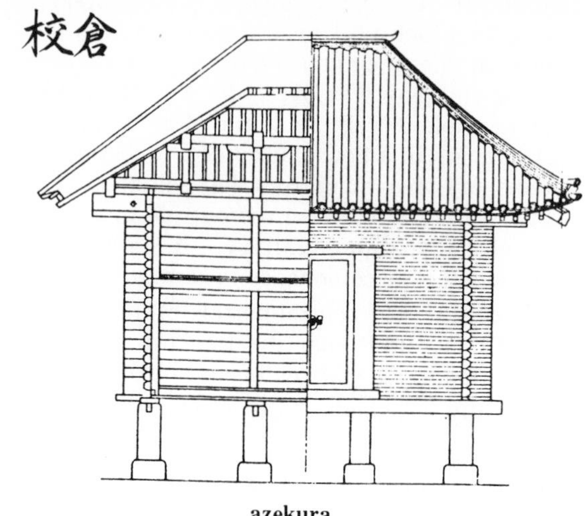

azekura

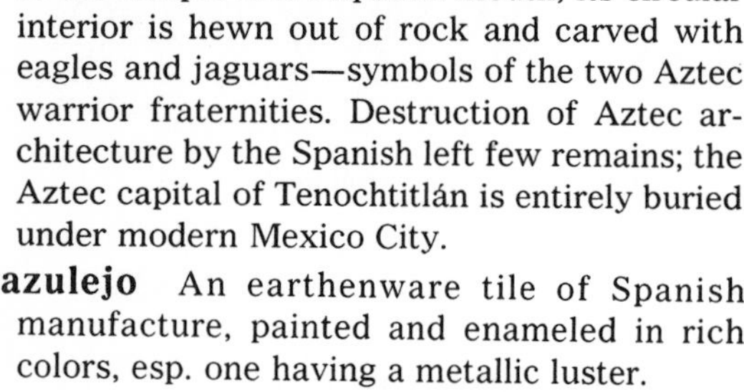
temple pyramid at the Aztec capital of Tenochtitlán (c. 1325)

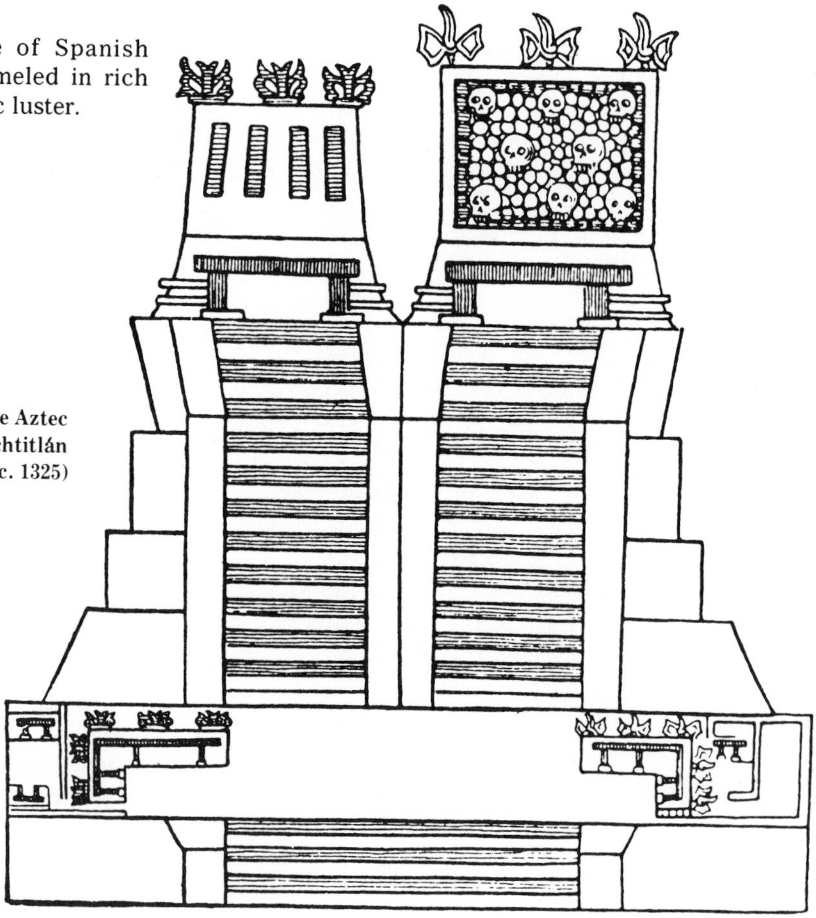

Baalbek The site of ruins of an important city in ancient times in the Bekaa valley of eastern Lebanon; contains a large temple compound, constructed in the 2nd and early part of the 3rd cent. A.D., which includes an enormous temple to the Syrian sun god Baal; hence it also carried the Greek name Heliopolis. The temple is set within a huge court and preceded by a hexagonal atrium and dodecastyle portico. Adjacent to the main temple stood a Temple of Bacchus and a circular Temple of Venus. The entire complex was built in the Baroque fashion of late imperial Rome.

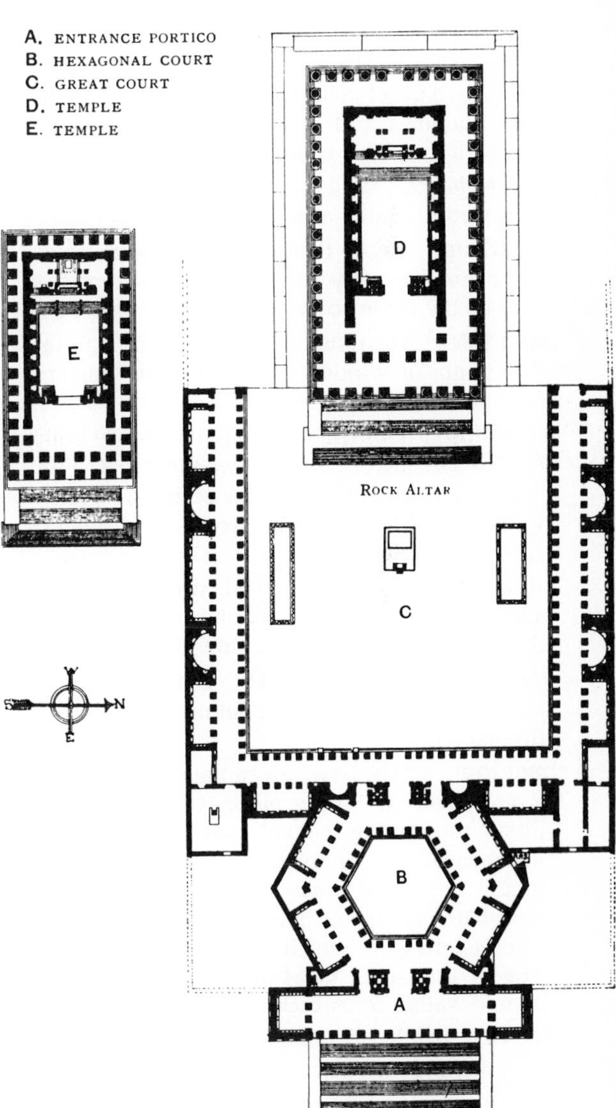

plan of Baalbek

bab In Muslim architecture, a gate or door.

Babylonian architecture In ancient Babylon, architecture characterized by: mud-brick construction; walls articulated by pilasters and recesses (for aesthetic and structural reasons), sometimes faced with burnt and glazed brick; narrow rooms, mostly covered with flat timber and mud roofs; and extensive use of bitumen in drain and pavement construction and as mortar. Elaborate palaces and temples have been unearthed which were built during the old Babylonian period (2000 to 1600 B.C.), although not in Babylon itself. The grandiose city of Babylon, capital of the Neo-Babylonian Empire, mostly was the creation of Nebuchadnezzar II (605 to 562 B.C.); planned as a huge rectangle and surrounded by a moat and a double fortification with eight gates, its center contained the holy precinct with the Temple of Marduk and the Tower of Babel, its famous **ziggurat,** from which a **processional way** led north to the Ishtar Gate, decorated with enameled blue brick and gold-colored friezes of dragons, bulls, and lions; to its west rose the Citadel, the enormous palace compound, and the vaulted terrace gardens known as the Hanging Gardens of Semiramis.

baccha In ancient Roman architecture, a lighthouse or beacon.

back **1.** The rear, reverse, unseen, more remote, or less important part of a structure, tool, or object. **2.** The support for a more prominent or visible element. **3.** The top or exposed side of a slate, tile, or the like, in contrast to the bed. **4.** The ridge or top of a horizontal member or structure like a joist, rafter, or roof. **5.** A principal rafter. **6.** The extrados or top surface of an arch, often buried in the surrounding masonry.

back arch An arch whose interior surface is different behind the face of a wall than it is at the face; a usual mode of construction in medieval buildings and in French architecture of the 17th and 18th cent.; an **arrière-voussure** or **rear arch.**

back choir Same as **retrochoir.**

backdrop On the theatre stage, a large, taut, flat canvas, usually hung from the grid at the rear of the stage to mask the backstage area.

back fillet The **return** of the margin of a groin, doorjamb, or window jamb when it projects beyond a wall.

backfilling, backfill **1.** Rough masonry built behind a facing or between two faces. **2.** Filling over the extrados of an arch. **3.** Brickwork in spaces between structural timbers. Also see **nogging.**

back gutter A gutter installed on the uphill side of a chimney on a sloping roof; used to divert water around the chimney.

back hearth, inner hearth That part of the hearth, or floor, which is contained within the fireplace itself.

backing **1.** The bevel given the upper edge of a **hip rafter.** **2.** Fitting pieces of furring onto joists to provide a level surface for laying floorboards. **3.** Shaping the back of **lining** so that it lies flat against a wall. **4.** The unexposed or unfinished inner face of a wall. **5.** Coursed masonry which is built over the extrados of an arch. **6.** Stone used for random rubble walls. **7.** A **backing brick.**

backing brick A relatively low-quality brick used behind face brick or other masonry.

backjoint In masonry, a rabbet such as that made on the inner side of a chimneypiece to receive a slip.

back-to-back house A house with a **party wall** at the rear as well as along the sides.

bada The base of a **sikhara** of a Hindu temple.

badigeon A filler or patching material used in masonry or wood work.

bagnette A **bead molding.**

bagnio **1.** A bathing establishment. **2.** A brothel. **3.** A Turkish prison.

bague An annular molding encircling the shaft of a column or pillar, either half-way between the base and capital or at lesser intervals.

baguette, bagnette, baguet **1.** A **bead molding.** **2.** A **chaplet.**

bahut **1.** In a masonry wall or parapet, the rounded upper course. **2.** A low wall surmounting a cornice to carry the roof structure.

baignoire A box in a theatre in the lowest tier.

bailey **1.** The open area within a medieval fortification; in complex sites the alley between the several layers of walls is called an "outer bailey"; the central area, the "inner bailey." **2.** The outer wall of a feudal castle.

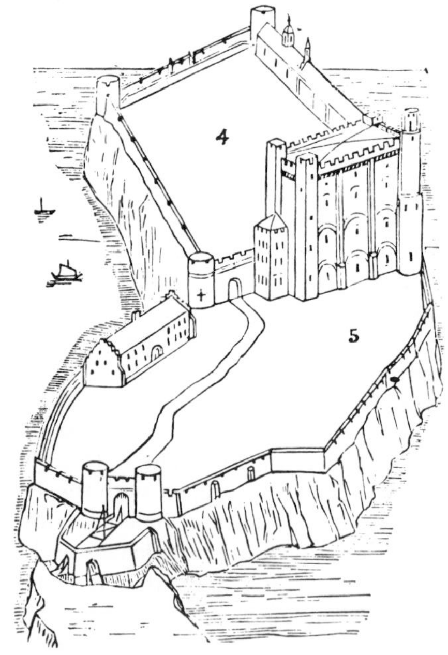

Norman castle: 4, inner bailey; 5, outer bailey

balanced step, dancing step, dancing winder One of a series of **winders** arranged so that the width of each winder tread (at the narrow end) is almost equal to the tread width in the straight portion of the adjacent stair flight.

balaneion A Greek term for a bath.

balconet A pseudo-balcony; a low ornamental railing to a window, projecting but slightly beyond the threshold or sill.

balcony **1.** A projecting platform on a building, sometimes supported from below, sometimes cantilevered; enclosed with a railing or balustrade. **2.** A projecting gallery in an auditorium; a seating area over the main floor. **3.** An elevated platform used in a permanent stage setting in a theatre.

balcony stage A balcony used as a playing area, as in the Elizabethan theatre.

baldachin, baldacchino, baldachino, baldaquin, ciborium An ornamental canopy over an altar, usually supported on columns, or a similar form over a tomb or throne.

balection molding See **bolection molding.**

balinea Same as **balnea.**

balistraria **1.** In medieval battlements, a loophole or aperture through which crossbowmen shot arrows. **2.** The room in which the *balistae* (crossbows) were kept.

two types of balistrariae

balk, baulk **1.** A squared timber used in building construction. **2.** A low ridge of earth that marks a boundary line.

balk-tie A **balk,** 1 which joins the wall posts of a timber roof, preventing the walls from spreading.

ball and flower See **ballflower.**

ballaster Same as **baluster.**

balconet to a window
above: front view; *left:* section of windowsill and balconet

baldachin

ballflower A spherical ornament composed of three conventionalized petals enclosing a ball, usually in a hollow molding, popular in the English Decorated style.

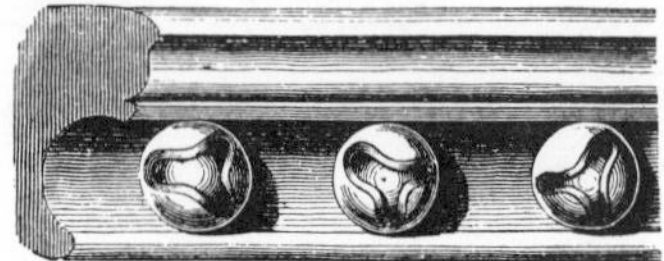
ballflower

ballistraria See **balistraria.**

ballium The court of open space within a medieval fortification; a **bailey.**

balloon A globe or round ball, placed on the top of a pillar, pediment, pier, or the like, which serves as a **crown,** 1.

balloon framing, balloon frame A system of framing a wooden building; all vertical structural elements of the exterior bearing walls and partitions consist of single studs which extend the full height of the frame, from the top of the soleplate to the roof plate; all floor joists are fastened by nails to studs.

balnea, *pl.* of **balneum** Roman baths, usually the great public ones.

balnearium, balneum In ancient Rome, a private bath.

balteus **1.** The band in the middle of the bolster of an Ionic capital. **2.** The band joining the volutes of an Ionic capital. **3.** One of the passages dividing the auditorium of ancient Roman theatres and amphitheatres horizontally into upper and lower zones.

baluster, banister **1.** One of a number of short vertical members, often circular in section, used to support a stair handrail or a coping. **2.** (*pl.*) A **balustrade.** **3.** The roll forming the side of an Ionic capital; a **bolster, pulvinus.**

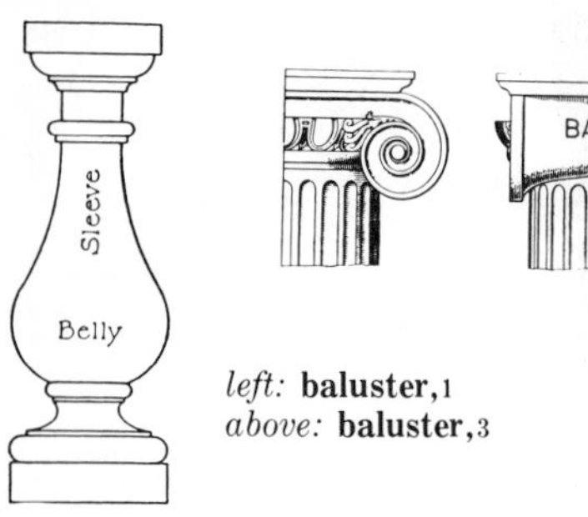

left: **baluster,**1
above: **baluster,**3

baluster column **1.** A column shaped somewhat like a baluster, with a short, massive shaft. **2.** A short, thick-set column in a subordinate position, as in the windows of early Italian campanili.

baluster column,1

baluster column,2

baluster shaft Same as **baluster column.**

baluster side On an Ionic capital, the return face (having the form of a concave roll), reaching from volute to volute.

balustrade An entire railing system (as along the edge of a balcony) including a top rail and its balusters, and sometimes a bottom rail.

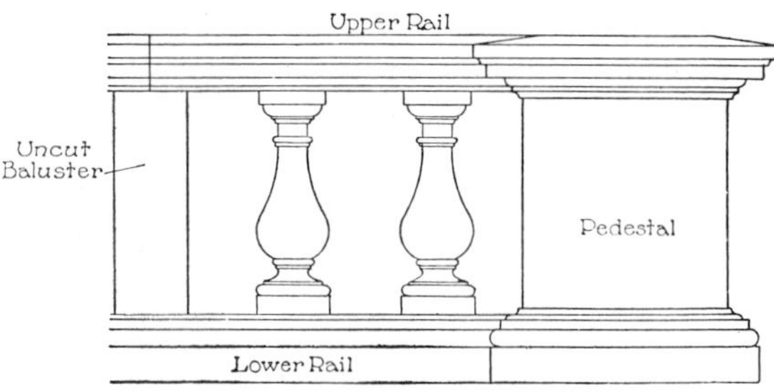

balustrade

balustrum A Latin term for a **chancel screen.**

bamli In the architecture of India, a court or courtyard.

band **1.** Any horizontal flat member or molding or group of moldings projecting slightly from a wall plane and usually marking a division in the wall. Also called **band molding** or **band course.** **2.** A small, flat molding, broad, but of small projection, rectangular or slightly convex in profile, used to decorate a surface either as a continuous strip or formed into various shapes. Also called **fillet, list.** **3.** A **fascia** on the architrave of an entablature.

band,1 of paneling

bandage A strap, band, ring, or chain placed around a structure to secure and hold its parts together, as around the springing of a dome.

band course **1.** A **stringcourse.** **2.** A **band,** 1.

banded architrave In late neoclassic architecture in England, Italy, and France, an **architrave** interrupted at intervals by smooth projecting blocks, between which are set the molded portions of the architrave.

banded column, ringed column, rusticated column In Renaissance architecture and derivatives, a column with **drums** alternately larger and smaller, alternately plainer and richer in decoration, or alternately protruding. The protruding drums may be smooth or textured.

banded column, Louvre, Paris

banded impost In medieval architecture, an impost with horizontal moldings, the section of the molding of the arch above being similar to that of the shaft below.

banded impost

banded pilaster A **pilaster** decorated in the manner of a banded column.

banded rustication Courses of masonry, alternating smooth ashlar with rustication, in Renaissance architecture and derivatives.

bandelet **1.** An **annulet.** **2.** A small flat molding.

banderol, banderole, bannerol A decorative representation of a ribbon or long scroll, often bearing an emblem or inscription.

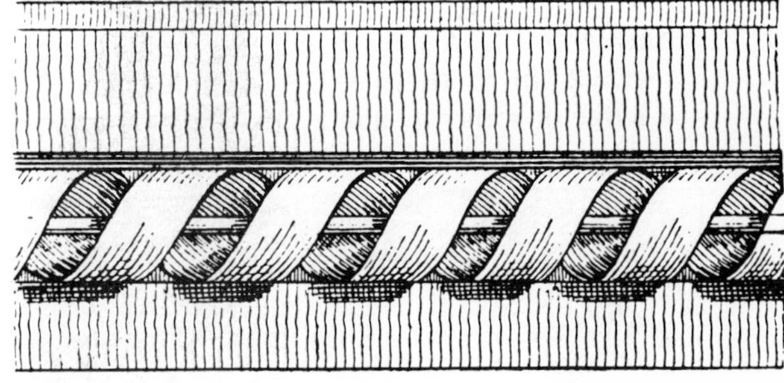
banderol

banding One or more decorative wood strips; decorative inlay.

bandlet Same as **bandelet.**

band molding A **band,** 1.

banister **1.** A handrail for a staircase. **2.** A **baluster.**

banker-mark In medieval construction, a mark cut in a dressed stone to identify the stonecutter.

bannerol See **banderol.**

banner vane, banneret A weather **vane** having the shape of a banner, balanced by a weight on the other side of the banner.

banner vane

banquette **1.** A long, bench-like upholstered seat. **2.** In southern U.S.A., a sidewalk. **3.** A ledge or walkway along the length of an aqueduct, canal, or ditch.

banquette,2

baphium In ancient Rome, an establishment for dyeing cloth.

baptisterium A cold bath, in the **frigidarium, 1.**

baptisterium

baptistery A building or part of one wherein the sacrament of baptism is administered.

baptistery

bar A gateway, as in the walls of a town or city.

bar: Temple Bar, London (1672)

baraban In early Russian architecture, same as **drum, 2.**

barai In Khmer architecture (Cambodia), a reservoir or artificial lake.

barbacan See **barbican.**

barbican, barbacan The outer defense work of a castle or town, frequently a watchtower at the gate.

left: barbican of a town
right: a detail of a barbican

bargeboard, gableboard, vergeboard A board which hangs from the projecting end of a roof, covering the gables; often elaborately carved and ornamented in the Middle Ages.

bargeboards, England (14th cent.)

barge couple **1.** One of the two rafters that support that part of a gable roof which projects beyond the gable wall. **2.** One of the rafters (under the barge course) which serve as grounds for the barge boards and carry the plastering or boarding of the soffits; also called a **barge rafter.**

barge course **1.** The coping of a wall, formed by a course of bricks set on edge. **2.** In a tiled roof, the part of the tiling which projects beyond the principal rafters **(bargeboards)** where there is a gable.

barge rafter Same as **barge couple, 2.**

barge spike, boat spike A long spike, square in cross section, used in timber construction.

barge stone One of the stones, generally projecting, which form the sloping top of a gable built of masonry.

barley-sugar column A spiral column.

Baroque A European style of architecture and decoration which developed in the 17th cent. in Italy from late Renaissance and Mannerist forms, and culminated in the churches, monasteries, and palaces of southern Germany and Austria in the early 18th cent. It is characterized by interpenetration of oval spaces, curved surfaces, and conspicuous use of decoration, sculpture, and color. Its late phase is called *Rococo*. The style prevailing in the restrained architectural climate of England and France can be called *Baroque* classicism.

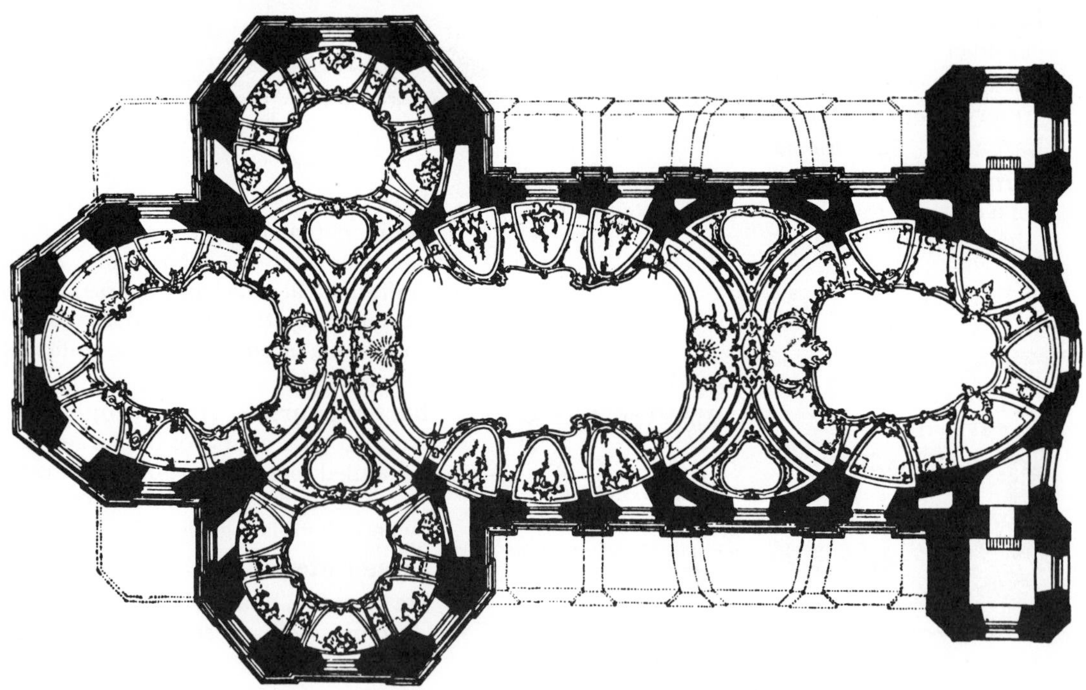

Pilgrimage Church, Vierzehnheiligen, Germany (1743 onwards)
above: **longitudinal section;** *below:* **plan of vaults**

bar post One of the posts driven into the ground to form the sides of a field gate.

barred-and-braced gate A gate with a diagonal brace to reinforce the horizontal timbers.

barred gate A gate with one or more horizontal timber rails.

barrel arch An arch formed of a curved solid plate or slab, as contrasted with one formed with individual curved members or ribs.

barrel bolt, tower bolt A door bolt which moves in a cylindrical casing; not driven by a key.

barrel ceiling A ceiling of semicylindrical shape.

barrel roof, barrel shell roof **1.** A roof of semicylindrical section; capable of spanning long distances parallel to the axis of the cylinder. **2.** A **barrel vault.**

barrel vault, barrel roof, cradle vault, tunnel vault, wagonhead vault, wagon vault A masonry vault of plain, semicircular cross section supported by parallel walls or arcades; a vault having a semicylindrical roof.

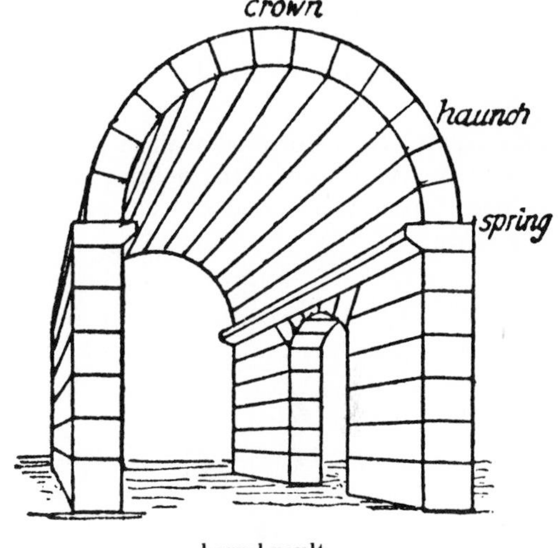

barrel vault

barrel vault, Temple of Venus and Rome, Rome (123–135 A.D.)

barrow An elongated artificial mound protecting a prehistoric chamber tomb or **passage grave.**

barstone One of two upright stones, placed on each side of a fireplace (before the invention of grates) to receive the ends of a metal bar.

bartizan On a fortified wall, a small overhanging structure with lookout holes and loops, often at a corner or near an entrance gateway.

bartizan

bar tracery A pattern formed by interlocking bars of stone within the arch of a Gothic window.

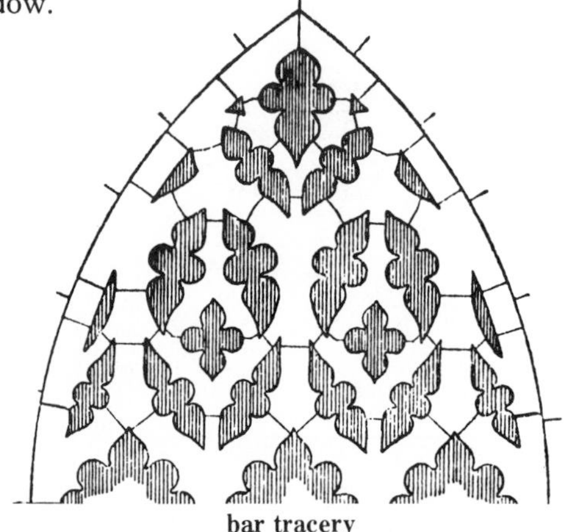
bar tracery

basadi A Jain temple or monastery (India).

bascule A structure that rotates about an axis, as a seesaw, with a counterbalance (for the weight of the structure) at one end.

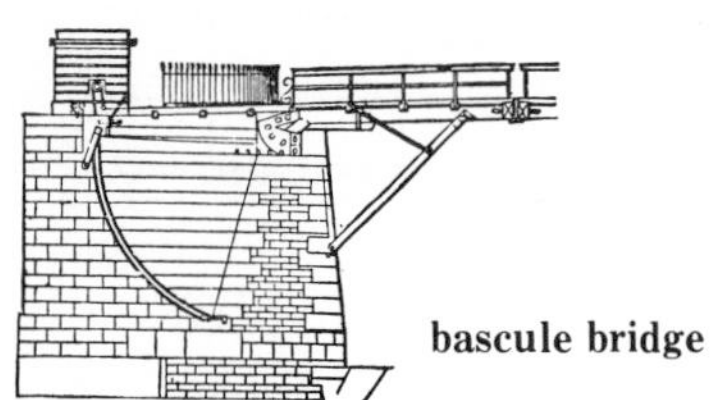
bascule bridge

base **1.** The lowest (and often widest) visible part of a building, often distinctively treated. A base is distinguished from a foundation or footing in being visible rather than buried. **2.** A low, thickened section of a wall; a **wall base.** Also see **socle.** **3.** Lower part of a column or pier, wider than the shaft, and resting on a plinth, pedestal, podium, or stylobate. Also see **Asiatic base, Attic base.**

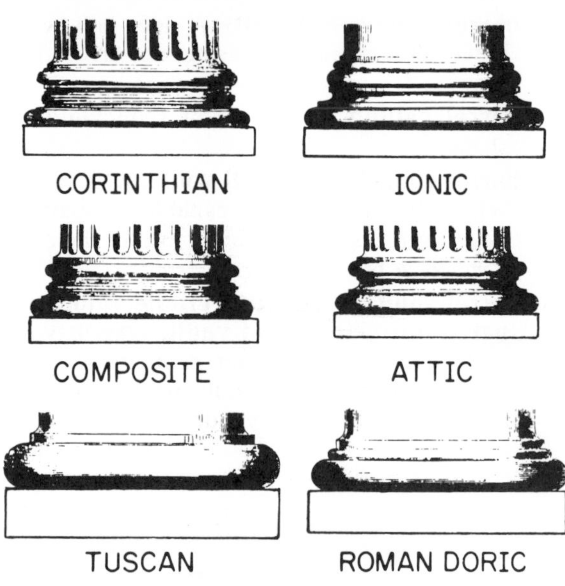

types of bases,3

Dodecagonal base,3: Temple of Apollo, Didyma, near Miletus (c. 330 B.C.–41 A.D.)

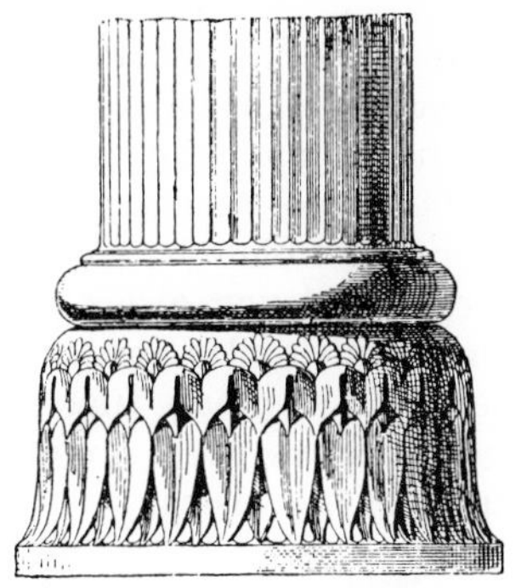

Persian

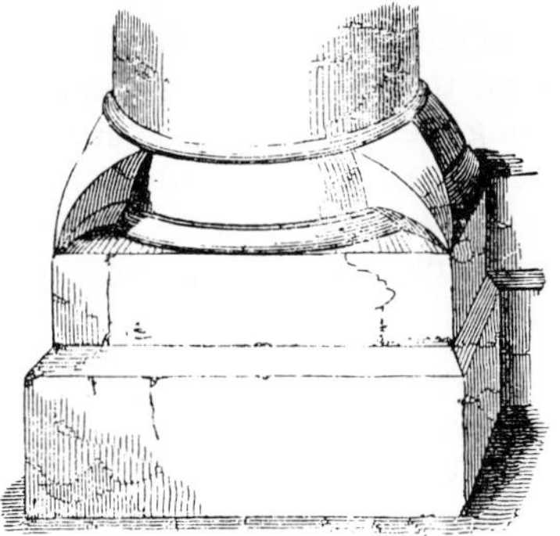

Norman

Transition

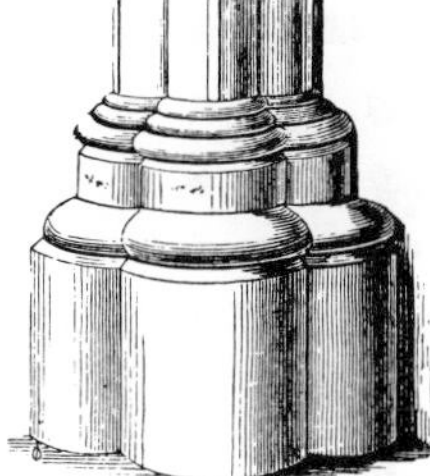

Early English

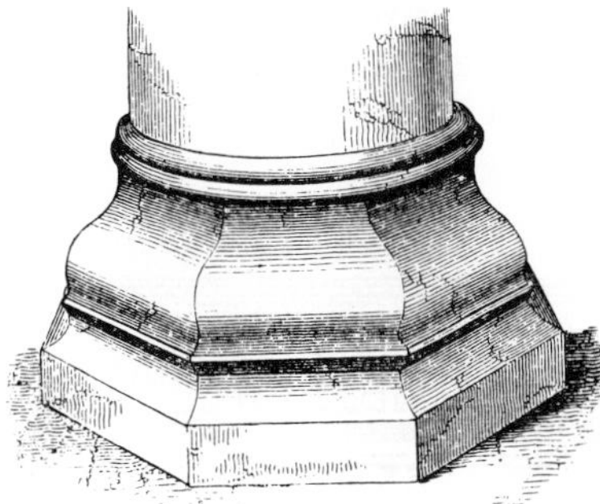

Decorated

Decorated

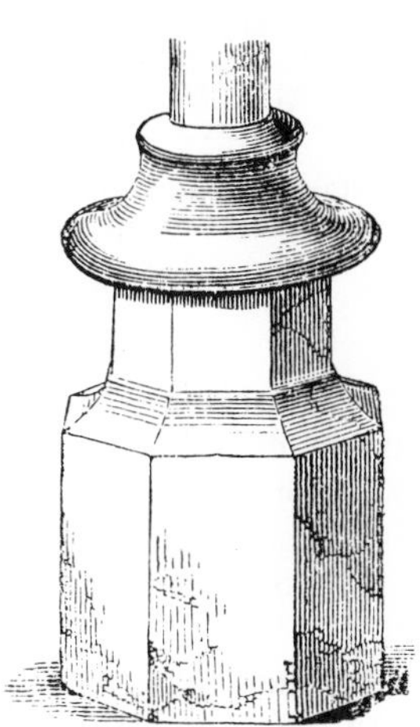

Perpendicular

base block **1.** A block of any material, generally with little or no ornament, forming the lowest member of a base, or itself fulfilling the functions of a base, as a member applied to the foot of a door or to window trim. **2.** A rectangular block at the base of a casing or column which the baseboard abuts.

base cap See **base molding, 1.**

base-court, basse-cour **1.** The outer court or yard of a castle or mansion. **2.** On a farm, a service yard often reserved for fowl. **3.** A lesser or service courtyard in any building.

basement **1.** Usually the lowest story of a building, either partly or entirely below grade. **2.** The lower part of the wall or walls of any building. **3.** The substructure of a column or arch.

basement,1 approximately the same height as principal story; Palazzo Stoppani, Rome

base molding **1.** Molding used to trim the upper edge of interior baseboard; a **base cap.** **2.** A projecting molding or band of moldings near the base of a wall, sometimes placed directly over the plinth or a short distance above it.

base shoe, base shoe molding, floor molding, shoe molding A molding used next to the floor on interior baseboard.

base table A **base molding, 2.**

base tile The lowest course of tiles in a tiled wall.

basilica **1.** A Roman hall of justice, typically with a high central space lit by a clerestory and lower aisles all around it, and with apses or exedrae for the seats of the judges. **2.** The form of the early Christian church, a central high nave with clerestory, lower aisles along the sides only, with a semicircular apse at the end. Often preceded by a vestibule (narthex) and atrium. In larger basilicas, there are often transepts, and sometimes five aisles.

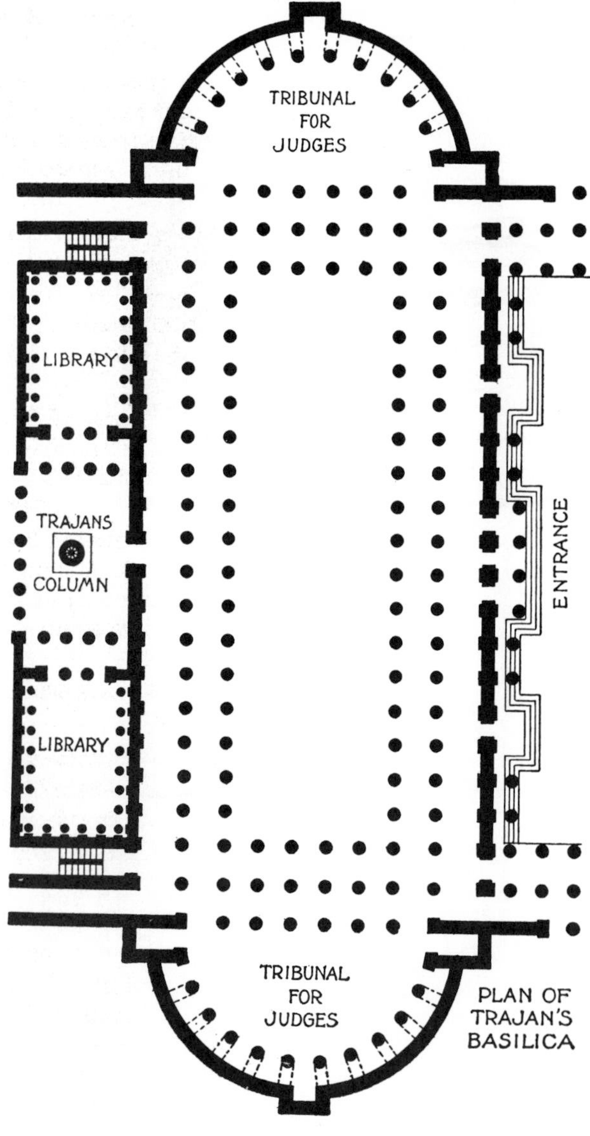

Basilica,1 of Trajan, Rome (98–113 A.D.)

Basilica of Sta. Maria Maggiore, Rome (432 A.D.)

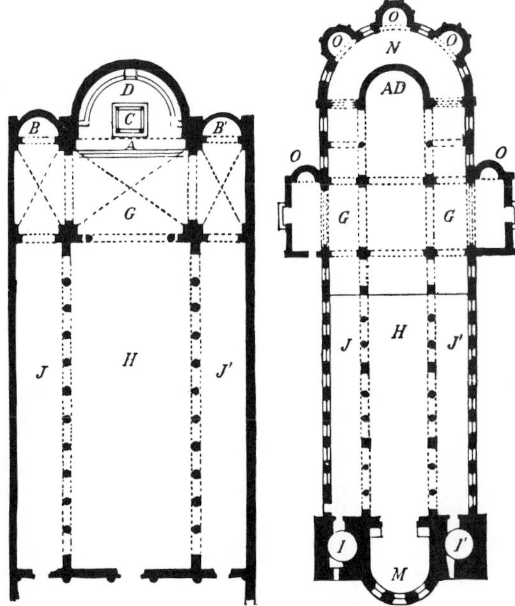

basilicas: *AD*, apse; *BB'*, secondary apses; *C*, high altar; *D*, bishop's throne; *G*, transept; *H*, nave; *I*, *I'*, towers; *J*, *J'*, aisles; *M*, western apse; *N*, aisle surrounding chief apse; *O*, *O*, apsidioles

Basilica of St. Peter See **St. Peter's Church.**

basket See **bell.**

basket capital A **capital** having interlaced bands resembling the weave of a basket; used in Byzantine architecture.

basket capital

basket-handle arch, basket arch, semielliptical arch A flattened arch designed by joining a quarter circle to each end of a false ellipse.

basket-handle arch

basket weave A checkerboard pattern of bricks, flat or on edge.

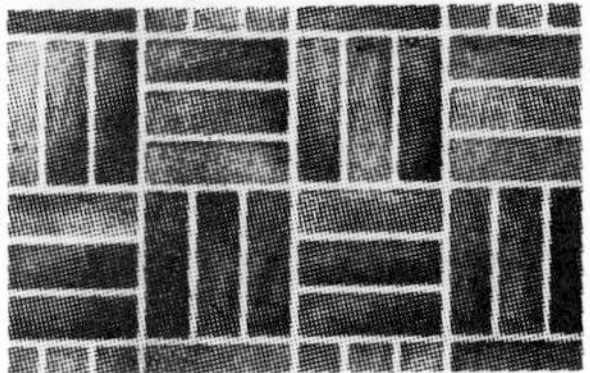
basket weave

bas-relief, basso-relievo, basso-rilievo A carving, embossing, or casting moderately protruded from the background plane; low relief.

bas-relief

basse-cour See **base-court.**

basso-rilievo, basso-relievo See **bas-relief.**

bas-taille Same as **bas-relief.**

bastard ashlar, bastard masonry **1.** Stone, in thin blocks, used to face a brick or rubble wall; square-hewn and laid to resemble **ashlar.** **2.** Ashlar stones which are only roughly dressed at the quarry.

bastard masonry See **bastard ashlar.**

bastel house, bastille house, bastle house A partly fortified house whose lowest story usually is vaulted.

bastide **1.** A medieval settlement built for defense purposes and generally laid out with a geometric plan, esp. in France. **2.** A small rural dwelling in southern France.

bastide,1

bastille, bastile **1.** A fortification or castle, frequently used as a prison. **2.** A tower or bulwark in the fortifications of a town.

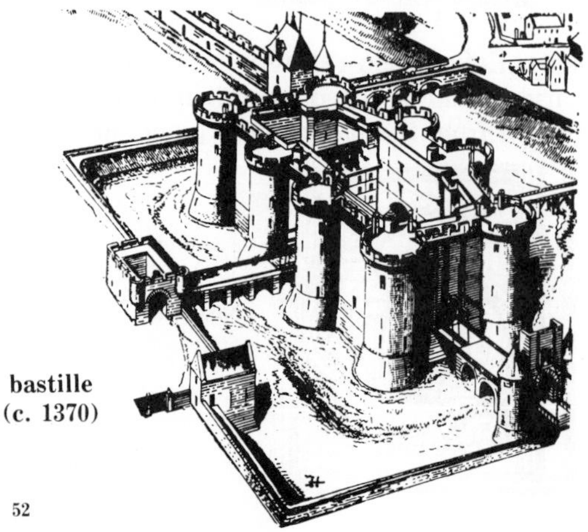

bastille (c. 1370)

bastille house A **bastel house.**

bastion A defense work, round, rectangular, or polygonal in plan, projecting from the outer wall of a fortification, principally to defend the adjacent perimeter.

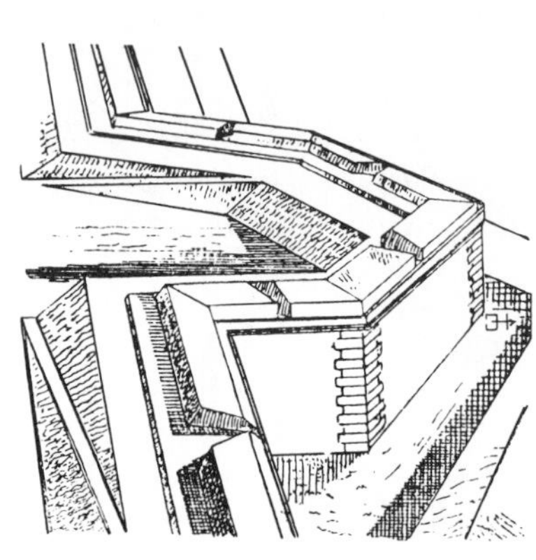

bastion

A, **bastion:** *a*, *a*, **curtain angles;** *b*, *b*, **shoulder angles;** *c*, **salient angle;** *ab*, *ab*, **flanks;** *bc*, *bc*, **faces;** *aa*, **gorge;** *ad*, *ad*, **parts of curtains**

bastle house See **bastel house.**

baston, baton, batoon **1.** A **torus.** **2.** A **batten.**

batement light A window with its lower edge cut diagonally rather than horizontally so as to fit an arch or rake below; esp. used in **perpendicular tracery.**

A, **batement light**

bath **1.** An open tub used as a fixture for bathing. **2.** The room containing the bathtub. **3.** *(pl.)* The Roman and Greek public bathing establishments, consisting of hot, warm, and cool plunges, sweat rooms, athletic and other facilities; **balnea, thermae.** The later Roman baths consisted of at least three chambers, each with separate compartments for the two sexes: **tepidarium,** a room heated with warm air, intended to promote perspiration after undressing; **caldarium,** where the hot bath was taken in a tub (*solium*) or basin; and **frigidarium,** where the final cold bath was taken.

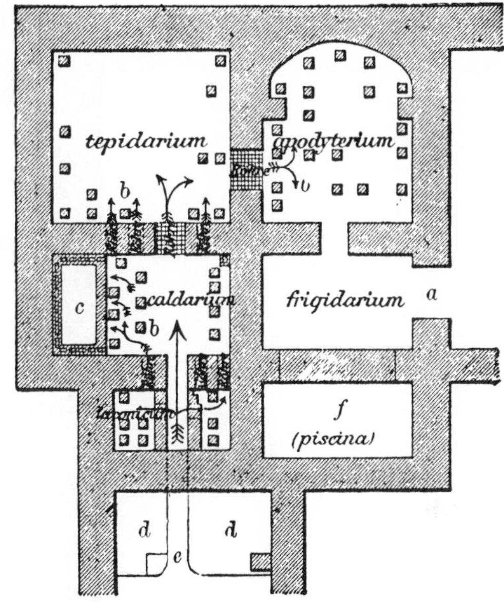

a, entrance; *b,b*, pipes; *c*, warm bath; *d*, furnace room; *e*, stove; *f*, cold bath

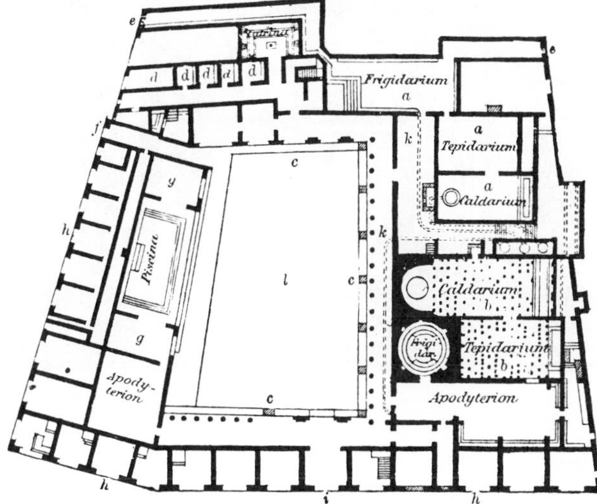

a,a,a, women's bath; *b,b*, men's bath; *c,c,c*, colonnade; *d,d,d,d,d*, single baths; *e,e*, entrance to women's bath; *f*, side entrance; *g,g*, waiting rooms; *h,h,h*, shops; *i*, chief entrance; *k,k*, heating apparatus; *l*, porticus

bath, 3

restored interior of the tepidarium,
Baths of Caracalla,
Rome (211–217 A.D.);
also see illustration
under tepidarium

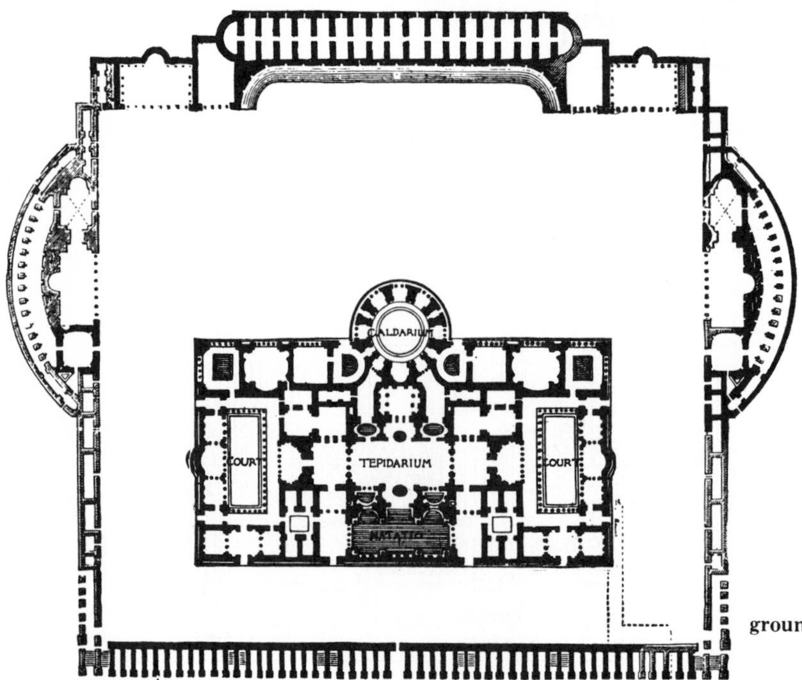

ground plan of the Baths of Caracalla

baton A **batten.**

bâtons rompus Short, straight pieces of convex molding, as those forming Norman or Romanesque chevrons and zigzags.

batoon A **batten.**

batted work, broad tooled A hand-dressed stone surface scored from top to bottom in narrow parallel strokes (usually 8 to 10 per inch) (approx. 3 to 4 per centimeter), by use of a batting tool. The strokes may be vertical or oblique.

batten **1.** A narrow strip of wood applied to cover a joint along the edges of two parallel boards in the same plane. **2.** A strip of wood fastened across two or more parallel boards to hold them together. **3.** A flat strip of wood attached to a wall as a base for lathing, plastering, etc. **4.** In roofing, a wood strip applied over boards or roof structural members; used as a base for the attachment of slate, wood, or clay-tile shingles.

batten door, ledged door, unframed door A wood door without **stiles** which is constructed of vertical boards held together by horizontal **battens, 2** on the back side.

battened column A column consisting of two longitudinal shafts, rigidly connected to each other.

battened wall, strapped wall A wall to which battens have been affixed.

battening Narrow battens or wood strips attached to a wall for the purpose of receiving lath and plaster.

batten seam A seam in metal roofing which is formed around a wood strip.

battered Inclined from the vertical. A wall is said to batter when it recedes as it rises.

battered wall A wall that is **battered.**

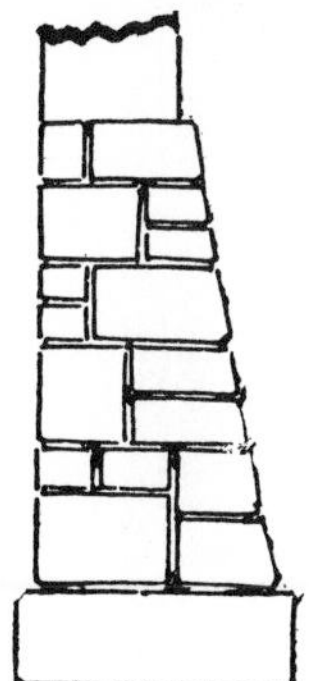

battered wall

battlement, embattlement **1.** A fortified parapet with alternate solid parts and openings, termed respectively "merlons" and "embrasures" or "crenels" (hence crenelation). Generally for defense, but employed also as a decorative motif. **2.** A roof or platform serving as battle post.

battlements: *above,* Verona; *below,* Yorkshire

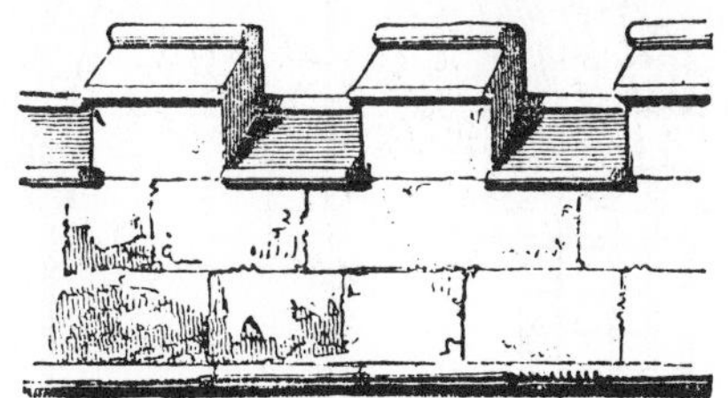

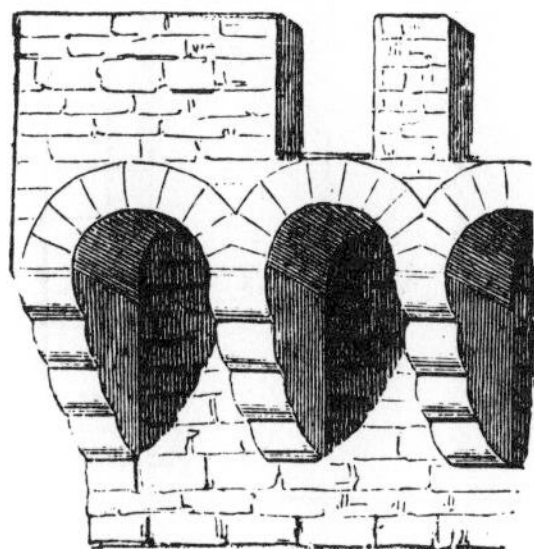

battlement at upper part of town wall, Avignon

Bauhaus A school of design established in Weimar, Germany, by Walter Gropius in 1919. The term became virtually synonymous with modern teaching methods in architecture and the applied arts, and with a functional aesthetic for the industrial age.

baulk Same as **balk.**

baulk-tie See **balk-tie.**

bawn A fortified enclosure, often of mud or stone, surrounding a farmyard or castle; esp. in Ireland.

bay **1.** Within a structure, a regularly repeated spatial element defined by beams or ribs and their supports. **2.** A protruded structure with a **bay window**. **3.** The free or light space between sash bars. **4.** In landscape architecture, a recess or alcove formed by plants in a design.

one bay of an arcade

bay at the nave, Notre Dame, Paris (1163–1220)

bayle The open space contained between the first and second walls of a fortified castle; a **bailey, 1.**

bay leaf A stylized laurel leaf used in the form of a garland to decorate torus moldings.

bayt **1.** A Muslim dwelling, generally for one family, e.g., a tent or house. **2.** In the early Muslim palace complex, a separate dwelling unit.

bay window **1.** The window of a protruded bay. **2.** Commonly, the windowed bay itself, rising from the ground for one or more stories. Also see **bow window, cant window, compass window, oriel, 1.**

examples of one- and two-story bay windows

bazaar A marketplace where goods are exposed for sale; esp. in the East, consisting either of small shops or stalls in a narrow street or series of streets, or of a certain section of town under one roof and divided into narrow passageways.

bead **1.** A **bead molding.** **2.** A narrow wood strip, molded on one edge, against which a door or window sash closes; a **stop bead.** **3.** A strip of metal or wood used around the periphery of a pane of glass to secure it in a frame, ventilator, or sash; a **stop.** **4.** A pearl-shaped carved decoration on moldings or other ornaments, usually in series, or in conjunction with other shapes; a **beading.** Also see **bead and reel.** **5.** A molding decorated with **beading;** an **astragal, 1** or **chaplet.** **6.** Used in combination with other terms to describe the function or position of a beaded molding, such as **quirk bead, corner bead,** etc.

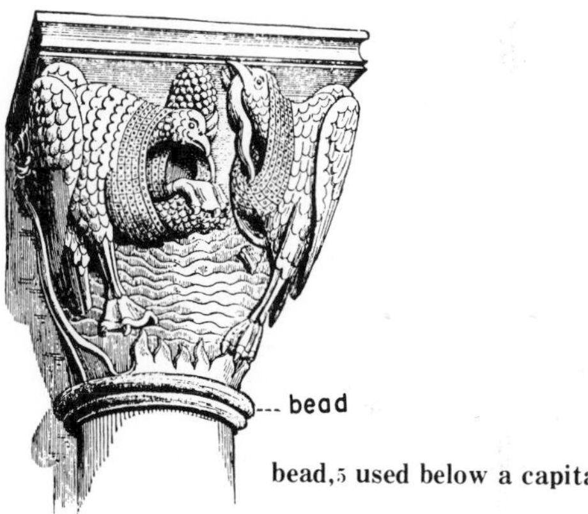

bead,5 used below a capital

bead and butt, bead butt, bead butt work Framed work in which the panel is flush with the framing and has a bead run on two edges in the direction of the grain; the ends are left plain.

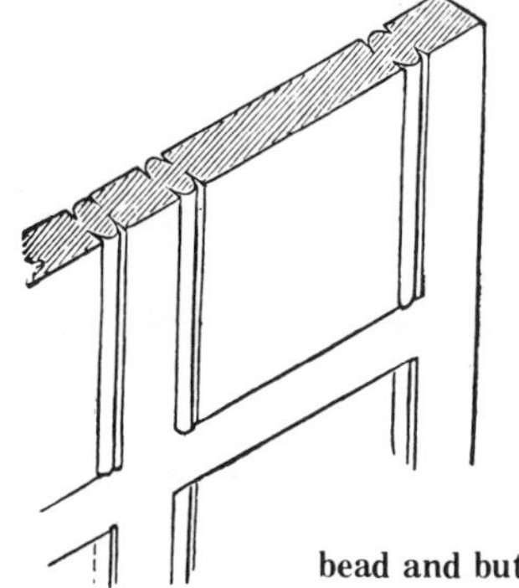

bead and butt

bead and flush panel See **beadflush panel.**

bead and quirk See **quirk bead.**

bead and reel, reel and bead A semiround convex molding decorated with a pattern of disks alternating with round or elongated beads.

bead and reel

bead butt, bead butt work See **bead and butt.**

bead, butt, and square Similar to **bead and butt** but having the panels flush on the beaded face only, and showing square reveals on the other.

beadflush panel, bead-and-flush panel A panel which is flush with the surrounding framing and finished with a flush bead on all edges of the panel.

bead house A dwelling for poor religious people, located near the church in which the founder was interred, and for whose soul the beadsmen or beadswomen were required to pray.

beading Collectively the bead moldings used in ornamenting a given surface; also see **bead.**

bead molding A small, convex molding of semicircular or greater profile; also called a **half round;** a **roundel,** 3; a **baguette,** 1.

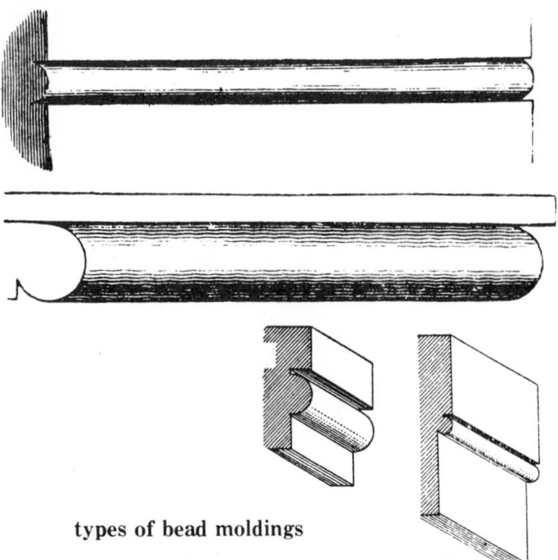

types of bead moldings

beadwork Same as **beading.**

beakhead An ornament; any of several fantastic, animal-like heads with tapered, down-pointed beaks; frequently used in richly decorated Norman doorways. Also see **catshead.**

beakheads: *lower right:* a beakhead combined with a tooth ornament

beakhead molding, bird's-beak molding Same as **beak molding,** 2.

beak molding **1.** A pendant fillet with a channel behind it on the edge of a corona, larmier, or stringcourse, etc., so called because in profile it resembles a bird's beak. **2.** A molding enriched with carved birds' heads or beaks.

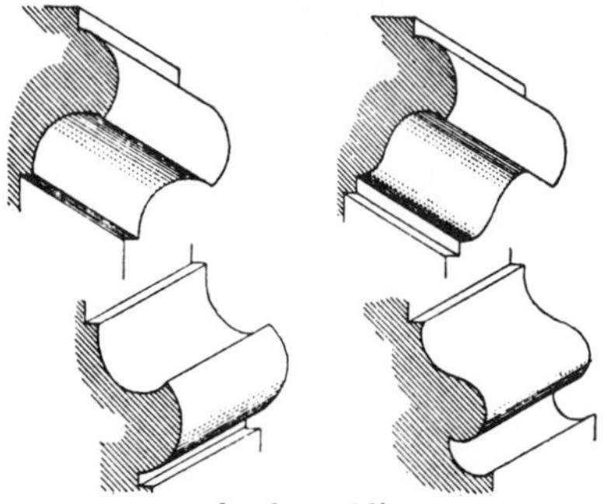

beak moldings

beam A structural member whose prime function is to carry transverse loads, as a joist, girder, rafter, or purlin.

beam anchor, joist anchor, wall anchor A metal **tie** used to anchor a beam or joist to a wall, or to tie a floor securely to a wall.

beam ceiling **1.** A ceiling, usually of wood, made in imitation of exposed floor beams with the flooring showing between. **2.** The underside of a floor, showing the actual beams, and finished to form a ceiling.

beam fill, beam filling Masonry, brickwork, or cement fill, usually between joists or horizontal beams at their supports; provides increased fire resistance.

beam iron Same as **beam anchor.**

beaumontage A resin, beeswax, and shellac mixture used for filling small holes or cracks in wood or metal.

Beaux Arts architecture Historical and eclectic design on a monumental scale, as taught at the Ecole des Beaux Arts in Paris in the 19th cent.

bed chamber An apartment or chamber intended for a bed, or for sleeping and resting.

bed molding **1.** A molding of the cornice of an entablature situated beneath the corona and immediately above the frieze. **2.** The lowest member of a band of moldings. **3.** Any molding under a projection, as between eaves and sidewalls.

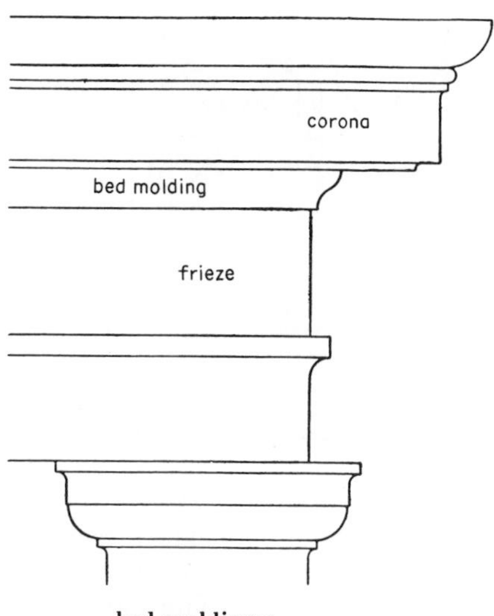

bed molding, 1

bed place In a Dutch Colonial house, an alcove into which a bed is built.

beehive tomb, tholos tomb A monumental underground tomb in the form of a beehive, used in the Mycenaean period.

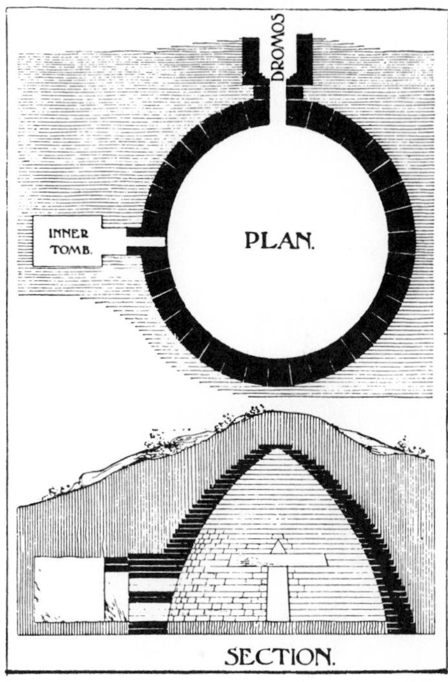

Beehive Tomb of Atreus at Mycenae (1325 B.C.)

bee house see **apiary.**

beggin, begging **1.** A dwelling of larger size than a cottage. **2.** In the north of England and in Scotland, a house; esp. applied to a hut covered with mud or turf.

beit See **bayt.**

beit hilani **1.** In northern Syria, a type of palace in the first millennium B.C. having a forward section with two large transverse rooms, a portico with one to three columns, and a throne room. **2.** In ancient Assyrian architecture, the pillared portico of a **beit hilani, 1.**

beki A stone slab between the **chapra** and **amalaka** of a Hindu temple.

belection See **bolection molding.**

Belfast roof A **bowstring roof.**

Belfast truss A **bowstring truss,** for large spans, which is constructed entirely of timber components; the upper member is bent, and the lower member is horizontal.

belfry **1.** A room at or near the top of a tower which contains bells and their supporting timbers. **2.** The bell tower itself.

belfry,2 at Ghent (1313–21)

Belgian block A type of paving stone generally cut in a truncated, pyramidal shape; laid with the base of the pyramid down.

bell The body of a Corinthian capital or a Composite capital, with the foliage removed; also called a **vase** or **basket.**

bell arch A round arch supported on large **corbels, 2**, giving rise to a bell-shaped appearance.

bell arch

bell cage The timber framework which supports the bells in a belfry or steeple.

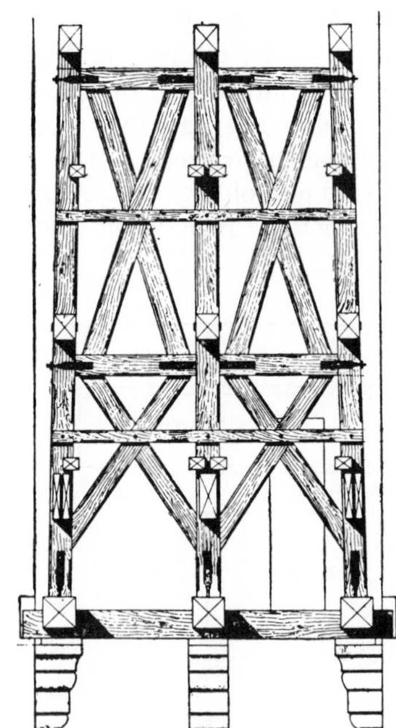

bell cage

bell canopy A gable roof to shelter a bell.

bell capital **1.** A bell-shaped **capital.** **2.** The bell-shaped core of a Corinthian capital to which the leaves and volutes appear to be attached.

bell chamber A room containing one or more large bells hung on their **bell cage.**

bell cot, bell cote A small belfry astride the ridge of a church roof, often crowned with a small spire.

bell cot

bell deck The belfry floor above the lower rooms in a tower.

bellexion molding See **bolection molding.**

bell gable A small turret placed on the ridge of a church roof to hold one or more bells.

bell gable

bell house A tower-like building for housing bells, esp. in Ireland.

bellied Having a convex or bulging form.

bell roof A roof whose cross section is shaped like a bell.

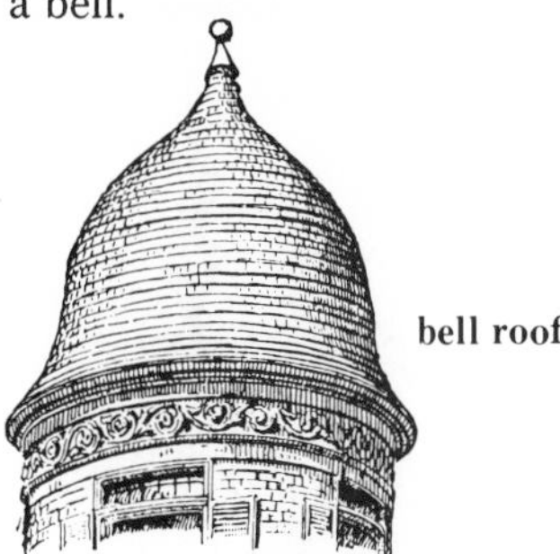
bell roof

bell tower A tall structure, either independent or part of a building, to contain one or more bells.

bell turret A small tower, usually topped with a spire or pinnacle, and containing one or more bells.

bell turret

belt course, belt **1.** A **stringcourse.** **2.** A **sill course.** **3.** A horizontal board across or around a building; usually a flat wood member with a molding.

belvedere 1. A rooftop pavilion from which a vista can be enjoyed. 2. A **gazebo.** 3. A **mirador.**

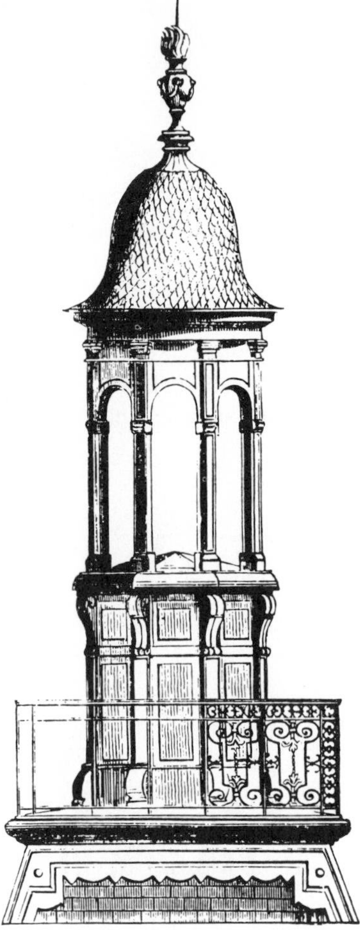

belvedere, 1

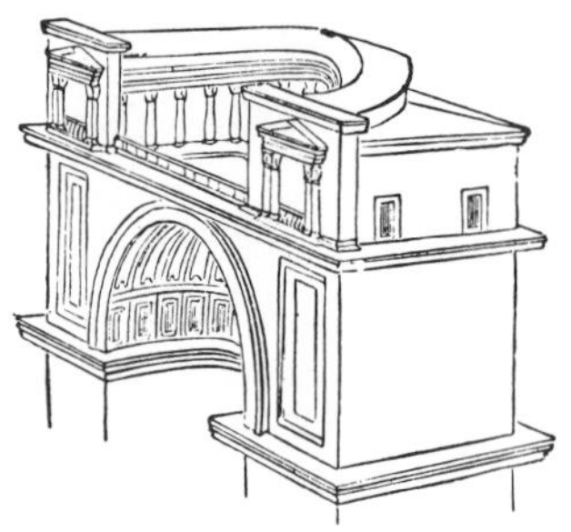

belvedere, 1 of the Vatican

bema 1. A transverse space in a church a few steps above the floor of the nave and aisles, and separating them from the apse. 2. In a synagogue, a raised pulpit from which the Torah (Holy Bible) is read. 3. The chancel of a Greek church.

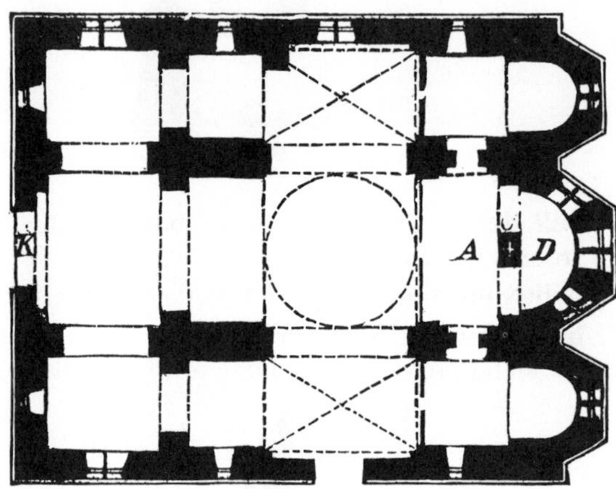

typical plan of Byzantine church: St. Theodore, Athens (1060–70); *AD*, bema

bematis Same as **diaconicon, 1.**

bench end A terminal wood facing on a church pew, often decorative.

bench ends

bench table A projecting course of masonry at the foot of an interior wall, or around a column; generally wide enough to form a seat.

bench table

bénitier A basin for holy water, usually set at the entrance to a church.

bénitiers

bent approach An arrangement of two gateways not in line, so that it is necessary to make a sharp turn to pass through the second; for privacy in houses or temples, for security in fortifications.

berliner, palladiana A type of terrazzo topping using small and large pieces of marble paving, usually with a standard terrazzo matrix between pieces.

berm **1.** The horizontal surface between a moat and the exterior slope of a fortified rampart. **2.** A continuous bank of earth piled against a masonry wall. **3.** A strip of ground, formed into a ledge to support beams or pipes.

besant See **bezant.**

bestiarium The place where wild beasts were kept before they fought in the ancient Roman amphitheatre.

bestiary In a medieval church, a group of carved or painted creatures, often highly imaginative and symbolic.

bethel A place of worship.

beth-knesset A Jewish house of assembly and prayer; a **synagogue.**

beth-midrash A traditional Jewish school.

beth-mikdash A **synagogue.**

beton A kind of concrete; a mixture of lime, sand, and gravel.

beveled siding See **clapboard.**

bevel siding See **clapboard.**

bezant, besant,, byzant An ornament shaped like a coin or disk; sometimes used in a series in decorative molding designs.

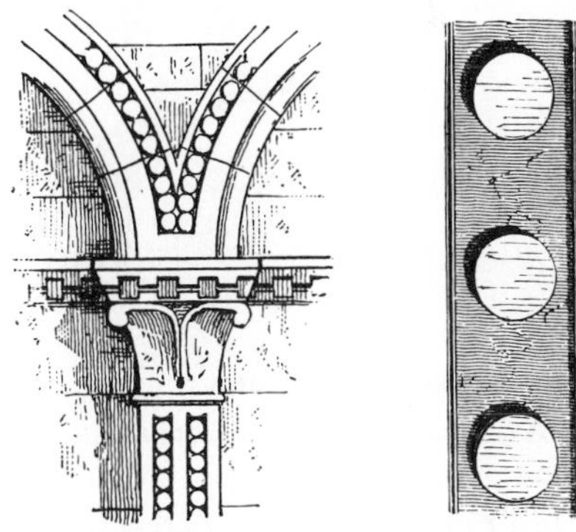

bezants

bhadra In Hindu architecture, a type of portico or building; a general term for a **ratha.**

bhoga-mandir A Hindu sacrificial pavilion.

bhumi In India, the site, floor, or story of a building.

bibliotheca A library; a place to keep books.

bicoca A turret or watchtower.

bidental A small Roman temple or shrine enclosing an altar, erected upon any spot which had been struck by lightning and consecrated by the official diviners (augurs).

remains of a bidental at Pompeii

biforis, biforus In ancient Roman construction, a term applied to doors and windows which opened in two leaves instead of in one piece; similar to a folding door or French window.

bifrons Having two fronts or faces looking in two directions, as a double **herm.**

bifrons

bifronted Same as **bifrons.**

biga A chariot similar to a **quadriga** but drawn by two horses.

bilection molding See **bolection molding.**

billet **1.** A common Norman or Romanesque molding formed by a series of circular (but occasionally square) cylinders, disposed alternately with the notches in single or multiple rows. **2.** A timber which is sawn on three sides and left rounded on the fourth.

billet, 1

binder A **binding stone.**

binding rafter A longitudinal timber which supports the roof rafters between the ridge and the eaves, as a **purlin.**

binding stone A stone which bonds masonry together, as a perpend; a **binder.**

bipeda An ancient Roman brick or thick tile which is two Roman feet long, one Roman foot wide, and one-third of a Roman foot thick; esp. used for pavements.

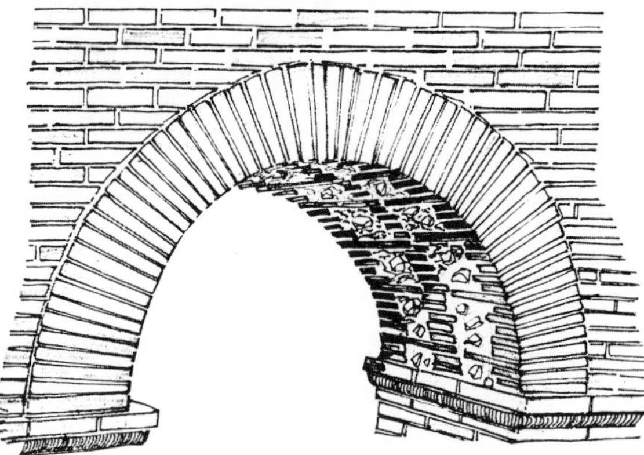

Roman arch faced with bipedales

bird's-beak molding See **beak molding, 2.**

bisellium In ancient Rome, a seat of honor, or a state chair, reserved for persons of note or persons who had done special service for the state.

bisomus A sarcophagus with two compartments.

bit hilani See **beit hilani.**

bivium **1.** The junction of two ancient roads which met at an angle. **2.** A plot of ground at the junction of two roads, which at Pompeii was always furnished with a fountain.

bivium, 1

blade One of the principal rafters of a roof.

blank arcade Same as **blind arcade.**

blank door **1.** A recess in a wall, having the appearance of a door; usually used for symmetry of design. **2.** A door which has been sealed off but is still visible.

blank wall, blind wall, dead wall A wall whose whole surface is unbroken by a window, door, or other opening.

blank window, blind window, false window **1.** A recess in an external wall, having the external appearance of a window. **2.** A window which has been sealed off but is still visible.

blind arcade A decorative row of arches applied to a wall as a decorative element, esp. in Romanesque buildings.

blind arcade

blind arch An arch in which the opening is permanently closed by wall construction.

blind arches in a nave wall

blind door **1.** Same as **blank door.** **2.** A louvered door.

blind joint A joint, no part of which is visible.

blind pocket A pocket in the ceiling at a window head to accommodate a Venetian blind when it is raised.

blindstory **1.** A floor level without exterior windows. **2.** The triforium of a Gothic church, or derivatives.

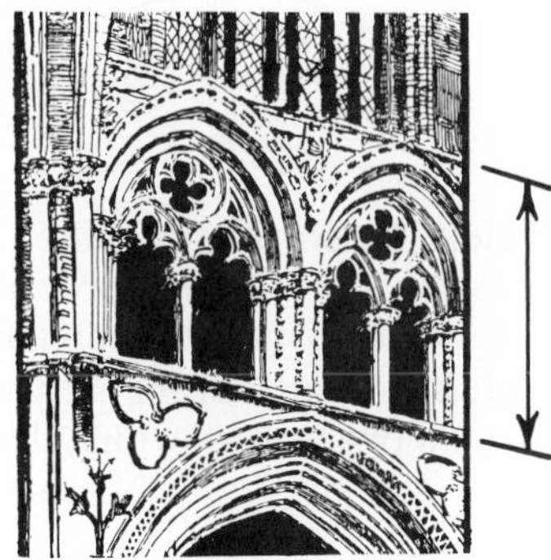
blindstory,2

blind tracery Tracery adorning a wall or panel but not pierced through.

blind wall A **blank wall.**

blind window See **blank window.**

block capital See **cushion capital.**

block cornice A cornice used in Italian architecture; usually consists of a bed molding, a range of block modillions or corbels, and a corona or cornice; the bed molding may be omitted. The block cornice differs from an **architrave cornice** in that the latter shows fascias only below the bed molding.

blockhouse A fortified log structure with loopholes in its sides which permit gunfire in all directions.

blockhouse

blocking course **1.** A plain finishing course of masonry directly above a cornice. **2.** A **stringcourse.**

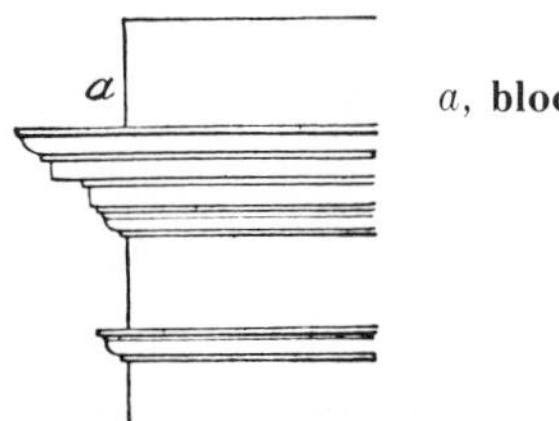

a, blocking course, 1

block modillion A **modillion** in the form of a plain block.

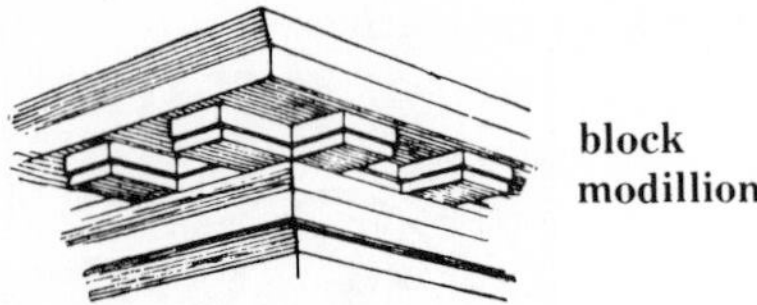

blue brick, Staffordshire blue A brick of high strength whose blue color results from firing in a kiln in a flame of low oxygen content.

blunt arch An arch rising to a slight point, struck from two centers within the arch.

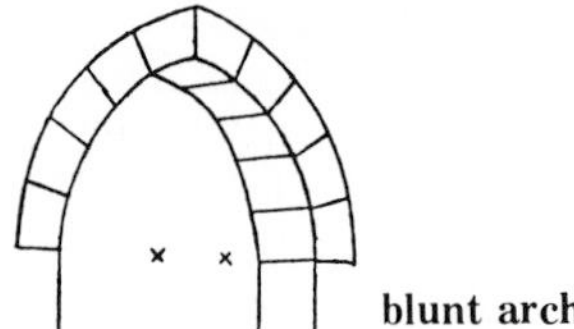
blunt arch

boardwalk A walkway made of boards or planks, often a promenade along a shore or beach.

boasted work A dressed (usually by hand) stone surface showing roughly parallel narrow chisel grooves, not uniform in width and not carried across the face of the stone.

boat spike Same as **barge spike.**

bobache See **bobeche.**

bobeche, bobache The collar fitted to a lamp holder as on a chandelier and from which glass prisms may be suspended.

bochka In early Russian architecture, a wooden roof whose peak has the shape of a horizontal cylinder with the upper side surface extended into a pointed ridge.

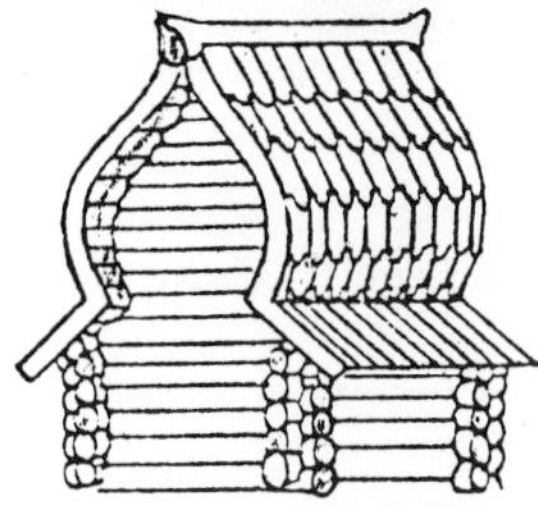
bochka

bodhika In Indian architecture, the capital of a column.

body The principal volume of a building, such as the nave of a church.

boiserie Wood paneling on interior walls, usually floor to ceiling; as a rule enriched by carving, gilding, painting, or, rarely, inlaying.

bolection molding, balection, belection, bellexion, bilection, bolexion A molding projecting beyond the surface of the work which it decorates, as that covering the joint between a panel and the surrounding stiles and rails; often used to conceal a joint where the joining surfaces are at different levels.

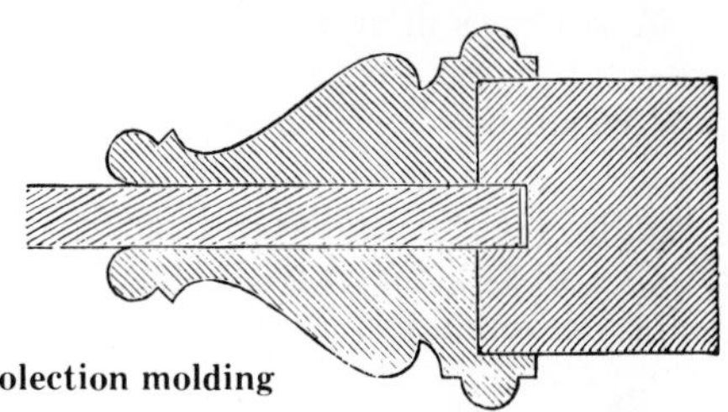
bolection molding

bollard A low single post, or one of a series, usually stone, set to prevent vehicles from entering an area.

bolster One of the rolls forming the sides of an Ionic capital, joining the volutes of the front and rear faces; a **baluster** or **pulvinus.**

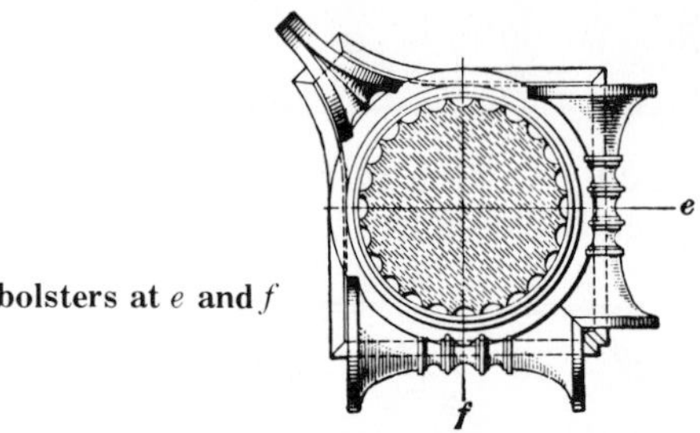

bolsters at *e* and *f*

bolster work A form of rusticated masonry; courses of masonry which are curved or bow outward like the sides of a **cushion, 1.**

boltel See **bowtell.**

bombé Swelling out; convex in shape.

bomon In ancient Greece, an altar to a god.

bond An arrangement of masonry units to provide strength, stability, and in some cases beauty through a setting pattern by lapping units over one another or by connecting with metal ties; some units may extend into adjacent courses, between withes, or through the wall, and vertical joints are not continuous.

bonder A masonry unit that bonds; also called a **bondstone.**

bond header In masonry, a **bondstone** that extends the full thickness of the wall; also called a **throughstone.**

bondstone, bonder In stone masonry, a stone usually set with its longest dimension perpendicular to the wall face so as to tie the masonry wall to the wall backing. A very large bondstone may be set with its long dimension parallel to the wall face and still serve as a bonder if its width is sufficiently large to tie to the wall backing.

bond timber A timber built into a brick or stone wall in a horizontal position, for the purpose of strengthening it or for tying it together during construction; serves as a bonding course and as a means for securing the battening and bracketing.

bone house See **ossuary.**

bonnet A **chimney cap.**

bonnet hip tile, cone tile A tile that resembles a woman's bonnet; used to cover the hip on a hip roof.

book matching, herringbone matching The assembling of wood veneers from the same flitch so that successive sheets are alternated face up and face down. In figured wood, side-by-side sheets show a symmetrical mirror image about the joints between adjoining sheets.

borning room In colonial New England houses, a small room (adjacent to the warm kitchen or **keeping room**) in which babies were born and sometimes kept during infancy.

Borobudur A colossal monument erected ca. 800 A.D., the only stupa in Java; atop a terraced hill which has been faced with stone, a large stupa surrounded by a series of square galleries. The inner faces of the galleries are decorated with a continuous frieze in relief, representing the life of Buddha and the bodhisattvas; the galleries are crowned with niches containing statues of Buddha.

bosket A grove; a thicket or small grouping of trees in a garden, park, etc.

bosquet Same as **bosket.**

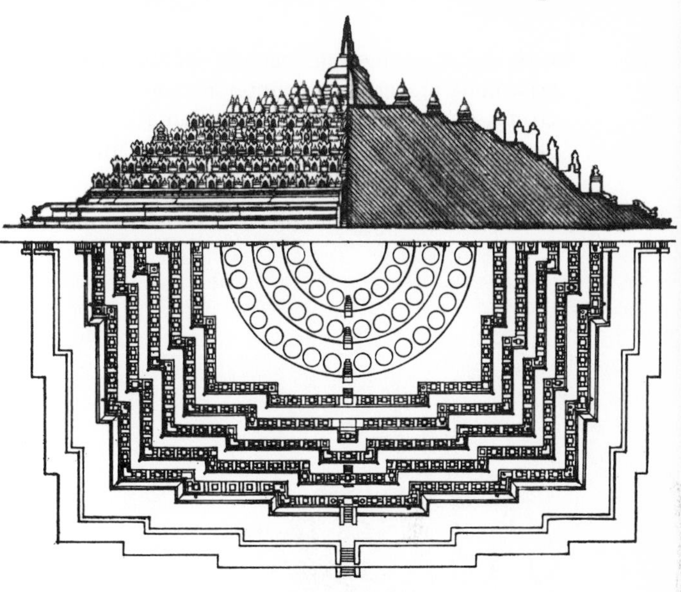

Borobudur (c. 850 A.D.): *upper left:* **elevation;** *upper right:* **section;** *below:* **plan**

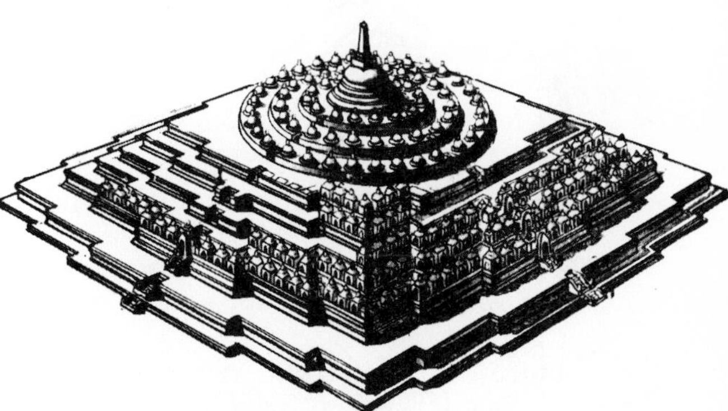

Borobudur: perspective

Borobudur: gateway

boss **1.** A projecting, usually richly carved ornament placed at the intersection of ribs, groins, beams, etc., or at the termination of a molding. **2.** In masonry, a roughly shaped stone set to project for carving in place.

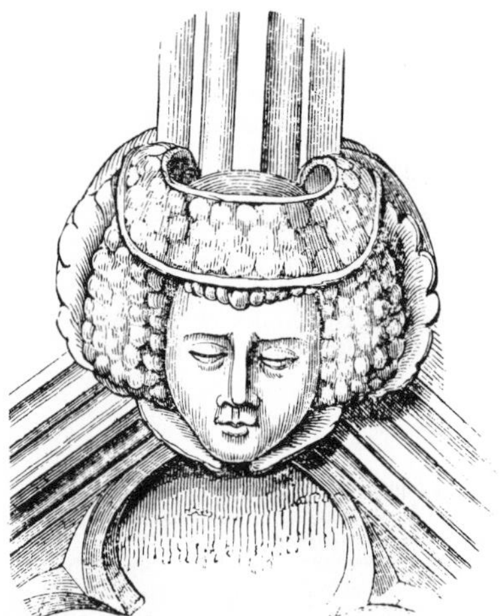

Cloisters, Oxford Cathedral

Merton College, Oxford

Chapter House, Oxford Cathedral

St. Albans Abbey Church, Hertford

York Cathedral

St. Stephen's Chapel, Westminster

Melrose Abbey

Warmington Cathedral

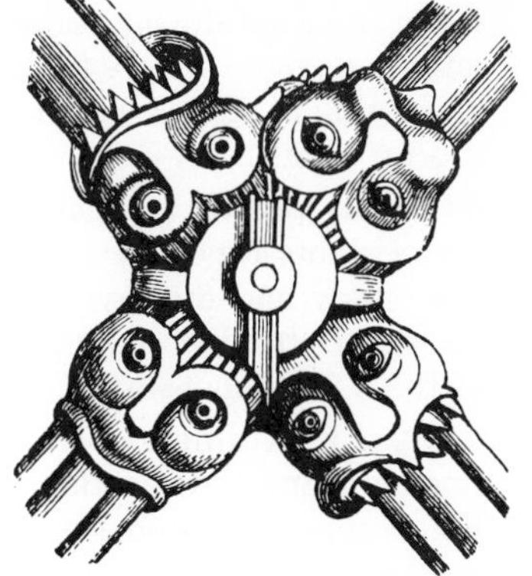

Church of Elkstone, Gloucestershire

French Gothic

French Gothic

French Gothic

Italian Renaissance

Italian Renaissance

Italian Renaissance

bossage 1. In masonry, projecting, rough-finished stone left during construction for carving later in final decorative form. 2. Rustic work, consisting of stones which project beyond the mortar joints.

botanical garden A garden in which a variety of plants are collected and grown for scientific study and display; often includes greenhouses for tropical material.

bothie Same as **bothy.**

bothy 1. A small cottage or hut, esp. in northern England, Scotland, or Ireland. 2. A house for accommodating a number of workers for the same company, farm, or employer.

botress, botras, botrasse, boterasse Same as **buttress.**

bottle Old English term for **bowtell.**

boudoir See **chamber,** 1.

bouleuterion In ancient Greece, a place of assembly, esp. for a public body.

boulevard An important thoroughfare, often with a center divider planted with trees and grass, or similarly planted dividers between curbings and sidewalks.

boultine, boultell See **bowtell.**

bouquet The floral or foliated ornament forming the extreme top of a finial, knob, hip, or the like.

bouteillerie See **buttery.**

boutel, boutell See **bowtell.**

bovile Same as **bubile.**

bow 1. The longitudinal curvature of a rod, bar, or piece of tubing or lumber. 2. An **archway.** 3. Old English term for **flying buttress.**

bower 1. A rustic dwelling, generally of small scale and picturesque nature. 2. In a large medieval residence, the private chamber of the lady. 3. A sheltered recess in a garden.

bowl capital A plain capital shaped like a bowl.

bowling green A carefully maintained, level piece of lawn, originally reserved for the game of bowls (bowling).

bow-shaped See **double-bellied.**

bowstring beam, bowstring girder, bowstring truss A **beam, girder,** or **truss** having one curved member in the shape of a bow (often circular or parabolic in shape) and a straight or cambered member which ties together the two ends of the bow.

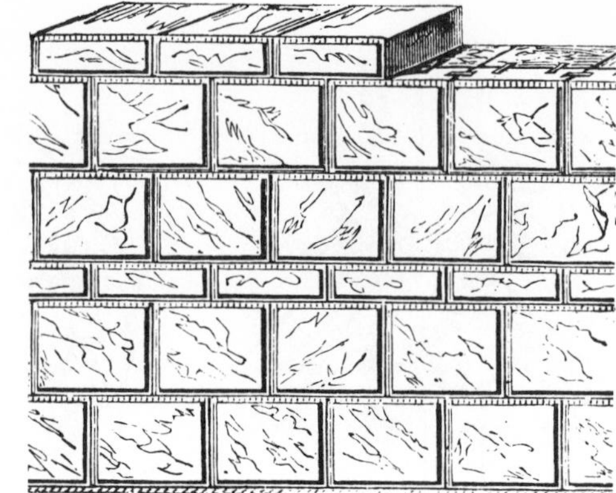

bossage

bouquets atop a finial

bower, 3

bowstring roof, Belfast roof A roof supported by bowstring trusses.

bowtell, boltel, boultine, boutell, bowtel, edge roll **1.** A plain, convex molding, usually an arc of a circle in section. **2.** A **torus** or **round molding.** **3.** The shaft of a clustered pillar. **4.** A **roll molding.** **5.** A **quarter round** or **ovolo.**

bow window, compass window A rounded **bay window;** projects from the face of a wall in a plan which is the segment of a circle.

English Renaissance bow window

box A private seating area for spectators in an auditorium, usually located at the front or side of a mezzanine or balcony; may contain movable, rather than fixed, chairs.

box cornice, boxed cornice, closed cornice A hollow cornice, built up of boards, moldings, shingles, etc.

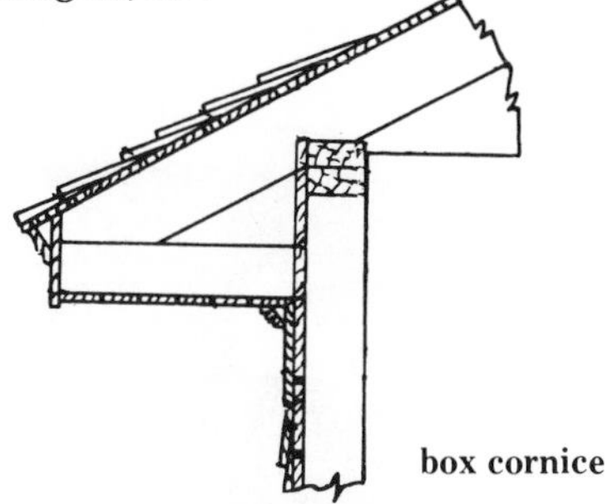

box cornice

box-head window A window constructed so that the sashes can slide vertically up into the head (or above it) to provide maximum opening for ventilation.

boxing A box-like enclosure or recess at the side of a window frame which receives a **boxing shutter** when it is folded.

boxing shutter, folding shutter A window shutter which can be folded into the **boxing** or recess at the side.

box pew A church pew screened or enclosed by a high back and sides.

box stoop A high **stoop** making a quarter turn, reached by a flight of stairs along a building front.

bracciale A projecting metal bracket, having a socket and ring for holding a flagstaff, torch, or the like; esp. used on Renaissance palaces in Florence and Siena.

brace **1.** A metal or wood member which is used to stiffen or support a structure; a strut which supports or fixes another member in position or a tie used for the same purpose. **2.** An **angle brace.**

braced arch An openwork truss in the form of an arch.

braced frame, braced framing Heavy, braced wood framing for a structure which uses **girts** that are mortised into solid posts; the posts are full frame height, with one-story-high studs between, usually diagonally braced.

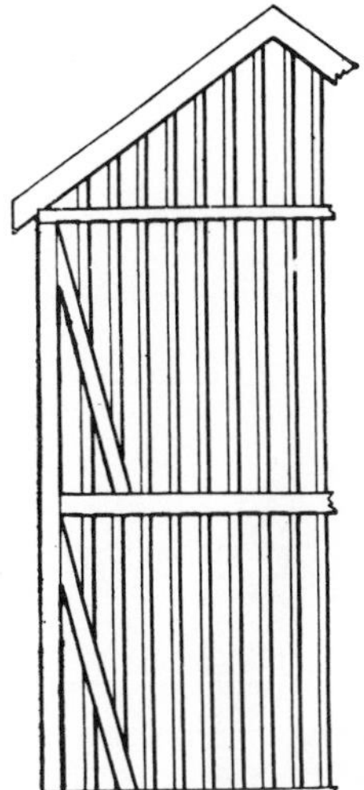

braced frame

brace molding The molding formed by joining two ogees with the convex ends together and in section resembling the brace used as a symbol in printing. Also see **keel molding.**

brace piece A **mantelpiece, 2.**

bracket **1.** Any overhanging member projecting from a wall or other body to support a weight (such as a cornice) acting outside the wall. **2.** A decorative detail attached to the spring of a stair under the overhanging edge of the treads.

brackets,1 supporting a projecting upper story

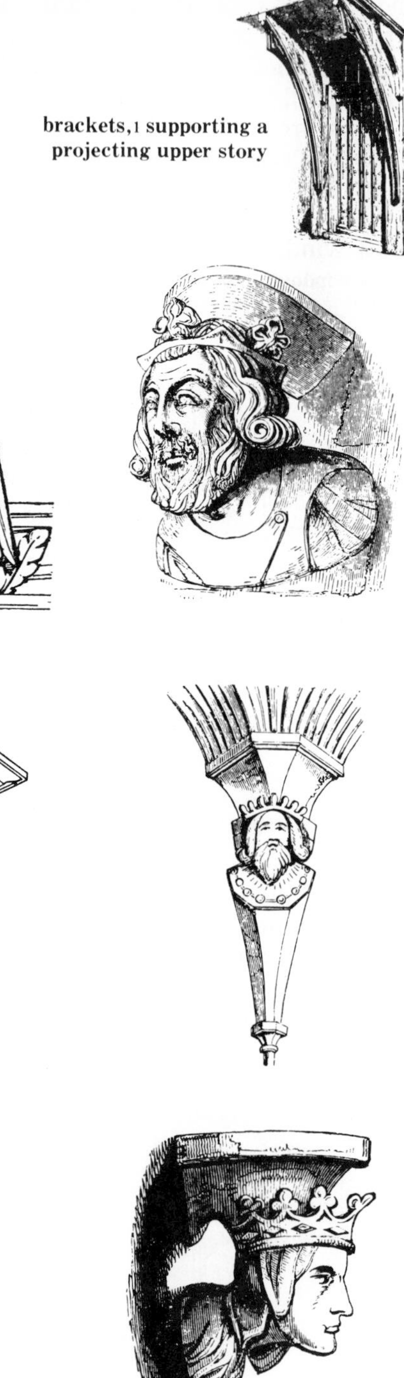

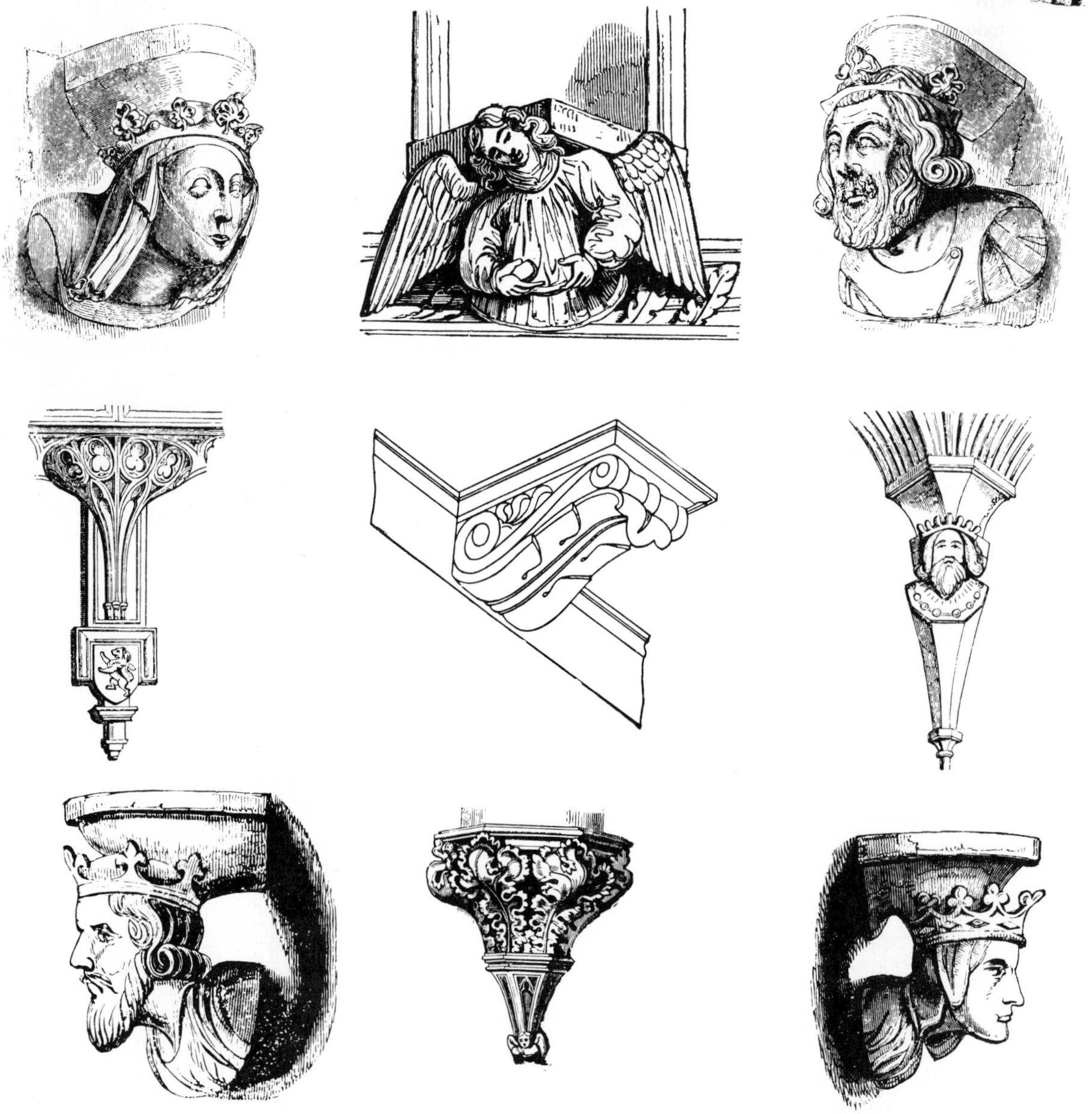

various types of brackets,1 projecting from a wall

bracket capital A capital extended by brackets, lessening the clear span between posts, often seen in Near Eastern, Muslim, Indian, and some Spanish architecture.

bracketed stair A flight of open string stairs; one with decorative brackets on the exposed outer string and under the return nosing of treads.

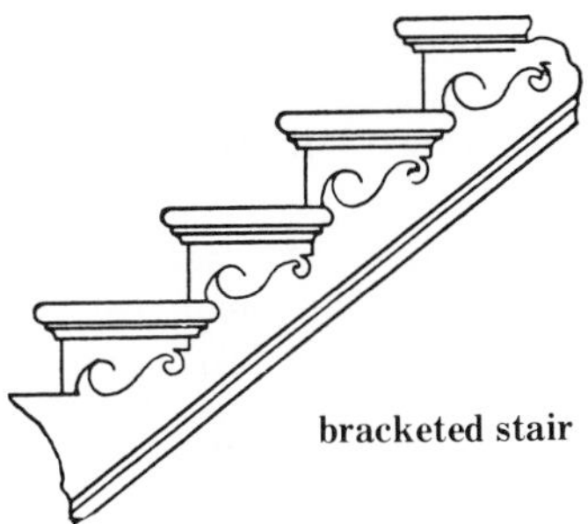
bracketed stair

bracketing 1. Any system of brackets. 2. An arrangement of wooden brackets employed as a skeleton support to plasterwork, moldings, or other plaster ornamental details.

bragger A **corbel.**

braid pattern Same as **guilloche.**

branch tracery A form of Gothic tracery in Germany in late 15th and early 16th cent.; made to imitate rustic work with boughs and knots.

brandishing Same as **brattishing.**

brandrith, bandreth A fence or rail around the opening of a well.

brass A plate of brass with memorial inscription and sometimes an effigy engraved on it, set into a church floor to mark a tomb.

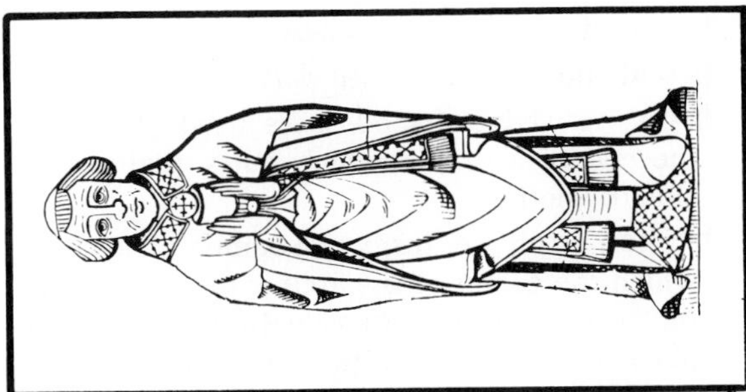
brass

brattice, bretessé, bretêche In medieval fortifications, a tower or bay of timber construction.

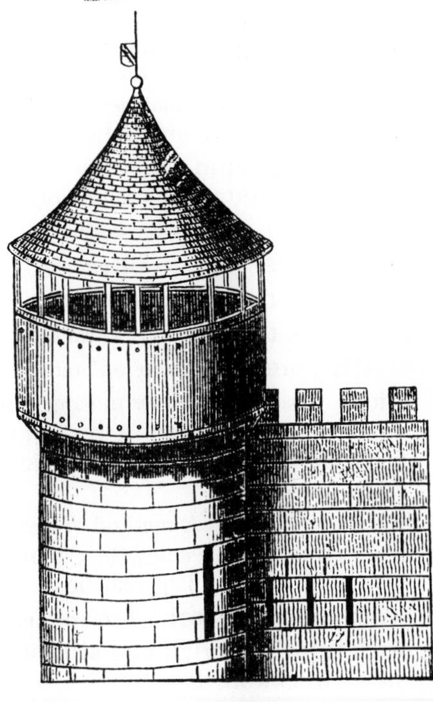
types of brattices

brattishing, brandishing, bretisement A decorative cresting at the top of a Gothic screen, panel, parapet, or cornice, generally in the form of openwork of a stylized floral design.

bread room A room fitted with shelves and bins for flour and loaves, biscuits, and confectionery; in medieval times it was part of the **buttery.**

breast **1.** A projecting part of a wall, as at a chimney. **2.** That portion of a wall between the floor and a window above. **3.** The underside of a handrail, beam, rafter, or the like.

breast beam See **breastsummer.**

breast molding **1.** The molding on a windowsill or on the breast of a wall. **2.** Paneling beneath a window.

breastsummer, breast beam, bressummer, brestsummer A horizontal beam which spans a wide opening (a **lintel**) in an external wall; a **summer, 3.**

breast wall, face wall **1.** A **retaining wall.** **2.** A parapet which is breast high.

breastwork **1.** Masonry work for a chimney breast. **2.** The parapet of a building. **3.** A defensive wall, hastily constructed, about breast high.

breccia Any stone composed of angular fragments embedded and consolidated in a finer ground. Numerous marbles owe their distinctive appearance to brecciation.

brephotropheum In ancient Greece and Rome, an institution for foundlings.

bressummer See **breastsummer.**

brestsummer See **breastsummer.**

bretêche, bretessé See **brattice.**

bretisement Same as **brattishing.**

brettiss, brettys Same as **brattice.**

brick A solid or hollow masonry unit of clay or shale, molded into a rectangular shape while plastic, and then burnt in a kiln. Also see **later.**

brick and brick A method of laying brick so that units touch each other; mortar is used only to fill surface irregularities.

brick-and-stud work See **brick nogging.**

brick nogging, brick-and-stud work, brick nog Brickwork laid in the spaces between timber in a wood-frame partition.

bridgeboard A notched board which supports the treads and risers of wooden stairs; an open or cut stringer.

brise-soleil A fixed or movable device, such as fins or louvers, designed to block the direct entrance of sun rays into a building.

broach **1.** To finish a stone surface with broad diagonal parallel grooves cut by a pointed chisel. **2.** A half pyramid above the corners of a square tower to provide a transition to an octagonal spire. **3.** A spire, sometimes springing from a tower without an intermediate parapet. **4.** Any pointed ornamental structure.

broached spire An octagonal spire surmounting a square tower, the transition between being made by broaches.

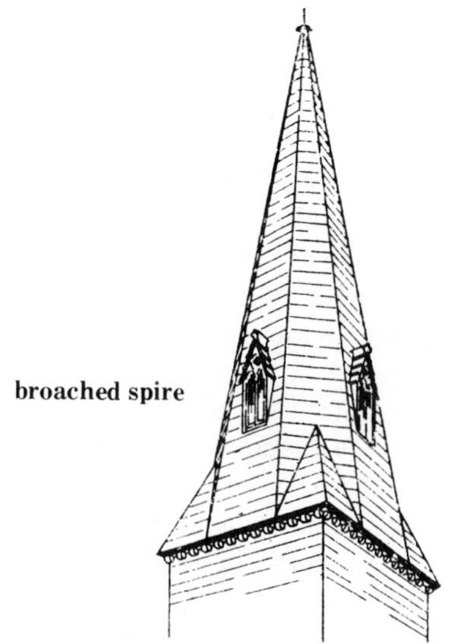

broached spire

broached work See **broach, 1.**

broach stop See **chamfer.**

broad stone Same as **ashlar.**

broad tooled See **batted work.**

brob A wedge-shaped spike used to secure the end of a timber which butts against the side of another.

broken arch A form of segmental arch in which the center of the arch is omitted and is replaced by a decorative feature; usually applied to a wall above the entablature over a door or window.

broken ashlar See **random work, 2.**

broken-color work See **antiquing.**

broken pediment A pediment in Roman and Baroque architecture that has been split apart at its apex or at the center of its base. When broken at its apex, the gap is often filled with an urn, a cartouche, or other ornament.

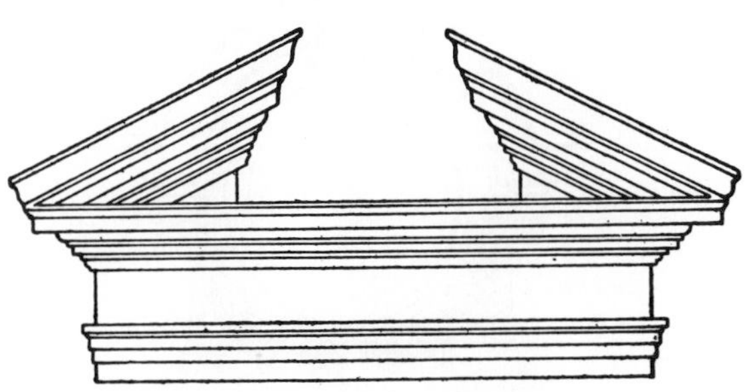

types of broken pediments

broken rangework Stone masonry laid in horizontal courses of different heights, any one course of which may be broken (at intervals) into two or more courses.

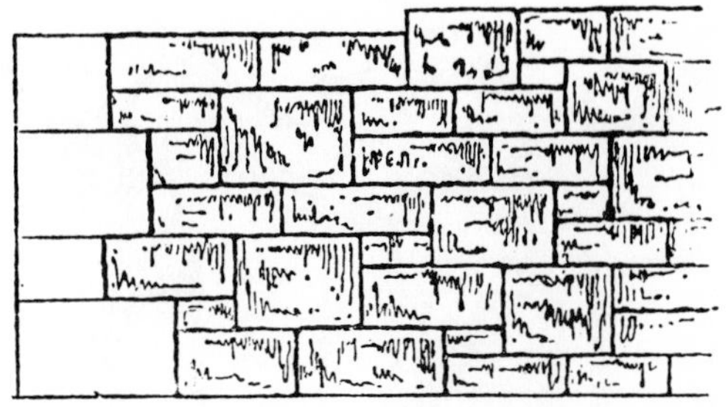

broken rangework

bronteum In ancient Greek and Roman theatres, a device for producing the noise of thunder, generated by the impact of stones against the inside of a heavy vase designed for this purpose.

brotch A thin piece of a tree branch which is bent in a U-shape; used for fastening thatch on roofs; also called a **buckle** or **spar.**

brownstone 1. A dark brown or reddish brown arkosic sandstone, quarried and used extensively for building in the eastern U.S.A. during the middle and late nineteenth cent. **2.** A dwelling faced with brownstone, often a **row house.**

Brutalism, New Brutalism Movement in modern architecture, emphasizing stark forms and raw surfaces, particularly of concrete.

bubile A structure to house cows.

buckle A **brotch.**

buckler An ornament used in the decoration of friezes; sometimes circular or lozenge-shaped.

buckler

bucranium, bucrane A sculptured ornament representing the head or skull of an ox, often garlanded; frequently used on Roman Ionic and Corinthian friezes.

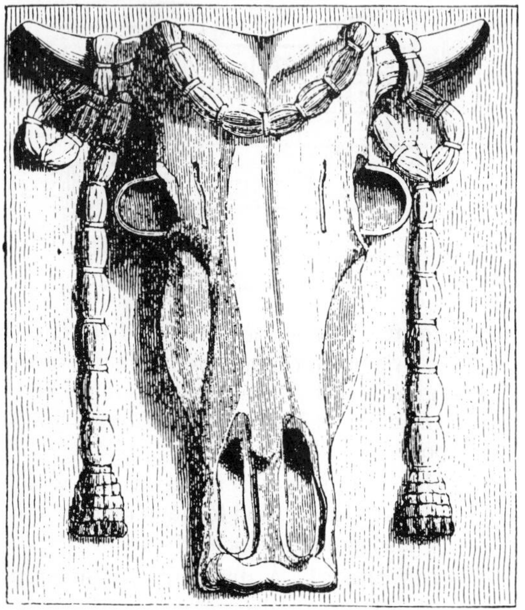

bucranium

bud An element in a Corinthian capital.

bud

bulla A circular metal boss used by the ancient Romans as a decoration and for fastening parts of doors; often highly ornamented.

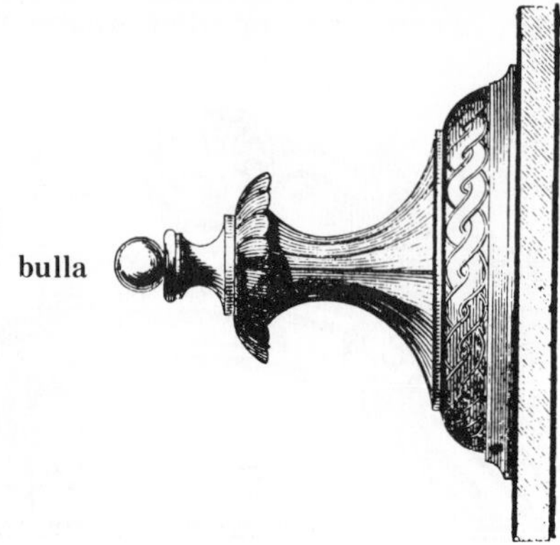

bulla

bullion Same as **bull's eye.**

bull-nosed step A step, usually lowest in a flight, having one or both ends rounded to a semicircle and projecting beyond the face of the stair string or strings. The semicircular projection extends beyond and around the newel post.

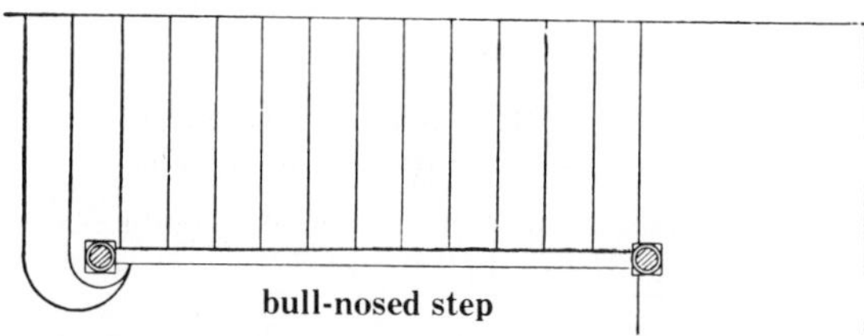

bull-nosed step

bull's-eye **1.** A figure or ornament of concentric bands. **2.** A round or oval aperture, open, louvered, or glazed; an **oculus** or **oeil-de-boeuf.** **3.** The enclosure of such an aperture, a double-arched frame with two or four key voussoirs. **4.** A glass disk formed with a raised center.

bull's-eye

bull's head 1. A **bucranium.** 2. In a frieze, the forepart of a bull employed in various ways.

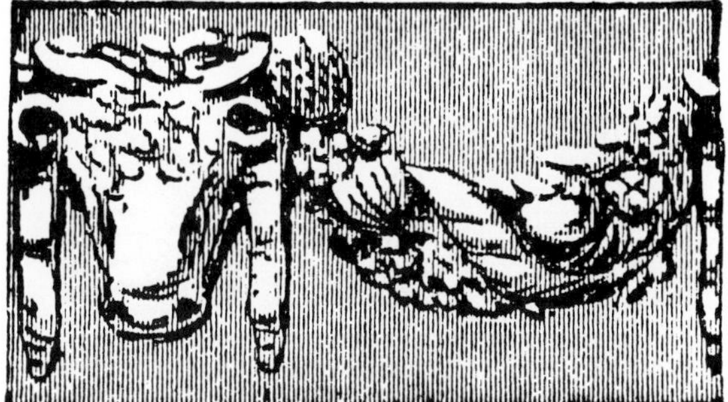

bull's head,1 and festoon

bulwark A strong defensive wall structure, generally low enough to permit defensive fire.

bundle pier A Gothic pier in which the plan takes a continuous undulating and breaking outline, giving the appearance of a dense bundle of rising forms rather than the distinct shafts of the **compound pier.**

buon fresco See **fresco.**

burj In the architecture of India, a tower.

bustum In ancient Rome, a vacant space of ground on which a funeral pyre was raised and the corpse burnt; esp. such an area when contained within a sepulchral enclosure and contiguous to the tomb in which the ashes were afterward deposited.

butment Same as **abutment.**

butsuden See **kondō.**

butterfly hinge A decorative hinge having the appearance of a butterfly.

buttery 1. Pantry or wine cellar; formerly a medieval storeroom for provisions (originally *bouteillerie*). 2. *(Brit.)* Dispensary of provisions, esp. food and drink, to college students. In former days a place where corporal punishment was inflicted.

buttery hatch Semiclosed screen between a buttery and the hall.

buttress An exterior mass of masonry set at an angle to or bonded into a wall which it strengthens or supports; buttresses often absorb lateral thrusts from roof vaults. Also see **flying buttress, hanging buttress.**

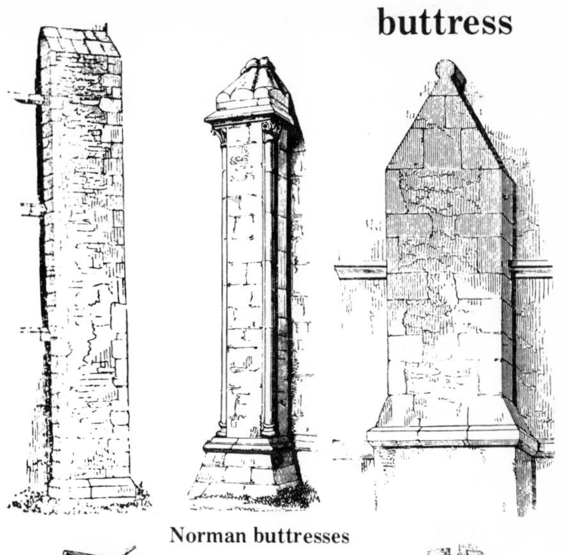

Norman buttresses

Early English buttresses

Decorated style buttresses

buttress pier **1.** A pier acting as a buttress by receiving lateral thrusts. **2.** The part of a buttress which rises above the point of thrust of a vault.

buttress tower A tower which flanks an arched entrance and acts, or appears to act, as a buttress.

by-altar A subordinate altar.

廟 **byō** In Japanese architecture, a mausoleum, often combined with a shrine (such as the **Tō-shōgū shrine** at Nikkō).

Byōdō-in A structure located at Uji, in the Kyōto prefecture of Japan; originally constructed as a villa for Fujiwara Michinaga (966–1027), converted into a temple in 1052. The original main hall of the building, known as Phoenix Hall (1053) or Hō-ōdō, is the best existing example of religious architecture of the Heian period.

byre A stable for livestock; a cow shed.

byzant See **bezant.**

Byzantine arch Same as **horseshoe arch.**

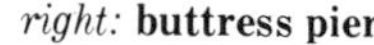

right: **buttress pier**

below: **Byōdō-in; Hō-ōdō also called "Phoenix Hall"**

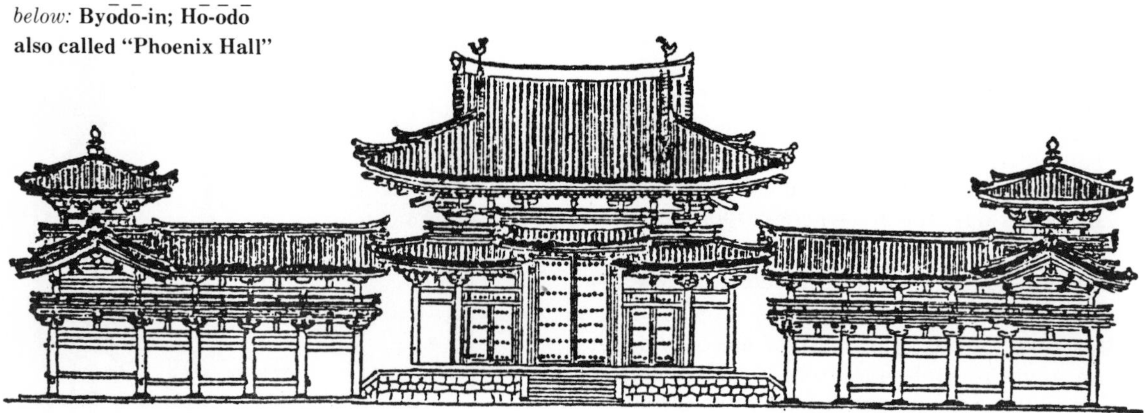

Byzantine architecture The architecture of the Byzantine or Eastern Roman Empire which developed from Early Christian and late Roman antecedents in the 4th cent., flourished principally in Greece, but spread widely and lasted throughout the Middle Ages until the fall of Constantinople to the Turks (1453). It is characterized by large pendentive-supported domes, round arches and elaborate columns, richness in decorative elements, and color. The most famous example is the **Hagia Sophia** in Istanbul (532–537).

running ornament, Hagia Sophia, Constantinople (532–36 A.D.)

section of Church of the Theotokos, Constantinople

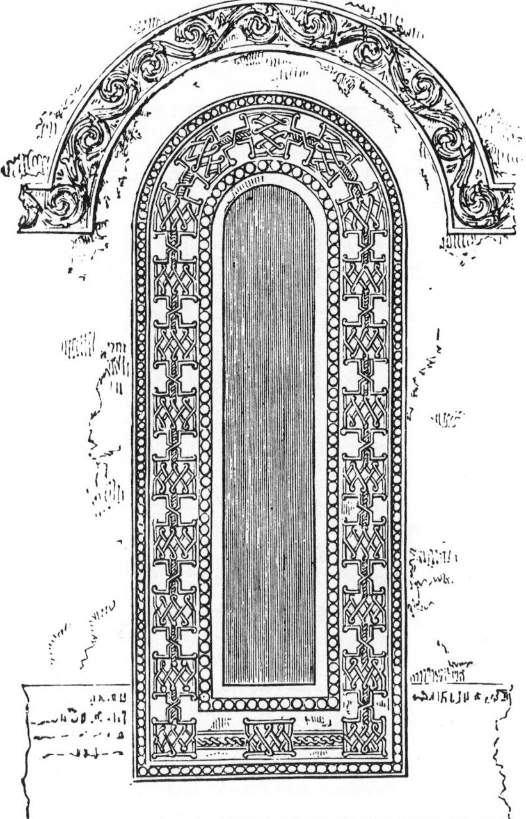

window at Kouthais

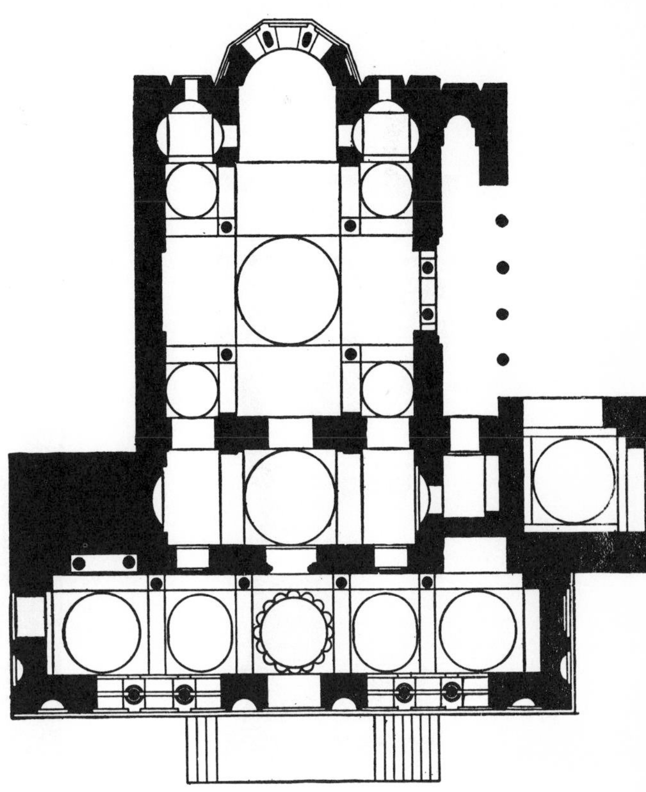

plan of Church of the Theotokos, Constantinople (10th cent.)

Byzantine architecture

elevation and section of Church of the Theotokos, Constantinople (10th–12th cent.)

wall decoration, Church of St. George, Thessalonica (c. 300 A.D.)

base and capital at Ravenna

Byzantine ornament, Church of St. Mark, Venice (1063–85)

Church of St. Mark, Venice (1063–85)

Ravenna

Church of the Theotokos, Constantinople (10th–12th cent.)

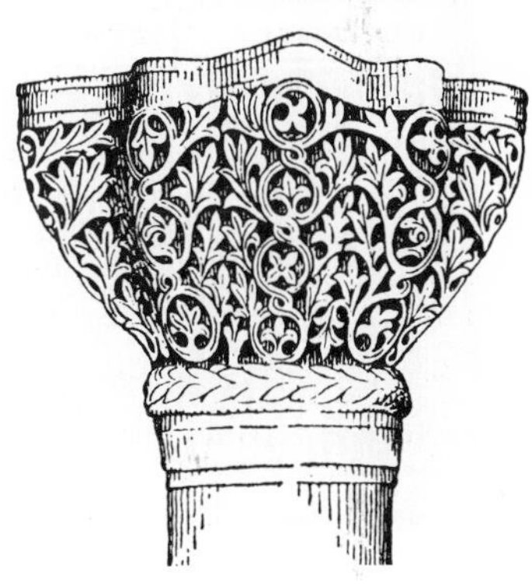

types of Byzantine capitals

Hagia Sophia, Constantinople (532–536 A.D.)

Byzantine type of foliage, El Barah, Syria

Byzantine Revival The re-use of Byzantine forms in the second half of the 19th cent., typically in churches, often characterized by multiple domes, round-arched windows, and ample decoration.

cabinet **1.** A private room for study or conference. **2.** A suite of rooms for exhibiting scientific and artistic curiosities.

cabinet window A type of projecting window or bay window for the display of goods in shops; much used early in the 19th cent.

cabinet window

cabinet work Joinery, often of fine quality, as in the construction of built-in cabinets and shelves.

cable One of the reedings which are set into the flutes of a pilaster or column.

cabled fluting, ribbed fluting, stopped flute A molding of convex section formed in the flutes of a column, usually in the lower third of the shaft.

cable molding See **cabling.**

cabling, cable molding **1.** An ornament formed like a cable, showing twisted strands. **2.** The convex filling of the lower part of the flutes of classical columns. Also see **rope molding, reeding.**

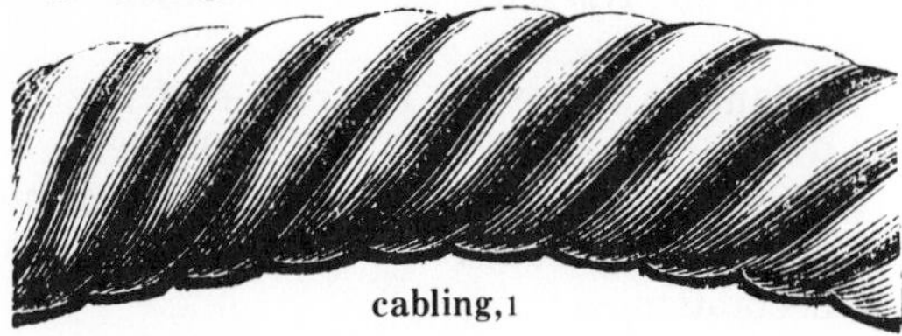

cabling,1

caementiciae structurae Concrete masonry walls constructed with caementa, of either of two types: **opus incertum** or **opus reticulatum.**

caementicium opus See **opus caementicium.**

caementum (usually *pl.* **caementa**) Rubble, or small undressed stones, used with mortar to form **caementiciae structurae.**

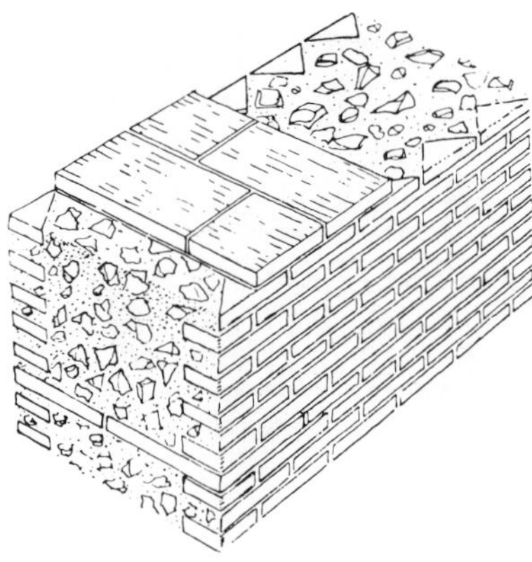

triangular brick and structural bonding showing a nucleus of caementum

caenaculum Same as **cenaculum.**

Caen stone A stone from Caen, in Normandy, used in some medieval buildings in England.

caer- A prefix signifying a fortified wall, castle, or city, occurring in place names in Wales and parts of western and northern England.

Caernarvon arch Same as **Carnarvon arch.**

cage A chantry or chapel screened by open **tracery.**

caher In Ireland, an ancient stone enclosure, often circular in plan, which was used as a field fortification; built of uncemented masonry enclosing an area of from 40 to 200 ft (approx. 12 to 60 m) in diameter and having subterranean chambers.

cairn A pile of stones heaped up for a landmark, memorial, or monument; a **tumulus.**

caisson A sunken panel, esp. in a vaulted ceiling or the inside of a cupola; a **coffer.**

calah See **Assyrian architecture.**

calathus The basket-shaped or bell-shaped core of a capital, esp. Corinthian.

calcatorium A raised platform of masonry in the cellar attached to an ancient Roman vineyard; ascended by two or three steps, it served as a passageway on a level with the tops of the large vessels in which wine was kept in bulk.

caldarium The vapor bath or hot plunge in Roman baths.

cairn, Isle de Gavr Inis, France, showing a slab-incised cistvaen

caldarium: the man pulling on a rope is adjusting the position of the clipeus

calefactory A heated common room in a monastery.

calendar A sculptured or painted emblematic series of the months.

calendar

calf's-tongue molding, calves'-tongue molding A molding consisting of a series of pointed tongue-shaped elements all pointing in the same direction or toward a common center when around an arch.

calf's-tongue molding

calidarium Same as **caldarium.**

caliduct In the ancient Roman systems of furnace heating, a hot-air flue, usually of terracotta or built up with brick partitions and tile facings.

calotte A dome, cupola, or structure of similar form, as a cup-shaped ceiling, the head of an alcove, etc.

Calvary **1.** In Roman Catholic countries, a representation of the passion of Christ, often of life size, erected on a hill near a city, sometimes near a church, in a chapel, or in a churchyard. **2.** A rocky mound or hill on which three crosses are erected; an adjunct to some religious houses.

Calvary,1

Calvary cross A cross mounted on three steps, which are intended to symbolize faith, hope, and charity.

calves'-tongue molding See **calf's-tongue molding.**

calyon Flint or pebble-stone; used in building walls, etc.

camara Same as **camera.**

camba The late Latin term for a place where brewing and sometimes baking were done.

camber arch A flat arch with a very slight upward curve in the intrados and sometimes also in the extrados.

camber beam A beam curved slightly upward toward the center.

camber piece, camber slip A slightly curved wood board used as a support in laying a brick arch having a small rise.

camber window A window arched at the top.

camboge A concrete masonry unit with transverse openings; used in tropical architecture, often decoratively, to permit ventilation while excluding sunlight, as in a **brise-soleil.**

came A slender rod of cast lead, with or without grooves, used in casements and stained-glass windows, to hold together the panes or pieces of glass.

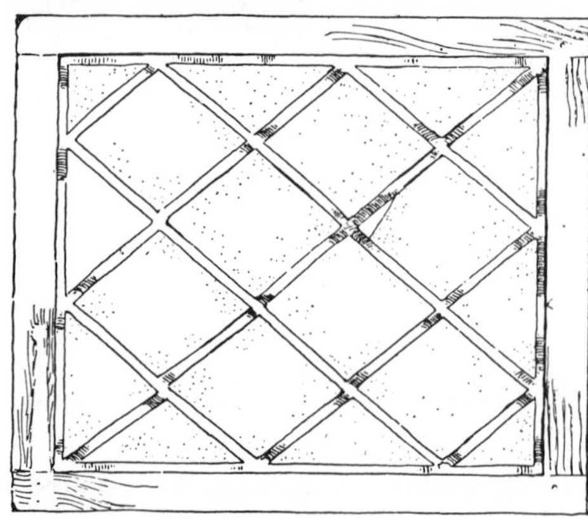
quarrels set in lead cames

camera **1.** In ancient architecture, an arched roof, ceiling, or covering; a vault. **2.** A room having an arched ceiling; a vaulted room. **3.** A small room, small hall, or chamber.

camerated Having an arched or vaulted appearance.

camera vitrea A vaulted ceiling, having its surface lined with plates of glass.

caminus **1.** An ancient Roman smelting furnace. **2.** A hearth or fireplace in a private house used for warmth.

campana The body of a Corinthian capital.

campaniform Bell-shaped.

campanile A bell tower, usually freestanding.

campanulated Bell-shaped.

camp ceiling **1.** A ceiling shaped like the interior of a truncated pyramid. **2.** The ceiling within the roof of a building, the sides of which are sloped, following the line of the rafters, but the center of which is flat.

canal See **canalis.**

canalis, canal **1.** A channel or groove, as a hollow between the fillets of the volutes of an Ionic capital. **2.** The sunk portions of the face of a triglyph. **3.** A narrow passage or alley in an ancient town. **4.** A pipe or gutter for conveying water. **5.** A designation for a particular area of the Roman Forum.

canaliculus A small channel or groove, as a fluting carved on the face of a **triglyph.**

cancelli **1.** Barred screens in a basilica, separating the clergy from the laity, in Early Christian architecture. **2.** In a Roman circus, gates of open woodwork which close the **carceres.**

candelabrum A movable candle lampstand with central shaft and, often, branches or a decorative representation thereof.

candle beam In old churches, a horizontal beam, bar, or rail furnished with prickets for holding candles, each of which has a saucer or tray to catch the drippings; placed over or near the altar, and also at the entrance to the choir or chancel, where the rood beam or rood screen was placed in richer churches.

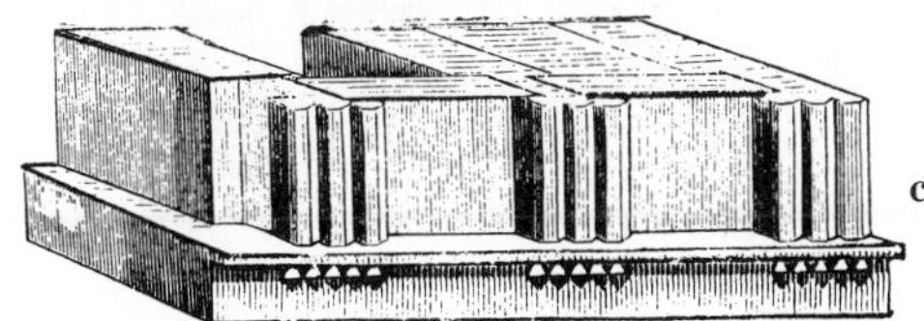

canaliculus

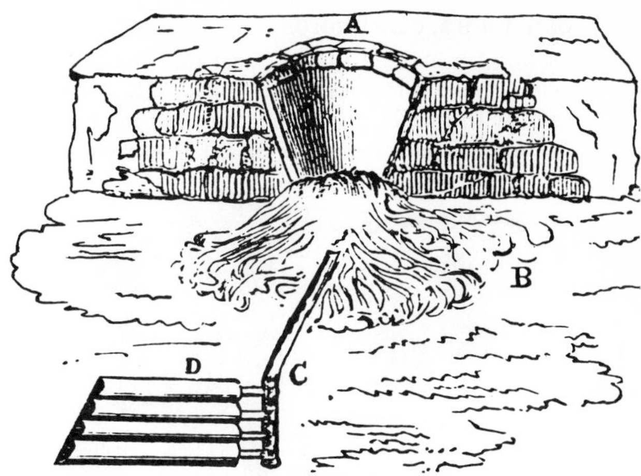

caminus,1: *A*, smelting furnace; *B*, slag overflow; *C*, channel conveying metal to the molds at *D*

campanile, Florence (1334–59)

canalis,4

cancelli,2

canephora, canephoros **1.** Ornament representing a maiden (youth) bearing a basket of ceremonial offerings on the head. **2.** A **caryatid** with basket on her head; used either as a support or as a freestanding garden ornament.

canephora

canephorae

canonnière A hole left in a retaining wall to permit water in the earth behind to drain through.

canopy **1.** A decorative **hood** above a niche, pulpit, choir stall, or the like. **2.** A covered area which extends from the wall of a building, protecting an entrance or loading dock.

canopy, 1

canopy, 1

altar with canopy, 1: France (14th cent.)

canopy of honor Same as **celure.**

cant **1.** A salient corner. **2.** A line or surface angled in relation to another, as a sloped wall.

cant bay A bay erected on a plan of canted outline.

cant-bay window A **cant window.**

canted Having a **cant, 2;** said of a wall, etc.

canted molding A wood **raking molding.**

canterius Same as **cantherius.**

cantharus A fountain or basin in the atrium or courtyard before ancient and some oriental churches, where persons could wash before entering the church.

cantherius The principal rafter in an ancient wooden roof.

cantilever **1.** A projecting bracket used for carrying the cornice or extended eaves of a building. **2.** A beam, girder, truss, or other structural member which projects beyond its supporting wall or column.

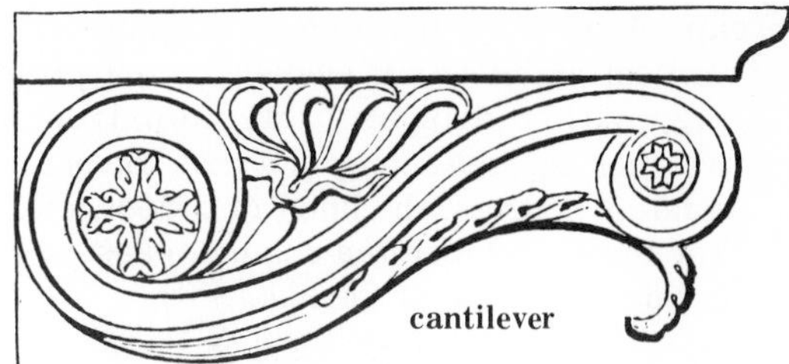
cantilever

cantilever supporting a cornice

cant molding A square or rectangular molding with the outside face beveled.

canton A corner of a building decorated with a projecting masonry course, a pilaster, or similar feature.

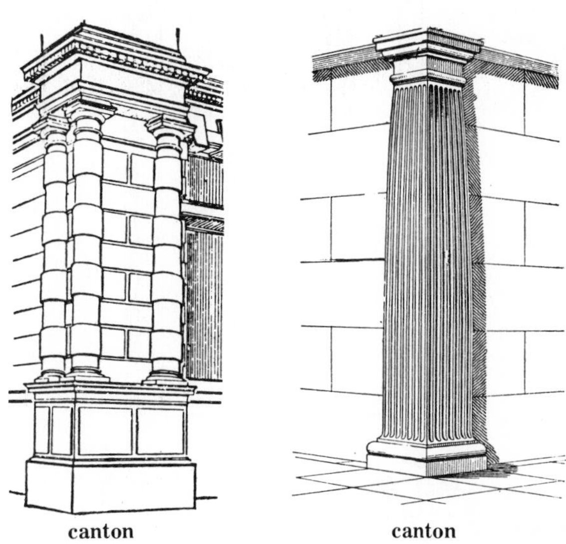
canton canton

cantoned **1.** Ornamented at the corners with projecting pilasters. **2.** Descriptive of a building which is decorated at the corners with columns, pilasters, rusticated quoins, etc., projecting from the face of the building.

cantoned pier Same as **pilier cantonné.**

cantoria A church choir gallery.

cantoris Of or belonging to the cantor or precentor, as the cantoris side of the choir, the side on the left or north as one faces the altar (as opposed to the **decani side**).

cant wall A wall canted on plan.

cant window A bay window erected on a plan of canted outline; the sides are not at right angles to the wall.

canvas wall A plastered wall to which a layer of canvas has been applied to serve as a base for wallpaper.

cap 1. Usually, the topmost member of any vertical architectural element, often projecting, with a drip as protection from the weather, e.g., the coping of a wall, top of a pedestal or buttress, the lintel of a door, etc. 2. The upper member of a column, pilaster, door cornice, molding, or the like.

door cap

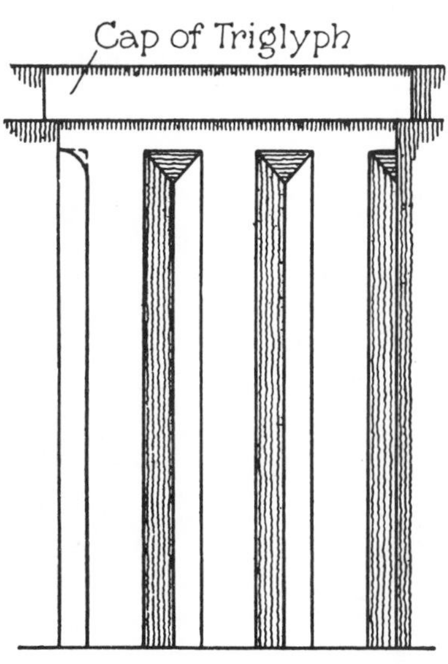

door cap

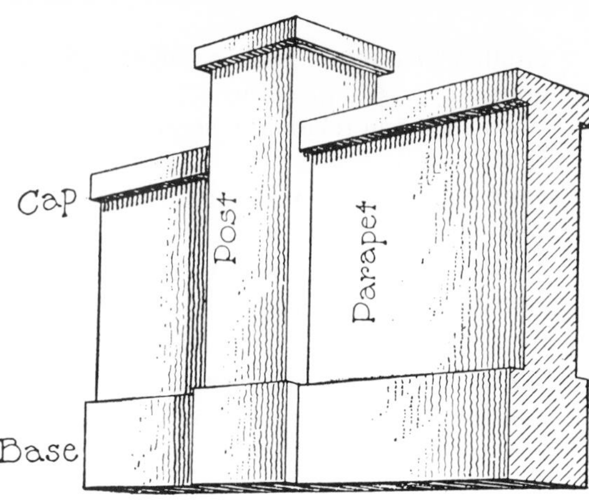

parapet cap

Cape Cod house A rectangular frame (1½-story) house having a pitched roof and usually no dormers; the roof and all sides were covered by long shingles, gray in appearance when weathered. A style which originated in colonial Cape Cod, Mass.; built in one of three types: **half house, three-quarter house,** and **full Cape house.**

Cape Cod house

capeleion 1. In ancient Greece, a place where wine and provisions were sold. 2. The bar in a public inn.

capellaccio A local **tufa** stone used for construction in ancient Rome.

capilla mayor The principal chapel in Spanish churches.

capital The topmost member, usually decorated, of a column, pilaster, anta, etc. It may carry an architrave or an arcade or be surmounted by an impost block (dosseret).

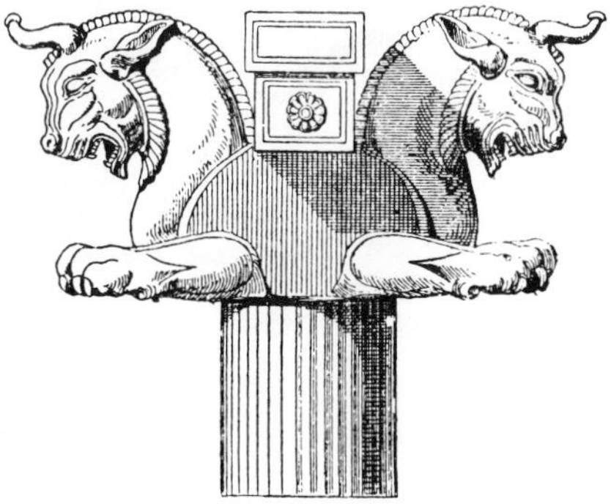

double unicorn, Persepolis

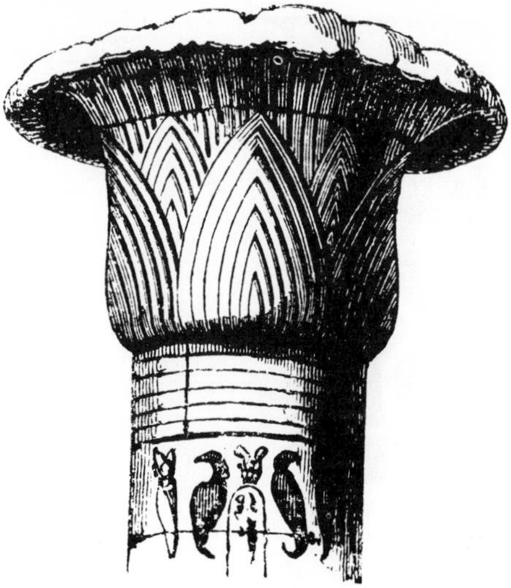

Egyptian

Assyrian

Tuscan

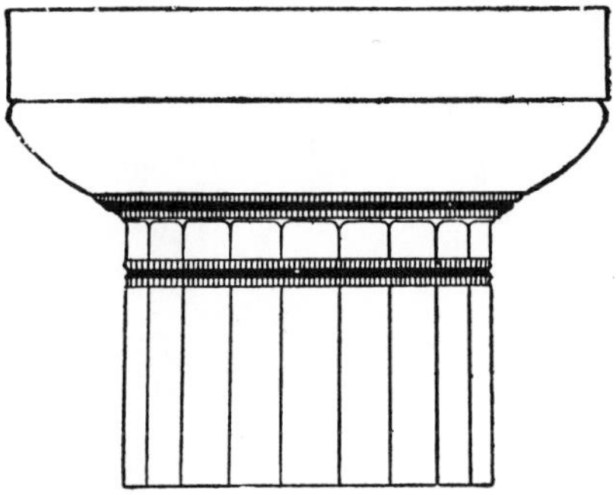

Doric

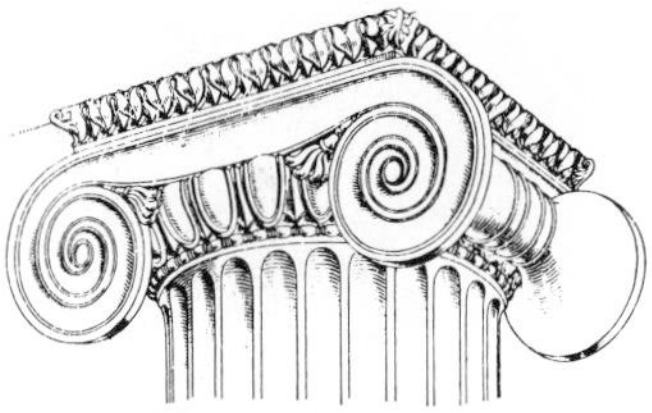

Ionic

Roman Corinthian

Roman Composite

Byzantine

capital

Moorish, the Alhambra

Khmere

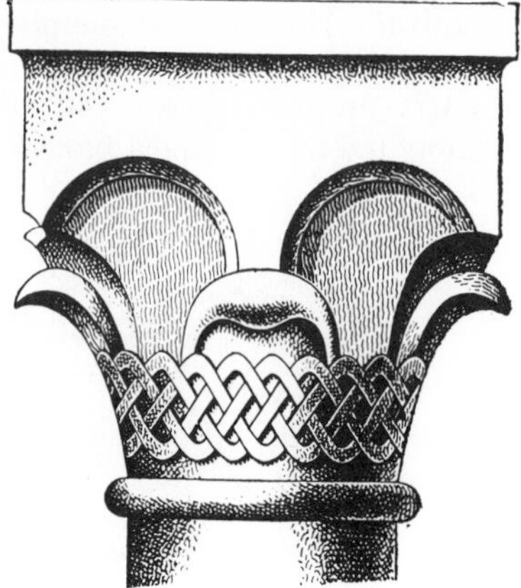
German Romanesque

early French Gothic

Rayonnant

Flamboyant

capital from house of Francis I, Orleans

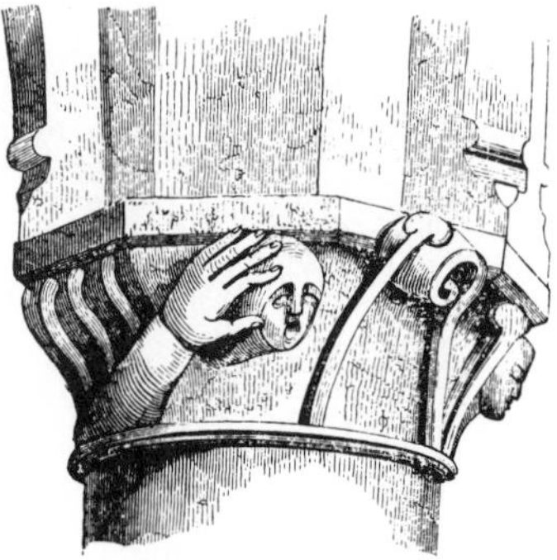
Transition

Transition

Norman | Norman | Norman

Early English | Early English | Decorated

Decorated | Perpendicular | Perpendicular

capitellum Same as **capitolium.**

capitolium **1.** (*cap.*) Originally, the site of the temple to Jupiter Optimus Maximus at Rome. **2.** (*cap.*) Later extended to include the adjacent citadel and the buildings within its precincts. **3.** (*cap.*) Still later, the entire hill was so designated. **4.** The chapter or the chapter house in a monastery.

capitolium vetus The old capitol; a small temple on the Quirinal hill, dedicated to Jupiter, Juno, and Minerva.

cap molding **1.** Molding or trim which embellishes the top of a dado. **2.** Molding at the head of a window or door, above the simple trim of the casing.

cappella del coro The **choir,** or chapel of the choir.

capping Any architectural member serving as a **cap, 1,** such as a **coping.**

capping piece, cap piece, cap plate A piece of timber covering the heads of a series of uprights or other vertical structure.

capreolus In an ancient timber roof, a brace or strut; a king post or tie beam.

caprile In ancient Rome, a structure to house goats.

capstone Any single stone in a **coping.**

captain's house Same as a **square-rigger house.**

captain's walk See **widow's walk.**

caracole, caracol **1.** A **spiral stair.** **2.** The astronomical observatory at Chichén Itzá, Yucatán; an example of classic **Maya architecture** with later Toltec additions; so-called because of its spiral inner staircase.

caravanserai, caravansary **1.** In the middle east, a building or inn for the overnight lodging of travelers by caravan; usually enclosed by a solid wall and entered through a large gate. **2.** By extension, any large inn or hotel.

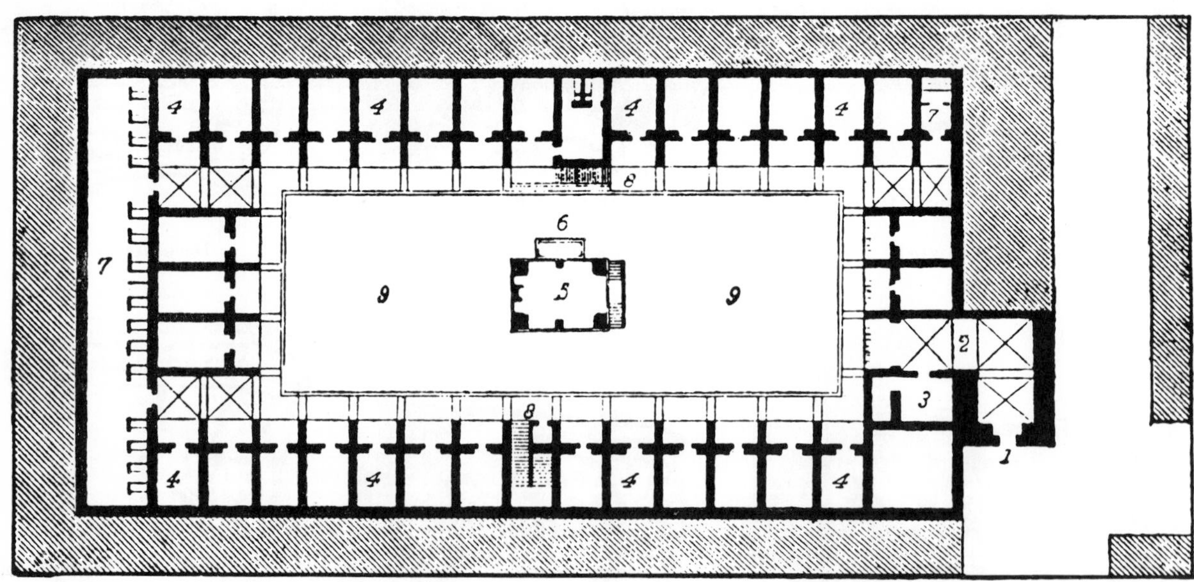

plan of a caravanserai: *1,* entrance; *2,* porch; *3,* porter's quarters; *4,* storerooms where the merchandise is placed; *5,* altar or little mosque; *6,* washbasin; *7,* toilets; *8,* stairways leading to the first floor; *9,* great courtyard

carcase Same as **carcass.**

carcass, carcase **1.** The framework of a building before the addition of sheathing or other covering. **2.** The frame or main parts of a structure unfinished and unornamented, lacking masonry, brickwork, floors, carpentry, plastering, inside trim, etc.

carcer **1.** A prison. **2.** A starting stall in a Roman circus for horse or chariot races. **3.** The dens for beasts in an amphitheatre.

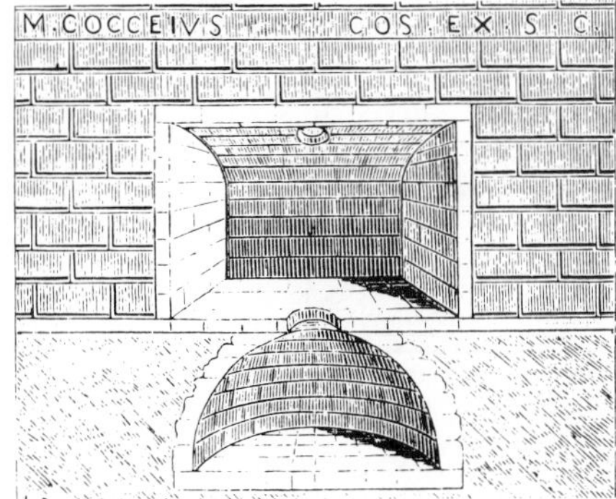

ancient Roman carcer,1

carcer,2

carcer rusticus Same as **ergastulum.**

cardo A hinge or pivot, used in ancient construction to hang a door.

carillon **1.** A bell tower; a **campanile.** **2.** A set of fixed bells, usually hung in a tower and struck by hammers.

carina In Roman antiquity, a building in the form of a ship.

Carnarvon arch A lintel supported on corbels.

carnel An embrasure of a **battlement.**

carnificina In ancient Rome, a subterranean dungeon in which criminals were tortured and in many cases executed.

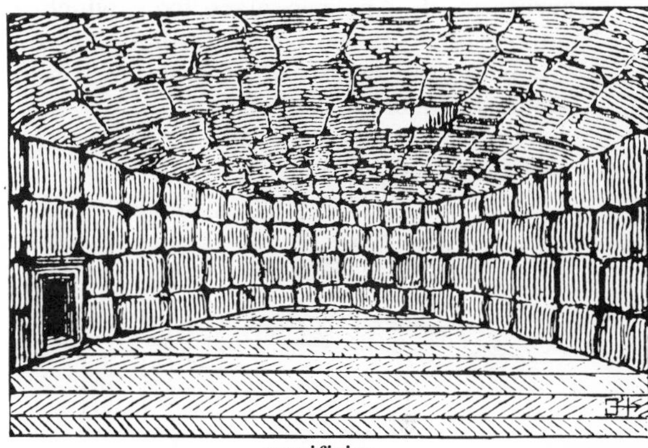

carnificina

carol **1.** An area in a cloister set off by screens, partitions, or railings; similar in use to a **carrel.** **2.** A **carrel.**

Carolingian architecture The pre-Romanesque architecture of the late 8th and 9th cent. in France and Germany. So called after the emperor Charlemagne (768–814). The cathedral of Aachen is the best-known example.

carolitic Decorated with branches and leaves, as a column.

Carpenter Gothic In 19th cent. U.S.A., the application of Gothic motifs, often elaborate, by artisan-builders in wood.

Carpenter Gothic

carreau A single glass or encaustic tile, usually square or diamond-shaped, used in ornamental glazing.

carrefour **1.** An open place from which a number of streets or avenues radiate. **2.** By extension, any crossroad or junction. **3.** A public square or plaza.

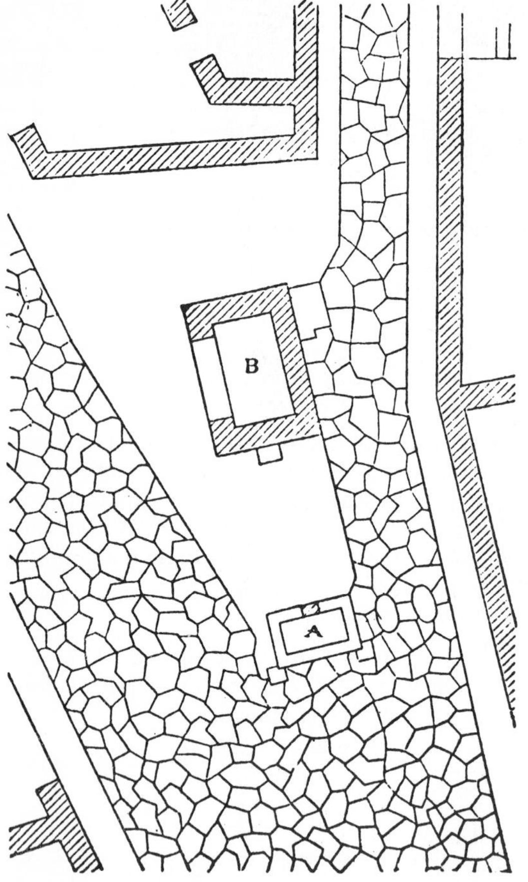

carrefour,2 in Pompeii: *A*, fountain; *B*, castellum

carrel, cubicle **1.** A small individual compartment or alcove in a library, used for semi-private study. **2.** A closet or pew in a monastery.

carrelage Terra-cotta decorative tiling in use in the Middle Ages for floors and the like.

carriage An inclined beam which supports the steps or adds support between the **strings** of a wooden staircase, usually between the wall and outer string.

carriage house See **coach house.**

carriage piece See **carriage.**

carriage porch A roofed structure over a driveway at the door to a building, protecting from the weather those entering or leaving a vehicle. Also see **porte cochère.**

cartibulum An oblong slab of marble supported on a single bracket or console, used as a table in the **atrium** of a Roman house.

cartibulum

carrol Same as **carrel.**

carton pierre A mixture of glue, whiting, paperpulp, and chalk; molded, dried, and finished to form durable, usually interior, architectural embellishments imitating stone, metal, etc.; a kind of **papier-mâché** used for making lightweight cast ornaments where plaster would be too heavy.

cartoon A drawing or painting made as a detailed model, often full-scale, of an architectural embellishment.

cartouche **1.** An ornamental tablet often inscribed or decorated, and framed with elaborate scroll-like carving. **2.** A modillion of curved form. **3.** In Egyptian hieroglyphics and derivatives, a frame around the Pharaoh's name.

cartouche

carved work **1.** In stonework, hand-cut ornamental features which cannot be applied from pattern. **2.** In brickwork, carving, usually on bricks of larger than ordinary size.

carvel joint A flush joint between adjacent planks.

caryatid A supporting member serving the function of a pier, column, or pilaster and carved or molded in the form of a draped, human, female figure.

caryatids

case bay That section of a floor or roof between two principals or girders.

cased beam A beam having a **casing, 2.**

cased glass, case glass, overlay glass Glass formed of two or more fused layers of different colors; the top layer may be cut, permitting a lower layer to show through.

cased-in timber Same as **cased beam.**

cased post A post having a **casing, 2.**

casemate A vault or chamber in a bastion, having openings for the firing of weapons.

casemate wall A city or fortress enclosure consisting of an outer and an inner masonry wall braced by transverse masonry partitions, which divide the interstitial space into a series of chambers for fill or storage.

caryatids at the Erechtheion, Athens (421–405 B.C.)

casement **1.** A window **sash** which swings open along its entire length; usually on hinges fixed to the sides of the opening into which it is fitted; see **casement window.** **2.** A deep hollow molding, used chiefly in cornices.

casement door A **French door.**

casement window A window having at least one **casement, 1;** may be used in any combination with **fixed lights.**

casework The aggregate assembled parts (including framework, finish, doors, drawers, etc.) which make up a case or cabinet.

casing **1.** The exposed trim molding, framing, or lining around a door or window; may be either flat or molded. **2.** Finished millwork, of uniform profile, which covers or encases a structural member such as a post or beam.

casing bead A **bead** applied to edges of a plaster surface to provide a stop or a separation between two dissimilar materials.

cassoon A deep panel or coffer in a ceiling or soffit.

castellated **1.** Bearing the external fortification elements of a castle, in particular, battlements, turrets, etc. **2.** Ornamented with a battlement-like or crenelated pattern.

castellum **1.** See **castellum aquae.** **2.** A small fortified town, or a fort surrounded by a village.

castellum aquae, castellum · A reservoir or building constructed at the terminus of an aqueduct, where it reached the city walls; water was distributed throughout the city from this location. Castella were of three kinds; domestic, private, and public.

castellum domesticum A lead cistern at the house of an individual for his own use.

castellum privatum A **castellum, 1** built by a number of individuals, living in the same neighborhood, who obtained a grant of water; the whole quantity allotted to them collectively was transmitted from the **castellum publicum.**

castellum publicum A **castellum, 1** which received water from a public duct to be distributed throughout the city for public purposes.

cast-iron front A load-bearing façade composed of prefabricated parts, commonly used on commercial buildings ca. 1850–1870.

castle A stronghold; a building or group of buildings intended primarily to serve as a fortified post; a fortified residence of a prince or nobleman.

castellum aquae

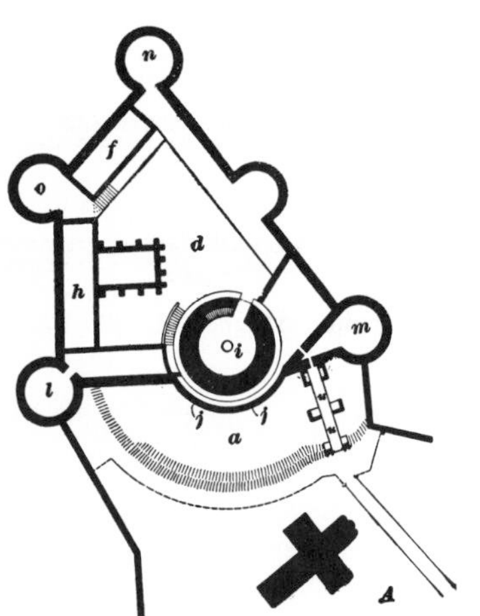

left and *above:* **Castle of Coucy, France:** *a*, **moat;** *A*, **outer bailey;** *d*, **inner bailey;** *f*, **fami apartments;** *h*, **great hall;** *i*, **keep;** *j*, **loopholes;** *l*, *m*, *n*, *o*, **chief towers**

castrum A castle, fort, or fortified town.

cast staff In plastering, a shape, usually decorative, made in a mold and then fastened in place.

catabasis, catabasion See **katabasis.**

catabulum **1.** A building or stable in which beasts of burden and carriages were kept for service in ancient times. **2.** A shed or common room in which the early Christians officiated.

catacomb Underground passageways used as cemeteries, with niches for sarcophagi or smaller ones for cinerary urns.

above: **Catacombes of Saint-Hermes; tomb of a saint converted into an altar;**

below: **catacombs**

catacumba The atrium or courtyard of a basilican church.

catadrome An ancient racecourse of any type; for chariots, for horses, or for men.

catafalque A draped and canopied stage or scaffold, usually erected in a church, on which is placed the coffin or effigy of a deceased person.

cataracta, cataractes **1.** An ancient Roman sluice, floodgate, or lock to regulate the flow of water. **2.** A **portcullis,** suspended over the entrance to a city or fortified place.

catenary The curve formed by a flexible cord hung between two points of support.

catenary arch An arch which takes the form of an inverted catenary.

catenated Decorated by a chain-like motif.

cathedra The bishop's throne, set at the end of the apse in Early Christian churches.

cathedra

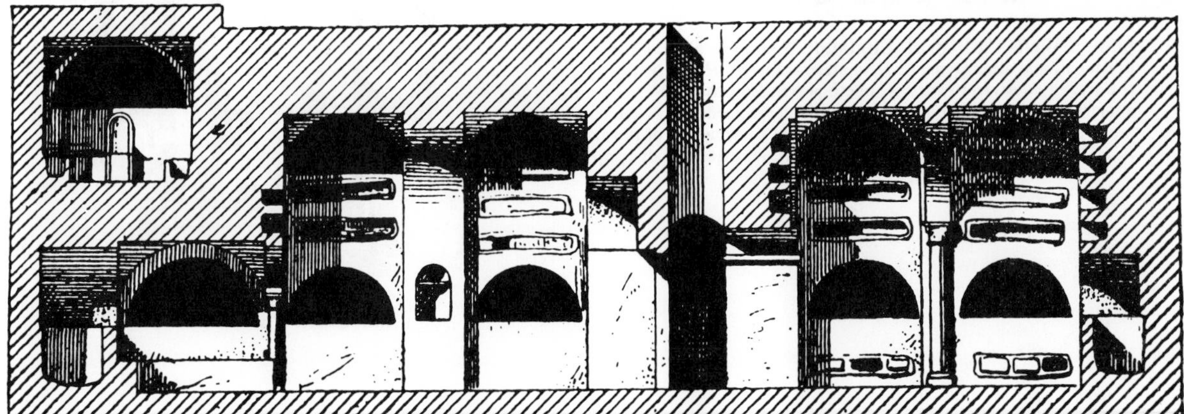

cathedral The home church of a bishop, usually the principal church in a diocese.

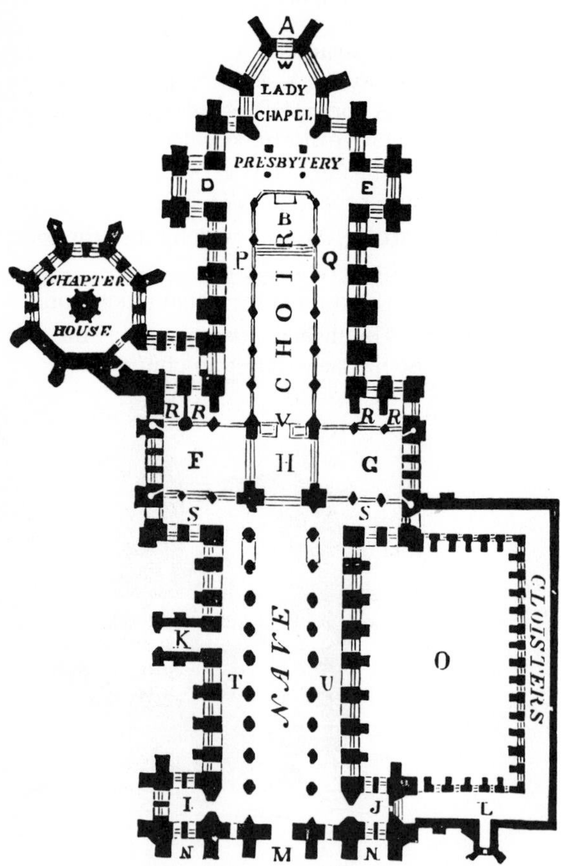

plan of Wells Cathedral, England: *A*, apse; *B*, altar, altar platform, and altar steps; *D*, *E*, eastern transept; *H*, central tower; *I*, *J*, western towers; *K*, north porch; *M*, principal doorway; *N*, *N*, western side doors; *O*, cloister yard; *S*, *S*, east and west aisles of transept; *T*, *U*, north and south aisles of nave; *R*, *R*, chapels; *V*, rood screen and organ loft; *W*, altar of lady chapel

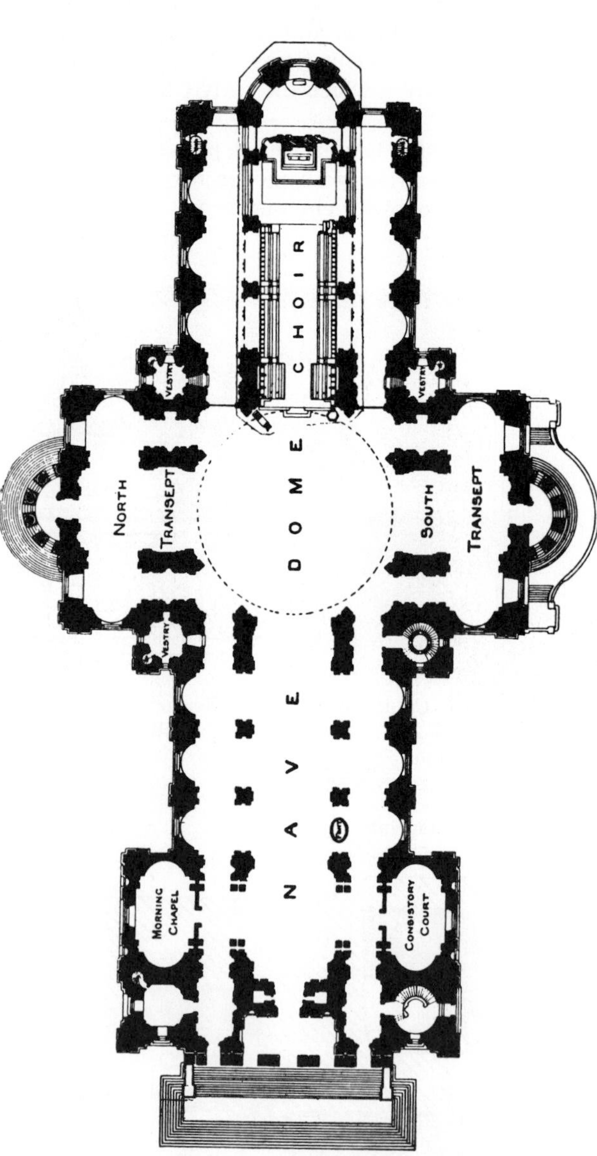

plan of St. Paul's Cathedral

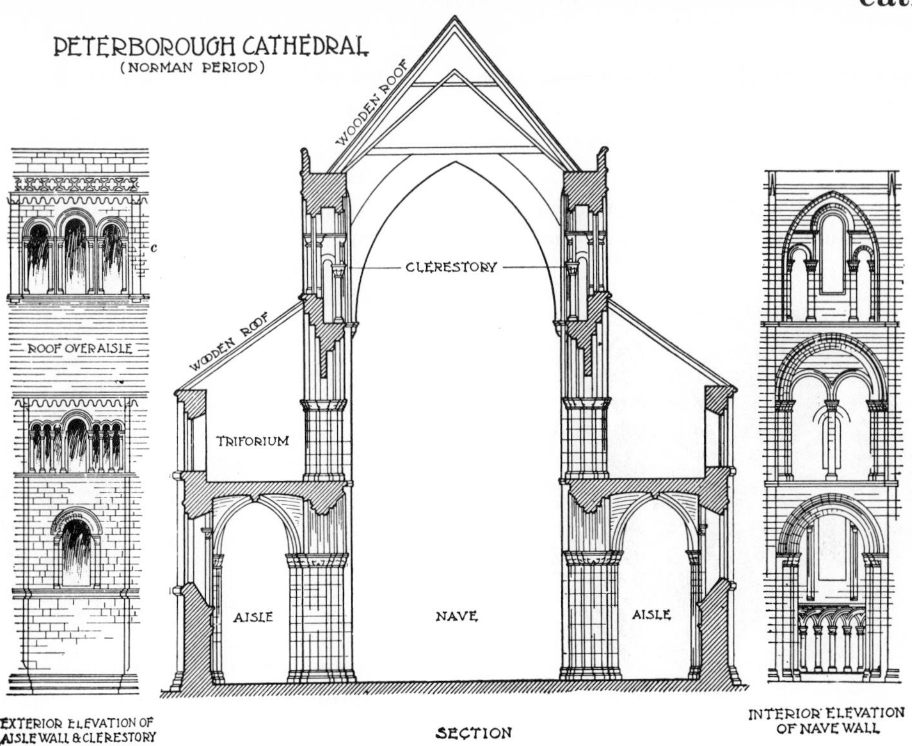
PETERBOROUGH CATHEDRAL
(NORMAN PERIOD)
WOODEN ROOF
CLERESTORY
WOODEN ROOF
ROOF OVER AISLE
TRIFORIUM
AISLE
NAVE
AISLE
EXTERIOR ELEVATION OF AISLE WALL & CLERESTORY
SECTION
INTERIOR ELEVATION OF NAVE WALL

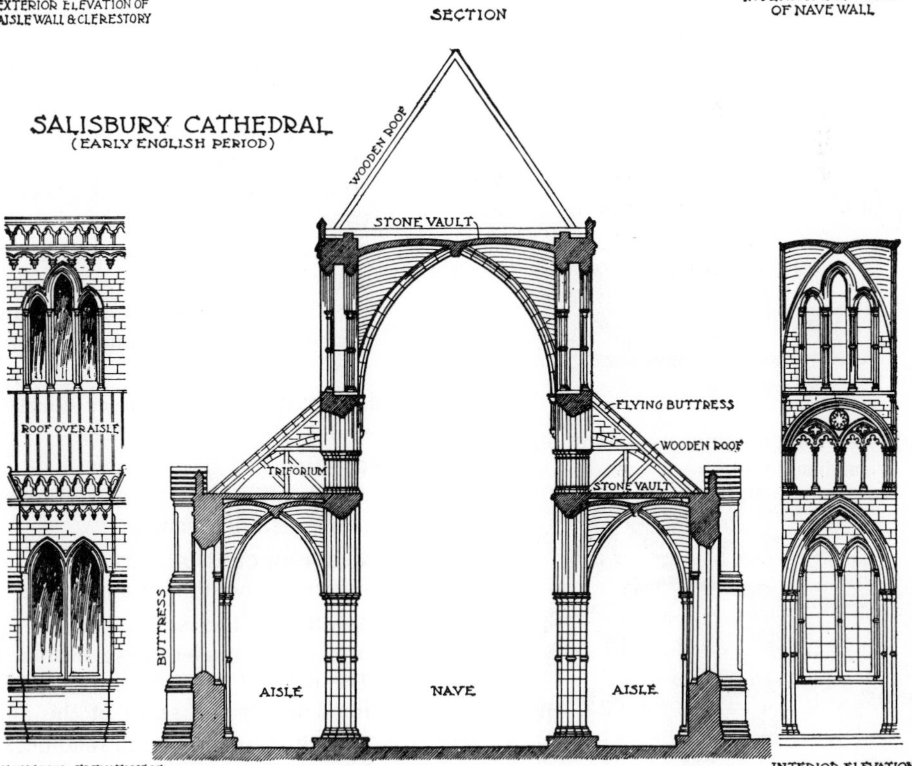
SALISBURY CATHEDRAL
(EARLY ENGLISH PERIOD)
WOODEN ROOF
STONE VAULT
FLYING BUTTRESS
WOODEN ROOF
TRIFORIUM
STONE VAULT
ROOF OVER AISLE
BUTTRESS
AISLE
NAVE
AISLE
EXTERIOR ELEVATION OF AISLE WALL & CLERESTORY
SECTION
INTERIOR ELEVATION OF NAVE WALL

Cathedral of Saint Basil the Blessed See **Saint Basil's Cathedral.**

catherii Rafters in ancient Roman construction.

Catherine-wheel window A round window with radial mullions. A **rose window, wheel window.**

Catherine-wheel window

cathetus The axis of a cylinder, esp. the axial line passing through the eye of an Ionic volute.

catholicon See **katholikon.**

catshead An ornament consisting of an animal-like head, similar to a **beakhead.**

catshead

catslide The long sloping roof at the rear of a **saltbox** or **catslide house.**

catslide house

catslide house Same as **saltbox;** the term is used in southern U.S.A.

catstep See **corbiestep.**

catstone Same as **barstone.**

cauliculus, caulicole Any one of the ornamental stalks rising between the leaves of a Corinthian capital, from which the volutes spring.

cauliculus

caulis One of the main stalks of leaves which spring from between the acanthus leaves of the second row on each side of the typical Corinthian capital, and which are carried up to support the volutes at the angles.

caupona **1.** In ancient Rome, a place where wine and provisions were sold. **2.** A tavern, seldom frequented by any but the commonest people. **3.** An inn for the accommodation of travelers.

causeway **1.** A paved road or passage raised above surrounding low ground. **2.** Such a passage ceremonially connecting the valley temple with the pyramid in Egyptian architecture.

cavaedium **1.** An inner courtyard in a Roman house. **2.** An **atrium.**

cavalier A raised portion of a fortress for commanding adjacent defenses or for the placement of weapons.

cavasion, cavtion, cavazion An excavation for the foundation of a building.

cavea **1.** The semicircular, tiered seating area of an ancient (esp. Roman) theatre. **2.** The dens of the wild beasts, which were confined under the seats of the ancient Roman amphitheatres, to be in readiness for the combats on the arena.

cavetto, gorge, hollow, throat, trochilus A hollow member or round concave molding containing at least the quadrant of a circle, used in cornices and between the tori of bases, etc.

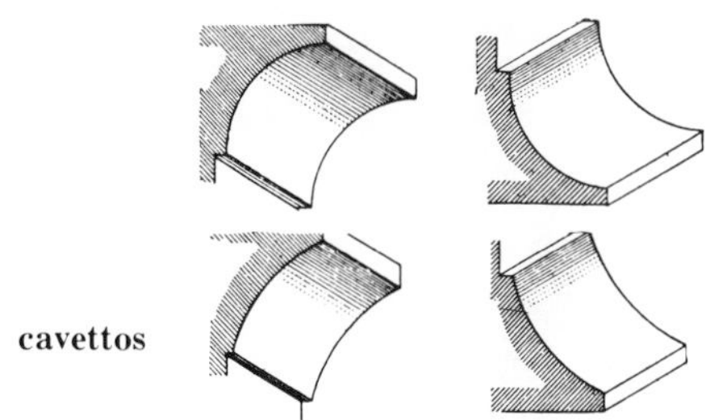

cavettos

cavetto cornice See **Egyptian gorge.**

cavo-rilievo, cavo-relievo See **sunk relief.**

ceele Old English for **canopy.**

ceil **1.** To provide with a ceiling. **2.** To provide with a wainscot finish; to sheathe internally.

ceiling The overhead surface of a room, usually a covering or decorative treatment used to conceal the floor above or the roof.

ceiling cornice Same as **cove molding.**

ceiling joist **1.** Any **joist** which carries a ceiling. **2.** One of several small beams to which the ceiling of a room is attached. They are mortised into the sides of the binding joists, nailed to the underside of these joists, or suspended from them by straps.

ceilure See **celure.**

celature Engraved, chased, or embossed decoration on metal.

cell **1.** Same as **cella.** **2.** A single small cavity surrounded partially or completely by walls. **3.** A segment of a ribbed vault. **4.** The small sleeping apartment of a monk or a prisoner.

cella **1.** The sanctuary of a classical temple, containing the cult statue of the god. Also called **naos.** **2.** Any one of a number of small rooms clustered together, such as were constructed for the dormitories of household slaves, for travelers' sleeping rooms at inns, as chambers occupied by public prostitutes, etc. **3.** A chamber containing the necessary conveniences for bathing in the ancient Roman baths.

cellarino In the Roman or Renaissance Tuscan or Doric orders of architecture, the neck or necking beneath the ovolo of the capital.

cellatio A suite of small rooms, such as those which might be applied for any ordinary purpose, as the **cellae, 2.**

cellula **1.** In ancient Rome, a small sanctuary in the interior of a small temple. **2.** Any small chamber or storeroom.

cellure See **celure.**

Celtic cross A cross with a long vertical shaft and short horizontal arms, and with a circle struck from their intersection, joining all four.

Celtic crosses

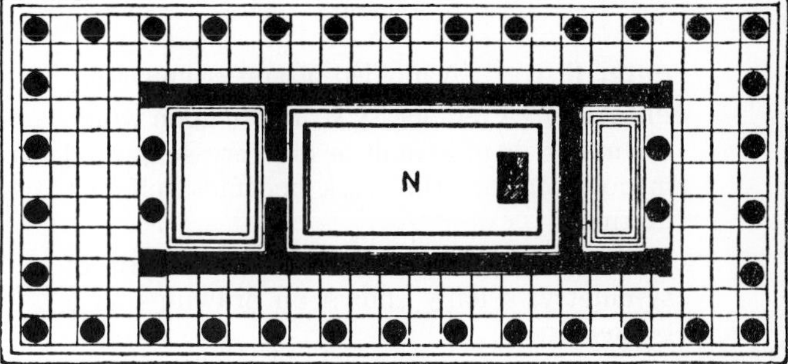

N, cella

celure, ceilure, cellure 1. A decorative ceiling, esp. over the chancel, in medieval church architecture or derivatives. 2. A paneled canopy above an altar or crucifix.

cemetery beacon A lighthouse, placed in graveyards on the European continent in the 12th and 13th cent., with an altar.

cenaculum Same as **coenaculum.**

cenatio In ancient Rome, the formal dining room in a house, sometimes even in a separate annex.

cenotaph A monument erected in memory of one not interred in or under it.

centaur In classical mythology, a monster, half man and half horse; a human torso placed on the body of a horse.

cenotaph at Udaypur, India

centaur

center flower A molded plaster **centerpiece.**

centering A temporary structure upon which the materials of a vault or arch are supported in position until the work becomes self-supporting.

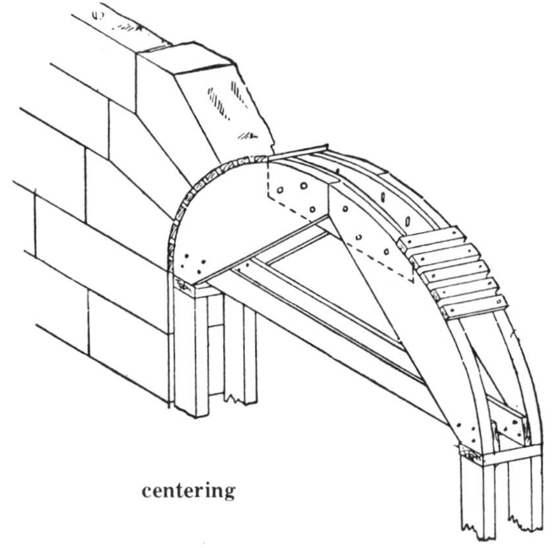

centering

center line A line representing an axis of symmetry; usually shown on drawings as a broken line.

centerpiece An ornament placed in the middle of something, as a decoration in the center of the ceiling.

centry-garth A burying ground or cemetery.

ceramic Any of a class of products, made of clay or a similar material, which are subjected to a high temperature during manufacture or use, as porcelain, stoneware, or terra-cotta; typically a ceramic is a metallic oxide, boride, carbide, or nitride, or a mixture or compound of such materials.

ceramic veneer Architectural terra-cotta with ceramic vitreous or glazed surfaces; characterized by large face dimensions and thin sections. The back is either scored or ribbed.

cercis The wedge-like or trapezoidal section of seats between two of the stepped passageways in a Greek theatre.

ceroma **1.** A plaster, with wax as the principal ingredient. **2.** A mixture of oil, wax, and earth, with which ancient Romans rubbed themselves before wrestling. **3.** The place where the wrestlers were anointed with this mixture.

certosa A monastery of the Carthusian monks, esp. in Italy.

刹 **ch'a** A Chinese temple of medium size; usually located in an isolated area.

chafer house Old English term for ale house.

chain bond Masonry construction which is bonded together by an embedded iron bar or chain.

chain course A bond course formed by stone headers which are held together by cramps.

chaînes A type of wall decoration used in 17th cent. French domestic architecture; consisted of vertical bands of rusticated masonry which divided the façades into panels or bays.

chain molding A molding carved with a representation of a chain.

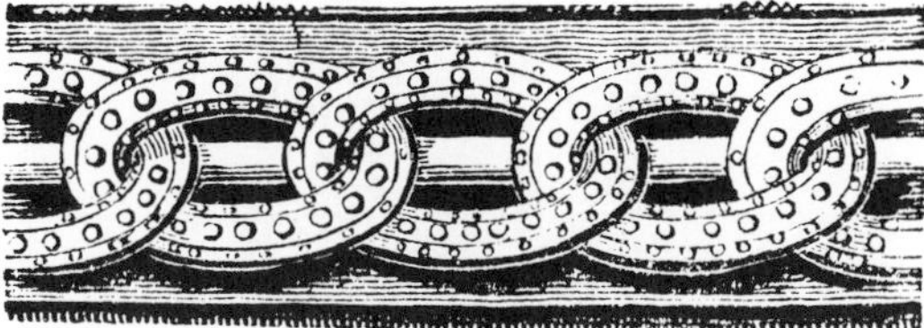

chain molding

chair rail A horizontal strip, usually of wood, affixed to a plaster wall at a height which prevents the backs of chairs from damaging the wall surface.

齋堂 **chai t'ang** In a Chinese religious establishment, a room which serves as a reception area for vegetarians.

chaitya **1.** Originally, a **tumulus.** **2.** Later, a Buddhist sanctuary, shrine, or place of religious worship.

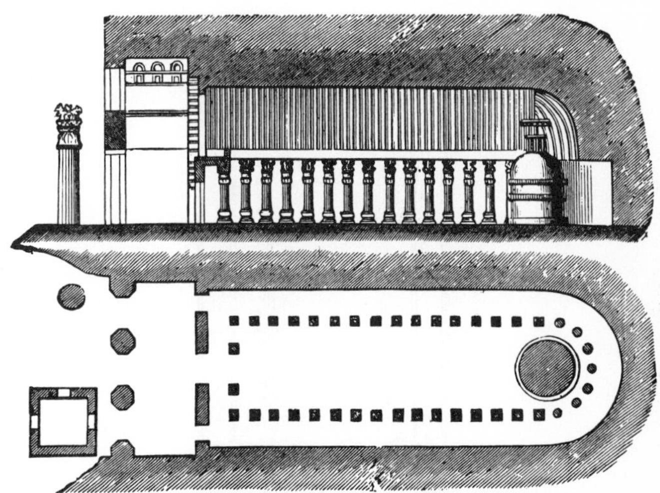

chaitya at Karli, India: section, plan, and interior view

宅院 **chai yüan** The courtyard of a traditional Chinese mansion.

chalcidicum, chalcidic **1.** A portico, or hall supported by columns, or any addition of like character connected with any ancient basilica; hence a similar addition to a Christian church. **2.** In a Christian basilica, the narthex. **3.** In ancient Roman architecture, a building for judicial functions.

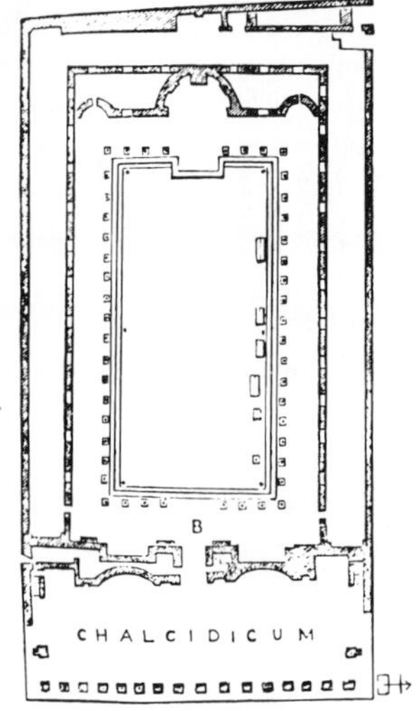

chalcidicum, 1

chalcidicum, 1

chambranle A structural feature, often ornamental, enclosing the sides and top of a doorway, window, fireplace, or similar opening. The top piece or lintel is called the *transverse* and the side pieces or jambs the *ascendants*.

chalcidium A committee room off the main part of an ancient Roman lawcourt (basilica).

chalet **1.** A timber house found in the Alps, distinguished by the exposed and decorative use of structural members, balconies, and stairs. Upper floors usually project beyond the stories below. **2.** Any building of a similar design.

chamber **1.** A room used for private living, conversation, consultation, or deliberation, in contrast to more public and formal activities. **2.** A room for such use which has acquired public importance, e.g., the senate chamber, an audience chamber. **3.** *(Brit., pl.)* A suite of rooms for private dwelling. **4.** (*pl.*) A suite of rooms for deliberation and consultation (juristic). **5.** A space equipped or designed for a special function, e.g., a torture chamber.

chamber tomb See **passage grave.**

chambranle

chamfer 1. A bevel or cant, such as a small splay at the external angle of a masonry wall. 2. A **wave molding.** 3. A groove or furrow. 4. An oblique surface produced by beveling an edge or corner, usually at a 45° angle, as the edge of a board or masonry surface.

chamfer,1 with an ornamental chamfer stop

chamfered rustication Rustication in which the smooth face of the stone parallel to the wall is deeply beveled at the joints so that, where two stones meet, the chamfering forms an internal right angle.

chamferet, chamfret 1. A hollow chamfer. 2. A hollow channel or gutter.

chamfer stop 1. Any ornamentation which terminates a **chamfer.** 2. A **stop chamfer.**

chamfret See **chamferet.**

champ A defined surface ready for carving.

champfer Same as **chamfer.**

chancel The sanctuary of a church, including the choir; reserved for the clergy.

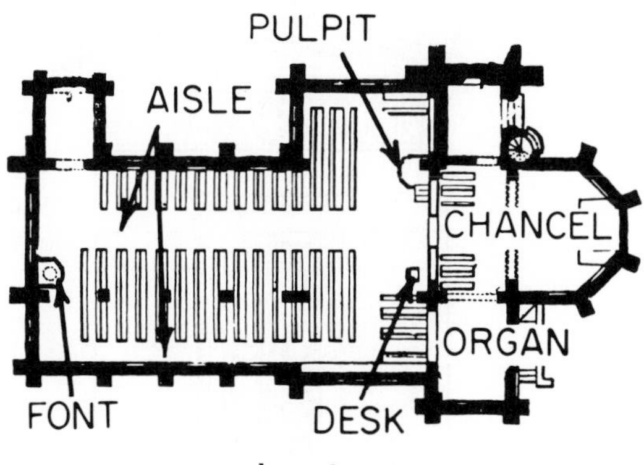

chancel

chancel aisle The side aisle of a chancel in a large church; it usually passes around the apse, forming a deambulatory.

chancel arch An arch which, in many churches, marks the separation of the chancel or sanctuary from the nave or body of the church.

Norman chancel arch

chancellery, chancellory 1. A chancellor's office or a building containing one. 2. The official premises of a diplomatic envoy abroad.

chancel rail The railing or barrier in place of a chancel screen by which the chancel is separated from the nave.

chancel screen Screen dividing the chancel from the nave.

chancery A building or suite of rooms designed to house any of the following: a lawcourt with special functions, archives, a secretariat, a chancellery.

chandi A Hindu sepulchral monument in Java, comprising a cella-like temple and pyramidal superstructure above a square base containing an urn with ashes.

chandlery, chandry A storage room for lighting supplies and devices, required before gas or electricity was available.

chandry See **chandlery.**

channel A decorative groove, in carpentry or masonry.

channeling A series of grooves in an architectural member, such as a column.

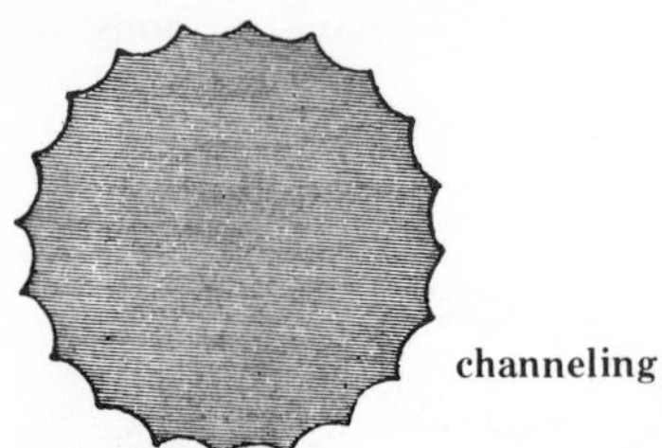
channeling

ch'an t'ang In Chinese architecture, a chamber set aside for meditation, mainly in the Zen sect in Buddhism.

chantlate A piece of wood fastened to the rafters at the eaves and projecting beyond the wall, so as to prevent rainwater from trickling down the face of the wall.

chantry A chapel within a church, endowed for religious services for the soul of the donor or others he may designate.

chantry chamber The room or rooms used by the priest or priests who were attached to a **chantry.**

chao ch'iang See **ying pi.**

chao pi See **ying pi.**

chapel **1.** A small area within a larger church, containing an altar and intended primarily for private prayer. **2.** A room or a building designated for religious purposes within the complex of a school, college, hospital, or other institution. **3.** A small secondary church in a parish.

chapel of ease A church built within the bounds of a parish for the attendance of those who cannot reach the parish church conveniently.

chapel royal The chapel of a royal castle or palace.

chapiter Same as **capital.**

chaplet An **astragal** or **bead molding,** sometimes enriched with carved foliage.

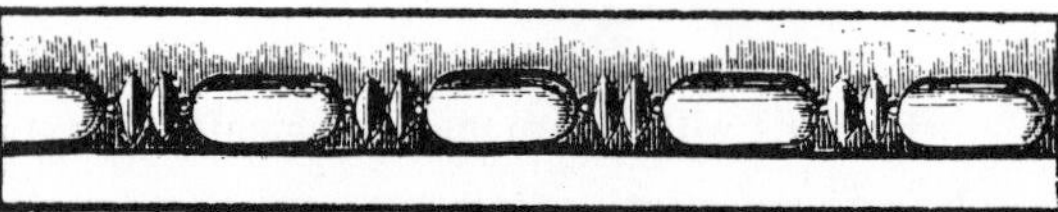

chaplet

chapra A tower having a parabolic outline of a **nagara** temple in India.

chapter house A place for business meetings of a religious or fraternal organization; occasionally also contains living quarters for members of such a group.

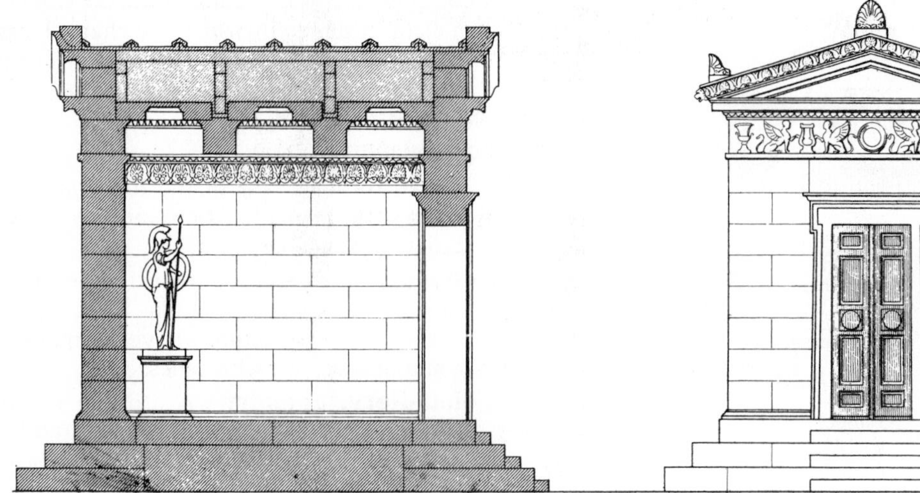
interior view and front elevation of a Hellenic chapel

chaptrel A small capital of a vaulting shaft.

a, chaptrel

charette, charrette **1.** The intense effort to complete an academic architectural problem within a specified time. **2.** The time in which this work is done.

charnel house A building or chamber for the deposit of the bones of the dead.

Charonian steps, Charon's staircase In the early Greek theatre, a flight of steps from the middle of the stage to the orchestra; used by characters from the underworld.

charterhouse A Carthusian monastery.

chartophylacium A place for the safe keeping of records and other valuable documents.

chartreuse A monastery of the Carthusian monks, esp. in France.

茶室 **chashitsu** A room or small elegantly rustic house equipped for the Japanese tea ceremony; usually has an area equal to 4½ **tatami.**

chasovnya In early Russian architecture, a chapel which is a detached structure.

chasse A container for a saint's relics.

château **1.** A castle or imposing country residence of nobility in old France. **2.** Now, any French country estate.

château d'eau At the termination of an aqueduct, a reservoir architecturally embellished as a public fountain.

chatelet A castle of small scale.

chattra On top of a **stupa,** a stone umbrella which symbolizes dignity; composed of a stone disk on a vertical pole.

chattravali Similar to a **chattra,** but having three stone disks; a triple umbrella.

chattrayashti The vertical rod of a **chattra.**

chaumukh In Indian architecture, four images (each facing a cardinal point) which are placed back-to-back.

chauntry Same as **chantry.**

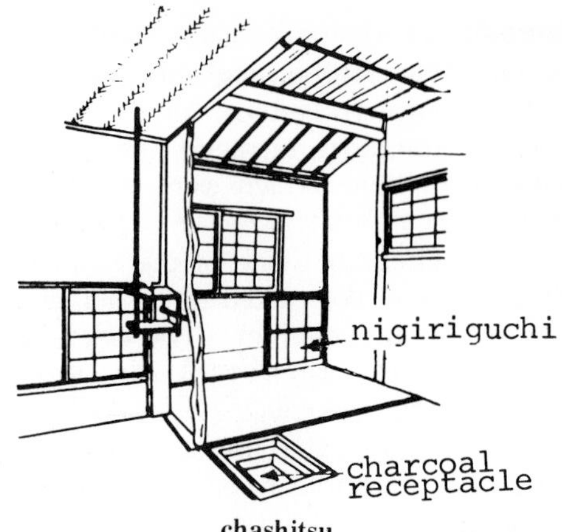

chashitsu

Renaissance château near Tours

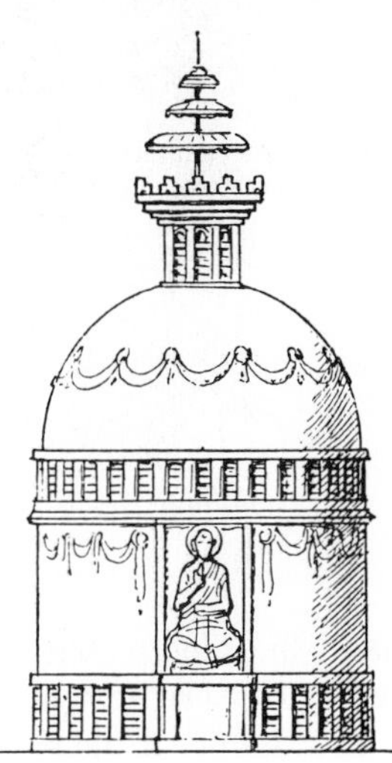
stupa with a chattravali

chavada In western India, a pavilion.

Chavín style The earliest of the architectural styles in northern Peru ca. 900 B.C.; characterized by grandiose terraced platforms, constructed of stone, which were grouped about large sunken plazas.

checker, chequer One of the squares in a check pattern, contrasted to its neighbors by color or texture; often only two effects are alternated, as in a chessboard. Also see **diaper.**

checkerwork In a wall or pavement, a pattern formed by laying masonry units so as to produce a checkerboard effect.

check fillet On a roof, a curb used to divert or control the flow of rainwater.

check throat A groove cut on the underside of a windowsill or doorsill to prevent the passage of drops of rainwater to the wall.

chedi A **stupa**-like Thai monument erected above a **cella** containing a relic.

cheek A narrow upright face forming the end or side of an architectural or structural member, or one side of an opening.

chemin-de-ronde A continuous gangway behind a rampart, providing a means of communication along a fortified wall.

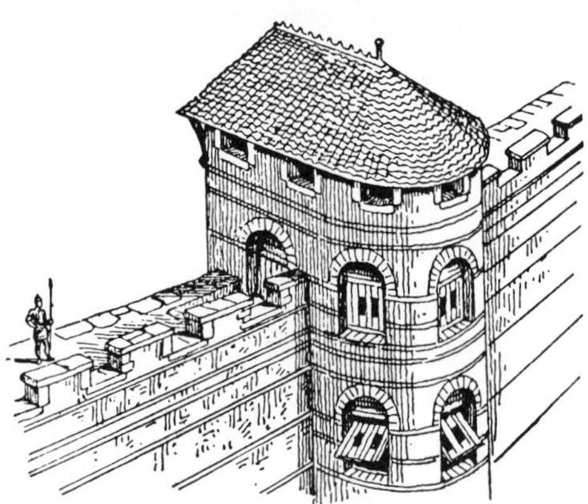

chemin-de-ronde

chên ch'üan In Chinese construction, a **semicircular arch** or **triangular arch.**

cheneau **1.** A gutter at the eaves of a building, esp. one that is ornamented. **2.** An ornamented **crest, 2** or cornice.

Chenes style A variant of **Rio Bec style** of Mayà architecture; characterized by doorways representing the gaping mouth of a serpent or earth monster; radiating from Hochob in Campeche, this style appears at Chichén Itzá (e.g., the Nunnery Annex) and at Uxmal (on the west temple entrance of the Pyramid of the Magician).

城隍廟

ch'êng huang miao A Chinese temple dedicated to a diety who acts as the city magistrate, in a supernatural way.

chên h'üan In Chinese architecture, a **triangular arch.**

chenoboscion An ancient term for a goose yard; placed near a running stream or a pond, with a good supply of herbage.

chequer See **checker.**

cherub A putto; see **putti** (*pl.*)

cheval-de-frise, *pl.* **chevaux-de-frise** Sharply pointed nails or spikes set into the top of a barrier.

chevet An apse having a surrounding ambulatory; usually opens into three or more chapels which radiate from the apse.

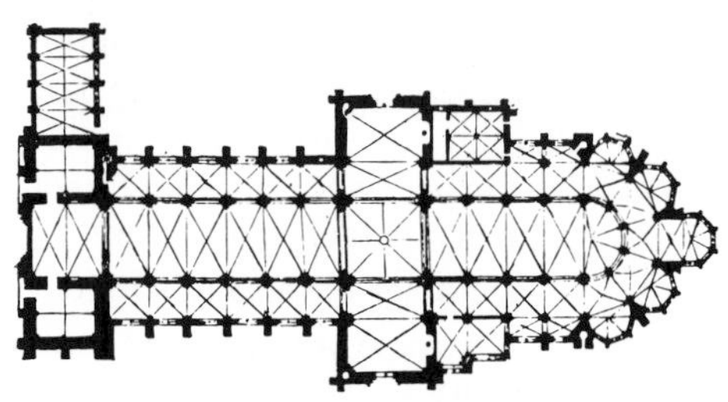

plan and elevation of an apse with chevets

chevron **1.** A V-shaped stripe pointing up or down, used singly or in groups in heraldry and on uniforms; hence, any ornament so shaped. **2.** A molding showing a zigzag sequence of these ornaments in Romanesque architecture or derivatives; a **dancette** or **zigzag molding.**

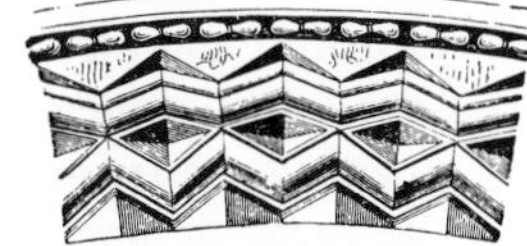
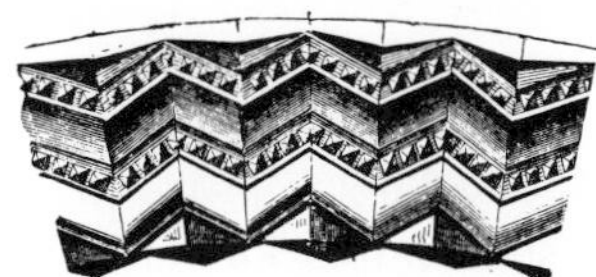

examples of chevron,2

chhattra Same as **chattra.**

chhattravali Same as **chattravali.**

chhattrayashti Same as **chattrayashti.**

chia ch'üan In Chinese architecture, a **corbel arch.**

架樑 **chia liang** A wood-beam roof framing system in a traditional Chinese building.

翹 **ch'iao** In traditional Chinese construction, the bracket member of the **tou kung** system of construction; located under the **ang** bracket.

橋 **ch'iao** In Chinese architecture, a bridge.

chiao chu See **chu.**

ch'iao ti A bracket, at right angles to a column, usually structural, providing extra support for lintels, but may be merely a decorative wood-carved grille.

Chichén Itzá In Yucatán, Mexico, the site of the largest postclassic center of Maya civilization whose architecture had its roots in the classic **Puuc style**; the Nunnery, the Annex of the Nunnery, the Iglesia, and the substructure of the Caracol are examples of this style. Structures showing the influence of Toltec architecture which was introducted from Mexico in the 10th cent. include: the largest of all Mesoamerican ritual ballcourts (to which is attached the Temple of the Jaguars) and the Great Plaza which is surrounded by the Pyramid of Kukulkan, the Temple of the Warriors, the Group of the Thousand Columns, and the Marketplace.

碣 **chieh** A stone pylon with an inscription which identifies and describes the location where it was erected; usually rectangular in cross section, although some are cylindrical; half the height of a **pei.**

chien A standard unit of floor space or bay in a Chinese dwelling.

chien-assis A small unglazed **dormer window** used to provide light and ventilation in an attic or space below a sloping roof; esp. used in buildings during the Middle Ages.

chien-assis

違棚 **chigai-dana** In the Shoin style of Japanese architecture, shelves which are placed in a step-like arrangement in an alcove.

right: **chigai-dana;** *left:* **toko-no-ma**

千木 **chigi** Originally, the projecting **barge couples,** at the ends of the ridge of a roof in a Shintō shrine; now usually a pair of crossed timbers which are placed at each end of the ridge; also called *forked finials.*

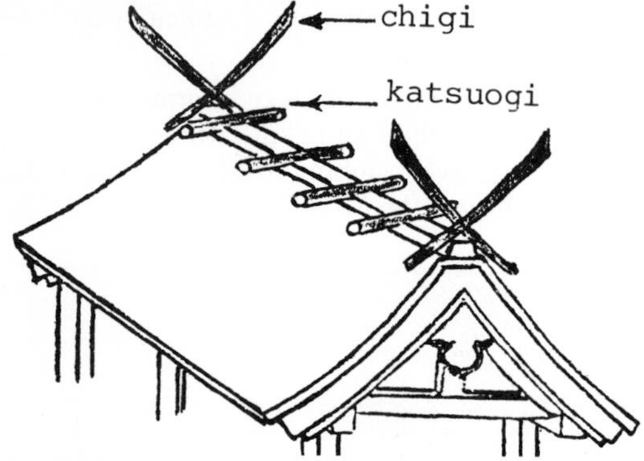

chimera A fantastic assemblage of animal forms so combined as to produce a single complete, but unnatural, design.

chimera

chimney arch The arch over the opening of a fireplace, supporting the breast.

chimney back See **fireback.**

chimney bar, turning bar A metal bar which is supported by the side walls and carries the masonry above the fireplace opening.

chimney breast, chimney piece A projection into a room of fireplace walls forming the front portion of the chimney stack.

chimney can A **chimney pot.**

chimney cap, bonnet An abacus or cornice forming a crowning termination of a chimney.

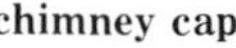

chimney cap

chimney cheek The sides of a fireplace opening which generally support the mantelpiece.

chimney corner, inglenook, roofed ingle An area adjacent to the hearth, usually provided with seating.

chimney crane A pivoted arm of cast iron attached to the rear wall of the fireplace upon which to hang pots for cooking.

chimney cricket A small false roof built over the main roof behind a chimney; used to provide protection against water leakage where the chimney penetrates the roof.

chimney crook, chimney hook In a fireplace, a cast-iron bar, hooked at the lower end and adjustable in length, upon which to suspend pots from a crane or other support.

chimneyhead The top of a chimney.

chimney hood A covering which protects a chimney opening.

chimney jamb One of the two vertical sides of a fireplace opening.

chimneypiece An ornamental embellishment above and/or around the fireplace opening.

chimney pot, chimney can A cylindrical pipe of brick, terra-cotta, or metal placed atop a chimney to extend it and thereby increase the draft.

chimney stack **1.** A group of chimneys carried up together. **2.** A very tall chimney, usually round in cross section.

chimney stalk Same as **chimney stack.**

chimney throat, chimney waist The narrowest portion of a chimney flue, between the "gathering" (or upward contraction above the fireplace) and the flue proper; often where the damper is located.

chimney waist, chimney waste Same as **chimney throat.**

chimney wing One of the sides or lateral cheeks of the gathering in of a chimney, immediately above a fireplace, by which the jambs are contracted toward the throat.

chimneypiece

Chimu architecture Architecture of a culture which was dominant in northern Peru from the 13th to 15th cent. The houses were built in rows, along symmetrically laid-out streets, within high city walls; the buildings were constructed of adobe with wood lintels; the walls, ramps, and chambers were decorated with wide carved moldings having geometric designs (typically birds and fish). Chan Chan, the capital of the Chimus, is famed for its adobe arabesques.

chinbeak molding One consisting of a convex followed by a concave profile, with or without a fillet below or between, as an inverted ogee, or an ovolo, fillet, and cove.

chin chu See **chu.**

Chinese architecture A highly homogeneous traditional architecture which repeated throughout the centuries established types of simple, rectangular, low-silhouetted buildings constructed according to canons of proportions and construction methods which varied with each dynasty and period and varied from one region to another. Stone and brick were used for structures demanding strength and permanence, such as fortifications, enclosure walls, tombs, pagodas, and bridges. Otherwise buildings were mostly constructed in a wooden framework of columns and beams supported by a platform, with nonbearing curtain or screen walls. The most prominent feature of the Chinese house was the tile-covered gabled roof, high-pitched and upward-curving with widely overhanging eaves resting on multiple brackets. Separate roofs over porches surrounding the main buildings or, in the case of pagodas, articulating each floor created a distinctive rhythmical, horizontal effect.

ch'ing chên ssŭ An Islamic temple in ancient China; follows designs similar to such temples in the Near East, but assimilated into the Chinese style since the Yan dynasty (14th to 17th cent.); usually constructed of wood but many are masonry.

紀念堂 **chi nien t'ang, chi nien kuan** In Chinese architecture, a memorial hall.

chink In a wall, a crack or fissure of greater length than breadth.

chin kang ch'iang 金剛墻 **1.** In Chinese masonry bridge construction, the abutment wall from which the arch of the bridge springs; usually submerged in water. **2.** Any load-bearing wall.

chinking Material used for filling a chink in a wall.

chinoiserie A Western European and English architectural and decorative fashion employing Chinese ornamentation and structural elements, particularly in 18th cent. Rococo design.

ch'in tien 寢殿 In an ancient Chinese royal cemetery, a ceremonial palace in which an emperor's coffin was placed.

chip carving Hand-decorating a wood surface by slicing away chips, forming incised geometric patterns.

chi shou 脊獸 Decorative glazed terra-cotta animals or figures along the ridge of a traditional Chinese roof.

choir That part of a church between the sanctuary and the nave reserved for singers and clergy.

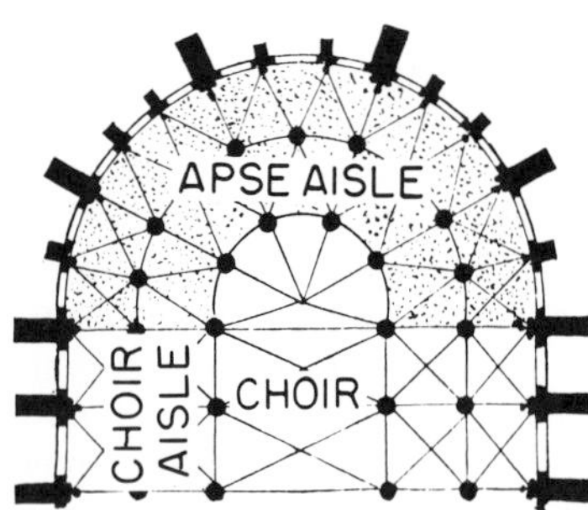

choir aisle An aisle parallel to and adjoining the choir.

choir loft A balcony choir area.

choir rail A railing separating the choir from the nave or the crossing.

choir screen, choir enclosure A screen wall, railing, or partition of any type dividing the choir from the nave, aisles, and crossing.

choir stall A seat with arms and a high back, often covered with a canopy, for clergy and singers.

choir wall A wall between piers and under an arcade screening the choir from the aisles.

choir

choltry Same as **choultry.**

choneion In the Greek Orthodox church, a **piscina.**

choragic monument In ancient Greece, a commemorative structure, erected by the successful leader in the competitive choral dances in a Dionysiac festival, upon which was displayed the bronze tripod received as a prize; such monuments sometimes were further ornamented by renowned artists.

Choragic Monument of Lysicrates, Athens (334 B.C.)

choragium In ancient Greece and Rome, a large space behind a theatre stage where the chorus rehearsed and where stage properties were kept.

choraula Rehearsal room in a church for a choir.

chord **1.** A principal member of a truss which extends from one end to the other, primarily to resist bending; usually one of a pair of such members. **2.** The straight line between two points on a curve. **3.** The span of an arch.

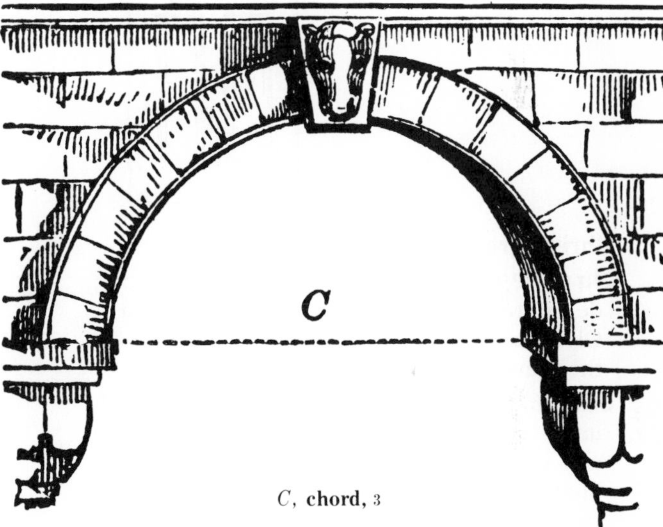

C, **chord,** 3

chorium Same as **chorus.**

chorten A Tibetan **stupa.**

chorus The Latin term for a **course** in regular masonry.

軸柱 **chou chu** In Chinese architecture, a stone abutment for a simple span bridge.

choultry **1.** A **caravanserai.** **2.** In India, a large village hall or place of assembly.

chresmographion The chamber between the pronaos and the nave or cella of a Greek temple where the oracles were delivered.

chrismatory A niche close to a church font which holds the consecrated oil for baptism.

chrismon Christ symbol composed of the first two letters of the Greek word for Christ, chi and rho; a "Christogram."

Christian door The front door of a colonial New England house in which the exterior paneling forms a cross.

Christian door

Christogram See **chrismon.**

chryselephantine Made of gold and ivory; descriptive of statues of divinities, like Zeus at Olympia, with ivory for the flesh and gold for the drapery, on a wooden armature.

柱 **chu** In traditional Chinese architecture, a column. Special types of columns include: *p'ing chu,* central bay column; *chiao chu,* corner column; *nei chu,* hypostyle column; *yen chu,* peripteral column; and *chung chu,* ridge column. Corresponds to **hashira** in traditional Japanese architecture.

chu

chua A Buddhist temple in Vietnam.

ch'üan In traditional Chinese construction, an arch.

ch'uang An octagonally shaped stone column serving as a religious monument in China since the 7th cent.; tipped with a roof-shaped covering; the column, usually 12 to 15 ft (approx. 4 to 5 m) high, is carved with Buddhist inscriptions.

ch'uang In Chinese architecture, a window. May be of the casement type with side hinges, it may have hinges along the top or bottom, it may be a sliding window, or it may be a fixed opening used to frame a landscape or filled with a decorative grille. Double glazing is used in the north; similar to **mado** in Japanese architecture.

ch'uang ling A wood grille, either carved or made in strips, formed in different patterns; used in fenestration in traditional Chinese architecture.

ch'uan tzŭ In traditional Chinese construction, a **purlin** on the exterior portion of the roof, projecting from a gable.

chūdō See **kondō.**

chullpa, chulpa A pre-Inca burial tower of the Peruvian and Bolivian highlands, constructed of **pirca** masonry; usually circular but occasionally rectangular in shape.

chullpa

chūmon In Japanese architecture, the middle gate between the main gate and the sacred area of a Buddhist temple.

chung chu See **chu.**

鐘楼

chung lou A structure which houses a bell; either a pavilion or a tower located at the right side of an entrance court of a Chinese temple or shrine, or at the right side of a city gate or palace entrance.

chū-nuri Same as **naka-nuri.**

church An edifice or place of assemblage specifically set apart for Christian worship.

church house A building used for the social and secular activities of a parish.

Church of Divine Wisdom, Church of Holy Wisdom Same as **Hagia Sophia.**

Church of St. Sophia See **Hagia Sophia.**

church stile Old English for **pulpit.**

churn molding Same as **zigzag molding.**

Churrigueresque architecture The lavishly ornamented Spanish Baroque style of the early 18th cent., named after the architect José Churriguera; a style also adopted in South America.

chymol See **gemel.**

chyngil Obsolete spelling of **shingle.**

ciborium A permanent canopy erected over a high altar; a **baldachin.**

ciele Old English for **canopy.**

cilery The ornamental carving, such as foliage, around the capital of a column.

cill British term for **sill.**

cillery Same as **cilery.**

cima See **cyma.**

cimbia A band or fillet around the shaft of a column.

cimborio A lantern or cupola above or nearly above the high altar in Spanish architecture.

cimeliarch The treasury of a church for storing valuables such as ceremonial garb and holy objects.

cincture, girdle A ring of moldings around the top or bottom of the shaft of a column, separating the shaft from the capital or base; a fillet around a post. Also see **necking.**

cinerarium A depository for urns containing the ashes of the dead.

ciborium

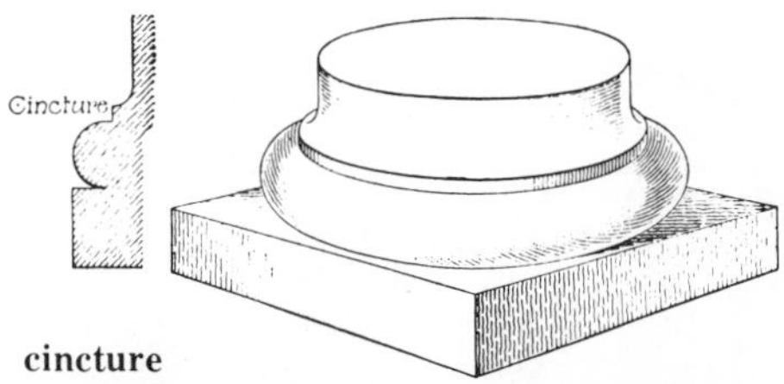

cincture

cinerarium

Cinquecento architecture Renaissance architecture of the 16th cent. in Italy.

above: **from the façade of Sta. Maria de' Miracoli, Brescia (c. 1350)**

chimneypiece

fragment from the Pelegrini Chapel, Verona (1557)

Palazzo Pompeii, Verona (1530–)

cinquefoil A five-lobed pattern divided by **cusps;** also see **foil.**

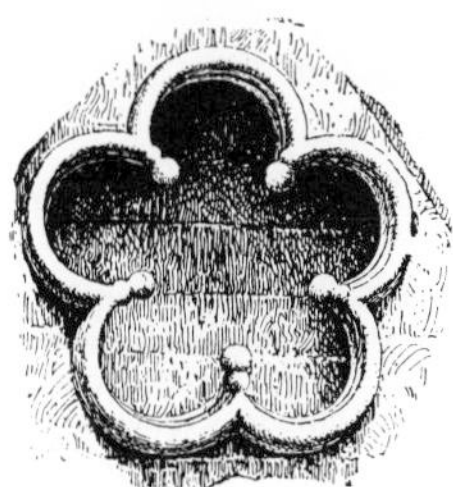

cinquefoil

cinquefoil arch A cusped arch having five foliations worked on the **intrados.**

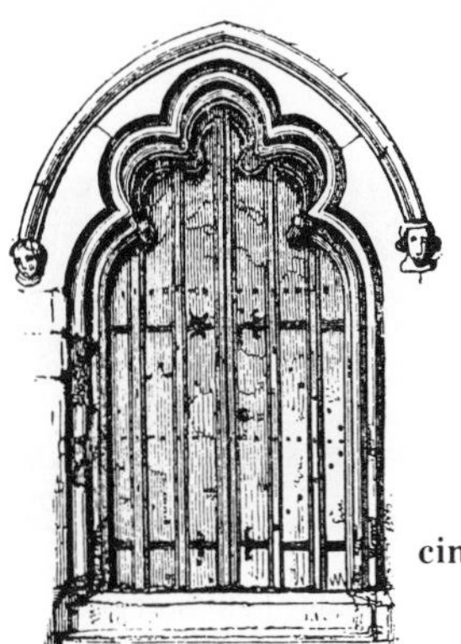

cinquefoil arch

cippus A small, low column or pillar, sometimes without a base or capital, usually bearing an inscription; used as a boundary marker, gravestone, or landmark.

circular arch An arch whose intrados takes the form of a segment of a circle.

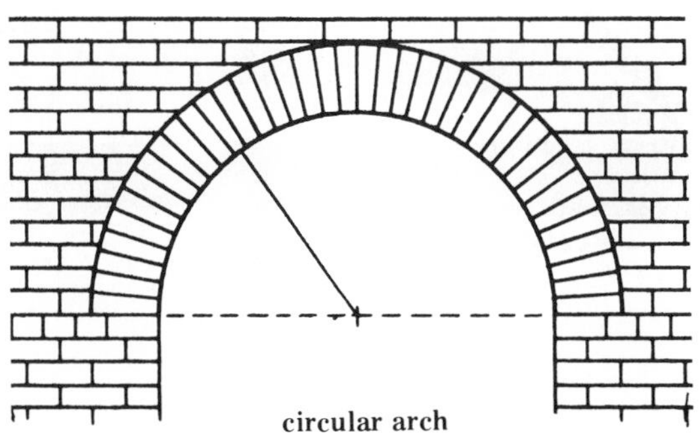

circular arch

cippus

SEX·ATILIVS·M·F·SARANVS·PROCOS
EX·SENATI·CONSVLTI
INTER·ATESTINOS·ET·VEICETIVOS
FINIS·TERMINOSVVE·STATVI·IVSIT

cippus

circular-circular face, circle-on-circle face In stonework, carpentry, and joinery: a face worked to convex spherical shape, presenting a curved outline in both plan and elevation.

circular-circular sunk face, circle-on-circle sunk face Same as **circular-circular face** but presenting a concave outline, in both plan and section.

circular face In stonework, a face worked to convex circular shape.

circular stair, spiral stair A stair having a cylindrical staircase.

circular sunk face In stonework, a face worked to concave circular shape; the opposite of **circular face.**

circular work See **compass work.**

circumvallate To surround an area with a wall or ramparts.

circumvolution One of the turns in the spiral of the **volute** of the Ionic column.

circus, hippodrome In ancient Rome, a roofless enclosure for chariot or horse racing and for gladiatorial shows; usually a long oblong with one rounded end and a barrier down the center; seats for the spectators usually on both sides and around one end.

cist Same as **cistvaen.**

cistern An artificial reservoir or tank for storing water at atmospheric pressure (such as rainwater collected from a roof) for use when required.

cistvaen, kistvaen A Celtic sepulchral tomb or chamber formed by placing huge flat stone slabs on end, set together like a box; if set below ground, it is covered by a **tumulus.**

citadel A fortress or castle in or near a city, intended to keep the inhabitants in subjugation, or, in case of a siege, to supply a final refuge.

civery See **severy.**

civic crown, civic wreath In ancient Rome, an honorary ornament, consisting of a garland of oak leaves, on a monument to one who had saved the life of a Roman citizen in battle.

clapboard, bevel siding, lap siding A wood siding commonly used as an exterior covering on a building of frame construction; applied horizontally and overlapped, with the grain running lengthwise; thicker along the lower edge than along the upper.

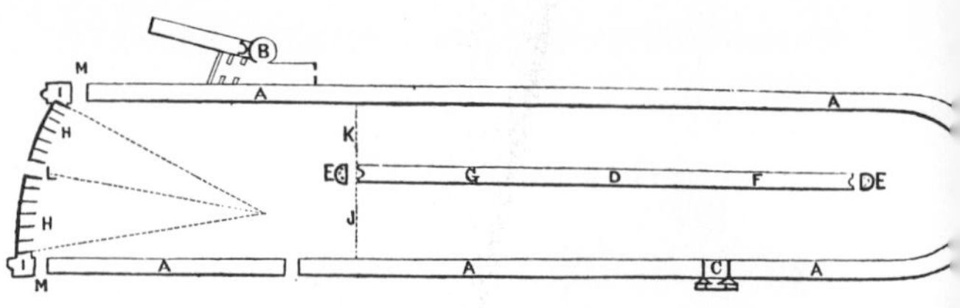

plan of the Circus of Romulus: *A, A,* seats (cavea); *B,* probably the pulvinar or station of the Emperor; *C,* seat for a person of distinction; *D,* spina; *E, E,* metae or goals; *F,* ova; *G,* delphinae; *H, H,* stalls for horses and chariots (carceres); *I, I,* two towers; *J,* starting line of race; *K,* goal line of return; *L,* entrance of procession; *M, M, O,* other entrances and exits

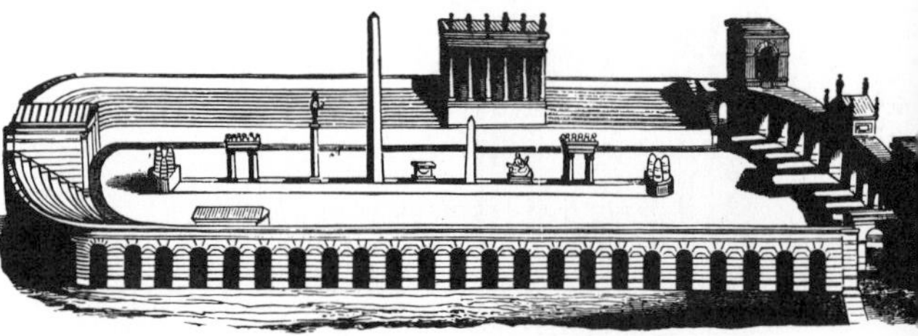

Circus Maximus, Rome: presumably built in the reign of Tarquin I (c. 616–c. 578 B.C.); rebuilt by Julius Caesar (from 46 B.C.), and further ornamented by later emperors

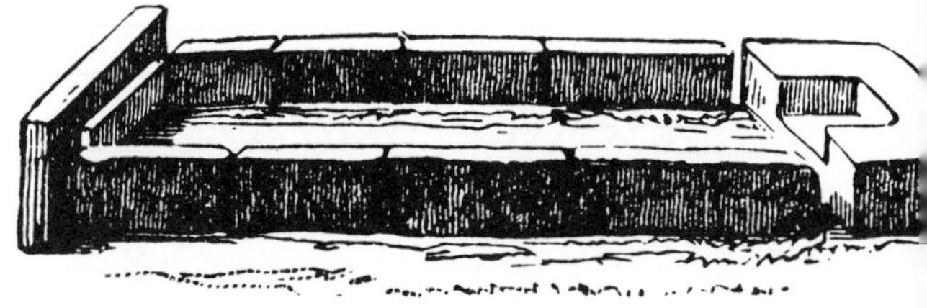

cistvaen

Classical architecture The architecture of Hellenic Greece and Imperial Rome on which the Italian Renaissance and subsequent styles such as the Baroque and the Classic Revival based their development. The Five Orders are a characteristic feature. (See illustrations under **order.**)

classical order See **order.**

classicism In architecture, principles that emphasize the correct use not only of Roman and Greek, but also of Italian Renaissance models.

Classic Revival An architectural movement based on the use of pure Roman and Greek forms, mainly in England and the U.S.A. in the early 19th cent., but in a wider sense in all of Western Europe in reaction to Rococo and Baroque design. One can distinguish between Greek Revival and Roman Revival.

Classic Revival

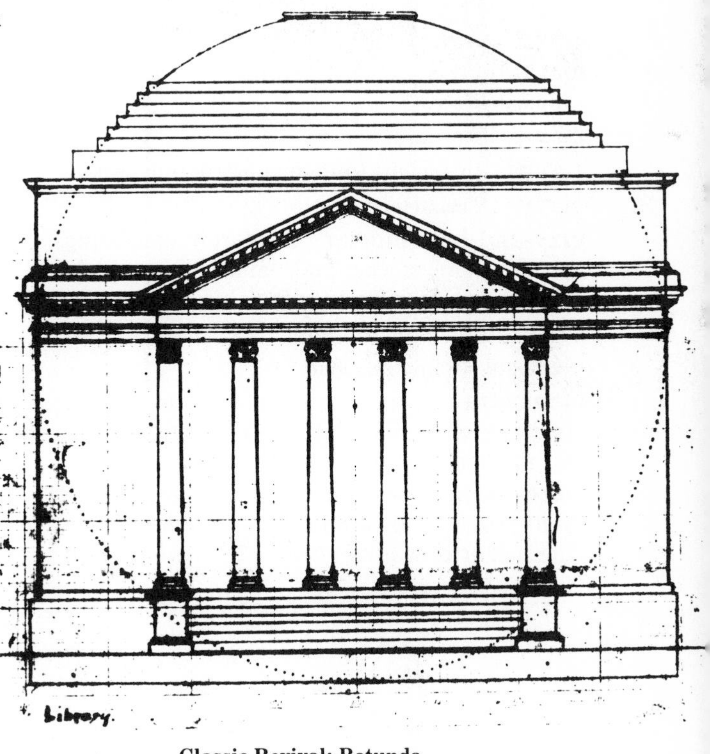

Classic Revival: Rotunda, University of Virginia; designed and drawn by Thomas Jefferson (1821)

Classic Revival

clathri A lattice of bars, as of cages for animals or gratings for windows.

clathri for a window

claustra See **repagula.**

claustral, cloistral Pertaining to a cloister.

clausura That part of a monastery or convent occupied by the monks or nuns, and not open to the public.

clavel, clavis **1.** A keystone of an arch. **2.** A **mantelpiece.**

clavis See **clavel.**

clavus In ancient Roman construction, a nail.

clavy A **mantelpiece.**

clay-and-hair mortar A mortar consisting of a mixture of clay and animal hair; widely used in construction in colonial U.S.A.

clearstory See **clerestory.**

cleithral Same as **clithral.**

clepsydra In ancient Greece, a device for measuring elapsed time by the quantity of water discharged through an opening.

clerestory, clearstory **1.** An upper zone of wall pierced with windows that admit light to the center of a lofty room. **2.** A window so placed.

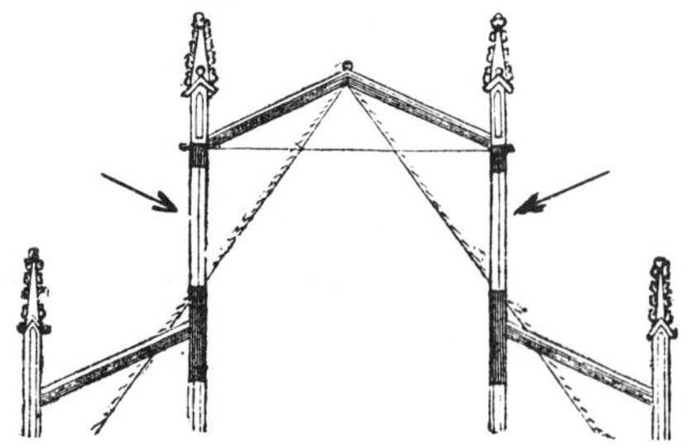

section through the upper part of a cathedral; location of the clerestory windows indicated by arrows

location of the clerestory in a large church

clipeus 1. An apparatus employed to regulate the temperature of a **laconicum** or ancient Roman vapor bath; consisted of a hemispherical metal plate suspended by chains under an opening in the dome of the ceiling at the circular end of the **caldarium;** by raising or lowering of the plate, the amount of cold air permitted to enter was controlled, thus regulating the temperature. 2. An ornamental disk of marble or other material, in the shape of a shield, often sculptured in relief, hung in the intercolumniations of the atria of Roman dwellings.

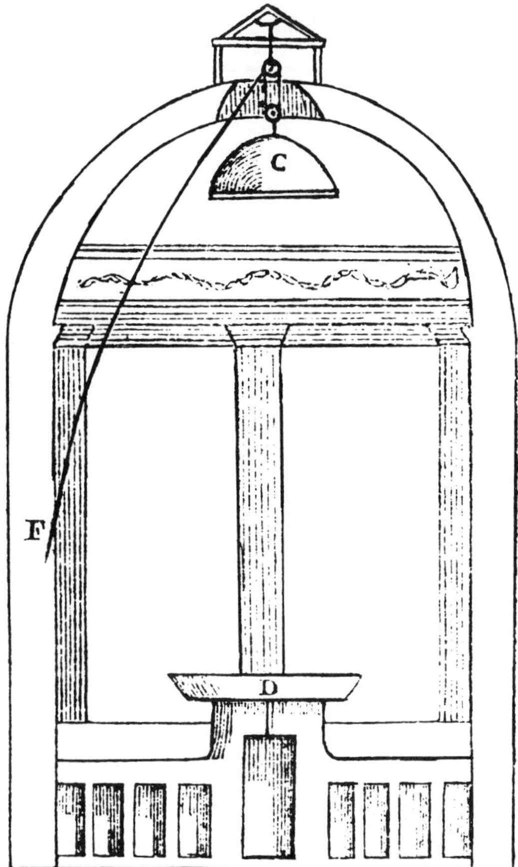

clipeus, 1: *C*, hollow metal hemisphere which closes opening; *D*, labrum; *F*, chain for raising or lowering

clipped gable See **jerkinhead.**

clithral In early Greek architecture, having a roof that forms a complete covering; said of certain temples, as distinguished from **hypaethral.**

cloaca An underground conduit for drainage; a sewer, esp. in ancient Rome.

cloaca

clochan A type of primitive building peculiar to Ireland, usually having a beehive form; the masonry usually is neither dressed nor cemented; a single stone covers the apex.

clochan houses in County Kerry

clocharium, clochier A building or tower in which clocks and bells were contained.

cloisonné A surface decoration in which differently colored enamels or glazes are separated by fillets applied to the design outline. For porcelain enamel, the fillets are wire secured to the metal body; for tile and pottery, the fillets are made of ceramic paste, squeezed through a small-diameter orifice.

cloister A covered walk surrounding a court, usually linking a church to other buildings of a monastery.

cloistered arch Same as **coved vault.**

cloistered vault A **coved vault.**

cloister garth The courtyard within a cloister.

cloistral See **claustral.**

close **1.** An enclosed space around or at the side of a building; esp. the neighborhood of a cathedral. **2.** A narrow lane leading from a street.

closed cornice **1.** A **box cornice.** **2.** A wood cornice which projects only slightly and has no soffit, having only a frieze board and crown molding.

closed eaves Eaves in which projecting roof members are not visible, being closed from view by boarding.

closed newel The central shaft of a turning stair when constructed as a continuous enclosing wall, either hollow or solid.

closing ring A metal ring fastened to a door; used to pull it shut.

clunch A stiff, rigid clay or a chalk, used in early British construction.

clustered column A number of columns which are grouped together and physically connected so they act as a single structural element.

clustered pier A **pier, 1** composed of a number of shafts grouped together, usually around a central, more massive, shaft or core.

cloister

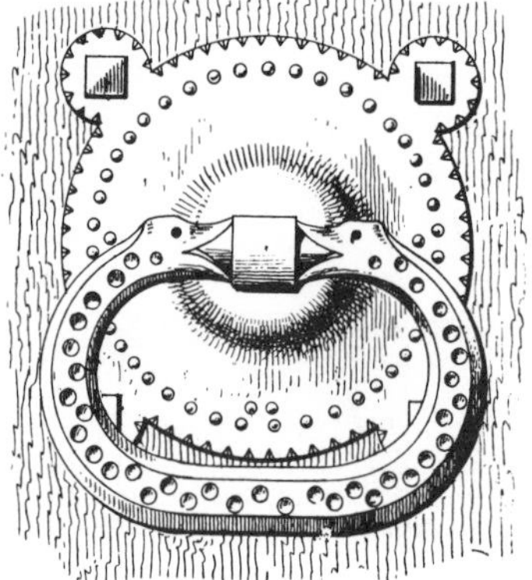

closing ring

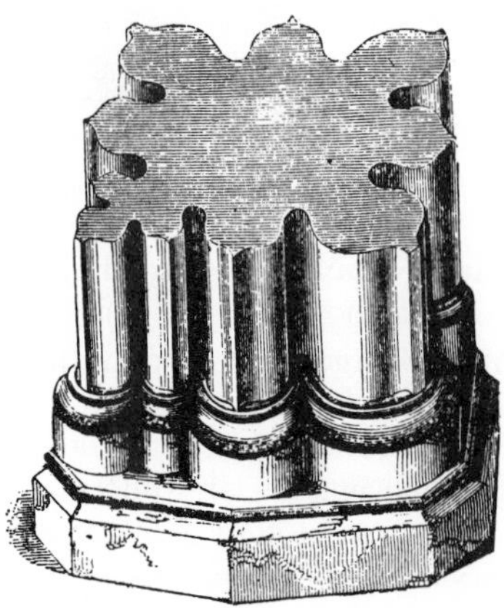

clustered pier

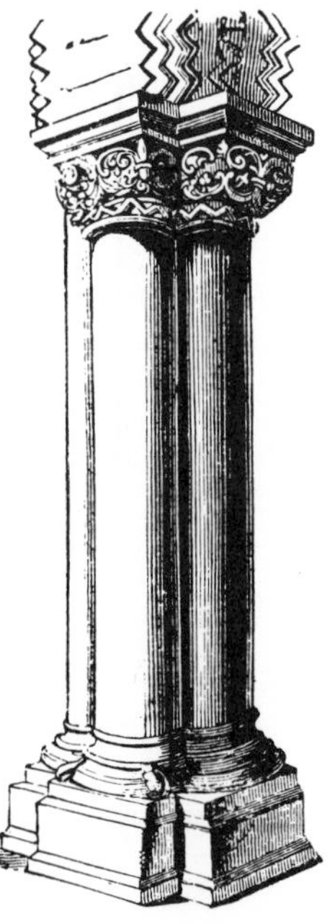

Norman clustered column

clypeus Same as **clipeus.**

Cnossus See **Knossos.**

coach house, carriage house A building or part thereof for housing carriages when not in use.

coakel Same as **cockle stair;** a **spiral stair.**

coaming A frame or curb around an opening in a roof or floor, raised above the surrounding level to prevent the flow of water into the opening.

coassatio In ancient Roman construction, anything made of boards joined together, as the flooring of a house.

coatepantli A carved wall featuring the serpent motif; introduced in **Toltec architecture** ca. 1000 A.D. at Tula (home of Quetzalcoatl, deified as the Feathered Serpent) and used extensively by the Aztecs thereafter.

cob A mixture of straw, gravel, and unburnt clay; used esp. for walls.

cob wall A wall formed of unburnt clay mixed with chopped straw, gravel, and occasionally with layers of long straw, in which the straw acts as a bond.

cochlea **1.** A tower for a spiral staircase. **2.** A **spiral stair.**

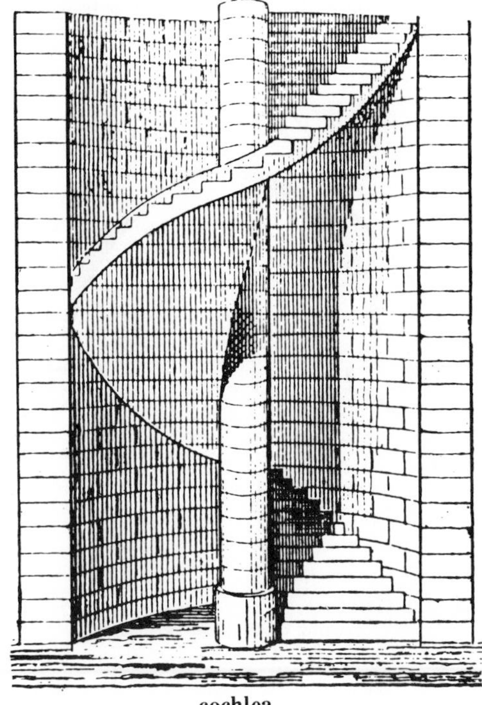

cochlea

cochleary, cochleated Spirally or helically twisted, as a spiral stair.

cock bead A bead which is not flush with the adjoining surface but is raised above it.

cocking Same as **cogging.**

cocking piece See **sprocket.**

cockle stair A **spiral stair.**

cockloft A garret under a roof, above the highest ceiling.

coctile Made by baking, as porcelain or a brick.

coctilis In ancient Roman construction, made of brick hardened by burning, as opposed to brick dried in the sun.

coctus Same as **coctilis.**

coelanaglyphic relief Carving in relief in which no part of the figure represented projects beyond the surrounding plane.

coelum An "inner" ceiling. The earliest Roman buildings were covered only by an outer roof, the inside of which served as a ceiling; the inner ceiling later was developed to provide better protection against changes in temperature and weather.

coemeterium A burying ground; a cemetery.

coenaculum **1.** In ancient Roman houses, the dining room or supper room, or any of the upper rooms in which food was eaten. **2.** Any of the rooms in the upper story.

coenatio Same as **cenatio.**

coenobium A community of monks living under one roof.

coffer, lacunar **1.** One panel in **coffering.** **2.** A **caisson.**

coffering **1.** Ceiling with deeply recessed panels, often highly ornamented. **2.** Similar effects executed in marble, brick, concrete, plaster, or stucco. Also see **caisson.**

coffering,1

cogging, cocking The joining of two timbers which are notched, cogged, or indented.

coign See **quoin.**

coillon Same as **quoin.**

coilon The Greek term corresponding to **cavea, 1.**

coin, quoin **1.** The corner of a building. **2.** The stones or bricks which form the corner. **3.** A wedge.

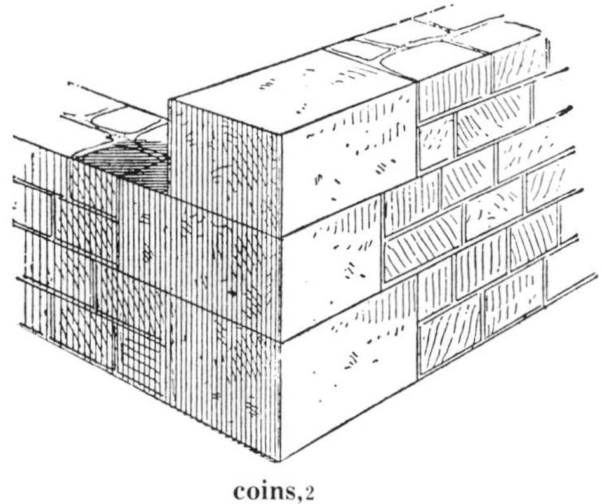

coins, 2

cokel Same as **cockle stair;** a **spiral stair.**

colarin, colarino Same as **collarino.**

coliseum See **colosseum.**

collar A **collarino.**

collar beam, spanpiece, sparpiece, top beam, wind beam A horizontal member which ties together (and stiffens) two opposite common rafters, usually at a point about halfway up the rafters in a collar beam roof.

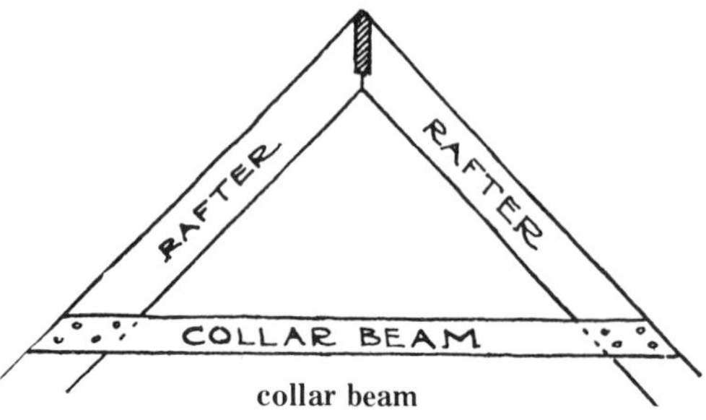

collar beam

collar beam roof, collar roof A roof supported by rafters tied together by collar beams.

collar brace A structural member which reinforces a collar beam in medieval roof framing.

roof with collar beams and collar braces

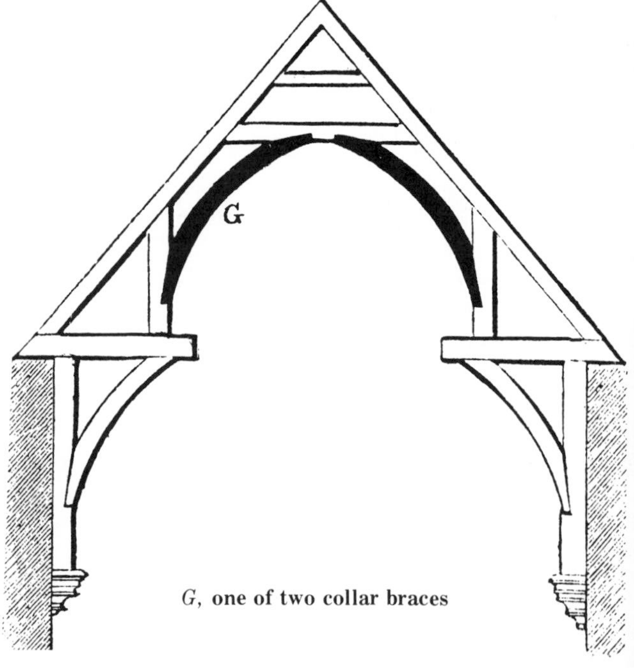

G, one of two collar braces

collarino 1. A **necking,** as on a classic Tuscan, Doric, or Ionic capital; also called a **collar.** 2. An **astragal.**

collar joint 1. The joint between a roof rafter and a **collar beam.** 2. The vertical joint between masonry **withes.**

collar tie In wood roof construction, a timber which prevents the roof framing from changing its shape.

collegiate Gothic A secular version of Gothic architecture, characteristic of the older colleges of Oxford and Cambridge.

colliciae, colliquiae Gutters, made with concave tiles, placed under the eaves of an ancient Roman house for the purpose of carrying away the rainwater and conducting it into the **impluvium.**

colliciaris A drain tile for making **colliciae.**

colluviarium In ancient Rome, an opening made at regular intervals in an aqueduct, for ventilation.

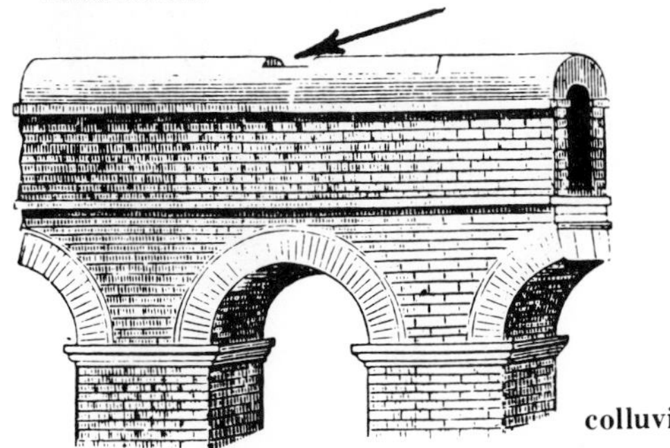

colluviarium

colombage Half-timber construction.

colonette, colonnette 1. A small column, usually decorative. 2. In medieval architecture, a thin round shaft to give a vertical line in elevation, or as an element in a compound pier.

Colonial architecture Architecture transplanted from the motherlands to overseas colonies, such as Portuguese Colonial architecture in Brazil, Dutch Colonial architecture in New York, and above all English Georgian architecture of the 18th cent. in the North American colonies.

colonial casing A type of decorative, exposed trim molding.

colonial panel door A door having stiles, rails, and a muntin which form frames around recessed panels.

Colonial Revival The reuse of Georgian and Colonial design in the U.S.A. toward the end of the 19th and into the 20th cent., typically in bank buildings, churches, and suburban homes.

colonial siding Wide, square-edged siding boards used extensively in early American construction.

colonica A term for an ancient Roman farmhouse.

colonnade A number of columns arranged in order, at intervals called **intercolumniation,** supporting an entablature and usually one side of a roof.

colonnette See **colonette.**

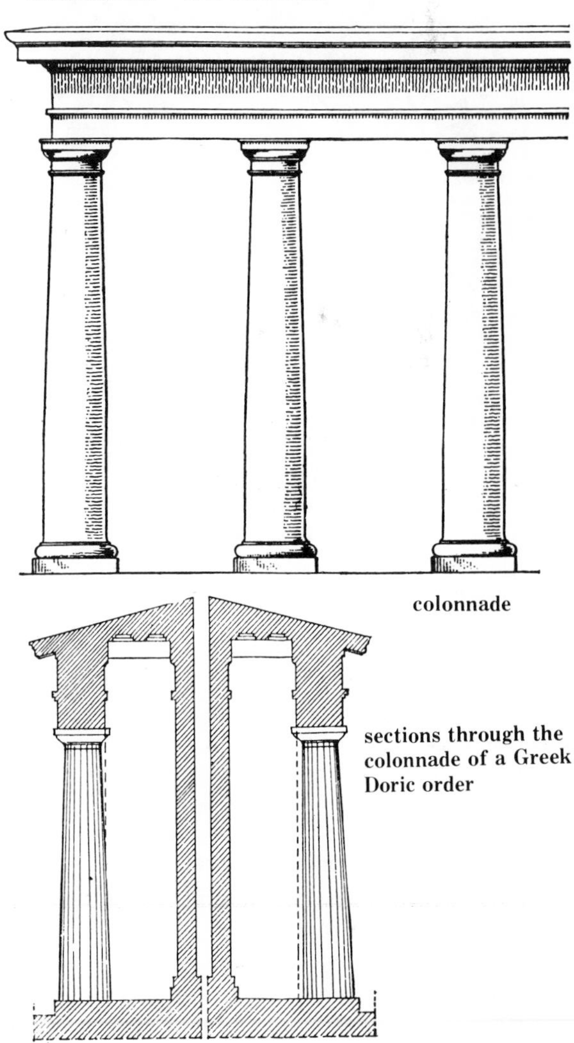

colonnade

sections through the colonnade of a Greek Doric order

colossal order, giant order An order more than one story in height.

colosseum, coliseum **1.** *(cap.)* The Flavian amphitheatre in Rome. **2.** Any large Roman amphitheatre. **3.** Now, any large sports arena, open or roofed.

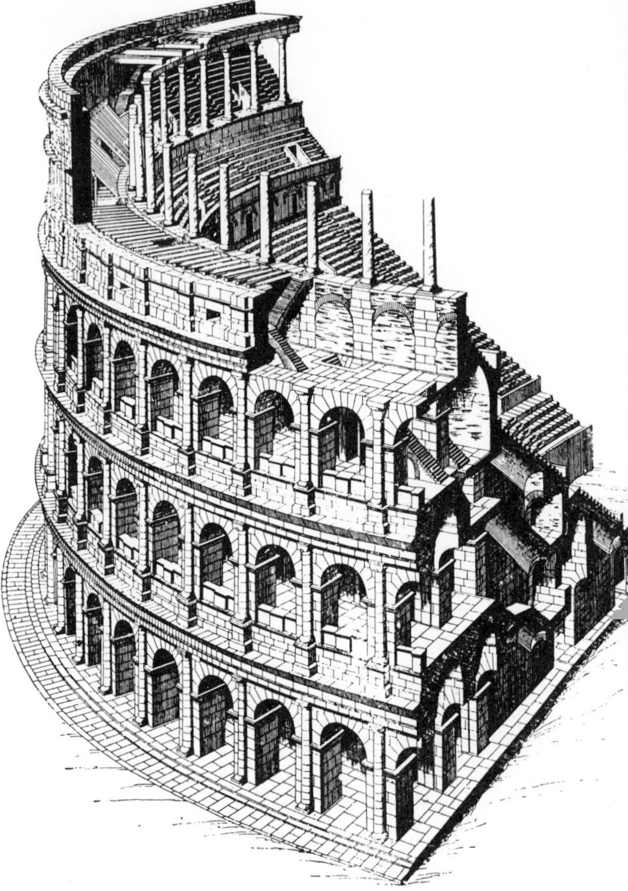

Colosseum, 1: isometric section

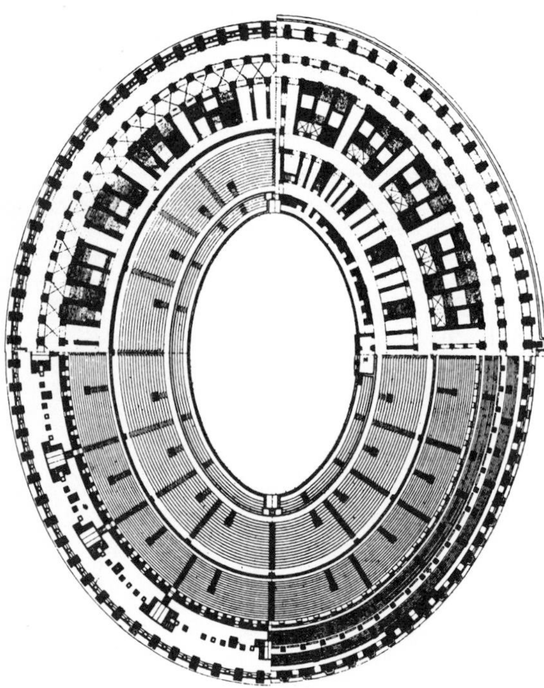

Colosseum, 1: quarterplan of seats and quarterplan of basement

columbarium, 1

columbarium **1.** One or a series of niches, intended to receive human remains. **2.** A putlog hole. **3.** A **dovecot** or one of the holes in a dovecot.

columbeion The Greek term for a fountain placed in the **atrium** of a church.

columbethra The Greek term for the piscina or pool in a baptistery.

columella Same as **colonette.**

columen, culmen In ancient Roman construction, the **ridgeboard** of a roof.

column **1.** In structures, a relatively long, slender structural compression member such as a post, pillar, or strut; usually vertical, supporting a load which acts in (or near) the direction of its longitudinal axis. **2.** In classical architecture, a cylindrical support consisting of a base (except in Greek Doric), shaft, and capital; either monolithic or built up of drums the full diameter of the shaft. **3.** A pillar standing alone as a monument.

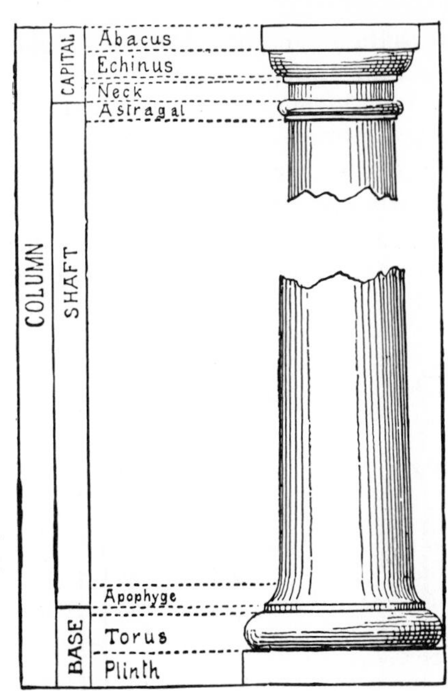

Tuscan order column, illustrating terms applied to its various parts

Tuscan

Doric

Ionic

Corinthian

Composite

Columna Bellica In ancient Rome, a short column near the Forum, from which the consul proclaimed war by hurling a spear into the surrounding field, toward the enemy's country.

columna caelata A column whose shaft was decorated with carved ornaments.

columna cochlis A column with a spiral staircase in its center for the purpose of ascending to the top.

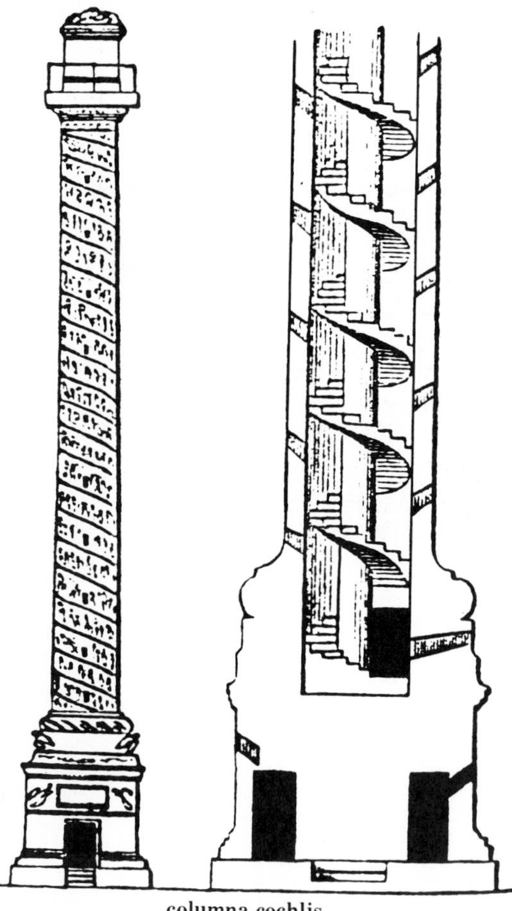
columna cochlis

Columna Maenia A column erected in the Roman Forum to which slaves, thieves, and other offenders were bound and publicly punished.

Columna Phocae A column erected at the center of the Forum in Rome in 608 A.D.

columna rostrata See **rostral column.**

column baseplate A horizontal plate beneath the bottom of a column; transmits and distributes the column load to the supporting material below the plate.

column head Same as **column capital.**

columniation Systems of grouping columns in classical architecture. Also see **intercolumniation.**

column of Trajan See **Trajan's column.**

colymbethra In a Greek church, the room or font for administering baptism.

comb Same as **combing.**

comb board A **saddle board** having notches along its upper edge.

combination stair A stair in which access to the first landing is provided by a supplementary service stair as well as the main flight.

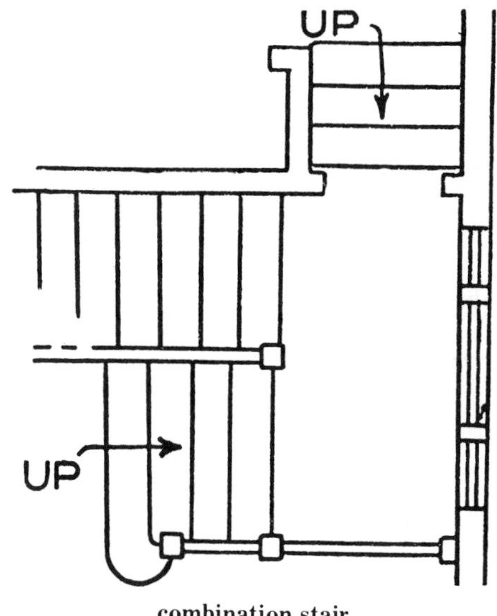

combination stair

combing In roofing, the topmost row of shingles which project above the ridge line; the uppermost ridge on a roof.

comitium An enclosed place abutting on the Roman Forum where the meetings were held and causes tried.

commode step One of two or more steps at the foot of a flight of stairs which have curved ends projecting beyond the string and surrounding the newel.

common ashlar A pick- or hammer-dressed block of stone.

common bond, American bond A bond in which every fifth or sixth course consists of **headers,** the other courses being **stretchers.** Widely used because such brickwork can be laid quickly.

common house That part of a monastery in which a fire was kept for the monks during the winter.

common rafter, intermediate rafter, spar A rafter which is at right angles to the **rafter plate** (at the eaves) of a roof and extends from the plate to the **ridgeboard** or **ridgepole.**

common room **1.** A room or lounge for the informal use of all members of a college. **2.** A room or lounge for the use of the patrons of an inn.

Communion table In Protestant churches, a table used instead of an altar in the Communion service.

compartment ceiling A ceiling divided into panels, which are usually surrounded by moldings.

compass brick An **arch brick.**

compass-headed arch A semicircular arch.

compass rafter A **rafter** which is curved on one or both sides.

compass roof **1.** A roof having curved rafters or ties. **2.** A form of timber roof in which the rafters, collar beams, and braces of each truss combine to form an arch.

compass window See **bow window.**

compass work, circular work Joinery which has circular forms within its overall design.

compitum A place where two or more ancient Roman roads met, as opposed to a **trivium** which is more applicable to the streets of a town. It was customary to erect altars, shrines and small temples at these places, at which religious rites in honor of the **lares compitales** (the deities who presided over the crossroads) were performed by the country people.

compluvium The aperture in the center of the roof of the atrium in a Roman house, sloping inward to discharge rainwater into a cistern or tank.

compitum in the Roman countryside

compitum near Pompeii

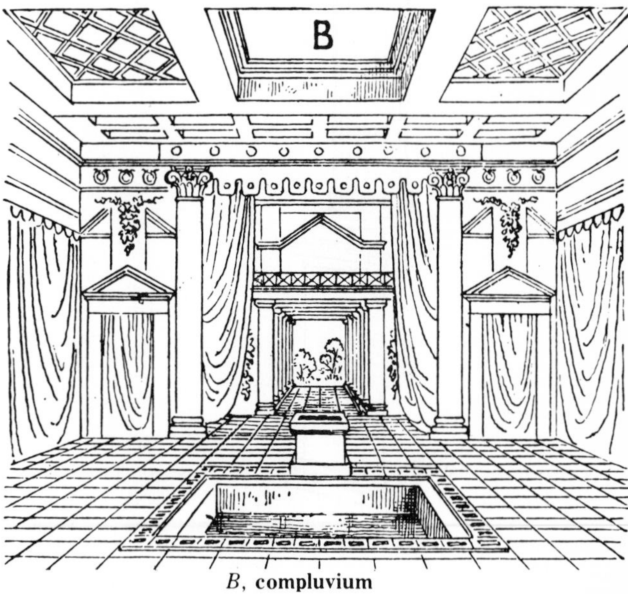

B, compluvium

Composite

Composite, Composite order One of the five classical orders. A Roman elaboration of the Corinthian order, having the acanthus leaves of its capital combined with the large volutes of the Ionic order, and other details also elaborated.

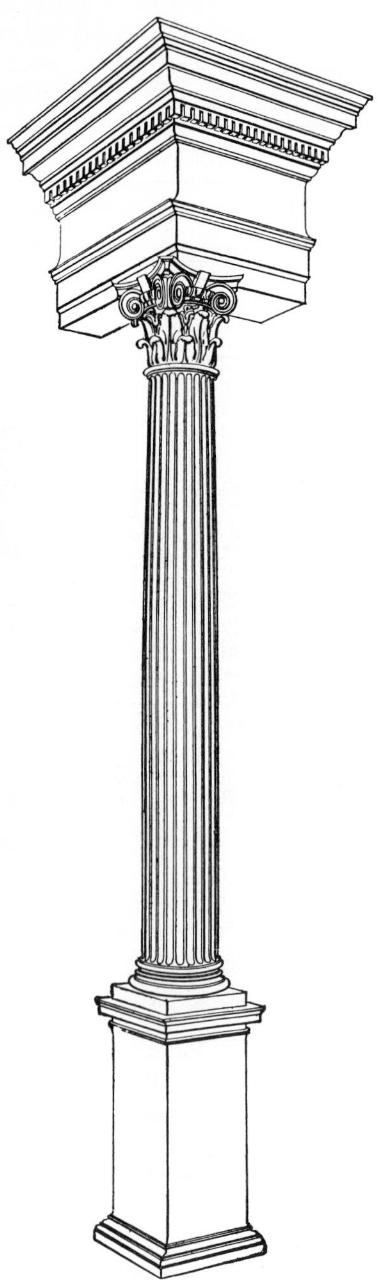

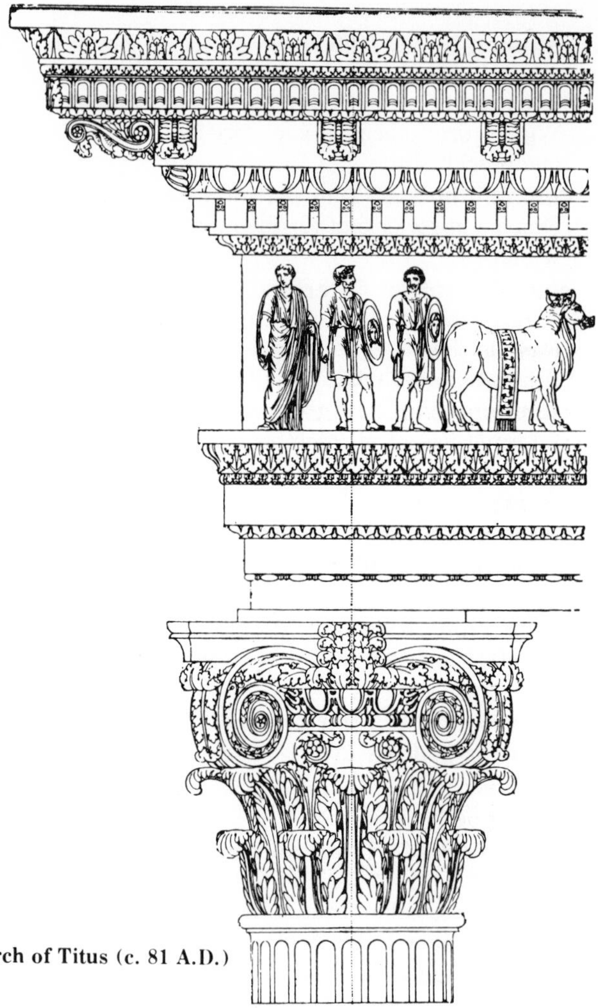

Arch of Titus (c. 81 A.D.)

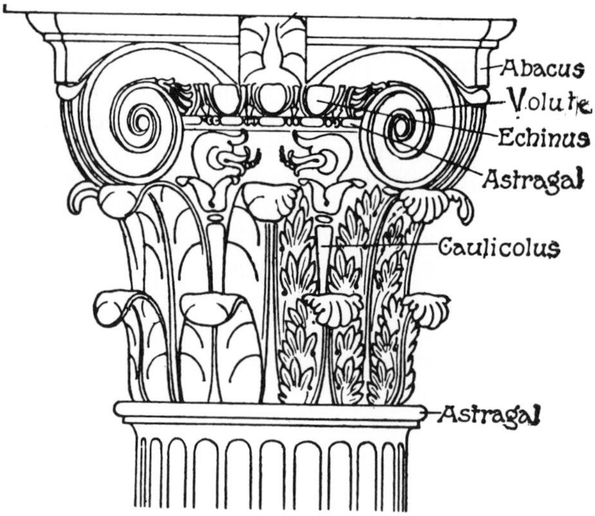

Abacus
Volute
Echinus
Astragal
Caulicolus
Astragal

composite arch An arch whose curves are struck from four centers, as in English Perpendicular Gothic; a **mixed arch.**

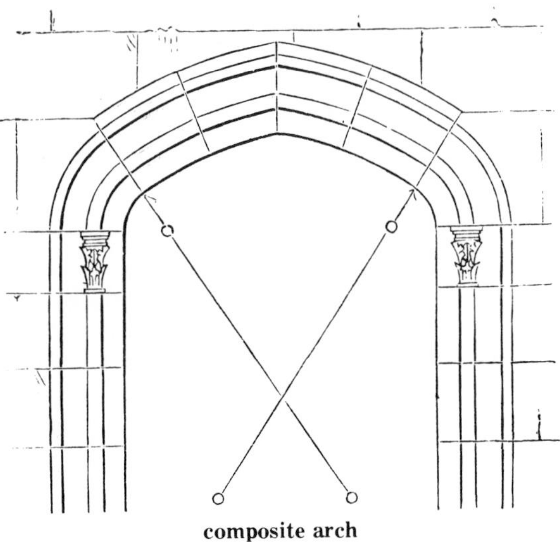
composite arch

Composite order See **Composite.**

compound arch An arch formed by concentric arches set within one another.

Compound order Same as **Composite.**

compound pier, compound pillar A pier composed of a conjunction of colonettes, generally attached to a central shaft; a **clustered column.** Also see **bundle pier.**

compound vault Any **vault** other than the simplest, e.g., a groined vault or fan vault.

concameration **1.** An arch or vault. **2.** An apartment; a chamber.

conch . A semicircular **niche** which is covered with a half-dome.

conch

concha Semidome vaulting of an apse.

conclavium In ancient Rome, any enclosed rectangular room; a dining room; a bedroom.

concourse **1.** An open space where several roads or paths meet. **2.** An open space for accommodating large crowds in a building, as in a railway terminal.

conditorium An underground vault or burying place in which a corpse was deposited in a coffin without being reduced to ashes, a practice prevalent among the Romans at the two extreme periods of their history, before the custom of burning had been initiated and after it had been discontinued.

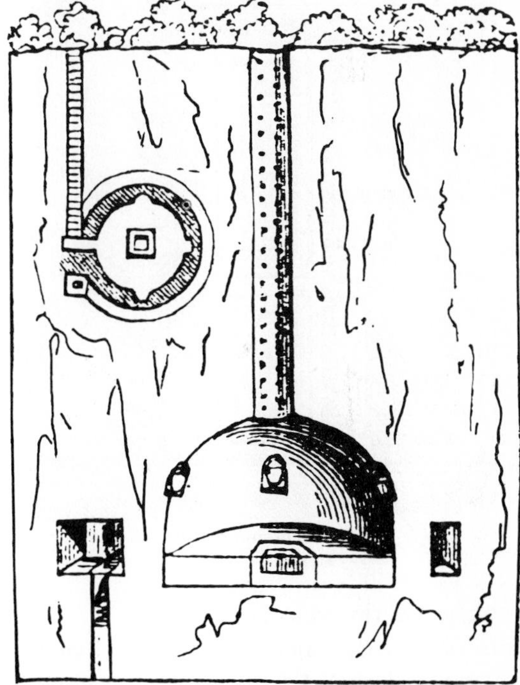
conditorium

conditory A repository for storing things.

cone mosaic A mosaic facing of glazed terracotta, in early Mesopotamian architecture.

cone tile, cone hip tile See **bonnet hip tile.**

confession, confessio The tomb of a martyr or confessor; if an altar was erected over the grave, the name was also extended to the altar and to the subterranean chamber in which it stood; in later times a basilica was sometimes erected over the chamber and the entire building was known as a confession.

confessional A small booth furnished with a seat for a priest and a screen or latticed window through which the penitent may talk to the priest, who is hidden; the penitent may or may not be visible to the public.

confessional

confornicatio A **vault.**

congé **1.** See **apophyge.** **2.** A cove base molding flush at the top with the wall above, but with a fillet between the cove and the floor. Hence any molding of similar profile.

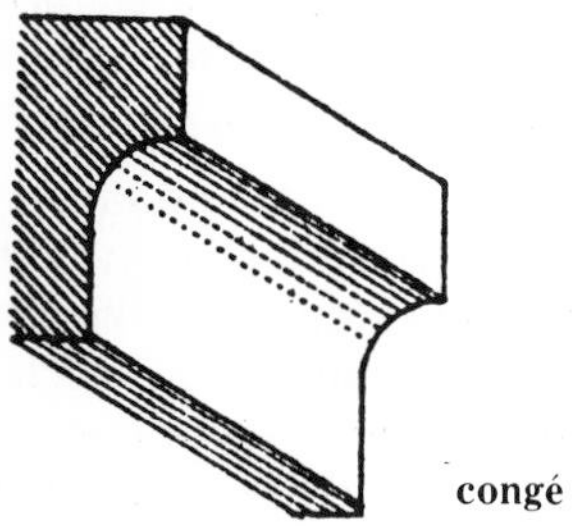

congé

conical vault A **vault** having a cross section in the form of a circular arc, which is larger at one end than the other.

conical vault

conisterium In ancient Greece and Rome, a room appended to a gymnasium or palaestra in which wrestlers were sprinkled with sand or dust after having been anointed with oil.

conservatory **1.** A school for the teaching of music, drama, or other fine arts. **2.** A house or glass-enclosed room of a house for the cultivation and display of plants.

conservatory, 2

consessus The apse or other presbytery in a church; a place for seats of the clergy.

consistorium **1.** A spiritual court, or assembly of the college of cardinals, at Rome. **2.** The privy councils of the Roman emperors, of kings, nobles, and abbots.

consistory, consistorium **1.** The meeting place of the privy council of the Roman emperors. **2.** The meeting place of the assembly of the college of cardinals at Rome. **3.** A place where a council meets or where an ecclesiastical or spiritual court is held.

console A decorative bracket in the form of a vertical scroll, projecting from a wall to support a cornice, a door or window head, a piece of sculpture, etc.; an **ancon, 1.**

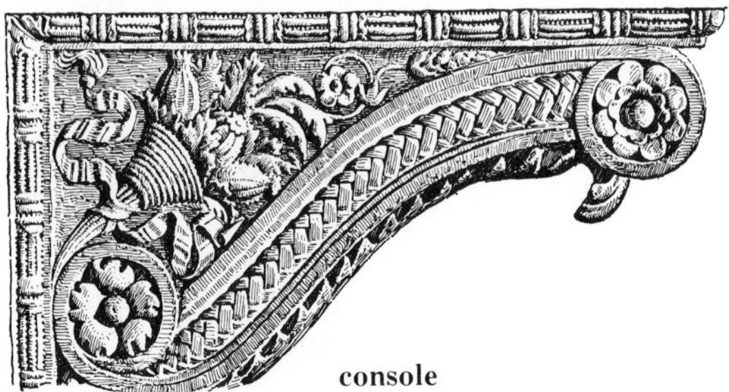
console

console table A table attached to a wall and supported on consoles.

console table

Constructivism A movement which originated in Moscow after 1917, primarily in sculpture, but with broad application to architecture. The expression of construction was to be the basis for all building design, with emphasis on functional machine parts. Vladimir Tatlin's project of a monument to the Third International in Moscow (1920) is the most famous example.

contignation, contignatio A framework, as of beams.

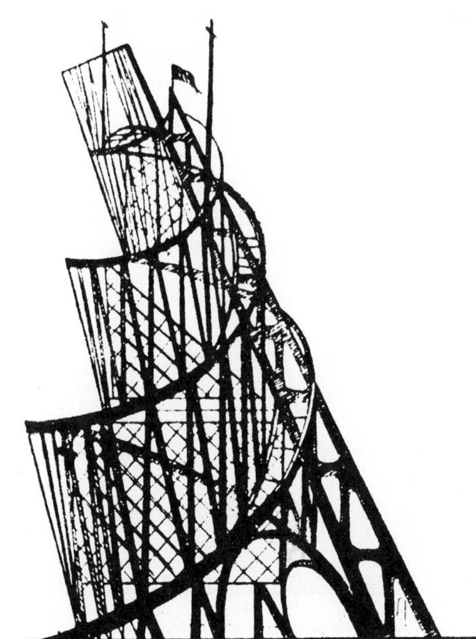
Constructivism: Tatlin's project

continuous impost In Gothic architecture, the moldings of an arch when carried down to the floor without interruption or anything to mark the impost point.

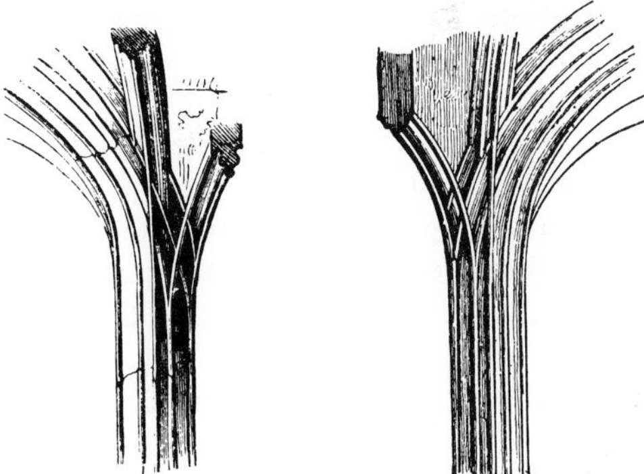
continuous imposts

contractura The tapering of a column from bottom to top; the opposite of **entasis.**

contramure Same as **countermure, 2.**

contrasted arch An **ogee arch.**

contravallation A series of redoubts and breastworks, either unconnected or united by a parapet, raised by the besiegers about the place invested, to guard against sorties of the garrison.

contrefort A brickwork revetment for ramparts on the side of a terreplein, or for counterscarps, gorges, and demigorges.

contre-imbrication An ornamental pattern on a surface formed by overlapping elements which are below the general plane of the surface; in **imbrication** the overlapping elements stand out and are above the general line of the surface.

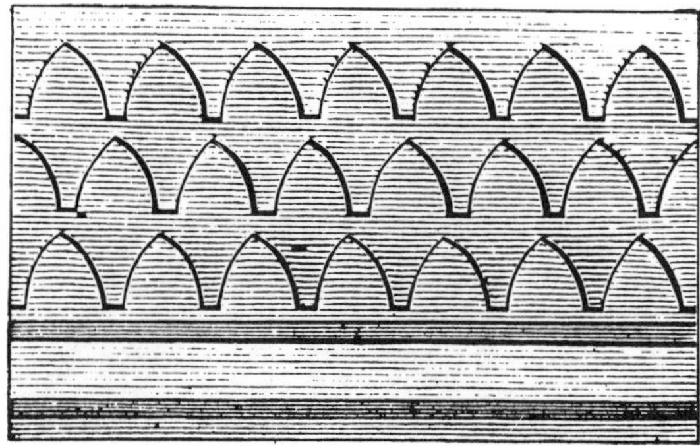

contre-imbrication

convent **1.** A religious community: friars, monks, or nuns (now usually nuns). **2.** A group of buildings occupied by such a community.

conventicle A room occupied by an assembly for secret (because illegal) worship or for nonconformist worship.

conventiculum A building used by a heretical congregation.

coolhouse A greenhouse which is maintained at a cool temperature above freezing.

cooperculum The cover of a **baldachin** or **ciborium.**

coopertorium Late Latin term for **roof.**

coped tomb A tomb whose top or covering slopes downward toward both sides.

copestone Same as **coping stone.**

coping A protective cap, top, or cover of wall, parapet, pilaster, or chimney; often of stone, terra-cotta, concrete, metal, or wood. May be flat, but commonly sloping, double-beveled, or curved to shed water so as to protect masonry below from penetration of water from above. Most effective if extended beyond wall face and cut with a drip.

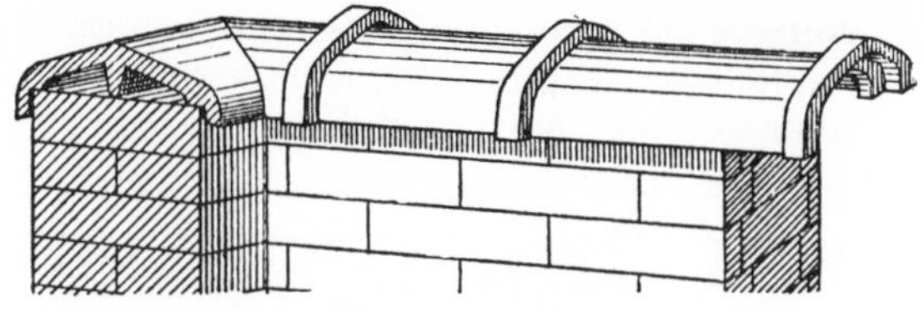

coping of terra-cotta

coping stone, capstone, copestone A stone which forms a coping.

coping stone

coquillage A representation of the forms of seashells and the like, as a decorative carving.

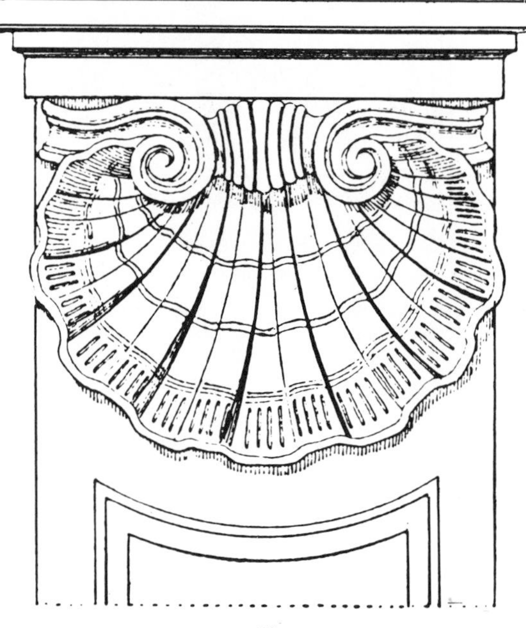

coquillage

coquina Coarse porous limestone composed of shells and shell fragments loosely cemented by calcite.

corbeil, corbeille An ornament resembling a basket, esp. a finial. Also see **calathus.**

corbel **1.** In masonry, a projection or one of a series of projections, each stepped progressively farther forward with height; anchored in a wall, story, column, or chimney; used to support an overhanging member above or, if continuous, to support overhanging courses; may support an ornament of similar appearance. **2.** A projecting stone which supports a superincumbent weight.

corbel, 1

early Renaissance corbel, 2

Romanesque corbel, 2

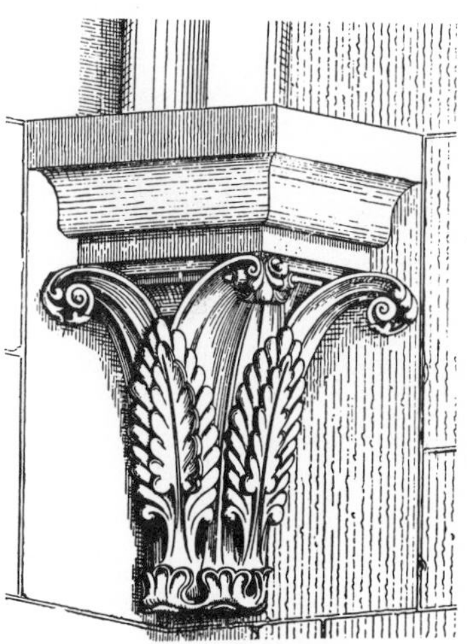

angle corbel, 2

corbel, 2: supporting a piscina

corbel, 2: Wells Cathedral

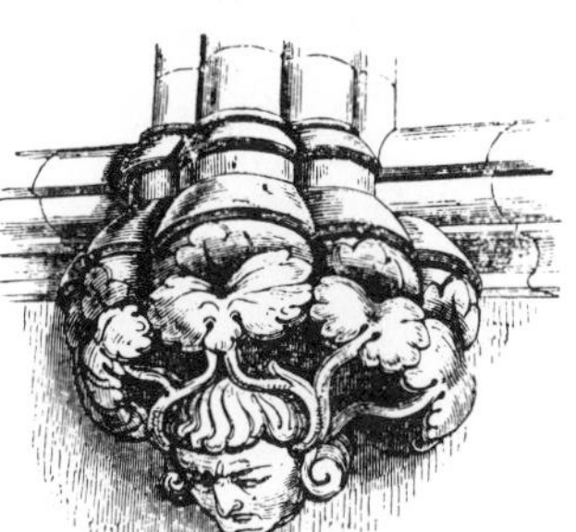

Merton College Chapel, Oxford (1277)

Christ Church, Oxford (1638)

corbel, 2

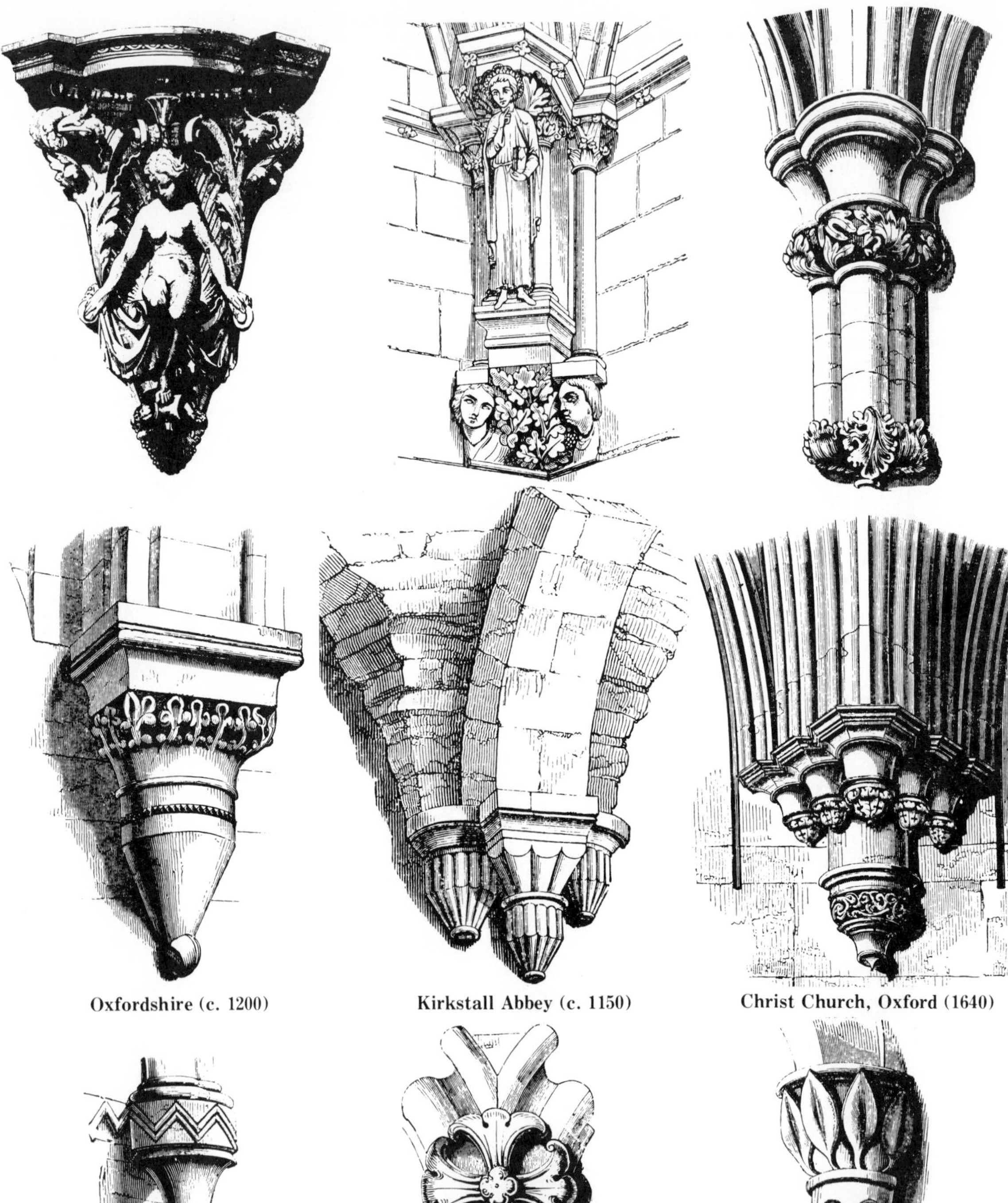

Oxfordshire (c. 1200)

Kirkstall Abbey (c. 1150)

Christ Church, Oxford (1640)

Broadwater, Sussex (c. 1250)

St. Benedict's Church, Lincoln (c. 1350)

Northmoor Church, Oxford (c. 1320)

corbel arch Masonry built over a wall opening by uniformly advancing courses from each side until they meet at a midpoint. The stepped reveals may be smoothed, even arcuated, but no arch action is effected—not a true arch.

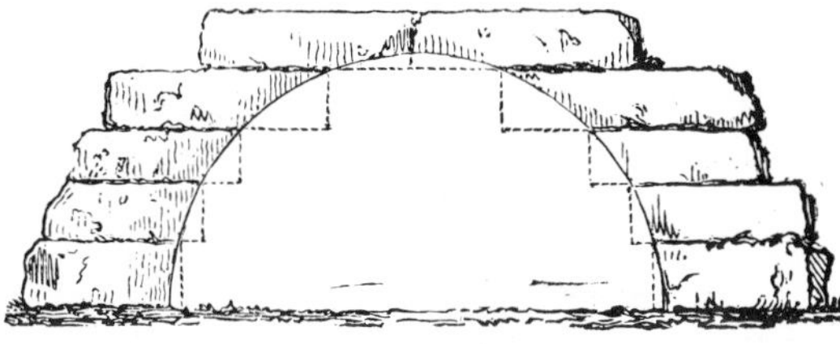

corbel arch

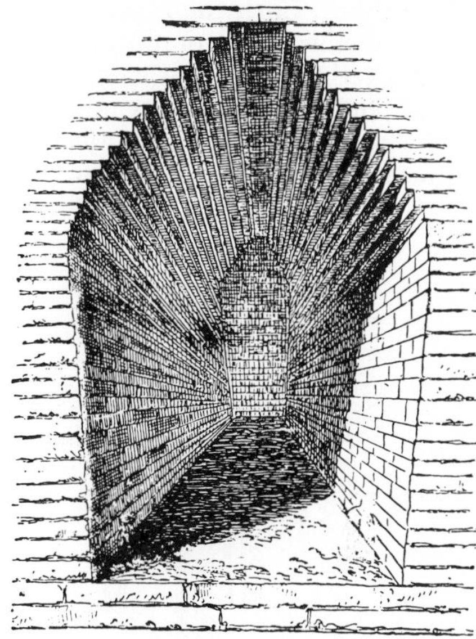

corbel arch

corbel course A masonry course acting as a corbel, or an ornament of similar appearance. Also see **stringcourse.**

corbel gable Erroneous for **corbie gable.**

corbel piece See **bolster.**

corbel-step Erroneous for **corbiestep.**

corbel table A projecting stringcourse or masonry strip supported by corbels. Also see **arched corbel table.**

corbel table, Romsey Church, Hampshire (c. 1180)

Early English style corbel table

corbel table, Salisbury Cathedral (c. 1260)

corbel vault, corbeled vault A masonry roof constructed from opposite walls, or from a circular base, by shifting courses slightly and regularly inward until they meet. The resulting stepped surface can be smoothed or curved, but no arch action is incurred.

corbie gable, crow gable, step gable A gable having a stepped edge.

corbiestep, catstep, crowstep The stepped edge of a gable masking a pitched roof, found in northern European masonry, 14th to 17th cent., and in derivatives.

corbiesteps

Córdoba See **Great Mosque of Córdoba.**

cordon A **stringcourse** or **belt course.**

coriceum Same as **corycaeum.**

Corinthian

Corinthian, Corinthian order The slenderest and most ornate of the three Greek orders, characterized by a bell-shaped capital with volutes and two rows of acanthus leaves, and with an elaborate cornice. Much used by the Romans for its showiness. Also see **order.**

Fleuron
Lip
Bell
Volute
Bud
Button
Caulicolus
Acanthus

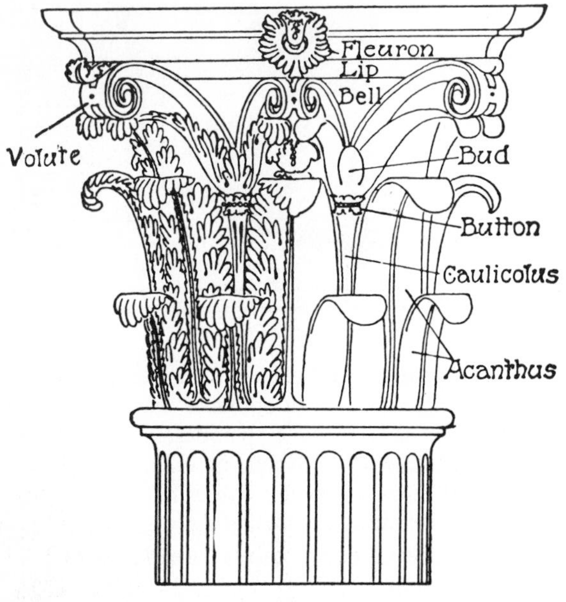

Roman Corinthian capital

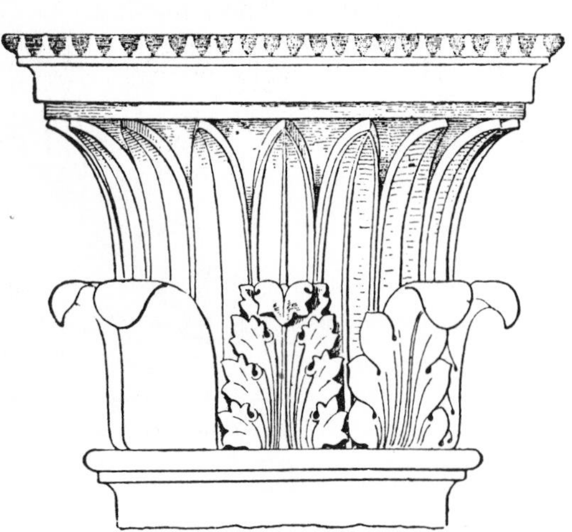

early form of Greek Corinthian capital

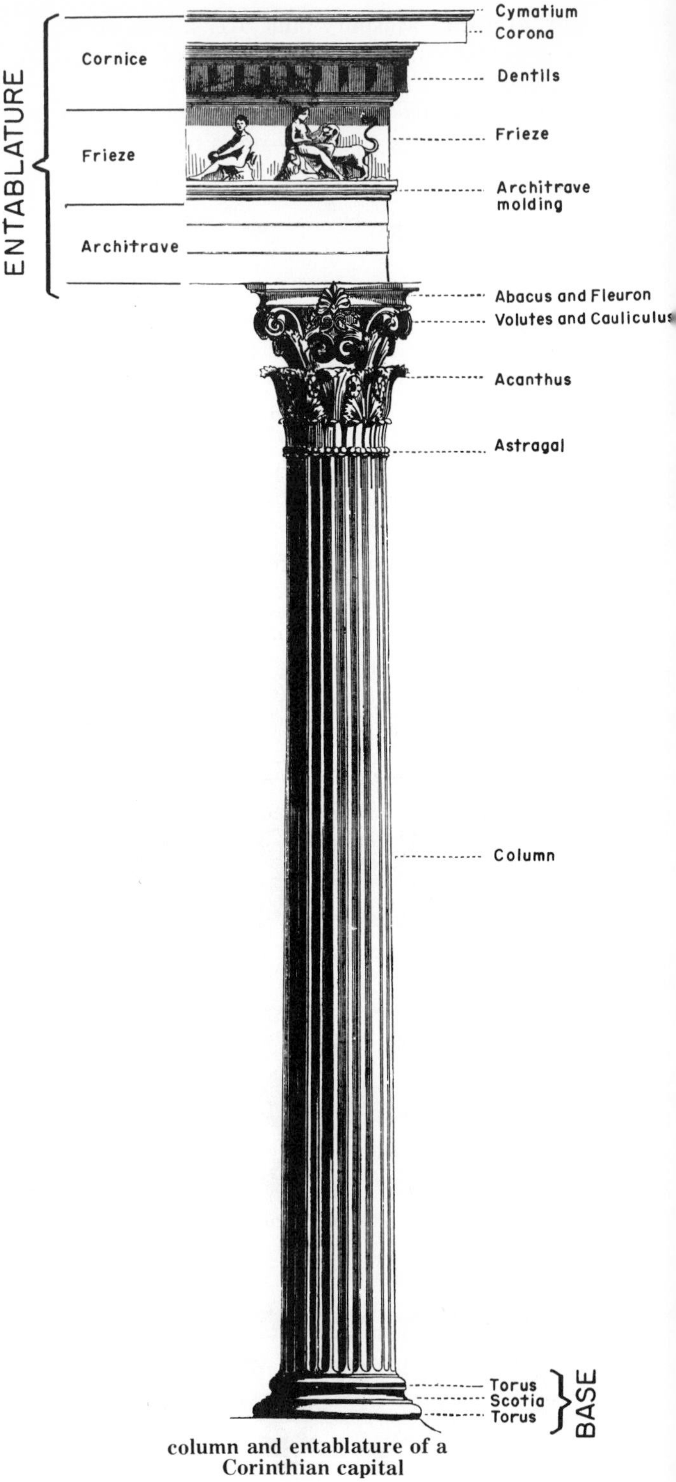

ENTABLATURE
Cornice
Frieze
Architrave
Cymatium
Corona
Dentils
Frieze
Architrave molding
Abacus and Fleuron
Volutes and Caulicolus
Acanthus
Astragal
Column
Torus
Scotia
Torus
BASE

column and entablature of a Corinthian capital

Greek Corinthian

Roman Corinthian

Corinthian order base,
Temple of Jupiter Stator

Corinthian entablature, Forum of Nerva, Rome
(c. 97 A.D.)

Corinthian

Corinthian entablature

Corinthian order ornament

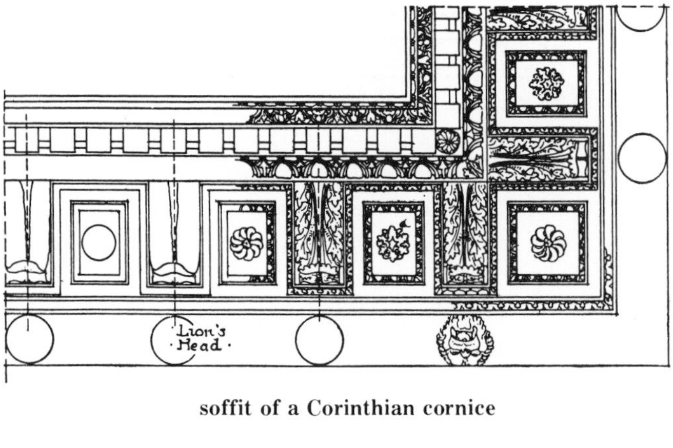

soffit of a Corinthian cornice

corkscrew stair A **spiral stair.**

corner bead, corner, corner molding Any vertical molding, usually a plain, filleted, or quirked bead, used to protect the external angle of two intersecting surfaces.

corner board A board which is used as trim on the external corner of a wood-frame structure and against which the ends of the siding are fitted.

corner capital Same as **angle capital.**

corner post In a timber structure, a post which is placed at a corner or return angle to provide for exterior or interior nailing.

cornerstone **1.** A stone that forms a corner or angle in a structure. **2.** A stone prominently situated near the base of a corner in a building, carrying information recording the dedicatory ceremonies, and in some instances containing or capping a vault in which contemporary memorabilia are preserved; a foundation stone.

cornice **1.** Any molded projection which crowns or finishes the part to which it is affixed. **2.** The third or uppermost division of an **entablature,** resting on the frieze. **3.** An ornamental molding, usually of wood or plaster, running round the walls of a room just below the ceiling; a **crown molding;** the molding forming the top member of a door or window frame. **4.** The exterior trim of a structure at the meeting of the roof and wall; usually consists of bed molding, soffit, fascia, and crown molding.

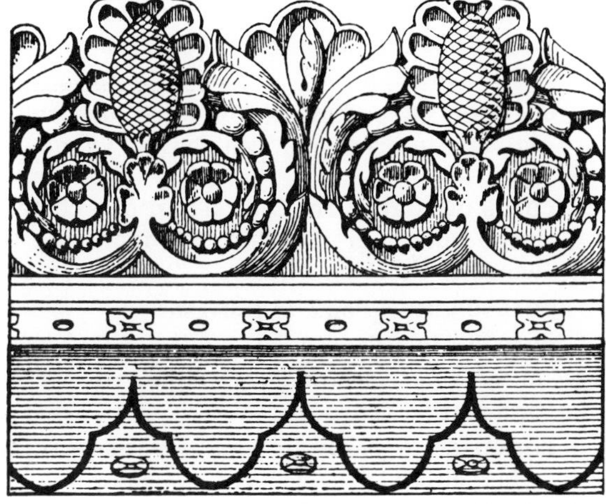

cornice,1

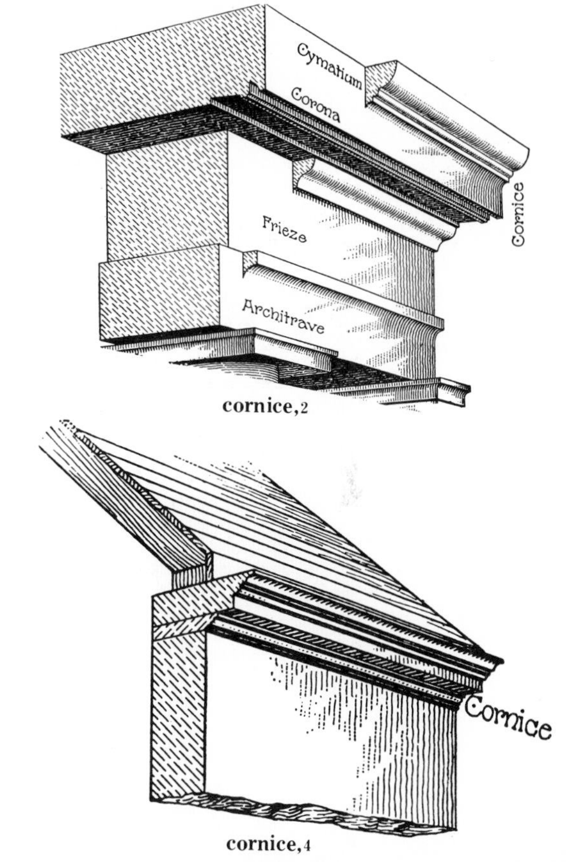

cornice,2

cornice,4

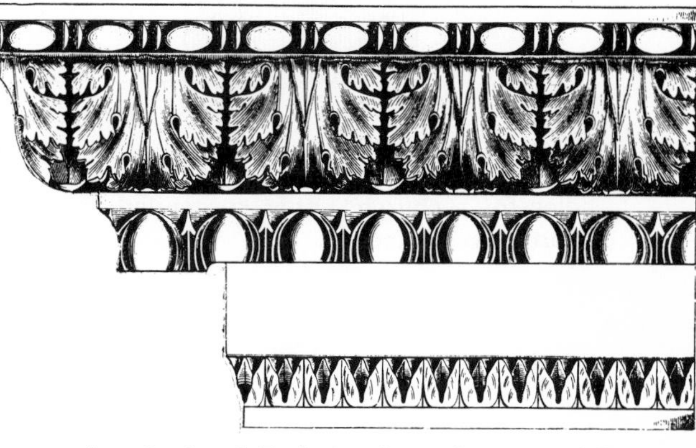

cornice of pedestal, Trajan's column, Rome (113 A.D.)

cornice return The continuation of a cornice in a different direction, usually at right angles, as at the gable end of a house.

coro An elaborate choir, at times almost an independent building, commonly placed to the west of the transept in a Spanish cathedral.

corona The overhanging vertical member of a cornice, supported by the bed moldings and crowned by the cymatium; usually with a **drip** to throw rainwater clear of the building. Also see **cornice.**

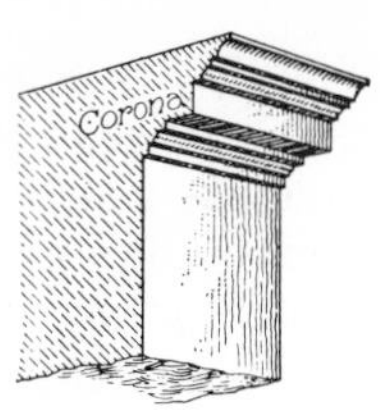

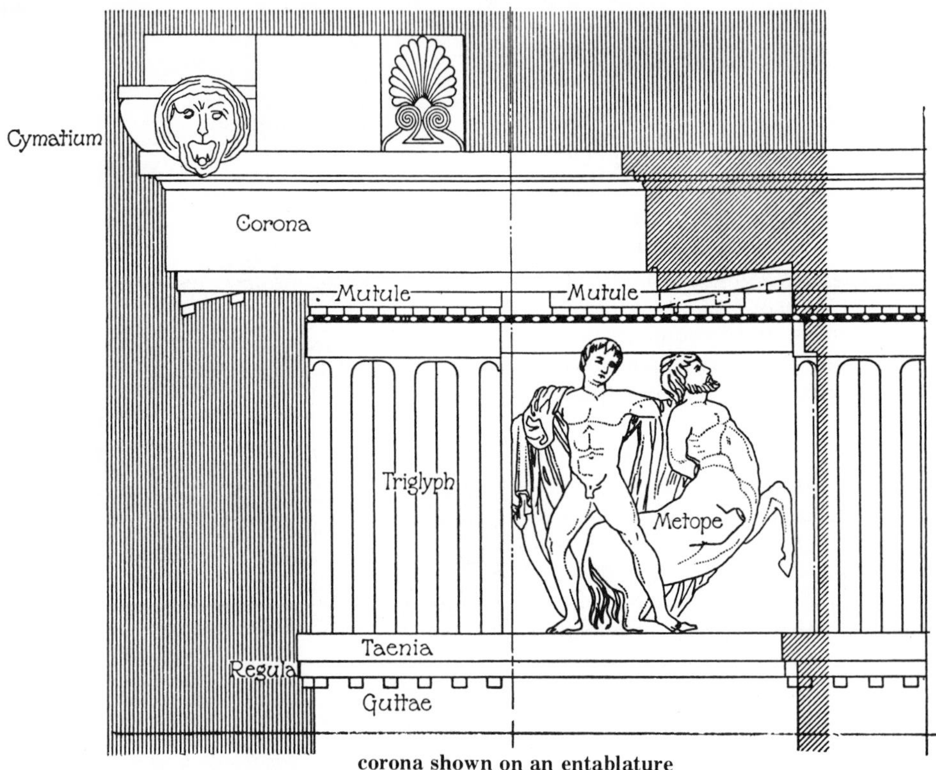

corona shown on an entablature

corona lucis A circle or hoop of lights or candles for a church, either suspended or supported on a stand.

corona lucis

coronarium In ancient Rome, stucco work applied to the decoration of a cornice or projecting molding.

coronet A pedimental or other decoration wrought in relief on a wall above a window or door.

corps de logis The central part of a château, large house, or mansion, not including the wings or subordinate parts.

corpse gate Same as **lych-gate.**

corsae In ancient Roman construction, fillets or moldings used to decorate the external face of a marble doorpost.

corseria A passage from one tower to another, either in the walls of a town or in a castle.

cortile An interior courtyard enclosed by the walls of a palace or other large building.

cortinale An ancient Roman cellar in which newly made wine was boiled down in caldrons.

cortis Same as **cortile.**

corycaeum A room in the **ephebeum** of a **palaestra** in which young men exercised by striking a large sack or bag filled with flour, sand, or fig seeds; the bag, at body height, hung from the ceiling in a manner similar to a punching bag. Derived from the Greek word *korykos* for "sack."

Cosmoto work Polychromatic patterns of stone, glass, or gilding set in marble; commonly applied in Italian Romanesque architecture.

cot, cote A small house or cottage.

cotloft Same as **cockloft.**

cottage orné, ferme ornée A small rustic country house of the late 18th and early 19th cent.

cottage roof A roof which has common rafters that rest on wall plates and are joined at their upper ends in a ridge; no principal beams are used.

coulisse, cullis A piece of channeled or grooved timber, as one in which a frame slides.

counter apse An **apse** opposite another; many double apses have a crypt below the western apse.

counter arch An arch used to counteract the thrust of another arch.

counterfort In masonry structures, a buttress, spur wall, pier, or projecting portion, extending upward from the foundation or from the inner face of a basement, abutment, or retaining wall to provide additional resistance to thrust.

counter-imbrication See **contre-imbrication.**

counterlight A light or window directly opposite another.

countermure **1.** In fortification, a wall raised behind another to supply its place when a breach is made. **2.** A wall raised in front of another partition wall to strengthen it; a **contramure.**

counterscarp In fortification: **1.** The exterior **talus** or slope of a ditch. **2.** The area between the **parapet** and **glacis.**

cortile

cortile of the Borghese Palace, Rome (begun 1590)

counterscarp gallery A framework covered with a sheeting, within the counterscarp at the salients, the entrance being by a narrow door.

counterscarp wall The revetment of the counterscarp, usually made of stone or brick, but sometimes of timber.

countertrench A trench made by the defenders of a place to render ineffectual one made by the besiegers.

countervault An **inverted arch.**

country seat A rural residence of some importance.

coupled columns Columns set as close pairs with a wider **intercolumniation** between the pairs.

coupled columns

coupled pilasters Two closely spaced pilasters forming a pair.

coupled windows Two closely spaced windows which form a pair.

coupled windows

couple roof, coupled roof A double-pitched roof, usually of narrow span, in which opposite rafters are not tied together; the walls resist the outward thrust.

cour d'honneur The **forecourt** of a building, esp. a monumental forecourt.

course **1.** A layer of masonry units running horizontally in a wall or, much less commonly, curved over an arch; it is bonded with mortar. **2.** A continuous row or layer of material, as shingles, tiles, etc.

coursed ashlar, range masonry, range-work, regular coursed rubble Ashlar masonry in which the stones are of equal height within each course; all courses need not be of the same height.

coursed masonry, course work Masonry construction in which the stones are laid in regular courses, not irregularly as in rough or random rubble.

coursed rubble Masonry construction in which roughly dressed stones of random size are used, as they occur, to build up courses; the interstices between them are filled with smaller pieces, or with mortar.

coursed rubble

coursed square rubble Same as **random ashlar.**

course work See **coursed masonry.**

court **1.** An open, uncovered, and unoccupied space partially or fully surrounded by walls or buildings. **2.** A courtroom. **3.** Residence of a dignitary or member of royalty and its enclosed grounds.

courtyard An open area partially or fully enclosed by buildings or other walls, adjacent to or within a castle, house, or other building.

coussinet **1.** The stone which is placed on the impost of a pier to receive the first stone of an arch. **2.** The part of the front of an Ionic capital between the abacus and echinus.

cove A concave or canted interior corner or molding, esp. at the transition from wall to ceiling or floor.

cove ceiling, coved ceiling A ceiling having a cove at the wall lines, or elsewhere.

cove ceiling, Louvre

coved vault, cloistered arch, cloistered vault A vault composed of four quarter-cylindrical surfaces or coves, meeting in vertical diagonal planes, the axial sections of the vault being arched, and the horizontal courses diminishing in length from spring to crown.

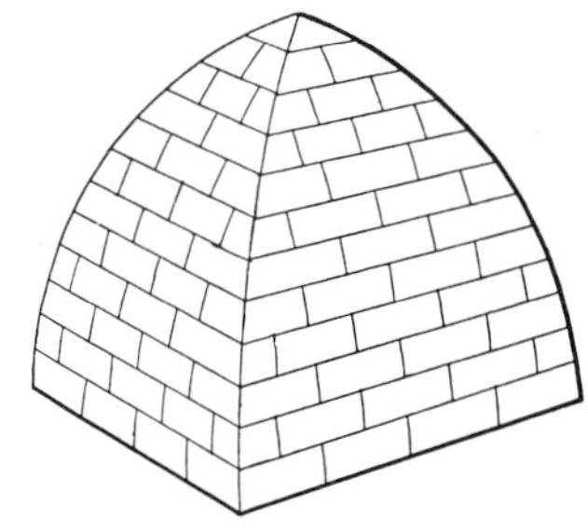
cove vault

cove molding, cavetto A molding having a concave face; often used as trim.

covent A convent or monastery.

cover fillet See **cover molding.**

cover molding, cover fillet Any plain or molded wood strip covering a joint, as between sections of paneling.

cover strip A thin strip used to cover a butt joint.

coving **1.** **Coves.** **2.** Vertical outward curve of an exterior wall, esp. to meet eaves or a jetty. **3.** A concave molding along a rood beam to support a loft or gallery. **4.** The curved or splayed jambs of a fireplace which narrows toward the back.

coyn, coyning Same as **quoin.**

cradle roof A **barrel roof, 1.**

cradle vault Same as **barrel vault.**

cradling Timber framing for supporting the lath and plaster or masonry of a dome or vaulted ceiling.

crail work Ornamental ironwork.

crease tile See **crest tile.**

creasing One or more courses of tiles or bricks laid upon the top of a wall or chimney with a projection to throw off water; if there is coping, it is placed above the creasing.

creasing course Same as **creasing.**

credence A small stand or shelf near an altar to hold the elements of the Eucharist: church vessels, service books, etc.

credence, church near Winchester (c. 1460)

credence, Woodford (c. 1350)

creeper **1.** A brick in the wall adjacent to an arch, cut to conform to the curvature of the extrados. **2.** *(pl.)* Same as **crocket.**

crematory, crematorium A building for the incineration of the human dead.

cremone bolt, cremorne bolt A type of hardware for locking French windows or the like; a rotating handle actuates sliding rods which move in opposite directions, extending from the edges of the window into sockets that are fixed in the frame.

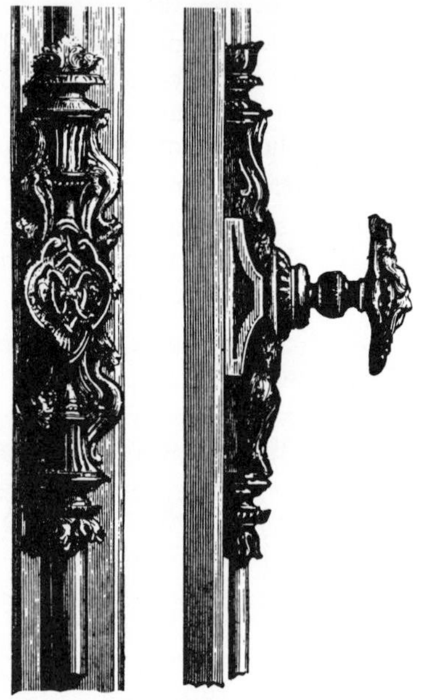

cremone bolt

cremorne bolt See **cremone bolt.**

crenation One of a series of rounded projections or teeth forming an edge.

crenel, crenelle An open space between the merlons of a **battlement.**

B, crenel

crenelated, crenellated **1.** Having battlements. **2.** Bearing a pattern of repeated indentations.

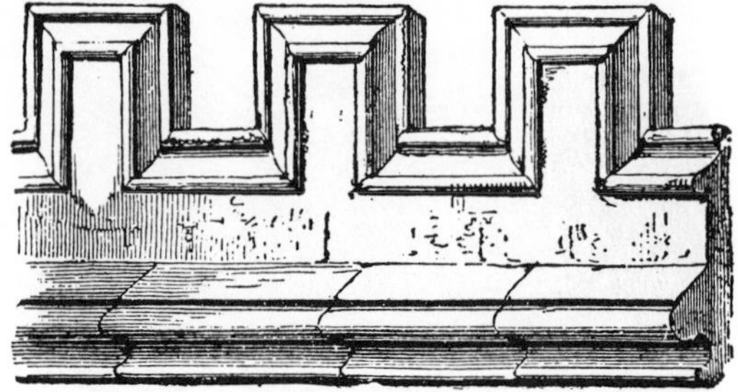

crenelated parapet

crenelated molding, crenellated molding, embattled molding A molding notched or indented to represent merlons and embrasures in fortification.

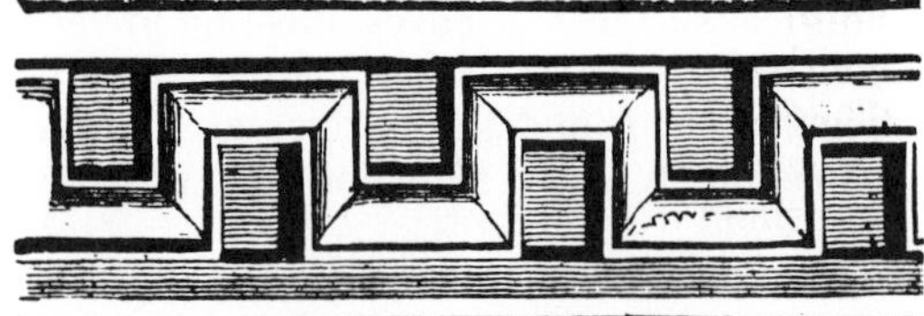

Norman crenelated molding

crenelet **1.** A small crenel, whether in an actual battlement or in a decorative design imitating one. **2.** A small **arrow loop.**

crenellation See **battlement.**

crepido **1.** Any raised base on which other things are built or supported, as of a Roman Temple, altar, obelisk, etc. **2.** A raised causeway for foot passengers on the side of a Roman road or street. **3.** The projecting members of a cornice, or other ornaments of a building.

ancient Roman street with a crepido on each side

crepidoma The base courses (a stepped platform) of a classical (esp. Greek) temple. Also see **stylobate.**

crescent A building or series of buildings whose façades follow a concave arc of a circle or ellipse in plan.

crescent arch A **horseshoe arch.**

cress tile See **crest tile.**

crest **1.** A finial. **2.** An ornament of a roof, a roof screen, wall, or aedicula, generally rhythmic and highly decorative, and frequently perforated; **cresting.**

Elizabethan crest, 2

cresting See **crest, 2.**

crest table A medieval term for a **coping** course.

crest tile, crease tile, cress tile **1.** Tile which fits like a saddle on the ridge of a roof. **2.** Tile forming a **crest, 2.**

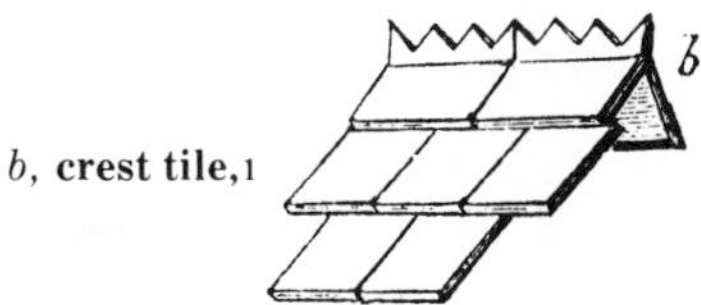

b, crest tile, 1

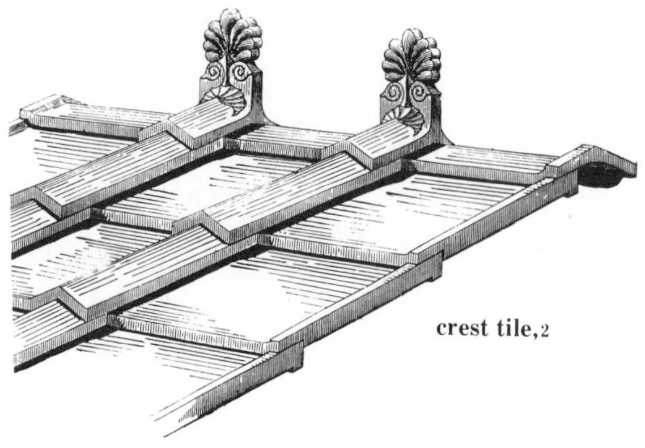

crest tile, 2

crinkle-crankle *(Brit.)* A serpentine wall, esp. in 18th cent. Suffolk.

cripple window A **dormer window.**

crocket In Gothic architecture and derivatives, an upward-oriented ornament, often vegetal in form, regularly spaced along sloping or vertical edges of emphasized features such as spires, pinnacles, and gables.

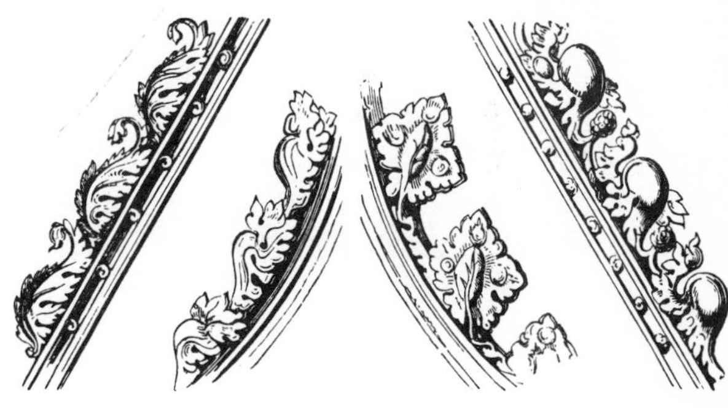

crockets

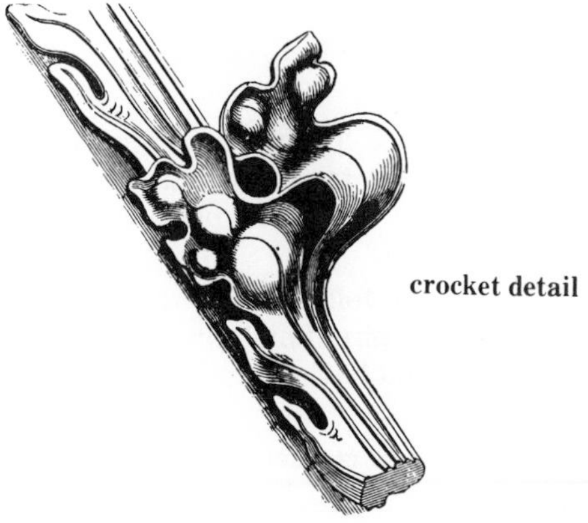

crocket detail

crocket arch An arch in which the intrados forms three or five foils.

crocket capital A capital having a series of **crockets.**

left: **crocket capital;** *right:* **a detail**

croft An **undercroft.**

croisette Same as **crossette.**

cromlech **1.** A monument of prehistoric or uncertain date consisting of an enclosure formed by huge stones planted in the ground in a circle. **2.** A **dolmen.**

cromlech,1

cromlech,2

crook A support consisting of a post or pile with a crossbeam resting on it; a bracket or truss consisting of a vertical piece, a horizontal piece, and a strut.

crop A bunch of foliage worked or sculptured at the top of a spire, finial, or similar decorative member, and having a resemblance to the top of a plant.

croquet Same as **crocket.**

crosette Same as **crossette.**

cross **1.** An object consisting primarily of two straight or nearly straight pieces forming right angles with one another; the usual symbol of the Christian religion. **2.** A monument or small building of any kind surmounted by a **cross, 1,** as a market cross.

Early English style crosses

Decorated style crosses

Perpendicular style crosses

cross aisle **1.** In a church, a transverse aisle between pews. **2.** In an auditorium, an aisle usually parallel to rows of seats, connecting other aisles or an aisle and an exit.

crossbeam **1.** A beam which runs transversely to the center line of a structure. **2.** Any transverse beam in a structure, such as a joist.

cross-church A cruciform church; one having a cross-shaped ground plan.

crossette, crosette **1.** A lateral projection of the architrave moldings of classical doors and windows at the extremities of the lintel or head. Also called an **ear,** or **elbow.** **2.** A small projecting part of an arch stone which hangs upon an adjacent stone.

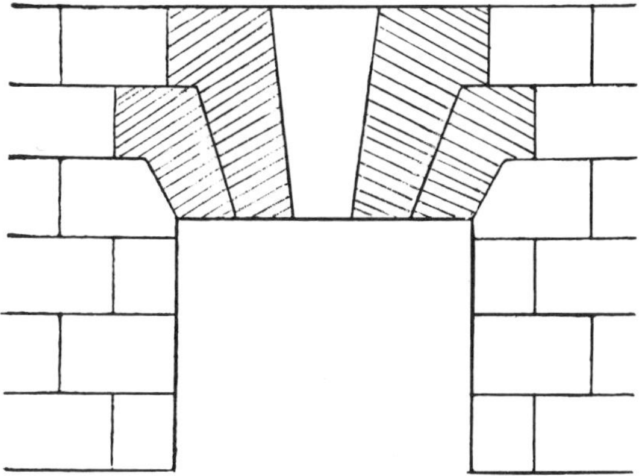

voussoirs with crossettes,2

cross-gable A **gable** which is set parallel to the ridge of the roof.

crossing In a church, the place where the nave and chancel cross the transept.

cross of Calvary See **Calvary cross.**

cross quarters A cross-shaped ornamental flower in tracery.

cross rib Same as **arch rib.**

cross springer **1.** The diagonal arch of a ribbed groin vault. **2.** A transverse rib of a groined roof.

cross vault, cross vaulting A vault formed by the intersection at right angles of two barrel vaults.

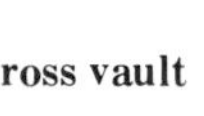

cross vault

cross window A window in which the combination of a single mullion and a transom presents the appearance of a cross.

crotchet Obsolete term for **crocket.**

croud Same as **crowde.**

croupe Obsolete term for **crop.**

crowde A crypt or cellar, esp. of a church.

crowfooted Having **corbiesteps.**

crow gable See **corbie gable.**

crown **1.** Any upper terminal feature in architecture. **2.** The top of an arch including the keystone, or of a vault. **3.** The corona of a cornice, sometimes including elements above it.

crown,1

crown,1

crown molding Any molding serving as a corona or otherwise forming the crowning or finishing member of a structure.

crown plate **1.** A **bolster.** **2.** A **ridge beam.**

crown post Any vertical member in a roof truss, esp. a **king post.**

crown steeple A decorative termination of a tower or turret, resembling a crown.

crown tile See **ridge tile.**

crow's-foot Same as **crowfoot.**

crowstep See **corbiestep.**

crowstep gable See **corbie gable.**

crowstone The top stone of the stepped edge of a gable.

cruciform **1.** Cross-shaped. **2.** The characteristic plan for Gothic and other large churches formed by the intersection of nave, chancel, and apse with the transepts.

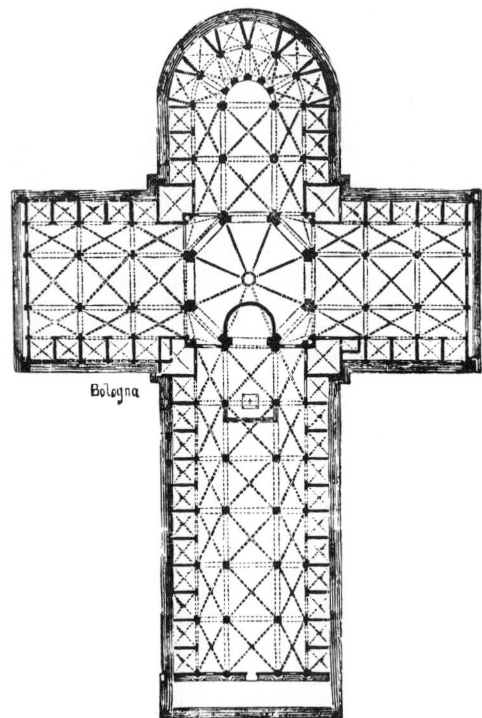

cruciform,2: San Petronio, Bologna (1390–1437)

cruck Same as **crutch.**

crusta Any veneer used in ancient Roman construction. It was common practice to cover large wall surfaces with veneers of marble.

crutch, cruck One of a pair of naturally curved timbers that rise from the outer walls to support the ridge beam, each crutch being called a **blade;** joined at the top and connected by one or two tie beams, the resulting arched frame forming the unit in the framework of old English houses or farm buildings; pairs of crutches were placed at approximately equal intervals.

crypt **1.** A story in a church below or partly below ground level and under the main floor, particularly of the chancel, often containing chapels and sometimes tombs. **2.** A hidden subterranean chamber or complex of chambers and passages.

crypt,1: Canterbury Cathedral (1070)

crypta **1.** Among the ancient Romans, any long narrow vault, whether wholly or partially below ground level; usually around the courtyard of a Roman villa or farmhouse; used to store grain, fruit, etc. **2.** A long narrow gallery, at ground level, enclosed by walls on both sides and receiving its light from rows of windows in one or both of the side walls which enclose it; somewhat resembles a **cloister.** Structures of this type were frequently built by the ancient Romans for the convenience and pleasure of the population; sometimes built as adjuncts to great mansions or to the promenades connected with a theatre, and commonly were attached to the side of an open colonnade. **3.** The stalls for horses and chariots in a circus.

cryptoporticus **1.** In ancient Roman architecture, a covered portico or arcade, not supported by open columns like the ordinary portico, but closed at the sides, with windows for the admission of light and air; frequented during summer for its coolness. **2.** An enclosed gallery, a common addition to a Roman villa or country house.

crystal palace **1.** An exhibition building constructed in large part of iron and glass in Hyde Park, London for the great exhibition of 1851. **2.** Any exhibition building similarly constructed.

cubicle **1.** A very small enclosed space. **2.** A **carrel.**

cubiculum **1.** In ancient Roman architecture, a bedchamber. **2.** A mortuary chapel attached to a church. **3.** A burial chamber having, on its walls, compartments for the reception of the dead. **4.** Same as **suggestus, 2.**

cubiform capital Same as **cushion capital, 2.**

Crystal Palace, New York (1852), inspired by the Crystal Palace in London (1851)

Ctesiphon A ruined city, the ancient capital of Parthia and later the Sassanian capital, located on the Tigris River near Baghdad. The site of a Sassanian palace of gigantic dimensions, built by Shapur I (241–272 A.D.); based on a Parthian prototype, it features an enormous **iwan** covered by a parabolic barrel vault which served as an audience hall. The originally symmetrical façade is articulated by horizontal bands, pilasters, and blind arches, all in brick. Both the exterior and interior originally were decorated with stucco, mosaics, and marble.

cubit **1.** A linear unit of measurement used by the ancients; in ancient Egypt, equal to 20.62 in. (52.4 cm). **2.** An ancient Roman measure of length equal to 17.5 in. (44.4 cm). **3.** An ancient Greek measure of length equal to 18.2 in. (46.2 cm).

cubitorium Same as **cubiculum.**

cubitus Same as **cubit, 2.**

cul-de-four A half-dome or quarter-sphere vault, as over an apse or niche.

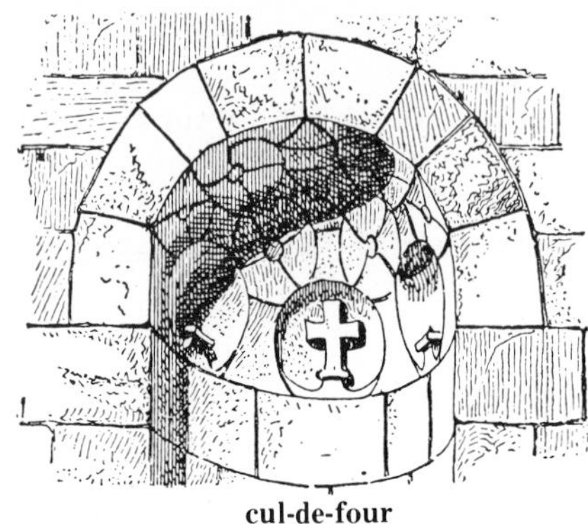
cul-de-four

cul-de-lampe **1.** A pointed, pendant ornament used at the apex of a vault and to terminate protruding, elevated structures. Also see **pendant.** **2.** An isolated corbel serving as a support for an oriel, column, statue, turret, or the like; esp. one resembling an inverted cone or pyramid.

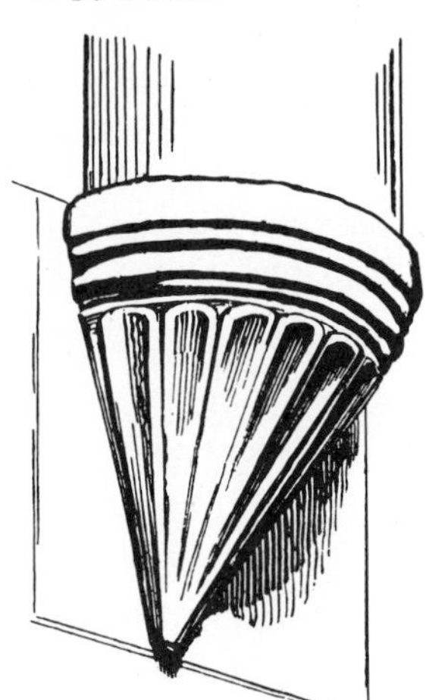
cul-de-lampe, 2

cul-de-sac A street, lane, or alley closed at one end, usually having an enlarged, somewhat circular area for turning around.

culina In ancient Rome, a kitchen.

cullis See **coulisse.**

culmen See **columen.**

cult temple A temple devoted to the worship of a divinity, as distinguished from a **mortuary temple.**

cum ceiling Same as **camp ceiling.**

cune An obsolete term for **quoin.**

cuneiform Having a wedge-shaped form; esp. applied to characters, or to the inscriptions in such characters, of the ancient Mesopotamians and Persians.

cuneus One of the wedge-shaped sections for spectators in an ancient theatre.

cuniculus A low underground passage.

cupola A domical roof on a circular base, often set on the ridge of a roof. Also see **dome.**

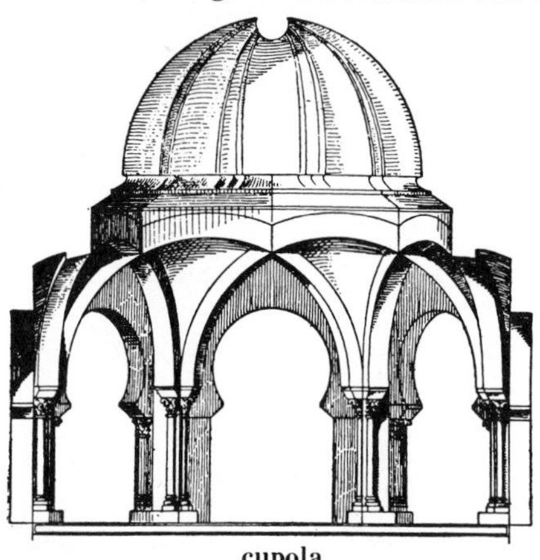
cupola

curb roof A pitched roof that slopes away from the ridge in two successive planes, as a **gambrel roof** *(U.S.A.)* or **mansard roof** *(Brit.)*.

curb roof

curia The council house in a Roman municipality.

curstable A course of stones with moldings cut on them. May be a **stringcourse** or part of a **cornice.**

curtail A spiral scroll-like termination of any architectural member, as at the end of a stair rail.

curtail step, scroll step A step, usually lowest in a flight, of which one end or both ends are rounded in a spiral or scroll shape which projects beyond the newel.

curtain wall In ancient fortifications, an enclosing wall or rampart connecting two **bastions** or towers.

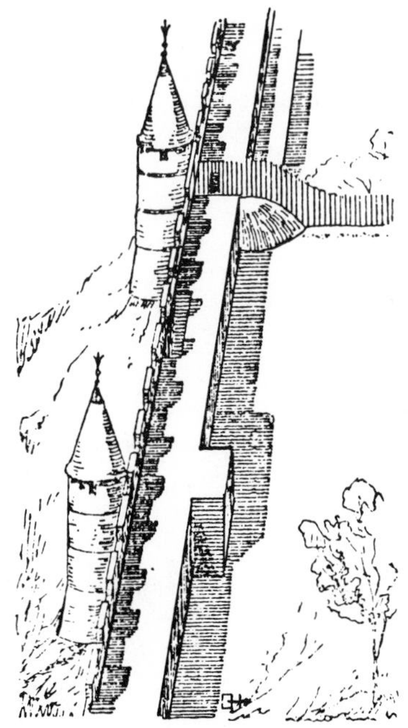

curtain wall

curtilage The ground adjacent to a dwelling and appertaining to it, as a yard, garden, or court.

Curvilinear style The later, richer period of the Decorated style of English Gothic architecture, in the second half of the 14th cent.

curvilinear tracery See **flowing tracery.**

cushion **1.** A convex element resembling a pad. **2.** A corbel for roofing, a padstone.

cushion capital **1.** A capital resembling a cushion that is pressed down because of weight on it. **2.** In medieval, esp. Norman, architecture, a cubic capital with its lower angles rounded off.

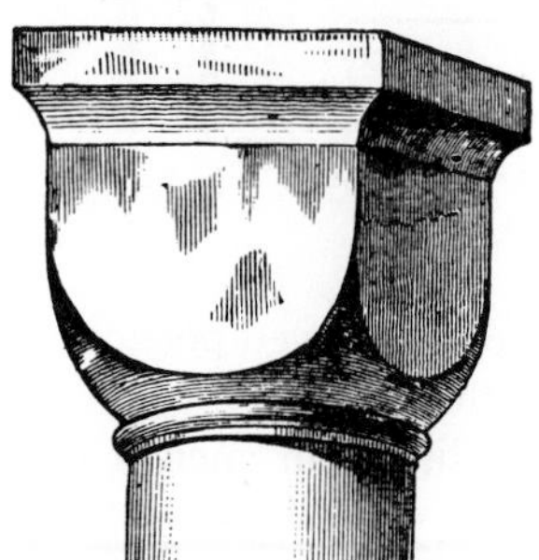

cushion capital

cushion course A convex **fascia.** Also see **torus.**

cusp **1.** The intersection of two arcs or foliations in a tracery. **2.** The figure formed by the intersection of tracery arcs. Also see **foil.**

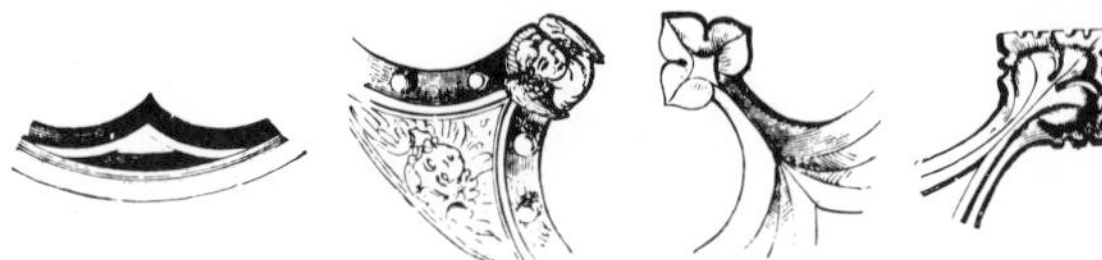

types of cusps

cusped arch An arch which has cusps or foliations worked on the intrados.

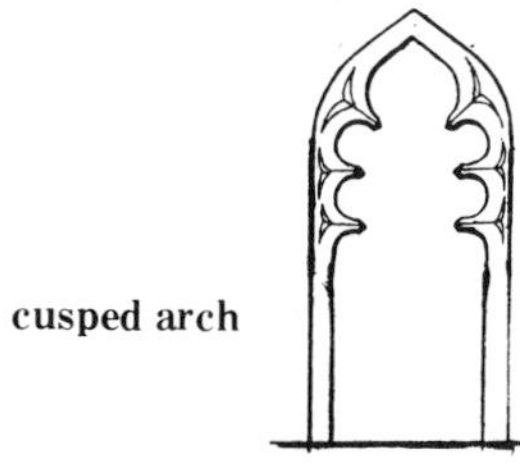

cusped arch

cuspidation A system of ornamentation consisting of or containing cusps.

cut string, cut stringer Same as **open string.**

cycloid A curve generated by a point in the plane of a circle when the circle is rolled along a straight line, keeping always in the same plane.

cycloidal arch An arch whose intrados forms a cycloid.

Cyclopean **1.** Describing prehistoric masonry, made of huge stone blocks laid without mortar. **2.** Megalithic.

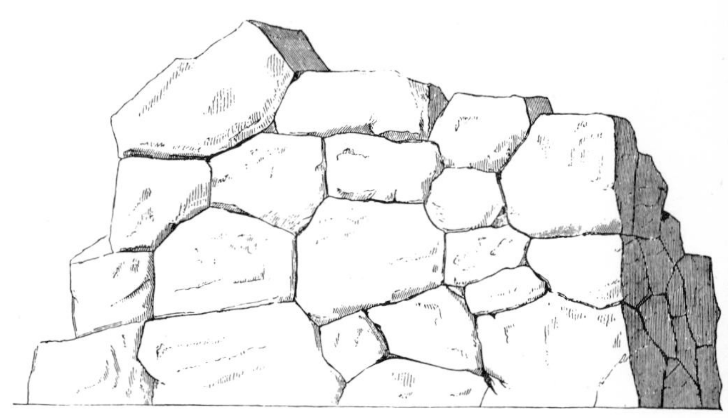

Cyclopean wall

cyclostyle A circular colonnade which is open at the center.

cylindrical vault A **barrel vault.**

cylindrical vault

cyma, cima A molding having a profile of double curvature; one having an ogee profile.

cyma recta, Doric cyma A molding of double curvature which is concave at the outer edge and convex at the inner edge.

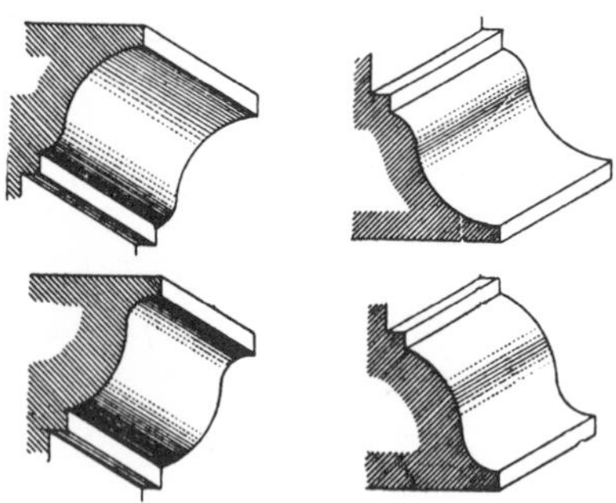

types of cyma rectas

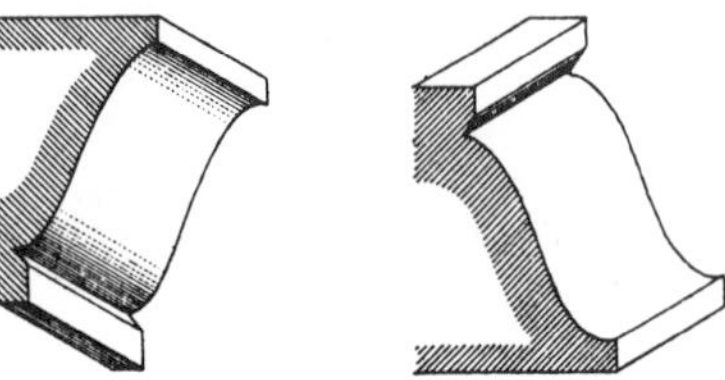

quirked cyma rectas

cyma reversa, Lesbian cyma A molding of double curvature which is convex at the outer edge and concave at the inner edge.

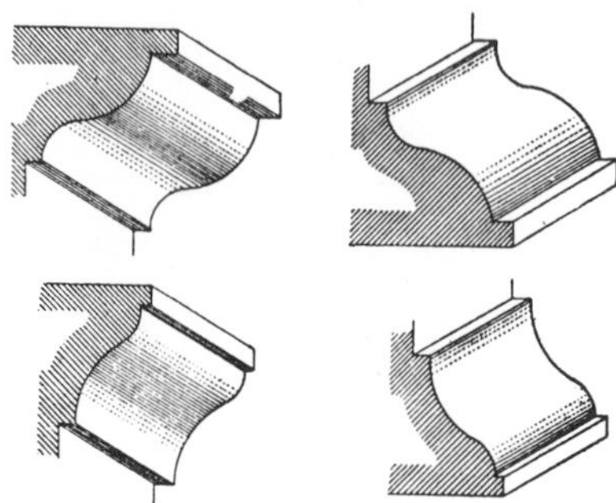

types of cyma reversas

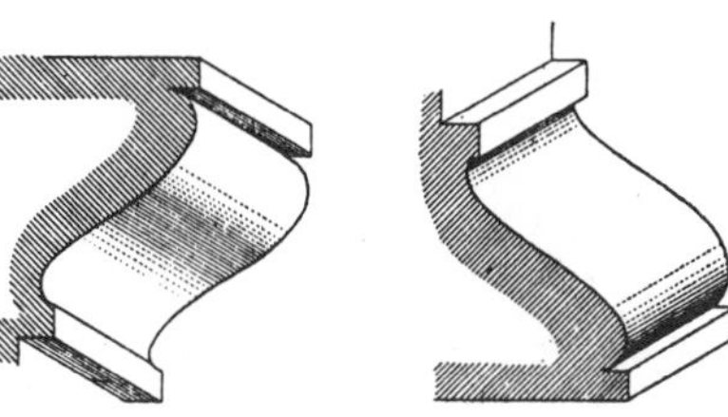

quirked cyma reversas

cymatium The crowning molding of a classical cornice, esp. when it has the form of a cyma, though it may also be an ovolo or cavetto; an **ogee.**

cymatium from a Syrian house (c. 400 A.D.)

cymbia See **cimbia.**

cyrtostyle A projecting, curved portico, usually semicircular, having columns.

cyzicene An apartment in an ancient Greek house, usually having a view of a garden, similar to the Roman **triclinium.**

D

dado **1.** The middle portion of a pedestal between the base (or the plinth) and the surbase (or the cornice, cap, or entablement); also called **die.** **2.** The middle part (sometimes all parts) of a protective, ornamental paneling applied to the lower walls of a room above the baseboard. **3.** A rectangular groove cut across the full width of a piece of wood to receive the end of another piece.

dagaba Same as **dagoba.**

dagger A small Decorated tracery motif in the form of a distorted cusped lancet, with the foot pointed; a pointed oval-shaped opening in the tracery.

dagoba In Buddhist architecture, a monumental structure containing relics of Buddha or of some Buddhist saint.

大黒柱 **daikoku-bashira** A heavy post placed at the center of a traditional Japanese house or farmhouse; often associated with the god of fortune.

dais A raised platform reserved for the seating of speakers or dignitaries.

dalan In Persian and Indian architecture, a veranda, or sometimes a more stately reception hall, more or less open to the weather, with a roof carried on columns, or the like.

dallan Same as **dalan.**

dalle A slab or large tile of stone, baked clay, etc., esp. a tile of which the surface is incised or otherwise ornamented, such as the medieval sepulchral slabs set in the pavement and walls of churches.

dancers Colloquial term for **stairs.**

dancette See **chevron, 2;** zigzag molding.

dancing step See **balanced step.**

dancing winder See **balanced step.**

Danish knot Same as **runic knot.**

danjōzumi See **kidan.**

dar **1.** In Indian and Persian architecture, a gateway. **2.** In Oriental architecture, a dwelling.

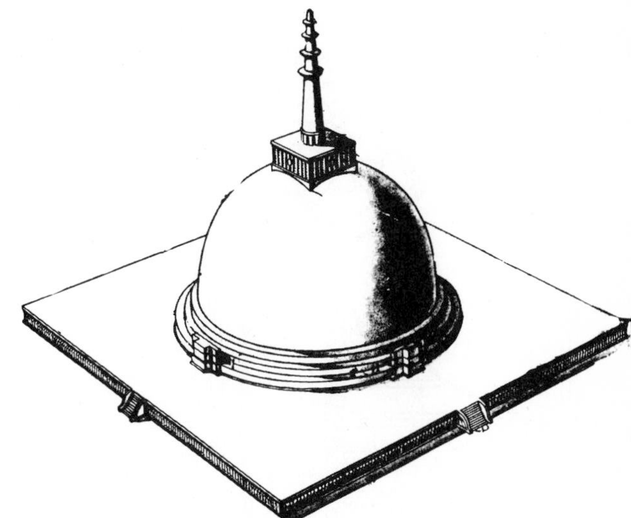

dagoba, Ceylon (2nd cent. B.C.)

dart See **egg and dart; anchor.**

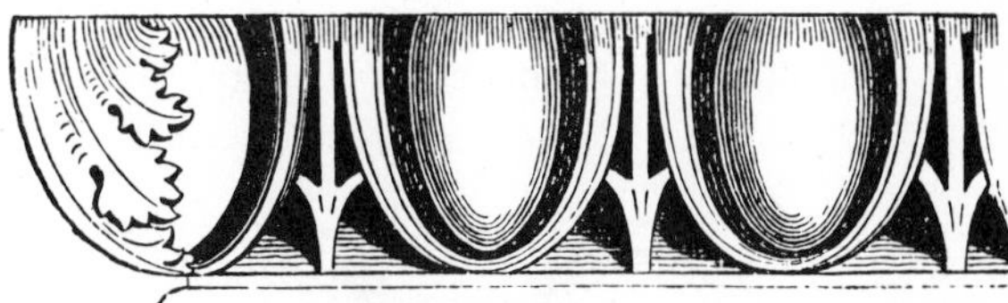

egg-and-dart molding

darwaza In the architecture of India, a door.

David's shield Same as **Star of David.**

day One division in a window, as in a large church window.

dead bolt A type of door lock; the bolt, which is square in cross section, is operated by the door key or a turn piece.

deadlight See **fixed light.**

dead wall A **blank wall.**

dead window Same as **blank window.**

dealbatus Covered with a coating of white cement or stucco (**albarium opus**), which the ancients employed extensively both in the interior and exterior of their buildings as an ornamental facing to conceal the rough stones or brickwork.

dealbatus

deambulatory **1.** An aisle extending around the apse of a church; an apse aisle. **2.** The ambulatory of a cloister, or the like.

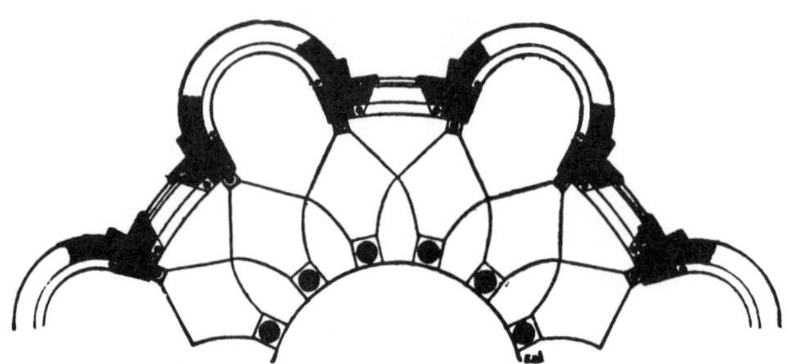

deambulatory, 1

debir The holy of holies in the **Temple of Solomon** which held the **ark** of the covenant.

decani side The south side of a church, or the side on the right of one facing the altar.

decanicum A prison in which ecclesiastical offenders were confined.

decastyle A building having a portico of ten columns, or rows of ten columns.

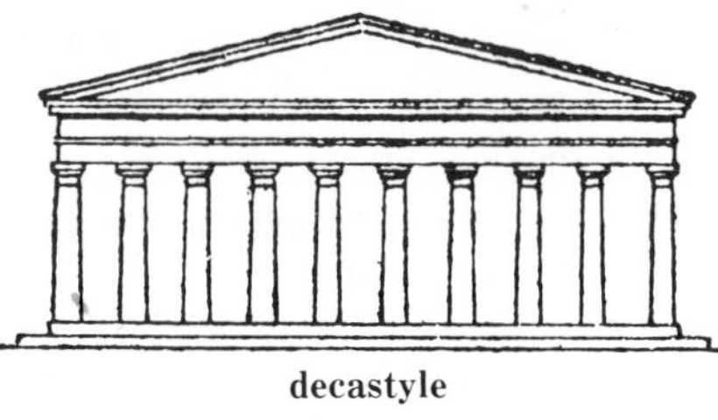

decastyle

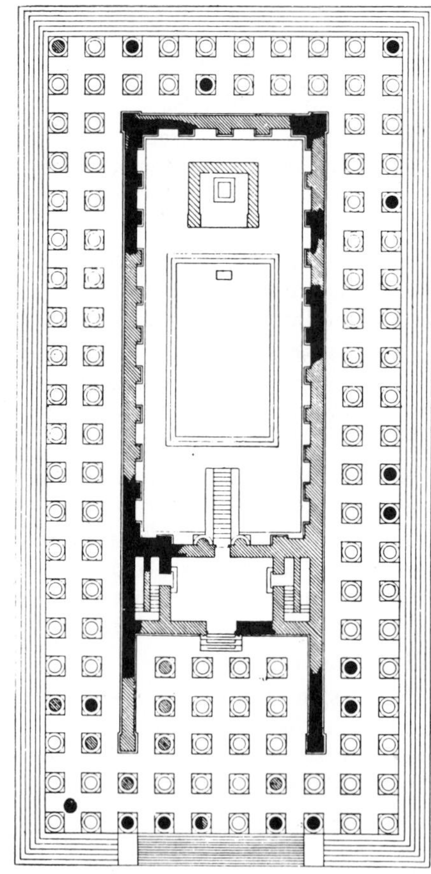

decastyle, dipteral

decempeda A rod equal in length to 10 **pedes** (Roman feet); used by ancient architects and surveyors for taking measurements.

decor The combination of materials, furnishings, and objects used in interior decorating to create an atmosphere or style.

Decorated style The second of the three phases of English Gothic architecture, from ca. 1280 to after 1350, preceded by Early English and followed by the Perpendicular; characterized by rich decoration and tracery, multiple ribs and liernes, and often ogee arches. Its early development is called *Geometric;* its later, *Curvilinear.*

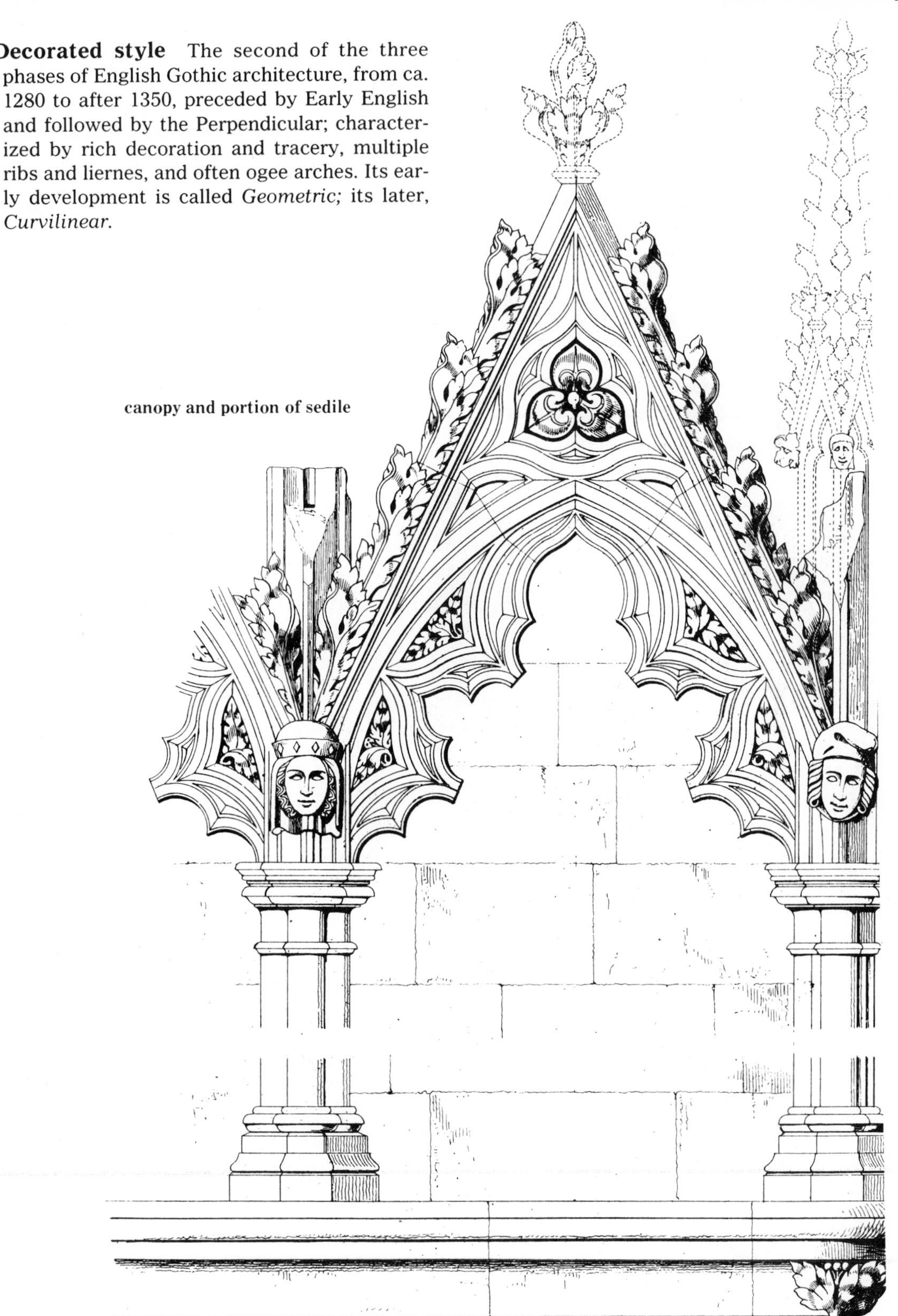

Decorated style

parapet, Beverly Minster (c. 1350)

parapet, Brailes Church, Warwickshire

Merton Chapel, Oxford (c. 1320)

Bloxham, Oxfordshire (c. 1320)

Broughton, Oxfordshire (c. 1320)

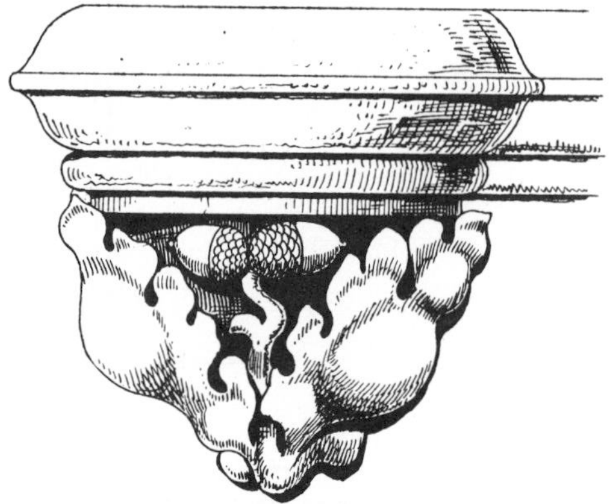

corbel, Winchelsea, Sussex

arcade, Lichfield Cathedral

Branbury, Oxfordshire (c. 1350)

Adderbury Church, Oxfordshire (14th cent.)

Flore Church, Northamptonshire

capital and base,
¼ full size

Dorchester, Oxford (c. 1300)

Garsington, Oxford (c. 1350)

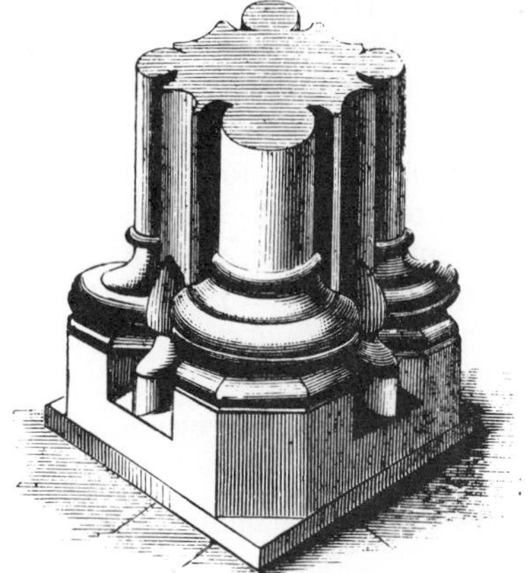

base of shaft

dedication cross A cross painted or carved on the wall of a church to indicate any one of the twelve spots touched with chrism by the bishop at the ceremony of the consecration of the church, which takes place on the day the debt for construction of the church is totally paid off. The cross usually has a bracket below it for a candle which is lit on the day of consecration and on subsequent anniversaries.

degree 1. A **step,** as of a **stair.** 2. A **stair,** or set of steps.

delphin, delphinus A dolphin. Also see **delphinorum columnae.**

delphins terminating an Attic pedestal

delphinorum columnae The two columns at one end of the spina of an ancient Roman circus, on which marble figures of dolphins were placed.

delubrum 1. In ancient Roman architecture, a sanctuary or temple. 2. The part of a classical temple containing the altar or a statue of the deity; the most sacred part of the temple. 3. A church furnished with a font. 4. A font or baptismal basin.

demicolumn Same as **half column.**

demilune See **ravelin.**

demimetope A half, or incomplete, **metope** in a Doric frieze.

demi-rilievo, demi-relievo Half relief. Also see **relief.**

denticulated, denticular Ornamented with **dentils.**

dentil One of a band of small, square, toothlike blocks forming part of the characteristic ornamentation of the Ionic, Corinthian, and Composite orders, and sometimes the Doric.

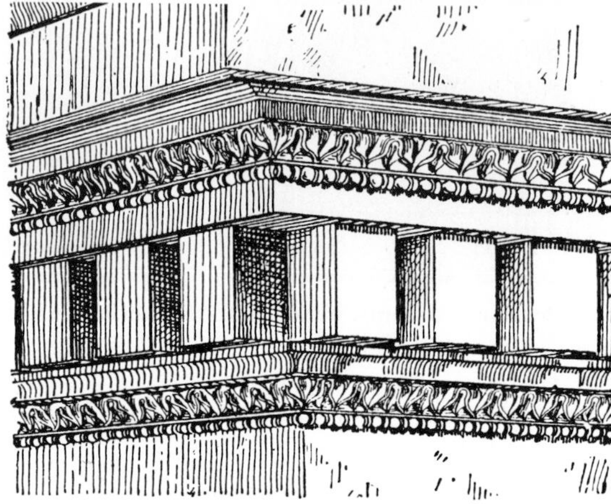

Ionic dentils

dentil band A plain, uncarved band occupying the position in a cornice where dentils would normally occur.

dependency A subsidiary building near or adjoining a principal structure.

depressed arch 1. A **drop arch.** 2. A flatheaded opening with the angles rounded off into segments of circles; frequently used in the **Perpendicular style.**

depressed arch,2

design 1. To compose a plan for a building. 2. The architectural concept of a building as represented by plans, elevations, renderings, and other drawings. 3. Any visual concept of a man-made object, as of a work of art or a machine.

destina **1.** A pillar or other support for a building. **2.** An aisle or small cell in a church.

destraria A late Latin term for **deambulatory.**

devagosta In the architecture of India, a niche.

deversorium In ancient Rome, an inn for travelers, or a private house used for their lodging.

deys Obsolete term for **dais.**

dhagobah Same as **dagoba.**

dharmsala A Hindu **caravanserai.**

dhvajastambham In the architecture of India, a high pillar in front of a temple.

dhwaja-stambha In Dravidian style architecture in India, a square pillar which bears the **trisula,** or symbol of the god Silva.

diaconicon **1.** Originally a place where the deacons kept the vessels used for the church service. **2.** In Greek churches, a sacristy to the right of the sanctuary.

diaconium Same as **aspasticum.**

diaeta **1.** The living quarters of an ancient Roman house (as opposed to those parts of the house used for other purposes). **2.** A dwelling.

diaglyph **1.** A relief engraved in reverse; an intaglio. **2.** A **sunk relief.**

diagonal buttress One extending at 45° from the right-angle corner of two walls.

diagonal joining Decorative work formed by bricks or tiles which are set obliquely and symmetrically with respect to a vertical or horizontal axis.

diagonal rib A rib crossing a bay or compartment of a vault on a diagonal.

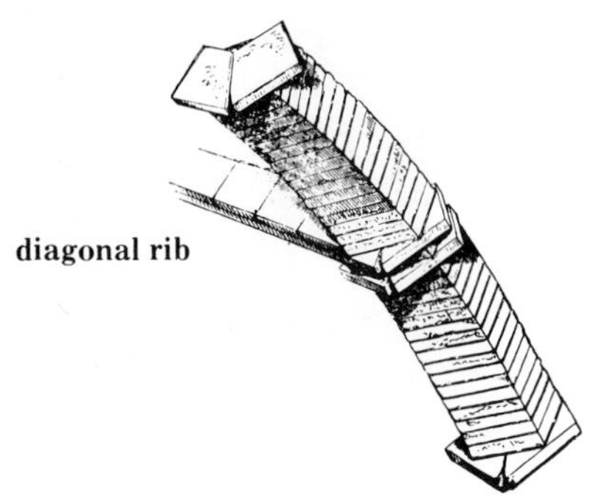

diagonal rib

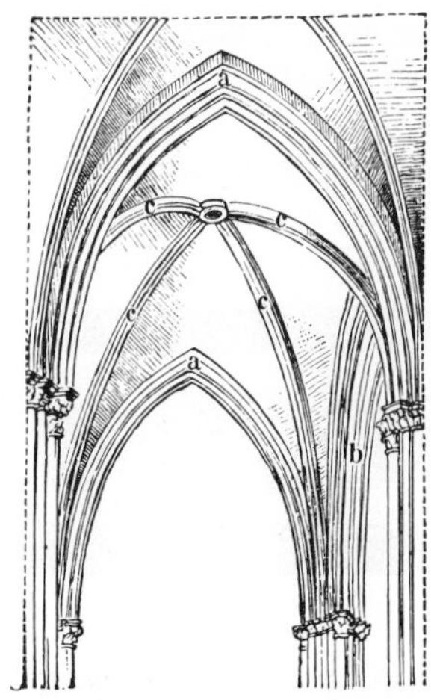

a, transverse rib;
b, pier arches;
c, diagonal ribs

diagonal slating, drop-point slating A method of laying shingles or slates so that the diagonal of each slate runs horizontally.

diamicton In ancient Roman architecture, a type of masonry wall construction having a hollow cavity filled with broken material of every description.

diamond fret, lozenge fret, lozenge molding A molding consisting of fillets intersecting so as to form diamonds or rhombuses.

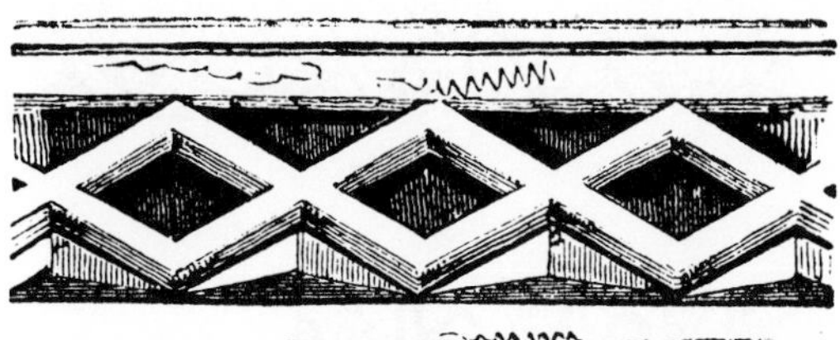

diamond frets

diamond matching, four-piece butt matching A method of cutting and piecing four adjacent, square-cut pieces of wood veneer so that a diamond pattern results at the center.

diamondwork Masonry construction in which pieces are set so as to form diamonds on the face of a wall.

diaper An allover pattern with motifs placed in a repeated design, esp. on a rectangular or diagonal grid.

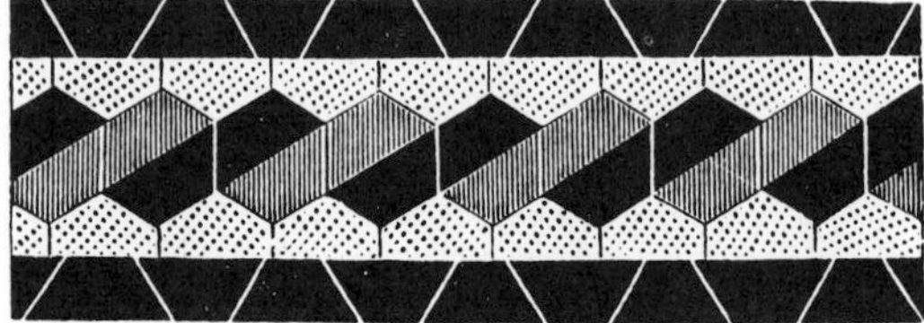

diaper

diaper

Egyptian diaper

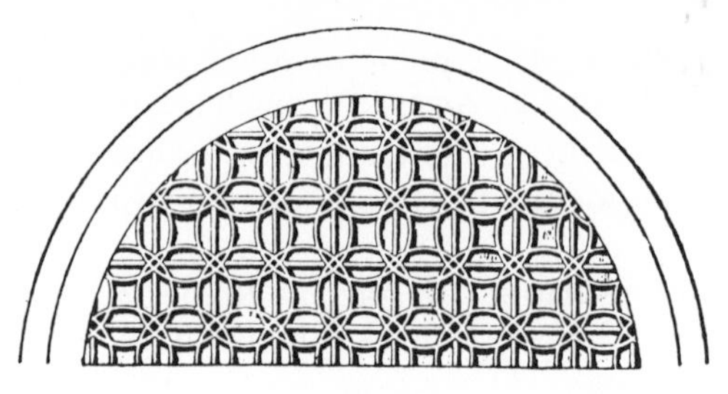

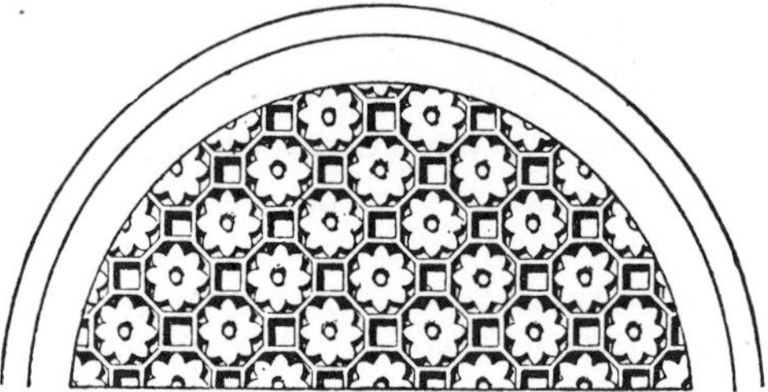

diaper

German Gothic diaper

early French diaper

diastyle See **intercolumniation.**

3

diastyle: separated by 3 column diameters

diathyros A vestibule in an ancient Grecian house with the street door at one end and the door to the courtyard at the other.

diatoni In ancient Greek and Roman masonry construction, stones which extend the full thickness of the wall; same as **through stones.**

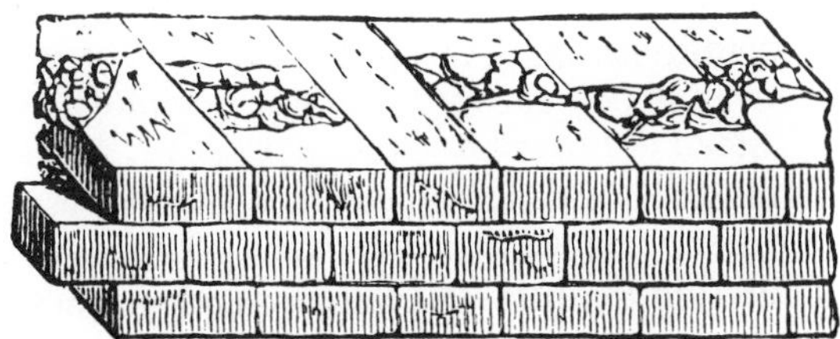

ancient construction with diatoni

diazoma The wide horizontal walkway between the lower and upper tiers of seats in a Greek theatre.

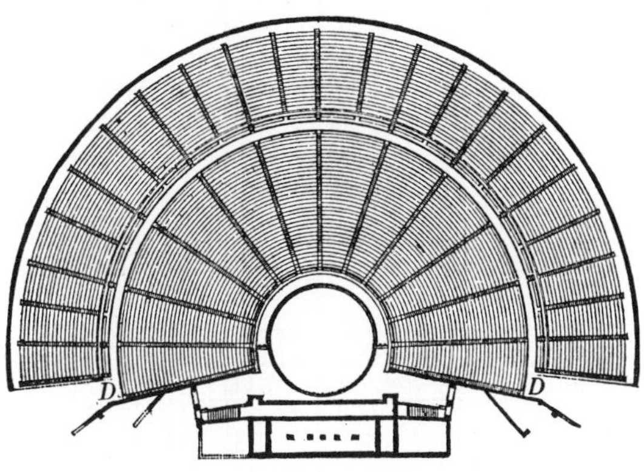

D, D, diazoma: Theatre at Epidaurus, Greece (350 B.C.)

dictorium Same as **ambo, 1.**

dictyotheton **1.** A type of masonry used by the ancient Greeks; composed of square-cut stones, forming a network or chessboard pattern; similar to the **opus reticulatum** of the Romans. **2.** Open lattice masonry to admit light and air.

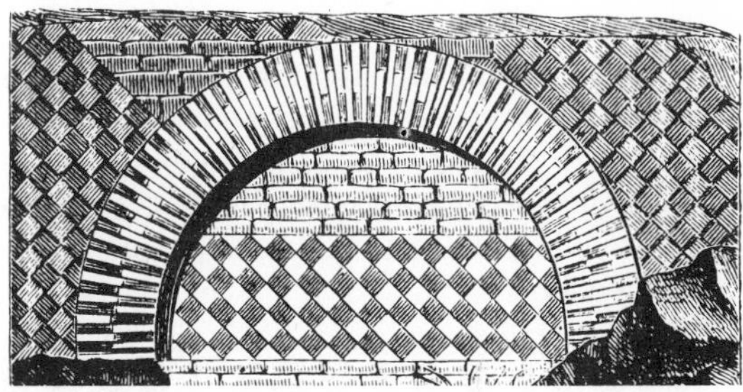

dictyotheton,1

didoron A type of ancient Roman brick; approx. 1 ft (30.5 cm) long and 6 in. (15.2 cm) in width.

die The middle portion of a pedestal between the base (or plinth) and the surbase; also called a **dado.**

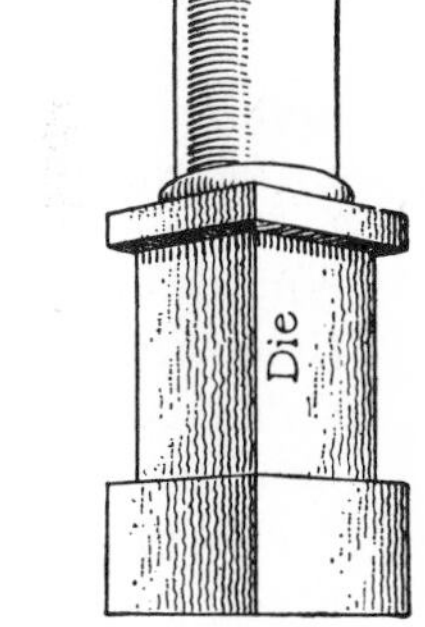

die

diglyph A member having two vertical channels or grooves, without the two lateral half grooves which characterize the **triglyph.**

dike, dyke A dry stone wall.

diminished arch, skeen arch, skene arch An arch having less rise or height than a semicircle.

diminished column A **column** having a greater diameter at its base than at its capital.

diminishing rule A template used to establish the **entasis** of a column.

dinh A communal hall in a Vietnamese village.

Diocletian window See **Venetian window.**

diorama 1. A large painting, or a series of paintings, intended for exhibition to spectators in a darkened room in a manner to produce by optical illusions an appearance of reality. 2. A building in which such paintings are exhibited.

diplinthius In ancient Roman construction, masonry which is two bricks thick.

dipmala In the architecture of India, a tall pillar or tower used to hold a festival light.

dipteral Said of a classical temple having two rows of free columns, rather than a single row, surrounding the **cella.** Also see **peripteral, pseudodipteral.**

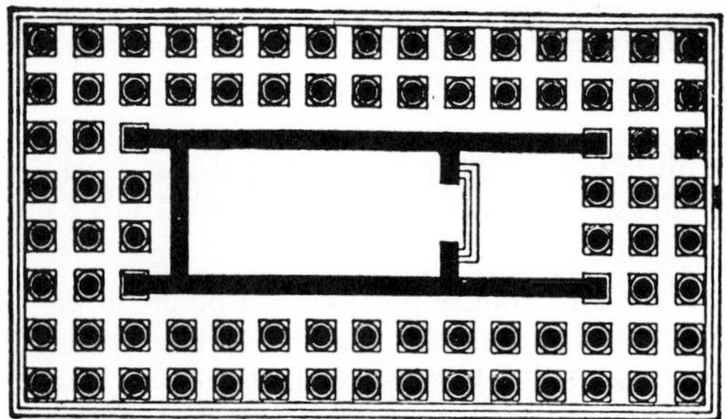

plan of a dipteral temple

dipylon 1. In ancient Greece, a gate consisting of two separate gates placed side by side. 2. *(cap.)* A gate of this type on the northwestern side of Athens.

Directoire style A transitional classicist style preceding the Empire style, named after the Directoire rule in France (1795–1799).

discharging arch, relieving arch, safety arch An arch, usually segmental and often a blind arch, built above the lintel of a door or window to discharge the weight of the wall above the lintel to each side.

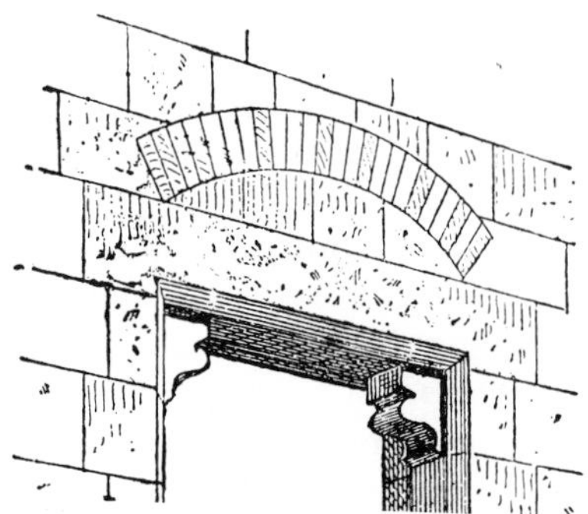

discharging arch

discontinuous impost A **shafted impost,** where the arch moldings are different from the moldings of the pier from which the arch springs.

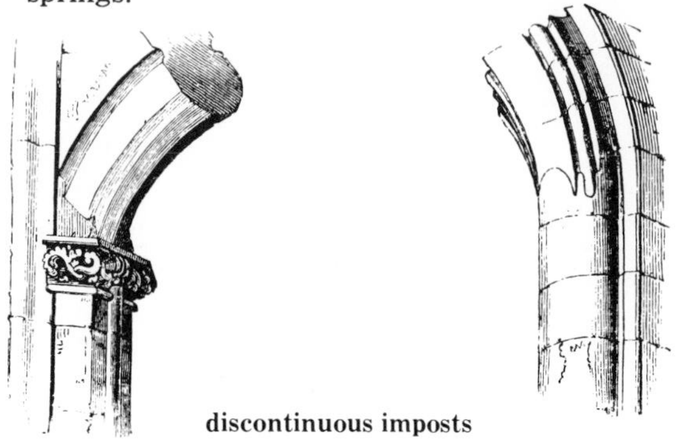

discontinuous imposts

displuviatum An atrium, the roof of which was sloped outward from the compluvium instead of toward it.

distyle Having two columns in front; used in describing a classical building.

distyle in antis Having two columns in front between **antae.**

distyle in antis

ditriglyph An interval between two columns such as to admit two triglyphs in the entablature instead of one, as usual.

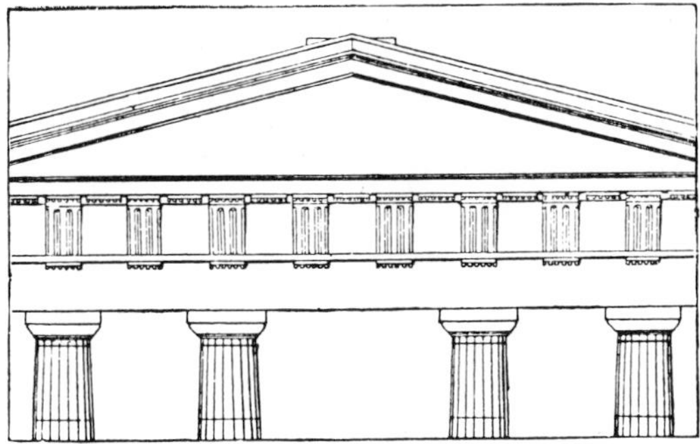

ditriglyph

divan 1. In Muslim countries, a council room or hall for a court of justice. 2. A smoking room.

divan-i-amm The great audience hall of a Mogul palace.

diversorium A lodging, hired or gratuitous, in ancient Rome.

dividiculum Earlier term for a **castellum aquae.**

diwan Same as **divan, 1.**

dodai In traditional Japanese architecture, the foundation sill (wooden) of a house.

dodai-ishi In traditional Japanese architecture, a foundation stone of a house.

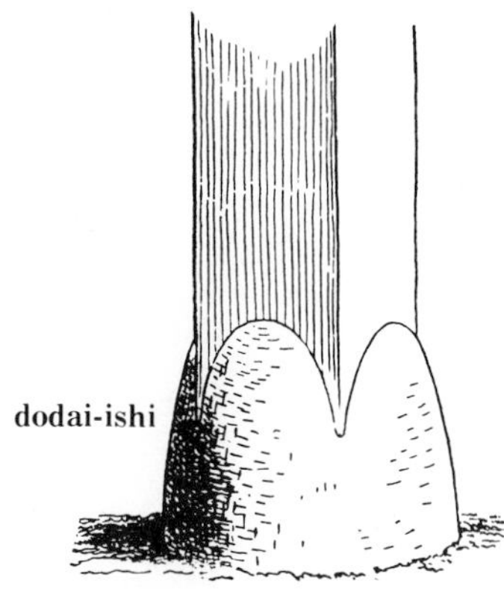

dodai-ishi

dodecastyle Having twelve columns in the front row; said of buildings of classical type.

dog's tooth Same as **dogtooth.**

dog's-tooth course Same as **dogtooth course.**

dogtooth, tooth ornament 1. An ornament in medieval architecture and derivatives, of more or less elaborate motif, usually pyramidal with notched sides, the diagonal portions usually resembling petals or leaves which radiate from the raised point. 2. A brick laid with its corners projecting from the wall face.

dogtooth

dogtooth course A stringcourse of bricks laid diagonally so that one corner projects from the face of the wall.

dolmen, table stone A prehistoric tomb of standing stones, usually capped with a large horizontal slab.

dolmens

dolphin column See **delphinorum columnae.**

dome **1.** A curved roof structure spanning an area; often hemispherical in shape. **2.** A vault substantially hemispherical in shape, but sometimes slightly pointed or bulbous; a ceiling of similar form.

Dome of the Rock The earliest extant monument of Islamic architecture, built (691 A.D.) by the ommiad caliph Abd al-Malik on the rock where, according to tradition, Mohammed ascended to heaven and where the Temple of Solomon stood. It was meant to compete with the Church of the Holy Sepulchre, the plan of which served as the basis for its scheme, and it has exactly the same dimensions. The central cylindrical space created around the sacred rock is covered by a wooden dome set on a drum, and is surrounded by two lower octagonal ambulatories. The interior is richly decorated with marble, mosaic, and metal repoussé work. Originally the exterior was faced with marble, mosaic, and gold. The present blue faïence panels date from the time of the renovation by Suleiman the Magnificent in 1552 A.D.

domical Pertaining to, resembling, or characterized by a dome, as a domical church.

domical vault A **coved vault.**

domus See **Roman house.**

donjon Same as **dungeon,** 1.

half section, half elevation, Dome of St. Irene, Constantinople (532 A.D.; rebuilt in 564 and 740)

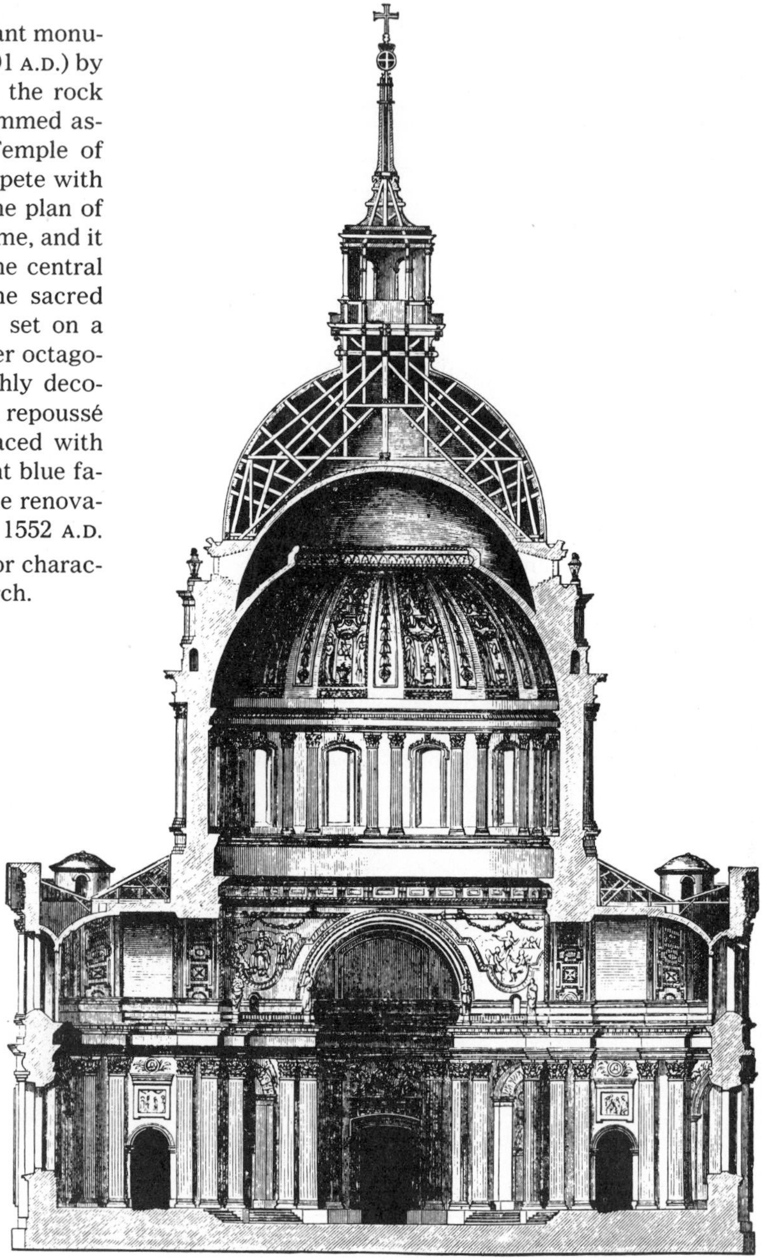

section of Dome of the Invalides, Paris (1679–1706)

door **1.** An entranceway. **2.** A barrier (usually solid) which swings, slides, tilts, or folds to close an opening in a wall or cabinet or the like.

Doric

Ionic: Erechtheion, Athens (421–405 B.C.)

door, House of Pansa, Pompeii

Anglo-Saxon (c. 900 A.D.)

door

Norman (c. 1120)

Early English (c. 1260)

Decorated (c. 1350)

Perpendicular

Tudor

Elizabethan (c. 1600)

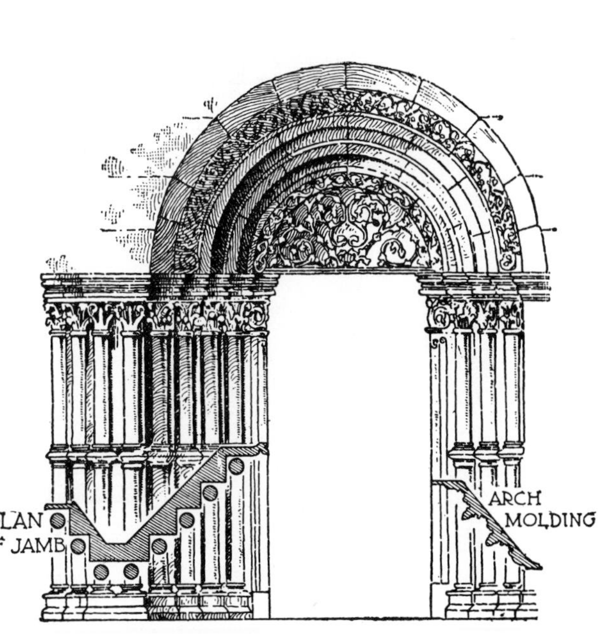

Romanesque

Gothic, Cologne Cathedral (1248–)

Renaissance

Baroque (c. 1760)

Rococo (c. 1730)

Neoclassic

doorcheek A **doorjamb.**

door head **1.** The uppermost member of a doorframe. **2.** A horizontal projection above a door.

door head, England (15th cent.)

doorjamb, doorcheek, doorpost The vertical member on each side of a door.

door knocker A knob, bar, or ring of metal, attached to the outside of an exterior door to enable a person to announce his presence; usually held by a hinge so that it can be lifted and allowed to strike a metal plate.

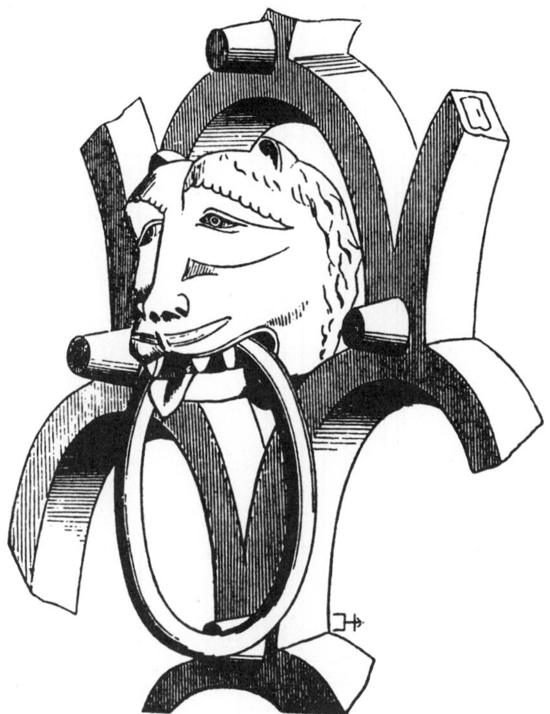

door knocker, St. Mark's, Venice

sculptured door head, Dorset

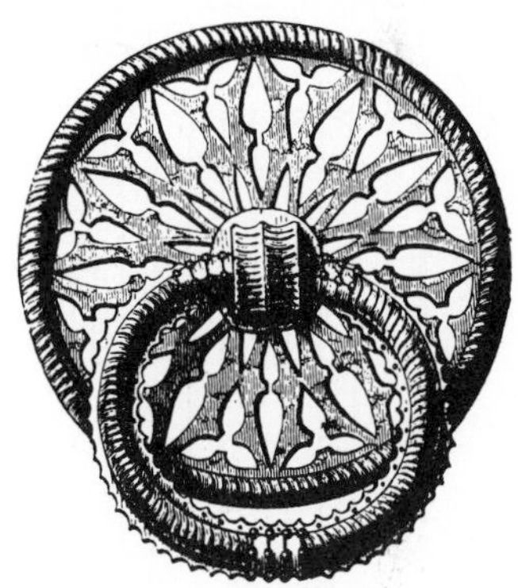

door knocker, England (15th cent.)

door mullion The center vertical member of a double-door opening, set between two single active leaves; usually forms the strike side of each leaf; may be removable. Also see **mullion.**

doorpost See **doorjamb.**

door rail A horizontal cross member which forms part of the framework of a door; connects the hinge stile to the lock stile, both at the top and bottom of the door and at intermediate locations; may be exposed, as in paneled doors, or concealed, as in flush doors.

doorsill, saddle The horizontal member, usually a board, covering the floor joint on the threshold of a door.

doorstone The stepstone at the threshold of a door.

door tree The jamb or sidepiece of a door.

door window A **French door.**

Doric cyma A **cyma recta.**

Doric order

Doric order The column and entablature developed by the Dorian Greeks, sturdy in proportion, with a simple cushion capital, a frieze of triglyphs and metopes, and mutules in the cornice.

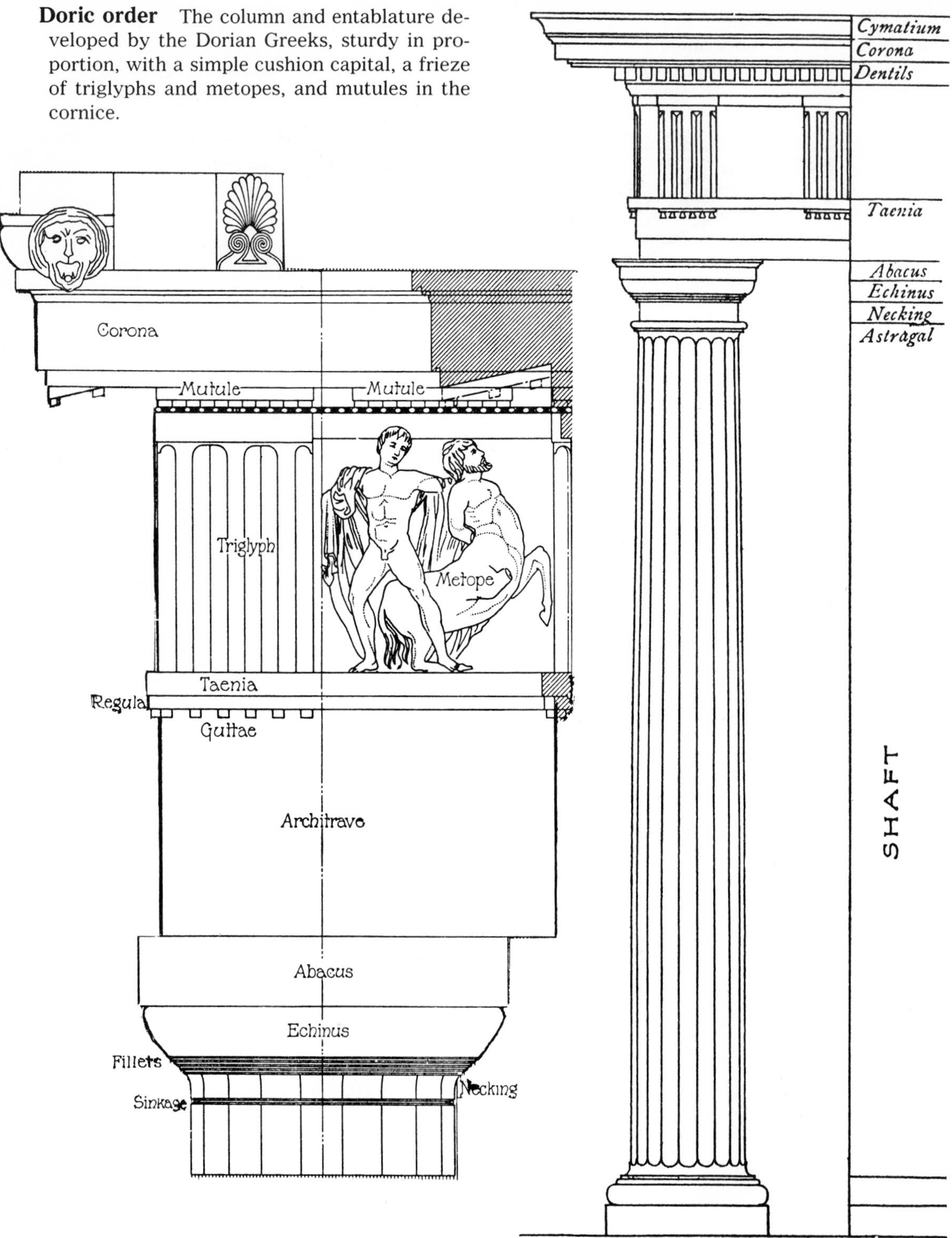

Doric order

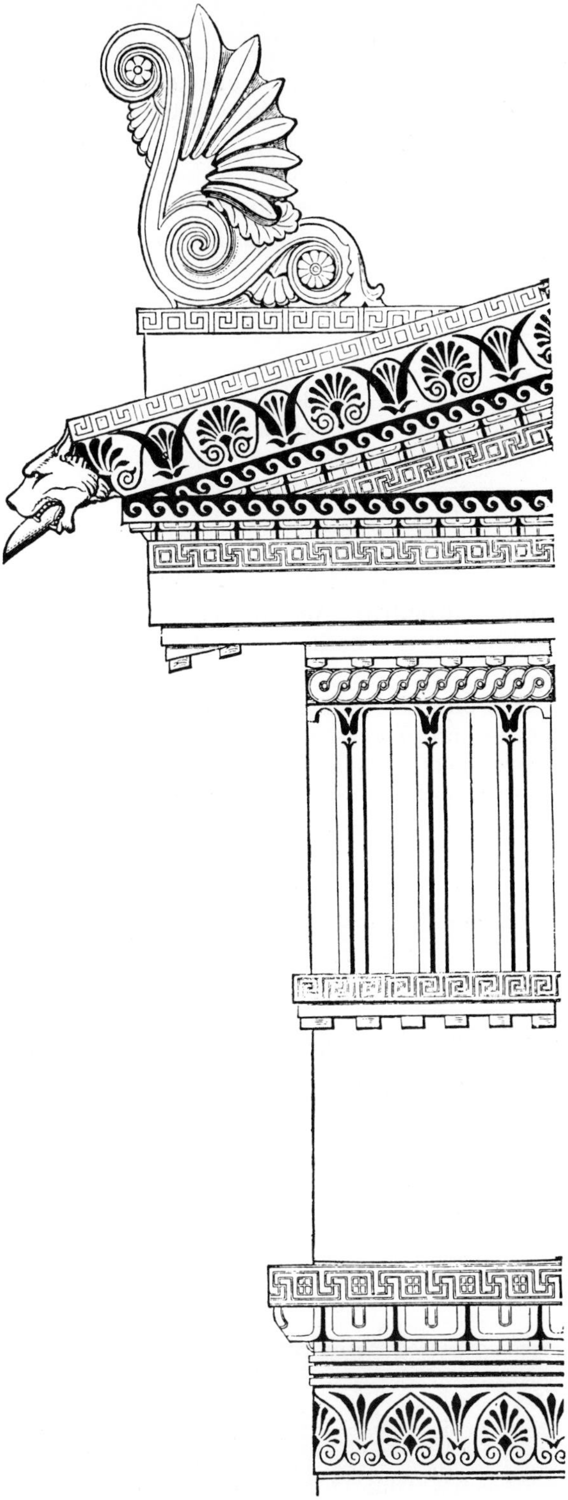

part of a painted Doric entablature

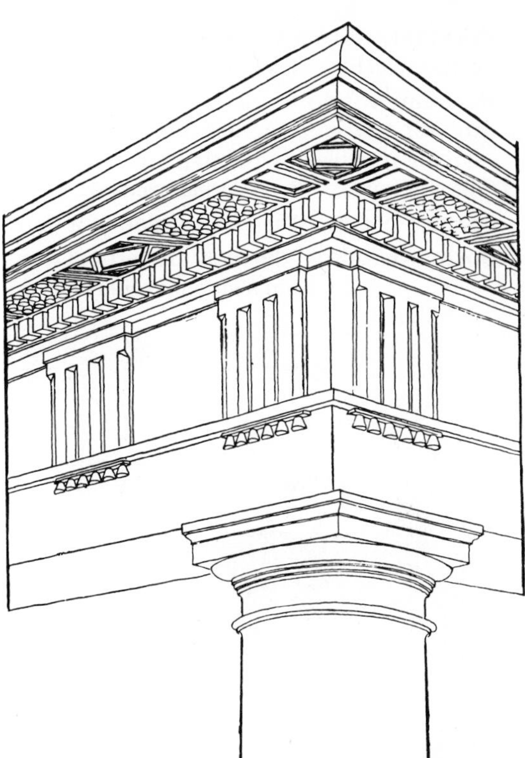

perspective of Roman Doric entablature

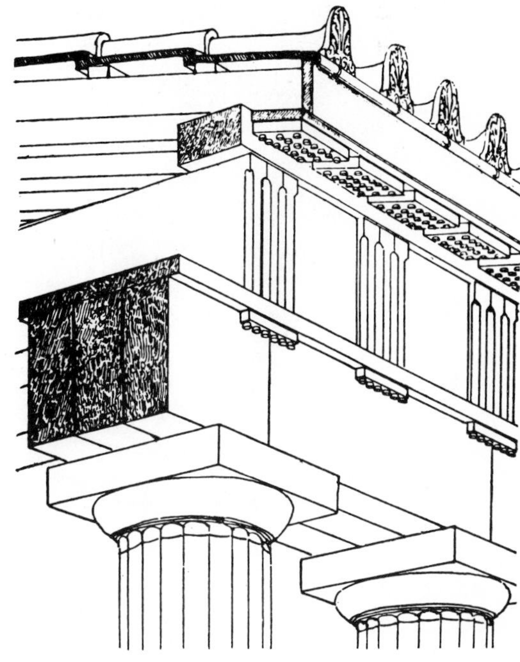

suggested origin of timber construction of the Doric order

dormant, dormant tree A large horizontal beam which carries lesser beams.

dormant window Same as **dormer window.**

dormer 1. A structure projecting from a sloping roof usually housing a window or ventilating louver. 2. A **dormer window.**

dormer cheek The vertical side of a dormer.

dormer window, dormer A vertical window which projects from a sloping roof, placed in a small gable.

dormer window, Bourges (1443)

dorse A **canopy.**

dorter, dortour A dormitory, esp. in a monastery.

dosel Same as **reredos.**

dossal Same as **dossel.**

dossel 1. Same as **reredos.** 2. A hanging of silk, satin, damask, or cloth of gold at the back of an altar of a church and sometimes also at the sides of the chancel.

dosseret See **impost block.**

double-bellied, bow-shaped Descriptive of a baluster whose profile is the same at both ends.

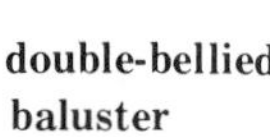

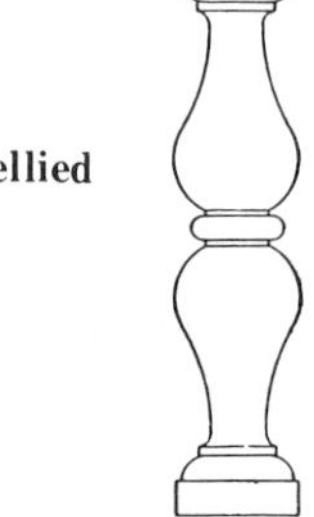

double-bellied baluster

double cathedral An Early Christian cathedral having two basilicas, usually on parallel axes.

double church A church constructed in two stories, affording two places of worship, one above the other; a large hole in the floor of the upper church enables the two congregations to hear the same service.

double church, Schwart-Rheindorff (1158)

double-cone molding A molding enriched with carved cones joined base to base and apex to apex.

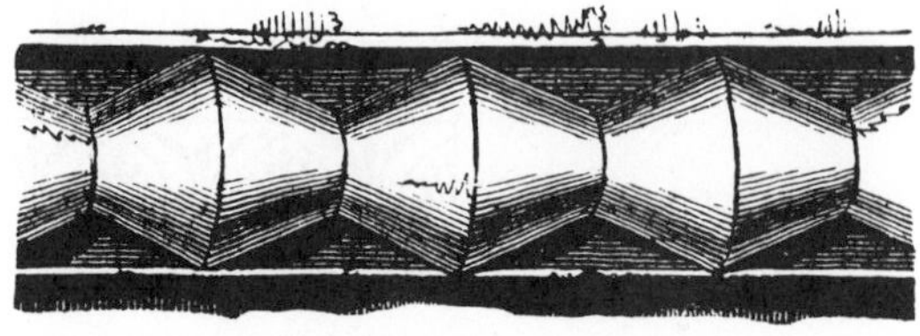

a Norman double-cone molding

double lancet window A window having a mullion which is so shaped as to form two **lancets.**

double lancet window

double monastery A monastery and a nunnery adjacent to each other, sharing the same church and under the rule of the same superior.

double raised panel See **raised panel.**

double-sunk Recessed or lowered in two steps, as when a panel is sunk below the surface of a larger panel.

double vault A vault, usually domical, consisting of an inner shell separated from a higher outer shell.

double vault, St. Peter's, Rome

double window Two windows, side by side, which form a single architectural unit.

double window

doucine A **cyma** molding.

dovecot, dovecote A pigeon house, generally round or square in plan, whose inner face is honeycombed with niches for nesting.

dovetail molding, triangular fret molding A molding decorated with fretwork in the form of dovetails.

dovetail molding

downcomer **1.** A **downspout.** **2.** Any pipe in which the flow is substantially vertical.

downpipe See **downspout.**

downspout, conductor, downcomer, downpipe, leader, rain leader, rainwater pipe A vertical pipe, often of sheet metal, used to conduct water from a roof drain or gutter to the ground or cistern.

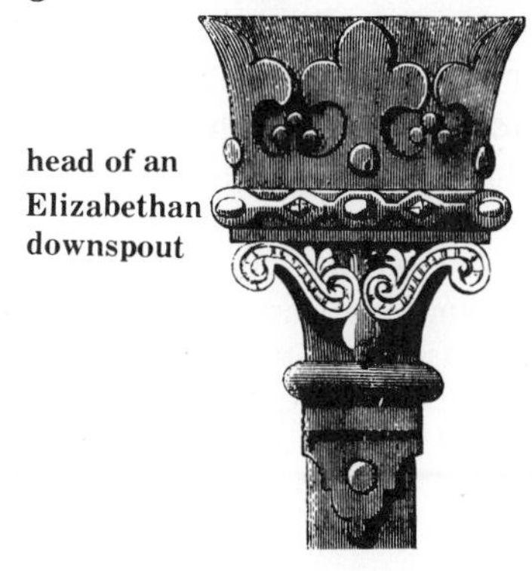

head of an Elizabethan downspout

draft, *Brit.* **draught** A narrow, dressed border around the face of a stone, usually about the width of a chisel edge; also called a **drafted margin** or **margin draft.**

drafted margin See **draft.**

dragging beam Same as **dragon beam.**

dragging piece Same as **dragon beam.**

dragon beam, dragon piece A short, horizontal piece of timber which bisects the angle formed by the **wall plate,** 1 at the corner of a wood-frame building; one end serves to receive and support the foot of a **hip rafter;** the other end is supported by a **dragon tie.**

dragon tie An **angle brace** which supports one end of a **dragon beam.**

drapery panel See **linenfold.**

draught Same as **draft.**

drawbolt Same as **barrel bolt.**

drawbridge At the entrance of fortifications, a bridge over the moat or ditch, hinged and provided with a raising and lowering mechanism so as to hinder or permit passage.

drawbridge

dressed lumber, dressed stuff Lumber having one or more of its faces planed smooth.

dressed stone Stone that has been worked to desired shape; the faces to be exposed are smooth; usually ready for installation.

dressing, dressings **1.** Projecting ornamental moldings and carved decorations of all kinds. **2.** Masonry or molding of better quality than the facing brick; used around openings or at corners of buildings; often made of gauged brick. **3.** Smoothing a stone surface.

drip, headmold, hoodmold, label, throating, weather molding **1.** The outermost projecting molding around the top of a door or window, to discharge rainwater. **2.** A **throat,** 2.

drip cap A horizontal molding, fixed to a door or window frame to divert the water from the top rail, causing it to drip beyond the outside of the frame.

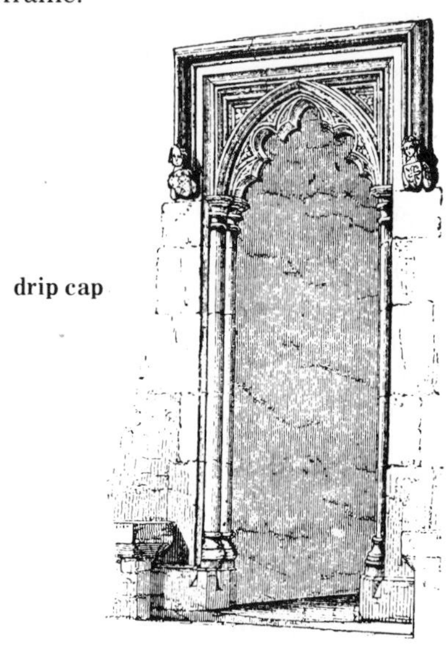

drip cap

drip channel A **throat,** 2.

drip course Same as **dripstone course.**

drip mold, drip molding Any molding so formed and located as to act as a **drip.**

dripping eaves Sloping eaves which project beyond a wall and are not provided with a gutter so that water on the roof falls directly to the ground.

dripstone A **drip** made of stone.

dripstone

dripstone course A continuous horizontal drip molding on a masonry wall.

dromos The long, deep entrance passageway to an ancient Egyptian tomb or a Mycenaean beehive tomb.

dromos

drop **1.** Any one of the guttae under the mutules or triglyphs of a Doric entablature. **2.** Same as **pendill.**

drop arch A pointed arch which is struck from two centers that are nearer together than the width of the arch, so that the radii are less than the span; a **depressed arch, 1.**

drop molding A panel molding recessed below the surface of the surrounding stiles and rails.

drop ornament A tear-shaped pendant, or a representation thereof.

drop-point slating See **diagonal slating.**

drop tracery Tracery hanging from the soffit of an arch.

drum **1.** One of the cylinders of stone which form a column. **2.** A cylindrical or polygonal wall below a dome, often pierced with windows. **3.** The bell of Composite or Corinthian capitals.

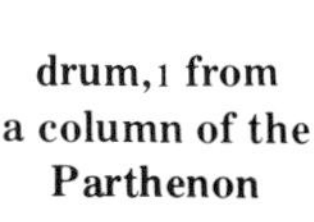

drum,1 from a column of the Parthenon

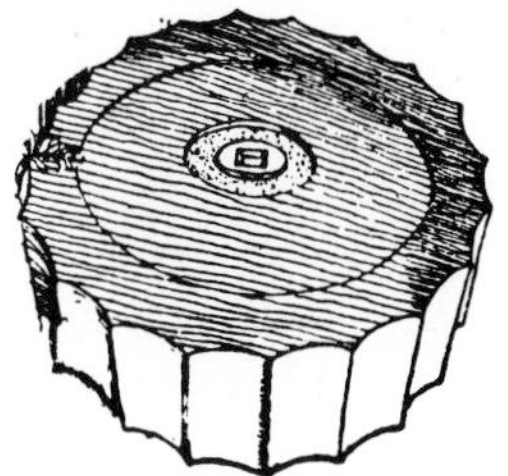

drum paneling A form of door construction in which the panels are flush on both sides and covered with cloth or leather.

dry masonry Masonry work laid without mortar.

dry rubble construction Masonry of rubble which is laid without mortar.

dry stone wall A wall composed of stones not cemented with mortar.

dry wall In masonry construction, a self-supporting rubble or ashlar wall built without mortar.

dumbbell tenement A five- to seven-story multiple dwelling built in New York City prior to 1901; characterized by a long, narrow plan with an indentation on each side (forming a shaft for light and air); hence its resemblance in plan to a dumbbell.

dungeon **1.** The principal and strongest tower of a castle; the **keep.** **2.** A dim chamber in a medieval castle, usually at the base of the keep. **3.** Any dark cell or prison, usually underground.

duomo The term for an Italian cathedral.

durbar In India, an audience hall in the palace of a prince.

durga In India, a fort or fortified city.

Dur Sharrukin See **Assyrian architecture.**

Dutch arch, French arch A flat arch in brick; most of the bricks slope outward from the middle of the arch (at the same angle on both sides of the centerline) and do not have radial joints. Properly not an arch.

Dutch barn An open-sided barn, sometimes sheltered only on the weather side, with a fixed roof or a roof which can be raised or lowered.

Dutch barn

Dutch bond 1. Same as **English cross bond.** 2. Same as **Flemish bond.**

Dutch brick A brick used in house construction in colonial U.S.A., 1½ in.by 3 in. by 7 in. (3.8 cm by 7.6 cm by 17.8 cm); smaller than the English brick which was adopted later.

Dutch Colonial architecture The style prevalent in the Dutch-settled parts of the North American colonies in the 17th cent., particularly in New York and the Hudson Valley. Characterized by gambrel roofs and overhanging eaves.

Dutch diaper bond Same as **English cross bond.**

Dutch door A door consisting of two separate leaves, one above the other; the leaves may operate independently or together.

Dutch gable A **gable, 2** each side of which is multicurved and which is surmounted by a pediment.

Dutch lap A method of applying shingles, slates, etc.; each shingle overlaps one below and one to the side.

Dutch stoop, Dutch stoep A small wooden porch, covered by a cantilevered hood, with a wood bench on both sides.

dvara A door or gate of a town, village, residential building, or temple in India.

dwarf gallery A passage on the external surface of a wall screened by a small-scale arcade.

dyakonik The **sacristy** in a Russian Orthodox church.

dyke See **dike.**

dynka In early Russian architecture, an ornamental band around the shaft of a column or pillar.

dyostyle Same as **distyle.**

Dutch Colonial architecture

eachea One of a number of earthen or bronze vases described by Vitruvius as being installed under the seats of open-air theatres for "reinforcing" the voices of the actors; it is doubtful that such vases were employed.

eagle A pediment of a Greek building.

ear Any small projecting member or part of a piece or structure, either decorative or structural.

Early Christian architecture The final phase of Roman architecture from the 4th to the 6th cent., primarily in church building. Coeval with and related to the rise of Byzantine architecture.

basilican Church of Sta. Maria Maggiore, Rome (432 A.D. with later alterations)

Basilica of S. Clemente, Rome (rebuilt 1099-1108 over a 4th cent. church)

Early English style The first of the three phases of English Gothic architecture, from ca. 1180 to ca. 1280, based on Norman and French antecedents and succeeded by the Decorated style. Often characterized by lancet windows without tracery.

window

window (c. 1220)

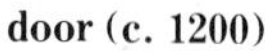

door (c. 1200)

door (c. 1220)

door

triforium and clerestory, New Shoreham Church, Sussex

Early English style

capital, Temple Church, London

capital, Lincoln Cathedral

base, Paul's Cray (c. 1230)

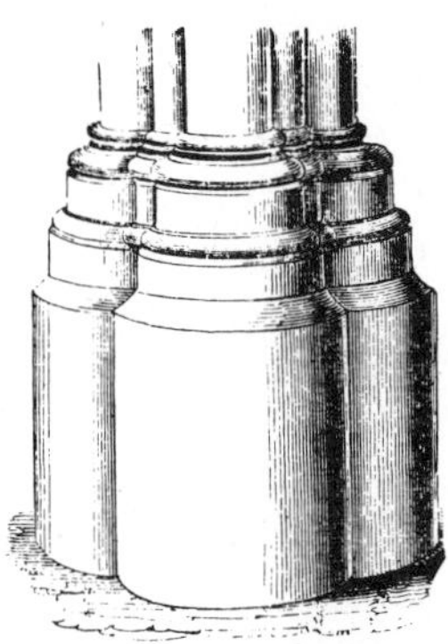

base, Temple Church, London (c. 1240)

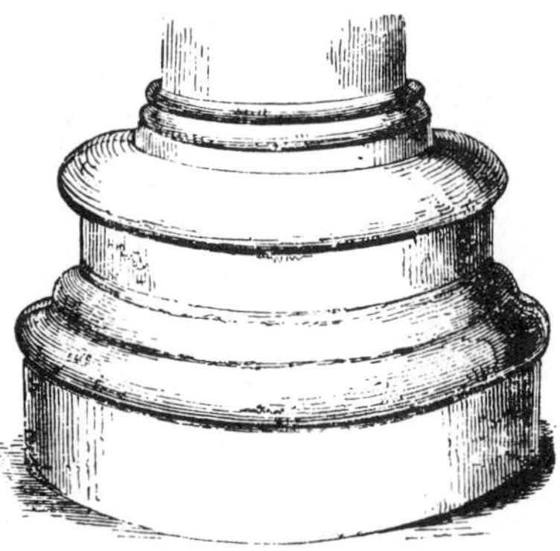

base, St. Albans (c. 1250)

font, St. Giles, Oxford (c. 1200)

arcade, Haddenham Church, Buckinghamshire (c. 1230)

vaulting shaft

vaulting shaft

corbel and capital

stone panel, Lincoln Cathedral

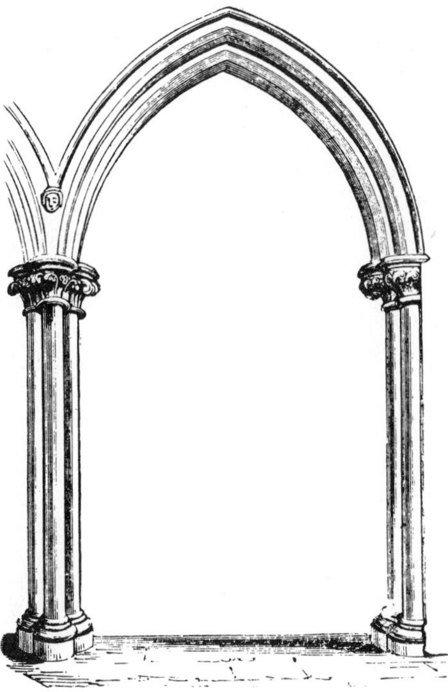

arch, St. Peter's, Oxford (c. 1250)

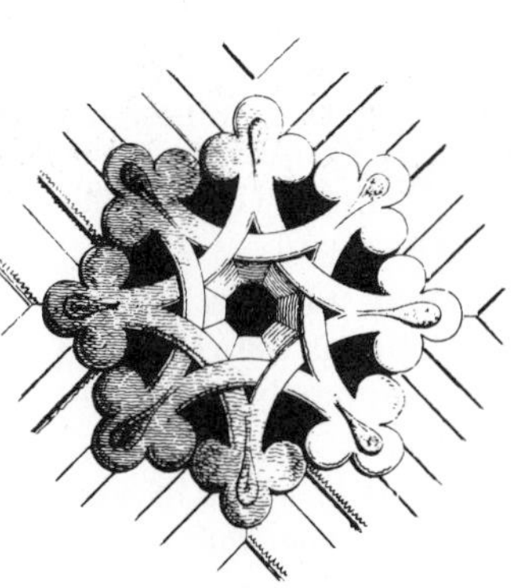

boss, Boxgrove Church, Sussex

earth table Same as **ground table.**

east end The end of a church where the principal altar is placed; so called because medieval churches almost invariably had their sanctuaries at the east end and the main doors at the west end.

eastern crown See **antique crown.**

Easter sepulcher In some churches, a shallow recess in which sacred elements are placed from Maundy Thursday to Easter.

Easter sepulcher, St. John's, Oxford

Eastlake style A forerunner of the **Stick Style** with rich ornamentation and heavy brackets, named after the English architect Charles Lock Eastlake (1833–1906), a pioneer of the Tudor Revival.

east window In church architecture, a window at the choir end of the church, which is commonly the **east end.**

eaves The lower edge of a sloping roof; that part of a roof of a building which projects beyond the wall.

eaves channel A channel or small gutter along the top of a wall; conveys the roof drippings to spouts or gargoyles.

eaves gutter See **gutter.**

eaves trough See **gutter.**

ecclesiasterion See **ekklesiasterion.**

ecclesiology The study of the furnishing and adornment of churches.

échauguette A **bartizan.**

echinus The convex projecting molding of eccentric curve supporting the abacus of the Doric capital. Hence the corresponding feature in capitals of other orders, which often had **egg-and-dart** ornamentation; any molding of similar profile or decoration. Also see **ovolo, bowtell.**

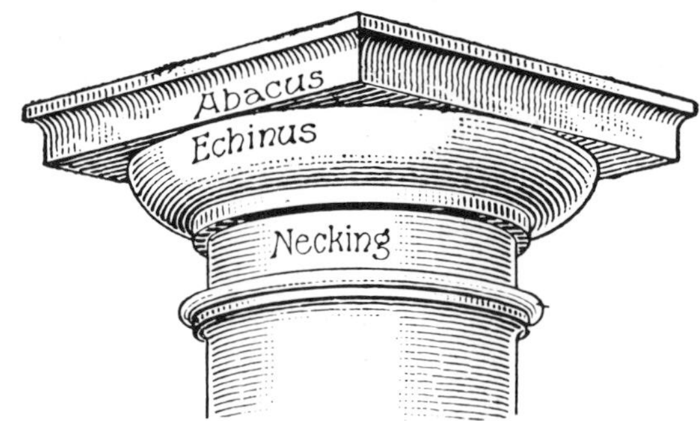

echinus in a Doric capital

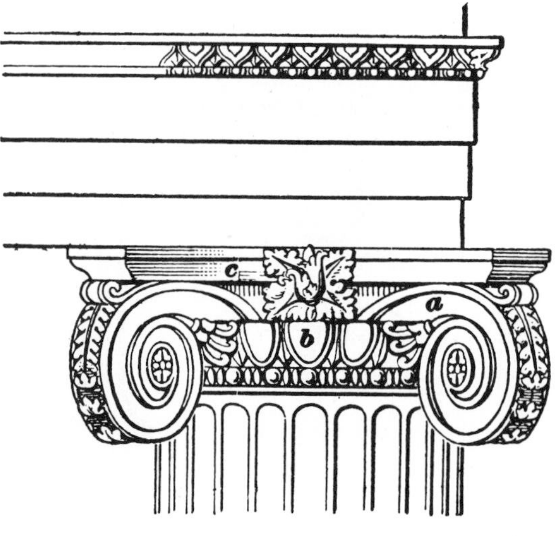

Ionic capital: *a*, volute; *b*, echinus; *c*, abacus

echinus and astragal An ornament similar to **egg and dart** with a **bead and reel** below it.

echinus and astragal, Pantheon, Rome

Eclecticism The selection of elements from diverse styles for architectural decorative designs, particularly during the second half of the 19th cent. in Europe and the U.S.A.

ecphora The projection of any member or molding beyond the face of the member or molding directly below it.

ectype A copy or image in relief or embossed.

edge roll See **bowtell.**

edge shafts Shafts which sustain arches, united by their sides and back to the nearest wall or arch, so they appear to support their edge only; abundantly used in Norman architecture.

edge shafts, St. John's Church, Chester (1075)

edicule An **aedicula.**

effigy A representation or imitation of a person, in whole or in part, as a likeness in sculpture.

effigy of the standard-bearer Pintaius

egg and dart, echinus, egg and anchor, egg and arrow, egg and tongue An egg-shaped ornament alternating with a dart-like ornament, used to enrich ovolo and echinus moldings and also on bands. In the **egg-and-anchor, egg-and-arrow,** and **egg-and-tongue** moldings, the dart-like ornament is varied in form.

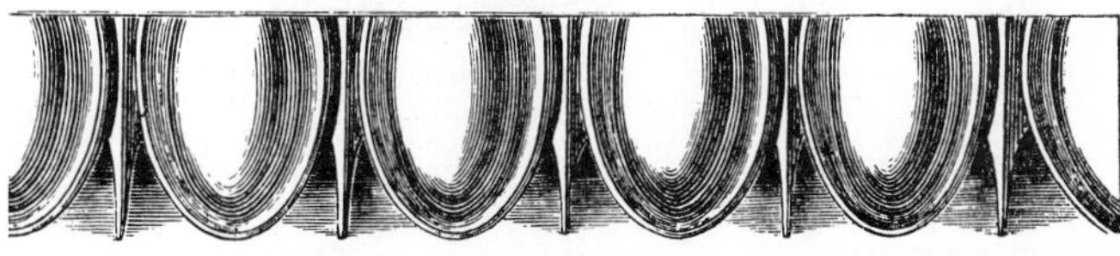

egg and dart

Egyptian architecture The architecture of Egypt from the 3rd millennium B.C. to the Roman period. Its most outstanding achievements are its massive funerary monuments and temples built of stone for permanence, featuring only post-and-lintel construction, corbel vaults without arches and vaulting, and pyramids.

restored views of an Egyptian temple

dromos leading to an Egyptian temple

façade (restored view), Temple of Horus (257-237 B.C.)

interior view (restored); Hypostyle Hall, Great Temple of Ammon, Karnak (1312-1301 B.C.)

Egyptian architecture

a restored façade, Great Temple of Ammon, Karnak (c. 1312–1301 B.C.)

section (restored) of the Hypostyle Hall, Great Temple of Ammon, Karnak (1312–1301 B.C.)

caryatid pillar

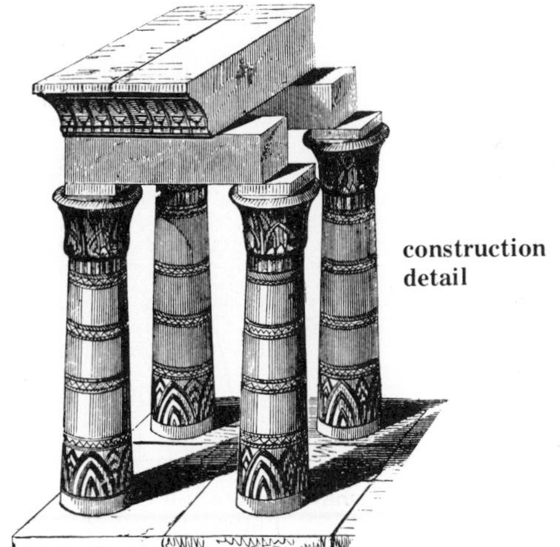

construction detail

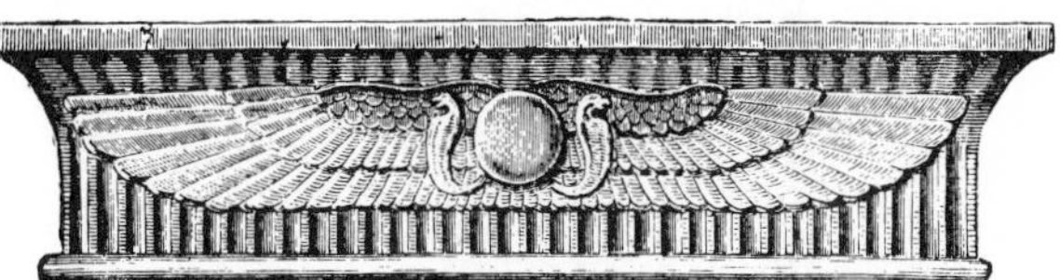

entablature over doorway, Temple of Isis, Philae (283–247 B.C.)

Egyptian architecture

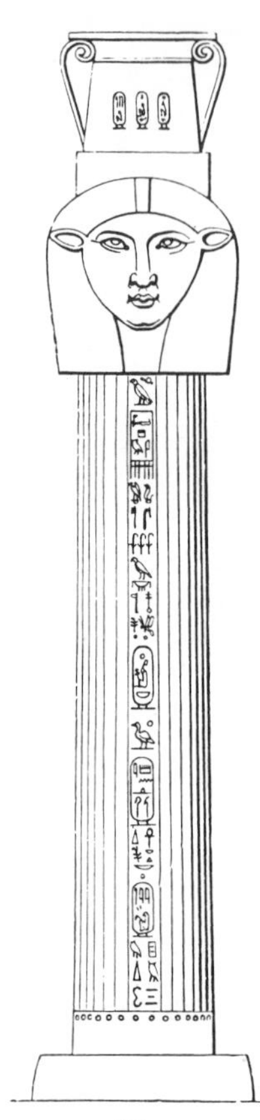
pillar

pillar, Temple of Hathor, Dendera (110 B.C.–68 A.D.)

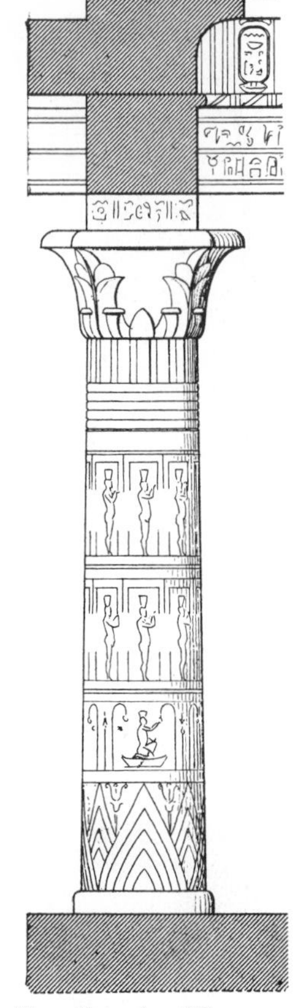
pillar, Temple of Rameses III, Luxor (1198 B.C.)

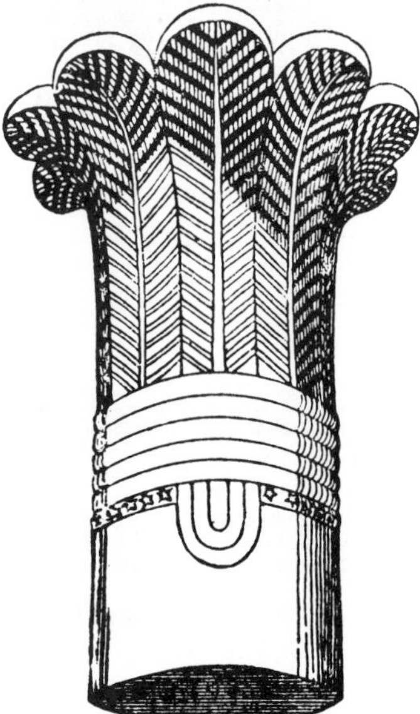
palm leaf capital, Philae

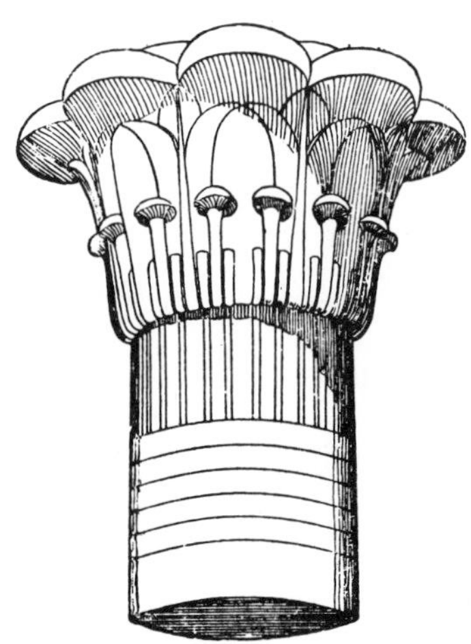
scalloped capital, Philae

mural decoration, Temple of Isis, Philae (283–247 B.C.)

Egyptian architecture (decorative elements)

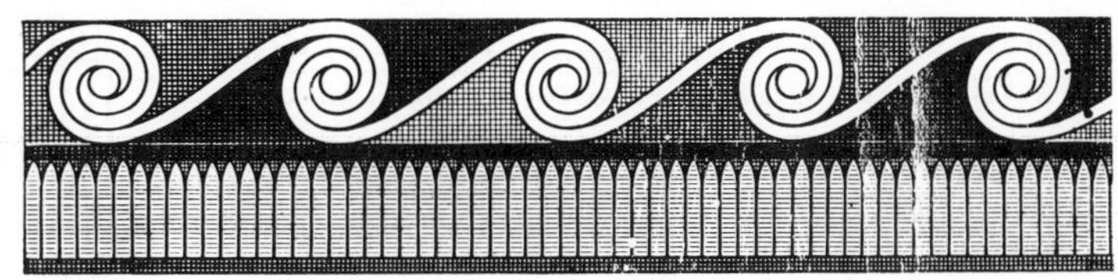

Egyptian gorge, cavetto cornice The characteristic cornice of most Egyptian buildings, consisting of a large cavetto decorated with vertical leaves, and a roll molding below.

Egyptian gorge, showing roll at angles

ekklesiasterion **1.** The public hall of a Greek town. **2.** The town's council chamber. **3.** A hall for religious meetings.

elaeothesium The place where oil was kept in a Roman bath, and where the bathers frequently were anointed.

elbow A **crossette, 1.**

electrum A natural alloy of gold and silver, sometimes employed in the decorations of ancient temples and palaces.

elevation A drawing showing the vertical elements of a building, either exterior or interior, as a direct projection to a vertical plane.

Elgin marbles A collection of sculptures, for the most part taken from the Parthenon at Athens by the Earl of Elgin; preserved in the British Museum since 1816; the finest surviving work of Greek sculptural decoration of the Classical age; includes a number of metopes, fragments of the pediment statues, and an extended series of the blocks carved in low relief of the cella frieze.

El Gizeh, El Giza See **Great Pyramid; Great Sphinx; Memphis.**

Elizabethan architecture The transitional style between Gothic and Renaissance in England, named after Elizabeth I (1558–1603); mainly country houses, characterized by large mullioned windows and strapwork ornamentation.

gable on an Elizabethan house

Elizabethan angle tower

Elizabethan architecture

Elizabethan house: front elevation

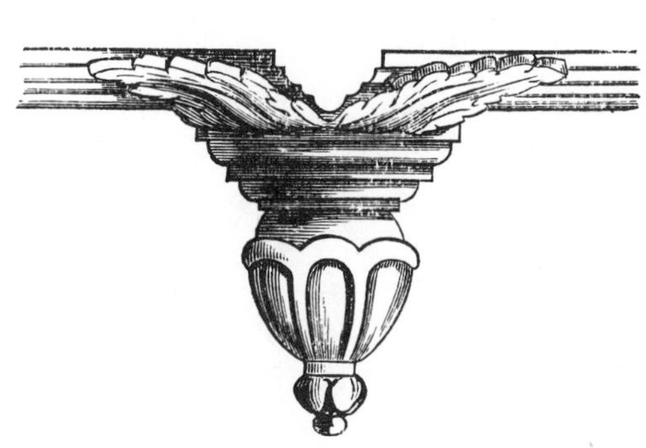

Elizabethan pendant

Elizabethan balustrade used to crown a cornice

Elizabethan architecture

carved stone doorway, Crewe Hall, Cheshire (1636)

ceiling decoration

ceiling decoration

ceiling decoration

ell, el A secondary wing or extension of a building at right angles to its principal dimension.

elliptical arch An arch having the form of a semiellipse.

elliptical stair A stair which winds about a solid elliptic **newel** or elliptically shaped well.

El Tajín style A style of Mesoamerican architecture of the Totonacs, ca. 200–900 A.D.; characterized by chiaroscuro effects achieved by flying cornices, recessed niches, many planes of geometric ornamentation, and elaborately carved sculptural decorations (as, for example, the reliefs on the walls of the courts used for ritual ballgames). At El Tajin, the capital of the Totonacs (located in the state of Vera Cruz, Mexico), the outstanding structure is the Pyramid of the Niches (600 A.D.) with its six tiers deeply niched in an adaptation of the **tablero,** and with a stairway flanked by balusters rising on its eastern slope.

emarginated Having the margin broken by a notch or notches.

embattled, embattlemented Having battlements.

embattled molding A **crenelated molding.**

embattlement See **battlement.**

embedded column A column that is partly built within the face of a wall.

embellishment Ornamentation; adornment with decorative elements.

emblemata, emblema A type of inlaid work used by the early Romans to embellish floors, panels, and the like.

emboss To raise or indent a pattern on the surface of a material; sometimes produced by the use of patterned rollers.

embow To form in a vault or arch.

embowed Having an outward-curving projection, as a bay window.

embrasure **1.** The crenels or intervals between the merlons of a battlement. **2.** An enlargement of a door or window opening, at the inside face of the wall, by means of splayed sides.

emissarium In ancient Roman construction, an artificial channel to drain a lake or a stagnant body of water.

elliptical arch

an embattled parapet

emblemata

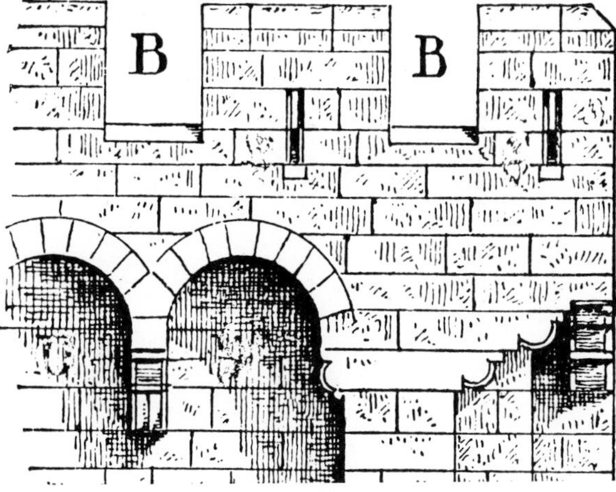

B, B, **embrasures,** 1

Empire style

Empire style The elaborate neoclassic style of the French First Empire (1804–1815).

design for a room in the Palais d'Aranjuez by Percier and Fontaine

emplecton A type of masonry commonly used by the Romans and Greeks, esp. in fortification walls, in which the exterior faces of the wall were built of ashlar in alternate headers and stretchers, and with the intervening space filled with rubble.

Roman emplecton

emporium In ancient Roman towns, a large building in which foreign merchandise, brought in by sea, was deposited until disposed of to retail dealers.

encarpus A sculptured festoon of fruit and flowers.

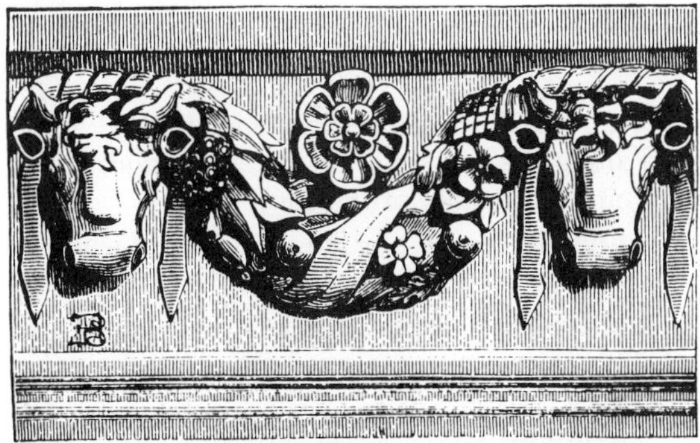

encarpus, Temple of Vesta, Tivoli (c. 80 B.C.)

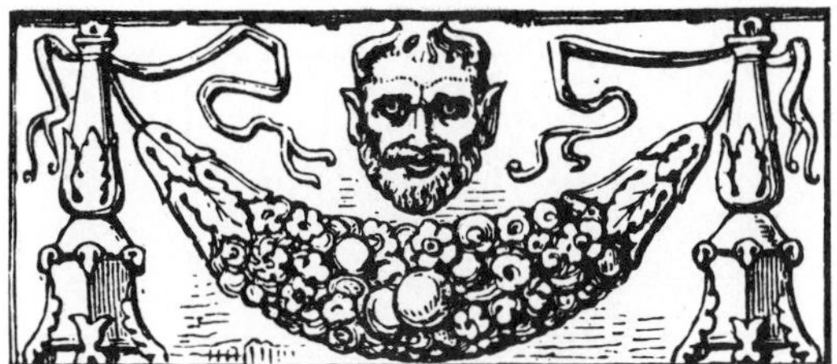

encarpus, Palazzo Niccolini, Rome

encastré Embedded.

encaustic **1.** Painted with a mixture of a paint solution and wax which, after application, is set by heat. **2.** Colors which have been applied to brick, glass, porcelain, and tile and set by the application of heat.

encaustic tile A tile for pavement and wall decoration, in which the pattern is inlaid or incrusted in clay of one color in a ground of clay of another color.

part of a medieval pavement of encaustic tiles, Church of St. Pierre-sur-Dives, Normandy

enceinte **1.** The fortification wall of a castle or town. **2.** The area so enclosed.

enchased Descriptive of a variety of hammered metalwork in which a pattern in relief is produced by hammering down the background or depressed portions of the design.

enfilade The alignment of a series of doors axially through a sequence of rooms.

engaged **1.** Attached, or apparently attached, to a wall by being partly embedded or bonded to it, as an **engaged column.** **2.** Framed into or fitting upon or within.

engaged column, attached column A column partially built into a wall, not freestanding.

engaged columns

engawa A veranda-like area beneath the eaves of a traditional Japanese building, constructed of finely finished boards; may be on one or all four sides of the building; its exterior side may be fitted with sliding doors.

English bond Brickwork with alternate courses of **headers** and **stretchers.**

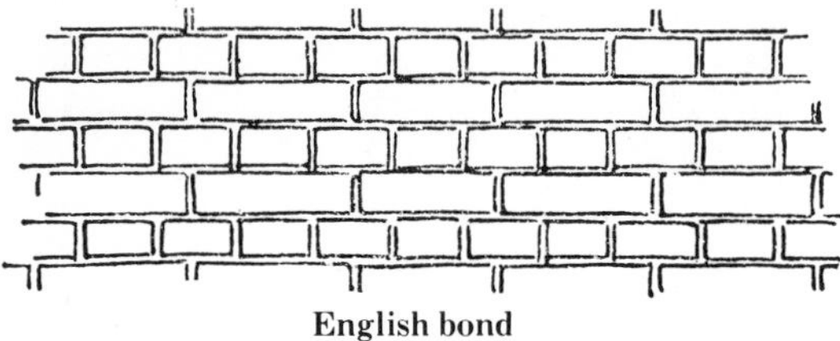

English bond

English cross bond, Saint Andrew's cross bond Similar to English bond, but the stretchers, in alternating courses, have their joints displaced by half the length of a stretcher.

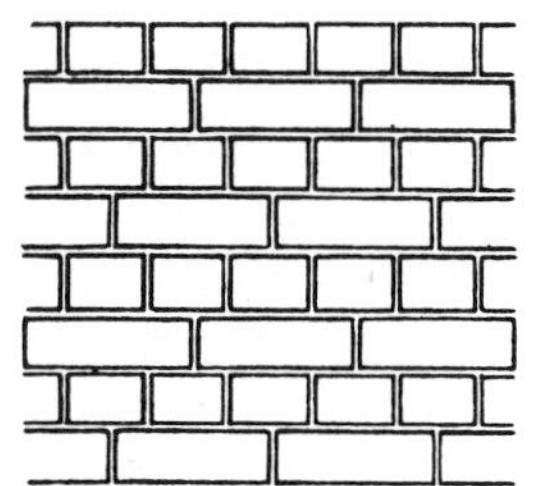

English cross bond

English garden wall bond Like **common bond** except that **headers** occur every fourth course.

English garden wall bond

engawa

engrailed Scalloped with concave lines; cut along the edge with a series of small concave curves, usually of the same size.

enneastyle A portico or temple façade having nine columns, in front or on each side.

enplecton Greek or Roman masonry consisting of cut stone facings with an infilling of rubble.

enriched Having **embellishment.** Also see **entail.**

an enriched Corinthian base

entablature **1.** In classical architecture, the elaborated beam member carried by the columns, horizontally divided into architrave (below), frieze, and cornice (above). The proportions and detailing are different for each order, and strictly prescribed. **2.** A similar feature as the crown of a wall.

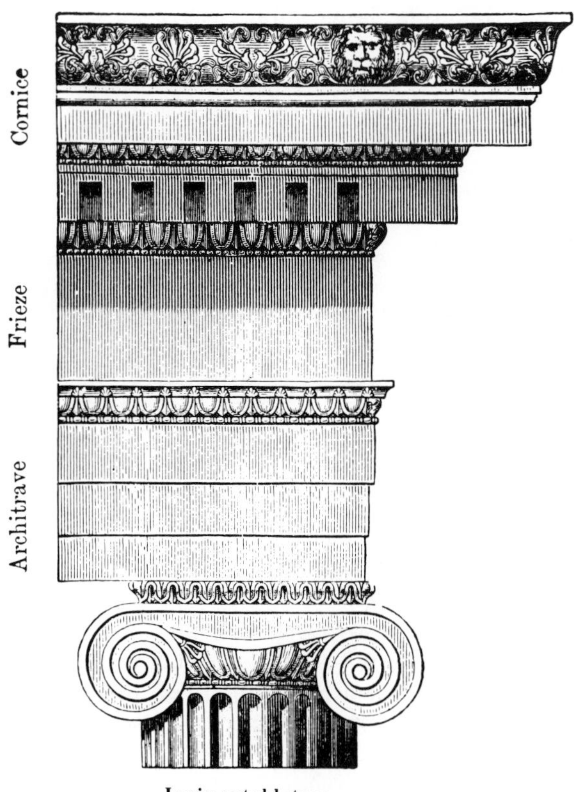

Ionic entablature

entablement **1.** The platform which is above the **dado** in a pedestal. **2.** An **entablature.**

entail **1.** Engraved or carved work. **2.** Intaglio; inlay.

entasis The intentional slight convex curving of the vertical profile of a tapered column; used to overcome the optical illusion of concavity that characterizes straight-sided columns.

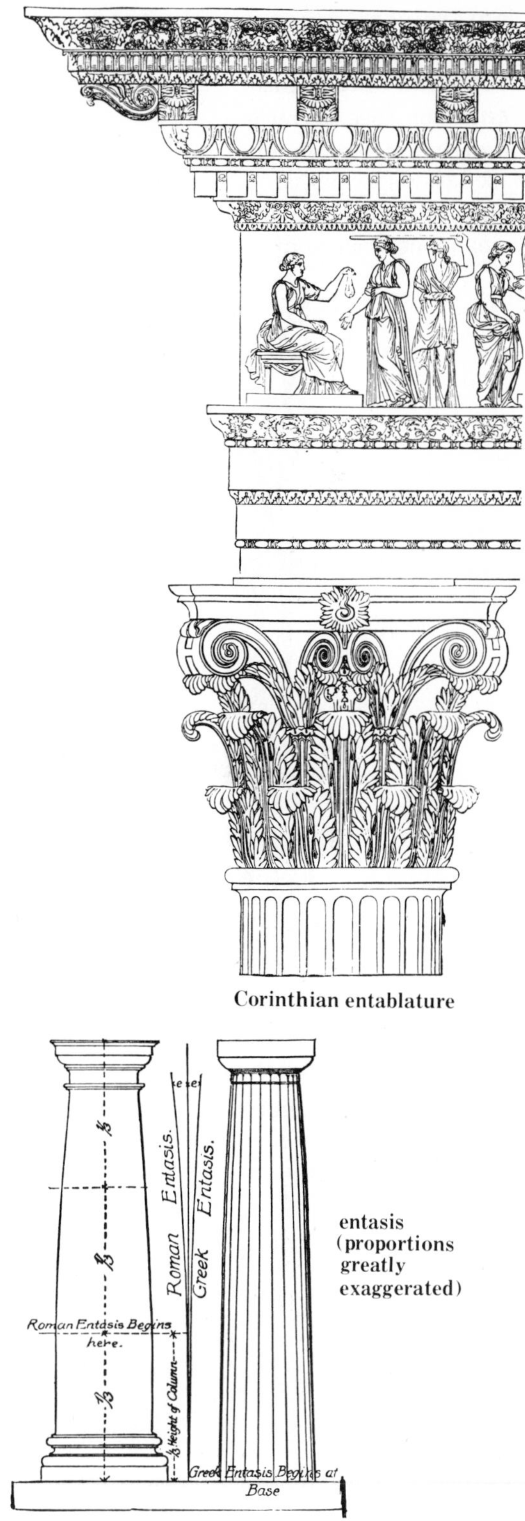

Corinthian entablature

entasis (proportions greatly exaggerated)

enterclose A passageway between two rooms or spaces in a building.

entrelacs See **interlace.**

entresol See **mezzanine.**

ephebeum, ephebeion In a **palaestra** a hall set aside for youths.

épi The spire-shaped termination of a projecting point or angle of a roof.

épi, Cathedral at Amiens (1220-88)

epicranitis, epikranitis **1.** A molding marking the top of a wall or forming the top member of a cornice. **2.** An interior cornice.

epicranitis, Temple of Aphaia, Aegina (c. 490 B.C.)

epinaos See **opisthodomos.**

episcenium Same as **episkenion.**

episkenion, episcenium The upper story of the scene building in an ancient Greek or Roman theatre.

epistle side The south side of a church when the altar is at the east end; the Epistle is read from that side of the altar.

epistomium In ancient Rome, a cock or faucet of a water pipe.

epistyle, epistylium The main beam or architrave laid horizontally over the capitals of a column, from one to the next, to form a continuous bed for a superstructure to rest on. When the architrave was made of timber, rather than stone or marble, it was called **trabes.**

epistyle

epithedes The upper member of the cornice of an entablature.

epiurus In ancient Roman construction, a wood peg used as a nail.

épure A full-scale, detailed drawing.

equilateral arch, equilateral pointed arch, three-pointed arch A **two-centered arch** in which the chords of the curves just equal the span of the arch.

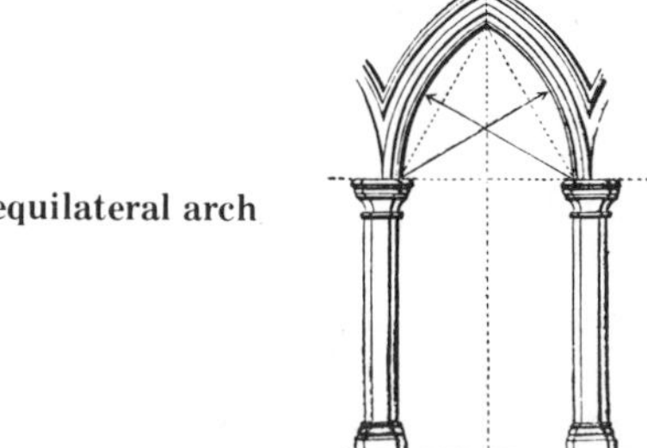

equilateral arch

equilateral roof A roof with sides sloping at 60°, forming an equilateral triangle in cross section.

Erechtheion, Erechtheum A temple on the Acropolis in Athens (421–405 B.C.); the most important monument of the Ionic style, including a fine example of a porch of caryatides.

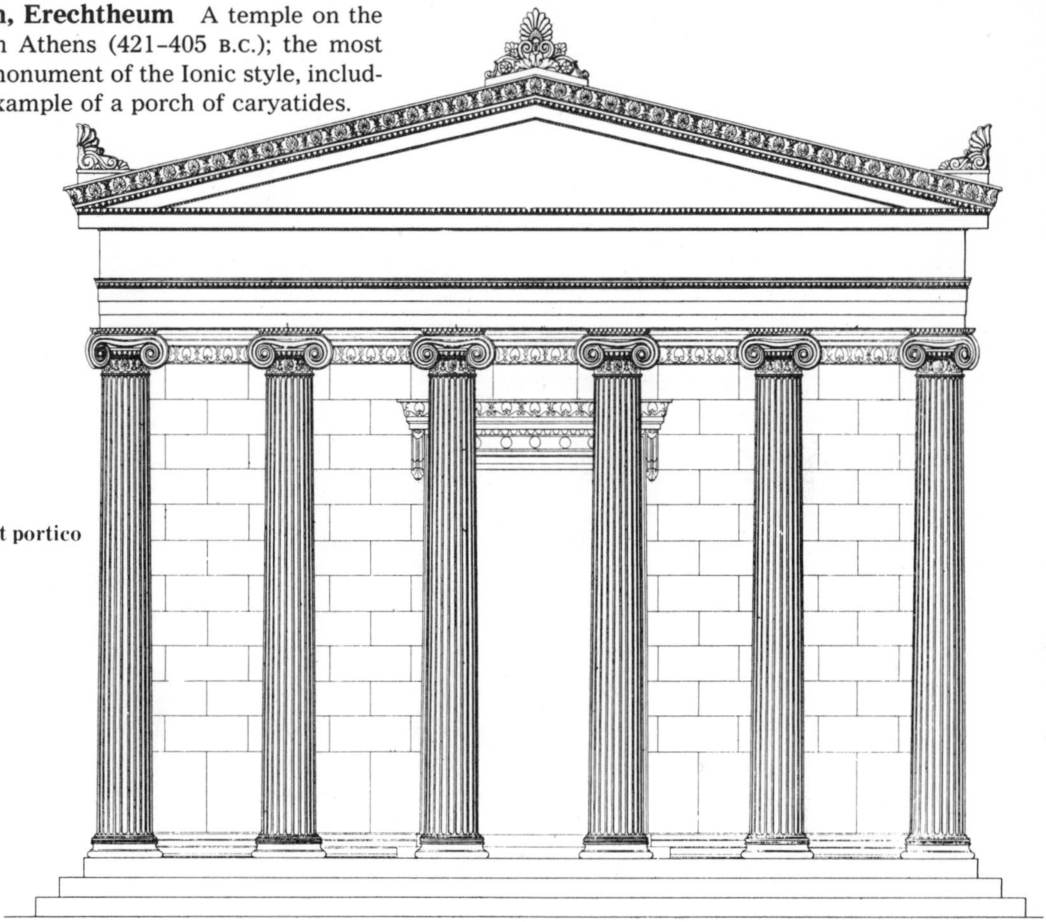

east portico

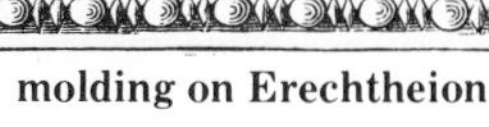

molding on Erechtheion

doorway

Erechtheion

west front of the Erechtheion

one of the caryatides on the Caryatid Porch

north portico

ergastulum On ancient Roman farms, a private prison where slaves were made to work in chains.

escape The curved part of the shaft of a column where it springs out of the base; the **apophyge, 1.**

escarpment A steep slope in front of a fortification to impede the approach of an enemy.

esconson Same as **sconcheon.**

Escorial A palace of the kings of Spain, built by Philip II in the 16th cent. near Madrid.

Escorial

escutcheon **1.** A protective plate surrounding the keyhole of a door, a door handle, etc.; also called a **scutcheon.** **2.** A shield on which armorial bearings are depicted; may be of any form, but the usual shape is that of a square or lozenge.

escutcheon,2

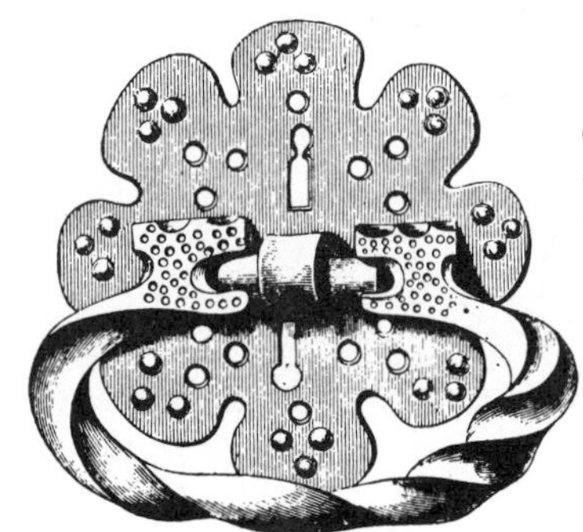

door handle escutcheon,1: Byarch Church, Kent (c. 1480)

escutcheon pin A small nail, usually brass, used for fixing an **escutcheon;** often ornamental.

esonarthex The second narthex from the entrance, when two are present.

espagnolette bolt Same as **cremone bolt.**

espalier **1.** A trelliswork of various forms on which the branches of fruit trees or fruit bushes are extended horizontally, in fan shape, etc., in a single plane, to secure a freer circulation of air for the plant and better exposure to the sun. **2.** A tree or plant so grown.

esplanade A level open space for walking or driving, often providing a view.

esquisse A first sketch or very rough design drawing showing the general features of a project.

estípite In Spanish and Latin-American Mannerist architecture and derivatives, a shaft of square cross section, tapering downward, frequently combined with other unusual elements, the whole used like an order.

estrade A platform or dais.

key plate escutcheon,1

Etruscan architecture The architecture of the Etruscan people in western central Italy from the 8th cent. B.C. until their conquest by the Romans in 281 B.C. Apart from some underground tombs and city walls, it is largely lost, but remains important for the influence of its construction methods on Roman architecture, e.g., the stone arch.

arch at Voltera

Arch of Augustus, Perugia (late 2nd cent. B.C.)

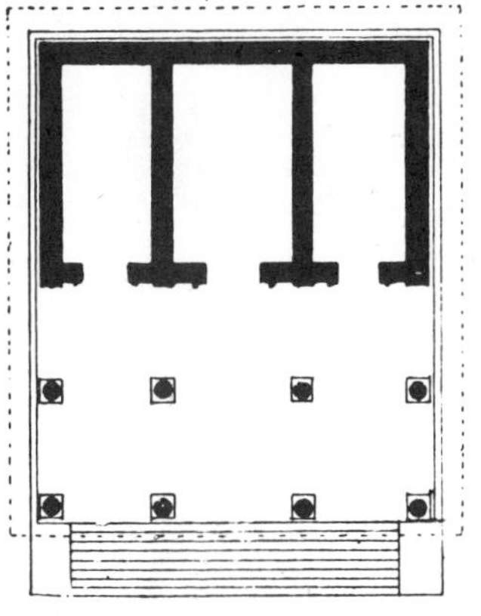

conjectural restoration of an Etruscan temple

Etruscan architecture

a terra-cotta antefix

façade of tomb at Castellacio

gateway at Arpino

relief on an Etruscan tomb

eucharistic window Same as **squint, 1.**

euripus **1.** A ditch around the arena of an amphitheatre or a circus to prevent wild animals from escaping; also see **podium, 3.** **2.** Any artificial pond or canal used to ornament an ancient Roman villa.

eurythmy Harmony, orderliness, and elegance of proportions.

eustyle See **intercolumniation.**

columns spaced 2¼ diameters apart

evasé Opened out, flared.

ewery A household service room where the ewers (pitcher-shaped jugs with handles) were kept.

exastyle Same as **hexastyle.**

exchequer To use or have a pattern of checkers.

excubitorium **1.** A gallery in a church where public watch was formerly kept at night on the eve of a festival. **2.** In a medieval monastery, an apartment for night watchers whose duty it was to call monks to their nocturnal devotions.

excubitorium, St. Albans Cathedral, England

exedra, exhedra **1.** A large niche or recess, usually with a bench or seats, semicircular or rectangular in plan and either roofed or unroofed. **2.** In a church, a large apsidal extension, normally on a main axis. **3.** An alcove, or semicircular extension of the colonnade, in a Greek gymnasium; furnished with seats on which the philosophers usually sat to talk with their disciples. **4.** In ancient Greek houses, a room intended for conversation, with a bench running around the wall. **5.** In a public place in the open air, a permanent bench having a high, solid back which is semicircular (or nearly so) in plan.

exedra, 5

exhedra Same as **exedra.**

exonarthex The narthex nearest the entrance, when two are present.

exostes A balconied **loggia.**

expanding vault A **conical vault.**

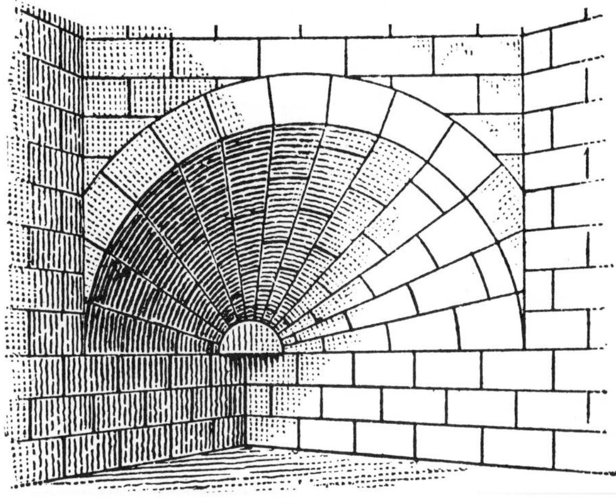

expanding vault

expiatory chapel A chapel erected to expiate a murder or other great crime.

expletive Something used to fill up, as a piece of masonry used to fill a cavity.

exposed masonry Any masonry construction having no surface finish other than paint applied to the wall face.

extension A wing or structure added to an existing building.

external dormer See **dormer window.**

extrados The exterior curve or boundary of the visible face of the arch.

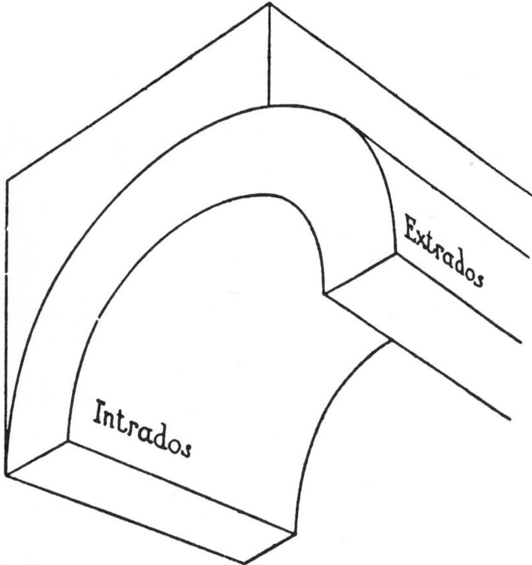

extradosed arch One which has the extrados clearly marked, as a curve exactly or nearly parallel to the intrados; has a well-marked archivolt.

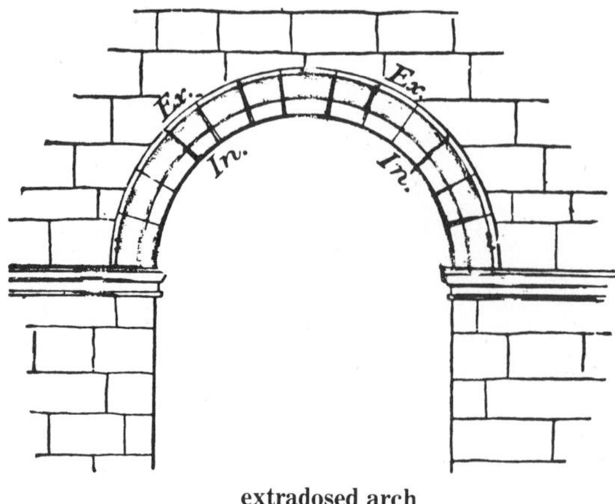

extradosed arch

eye **1.** The central roundel of a pattern or ornament. **2.** The circular (or nearly circular) central part of a volute, as in an Ionic capital. **3.** One of the smaller, more or less triangular, openings between the bars of Gothic tracery. **4.** An **oculus,** esp. one at the summit of a dome.

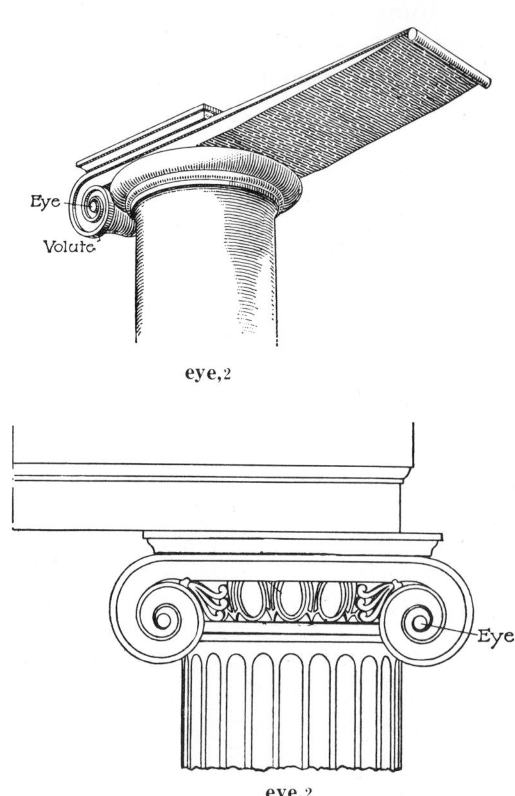

eye,2

eye,2

eyebrow A low dormer on the slope of a roof. It has no sides, the roofing being carried over it in a wavy line.

eyebrow window **1.** A bottom-hinged, inward-opening sash in the uppermost level of a Greek Revival house, or the like. **2.** A window in an **eyebrow.**

eye-catcher See **folly.**

eyelet **1.** In a medieval castle, a small opening for light, air, or the discharge of missiles, in a wall or parapet; a small **loophole.** **2.** A small hole in a wall.

fabric The basic elements making up a building; the carcass without finishings or decoration.

façade The exterior face of a building which is the architectural front, sometimes distinguished from the other faces by elaboration of architectural or ornamental details.

face string, finish string An **outer string,** usually of better material or finish than the roughstring which it covers; may be part of the actual construction or applied to the face of the supporting member.

facet **1.** One surface of a polyhedron. **2.** A flat surface between two column flutes, a fillet.

principal façade of the Church of San Giovanni in Laterano, Rome (330 A.D.)

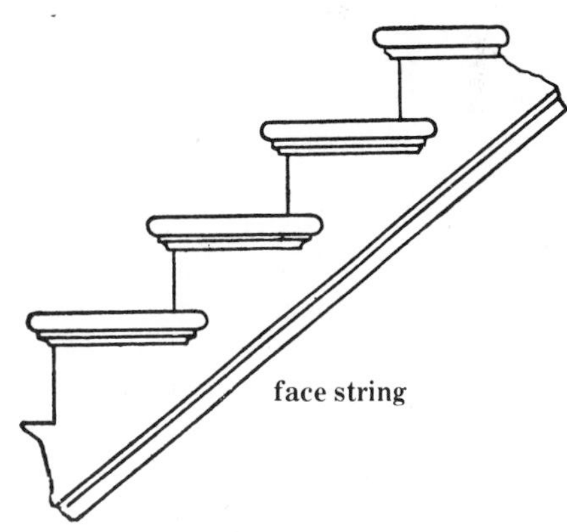

facette Same as **facet.**

face wall **1.** A **retaining wall.** **2.** The front wall of a building.

發券 **fa ch'üang** In traditional Chinese architecture, a masonry arch.

facia See **fascia.**

facing, facework **1.** A veneer of nonstructural material such as stone, terra-cotta, metal, stucco, plaster, and wood used to finish the surface of a rougher or less attractive material. **2.** Any material, forming a part of a wall, used as a finished surface; a **revetment.**

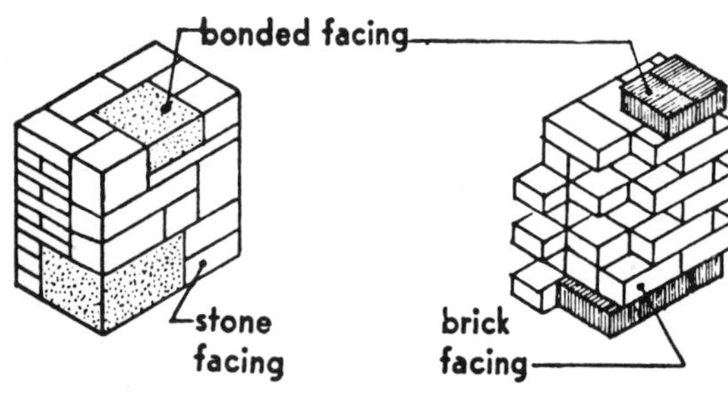

facing

factabling Same as **coping.**

faïence, faïence ware Any earthenware having a transparent glaze; formerly, any decorated earthenware with an opaque glaze.

faïence mosaics Ceramic faïence tile, less than 6 sq in. (38.7 sq cm) in facial area, usually about 3/8 in. (0.95 cm) thick.

faïence tile Glazed or unglazed ceramic tile which shows characteristic variations in the face, edges, and glaze that give a handicrafted, nonmechanical, decorative effect. Also see **majolica.**

fair-faced brickwork A neatly built, smooth surface of brickwork.

fall-pipe Same as **downspout.**

false arch One having the appearance of an arch, though not of arch construction, as a **corbel arch.**

false attic An architectural construction above the main cornice, concealing a roof, but not having windows or enclosing rooms.

false door, blind door The representation of a door, inserted to complete a series of doors or to give symmetry; a **blank door.**

false ellipse A curve struck from three or five foci, preferred in the design of prefabricated parts for arches since fewer different elements are required. Also see **basket-handle arch.**

false front **1.** A front wall which extends beyond the sidewalls of a building to create a more imposing façade. **2.** A front wall that extends above the roof of a building; a **flying façade.**

false window, blind window The representation of a window inserted to complete a series of windows or to give symmetry; a **blank window.**

fane A temple, esp. one devoted to pagan worship.

枋 **fang** **1.** A wall plate, rectangular in cross section, which lies along the top of a main lintel on peripteral columns in traditional Chinese architecture. **2.** A member which interconnects and ties together clusters of **tou kung.**

舫 **fang** In traditional Chinese architecture, a permanent structure, usually of wood but sometimes of stone, built in the shape of a barge and located adjacent to a lake or pond as a feature of landscape architecture; used for dining, drinking, and relaxation.

方丈 **fang chang** A building, within a Chinese temple compound, used as the abbot's quarters.

fan groining Same as **fan vaulting.**

fanlight **1.** A semicircular window over the opening of a door, with radiating bars in the form of an open fan. Also called a **sunburst light.** **2.** Any window occupying a similar position.

fanlight,1

fantail Any member or construction having a form resembling the construction of a fan, esp. applied to **centering** having radiating struts.

fan tracery,
vault of cloisters, Gloucester (1351–1412)

fan vaulting, King's College Chapel, Cambridge (1508–15)

fan vault, Chapter House, Wells

fan tracery, fanwork Tracery on the soffit of a vault whose ribs radiate like the ribs of a fan.

fanum **1.** An ancient Roman plot of ground which had been consecrated to some divinity. **2.** A temple that was erected on such a plot of ground.

fan vault A concave conical vault whose ribs, of equal length and curvature, radiate from the springing like the ribs of a fan.

fan vaulting A system of **fan vaults.**

fan window A **fanlight.**

fanwork See **fan tracery.**

farrarium An ancient Roman barn for storing grain.

fartura The mass of rubble employed for filling up the internal part of a Roman wall between the outside surfaces when the wall was not constructed of solid masonry.

fasces A symbol of Roman authority consisting of a bundle of rods with an ax blade projecting from them.

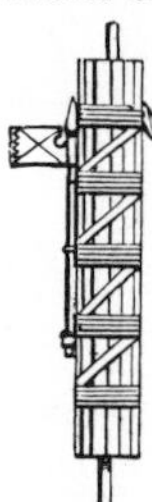

fasces of a Roman magistrate

fascia, facia **1.** Any flat horizontal member or molding with little projection, as the bands into which the architraves of Ionic and Corinthian entablatures are divided. **2.** Any relatively narrow vertical surface (but broader than a fillet) which is projected or cantilevered or supported on columns or element other than a wall below. Also see **platband.**

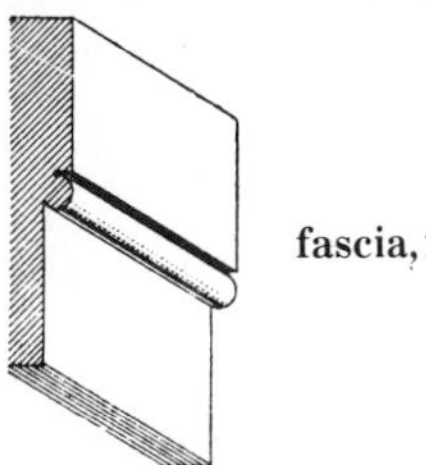

fascia,1

fasciated Composed either of bands of molded fasciae, as in the Ionic architrave, or of bands of color.

fastigium **1.** The pediment of a portico, so-called in ancient architecture because it followed the form of the roof. **2.** The crest or ridge of a roof.

fastigium,1 from an ancient Roman coin

fauces Plural of **faux.**

fauwara The fountain in the court of a **mosque.**

faux A narrow passageway between the two principal divisions of an ancient Roman house (atrium and peristylium); located by the side of the tablinum.

favissa In ancient Rome, a crypt, cellar, or underground treasury.

favus A tile or slab of marble cut into a hexagonal shape, so as to produce a honeycomb pattern in pavements.

featheredge board A board made thin on one edge, to overlap a part of the one next to it; also called a **clapboard.**

featheredge brick Same as **arch brick.**

featheredged coping, splayed coping, wedge coping Coping that slopes in only one direction (not ridged or gabled).

Federal style In the U.S.A., the Classic Revival style, from ca. 1790 to 1830.

Federal style house

femerall See **femerell.**

femerell A ventilator, often louvered, drawing smoke through a roof when no chimney is provided. Also see **louver.**

femur The long projecting face between each channel of a triglyph.

fenestella **1.** A small glazed opening in a shrine to afford a view of the relics. **2.** A small niche above a **piscina, 1** or **credence.** **3.** A small aperture made in altars and confessions to permit their contents to be visible at certain times. **4.** A small window.

fenestra,2

fenestella,2

fenestra **1.** A **loophole** in the walls of a fortress, from which missiles were discharged. **2.** Ancient equivalent of a window.

fenestra, 2: two such windows on the street side of a house in Pompeii

fenestra biforis The ancient equivalent of a French window.

fenestral **1.** A small window. **2.** A framed window blind of cloth or paper used prior to the introduction of glass.

fenestration The arrangement and design of windows in a building.

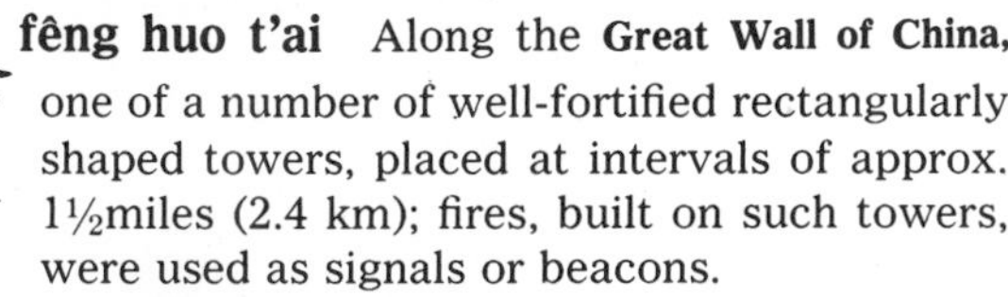

fêng huo t'ai Along the **Great Wall of China,** one of a number of well-fortified rectangularly shaped towers, placed at intervals of approx. 1½miles (2.4 km); fires, built on such towers, were used as signals or beacons.

fenyaille Same as **finial.**

feretory In a church, a space where major relics are kept, often treated as a chapel behind the main altar.

ferme ornée See **cottage orné.**

ferriterium An ancient Roman prison where slaves were kept in chains.

fertre Same as **feretory.**

festoon A festive decoration of pendant semiloops with attachments and loose ends, esp. a swag of fabric, or representations of such decorations. Also see **garland.**

festoons

feyra A druidical spherical rock placed at the center of a Celtic monument consisting of a number of **menhirs** arranged in a circle.

fielded panel See **raised panel.**

filet Same as **fillet.**

fillet 1. A molding consisting of a narrow flat band, often square in section; the term is loosely applied to almost any rectangular molding; usually used in conjunction with or to separate other moldings or ornaments, as the stria between the flutes of columns. Also see **annulet, band, cimbia, cincture, fascia, fret, lattice molding, platband, reglet, supercilium,** and **taenia;** a **list,** or **tringle.** 2. A carved ornament representing a flowing band or ribbon.

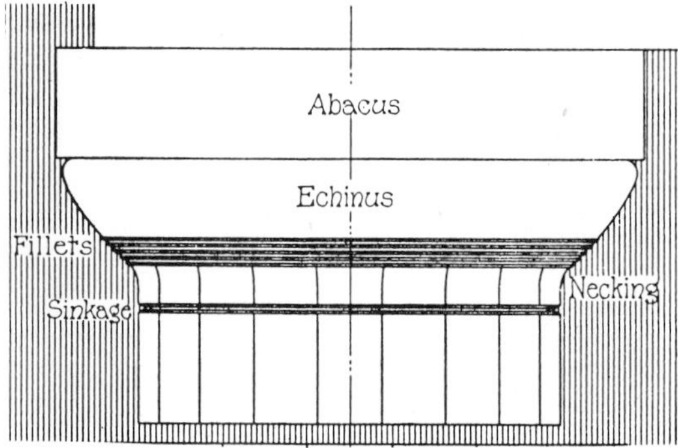

fillets between the echinus and necking of a column

fillet gutter A narrow gutter on the slope of a roof against a chimney or the like.

finial An ornament which terminates the point of a spire, pinnacle, etc. Also see **acroterion, crop, knob, pineapple, pommel.**

finish string See **face string.**

finol Same as **finial.**

fire altar An open-air stone structure for the cult of the sacred fire in ancient Persia.

fireback, chimney back The back wall of the fireplace, constructed of heat-resistant masonry or ornamental cast or wrought metal, which not only is decorative but radiates heat into the room.

fireback

Early English style

Decorated style

Perpendicular style

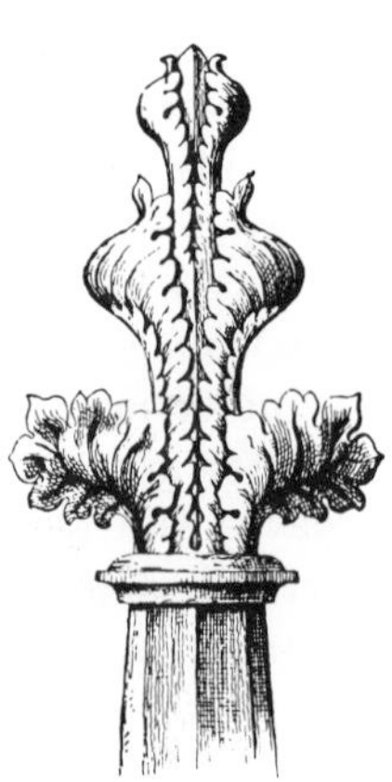

French (15th cent.)

fireplace An opening at the base of a chimney, usually an open recess in a wall, in which a fire may be built.

Rochester Castle (c.1130)

Coinsborough Castle (c.1170)

Aydon Castle, Northumberland (c. 1270)

Aydon Castle, Northumberland (c. 1270)

Edlingham Castle, Northumberland (c. 1330)

Sherborne Abbey, Dorset (c. 1470)

fireplace cheeks The splayed sides of a fireplace.

fireplace throat Same as **chimney throat.**

fire screen Any screen set in front of a fireplace to prevent flying sparks or embers from entering the room.

fire screen, Louis XVI style

fire temple A tower built for the maintenance of the sacred fire in ancient Persia.

fish bladder (fischblase) An ornamental motif of late Gothic tracery, reminiscent in form of the air-bladder of fish.

fish bladder tracery

fistuca A device used by the ancient Romans to ram down pavements and the foundations of buildings.

fistula In ancient Roman construction, a water pipe of lead or earthenware.

five-centered arch An arch whose intrados is struck from five centers.

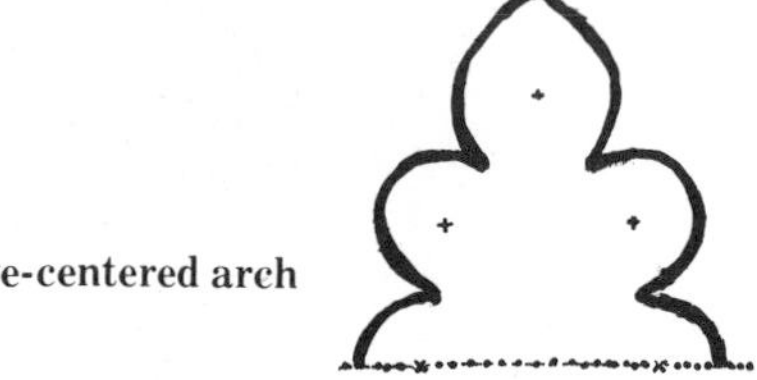

five-centered arch

fixed light, deadlight A window or an area of a window which does not open; glazed directly in a fixed frame that does not open.

flabelliform Fan-shaped; said of an ornament composed of palm leaves, or the like.

flabelliform ornament

flambeau A luminaire resembling a flaming torch.

flambé glaze A flow ceramic glaze with copper, which produces a variegated effect.

flamboyant finish A decorative coating achieved by applying transparent colored varnish or lacquer over a polished metal substrate.

Flamboyant style The last phase of French Gothic architecture in the second half of the 15th cent., characterized by flowing and flame-like tracery.

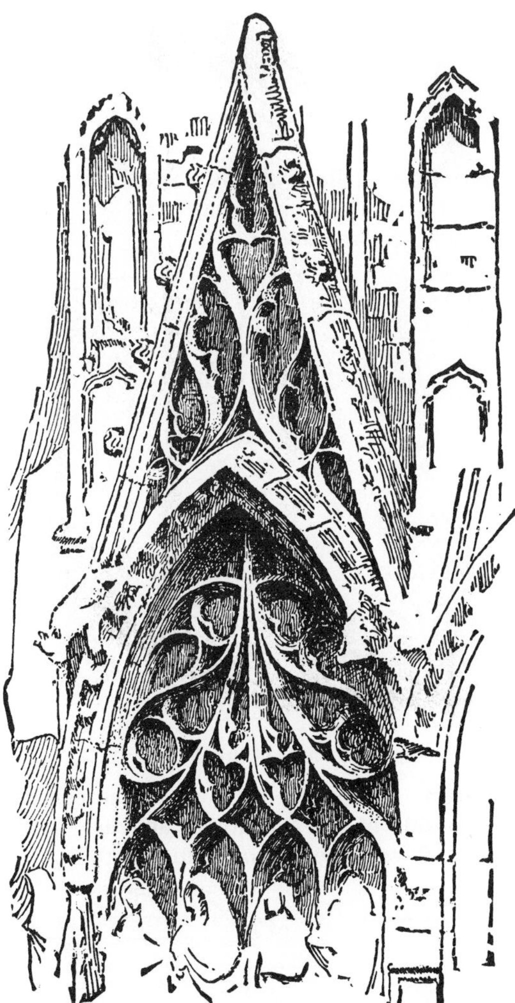

Flamboyant tracery, Rouen Cathedral, France

Flamboyant window, St. Jean à Caen

Flamboyant window, St. Ouen, Rouen

flanch, flaunch To widen and slant the top of a chimney stack so that water is directed away from the flue.

flank A side, as of a building or arch.

flanking window See **side light.**

flat arch, jack arch, straight arch An arch with a horizontal or nearly horizontal intrados; has little or no convexity.

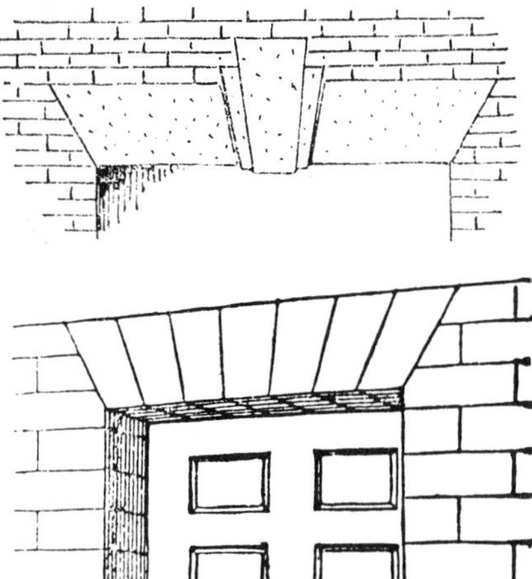

flat arches

flaunch Same as **flanch.**

flèche A spire, usually comparatively small and slender, above the ridge of a roof, particularly one rising from the intersection of the nave and transept roofs of Gothic churches.

Flemish bond In brickwork, a bond in which each course consists of **headers** and **stretchers** laid alternately; each header is centered with respect to the stretcher above and the stretcher below it.

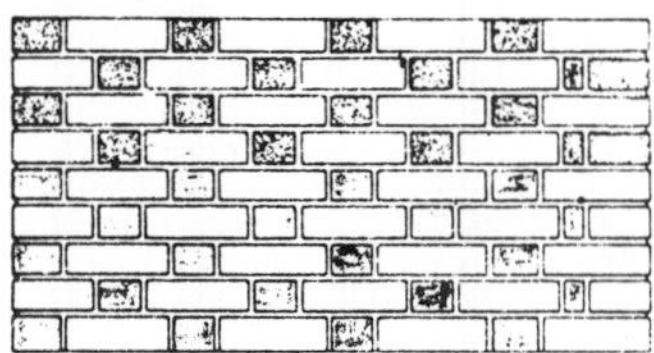

Flemish bond

Flemish cross bond Similar to **Flemish bond** but with two additional headers in place of a stretcher at intervals.

Flemish diagonal bond A bond in which a course of alternate **headers** and **stretchers** is followed by a course of stretchers, resulting in a diagonal pattern.

Flemish garden wall bond, Sussex garden wall bond A bond similar to **Flemish bond** except that in each course a **header** is followed by three **stretchers.**

Flemish garden wall bond

fleur-de-lys, fleur-de-lis The French royal lily, conventionalized as an ornament in Late Gothic architecture.

various forms of the fleur-de-lys

fleuron **1.** The small flower at the center of each side of the Corinthian abacus. **2.** Any small flower-like ornament in general.

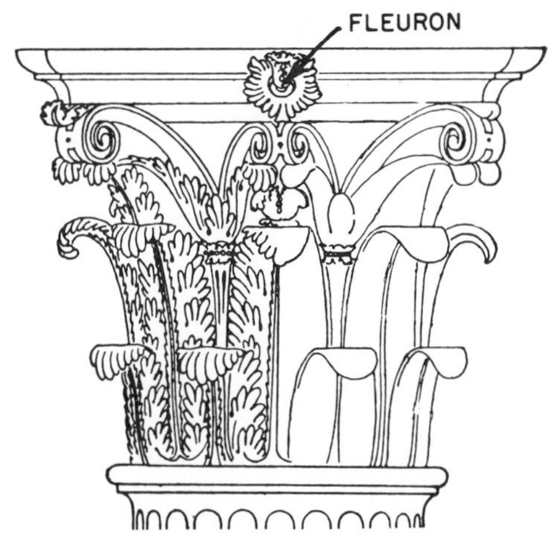

flier, flyer Any of the steps in a straight flight of stairs, each tread of which is of uniform width (as distinguished from the treads in a winding stair).

flight A continuous series of steps with no intermediate landings.

flights of steps, Scala Regia, Vatican (1663-66)

flint A dense, fine-grained stone; a form of silica; naturally occurs in the form of nodules; usually gray, brown, black, or otherwise dark in color, but nodules and other chunks tend to weather white or light shades from the surface inward. Broken "flints," as the nodules are called, are used in cobble size, either whole or split (knapped) in mortared walls, esp. in England.

flooring Any material used in laying a floor.

floor molding See **base shoe.**

Florentine arch An arch whose extrados is not concentric with its intrados and whose voussoirs are therefore longer at the crown than at the springing; common in the region of Florence in the late Middle Ages and early Renaissance.

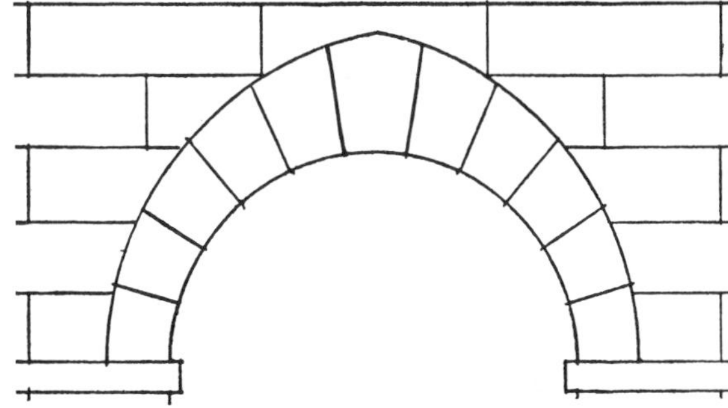

Florentine arch

Florentine lily Same as **giglio.**

Florentine mosaic A kind of mosaic made with precious and semiprecious stones, inlaid in a surface of white or black marble or similar material, generally displaying elaborate flower patterns and the like.

floriated, floreated Decorated with floral patterns.

floriated Romanesque capitals, France

florid Highly ornate; extremely rich to the point of overdecoration.

flos Same as **fleuron,** 1.

Flowing style An old term for the later phases of the English Decorated and the French Flamboyant styles of Gothic architecture. The term was derived from the flowing quality of the tracery.

flowing tracery, curvilinear tracery, undulating tracery Tracery in which continuous, curvilinear patterns (largely ogees) dominate. A characteristic feature of the Decorated and Flamboyant styles.

flowing tracery, Lincoln Cathedral

below: **flowing tracery, Little St. Mary's, Cambridge (c. 1350)**

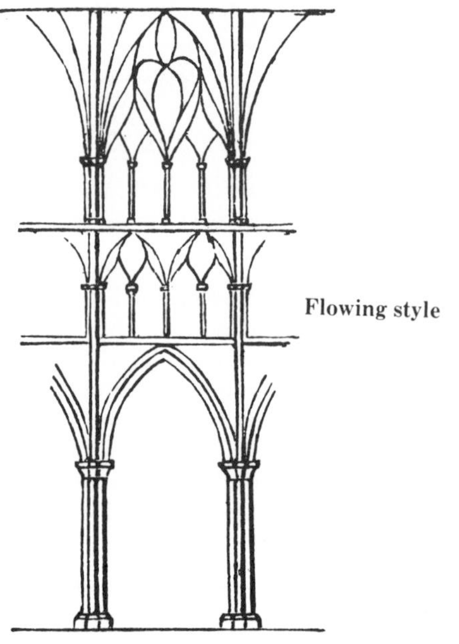

Flowing style

flue, chimney flue **1.** An incombustible and heat-resistant enclosed passage in a chimney to control and carry away products of combustion from a fireplace, furnace, or boiler to the outside air. **2.** The chimney itself, if only one such passage is enclosed.

flush Having the surface or face even or level with the adjacent surface.

flush bead See **quirk bead, 2.**

flushwork *(Brit.)* Masonry which contrasts smooth ashlar with knapped flint; the split side is set flush with the wall face.

flute A groove or channel, esp. one of many such parallel grooves, usually semicircular or semielliptical in section; used decoratively, as along the shaft of a column.

fluted column, Canterbury Cathedral

fluting A series of **flutes,** as on a column.

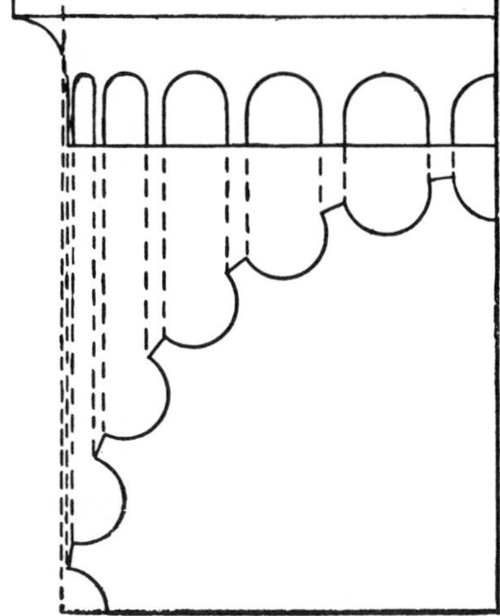

Ionic fluting: part plan and part elevation

flyer See **flier.**

flying buttress A characteristic feature of Gothic construction, in which the lateral thrusts of a roof or vault are taken up by a bar of masonry, usually sloping, carried on an arch, and a solid pier or buttress sufficient to receive the thrust.

A, flying buttress; *B*, vaulted roof of aisle; *C*, outside buttress; *D*, division between aisle and nave; *E*, vaulted roof of nave; *F*, pillar between aisle and nave

flying buttress

Decorated style, Caythorpe, Lincolnshire (c. 1320)

Louth Church, Lincolnshire (c. 1500)

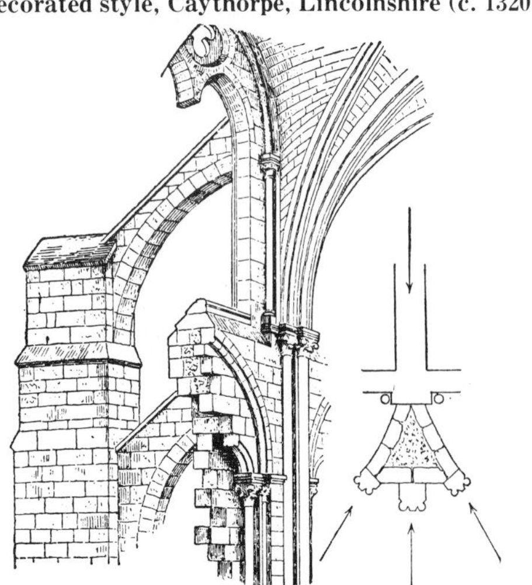

right: **plan taken at the level of the flying buttress; arrows show direction of thrusts**

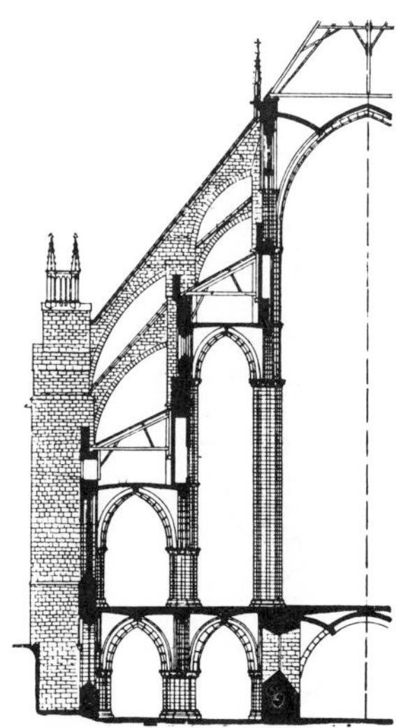

half-section, Bourges Cathedral (13th cent.)

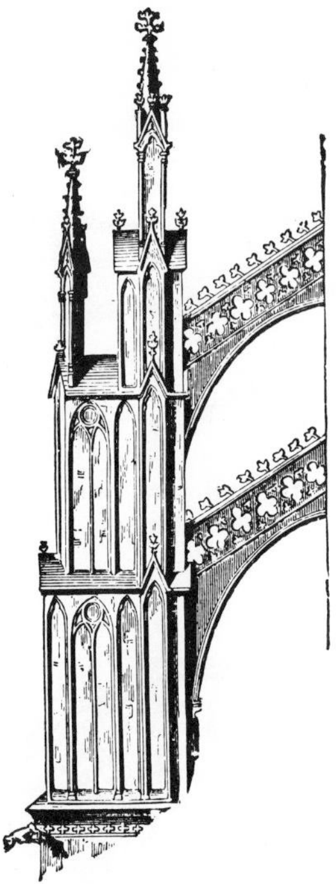

Cologne Cathedral (1248 onward)

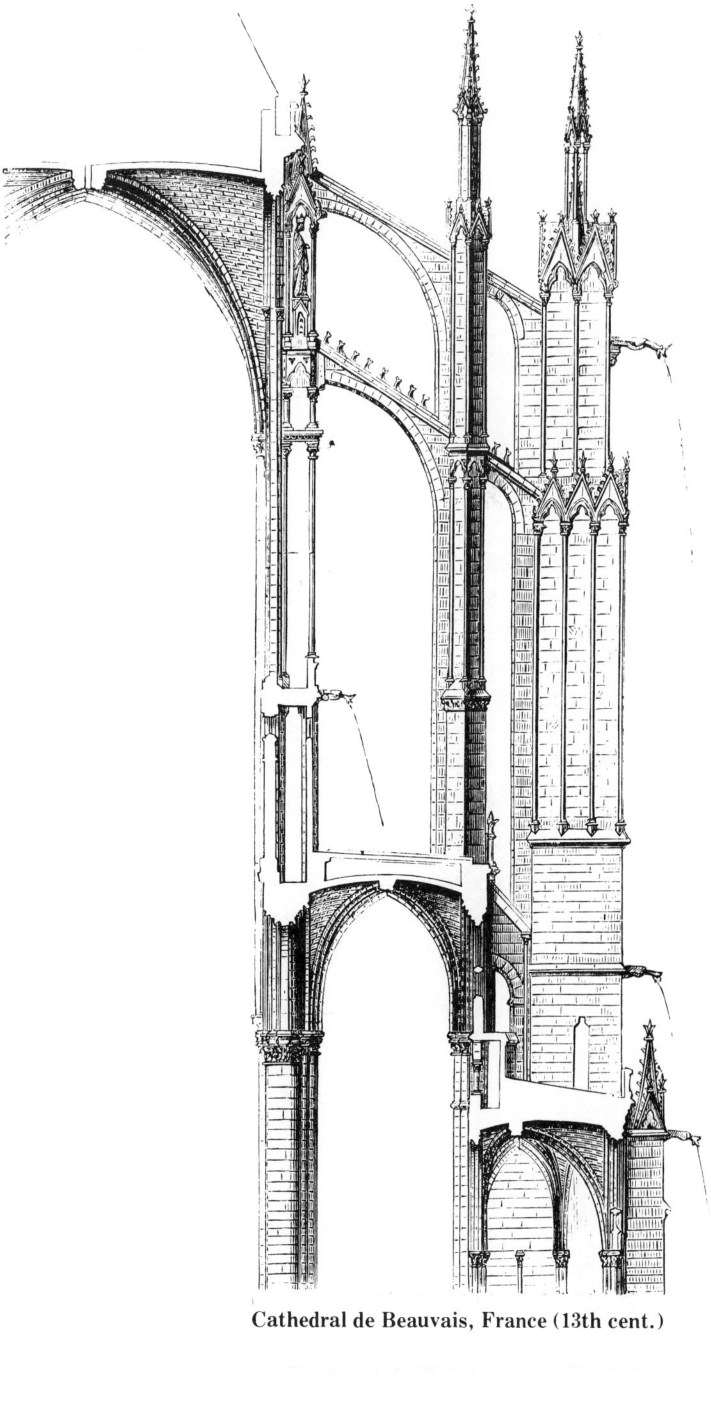

Cathedral de Beauvais, France (13th cent.)

left: buttress and flying buttress of Notre Dame, Paris (late 12th cent.)

flying façade See **false front.**

fly rafter A **rafter** in the projecting portion of a gabled roof.

foil In tracery, any of several lobes, circular or nearly so, tangent to the inner side of a larger arc, as of an arch, and meeting each other in points, called **cusps,** projecting inward from the arch, or circle. Three such lobes make a **trefoil,** etc.

opening with five foils (cinquefoil)

foliated sculpture, Notre Dame, Paris (13th cent.)

foiled Decorated with foils.

foiled arch Same as **cusped arch.**

folding shutter See **boxing shutter.**

foliated 1. Adorned with foils, as on tracery. 2. Decorated with conventionalized leafage, often applied to capitals or moldings.

foliation 1. The cusps or foils with which the divisions of a Gothic window are ornamented. 2. Leaf-like decoration.

foliated capital

foliated arch, Beverley Minster

Moorish foliated arch

folly, eye-catcher A functionally useless structure, often a fake ruin, sometimes built in a landscaped park to highlight a view.

foliation in tracery, Sainte Chapelle, Paris (1240)

Medieval conventionalized foliation, Notre Dame, Paris (end of 13th cent.)

folly, Louis XVI (1774–1789)

fonar In early Russian architecture, a type of **lantern** consisting of a cupola having many small windows.

fons **1.** A natural spring. **2.** An artificial fountain, made either by covering and decorating a spring with a structure or sculpture, or by making a jet of water, supplied from an elevated cistern, play into an artificial basin.

font A basin, usually of stone, which holds the water for baptism.

Anglo-Saxon, Deerhurst

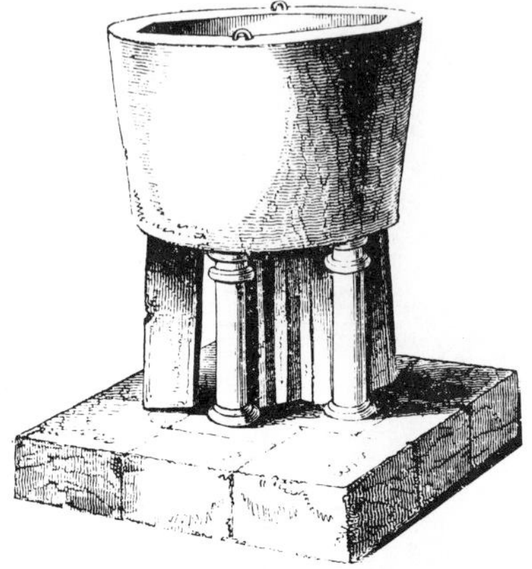

Norman

Norman

Cathedral of Langres, France (end of 13th cent.)

Early English style

Decorated style (c. 1320)

late Decorated style (c. 1360)

Perpendicular style

foot base A molding above a plinth.

footpace **1.** A dais. **2.** A **halfpace.**

footstall **1.** The plinth or base of a pillar or pier, usually having a distinctive architectural treatment. **2.** A pedestal which supports a pillar, statue, etc.

footstone A **kneeler,** 1; a **gable springer.**

foramen Same as **fenestella.**

fore choir Same as **antechoir.**

forechurch A consecrated extension in front of a larger church.

forecourt A court forming an entrance plaza for a single building or several buildings in a group.

fores Plural of **foris.**

fores carceris In the ancient Roman circus, the doors which close the front of a stall, in which horses and chariots were stationed before the start of a race.

foreyn An ancient term for a cesspool or drain.

forica A set of public privies in ancient Rome, distributed in various parts of the city for the convenience of the population.

foris One of the two leafs of a door to a sacred classical edifice; usually used in the plural (**fores**).

forked finial See **chigi.**

formal garden A garden whose plantings, walks, pools, fountains, etc., follow a definite, recognizable plan, frequently symmetrical, emphasizing geometrical forms.

formeret, wall rib One of the ribs against the walls in a ceiling vaulted with ribs.

form-pieces A medieval term for **tracery.**

fornacula Diminutive of **fornax.**

fornax In ancient Roman construction, a kiln.

forniciform In the shape of a vaulted roof or ceiling.

fornix **1.** In ancient Roman construction, a vaulted surface. **2.** In ancient Rome, an early type of **triumphal arch.**

fornus Same as **furnum.**

fort A fortified place of exclusively military nature.

fortress **1.** A fortification of massive scale, generally of monumental character and sometimes including an urban core; also called **stronghold.** **2.** A protected place of refuge.

fores carceris

Roman fornax

fornices (pl. fornix, 1)

forum A Roman public square surrounded by monumental buildings, usually including a basilica and a temple; the center of civic life. A forum sometimes was purely commercial in aspect.

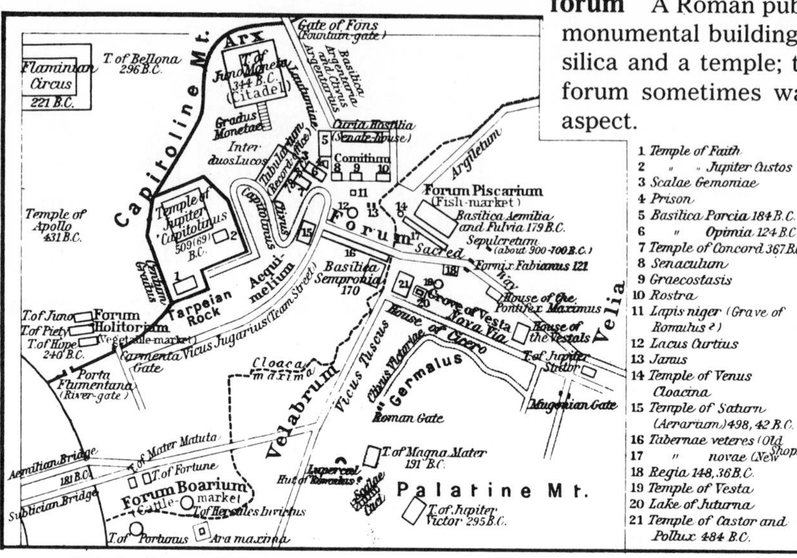

plan of the Roman Forum and its vicinity at the time of the Republic.
Scale: 1:10,000

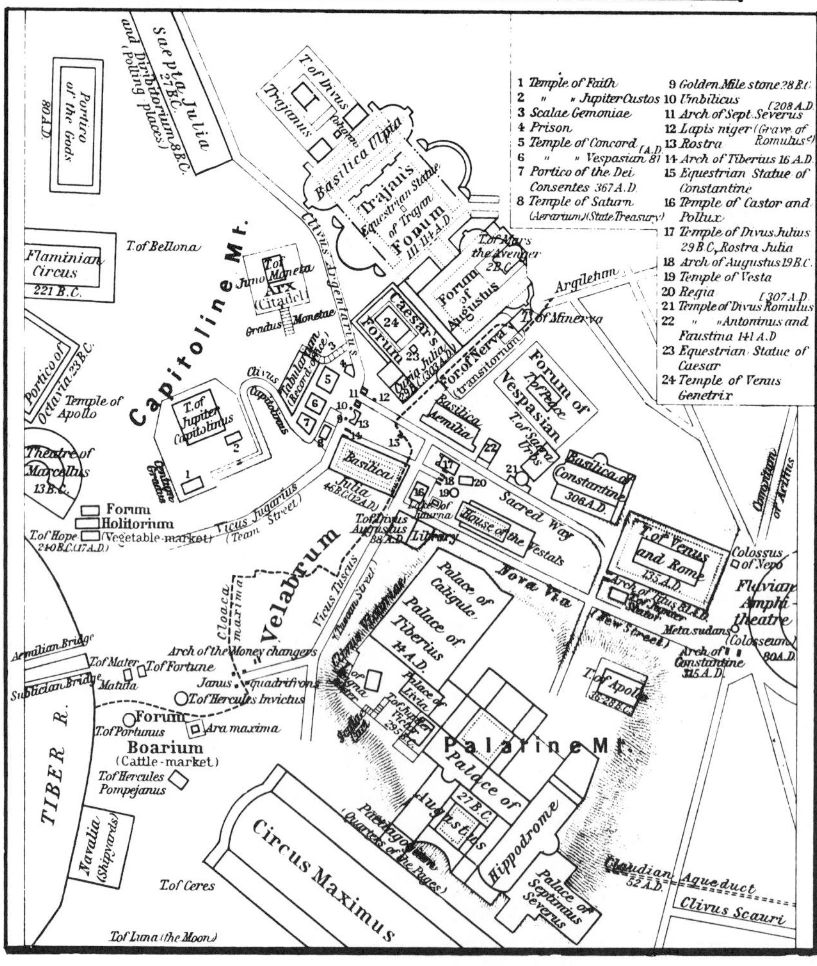

plan of the Imperial Forums and their vicinity.
Scale: 1:10,000

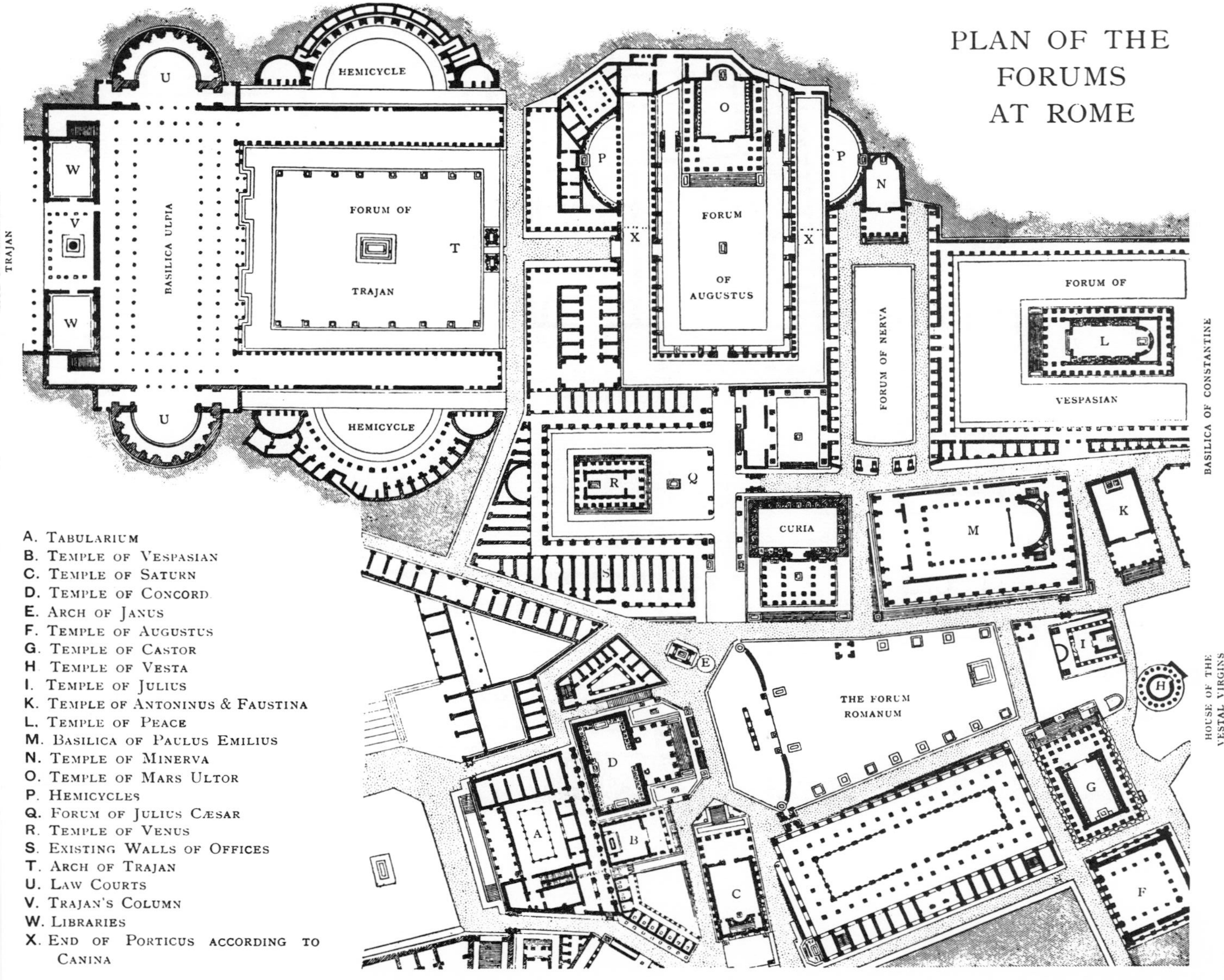
PLAN OF THE FORUMS AT ROME
SITE OF TEMPLE OF TRAJAN
BASILICA ULPIA
FORUM OF TRAJAN
HEMICYCLE
HEMICYCLE
FORUM OF AUGUSTUS
FORUM OF NERVA
FORUM OF VESPASIAN
BASILICA OF CONSTANTINE
CURIA
THE FORUM ROMANUM
HOUSE OF THE VESTAL VIRGINS
A. Tabularium
B. Temple of Vespasian
C. Temple of Saturn
D. Temple of Concord
E. Arch of Janus
F. Temple of Augustus
G. Temple of Castor
H Temple of Vesta
I. Temple of Julius
K. Temple of Antoninus & Faustina
L. Temple of Peace
M. Basilica of Paulus Emilius
N. Temple of Minerva
O. Temple of Mars Ultor
P. Hemicycles
Q. Forum of Julius Cæsar
R. Temple of Venus
S. Existing Walls of Offices
T. Arch of Trajan
U. Law Courts
V. Trajan's Column
W. Libraries
X. End of Porticus according to Canina

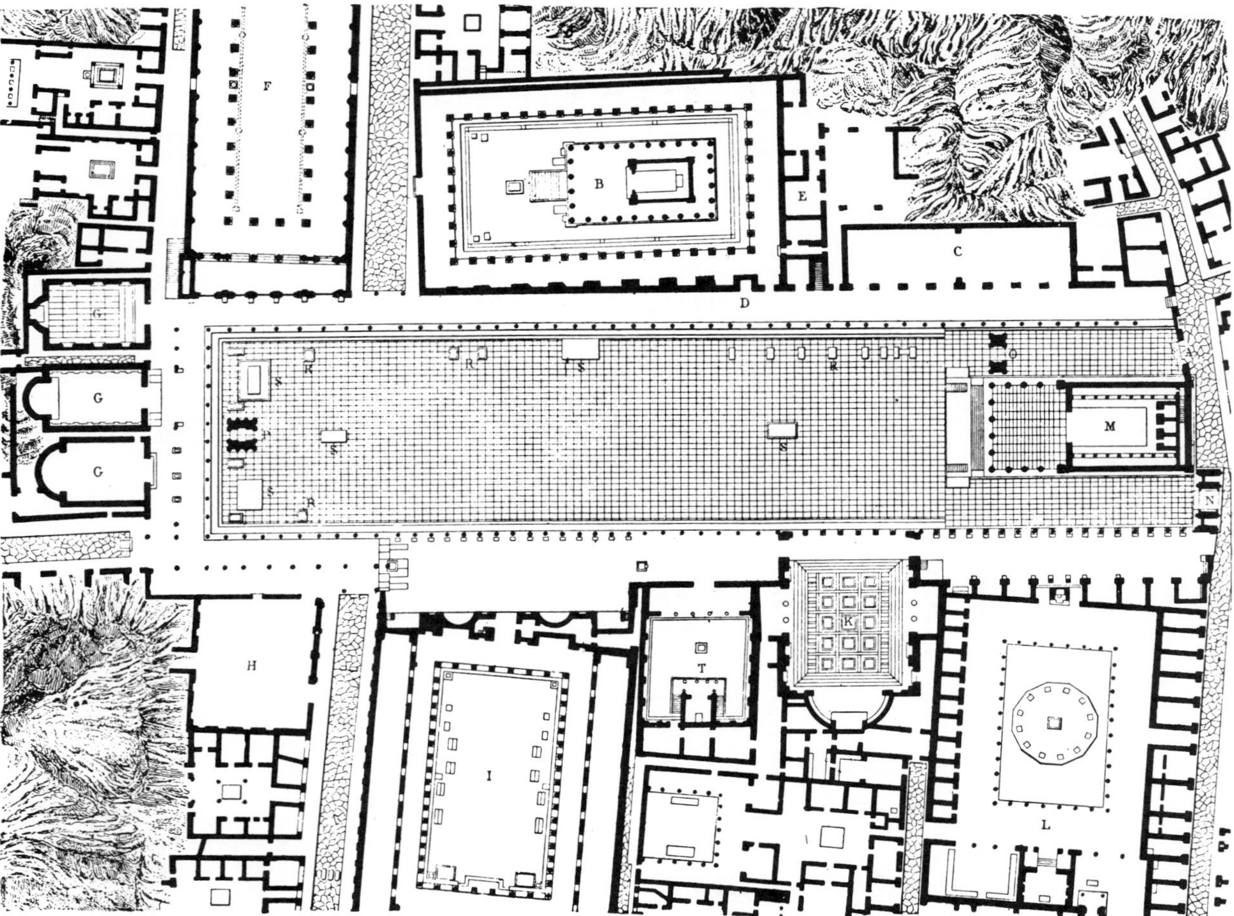

FORUM OF POMPEII, WITH SURROUNDING BUILDINGS.

A. Archway (disputed), with steps descending into forum.

B. Temple of Apollo.

C. Market buildings.

D. Table of standard measures.

E. Rooms dependent upon the Temple, B.

F. Basilica.

G. Municipal buildings.

H. Comitium, or place for boating.

I. Building of Eumachia: a late building of unknown purpose.

K. Sanctuary of the city Lares; unroofed, except for apse and niches.

L. Macellum (market for provisions).

M. Temple of Jupiter.

N. Triumphal Arch of Tiberius.

O. Triumphal arch of unknown significance.

P. Substructure of what was once thought an arch; now known as the pedestal of the statue of Augustus.

R. Pedestals, mostly of unknown destination.

S. Pedestals: of Claudius and Agrippa on each side of *P*; of Nero in front of *P*; of Caligula in front of *M*.

T. Temple of Vespasian.

foss, fosse A moat or ditch.

fossa In ancient Rome, a trench, esp. one outside a city wall.

fo ssŭ See **ssŭ.**

foundation stone Same as **cornerstone.**

fountain See **architectural fountain.**

four-centered arch An arch whose intrados is struck from four centers.

four-centered pointed arch See **Tudor arch.**

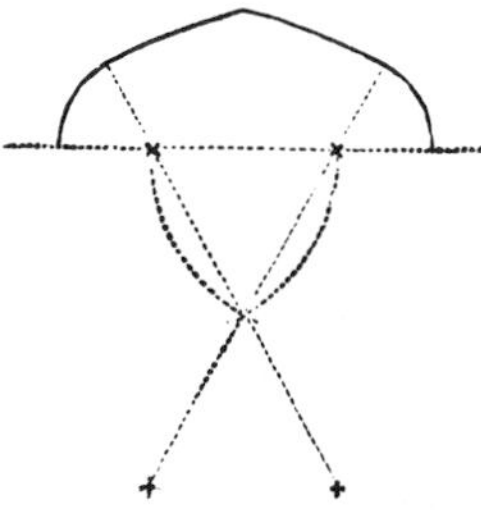

four-centered arch

fourches patibulaires Gallows which could accommodate simultaneously a number of victims; consisted of stone pillars connected by wooden beams, constructed in the Middle Ages by the French nobility on their lands at the behest of the King; the number of pillars in the gallows depended on the rank of the noble. The King himself had as many pillars on the Royal Gallows as he thought necessary. Criminals were either hanged there, ascending to their nooses on inside ladders, or brought there after execution for public display. The gallows were used not only for human beings but also for animals, particularly for pigs that had been condemned to death for eating children.

fourches patibulaires

four-leaved flower An ornament used in hollow moldings, resembling a flower with four petals.

four-leaved flower, St. Albans

four-piece butt match See **diamond matching.**

foyer **1.** An entranceway or transitional space from the exterior to the interior of a building. **2.** The area between the outer lobby and an auditorium. **3.** The lobby itself.

fractable A coping on the gable wall of a building, when carried above the roof; esp. when broken into steps or curves forming an ornamental silhouette.

fractables

fraiter, fraitor Same as **frater.**

framed overhang An **overhang, 1** of the upper section of a house over the vertical face of the section below.

frame house A house of wood frame construction, usually sheathed and covered with lap or panel siding or shingles.

framing **1.** A system of structural woodwork. **2.** The rough timber structure of a building, such as partitions, flooring, and roofing. **3.** Any framed work, as around an opening in an exterior wall.

François I (Premier) style The culmination of the early phase of French Renaissance architecture named after Francis I (1515–1547), merging Gothic elements with the full use of Italian decoration. Fontainebleau and the châteaux of the Loire, among them Chambord, are outstanding examples.

dormer, Chambord

salamander: emblem of Francis I

villa at Moret, court front (now rebuilt in Cours la Reine, Paris)

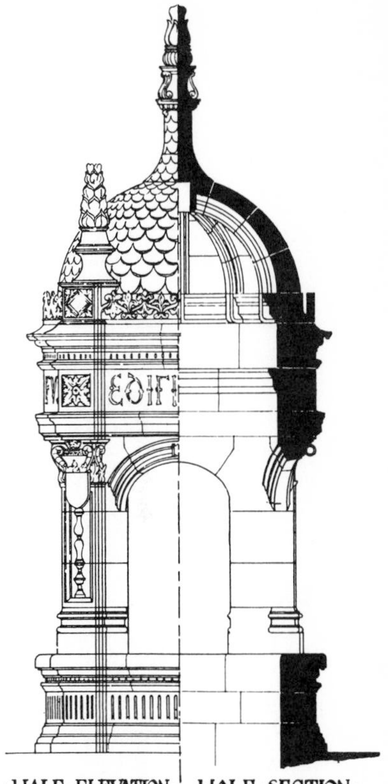

well house, St. Jean d'Angely

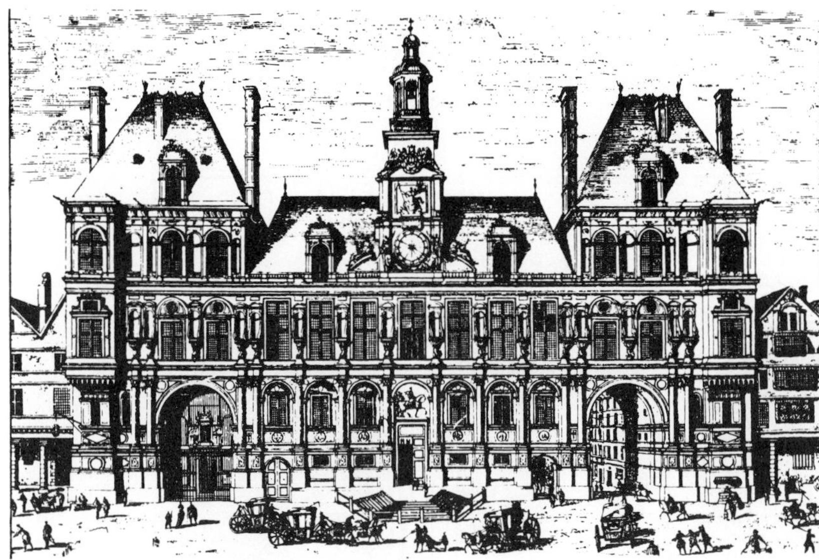

Hotel de Ville, Paris, by Domenico Bernabei of Cortona ("Boccador") (begun 1532, burnt down 1871)

initial of Francis I

François I (Premier) style

house of
Agnès Sorel,
Orleans

Franklin stove A metal stove, resembling an open fireplace, which is freestanding in the room.

frater, frater house A common eating room or hall in a monastery.

fratery Same as **frater.**

freedstool Same as **frithstool.**

freestanding Said of a structural element which is fixed by its foundation at its lower end, but not constrained throughout its vertical height.

French arch A **Dutch arch.**

French door, casement door, door window A door having a top rail, bottom rail, and stiles, which has glass panes throughout (or nearly throughout) its entire length; often used in pairs.

French flier, French flyer A **flier** of a three-quarter-turn stair, around an open well.

French roof A mansard roof whose sloping sides are nearly perpendicular.

French stuc An imitation stone formed by plasterwork.

French tiles A type of interlocking roof tiles.

French window A casement window extending down to the floor; also called a **French door.**

fresco, buon fresco A mural painted into fresh lime plaster; in such work water-based colors unite with the base; retouching is done *a secco* (dry).

fresco secco, secco A mural, often fugitive, painted with water-based colors on dry plaster.

French roof

fret 1. An ornament, sometimes painted, incised, or raised and formed of short fillets, bands, or reglets variously combined, frequently consisting of continuous lines arranged in rectangular forms; a **meander;** a **Greek key.** 2. Similar ornamentation in which the fillets intersect at oblique angles, as often in Oriental designs.

fretwork Ornamental openwork or interlaced work in relief, esp. when elaborate and minute in its parts and in patterns of contrasting light and dark.

fretwork pavement design, Pompeii

examples of Greek fretwork

Early Greek mosaic pavement

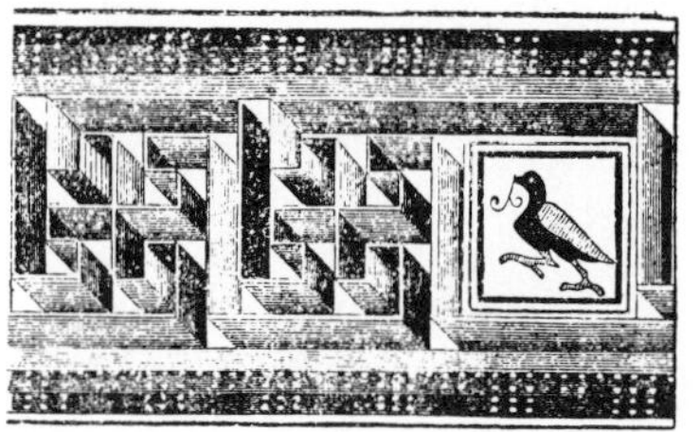

fretwork, Poitiers (12th cent.)

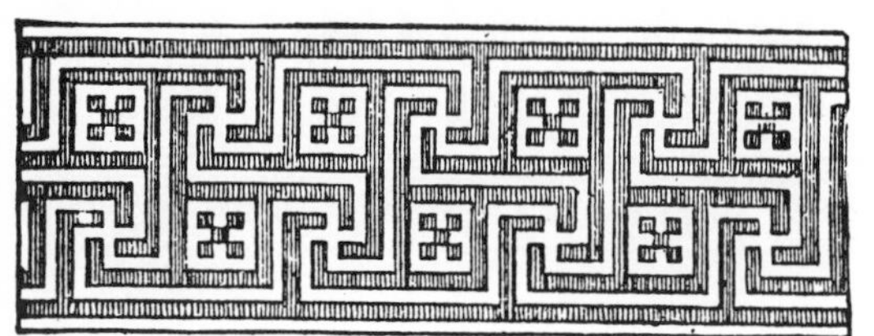

fretwork above cella frieze, Parthenon

friary A religious establishment consisting of various ecclesiastical and domestic buildings for the use of friars.

fridstool Same as **frithstool.**

frieze **1.** The middle horizontal member of a classical entablature, above the architrave and below the cornice. **2.** A similar decorative band in a stringcourse, or near the top of an interior wall below the cornice. Also see **order.**

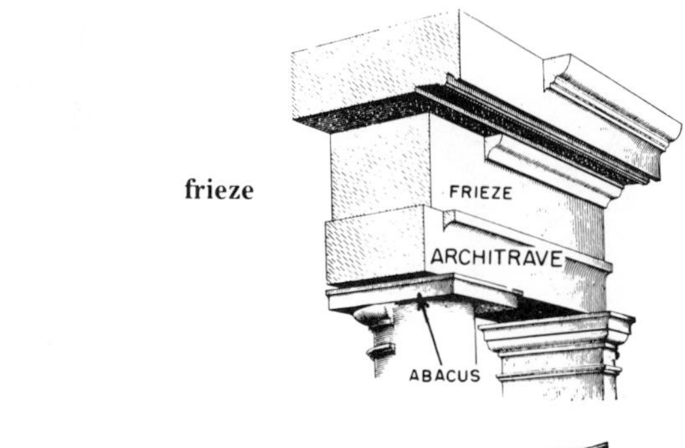

frieze

Doric entablature, *E*, **showing:** *a*, **architrave;** *b*, **frieze;** *c*, **cornice**

frieze along stairway, great altar at Pergamon

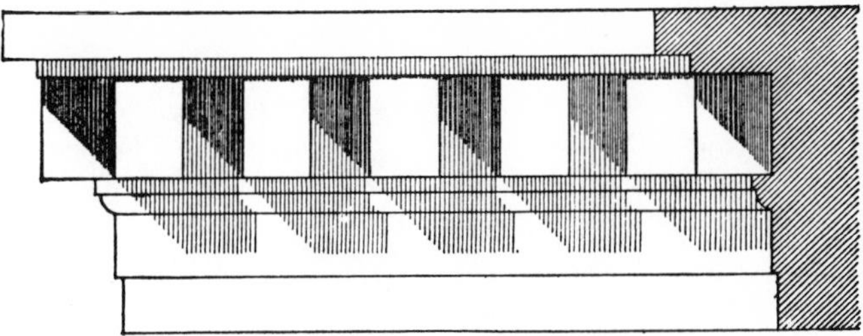

dentil frieze

east frieze of the Parthenon. *left to right:* **Poseidon, Apollo, Demeter, Aphrodite, and Eros**

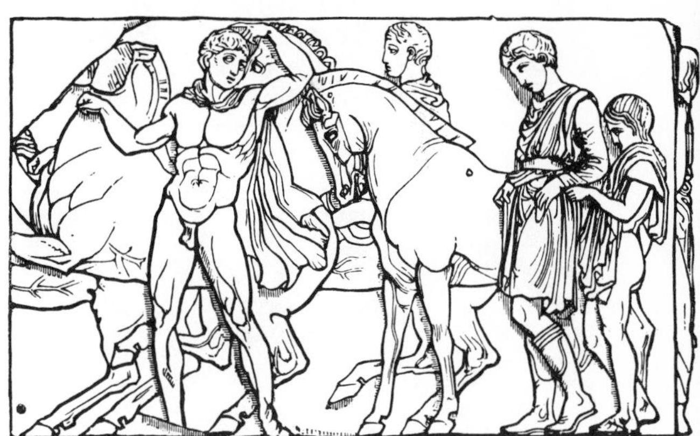

frieze from the Parthenon

frieze from the principal Ionic temple, the Erechtheion

frieze, Forum of Trajan, Rome (98–113 A.D.)

German Romanesque (12th cent.)

Early Gothic frieze, Chartres (13th cent.)

Italian Renaissance frieze

frieze panel The topmost panel in a multi-paneled door.

frieze rail A door rail which is just below the frieze panel.

frigidarium **1.** The cold section of a Roman bath, sometimes including a swimming pool (piscina). Also see **bath, 3.** **2.** In an **ahenum,** the uppermost boiler, which was filled directly from the cold cistern and was completely removed from the heat of the furnace.

frigidarium,2. *left:* **the uppermost boiler in the ahenum**

frigidarium,1

frithstool A seat, usually of stone, placed near the altar in some churches as a sacred refuge for those who claimed the privilege of sanctuary.

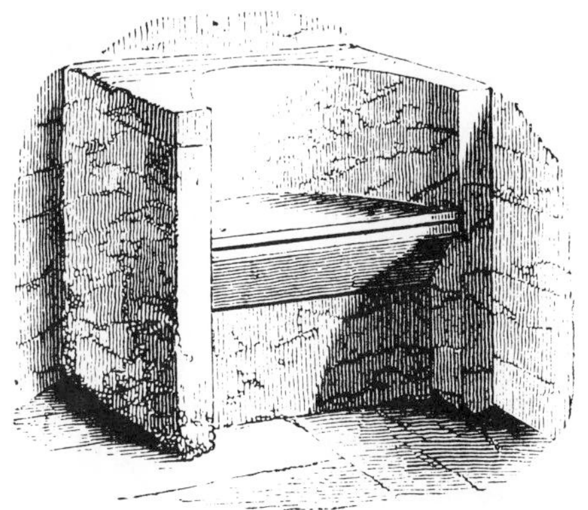

frithstool

frontal **1.** The textile or panels which form the decorative front of an altar. **2.** Same as **fronton.**

frontal

front hearth, outer hearth That part of the hearth or hearthstone which is on the room side of the fireplace opening.

frontispiece **1.** The decorated front wall or bay of a building. **2.** An ornamental porch or chief pediment.

fronton A small pediment placed over a door, niche, porch, etc.

fronton, Sweden (16th cent.)

frosted **1.** Rusticated, with formalized stalactites or icicles. **2.** Given an even, granular surface to avoid shine; matted. **3.** Closely reticulated or matted to avoid transparency.

frosted work A type of ornamental rusticated work, having an appearance like that of frost on plants.

栿 **fu** In Sung architecture (China, 11 to 13th cent.), a beam which supports purlins that are perpendicular to the longitudinal side of a building.

fu hsüeh See **k'ung miao.**

full Cape house A **Cape Cod house** with two windows on both sides of the front door.

full-centered Descriptive of an architectural feature whose outline follows an arc of a circle.

fumarium **1.** A chamber into which the flues of a house conduct the heated air and smoke before they are vented to the open air. **2.** Same as **femerell.**

fummerell See **femerell.**

Functionalism A philosophy of architectural design, emerging in the 20th cent., asserting that the form of a building should follow its function, reveal its structure, and express the nature of the material.

fundula In the ancient Roman Empire, a blind alley; a **cul-de-sac.**

fundula

furnus **1.** A vapor bath, as distinguished from an ancient **bath, 3.** **2.** A baker's shop.

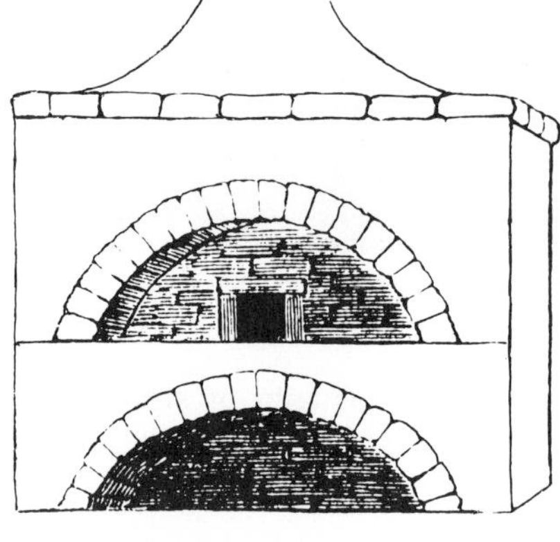

furnus, 2, Pompeii. *above:* the door where the baking was done

fusarole A molding of convex rounded section, commonly carved into beads and the like.

fusorium In ancient Roman construction, a drain.

fusuma A sliding interior partition used in Japanese domestic or temple architecture; its exterior frame is plain or lacquered wood; its core is composed of a wood lattice framework which is covered with heavy paper or cloth; the surface may be decorated with an all-over pattern or with ink paintings. 襖

fusurole Same as **fusarole.**

fymrell Same as **femerell.**

fynial Same as **finial.**

gable **1.** The vertical triangular portion of the end of a building having a double-sloping roof, from the level of the cornice or eaves to the ridge of the roof. **2.** A similar end when not triangular in shape, as of a gambrel roof or the like.

gable,1: Shrewsbury Abbey (c. 1360; the window c. 1600)

gable,2

gableboard A **bargeboard.**

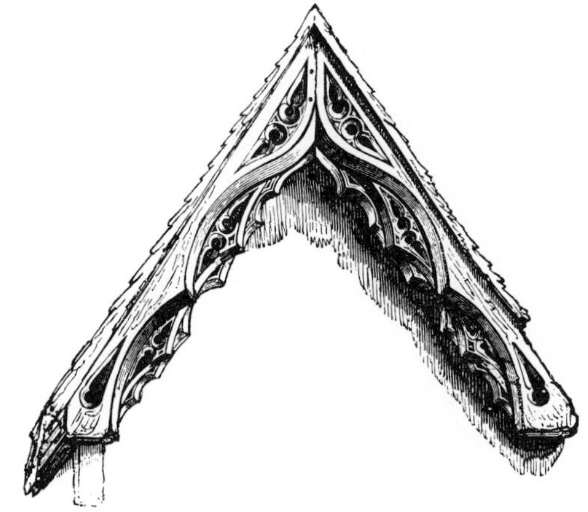

gableboard

gabled tower A tower finished with a gable on two sides or on all sides, instead of terminating in a spire, or the like.

gabled tower, Dormans, France

gable end **1.** An end wall having a **gable.** **2.** A **gable.**

gable post A short post located at the peak of a gable into which the **bargeboards** are fixed.

gable roof A roof having a gable at one or both ends.

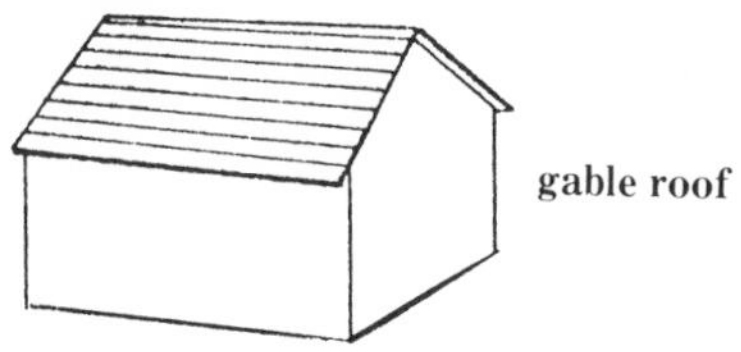
gable roof

gable shoulder Projecting brickwork or masonry which supports the foot of a gable.

gable springer, skew block, skew butt A **kneeler, 1** (esp. a projecting one) which is at the foot of a gable or the like.

gablet A small ornamental gable.

gablet

gable wall A wall which is crowned by a gable.

gable window 1. A window in a gable. 2. A window shaped like a gable.

gadroon, godroon An ornament composed chiefly of ovoid or more elongated bosses regularly repeated, side by side.

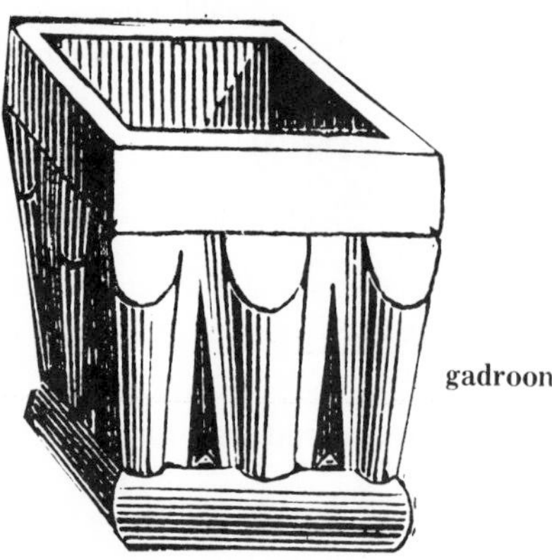
gadroon

gaine 1. A decorative pedestal, esp. one tapered downward and rectangular in cross section, forming the lower part of a **herm.** 2. Such a pedestal on which a human bust is mounted, often with a capital above, which takes the place of a pilaster or column.

gaine

galilee, Durham Cathedral (end of 12th cent.)

galilee **1.** A narthex or chapel for worship at the west end of a church. **2.** A chapel connected with some early medieval churches, to which monks returned after processions, in which ecclesiastics were allowed to meet women who were related to them, and where the worthy dead were buried.

galilee porch A galilee when it has direct communication with the exterior, and thus can be considered as a vestibule to the main church.

gallery 1. A long, covered area acting as a corridor inside or on the exterior of a building, or between buildings. 2. An elevated area, interior or exterior, e.g., minstrel gallery, music gallery, roof gallery. 3. An elevated section of the seating area of an auditorium, esp. the uppermost such space. 4. In buildings for public worship, a similar space, sometimes set apart for special uses. 5. A service passageway within a building, or linking a building underground to exterior supplies or exits. Some service galleries also serve sightseers, e.g., the lighting gallery in the base of the dome at St. Peter's, Rome. 6. A long, narrow room for special activities. 7. A room, often top-lit, used for the display of art works. 8. A building serving such art needs. 9. See **long gallery.** 10. An **arcade,** 2.

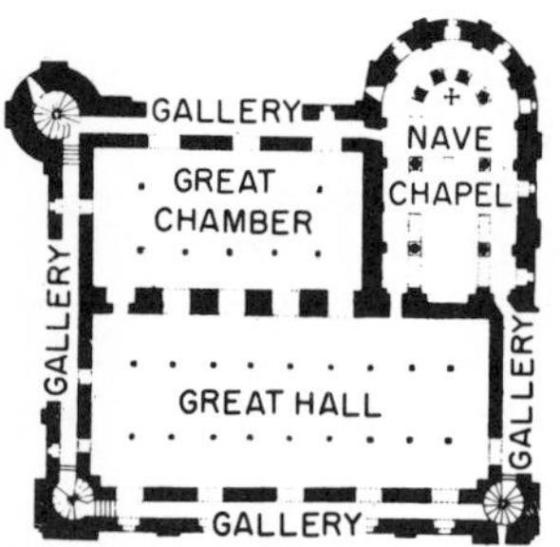

gallery, 1: plan of the keep, White Tower, Tower of London (late 11th cent. onward)

gallery, 4: Exeter Cathedral (c. 1300)

gallery, 1: Jardin de Montargis

galleries, 4: Cathedral of Amiens (13th cent.)

gallery grave A prehistoric burial place in which the entrance passage and burial chamber were merged, forming a long stone-lined gallery.

gallet A stone chip or **spall.**

galleting, garreting The insertion of stone chips into the joints of rough masonry to reduce the amount of mortar required, to wedge larger stones in position, or to add detail to the appearance.

gallows See **fourches patibulaires.**

gambhara In Jain architecture (India), a sanctuary cell.

gambrel roof, gambrel **1.** *(U.S.A.)* A roof which has two pitches on each side; in Great Britain called a **mansard roof.** **2.** *(Brit.)* A roof which has a small gable near the ridge on one end; the part of the roof below the gable is inclined.

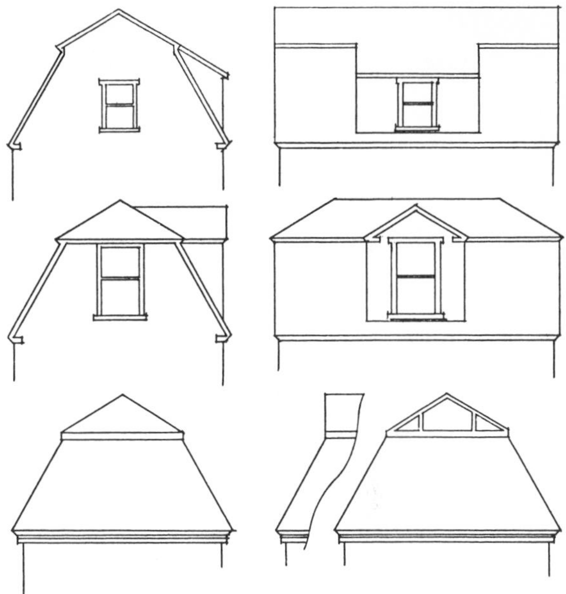

types of gambrel roofs

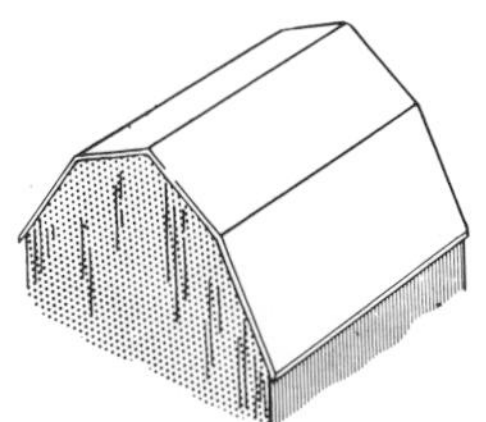

gambrel roof,1

gami Same as **jami.**

garbha-griha The dark, innermost sanctuary of a Hindu temple, where the statue of the deity is placed.

garden house A summer house in a garden or a garden-like situation.

garden house: pavilion, Baux (16th cent.)

garden wall bond See **English garden wall bond, Flemish garden wall bond, mixed garden wall bond.**

garden wall cross bond In brickwork, a bond in which a course of **headers** alternates with a course consisting of a header followed by three **stretchers.**

garderobe **1.** See **wardrobe.** **2.** A small bedroom or study. **3.** Euphemism for a latrine in medieval buildings.

garetta Same as **garretta.**

gargoyle (Gothic examples)

gargoyle A waterspout projecting from the roof gutter of a building, often carved grotesquely.

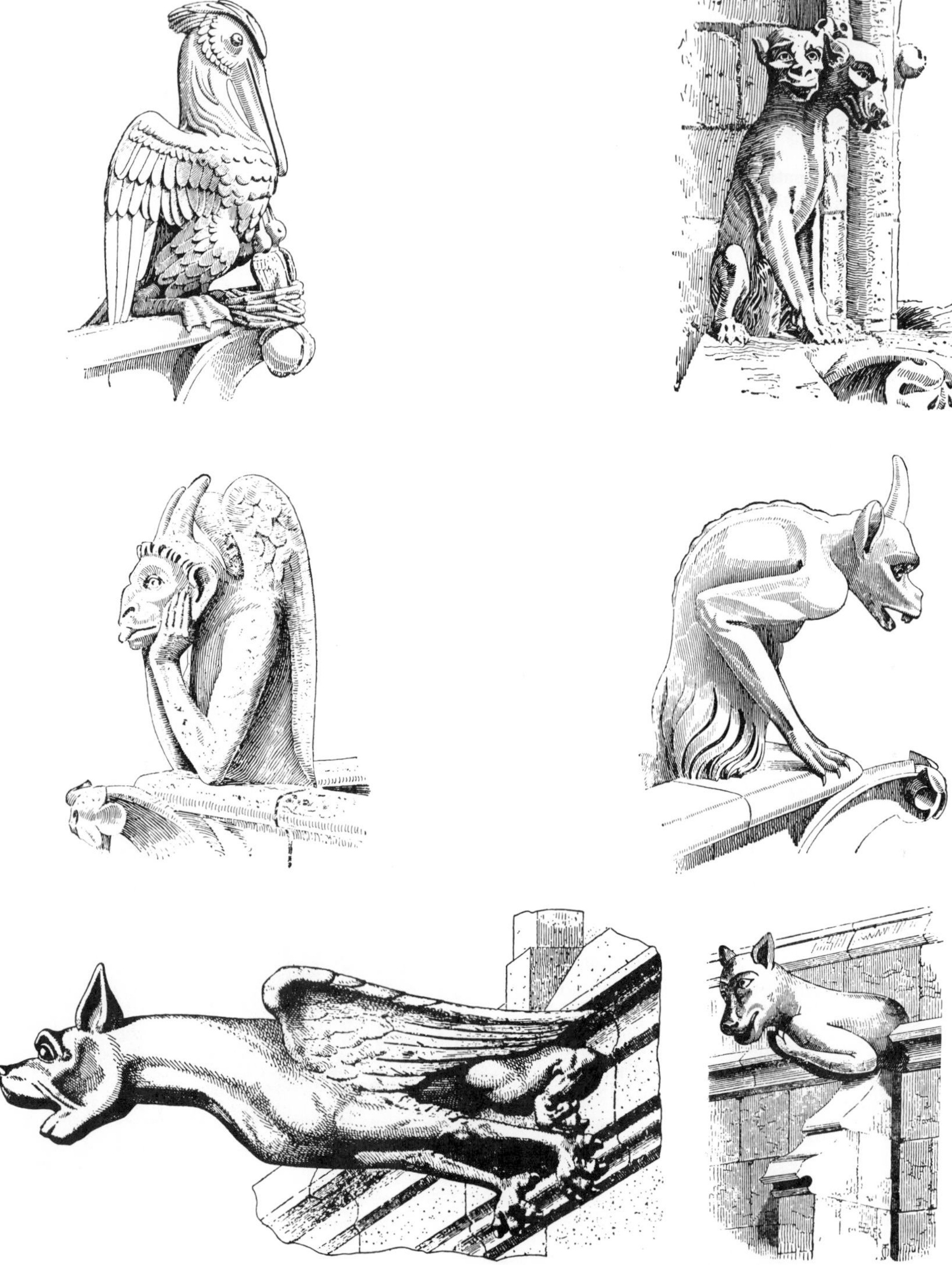

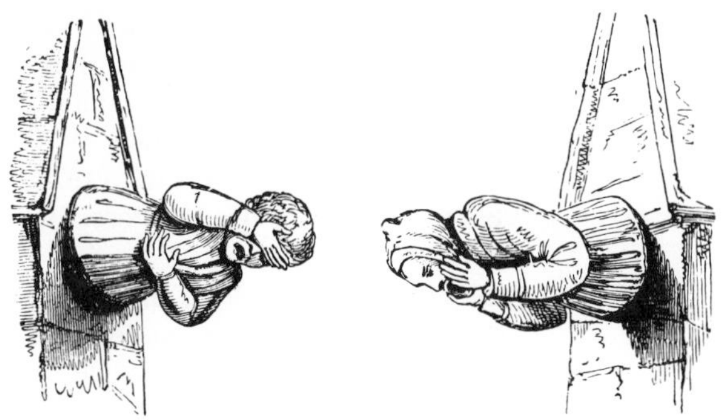

Merton College Chapel, Oxford (c. 1277)

Horsley Church, Derbyshire (c. 1450)

Merton College Chapel, Oxford (c. 1277)

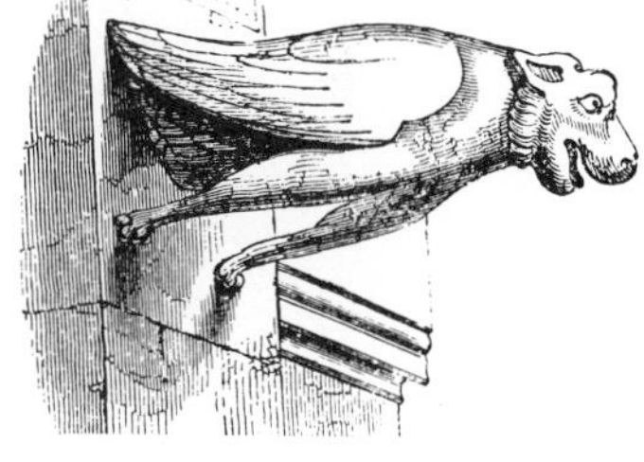

Howden, Yorkshire (c. 1350)

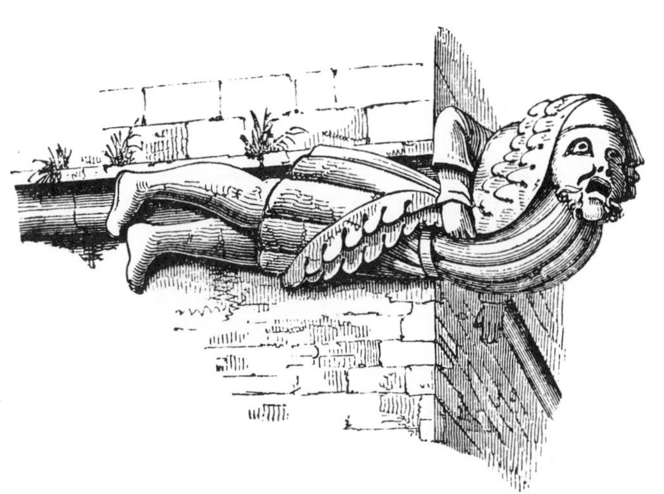

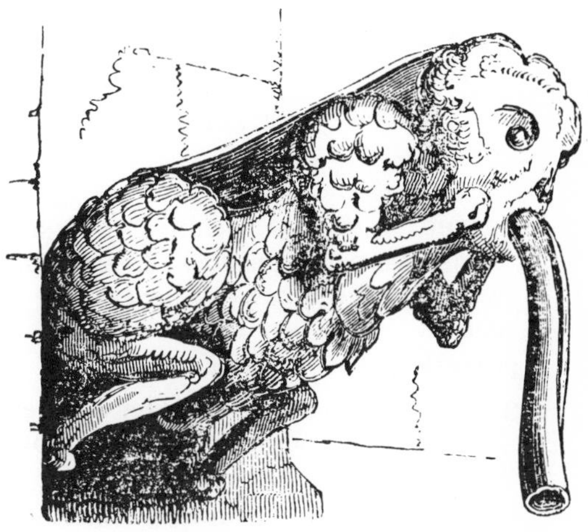

St. Alkmund's, Derby

garland An ornament in the form of a band, a wreath, or a **festoon** of leaves, fruits, or flowers.

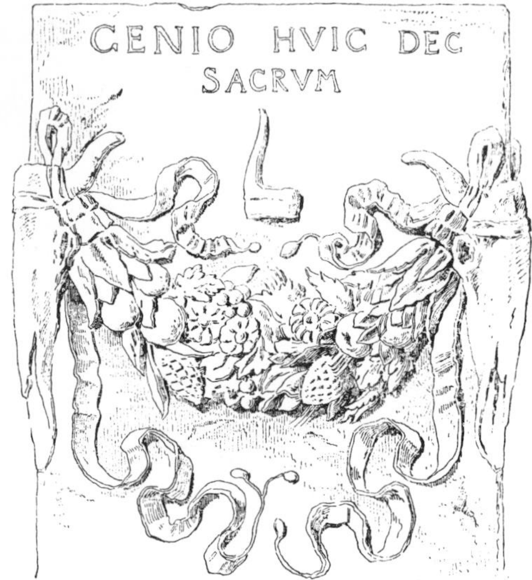

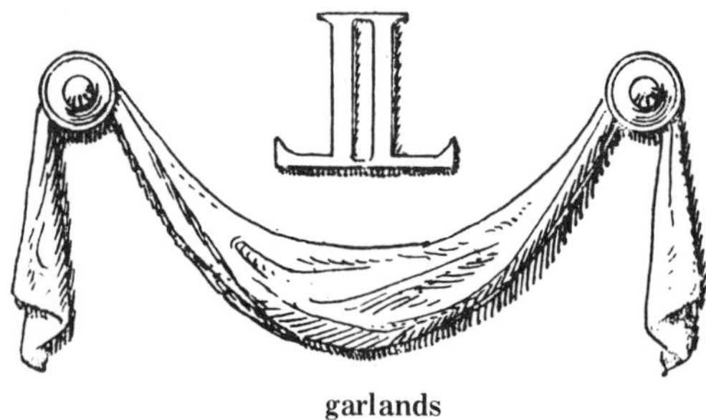

garlands

garret **1.** Space within a roof structure; sometimes called an **attic.** **2.** A room, usually with sloping ceilings, just beneath the roof of a house.

garreting See **galleting.**

garretta A medieval term for a turret on the battlements of a castle or house to provide protection for a soldier.

garrison house **1.** An early American fort to protect settlers from the Indians. **2.** A colonial house, of logs or heavy timber, whose second story projected beyond the first-story façade.

garth The open courtyard of a cloister, often a lawn.

gasshō style, gasshō-zukuri A type of construction associated with farmhouses in Japan; consists of an A-frame in which the roof rafters are joined at the ridge of the roof and spread widely apart at their lower ends.

gatch Plaster as used in Persia for decorative purposes.

gatehouse A building, enclosing or accompanying a gateway for a castle, manor house, or similar buildings of importance.

gatehouse

gate pier A brick, concrete, or stone **hanging post.**

gatepost See **hanging post.**

gate tower A tower containing a gate to a fortress.

gate tower, Walmargate Bar, York (c. 16th cent.)

gateway **1.** A passage through a fence or wall. **2.** A frame, arch, etc., in which a gate is hung. **3.** A structure at an entrance or gate designed for ornament or defense.

gateway, Merton College, Oxford (1416)

gauged arch An arch of wedge-shaped bricks which have been shaped so that the joints radiate from a common center.

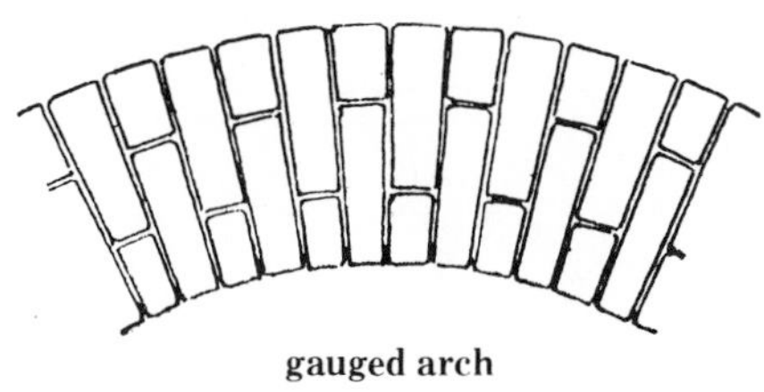

gauged arch

gauged work A precise brickwork in which bricks are cut or sawn to shape and then rubbed to an exact size and smooth finish.

gavaksa, gavaksha A **dormer** or latticed window in Buddhist and Hindu structures.

gazebo **1.** A summerhouse with a view. **2.** A **belvedere.**

gazebo

gazophylacium A place where precious items were deposited, as a treasury in a palace or in a church.

gegyō In a traditional Japanese structure, a decorative pendant which hangs from the intersection of the bargeboards at the peak of the gable.

geison A cornice.

gelbai In Indian architecture, the carving around a doorway.

gemel, chymol, gimmer, gymmer, jimmer **1.** Two corresponding elements of construction considered as a pair. **2.** Ancient term for a hinge.

gemel window A window built into a pair of openings; a window having two bays.

geminated Coupled, as in **coupled columns.**

geminated capitals, Sicily (12th cent.)

gemmel Same as **gemel.**

玄関 **genkan** In a traditional Japanese structure, a vestibule or entrance hall where shoes are removed before entering the building.

genkan

gentese In Early English architecture, cusps in the arch of a doorway.

geometrical stair A stair constructed around a stairwell without the use of newels at the angles or turning points.

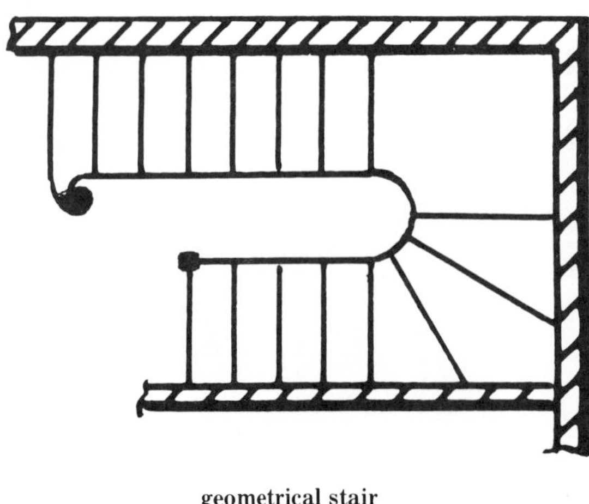

geometrical stair

Geometric style The early development of the Decorated style of English Gothic architecture, in the first half of the 14th cent., characterized by the geometrical forms of its window tracery.

Geometric style

geometric tracery Gothic openwork in the form of simple geometrical patterns, principally circles and multifoils.

geometric tracery

Georgian architecture The prevailing style of the 18th cent. in Great Britain and the North American colonies, so named after George I, George II, and George III (1714–1820), but commonly not including George IV. Derived from classical, Renaissance, and Baroque forms.

gesso A mixture of gypsum plaster, glue, and whiting; applied as a base coat for decorative painting.

ghanadvara A solid door through which the deity enshrined in a Hindu temple manifests itself.

ghat In India, a flight of steps leading to a river or other body of water.

Ghizeh See **Great Pyramid** and **Great Sphinx.**

giant order See **colossal order.**

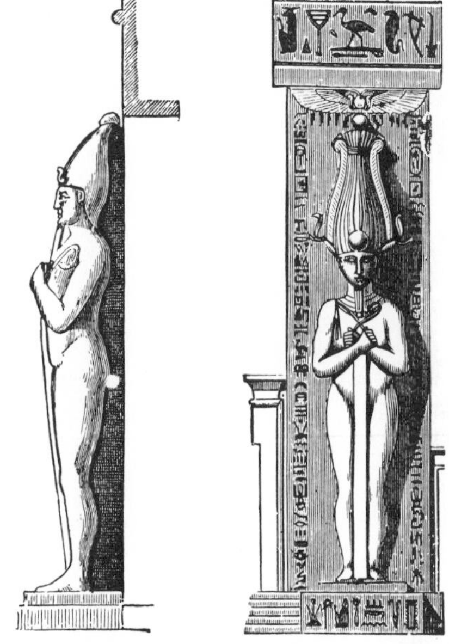

giant order statue (more than one story high) on a pier, Temple at Luxor

Ghusla ghat, Benares

Gibbs surround The **framing, 3** of a door or window by a head composed of a triple keystone and by jambs that are bordered by protruding blocks of stone; also see **surround, 1.**

gib door See **jib door.**

giglio A Florentine emblem like a **fleur-de-lys.**

gilding **1.** Gold leaf, gold flakes, brass, etc., applied as a surface finish. **2.** The surface so produced.

gimmer See **gemel.**

gingerbread The highly decorative woodwork applied to Gingerbread style houses, or the like.

Gibbs surround

Gingerbread style A richly decorated American building fashion of the 19th cent.

girandole A branched light holder, either standing on a base or projecting from a wall.

girder A large or principal beam used to support concentrated loads at isolated points along its length.

girdle A band, usually horizontal; esp. one ringing the shaft of a column.

girt, girth **1.** In a **braced frame,** a horizontal member at intermediate level between columns, studs, or posts. **2.** A heavy beam, framed into the studs, which supports the floor joists. **3.** One of the horizontal members, from column to column, which carry wall sheaths.

Giza See **Great Pyramid** and **Great Sphinx.**

glacis **1.** A sloped embankment in front of a fortification, so raised as to bring an advancing enemy into the most direct line of fire. **2.** The inclined surface of a cornice or projecting molding.

glaze **1.** A ceramic coating, usually thin, glossy, and glass-like, formed on the surface of pottery, earthenware, etc. **2.** The material from which the ceramic coating is made.

glazed work Brickwork built with enameled brick or glazed brick.

glory The luminous halo encircling the head of a sacred person and the radiance or luminous emanation encompassing the whole.

glory, Italy (14th cent.)

glukhaya glava In early Russian architecture, a blind cupola.

glukhie shatry In early Russian architecture, any blind building element, as a **blind window.**

glyph **1.** A sculpted pictograph. **2.** A groove or channel, usually vertical, intended as an ornament.

glyptic Pertaining to carving or engraving.

glyptotheca A sculpture gallery.

godown In India and the Far East, a storehouse of any description.

godroon See **gadroon.**

gojū-no-tō A five-storied pagoda. See **tō.**

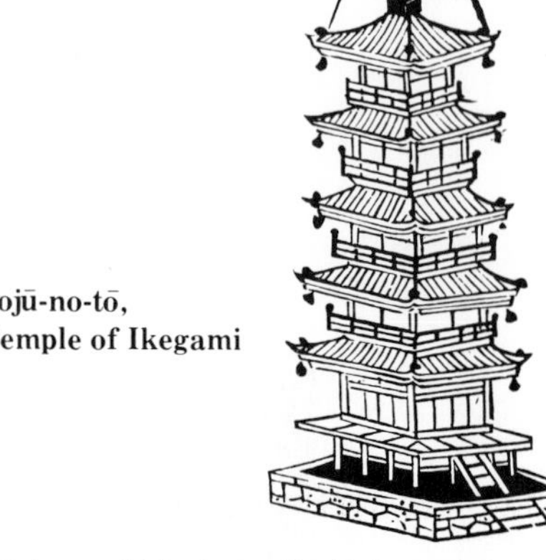
gojū-no-tō, Temple of Ikegami

gokhala In Jain architecture (India), a niche.

gola An **ogee.**

Golden Pavilion See **Kinkakuji.**

gold foil See **gold leaf.**

gold leaf Very thin sheets of beaten or rolled gold, used for gilding and inscribing on glass; usually contains a very small percentage of copper and silver. Sometimes heavy gold leaf is classified as gold foil.

gold size A varnish used to attach gold leaf or foil to a surface; it turns sticky quickly on application, and then sets slowly.

golosniki In early Russian architecture, acoustic resonators, made of clay, which were set into the upper portion of the walls of some churches; the mouth of the resonator faced the interior of the church and was flush with the wall surface. Such resonators also are found in some Greek Orthodox churches and early Scandinavian churches.

gomphi In ancient Roman construction, curbstones of greater size than usual; placed at regular intervals in a line of umbones (see **umbo, 2**).

gonge The Anglo-Saxon term for a privy.

gont A thin wood shingle, used for roofing in early Russian architecture.

good morning stairs In a **full Cape house,** the front stairs leading from the front hall to the attic rooms; at the chimney block the stairs turn both right and left, serving both sides of the house.

goose neck A curved section of a handrail which forms its termination at the top of a newel post.

gophus **1.** A large wedge-shaped pin driven between two objects to increase the tightness of contiguous members. **2.** Large, round-headed, wedge-shaped stones, placed at intervals between the ordinary curbstones bounding the foot pavements of ancient Roman roads and streets.

gopuram In Indian architecture, a monumental gateway.

gopuram at Kumbakonam

gore Same as **lune.**

gorge **1.** In some orders of columnar architecture, a narrow band around the shaft near the top, or forming part of the capital near the bottom; a fillet or narrow member which seems to divide the capital from the shaft. **2.** A **cavetto** or hollow molding. **3.** A narrow entry into a bastion.

gorge cornice Same as **Egyptian gorge.**

gorgerin See **hypotrachelium.**

gorgoneion In classical decoration, the mask of a Gorgon, a woman with snakes for hair, to avert evil influences.

御所 **Gosho** The imperial palace in Kyōto, Japan, rebuilt in the mid-nineteenth century in a style resembling that of the Heian period **Shinden style.** Important structures include: The Shishinden (official ceremonial hall); the Seiryōden (emperor's residence); the Kogosho (meeting place for poetry recitation, etc.); the Higyōsha (empress's quarters).

gospel hall House for Protestant Christian worship.

Gospel side The north side of a church (when the main altar is at the east), from which the Gospel is read.

Gothic arch A loose term denoting a **pointed arch.**

Gothic architecture

Gothic architecture The architectural style of the High Middle Ages in Western Europe, which emerged from Romanesque and Byzantine forms in France during the later 12th cent. Its great works are cathedrals, characterized by the pointed arch, the rib vault, the development of the exterior flying buttress, and the gradual reduction of the walls to a system of richly decorated fenestration. Gothic architecture lasted until the 16th cent., when it was succeeded by the classical forms of the Renaissance. In France and Germany one speaks of the Early, High, and Late Gothic; the French middle phase is referred to as Rayonnant, the late phase as Flamboyant. In English architecture the usual divisions are Early English, Decorated, and Perpendicular.

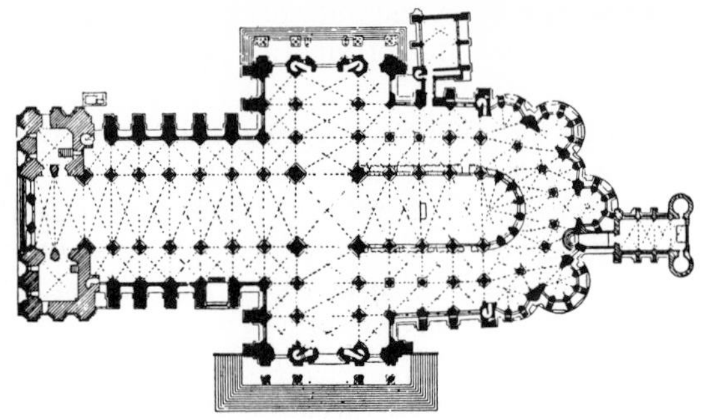

plan, Chartres Cathedral (1194-1260)

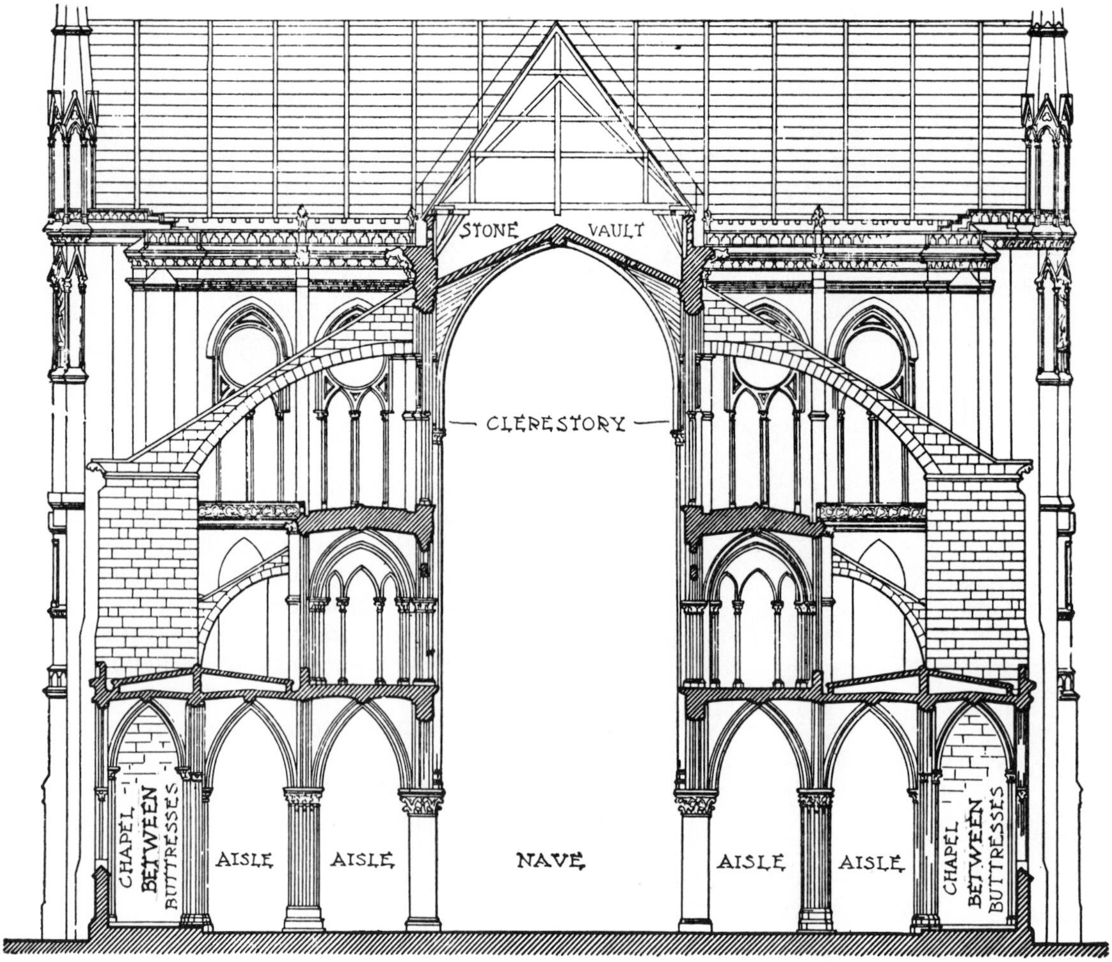

Notre Dame, Paris: section

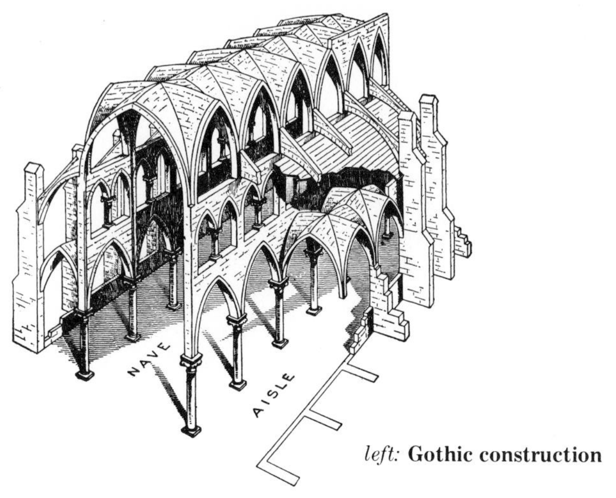

left: **Gothic construction**

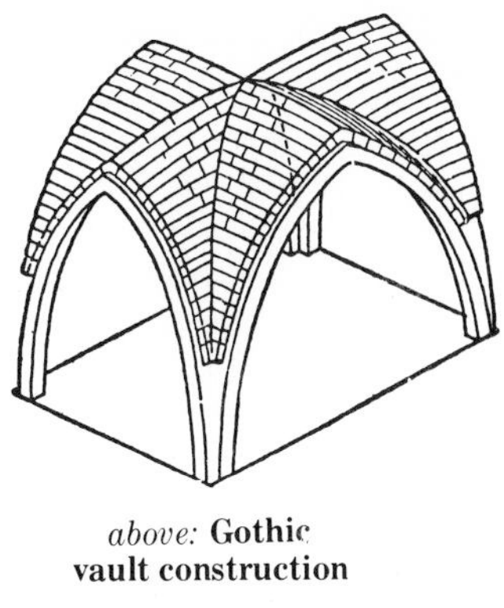

above: **Gothic vault construction**

façade, west front, Notre Dame (1214)

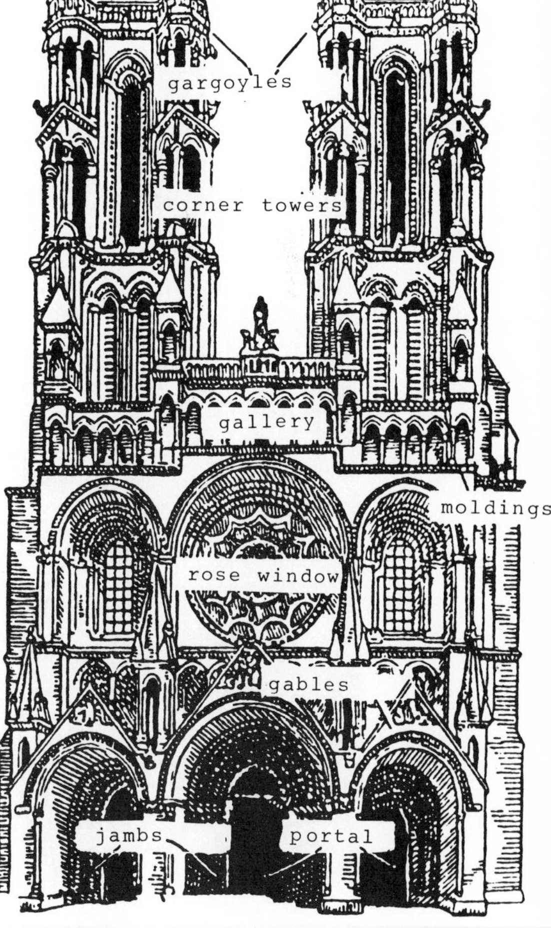

terminology: Gothic church, west front

late Gothic: east end, Church of St. Barbara, Kuttenberg (1358–1548)

Gothic architecture

German Gothic 5-aisle cathedral, Cologne (1248 onward)

left: **exterior elevation of aisle wall and clerestory**
center: **section**
right: **interior elevation of nave wall**

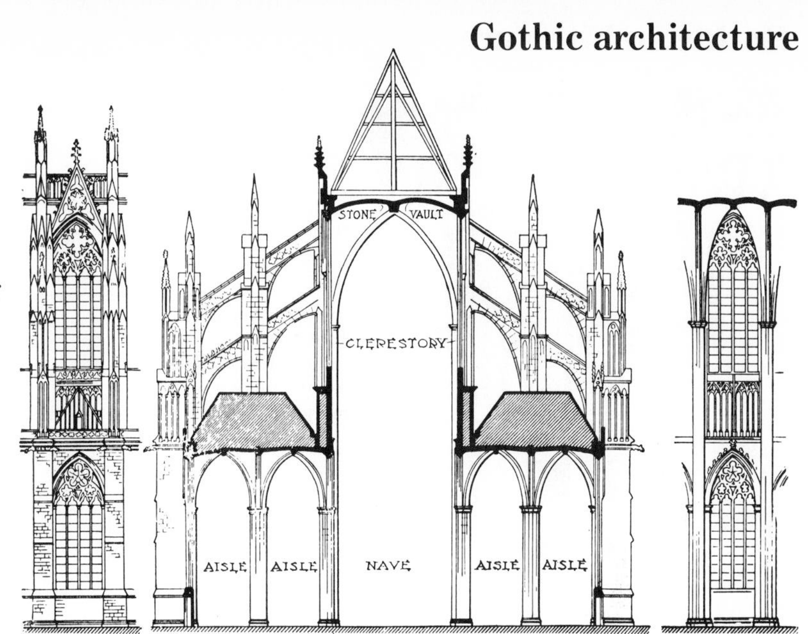

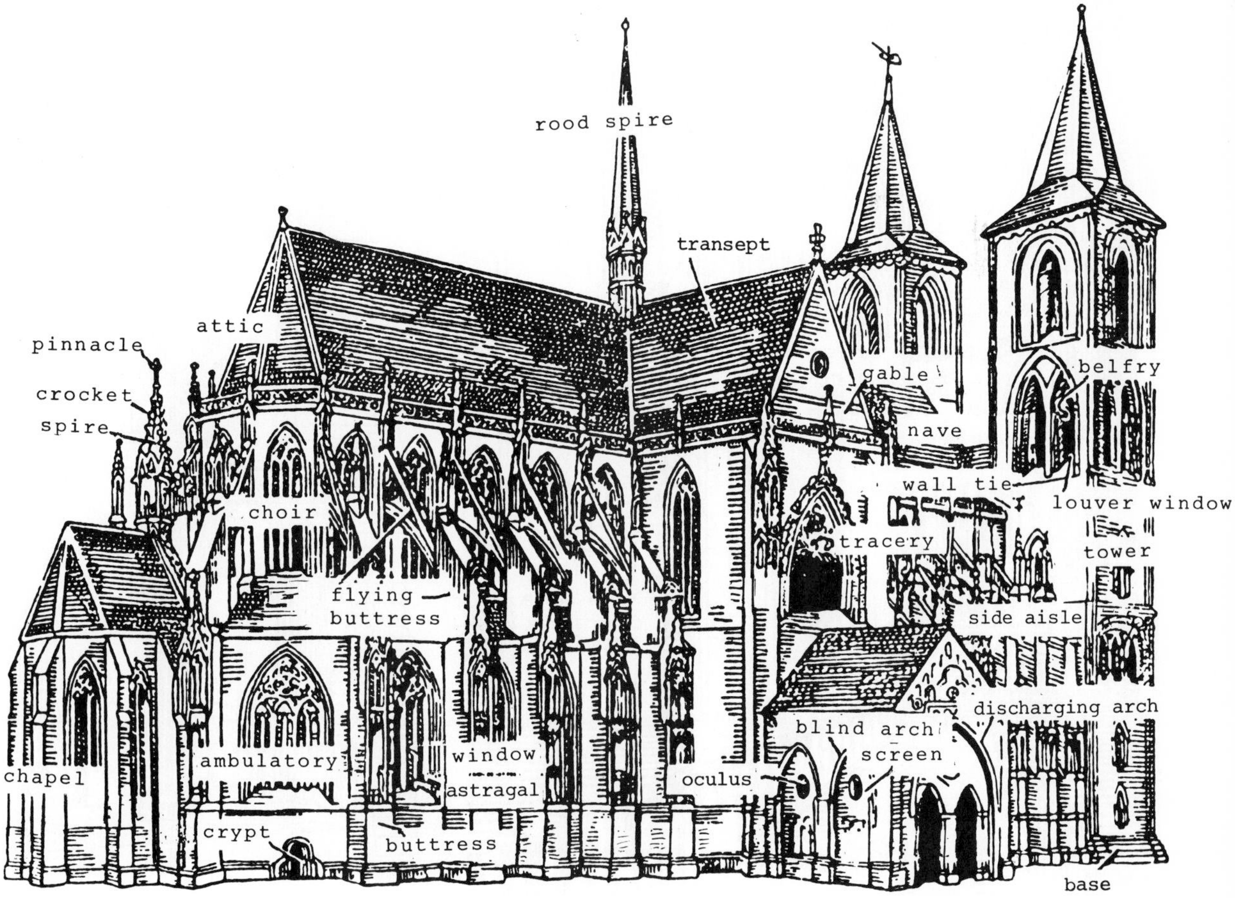

rood spire
transept
attic
pinnacle
crocket
spire
choir
gable
belfry
nave
wall tie
louver window
tracery
tower
flying buttress
side aisle
discharging arch
blind arch
screen
window
chapel
ambulatory
oculus
astragal
crypt
buttress
base

terminology: Gothic cathedral

Gothic architecture

left: **secular Gothic architecture. Façade of Knight Hall, Castle of Marienburg (completed 1360)**

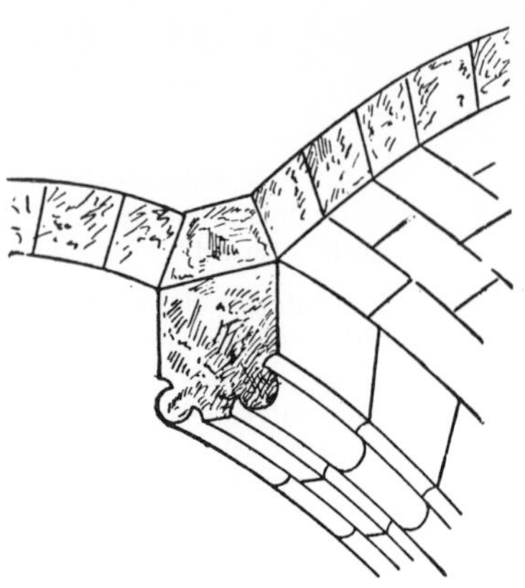

relation of rib to shell of vault

terminology: interior of Gothic church

construction, Amiens Cathedral (1220–88)

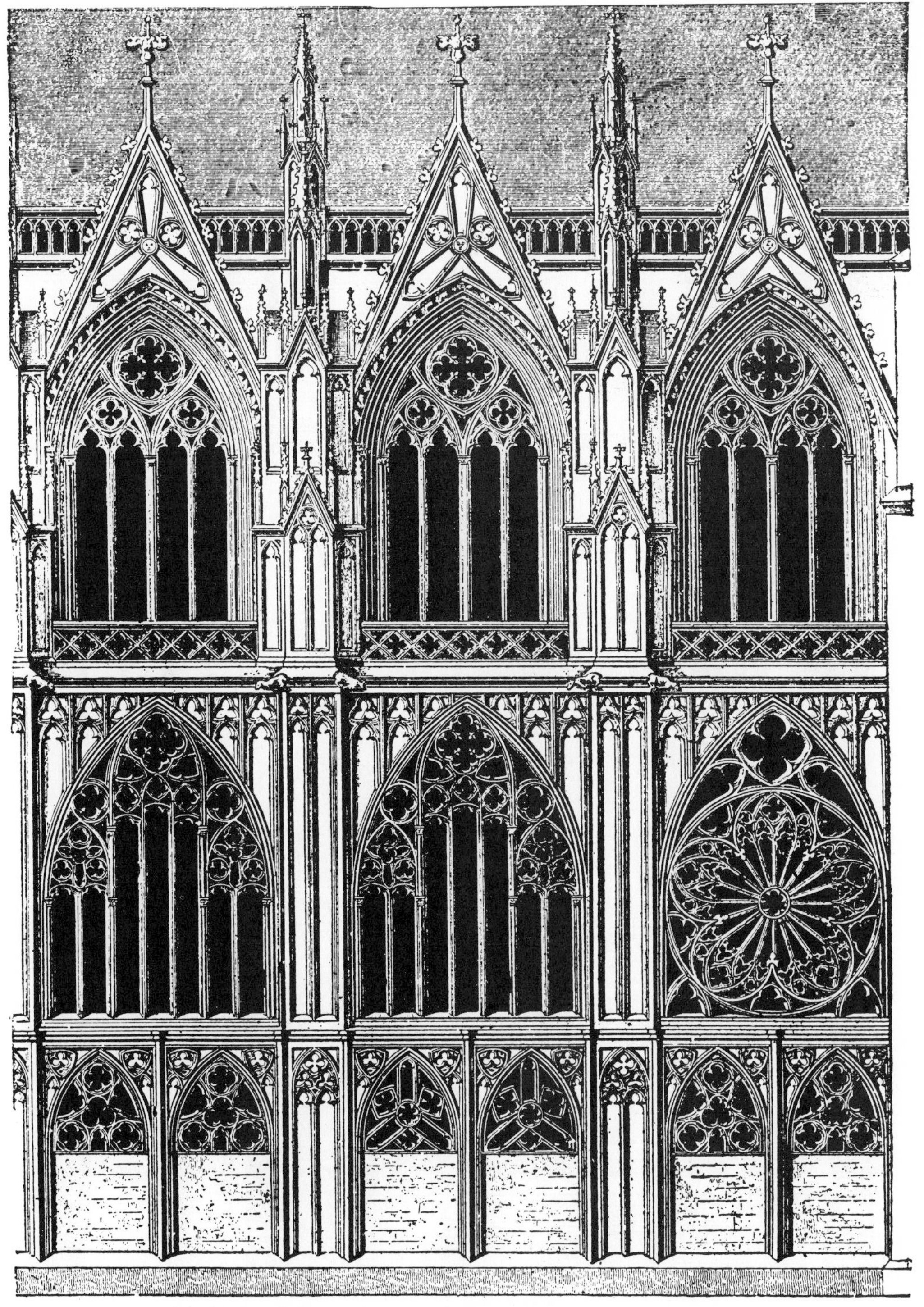

Gothic tracery, Church of St. Katherine, Oppenheim, Germany
(early 14th cent.)

Italian Gothic: part of façade of Florence Cathedral
(1296–1462)

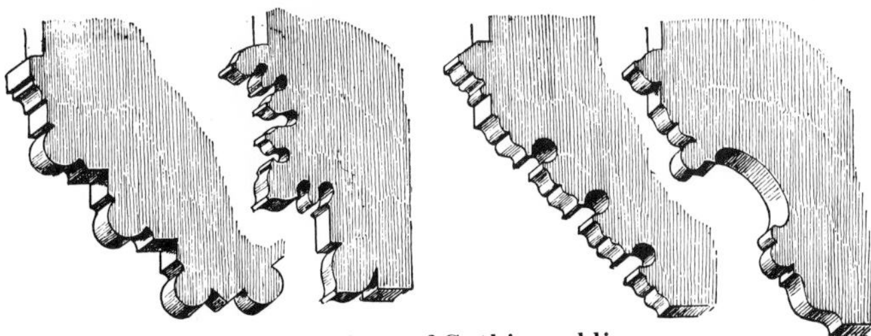

sections of Gothic moldings

cornice and capital, Notre Dame, Paris

portal, Church of Thann (14th cent.)

gable, Rouen Cathedral (1202–30 and later)

Gothic Revival A movement originating in the 18th and culminating in the 19th cent., flourishing throughout Europe and the U.S.A., which aimed at reviving the spirit and forms of Gothic architecture.

Gothic Revival cottage

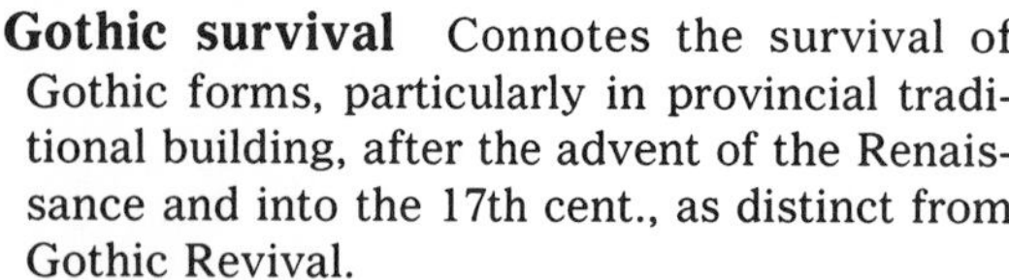

Gothic survival Connotes the survival of Gothic forms, particularly in provincial traditional building, after the advent of the Renaissance and into the 17th cent., as distinct from Gothic Revival.

gouache **1.** A method of painting, using opaque pigments pulverized in water and mixed with gum. **2.** A painting so made. **3.** An opaque color used in the process.

government house **1.** Building for the offices of the main departments of government, esp. in English colonies or Commonwealth nations. **2.** Governor's state home, esp. in a Crown colony.

gradetto Same as **annulet.**

gradine, gradino **1.** A step. **2.** A raised shelf above and at the back of an altar.

gradino Same as **predella.**

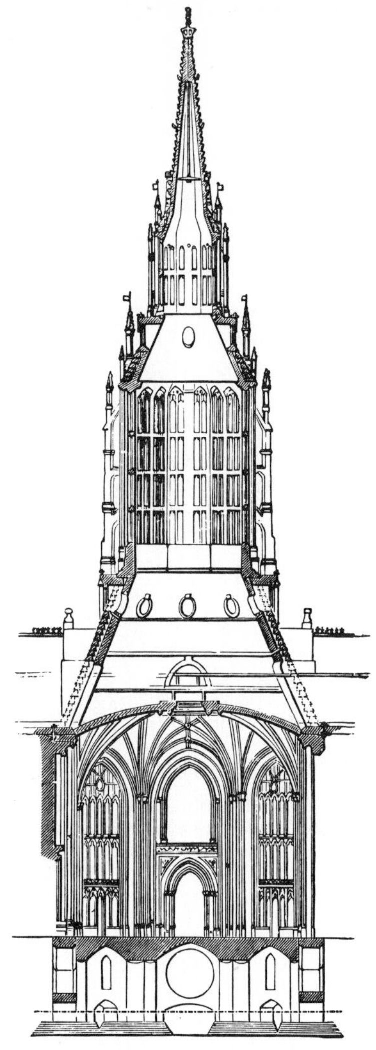

Gothic Revival: section of Central Hall, Houses of Parliament

Graecostasis In the Roman Forum, a platform where the ambassadors from foreign states stood to hear debates and attend ceremonies.

graffito Casual remark or depiction drawn on a wall; not synonymous with **sgraffito.**

grass table Same as **ground table.**

gre See **grees.**

great house The main or central residence of an estate or plantation.

Great Mosque of Córdoba An outstanding example of Islamic architecture, begun in 780 A.D. Originally a mosque having 11 naves and 12 bays, with a courtyard of the same size. To increase the height of the interior, a second arcade was superimposed on the first, carried by brackets on impost blocks over the column capitals. More than 600 columns support its arches; these columns, of various colors, were spoils from Roman and Christian churches; adjacent voussoirs are alternately brick and stone. Colorful mosaics, carved stucco friezes, marble revetments, and richly carved wood ceilings added to the brilliance of the interior. The mosque underwent a number of extensions, increasing its size to its present length of 32 bays. The original arches were horseshoe-shaped in the lower tiers and semicircular in the upper tiers; the new construction added an array of variously decorated cinquefoil arches and intersecting arches as well as horseshoe arches.

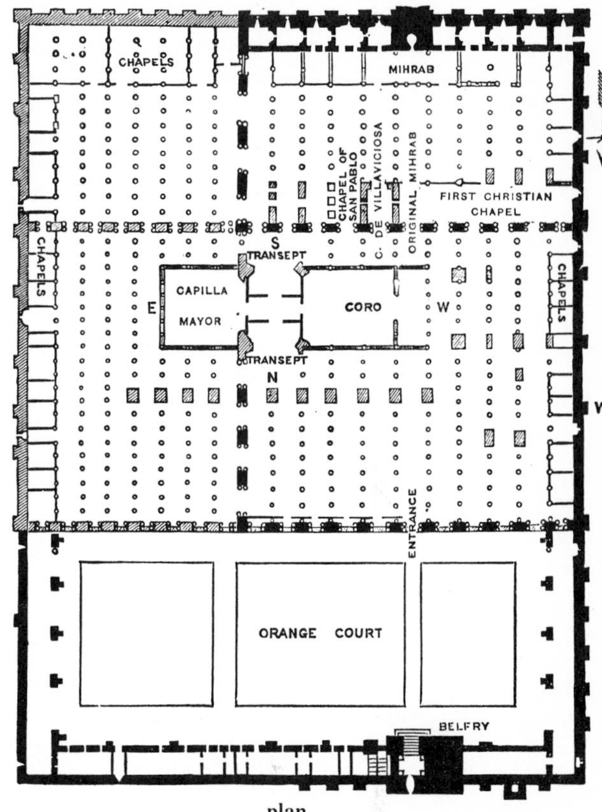

plan

interior view

screen of Chapel de Villa Viciosa

Great Pyramid The largest of three **pyramids** at El Gizeh near Cairo, which were built as tombs for royalty. The square base averages 756 ft (230.4 m) on a side; it rose in 201 steps to a height of 481 ft (146.6 m); more than 2,500,000 blocks of granite and limestone were used in its construction. Believed to have been built for King Khufu (Cheops) of the IVth dynasty. The only one of the Seven Wonders of the World still in existence.

Great Sphinx The most celebrated example of a **sphinx,** near the **Great Pyramid** of El Gizeh, hewn from a single sandstone knoll, with the recumbent body of a lion and a man's head; 244 ft (74.4 m) long, 66 ft (20.1 m) high, and 13 ft 8 in. (4.2 m) broad at its widest point; the head is 28½ ft (8.7 m) high from chin to crown. At one time a small temple stood between the forepaws.

Great Sphinx (c. 2600 B.C.)

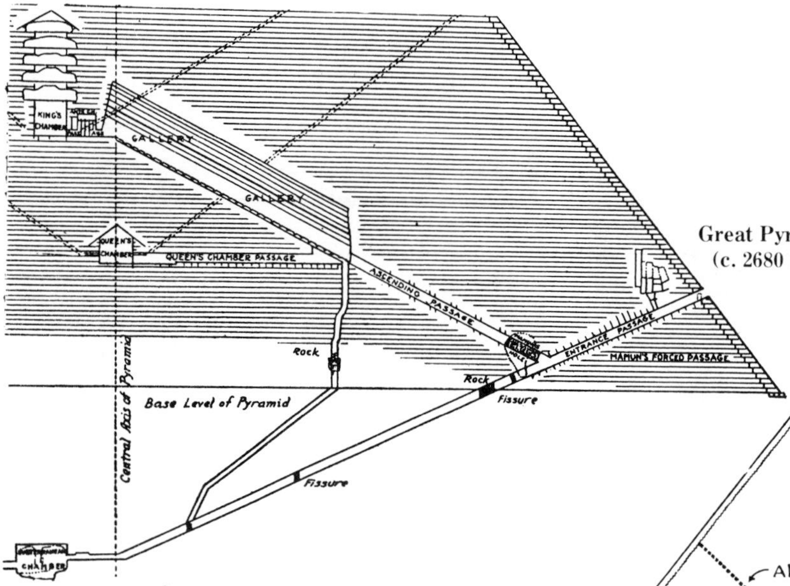

Great Pyramid of Cheops (c. 2680 B.C.): section detail

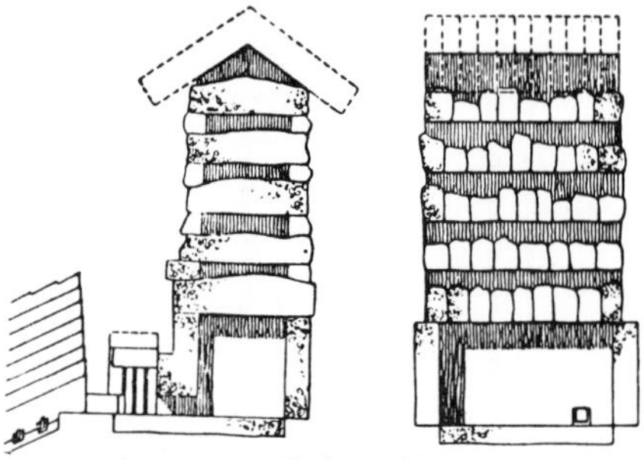

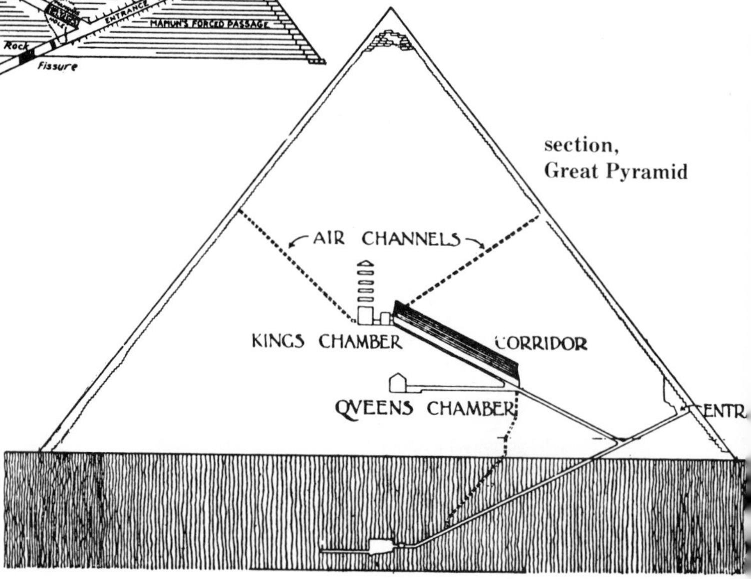

section, Great Pyramid

transverse *(left)* and longitudinal sections through the king's chamber

Great Wall of China A wall with crenelated parapets over 1,500 miles (2,400 km) long, between China and Mongolia, providing a massive system of fortifications with watchtowers at regular intervals, protecting China against nomads from the north; built in 3rd cent. B.C., rebuilt and refaced repeatedly. The only man-made structure visible from outer space. See **fêng huo t'ai.**

grece Same as **grees.**

Greek cross A cross with four equal arms.

Greek cross

Greek foot An ancient Greek measure of length, equal to 12.15 in. (30.9 cm).

Greek house The ancient Greek house varied in design according to the period and the wealth of the owner, but there were common features. The house was divided into two parts; the men's apartments (**andron**) and the women's apartments (**gynaeceum** or **gynaekonitis**). The entrance door of the house opened into a vestibule (**prothyron**); on both sides of the vestibule, in the interior, were the doorkeeper's room and shops for business and work. The vestibule led to an open court (**aula**) which was surrounded on three sides by columns, in the middle of which was the altar of Zeus Herkeios, the patron deity of domestic life. Large houses usually had a second court entirely surrounded by columns. At the sides of the aula were rooms for eating, sleeping, and storage, as well as cells for the slaves. On the sides of the court opposite the vestibule there were no columns, but two pilasters which marked the entrance to an open room or vestibule called the **prostas** or **parastas.** On one side of the parastas was the sleeping room of the master and mistress of the house (**thalamos**). Some houses had an upper story, usually smaller in area than the lower story. The roof of the Greek house usually was flat. The rooms usually were lighted through doors which opened into a court.

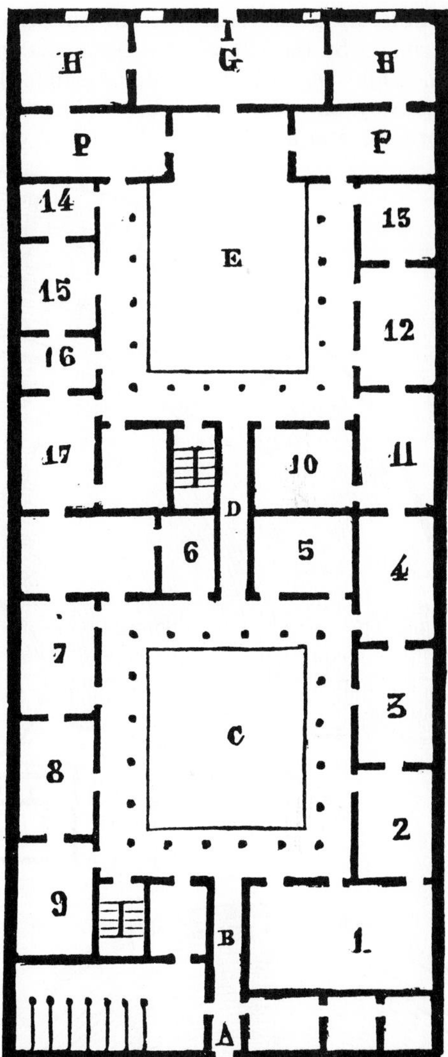

Greek house: *AB*, entrance passage with stables on the left and the porter's lodge on the right; *C*, aula of the men's quarters, surrounded by porticoes and the men's apartments, 1–9; *D*, passage which led to the aula of the gynaeceum, the chambers for the women (10–19); *E*, aula; *G* and *HH*, rooms for working in wool; *I*, garden gate; and *PP*, thalamos and amphithalamos

Greek key See **fret.**

Greek masonry See **isodomum.**

Greek Revival See **Classic Revival.**

Greek theatre

Greek theatre An open-air theatre constructed by the ancient Greeks; usually built on a hillside, with no outside facade. The **orchestra,** 1, on which the actors and chorus performed, was a full circle; behind it was the **skene,** a temporary or permanent building for the actors' use. In the classic theatre, the seating area (around and facing the orchestra) usually occupied approx. three-fifths of a circle. Also see **Roman theatre.**

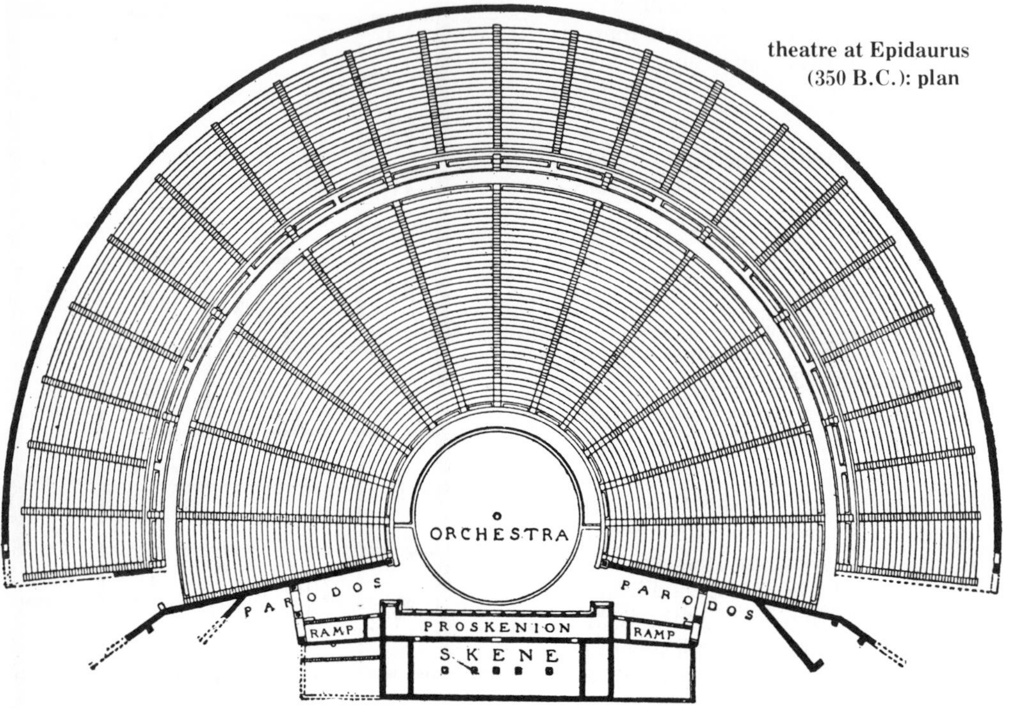

theatre at Epidaurus (350 B.C.): plan

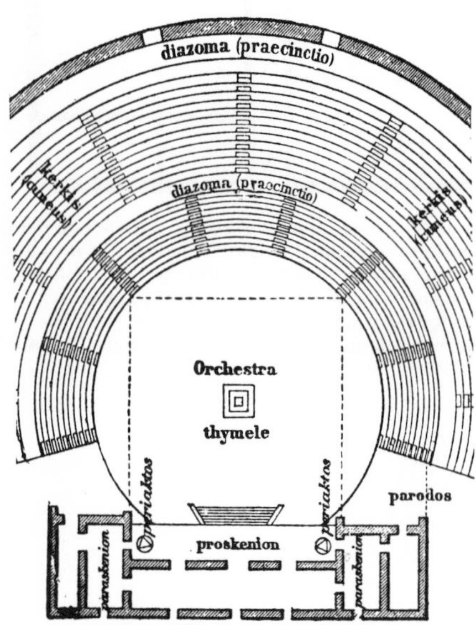

portion of theatre showing the diazoma and thymele

theatre at Oeniadae (c. 219 B.C.) showing the orchestra, stage building, and a portion of the seating

green **1.** An open space or public park in the center of a town or village. **2.** A bowling green or putting green.

grees, gre, greese, gryse In medieval architecture, a step or flight of steps.

griffe See **spur, 1.**

griffin, griffon, gryphon A mythological beast having a lion's body with an eagle's head and wings; used decoratively.

griffin

grille A grating or openwork barrier, usually of metal but sometimes of wood or stone; used to cover, conceal, decorate, or protect an opening, as in a wall, floor, or outdoor paving.

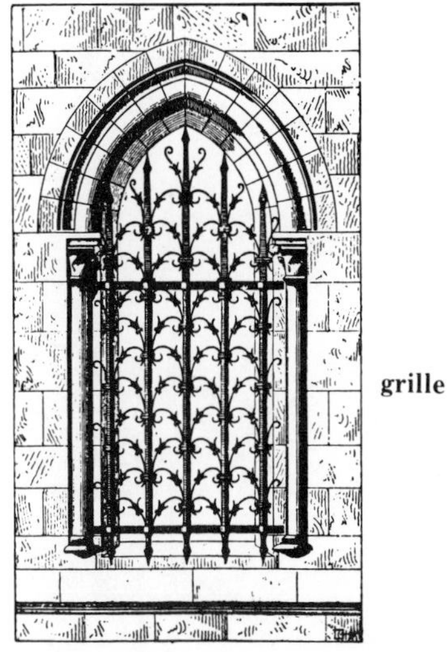

grille

grillwork Material which functions as, or has the appearance of, a **grille.**

grisaille **1.** A system of painting in grey tints of various shades; used either for decoration or to represent objects, as in relief. **2.** A stained glass window executed according to this method.

groin The ridge, edge, or curved line formed by the intersection of the surfaces of two intersecting vaults.

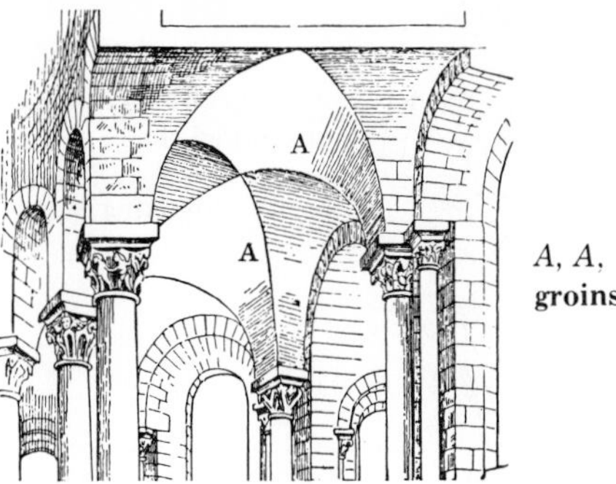

A, A, groins

groin arch, **1.** One arched division of a **cross vault.** **2.** An arch formed by the intersection of two simple vaults. **3.** A transverse arch which separates each bay in a vault.

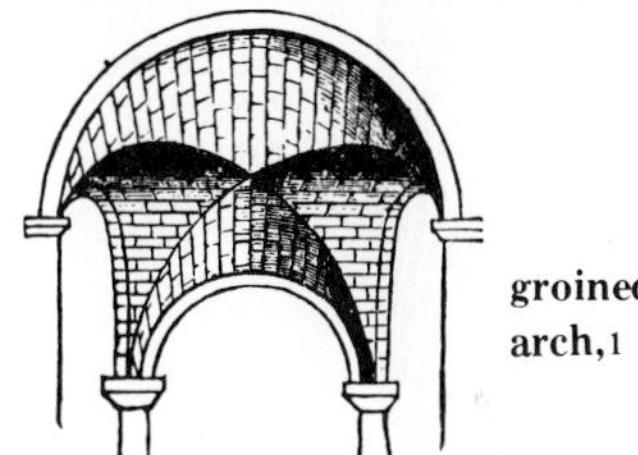

groined arch, 1

groin centering **1.** In groining without ribs, the **centering** of timber extended during construction under the whole surface. **2.** In ribbed or groined work, the centering for the stone ribs, which need support until their arches are closed, after which the supports for the filling of the spandrils are sustained by the ribs themselves.

groined **1.** Having groins. **2.** Showing the curved lines resulting from the intersection of two semicylinders or arches.

Norman groined roof

groined rib A rib under the curve of a groin, either to mask the groin or to support it.

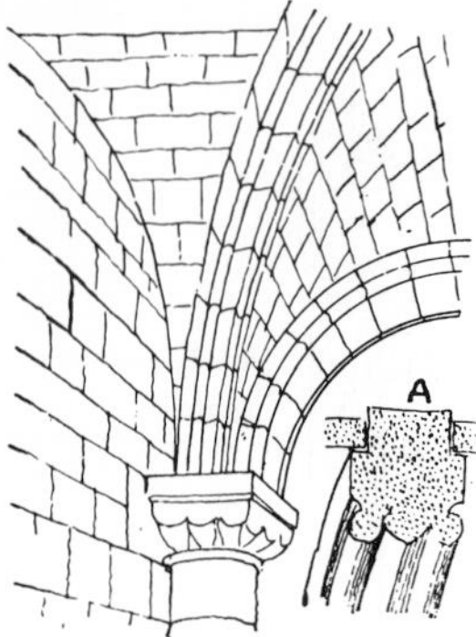

A: enlarged section of groined rib and vaulting surface abutting it

a, transverse ribs;
b, pier arches;
c, groined ribs

groined vault, groin vault A compound vault in which **barrel vaults** intersect, forming arrises called **groins.**

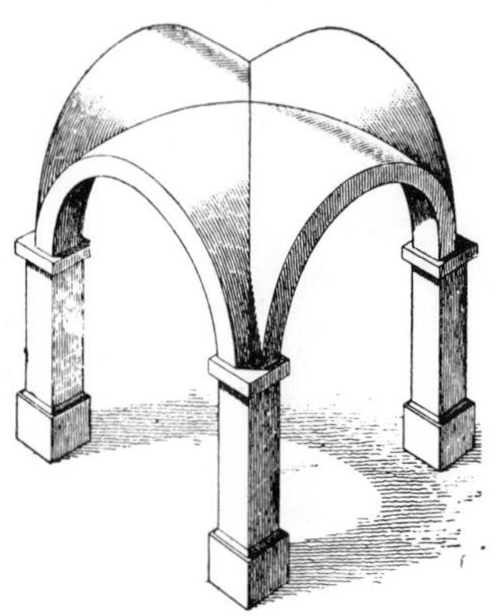

groined vault

groining Any system of vaulting implying the intersection, at any angle, of simple vaults.

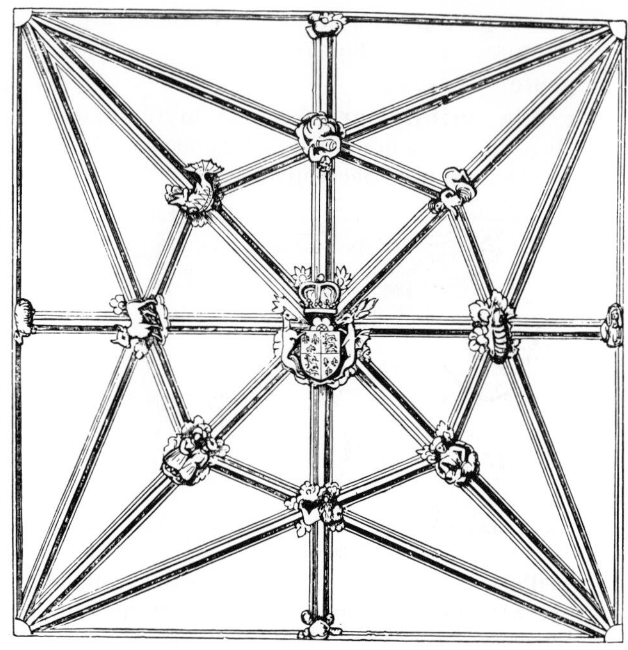

ceiling plan, groining, Merton College, Oxford (1490)

groining, aisle of Kirkstall Abbey (1052)

groin rib See **groined rib.**

groin vault Same as **groined vault.**

grotesque Sculptured or painted ornament involving fanciful distortions of human and animal forms, sometimes combined with plant motifs, esp. a variety of arabesque which has no counterpart in nature.

grotesque capitals, Saint-Etienne, Caen: Romanesque (c. 1068–1115)

grotto A natural or artificial cave, often decorated with shells or stones and incorporating waterfalls or fountains.

ground beam See **groundsill.**

ground niche A **niche** whose base is on a level with the floor.

ground plate A **groundsill.**

groundsill, ground beam, ground plate, mudsill, sole plate In a framed structure, the sill which is nearest the ground or on the ground; used to distribute concentrated loads.

ground table, earth table, grass table A projecting course or plinth resting immediately upon the foundation; the lowest course visible above the ground.

grouped columns Three or more closely spaced columns forming a group, often on one pedestal.

grouped pilasters Three or more closely spaced pilasters forming a group, often on one pedestal.

group house, row house One of an unbroken line of houses having a common wall or party wall with its neighbors.

grotesque forms, France (14th cent.)

gryphon A **griffin.**

gryse See **grees.**

gudgeon A metal pin used to hold together two blocks or slabs, as of stone.

gueula Same as **gula.**

guglia An elongated finial.

guildhall The place of assembly for a guild or corporation.

guilloche An ornament formed by two or more bands twisted over each other in a continuous series, leaving circular openings which are often filled with round ornaments.

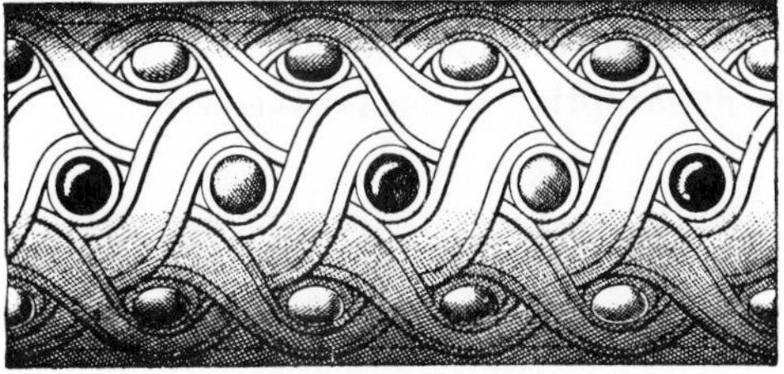

types of guilloches

gula 1. A molding having a large hollow. 2. A **cyma.** 3. A **gorge.**

gulbishche In early Russian architecture, a terrace which surrounds a building.

guldasta In Indian architecture, a pinnacle.

gumbad A mausoleum or tomb tower in Muslim Persia and India.

gumpha In Indian architecture, a monastery.

gurgoyle Same as **gargoyle.**

gutta One of a series of pendant ornaments, generally in the form of the frustum of a cone, but sometimes cylindrical; usually found on the underside of the mutules and regulae of Doric **entablatures.**

guttae, Parthenon (indicated by arrows)

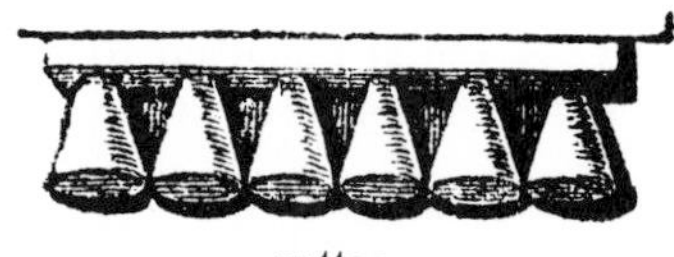

guttae

guttae band Same as **regula** in the Greek Doric entablature.

gutter A shallow channel of metal or wood set immediately below and along the eaves of a building to catch and carry off rainwater from the roof; also called **eaves gutter, eaves trough, roof gutter.**

gymmer See **gemel.**

gymnasium In Greek and Roman architecture, a large open court for exercise, surrounded by colonnades and rooms for massage, lectures, etc.; a **palaestra, ephebeum.**

gymnasterium See **apodyterium.**

gynaeceum That part of a Greek house or a church reserved for women.

gynaekonitis Same as **gynaeceum.**

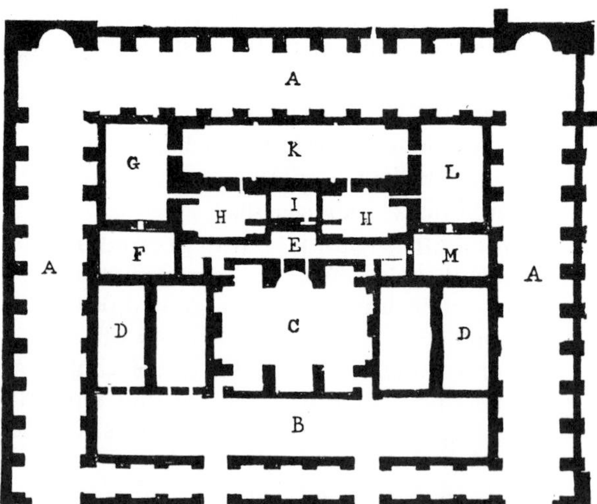

gymnasium at Ephesus: *A*, portico; *B*, palaestra; *C*, ephebeion; *D*, dressing rooms; *E*, passage; *F*, *G*, cold baths; *H*, *H*, hot baths; *L*, *M*, warm baths; near *I*, staircase to laconicum; *K*, ball alley

H

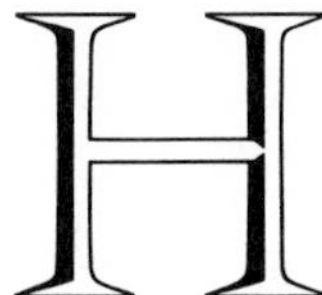

habitacle **1.** A dwelling or habitation. **2.** A niche for a statue.

hacienda **1.** A large estate in North and South American areas once under Spanish influence. **2.** The main house on such an estate or ranch.

hadish A palace built by Xerxes at **Persepolis.**

Hadrian's Villa Built by Hadrian in 124 A.D., the Villa includes a vast complex of buildings in the Imperial Roman style; covers a hilly area of 7 sq miles (18 sq km) at Tivoli, near Rome.

Hafner ware In northern European decorative arts of the Renaissance and derivatives, modeled, lead-glazed earthenware often used for tiled heating stoves.

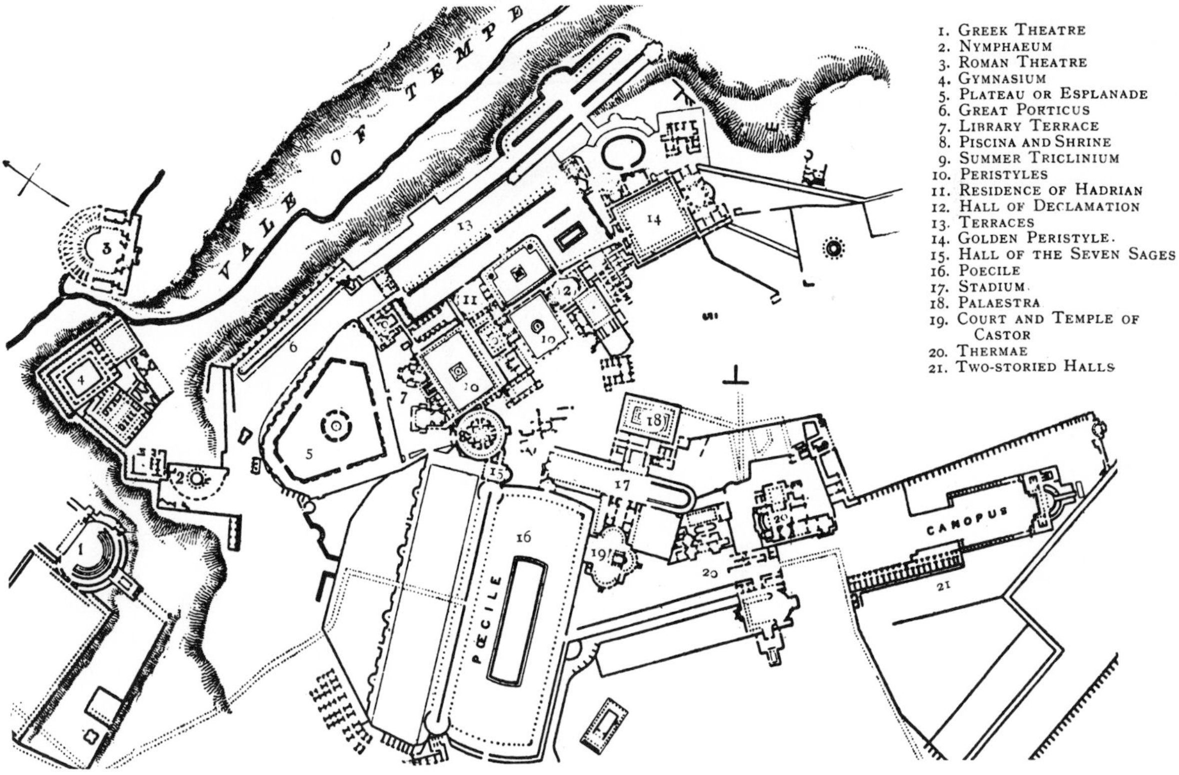

VALE OF TEMPE
CANOPUS
PŒCILE
1. Greek Theatre
2. Nymphaeum
3. Roman Theatre
4. Gymnasium
5. Plateau or Esplanade
6. Great Porticus
7. Library Terrace
8. Piscina and Shrine
9. Summer Triclinium
10. Peristyles
11. Residence of Hadrian
12. Hall of Declamation
13. Terraces
14. Golden Peristyle.
15. Hall of the Seven Sages
16. Poecile
17. Stadium.
18. Palaestra
19. Court and Temple of Castor
20. Thermae
21. Two-storied Halls

plan, Hadrian's Villa at Tivoli (124 A.D.)

Hagia Sophia The outstanding example of **Byzantine architecture** (Constantinople); originally built as a church by Emperor Constantine in 360 A.D., rebuilt in 537 and then again in 563 in a form probably very nearly as it is today; became a mosque in 1453 with the Turkish conquest of the city. Has a huge dome, approx. 107 ft (32.6 m) in diameter, rising 184 ft (56 m) above the floor, which is carried on pendentives, with half-domes at two ends which are, in turn, carried by smaller semidomed exedrae. The interior surface of the edifice is richly decorated.

elevation façade

running ornament

Byzantine capital

section, east to west

Hagia Sophia

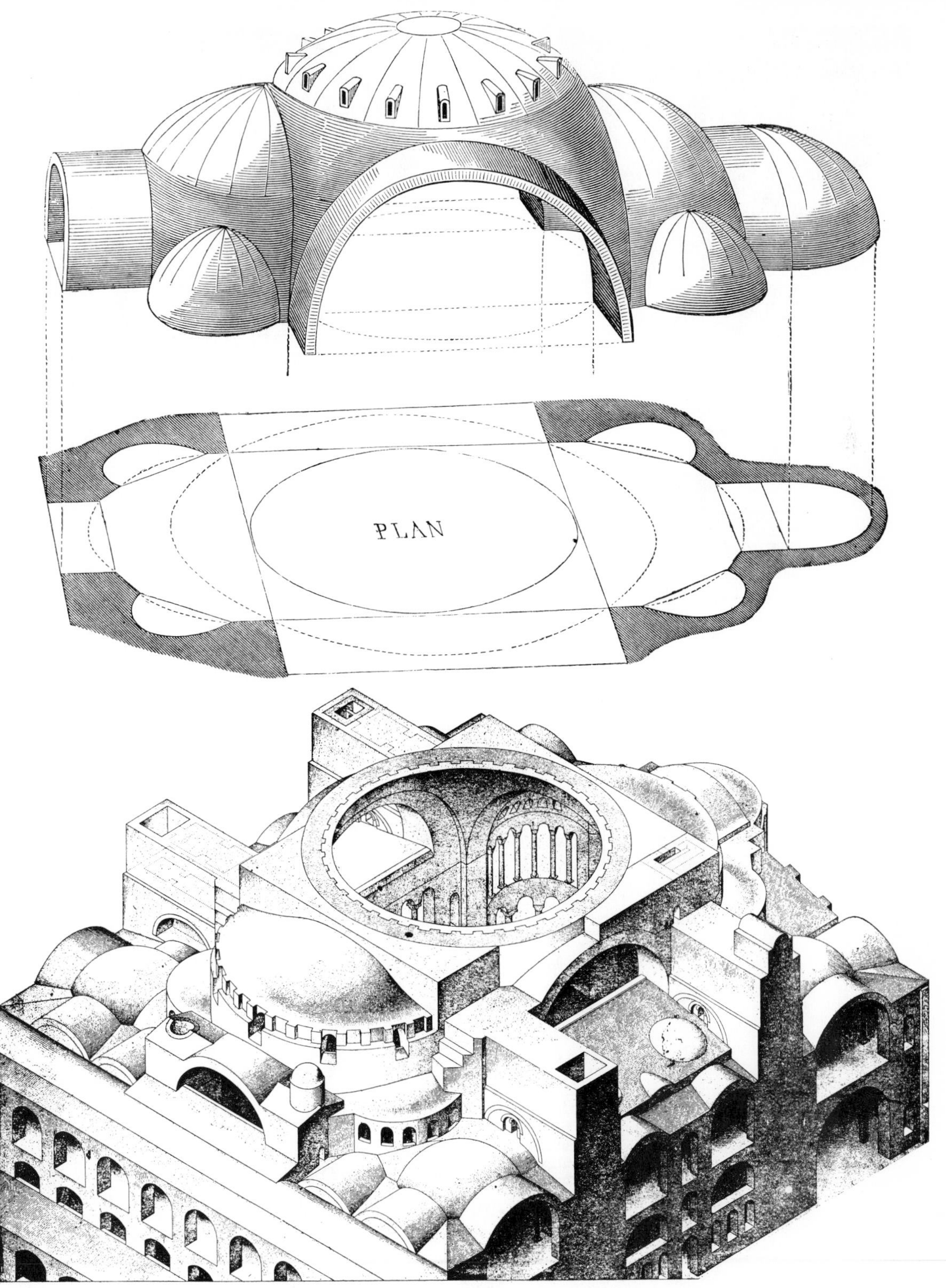

Hagia Sophia

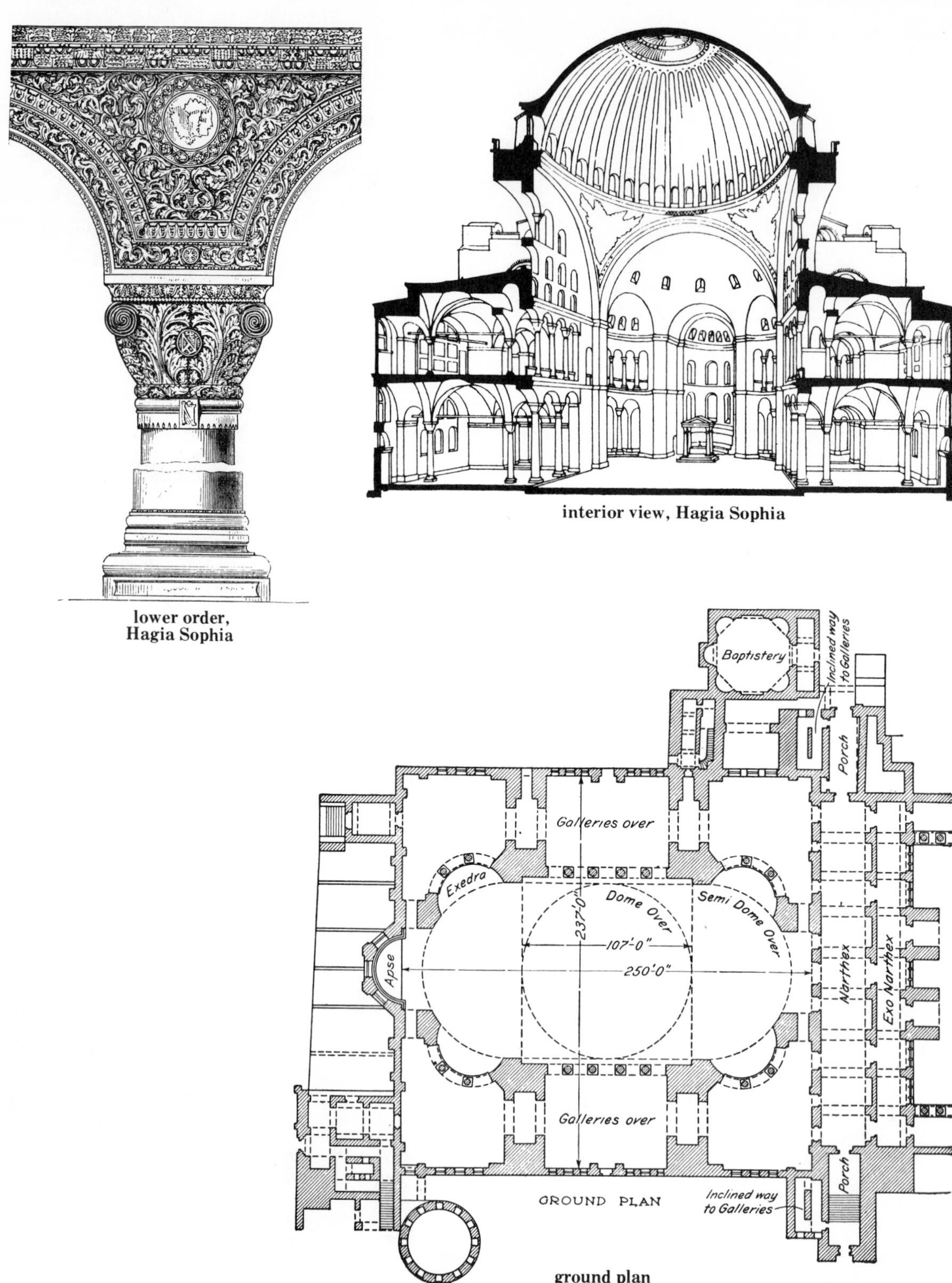

interior view, Hagia Sophia

lower order, Hagia Sophia

ground plan

hagiasterium A sacred place; a baptismal font.

hagioscope A **squint, 1.**

ha-ha A barrier in the form of a trench; usually used to prevent livestock from crossing; a sunken fence.

拝殿 **haiden** A hall of worship, usually in front of the **honden** of a Shintō shrine.

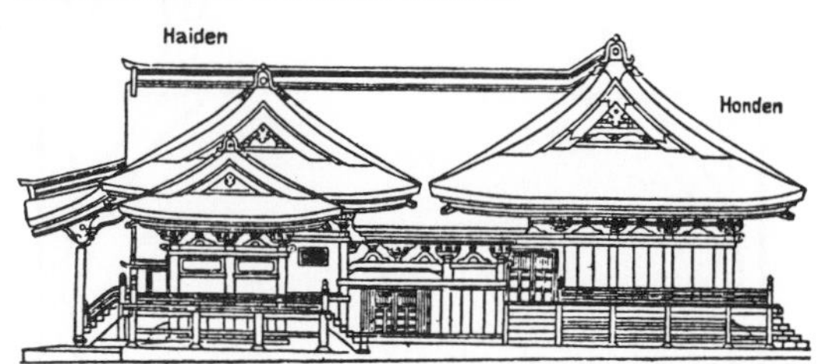

haikal The central chapel of the three forming the sanctuary of a Coptic church.

half baluster An engaged **baluster,** projecting about half of its diameter.

half column An **engaged column** projecting approx. one half its diameter, usually slightly more.

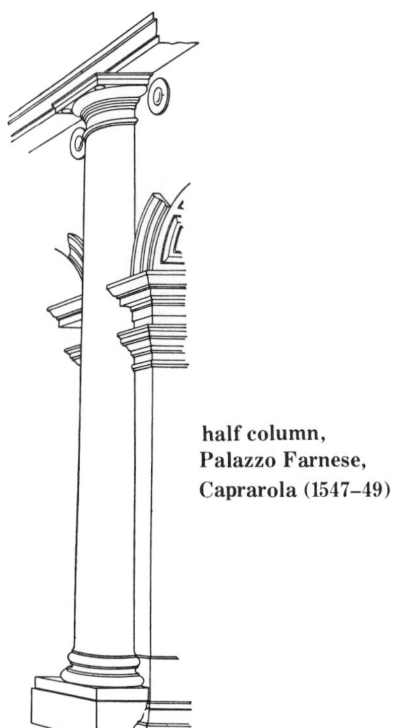

half column, Palazzo Farnese, Caprarola (1547–49)

half house A **Cape Cod house** or **saltbox** having two windows on one side of the front door and none on the other.

half-moon A roughly crescent-shaped fortification outwork. Also see **ravelin.**

halfpace, half-space landing **1.** A stair landing at the junction of two flights which reverses the direction of horizontal progress, making a turn of 180°. Such a landing extends the width of both flights plus the well. **2.** A raised floor in a bay window, in front of a fireplace, etc.; raised a step higher than the general floor area.

halfpace stair A stair making a 180° turn, usually having a **halfpace** landing.

half principal A roof member or rafter that does not reach to the ridgepole but is supported at its upper end by a purlin.

half round, half-round molding A convex strip or molding of semicircular profile.

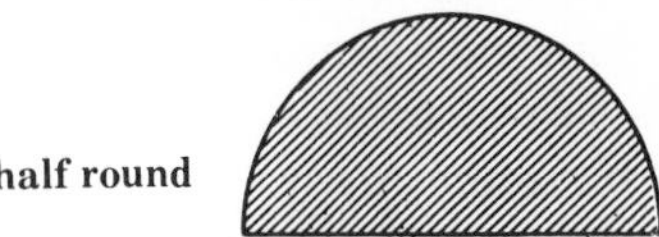

half round

half-space stair Same as **halfpace stair.**

half-timbered Descriptive of buildings of the 16th and 17th cent. which were built with strong timber foundations, supports, knees, and studs, and whose walls were filled in with plaster or masonry materials such as brick.

half-timbered house

hall **1.** A large room for assembly, entertainment, etc. **2.** An entrance room or corridor. **3.** A royal or noble castle, a manor house, a public or university building, etc. Commonly used in the proper names of such buildings (City Hall). **4.** The principal and most spacious room in a medieval residence, communal and multipurpose.

hall church A church with aisles but without clerestories, the interior of which is a hall of approximately uniform height throughout.

hall keep A rectangular **keep** in which the great hall and bed chamber were adjacent.

halo See **nimbus.**

halpace Same as **halfpace.**

hammam An establishment for bathing in the Oriental way, with steam rooms, etc.; a Turkish bath.

hammer beam One of a pair of short horizontal members attached to the foot of a **principal rafter** in a roof, in place of a **tie beam.**

hammer-beam roof A roof supported by **hammer beams.**

hammer brace A bracket under a hammer beam to support it.

hammer post A **pendant** which is in the shape of a pilaster; serves as an impost for a **hammer brace.**

hance The curve of shorter radius which adjoins the impost at each side of a three- or four-centered arch, of an elliptical arch, or similar arch. **2.** A small arch which joins a lintel to a jamb. **3.** Same as **haunch, 1.**

hance arch Same as **hanse arch.**

hanging buttress In later Gothic architecture and derivatives, a freestanding vertical rib or buttress which is supported from a wall by a corbel rather than by its own foundation.

Hanging Gardens A series of terraced, irrigated gardens built on a vaulted substructure in the citadel of ancient Babylon; traditionally attributed to Queen Semiramis, but probably built by Nebuchadnezzar; one of the Seven Wonders of the World. Also see **Babylonian architecture.**

hanging post, gatepost, hinge post, swinging post The post on which a gate is hung.

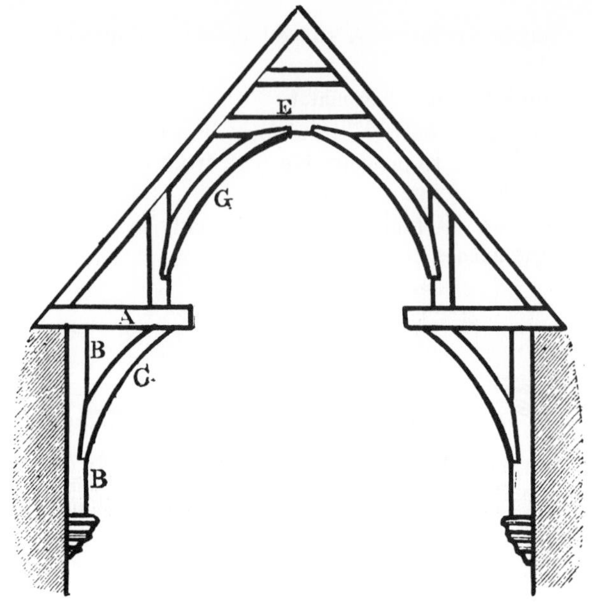

hammer-beam roof: *A*, **hammer beam;** *BB*, **pendant post;** *C*, **hammer brace;** *E*, **collar;** *G*, **collar brace**

hammer-beam roof

hanse arch, haunch arch An arch having a crown of different curvature than the haunches, which are thus strongly marked; usually a **basket-handle** or **three-centered** or **four-centered arch.**

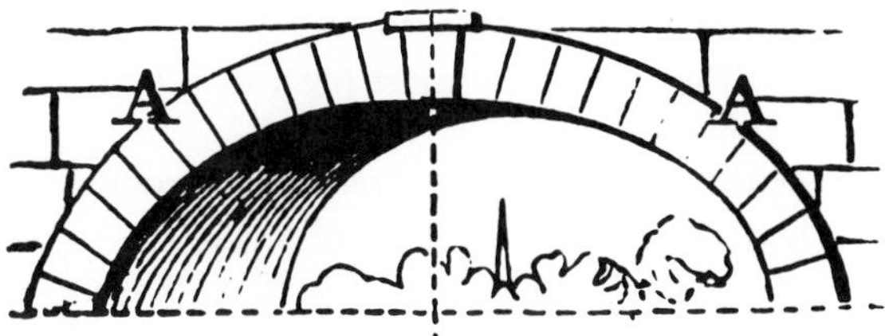

hanse arch: *A*, *A*, haunches

haram A **temenos** or sacred area in **Muslim architecture.**

harem In Muslim architecture, the women's quarters in a palace or house.

梁 **hari** In traditional Japanese architecture, a beam similar to **liang** in traditional Chinese architecture.

harim Same as **harem.**

harmika A shrine or relic receptable on top of the dome of a Buddhist **stupa,** surrounded by a railing and surmounted by a **chattravali.**

柱 **hashira** A column, post, or pillar; the basic vertical member of a traditional Japanese wooden structure.

hastarium In ancient Rome, a room in which sales were made by public auction, under public authority.

hatched molding Same as **notched molding.**

hatchet door Same as **Dutch door.**

Hathoric, Hathor-headed Pertaining to an Egyptian column with a capital which bears masks of the Egyptian cow-head goddess Hathor.

hathpace Same as **halfpace.**

hatto A rectangular, one-story building used as a lecture hall for the instruction of monks in a Japanese Zen temple.

haunch **1.** The middle part between the crown and the springing of an arch. **2.** The part of a beam projecting beneath a roof slab or floor.

haunch arch See **hanse arch.**

Hathoric capital

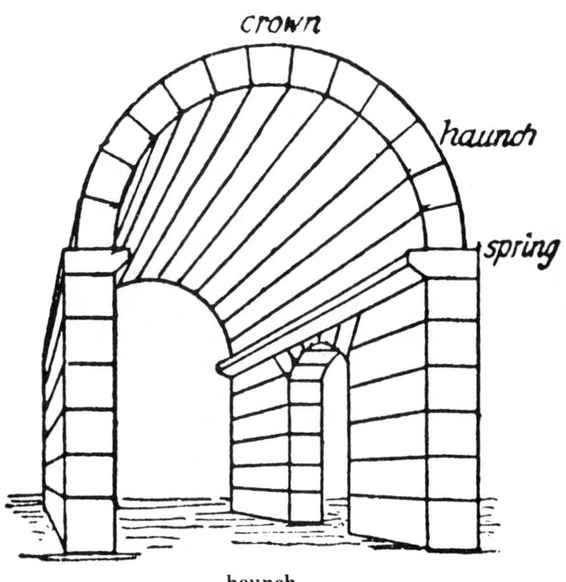

haunch

haunched beam A beam whose cross section thickens toward its supports.

hautepace, hautpace Same as **halfpace.**

haw-haw Same as **ha-ha.**

hawksbeak A **beak molding, 2.**

head **1.** In general, the top or upper member of any structure; the top or end (esp. the more prominent end) of a piece or member. **2.** The upper horizontal cross member, between the jambs, which forms the top of a door or window frame; may provide structural support for construction above if required. **3.** A stone that has one end dressed to match the face because the end will be exposed at a corner or in a reveal. **4.** A roofing tile of half the usual length but of the same width; for forming the first course at the eaves.

header **1.** A masonry unit, laid so that its ends are exposed, overlapping two or more adjacent withes of masonry and tying them together; a **bondstone;** a **bonder.** **2.** A **header joist.** **3.** A framing member which crosses and supports the ends of joists, rafters, etc., transferring the weight of the latter to parallel joists, rafters, etc.

header joist, header, lintel, trimmer joist A short structural member (as used in framing an opening) which is fastened between parallel full-length framing members at right angles to them and supports cut-off members, e.g., the common joists in framing around a rectangular opening in a wood floor.

headmold, dripstone, head molding, hoodmold, weather molding The molding carried around or over the head of a door or window.

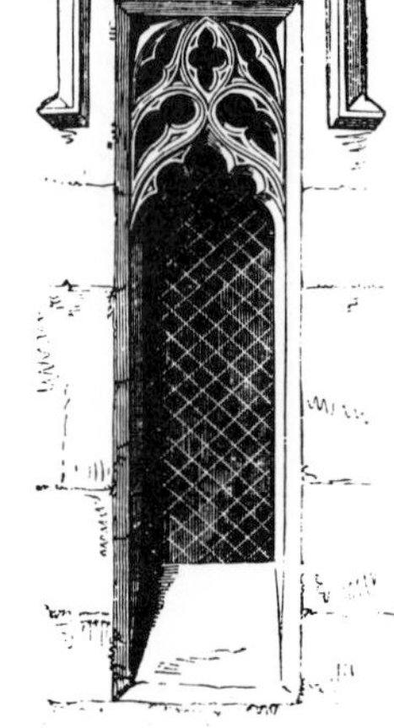

headmold:
Decorated style
window,
Marcham, Berkshire
(c. 1400)

headstock A supporting beam for a church bell.

headstone The principal stone in a foundation, as the cornerstone of a building or the keystone of an arch.

headwork The heads and other ornaments on the keystone of an arch.

healing The outermost layer of the roof of a building.

healing stone A roofing slate or roofing tile.

hearse **1.** A framework of metal bars or rods placed over a tomb or coffin of a noble or very important person. **2.** A canopy, usually of openwork or trellis, set over a bier, or more rarely over a permanent tomb, and used especially to support candles which were lighted at times of ceremony.

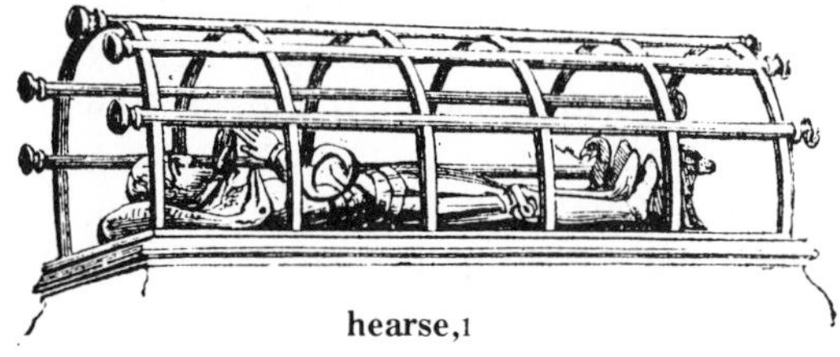

hearse,1

hearse,2

heart and dart See **leaf and dart.**

hearth The floor of a fireplace (usually brick, tile, or stone) together with an adjacent area of fireproof material.

hearthstone **1.** A single large stone forming the floor of a fireplace. **2.** Materials such as firebrick, fireclay products, etc., used to form a hearth.

hecatompedon A building 100 Greek ft in length or width; esp. the cella of the great temple of Athena, the Parthenon, at Athens.

hecatonstylon A building having a hundred columns.

heck **1.** A door having its upper part hinged independently of its lower part, or one with an open or latticework panel. **2.** A latticed gate.

hectastyle Same as **hexastyle.**

heelpost **1.** A post or stanchion at the free end of the partition of a stall. **2.** A post to receive the hinges of a gate (either part of the gate or the stationary support).

heel stone A stone at the bottom of a gate pier; used to mount the bottom hinge pin for the gate.

heil Same as **hiling.**

hekhal The sanctuary or largest main room in the **Temple of Solomon.**

heliakon A sun terrace.

helical stair A **spiral stair.**

heliocaminus A room with a southern exposure, which received sufficient heat from the natural warmth of the sun so no other source of heat was required.

helix **1.** Any spiral, particularly a small volute or twist under the abacus of the Corinthian capital. **2.** The volute of an Ionic capital.

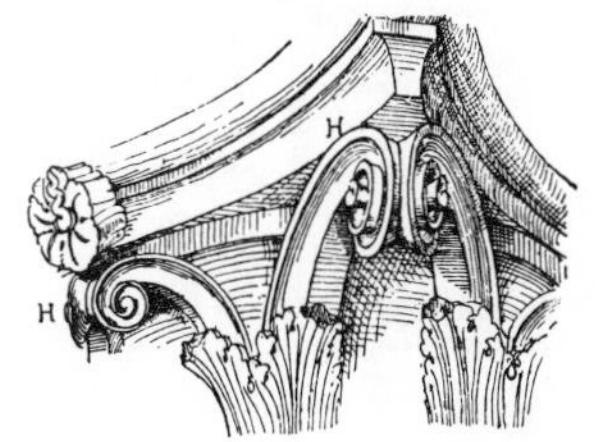

helix,1 used in a Corinthian capital

Hellenic Pertaining to the classical Greek period, roughly from 480 B.C. to the death of Alexander in 323 B.C.

Hellenistic Characteristic of the style of Greek art after the death of Alexander in 323 B.C.

helm roof A roof having four faces, each of which is steeply pitched so that they form a spire; the four ridges rise to the point of the spire from a base of four gables.

helm roof

hem The projecting spiral of a volute of an Ionic capital.

hemicycle **1.** A semicircular arena. **2.** A room or division of a room in the form of a semicircle. **3.** A semicircular recess.

hemicyclium A semicircular alcove, sufficiently large to provide seating for several persons; the ancient Romans built such places in different parts of town for the accommodation of its inhabitants and also in their pleasure gardens.

hemicyclium

hemiglyph The half channel on each of the two sides of a triglyph.

hemitriglyph The portion of a triglyph which sometimes occurs in an internal angle of a returned frieze which has triglyphs in it.

桁 **hêng** A **purlin** within an enclosed roof.

Henri II (Deux) style The second phase of the early French Renaissance, named after Henri II (1547–1559) who succeeded Francis I. Italian classic motifs began to supplant the Gothic elements, both in architecture and in decoration. The West Side of the Court of the Louvre (1546–59) is an outstanding example.

Ancy-le-Franc, Burgundy (c. 1546): balcony over entrance door

west side of the Court of the Louvre

Henri IV (Quatre) style The early phase of the Classical period of French architecture, named after Henry IV (1589–1610), preceding the architecture of Louis XIII and Louis XIV. It is particularly strong in domestic architecture and town-planning arrangements. The Place des Vosges in Paris is the outstanding example.

Place des Vosges, Paris (1605–12)

Henri IV (Quatre) style

wall decoration with painting in the style of Henri IV

heptastyle A portico having seven columns, at one or at each end.

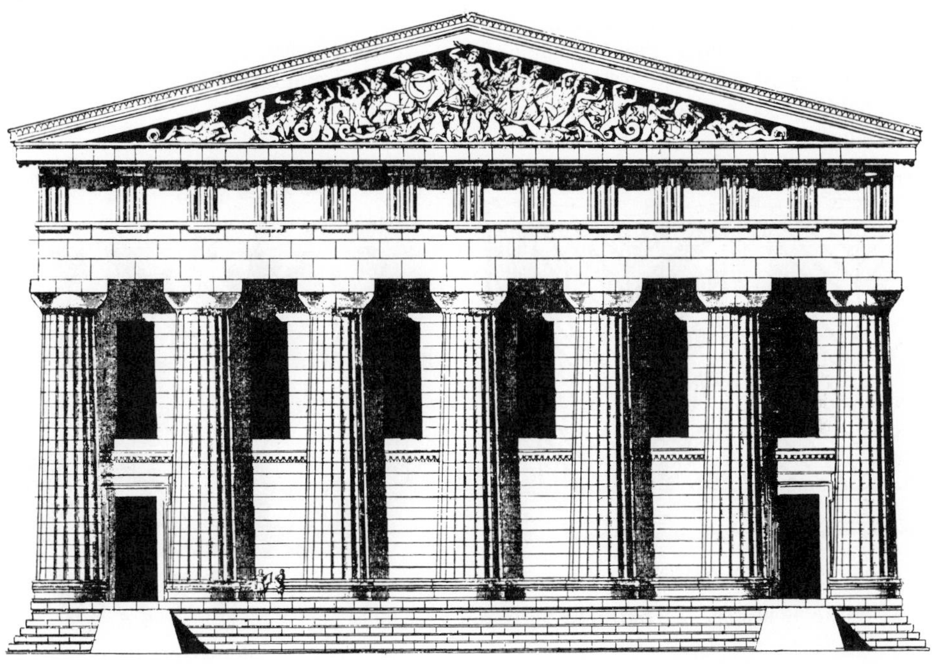

Heraclium A temple dedicated to Hercules.

Heraeum A temple or sacred enclosure dedicated to the goddess Hera.

Herculaneum An ancient Roman city near Naples, buried at the same time with Pompeii by the eruption of Vesuvius in 79 A.D.

herm A rectangular post, usually of stone and tapering downward, surmounted by a bust of Hermes or other divinity, or by a human head.

maiden decorating a herm: from an attic relief found near Naples

heroum A building or sacred enclosure dedicated to a hero, usually erected over a grave.

heroum: monument of ancient Greek lady

herringbone matching See **book matching.**

herringbone pattern A way of assembling, in diagonal zigzag fashion, brick or similar rectangular blocks for paving and for masonry walls; also strips of wood or other finishing materials having rectangular shapes for facing walls or ceilings.

herringbone patterns

herse 1. Same as **hearse.** 2. Same as **portcullis.**

Hertfordshire spike Same as **needle spire.**

hexapartite vault Same as **sexpartite vault.**

hexastyle, exastyle Having six columns, as at one end or at both ends of a portico.

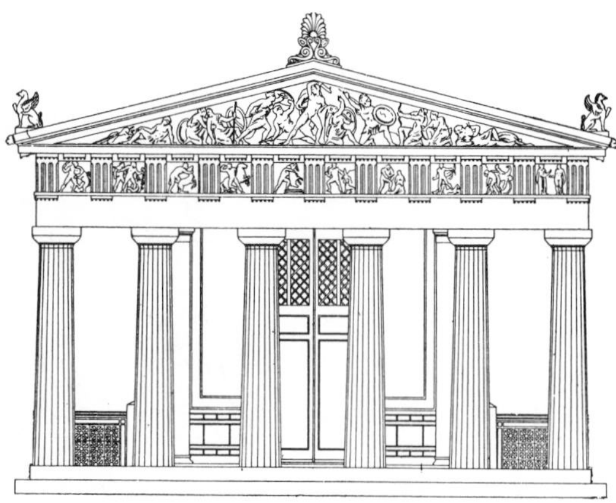

hexastyle, Temple of Theseion, Athens (449-444 B.C.)

hibernacula Ancient apartments in a house intended for winter occupancy; less decorated than other apartments because of the dirt caused by the smoke from the fires and lamps burnt in them.

hieroglyph A figure representing (*a*) an idea, and intended to convey a meaning, (*b*) a word or root of a word, or (*c*) a sound which is part of a word; esp. applied to the engraved marks and symbols found on the monuments of ancient Egypt.

hieroglyphs from an ancient Egyptian manuscript on papyrus

hieron The sacred enclosure of a temple or shrine.

high altar The primary altar in a church.

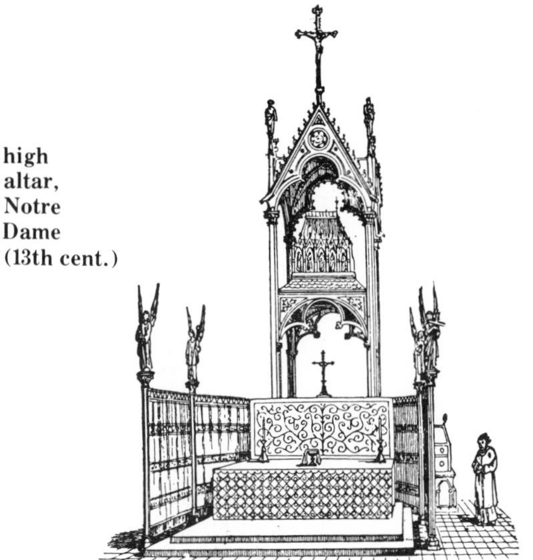

high altar, Notre Dame (13th cent.)

high relief, alto-relievo, alto-rilievo Sculpture relief work in which the figures project more than half their thickness.

High Renaissance A term referring primarily to the culmination of the Italian Renaissance style in the 16th cent. (*cinquecento*). St. Peter's in Rome is the most famous example.

interior of St. Peter's, Rome

high tomb Same as **altar tomb.**

hilammar A portico having a roof supported by columns, leading to the sanctuary of a Hittite temple.

hiling The covering or roof of a building.

姫路城 **Himeji Jō** Located in the city of Himeji, in the Hyōgo prefecture of Japan, the Himeji Castle is a stronghold which dates back to the 14th cent. It is the best and most beautiful example of castle architecture in Japan. Although completely repaired in 1964, it retains many original structures of the late 16th and early 17th cent.; representative of the late Momoyama and early Edo periods.

hinge A movable joint used to attach, support, and turn a door (or cover) about a pivot; consists of two plates joined together by a pin which support the door and connect it to its frame, enabling it to swing open or closed.

wrought iron hinge, Notre Dame

hinge post See **hanging post.**

hip 1. The external angle at the junction of two sloping roofs or sides of a roof. 2. The rafter at the angle where two sloping roofs or sides of roofs meet.

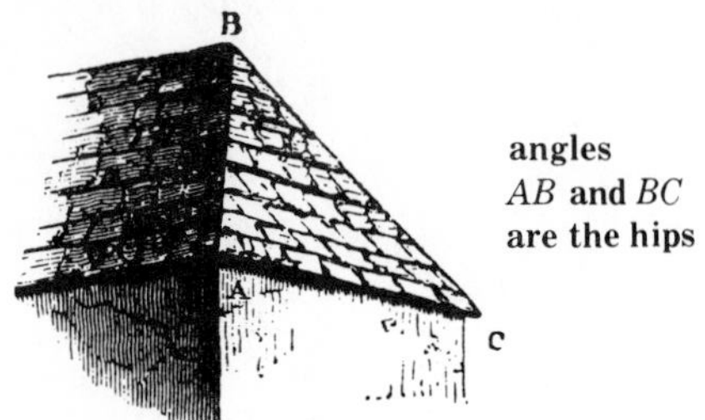

angles *AB* and *BC* are the hips

hip knob A finial or other similar ornament placed on the top of the hip of a roof or at the apex of a gable.

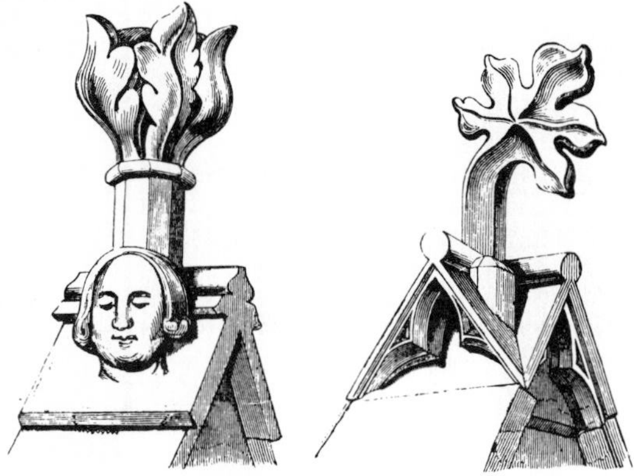
English hip knobs

hip molding A molding on the rafter that forms the hip of a roof.

hipped end The sloping triangularly shaped end of a hipped roof.

hipped gable See **jerkinhead.**

hipped roof See **hip roof.**

hippodrome The Greek term for a racecourse for horses and chariots; much wider than the Roman **circus** in which only four chariots ran at a time; the Greeks raced as many as ten or more.

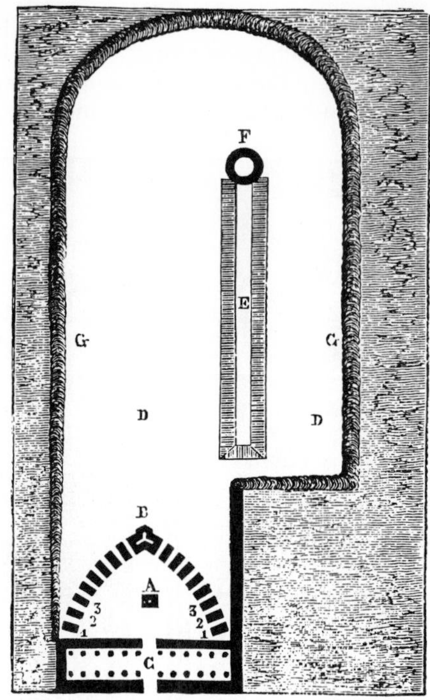

a Greek hippodrome: *1, 2, 3,* carceres; *A,* space between the carceres; *B,* starting place for the chariots; *C,* colonnade; *D,* arena; *E,* barrier; *G,* area occupied by spectators

hippodromus 1. A plot of ground in a Roman garden or villa, planted with trees and laid out into a variety of avenues designed for equestrian exercises. 2. A **hippodrome.**

hip rafter, angle rafter, angle ridge A rafter placed at the junction of the inclined planes forming a hipped roof.

hip roll, ridge roll A rounded strip of wood, tile, metal, or composition material which is used to cover and finish the **hip** of a roof.

hip roof, hipped roof A roof which slopes upward from all four sides of a building, requiring a hip rafter at each corner.

hip roof

hip tile A saddle-shaped tile used to cover the hips of a roof.

hiragawara See **hongawara-buki.**

庇 **hisashi** The eaves area, usually one **ken** in width which runs parallel to one or more sides or corridors of a traditional Japanese wooden building.

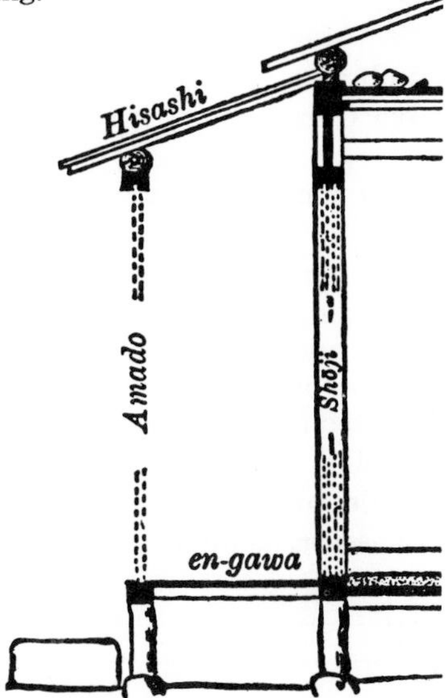

Hispano-Moresque architecture The Moorish architecture of the regions of Spain under Islamic domination from the 8th to the 15th cent. The **Alhambra** is the most famous example.

Hittite architecture The distinctive rugged architecture created in central Anatolia at the time of the Hittite Empire (14th to 13th cent. B.C.), preeminent for its fortifications, citadels, and temples.

hiwada-buki A roof of a Japanese building covered with many layers of thin, precisely cut shingles of cypress bark.

hoarding, hoard A covered wooden gallery projecting from the top of the wall of a medieval fortress to shelter the defenders and to increase facilities for defense.

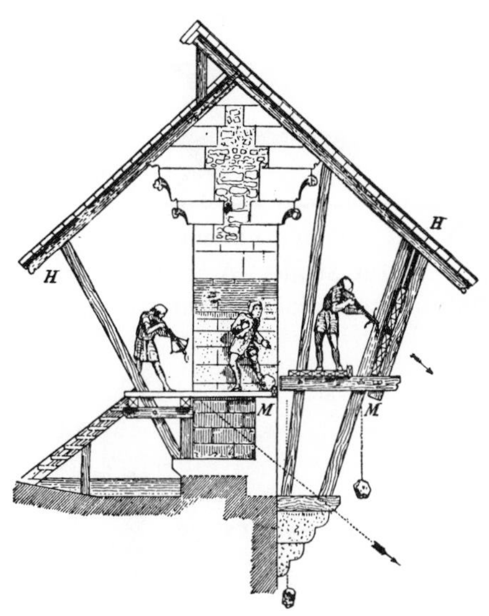

H, *H*, **hoarding;** *M*, *M*, **machicolations**

hob A flat projecting shelf at the side of a fireplace where pots or pans may be placed to keep warm.

方形屋根 **hōgyō-yane** In a traditional Japanese structure, a roof which is pyramidal in shape; usually has four sides which join at the top, but may also have six or eight sides; has no ridgepole.

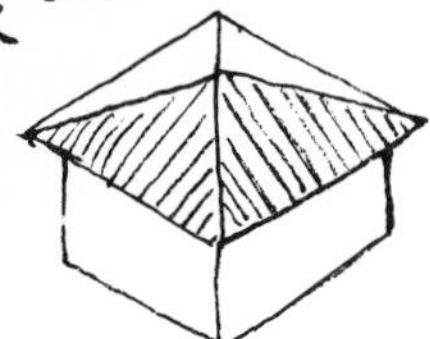

hōgyō-yane

方丈 **hōjō** The abbot's quarters in a Japanese Zen temple.

hollow chamfer A **chamfer** which is concave.

hollow gorge Same as **Egyptian gorge.**

hollow molding, gorge, trochilus A concave, often circular molding; a **cavetto** or **scotia.**

hollow newel, hollow newel stair **1.** The newel or central shaft of a winding stair built as a hollow cylinder. **2.** The open well in such a stair when built without the hollow enclosure.

hollow newel stair See **open-newel stair.**

hollow relief Same as **sunk relief.**

hollow square molding A common Norman molding consisting of a series of indented pyramidal shapes having a square base.

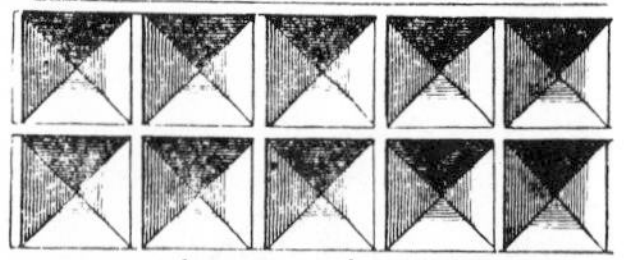

hollow square molding

holy loft Same as **rood loft.**

holy-water stone A stone basin for holding holy water, placed near the entrance of a church.

holy-water stone

homestall See **homestead, 2.**

homestead **1.** A piece of land, limited to 160 acres, deemed adequate for the support of one family. **2.** *(Brit.)* A group of buildings and the land forming the home of a family; a **homestall.**

本殿 **honden** In Shintō architecture, the main inner shrine.

hondō See **kondō.**

honeycomb Any hexagonal structure or pattern, or one resembling such a structure or pattern.

honeycomb vault, honeycomb work See **muqarnas.**

honeycomb wall A brick wall having a pattern of openings; equal in thickness to the width of one brick; either gaps are left between stretchers or bricks are omitted to provide openings; used to support floor joists and provide ventilation under floors.

honeysuckle ornament A common name for the **anthemion,** common in Greek decorative sculpture.

honeysuckle ornament

本瓦葺 **hongawara-buki** In traditional Japanese architecture, clay roofing tile; consists of half-round tiles (*marugawara*) and broad, slightly curved, flat tile (*hiragawara*) laid alternately; the eave-end tiles are capped and decorated.

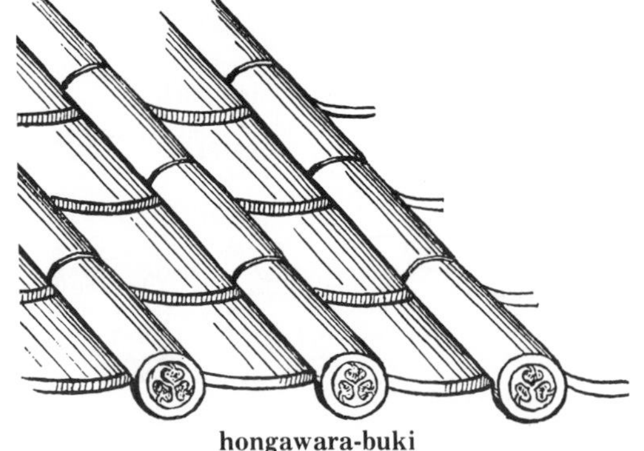

hongawara-buki

hon-kaerumata See **kaerumata.**

hood **1.** A cover placed above an opening or an object to shelter it. **2.** A cover placed over a fire or chimney to create a draft and to direct the smoke, odors, or noxious vapors into a flue; may be supported or hung in space, or attached to a wall.

hood,1 over a door in Syria (5th or 6th cent.)

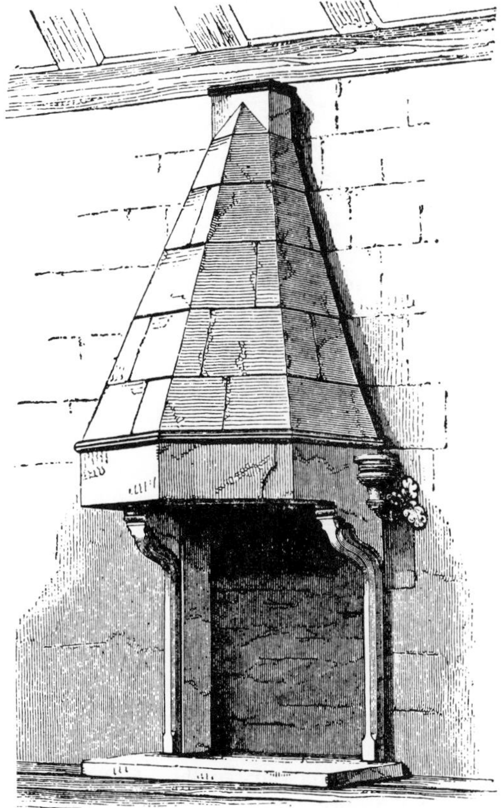

hood,2

hoodmold, hood molding The projecting molding of the arch over a door or window, whether inside or outside; also called a **dripstone.**

Early English style window with hoodmold, Oxford (c. 1300)

horizontal cornice The level cornice of the pediment under the two inclined cornices.

hornwork Fortress outwork with two half bastions.

a, hornwork

horreum **1.** An ancient Roman granary, barn, or other building in which agricultural products were stored. **2.** A storeroom for bottled wine on the upper floor of a house.

hors concours Describing an invited exhibit or exhibitor, ineligible for an award in a competition owing to acknowledged superiority.

horse block A block or platform, often set near a door, on which one steps when mounting or dismounting from a horse.

horseshoe arch, Arabic arch, Moorish arch A rounded arch whose curve is a little more than a semicircle so that the opening at the bottom is narrower than its greatest span.

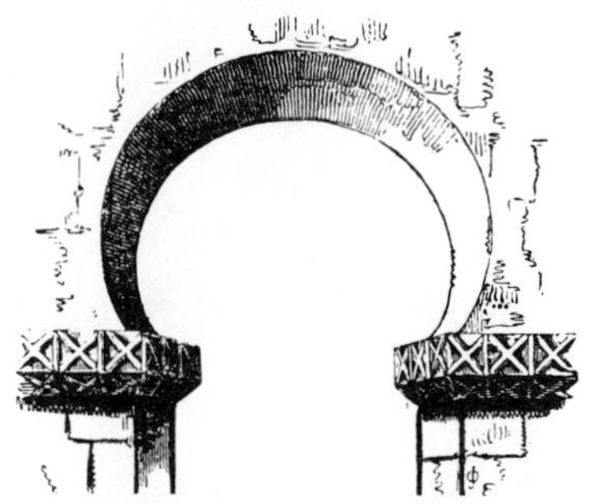

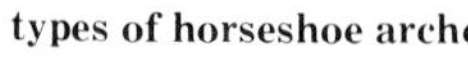
types of horseshoe arches

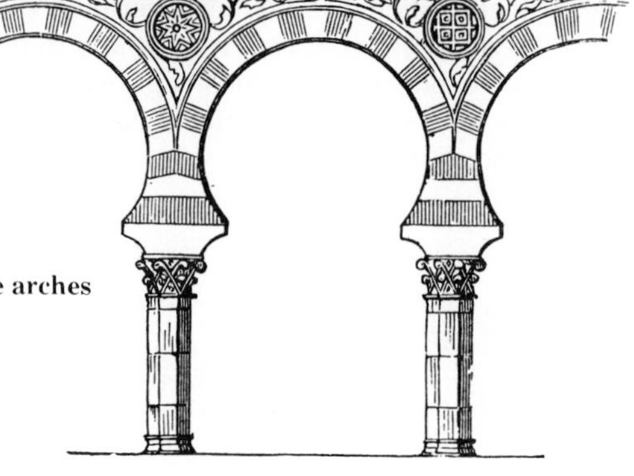

hortus **1.** A pleasure garden or pleasure ground of the ancients, similar in style and arrangement to the garden of a modern Italian villa. **2.** Any type of garden in ancient Rome.

below: **hortus**

法隆寺 **Hōryūji** A temple, located near Nara, Japan, said to have been built at the end of the 6th cent. The original temple burned in 670; the present compound was rebuilt in the year 693. Contains the oldest existing wooden structure in the world, a five-storied pagoda (gojū-no-tō); see **tō**. Also contains important structures of the Nara, Heian, and Kamakura periods (7th and 8th cent.).

hospice A resort for travelers which includes lodging and entertainment.

hospitalium **1.** A guest chamber in a Roman house. **2.** A conventional entrance for strangers in a dramatic performance.

hospitium An inn or a place for the reception of strangers.

hostry An inn.

hourd Same as **hoard.**

house See **Greek house, Roman house.**

hovel **1.** A shed open at the sides and covered overhead for sheltering livestock, produce, or people. **2.** A poorly constructed and ill-kept house.

höyük The Turkish equivalent of a **tell.**

小式大木 **hsiao shih ta mu** Any timber construction in Chinese traditional architecture which does not employ the **tou kung** system of construction; usually used for common dwellings and less important buildings.

戲楼 **hsi lou** A structure used for performances in a Chinese courtyard; includes a stage, changing room, storage facilities for scenery, and sometimes a playing area for an orchestra.

杏檀 **hsing tan** The podium in a Confucian temple.

花磚 **hua chuan** A decorative grille, usually made of flat or curved terra-cotta tiles; used to lessen the weight of masonry walls; a feature of traditional Chinese landscape architecture. Also called **lou ch'uang.**

華表 **hua piao** A monumental stone pylon at the entrance of a Chinese palace; a symbol of welcome.

hüyük See **höyük.**

hylying Same as **hiling.**

hymn board A notice board in a church, on which the numbers of hymns and psalms are posted.

hypaethral, hypethral Describing a building which is open, or partly open, to the sky.

hypaethron An open court or enclosure; a place or part of a building that is roofless.

hypaethrum A latticed window constructed over the door of an ancient building.

hypaethrum above door

hypermensul A "sun-stone" placed at the center of a Celtic monument consisting of a number of **menhirs** arranged in a circle.

hyperthyrum A frieze and cornice arranged and decorated in various ways for the lintel of a door.

hypobasis **1.** The lower base or the lowermost division of a base. **2.** A lower base which is below a more important one.

hypocaustum A central heating system of ancient Rome; hot gases from a furnace were conducted to rooms above, through a hollow floor and through tile flues within walls.

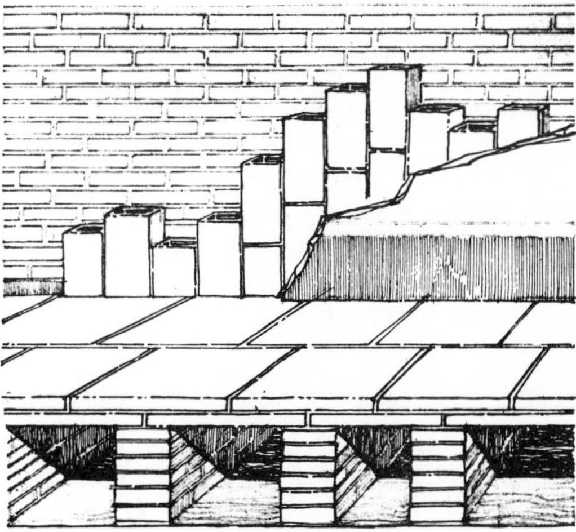

hypocaustum in bath, Pompeii

hypocaustum in Roman villa, Tusculum

hypodromus In ancient Rome, a shady or covered walk or ambulatory.

hypogeum In ancient architecture, any underground chamber or vault, esp. an underground burial chamber.

hypophyge A depression of curved profile beneath some feature, such as the hollow molding beneath some archaic Doric capitals.

hypopodium Same as **hypobasis, 2.**

hyposcenium In the ancient Greek theatre, the low wall beneath the front part of the **logeion.**

hypostyle hall **1.** A large space with a flat roof supported by rows of columns. Prevalent in ancient Egyptian and Achaemenid architecture. **2.** A structure whose roofing was supported, within the perimeter, by groups of columns or piers of more than one height; clerestory lights sometimes were introduced.

hypotrachelium, gorgerin In some columns, that part of the capital between the termination of the shaft and the annulet of the echinus, or the space between two neck moldings.

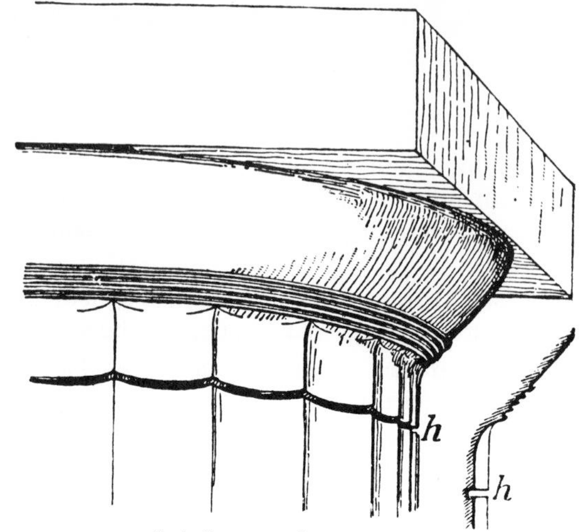

h, h, **hypotrachelium from a column of the Parthenon**

Hypostyle Hall at Karnak (1312–1301 B.C.), showing the clerestories; pylons can be seen in the background

I

ianua In ancient Rome, the outer door of a house. Same as **janua.**

ice house A structure, usually with double walls, packed between with sawdust or some similar material which does not conduct heat; used for the storage of ice; usually encloses a pit which has a drain to carry off the water resulting from melting ice.

ice house: front elevation

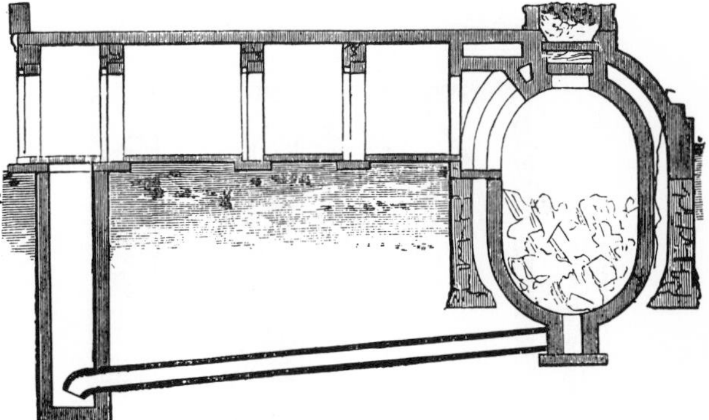

section through ice house

ichnographia A ground plan made by ancient architects and surveyors for the use of builders or for use as a map of reference.

iconostasis A screen in a Greek or Russian Orthodox church, on which icons are placed, separating the chancel from the space open to the laity.

igloo, iglu An Eskimo house, constructed of snow blocks or various materials such as wood, sod, poles, and skins; when of snow, a domed structure.

image Any representation of form or features, but esp. one of the entire figure of a person; a statue, effigy, bust, relief, intaglio, etc.

image, All Souls College, Oxford (1715–40)

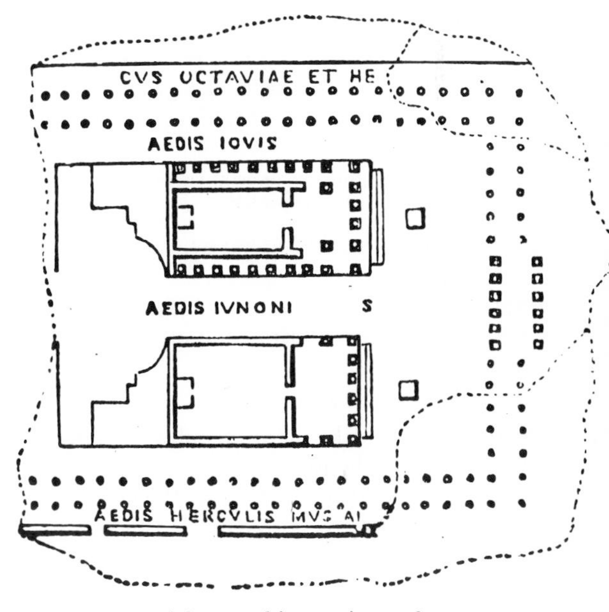

ichnographia: specimen of ancient Roman mapping from an engraving on a marble slab

imagines Roman portrait masks of deceased members of a family; made of wax and painted, and probably fastened onto busts. They were kept in small wooden shrines set into the inner walls of the atrium; beneath the shrines were inscriptions which recorded the names, merits, and exploits of the individuals. The images were arranged and connected with one another by means of colored cords, in such a way as to exhibit the pedigree of the family.

imagines: memorial bust of a Roman lady

imam-zadeh In Muslim Persia, a saint's mausoleum.

imaret A type of hostelry for the accommodation of Muslim pilgrims and other travelers in the Turkish empire.

imbowment An **arch** or **vault.**

imbrex **1.** A tile, semicircular in shape, which fits over the joints in a tile roof. **2.** One of the scales in ornamental **imbrication.**

imbrex supinus A gutter formed by a series of ridge tiles fitted into one another and laid on their backs.

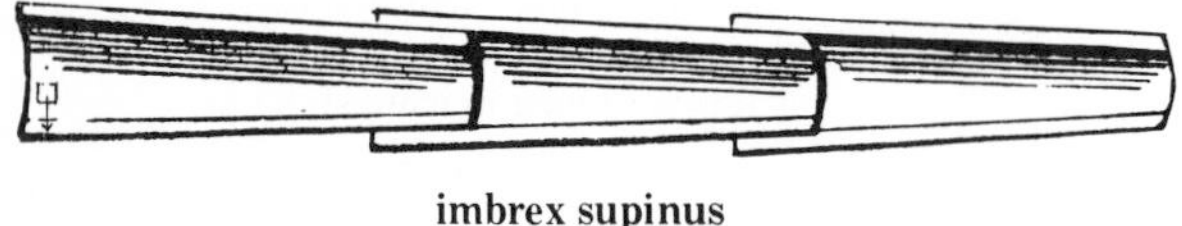

imbrex supinus

imbricate To overlap in regular order, as shingling, tiles, etc.

imbrication **1.** A weathertight covering, formed by overlapping rows of shaped tiles, shingles, or the like, using discontinuous joints perpendicular to the lap. **2.** A pattern on a surface that resembles imbrication.

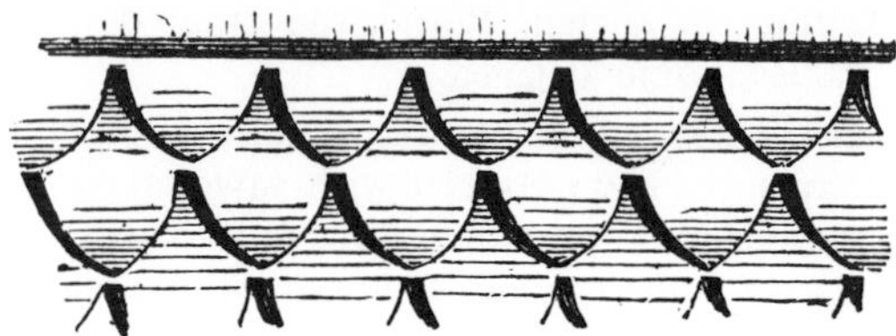

imbrication

immissarium A basin, trough, or other contrivance built on the ground, of stone or brick, to contain a body of water flowing from a reservoir (**castellum**) of an aqueduct, to accommodate the adjacent neighborhood.

immissarium at Pompeii: the high vaulted building is the reservoir; water flowed through the hole to the immissarium

impages **1.** The broad transverse band on a door, which stretches from stile to stile and divides the panels horizontally from one another; a **door rail.** **2.** The border or framework of a panel of a door.

impasto In painting, the thick laying of pigments.

imperfect arch A **diminished arch.**

impetus The span of a building, roof, or arch.

impluvium In ancient Roman dwellings, a cistern set in the **atrium** or **peristyle** to receive water from the roofs.

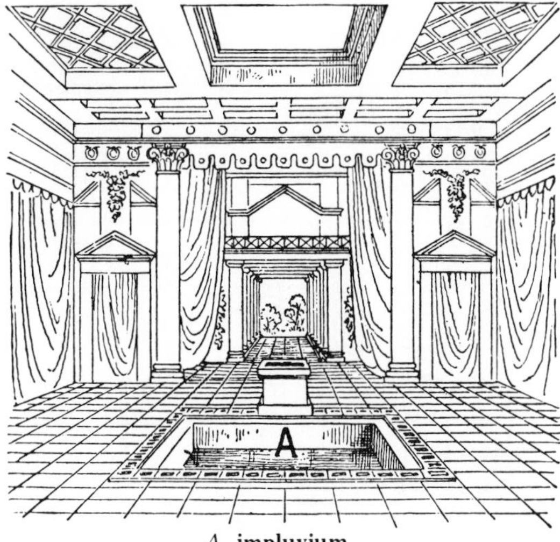

A, impluvium

impost 1. A masonry unit or course, often distinctively profiled, which receives and distributes the thrust at each end of an arch. Also see **abutment, springer.** 2. A vertical member in a gemel or double window taking the place of a mullion; an **integral mullion.**

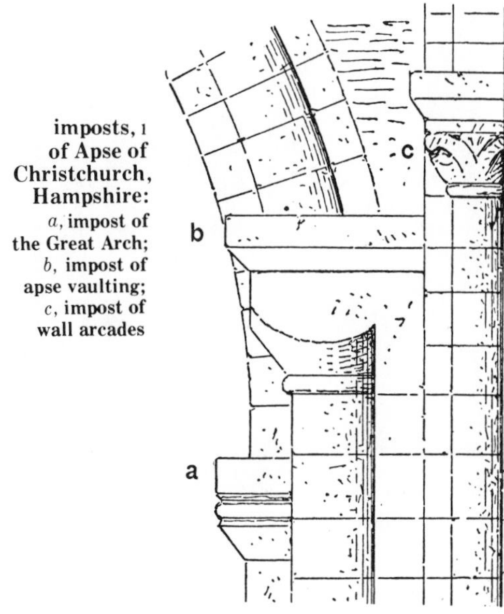

imposts, 1 of Apse of Christchurch, Hampshire: *a*, impost of the Great Arch; *b*, impost of apse vaulting; *c*, impost of wall arcades

impost block, dosseret, supercapital A transitional member, often tapered, placed above a column capital to receive the thrust of vaults or arches.

impost block: the block above the capital, St. Demetrius, Thessalonica (500–520 A.D.)

in-and-out bond In masonry, a **bond,** formed by headers and stretchers alternating vertically, esp. when formed at a corner, as by quoins.

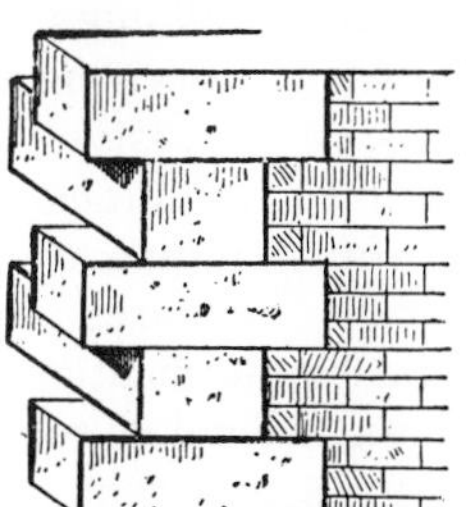

in-and-out bond formed of cut stones inserted in a brick wall

in antis Between **antae;** said of columns in a portico, or of the portico itself.

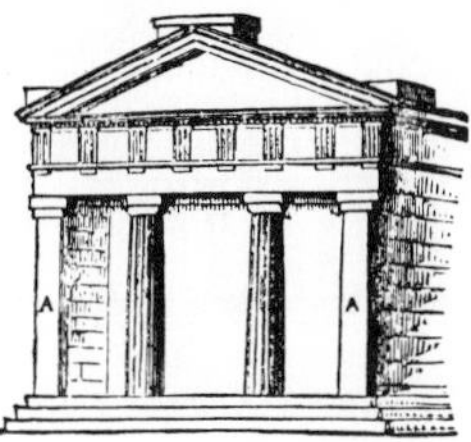

in antis, between antae, *A*, *A*

Inca architecture The architecture of the Inca Empire in Peru from the 12th cent. until the Spanish conquest in the 16th cent., particularly fortified towns with massive stonework.

in cavetto The reverse of relief, differing from intaglio in that the design is impressed into plaster or clay.

incavo The hollowed or incised part of an intaglio.

incertum opus See **opus incertum.**

indented molding, indenting A molding with the edge toothed or indented in triangular tooth-like shapes.

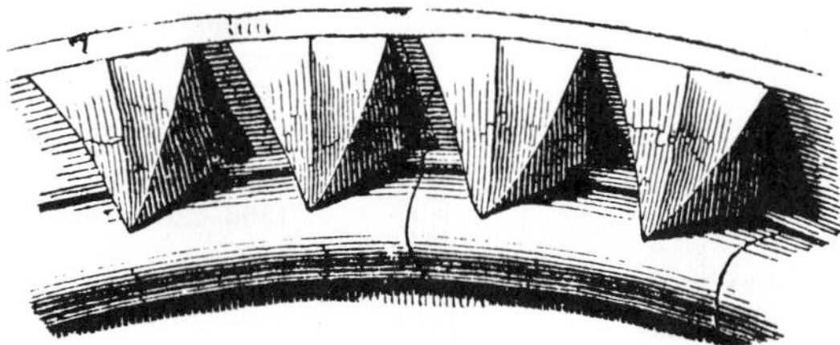

indented molding

Indian architecture The architecture of the Indian subcontinent, originally a timber and mud-brick architecture of which nothing survives. Early Buddhist monuments, chaitya halls, stupa rails, and toranas clearly imitate wood construction, and timber buildings appear on relief representations. All surviving architecture is of stone, using exclusively a structural system of post and lintel, brackets, and corbels. The basically simple Indian architectural forms are generally obscured and overwhelmed by a rhythmical multiplication of pilasters, cornices, moldings, aediculae, roofs, and finials, and an exuberant and sensuous overgrowth of sculptural decoration.

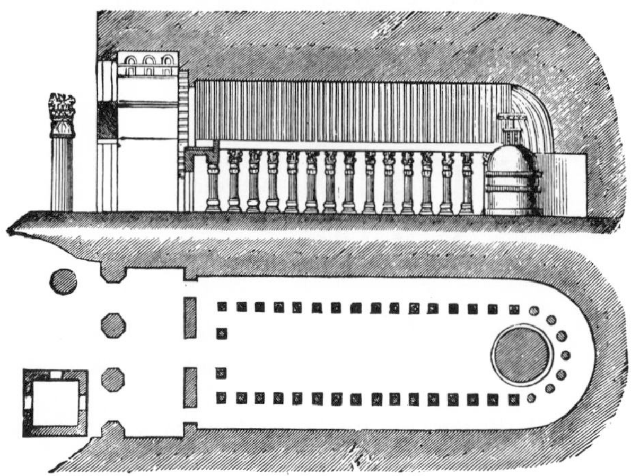

interior of rock-cut chaitya at Ajanta (250 B.C.)

Buddhist rock-cut cave at Nasik (129 B.C.)

left: rock-cut chaitya, ground plan and section; Karli (78 B.C.)

Buddhist rock-cut dagoba
at Ajanta (250 A.D.)

sikhara at Benares:
Temple of Visveswar

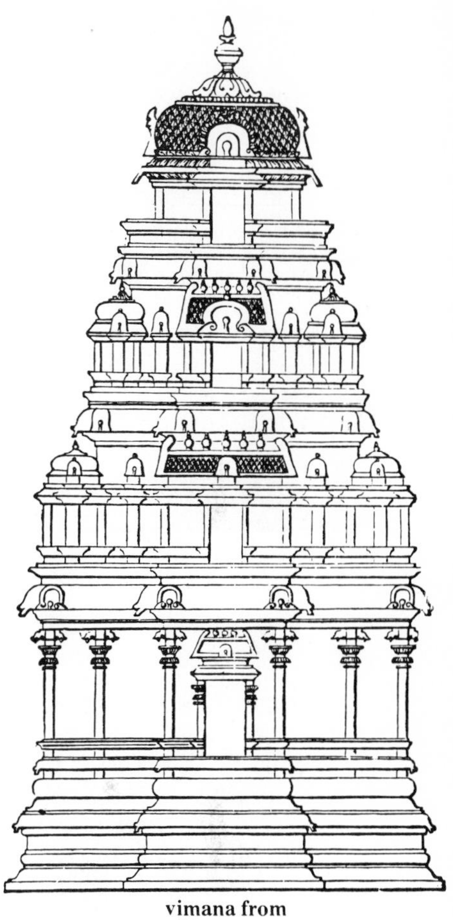
vimana from
Manasara

amalaka: the fluted crowning
of an Indo-Aryan sikhara

cross section, Gondesvara Temple
at Sinar (12th cent.); Indo-Aryan style

Indian architecture

interior of rock-cut Temple of Indra, Ellora; southern Dravidian style

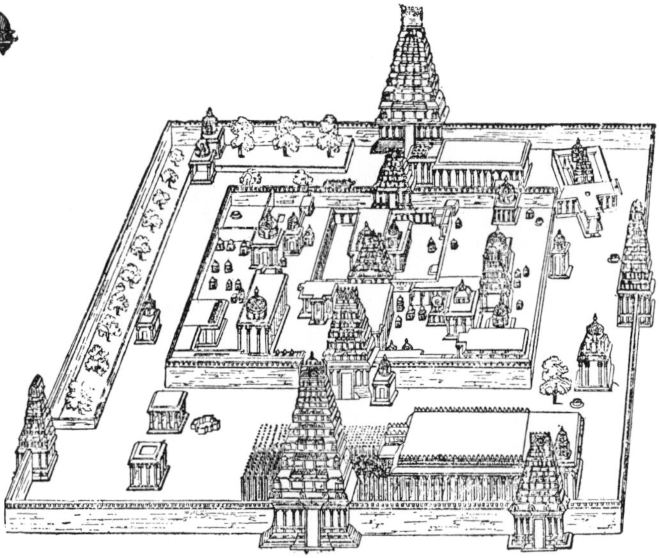

Hindu temple at Tiruvarur; later Dravidian style

one of the pillars in a pillared hall attached outside a Dravidian temple

inflected arch Same as **inverted arch.**

in-glaze decoration A ceramic decoration applied on the surface of an unfired glaze and then matured with the glaze.

ingle A fireplace; a hearth.

inglenook A **chimney corner.**

inlay, intarsia, marquetry **1.** A shaped piece of one material embedded in another as part of a surface ornamentation. **2.** Such ornamentation as a whole. Also see **encaustic tile.**

inlay: black and white marble pavement of Baptistery, Florence (c. 1200)

inn **1.** A place which provides eating and drinking, but no lodging, for the public; a tavern. **2.** A hotel. **3.** A student hostel or residence. **4.** A **hospice.**

inner hearth See **back hearth.**

inner sanctum A most sacred place.

inosculating column Same as **clustered column.**

inserted column A column which is partially inserted in a wall; an **engaged column.**

insula In Roman town planning, a block of buildings surrounded by streets.

insulated column A column which is entirely detached from a building or structure.

intaglio **1.** Incised engraving, as opposed to carving in relief. **2.** The work producing such an object.

intaglio rilevato See **sunk relief.**

intarsia Mosaic inlay, esp. the Italian Renaissance wooden form.

integral mullion See **impost, 2.**

intercapedo The passage between the **caldarium** and the **laconicum** in a Roman bath; the flooring of the passage was over the **hypocaustum.**

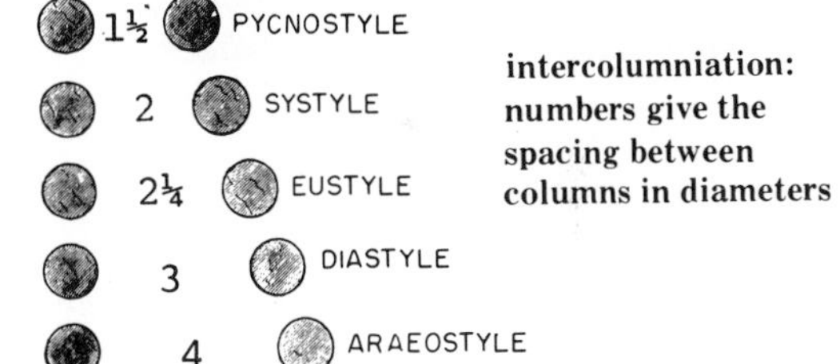

intercolumniation: numbers give the spacing between columns in diameters

intercolumniation **1.** The clear space between two adjacent columns, usually measured at the lower parts of the shafts. **2.** The system of spacing between columns which determines the style: *pycnostyle,* 1½ diameters; *systyle,* 2 diameters; *eustyle,* 2¼ diameters; *diastyle,* 3 diameters; *araeostyle,* 4 diameters.

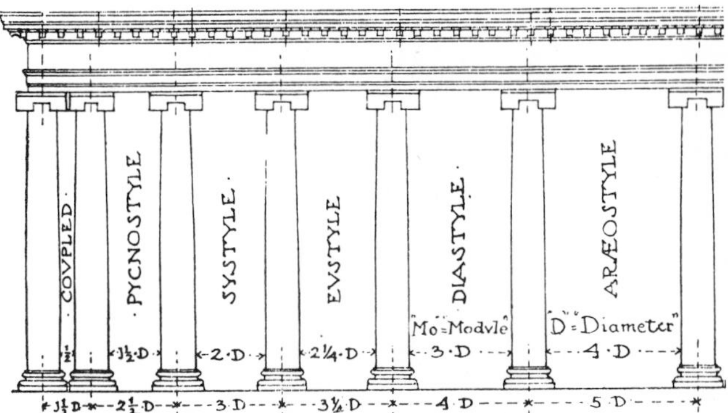

Roman Ionic intercolumniation

intercupola **1.** The space between two cupolas. **2.** The space between two shells of a cupola.

interdentil The space between two dentils.

interdome The space between the inner and outer shells of a dome.

interfenestration The space between windows in a façade consisting chiefly of the windows with their decorations.

interglyph The space between two grooves or cuts, as in a triglyph; usually a flat surface below which the groove itself has been sunk.

interlace, entrelacs An ornament of bands or stalks elaborately intertwined, sometimes including fantastic images. Also see **knot.**

interlace

interlaced arches See **interlacing arcade.**

interlacement band Same as **guilloche.**

interlacing arcade Arches resting on alternate supports in one row, the arches overlapping in series where they cross. Also see **intersecting arcade.**

interlacing arcade, St. John's, Devizes (c. 1150)

intermediate rafter See **common rafter.**

intermediate rib **1.** A rib in vaulting subordinate to the primary ribs. **2.** In a sexpartite vault, the transverse rib in the middle of the bay, above the intermediate and smaller piers.

internal dormer A vertical window in a sloped roof; unlike the usual **dormer window,** it is not covered by a small pitched roof, but projects down from (and is set below) the slope of the main roof.

International style The functional architecture devoid of regional characteristics, created in Western Europe and the U.S.A. during the early 20th cent. and applied throughout the world.

interrupted arch A segmental pediment whose center has been omitted, often to accommodate an ornament.

interrupted arched molding A common Norman molding consisting of a series of interrupted arches.

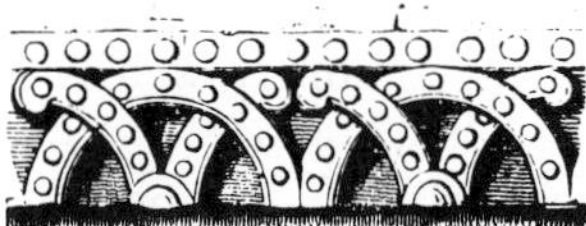

interrupted arched molding

intersecting arcade Arches resting on alternate supports in one row, the arches meeting on one plane at the crossings. Also see **interlacing arcade.**

intersecting arcade: Christ Church, Oxford (end of 12th cent.)

intersecting tracery Tracery formed by the curving upward, forking, and continuation of the mullions, springing from alternate mullions or from every third mullion and intersecting each other.

interstitium The crossing in a cruciform church.

intertignium The space between the ends of the tie beams (**tigna**) which rest upon the architrave (**trabes**) of a roof.

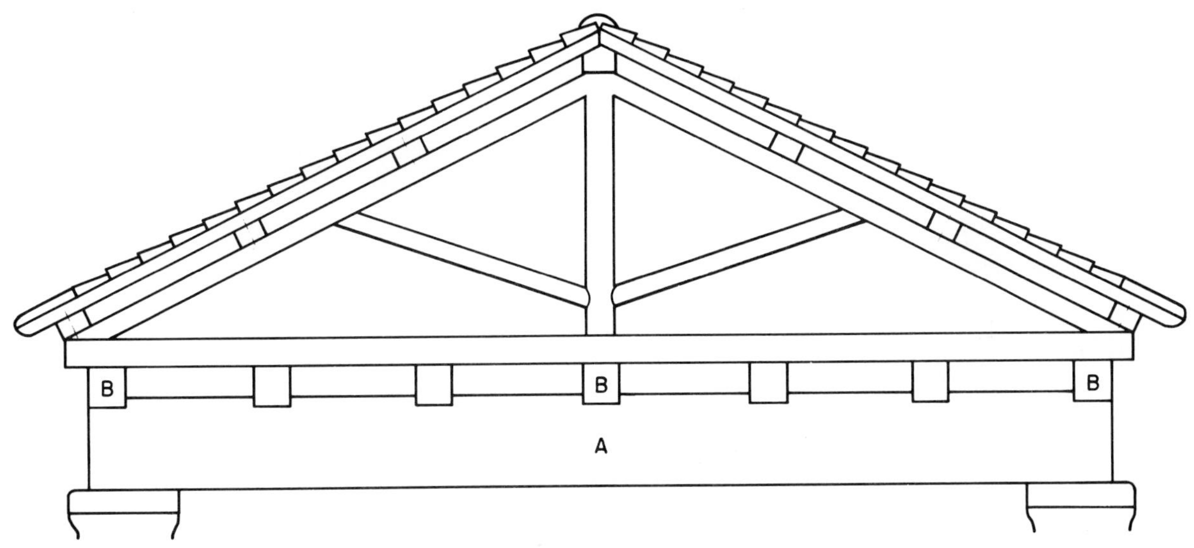

intertignium
in Roman roof construction: *A*, **architrave (trabes);**
B-B-B, **tigna (tie beams); six of the spaces are shown here**

intertriglyph The space between two triglyphs in a Doric frieze; a **metope.**

intonaco The fine finish coat of plaster made with white marble dust to receive a fresco painting.

intrados The inner curve or face of an arch or vault forming the concave underside.

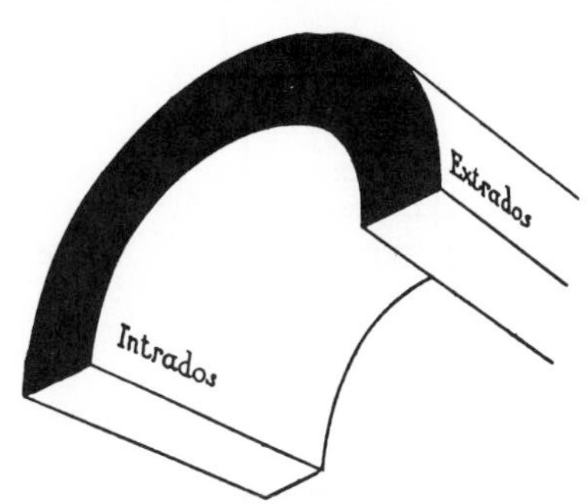

inverted arch An arch with its intrados below the springing line; esp. used to distribute concentrated loads in foundations.

inverted arch

involute **1.** A curve traced by a point at the end of a string as the string is unwound from a stationary cylinder. **2.** Curved spirally.

inwrought Closely combined or profusely embellished.

Ionic 1. Pertaining to, or characteristic of, Ionia. Same as **Ionic Order.**

Ionic order The classical order of architecture, originated by the Ionian Greeks, characterized by its capital with large volutes, a fasciated entablature, continuous frieze, usually dentils in the cornice, and by its elegant detailing, less heavy than the Doric, less elaborate than the Corinthian.

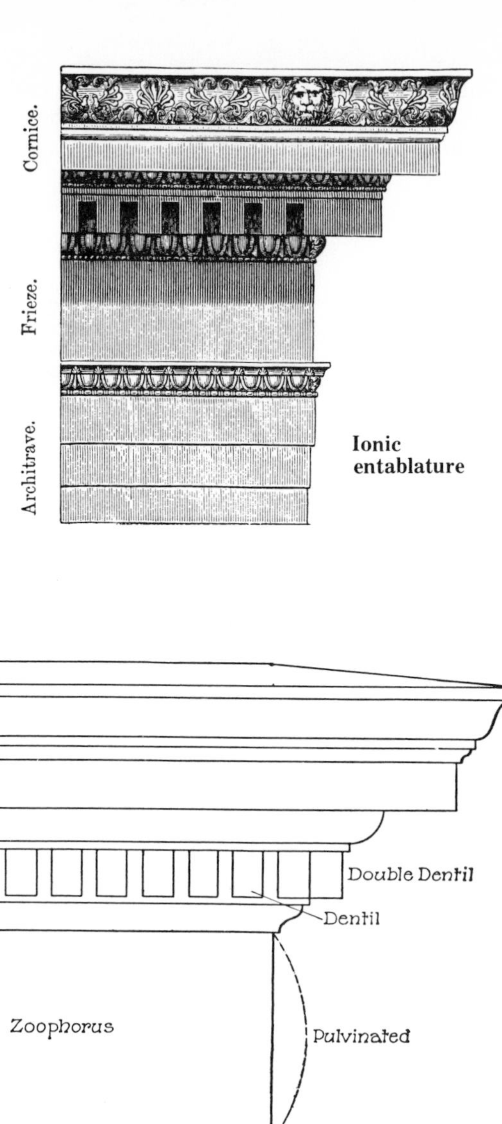

Ionic entablature

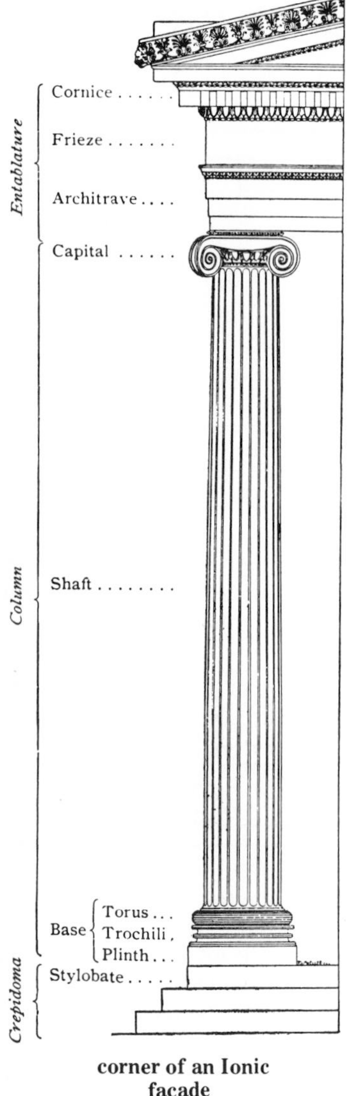

corner of an Ionic façade

Ionic order

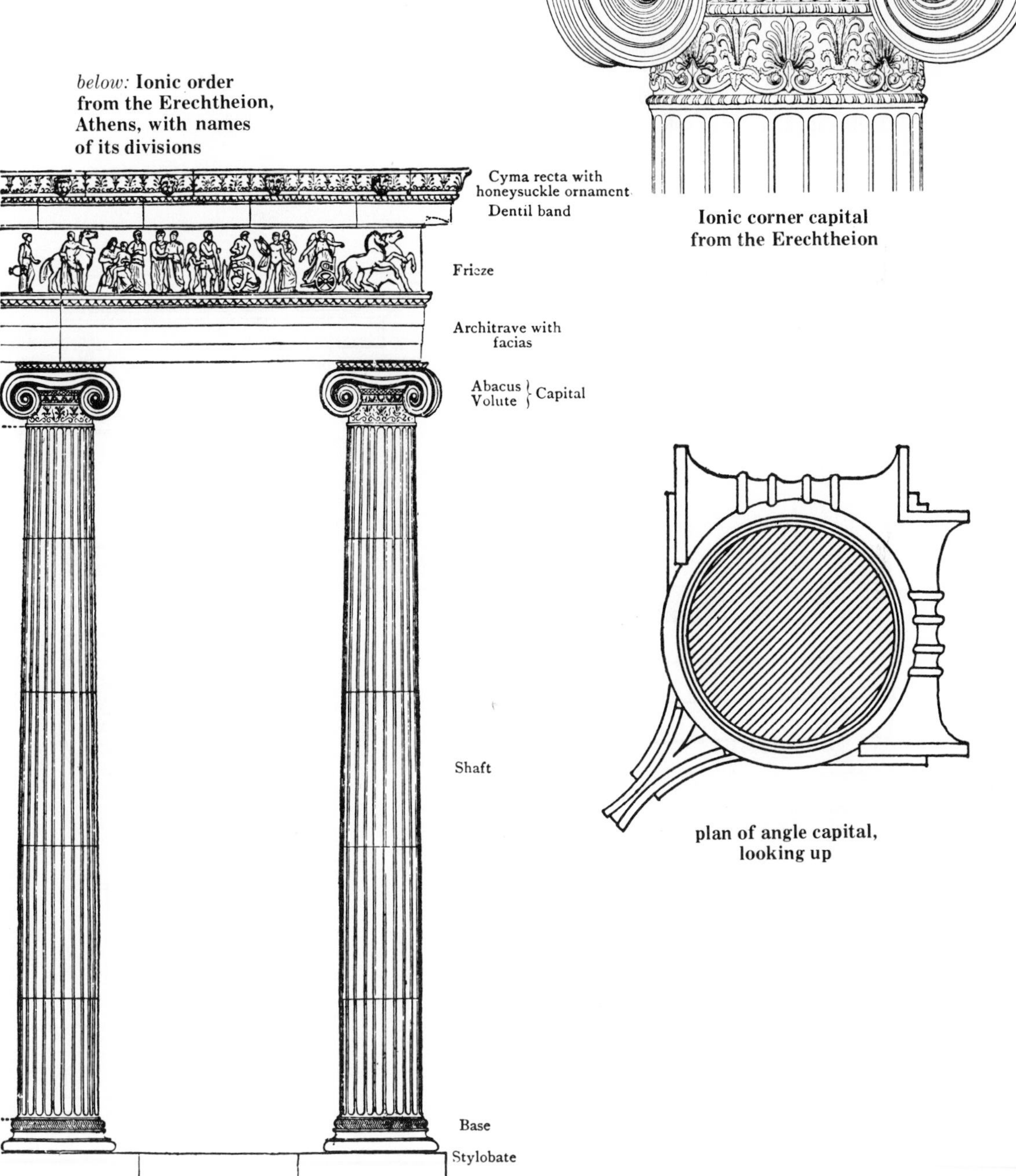

below: **Ionic order from the Erechtheion, Athens, with names of its divisions**

Ionic corner capital from the Erechtheion

plan of angle capital, looking up

Ionic order

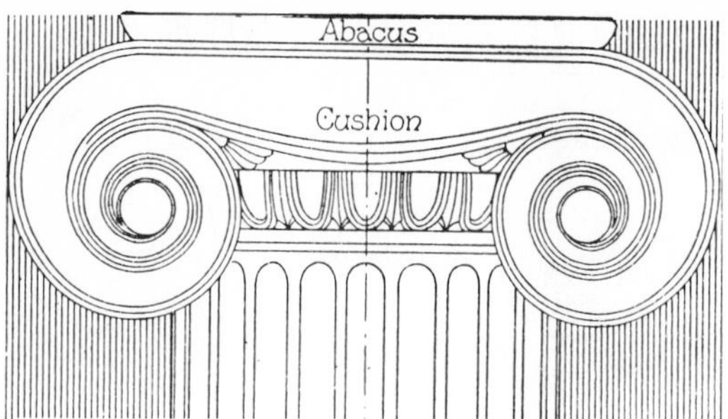

Ionic capital, cushion side

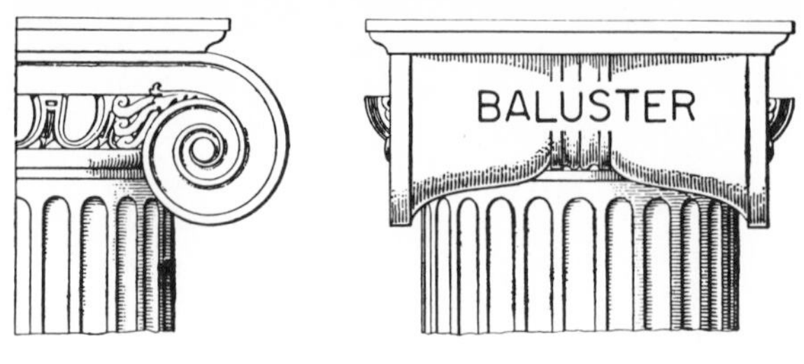

Ionic capital, baluster side

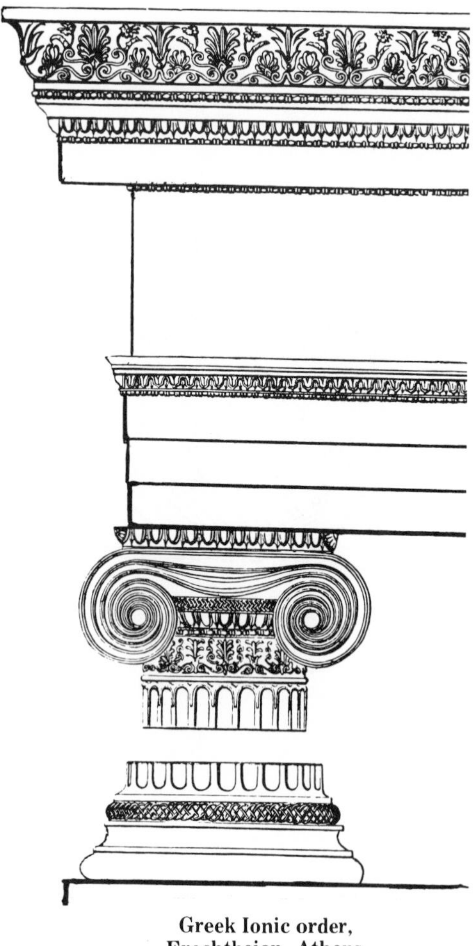

Greek Ionic order,
Erechtheion, Athens

Roman Ionic order

irimoya-yane A hipped and gabled roof of a traditional Japanese structure; the upper section is sloped on two sides, and the lower section is sloped on all four sides.

irimoya-yane
入母屋屋根

ironwork Wrought iron or cast iron; usually decorative, often elaborate.

Isabelline architecture See **Plateresque architecture.**

Ise Jingu 伊勢神宮 Located in Mie prefecture of Japan, the most sacred shrine dedicated to the Sun Goddess. Every twenty years a completely new set of buildings is reconstructed in the Shimmei style, on alternate sites adjacent to the existing structures. Hence the original style has continued at least from the Nara period, if not earlier, representing an unadulterated Japanese style of architecture.

Ishtar Gate See **Babylonian architecture.**

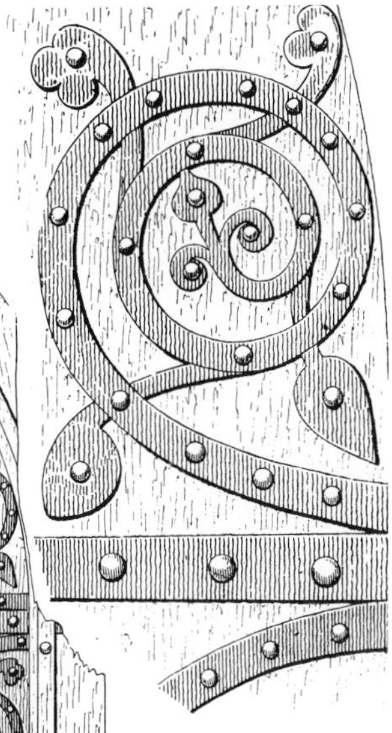

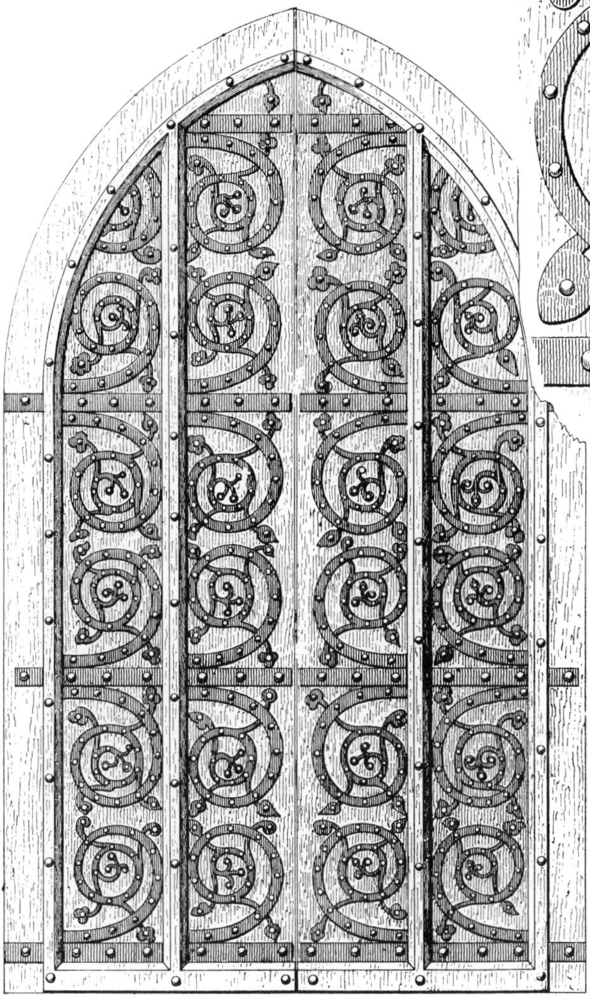

ironwork, Blocking Church, Essex; *above:* **detail**

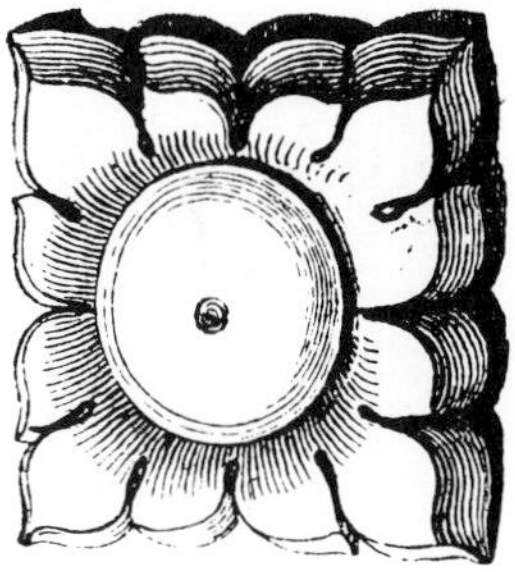

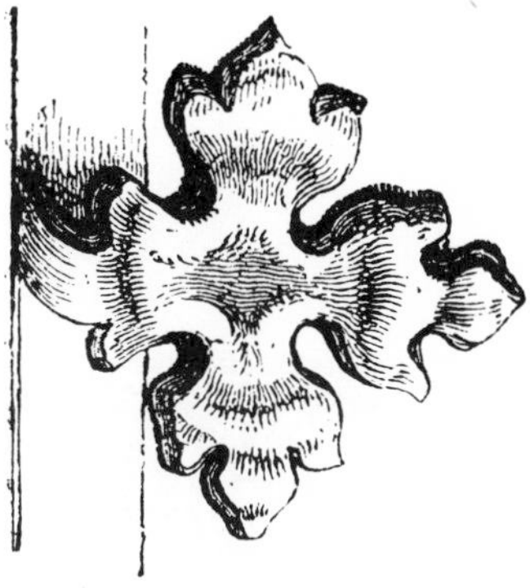

ironwork, Henry VII Chapel, Westminster Abbey (1503–19)

Islamic architecture

Islamic architecture, Muslim architecture The architecture of the peoples of Islamic faith, also called Mohammedan, which from the 7th cent. onward expanded throughout the Mediterranean world and as far as India and China, producing a variety of great regional works and local decorative styles. It is characterized by domes, horseshoe and round arches, tunnel vaults and rich ornaments, geometric because of the ban on human and animal representation. Also see **Muslim architecture.**

façade, Mosque of Sultan Ahmed, Constantinople (1610–16)

portal, Mosque of Ispahan (Isfahan), Persia

Islamic horseshoe arch

Islamic decoration (1st cent.)

isocephalic In bas-relief, having the heads nearly on a horizontal line; esp. said of the heads of human figures in a frieze or band.

isocephalic frieze at the Parthenon

isodomum In ancient Roman and Greek masonry, an extremely regular masonry pattern in which stones of uniform length and uniform height are set so that each vertical joint is centered over the block beneath. Horizontal joints are continuous, and the vertical joints form discontinuous straight lines; **opus isodomum.**

isodomum

ita-kaerumata See **kaerumata.**

Italian roof Same as **hip roof.**

Italian tiling Same as **pan-and-roll roofing tile.**

Italian villa style, Italianate style The eclectic form of country-house design, fashionable in England and the U.S. in the 1840s and 1850s, characterized by low-pitched, heavily bracketed roofs, asymmetrical informal plan, square towers, and often round-arched windows.

Italian villa style

iugumentum The **lintel** of an ancient Roman door.

iwan A large vaulted hall having one side open to a court; prevalent in Parthian, Sassanian, and Muslim architecture.

izba A Russian **log cabin,** log house, or hut.

J

jack arch Same as **flat arch.**

jack rafter Any rafter that is shorter than the usual length of the rafters used in the same building; esp. occurs in hip roofs.

jack rib Any rib in a framed arch or dome shorter than the others.

Jacobean architecture English architectural and decorative style of the early 17th cent., adapting the Elizabethan style to continental Renaissance influences; named after James I (1603–1625), but continuing beyond his death.

Jacobean architecture

jagamohan An enclosed square assembly porch in a Nagara-style temple, corresponding to the **mandapa** in southern India.

jagging Notching or indenting, as on beams.

jamb A vertical member at each side of a doorframe, window frame, or door lining.

jamb post An upright timber at the side of an opening; a wood **jamb.**

J, *J*, jambs: Church of St. Genest, France (12th cent.)

jamb shaft A small shaft having a capital and a base, placed against or forming part of the jamb of a door or window; occurs mostly in medieval architecture.

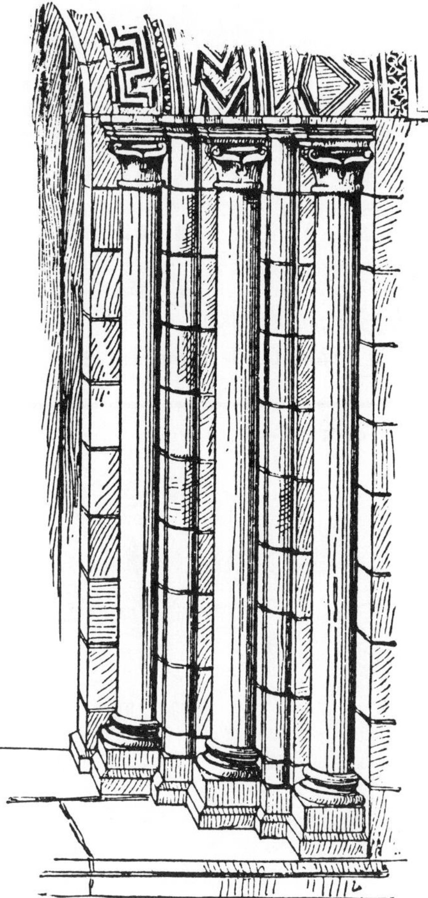

jamb shafts, galilee porch, Durham Cathedral (1093–1133)

jambstone A stone which forms a **jamb** of a door.

jamb stove An 18th cent. cast-iron stove at the back wall of a fireplace; projects into and heats the room adjoining the back of the fireplace.

jami A **mosque** intended for large congregations.

janua **1.** In ancient Roman architecture, the door of a house or any covered edifice. **2.** The front door which opens on the street; also called **anticum.**

janua,2: doorway to house in Pompeii

Janus A divinity regarded by the ancient Romans as the doorkeeper of heaven and the special patron of the beginning and ending of all undertakings; as god of the sun's rising and setting, he had two faces, one looking east, the other looking west.

Japanese architecture Architecture of timber construction exclusively, from the 5th cent. A.D. under the strong influence of China. Simple pavilion-like structures consist of a wooden framework of uprights and tie beams supported by a platform, with nonbearing plaster or wood panel walls, sliding partitions, and doors and windows of lightweight material—often paper. The tiled, hipped roofs are widely projecting and upward-turning, on elaborate bracket systems. Stone is used only for pillar bases, platforms, and fortification walls. Great emphasis is put on the integration of buildings with their surroundings, with verandas providing the transition. Proportions of floor dimensions, height, and length of walls follow fixed standards.

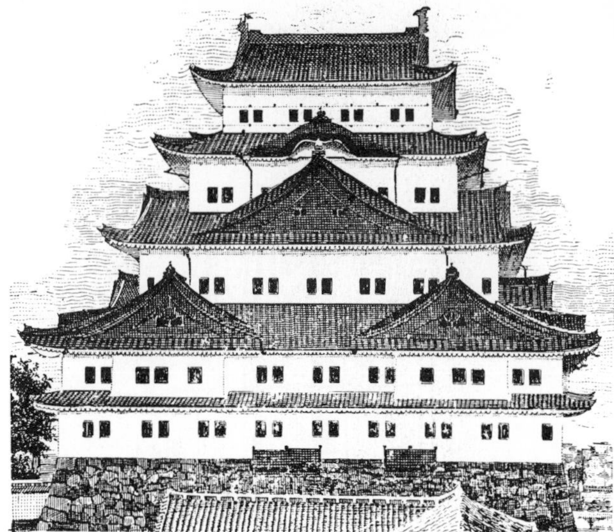

Nagoya Castle (completed 1612)

1. The *Honden*, or Main Shrine
2. The *Haiden*, or Oratory
3. The *Ai-no-ma*, or Corridor
4. The *Mitarashi*, or Cistern for Purification before Prayer
5. The *Tama-gaki* (Jewel Hedge), a wall inclosing the principal buildings
6. The *Ita gaki*, or board Hedge
7. The *Torii*
8. The *Shamusho*, or Temple Office
9. The *Sessha*, or Secondary Shrines
10. The *Bunko*, or Library
11. The *Hozo*, or Treasure House
12. Places for Offerings
13. The *Kwairo*, or Gallery
14. The *Kagura-do*, or Dancing Stage
15. Stable for the Sacred Horse
16. Assembly Hall
17. Gates

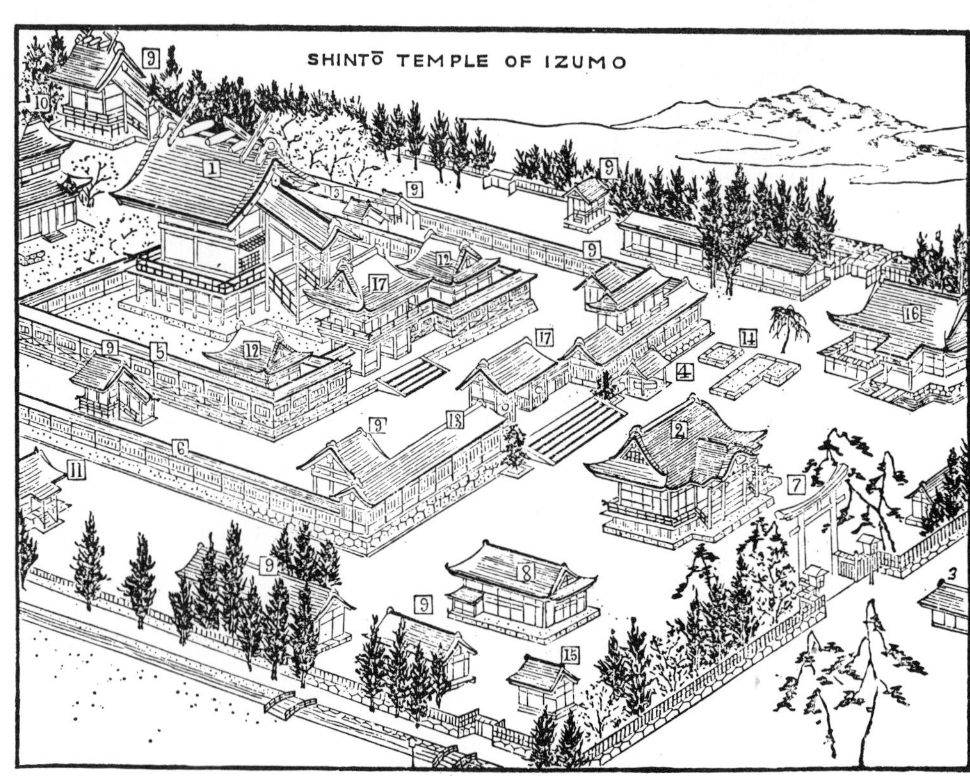

Izumo Taisha (Great Shrine of Izumo), rebuilt in 1874, is the oldest in Japan; dedicated to a Shintō deity

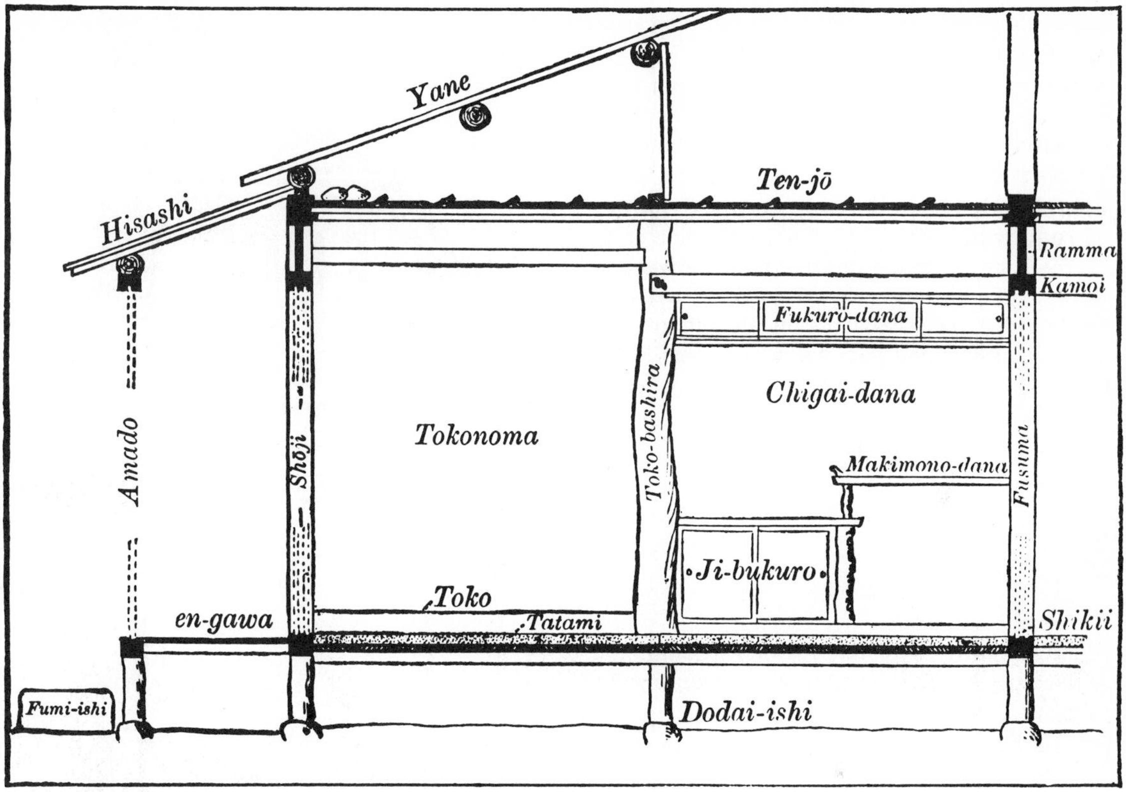

Yane
Hisashi
Ten-jō
Ramma
Kamoi
Fukuro-dana
Chigai-dana
Toko-bashira
Tokonoma
Amado
Shōji
Makimono-dana
Fusuma
Ji-bukuro
Toko
Tatami
en-gawa
Shikii
Fumi-ishi
Dodai-ishi

section through a Japanese house

types of ridges of thatched roofs

jaspé Mottled and marbled to resemble variegated stone, and to mask signs of use.

jawab A false building or structure, set in a complex of other structures, which is constructed solely to achieve a desired balance or proportions.

jerkinhead, clipped gable, hipped gable, shreadhead The end of a roof when it is formed into a shape intermediate between a gable and a hip; the gable rises about halfway to the ridge, resulting in a truncated shape, the roof being inclined backward from this level.

jerkinhead

Jerusalem cross A Greek cross with a smaller Greek cross inscribed in each of the four spaces between the arms.

Jerusalem cross

Jesse window A painted window containing a decorative genealogical tree representing the genealogy of Christ.

jesting beam A beam introduced for the sake of appearance and not for use.

jetty A projecting part of a building, as a bay window or the upper story of a timber house.

jib door, gib door A door which is flush with, and treated in the same manner as, the surrounding wall so as to be concealed; has no visible hardware on the room side.

食堂

jikidō The refectory in an ancient Buddhist Temple.

軸組

jikugumi The construction and assembly of the basic framework of a traditional Japanese building, including joists, pillars, rafters, crossbeams, etc.

jimmer See **gemel.**

jinja, jinsha A Shintō shrine.

jinsha See **jinja.** 神社

joggle: hood over fireplace. The lintel is constructed of stones supporting each other by joggles

joggle A notch or projection in one piece of material which is fitted to a projection or notch in a second piece to prevent one piece from slipping on the other.

joggle joint A joint between two blocks of material (such as masonry) which fit one into the other by a **joggle.**

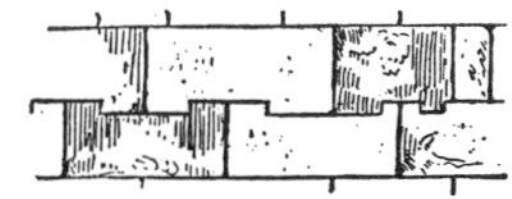

joggle joints

joggle post **1.** A post made of two or more pieces of timber joggled together. **2.** A **king post** having shoulders or notches at its lower end to support the feet of struts.

joggle work In masonry, construction in which stones are keyed together by **joggles.**

joist One of a series of parallel timber beams used to support floor and ceiling loads, and supported in turn by larger beams, girders, or bearing walls; the widest dimension is vertically oriented.

joist anchor A **beam anchor.**

城郭 **jōkaku** The stronghold or citadel of an ancient Japanese castle.

jopys, jopies The **collar beams** of a roof.

jube A screen separating the chancel from the nave or aisles, or both. Also see **rood screen.**

judas, judas-hole, judas window A small trap or hole in a door for peering or watching, as in a prison door.

Jugendstil "Youth style"; the German version of Art Nouveau.

jutty A **jetty.**

jut window Any window that projects from the line of the building, as a **bow window** or **bay window.**

judas

jube, Albi Cathedral, France (1282–1390)

ka'a, qa'a The reception room of a palace or house in the Near East.

Kaaba A cube-shaped, flat-roofed building in the center of the Great Mosque at Mecca; the most sacred shrine of the Muslims.

Kabah Same as **Kaaba.**

壁 **kabe** In traditional Japanese architecture, a wall.

蟇股 **kaerumata** A decorative strut placed between two horizontal plates; the shape of the strut resembles the outstretched legs of a frog; in one type, the shape is outlined **(hon-kaerumata)**; in the other type, a solid plank is cut to a specific shape **(ita-kaerumata)**.

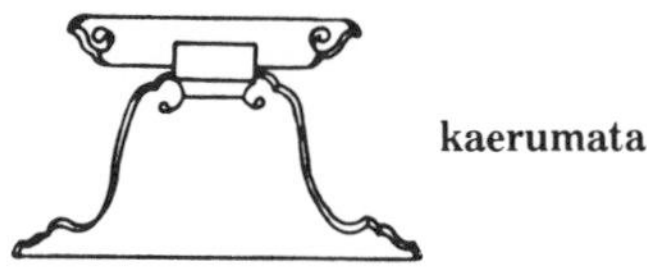

kaerumata

階段 **kaidan** Steps or stairs in Japanese architecture.

Kailasa A multistoried Brahmanical temple, constructed as an allegory of the sacred mountain, Kailasa, favorite abode of Hindu god Shiva. Located at Ellora, India, an outstanding example of an ancient **rock-cut** temple.

kairō A covered corridor surrounding the central core of a Buddhist temple or Shintō shrine.

kala A monster head, intended to avert evil, which was featured over entrances and in niches of Hindu temples.

kal'a, qala'a An Arab fortress or stronghold built on a hill.

kalasa In Indian architecture, an ornamental pot, usually a crowning feature on a sikhara.

kale A Turkish citadel or fortress.

kamebara See **kidan.**

kamoi In traditional Japanese architecture, the upper grooved beam which holds a sliding partition or screen (shōji). Also see **shikii** (lower grooved beam).

龕 **k'an** In ancient Chinese architecture, a niche for the storage of manuscripts; later such niches were used as shrines for the tablets of ancestors or for statues; the more elaborate niches include pedestals and columns; the less elaborate niches (in small houses) were used to display works of art or to house incense burners.

炕 **k'ang** In dwellings and palaces in northwest China and Korea, a radiant heating system in which hot air is supplied from a central furnace to hollow clay-tile blocks set in the floor.

Karnak See **Thebes.**

kasr, qasr An Arabic palace, castle, or mansion.

katabasis In the Greek Orthodox church, a place under the altar for relics.

katholikon **1.** The central nave of a church. **2.** The church of a monastery.

katolikon See **katholikon.**

鰹木 **katsuogi** On certain Shintō shrines, short circular billets placed at right angles to the ridge of the roof; may be as many as ten in number.

Katsura Rikyū A detached palace for imperial princes of Japan, located in Kyōto; constructed in the Edo period, a superlative example of the **Shōin style.** The grounds contain numerous buildings, including one with a famous tea room, noted for its unusually good lighting. Its magnificent gardens and the buildings are superbly interrelated.

茅葺 **kaya-buki** On a Japanese structure, a roof thatched with grass called *kaya.*

keblah See **kiblah.**

keel An appendage of a molding, usually a fillet, on the furthest projection of a molding.

keel arch Same as **ogee arch.**

keel molding A **brace molding** in which the ogee curves meet sharply at a point or fillet more or less resembling the shape of a ship's keel.

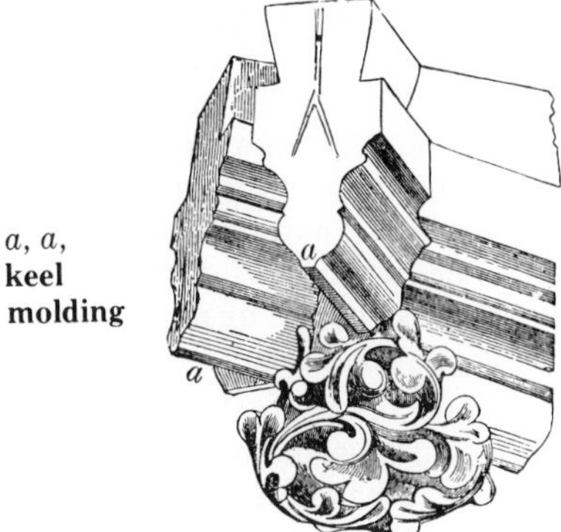

a, *a*, **keel molding**

keep, donjon The stronghold of a medieval castle, usually in the form of a massive tower, and a place of residence, esp. in times of siege.

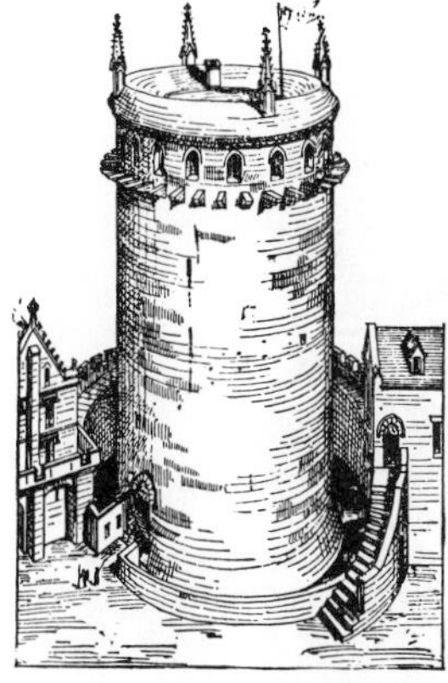
keep, Castle of Cousy, Aisne, France, as seen from the inner court

keeping room A room (often rectangular) at the back of a colonial New England house, which served as a combination kitchen, living room, and workroom.

間 **ken** A unit of linear measurement equal to 5.96 ft (1.818 m); the dimension most commonly used for spacing the centers of pillars in traditional Japanese structures.

Kentish tracery Circumscribed tracery motif, with foils separated by barbs or with forked cusps.

kepe Same as **keep.**

kercis Same as **kerkis.**

kerkis In an ancient Greek theatre, one of the wedge-shaped sections of seating of the theatre, divided by radiating staircases.

kernel Same as **crenel.**

Kentish tracery

桁 **keta** A beam of a traditional Japanese structure; similar to **lin tzŭ** in traditional Chinese construction.

key block A **keystone.**

key brick A brick which is tapered toward one end; used in brick arches.

key console A **console** which acts as the **keystone** of an arch.

key course **1.** A course of keystones in an arch; used in a deep archway where a single keystone will not suffice. **2.** A course of keystones used in the crown of a barrel vault.

key pattern See **labyrinth fret.**

keystone, key block **1.** In masonry, the central, often embellished, voussoir of an arch. Until the keystone is in place, no true arch action is incurred. **2.** An element resembling a keystone in function or in shape.

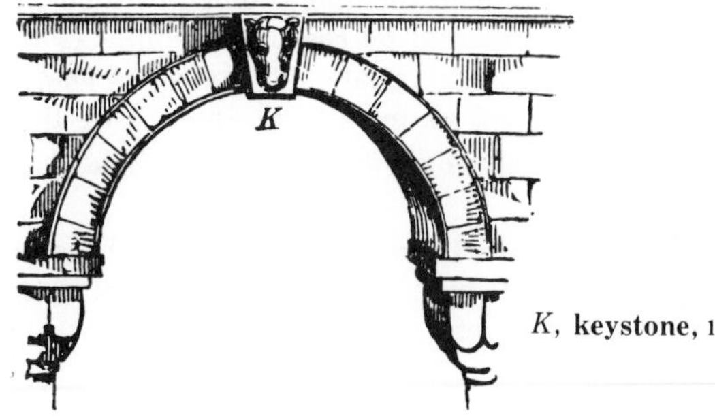

K, **keystone,** 1

khan Same as **caravanserai.**

khangah, khanka The Muslim equivalent of a monastery; a retreat for dervishes.

khirbeh A ruin, in Muslim architecture.

Khorsabad See **Assyrian architecture.**

khory In early Russian architecture, a gallery.

kiblah, keblah, qibla In Islam, the required orientation of the prayer niche, toward Mecca.

基壇 **kidan** The foundation or podium of a Buddhist temple building. May be of three types: hard-packed earth covered with rectangular blocks of stone *(danjōzumi)*; hard-packed earth covered with dressed stone having natural shapes and smooth finishes *(ranzumi)*; an earthen mound covered with thick plaster *(kamebara)*.

killesse Same as **coulisse.**

kingbolt A tie rod or long bolt which takes the place of a **king post.**

king post **1.** In a truss, as for a roof, a vertical member extending from the apex of the inclined rafters to the tie beam between the rafters at their lower ends. **2.** See **joggle post, 2.**

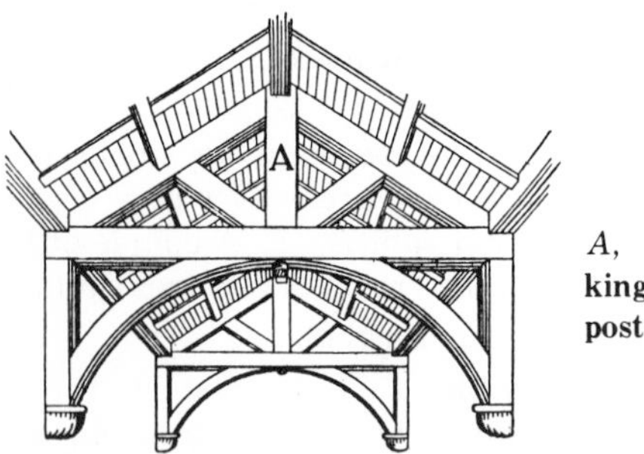

A, king post

king-post truss A triangular frame formed by two inclined members joined at their apex and a horizontal **tie beam** that connects their lower ends; a vertical central strut (a **king post** or a **kingbolt**) extends from apex to tie beam.

King Solomon's Temple See **Temple of Solomon.**

king-table In medieval architecture, the **stringcourse,** with ballflower ornaments, usual under parapets.

Kinkakuji Formerly the villa of Ashikaga Yoshimitsu, the third Shōgun of the Muromachi period in Japan, located in Kyōto city; converted into a Zen temple after he died. Its most important structure is the Kinkaku (Golden Pavilion) of the Muromachi period, 1398, which was destroyed by fire in 1950 but reconstructed, exactly as it had been, in 1954. Also called **Rokuonji.**

kiosk **1.** A small pavilion, usually open, built in gardens and parks. **2.** In Turkish architecture, a pavilion.

kiosk,1: Paris

kiot In early Russian architecture, a niche to house one or more icons.

kirizuma-yane A gabled roof of a traditional Japanese structure; has two sloping sides which are connected at the ridge of the roof.

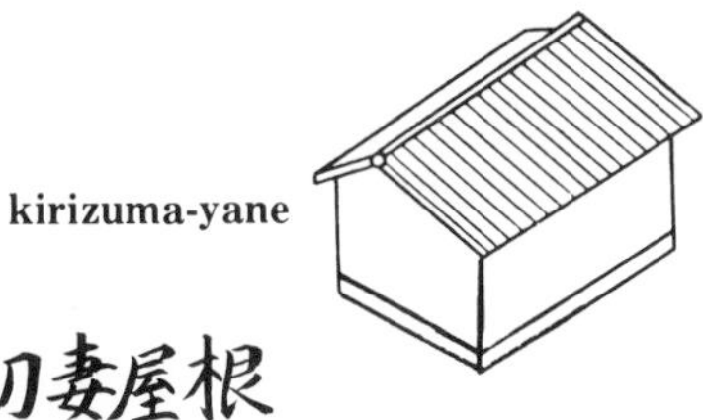

kirizuma-yane

切妻屋根

kirk, kirke A church, esp. in Scotland.

kirnel Same as **crenel.**

kirtimukha A grotesque mask appearing as an ornament on Hindu temples.

kiryah In ancient Israel, a city.

kistvaen See **cistvaen.**

kliros The choir platform in a Russian Orthodox church.

knee **1.** A piece of wood having a bend, either natural or artificially set; a **crook.** **2.** A part of the back of a handrail having a convex upper surface. **3.** See **label stop, 2.**

kneeler, kneestone, skew **1.** A building stone which is sloped on top and flat on the bottom, as the stone that supports inclined coping on the slope of a gable. Also see **footstone; gable springer.** **2.** The stone that breaks the horizontal-vertical unit-and-joint pattern of a normal masonry wall to begin the curve or angle of an arch or vault.

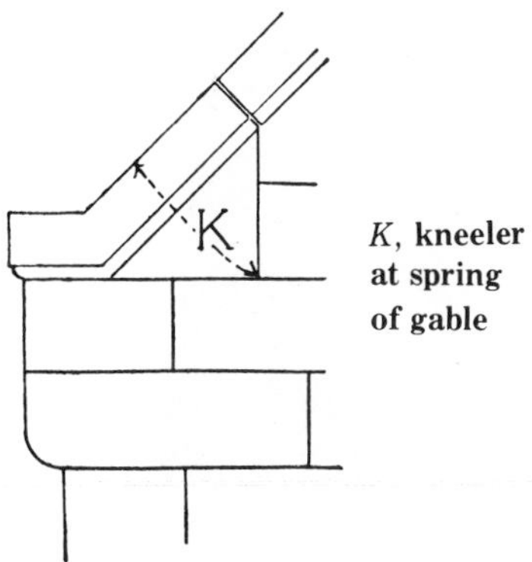

***K*, kneeler at spring of gable**

knob **1.** A handle, more or less spherical, usually for operating a lock. **2.** A protuberance, useful or ornamental, which forms the termination of an isolated (usually slender) member.

knob,2

knocker A knob, bar, or ring of metal, attached to the outside of an exterior door to enable a person to announce his presence; usually held by a hinge so that it can be lifted and allowed to strike a metal plate.

knocker from a 16th cent. palazzo, Bologna

Knossos The site of a large palace on the Island of Crete, site of a large palace traditionally associated with King Minos. Mainly constructed during the middle of the Minoan III period (1700–1550 B.C.) above the remains of an earlier palace; destroyed in 1500 B.C., rebuilt, and then destroyed again ca. 1400 B.C. As in all **Minoan architecture,** groups of rectangular rooms are clustered around a large central courtyard, which served as a theatrical area. To the east were located the domestic quarters; to the west the official palace chambers with the throne room; behind long connecting corridors were deep, narrow storage rooms. An excellent drainage system served the palace complex; open shafts provided light and ventilation to the interior spaces. Exquisite frescoes decorate the walls.

knot **1.** In medieval architecture, a bunch of leaves, flowers, or similar ornament, as the bosses at the intersections of ribs, and bunches of foliage in capitals. **2.** An ornamental design resembling cords which are interlaced.

knotted pillar, knotted shaft A form of pillar, occurring in Romanesque architecture, so carved as to appear knotted in the middle.

knotted pillar, Basilica of St. Mark, Venice (1063–1085)

knotwork A carved ornamental arrangement of cord-like figures knotted together as in some kinds of fringe, used to decorate voussoirs, moldings, etc.

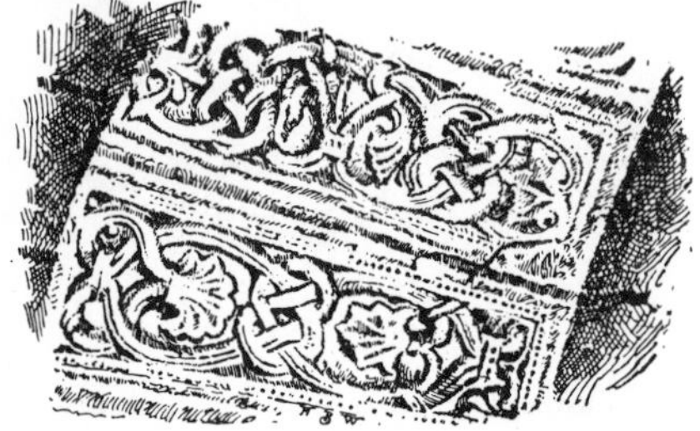

knotwork, Angers Cathedral (1149–1274)

knulling, knurling A convex rounded molding of slight projection, consisting of a series of more or less elaborate members separated by indentations.

講堂 **kōdō** A rectangular one-story building used as a lecture hall for the instruction of Buddhist monks.

koil, kovil A Hindu temple in southern India.

杮葺 **kokera-buki** In traditional Japanese roof construction, a roof covering composed of wood shingles, used in multiple layers.

kokoshniki **1.** In early Russian architecture, a series of corbeled arches (usually one of two or three tiers, one above the other); esp. used around the drum supporting a cupola. **2.** Any similar decorative feature.

kokoshniki,1

kolokolnya In Early Russian architecture, a **bell tower.**

kondō A sacred hall (literally, "golden hall"), the sanctuary where the main image of worship is kept in a Buddhist temple. This term was used during ancient times of Japanese history, but the Jōdo, Shinshū, and Nichiren sects used the term *hondō,* the Shingon and Tendai sects used the term *chūdō,* and the Zen sect used the term *butsuden.*

konistra In the ancient Greek theatre, the **orchestra.**

格子戸 **kōshi-do** In traditional Japanese construction, a door latticed with wood or bamboo.

köshk Same as **kiosk, 2.**

kovil See **koil.**

path flanked by stone lanterns leads to the kondō

kokoshniki, 2

kondō (hondō) at Horiuji

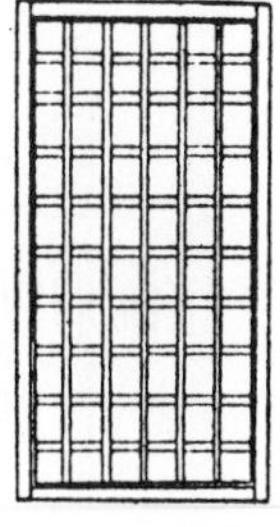

kōshi-do

kremlin **1.** In Russia, the citadel of a town or city, serving as an administrative and religious center. **2.** (*cap.*) The citadel of Moscow, a 90-acre (36-ha) area surrounded by 15th-cent. crenelated walls, entered by five steepled gate towers; bounded on the south by the Moscow River and on the east by Red Square. The buildings within its walls include: Arkhangelski Cathedral (Cathedral of the Archangel), 14th–17th cent., which contains tombs of the tsars; Uspenski Sobor (Cathedral of the Assumption), late 15th cent., where tsars were crowned and Moscow's metropolitans and patriarchs of the church were buried; Blagoveshchensky Cathedral (Cathedral of the Annunciation), 15th–16th cent., smallest of the Kremlin churches; Granovitaya Palata (Palace of the Facets), 15th cent., the oldest public building extant in Moscow; Bell Tower of Ivan the Great, erected in 1600 by Boris Godunov, 266 ft (81 m) high, containing 33 bells; Terem Palace; Senate Building, added during the reign of Catherine the Great in the 18th cent.; and the Bolshoi Dvorets (Grand Palace), 19th cent., in old Russian style of architecture, now housing the Supreme Soviet of the U.S.S.R.

Borovitskaya Tower, along wall of the Kremlin

Cathedral of the Assumption

Arkhangelski Cathedral

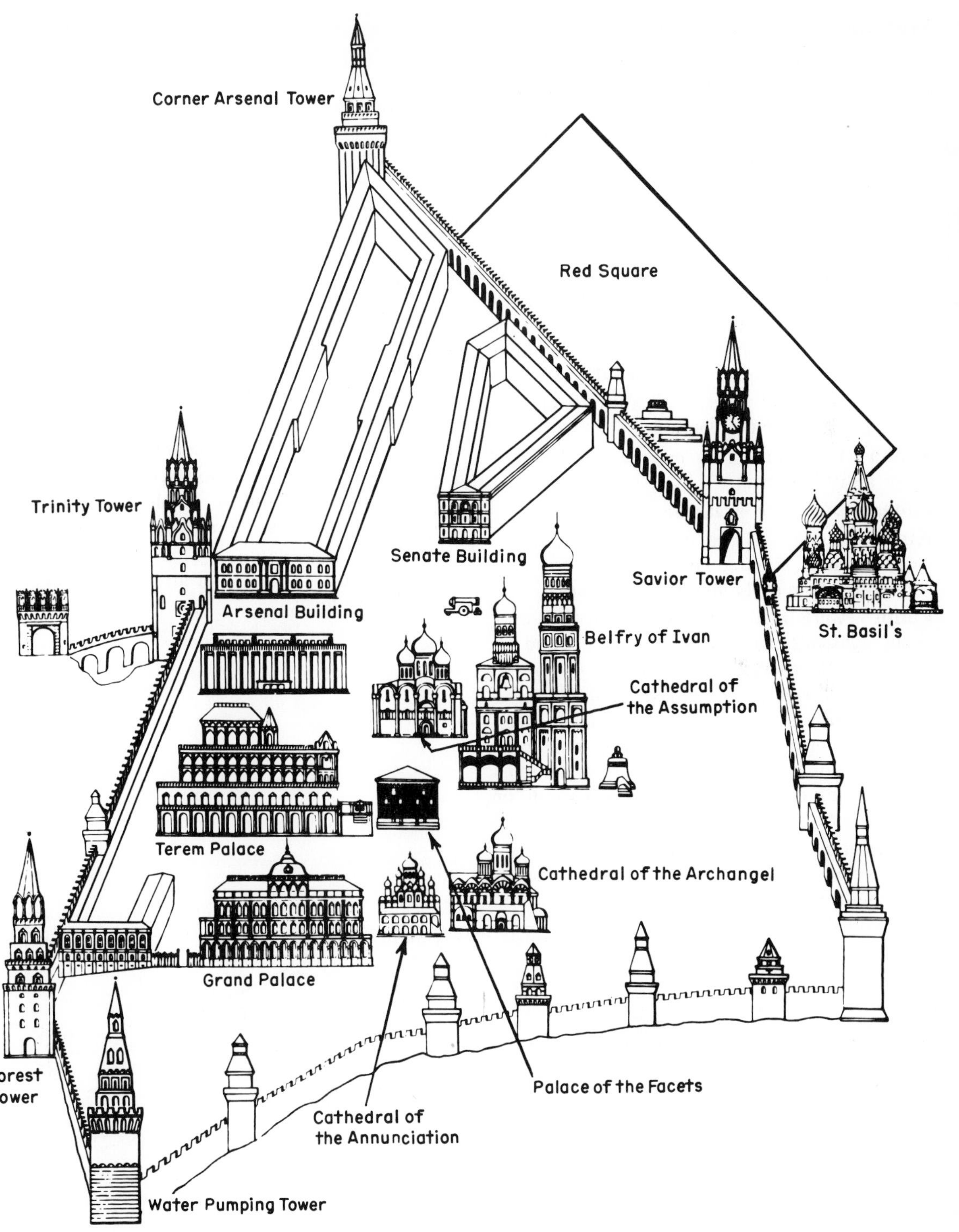
Corner Arsenal Tower
Red Square
Trinity Tower
Senate Building
Savior Tower
Arsenal Building
St. Basil's
Belfry of Ivan
Cathedral of
the Assumption
Terem Palace
Cathedral of the Archangel
Grand Palace
Forest
Tower
Palace of the Facets
Cathedral of
the Annunciation
Water Pumping Tower

krepidoma Same as **crepidoma.**

krest In Russian architecture, a cross.

krestokupolnyi A Russian Orthodox church having a dome over the crossing.

觀 **kuan** A Taoist monastery consisting of twin main halls connected by a covered corridor, forming an H-shape.

kuang t'a See **pang k'o lou.** 光塔

關帝廟 **kuan ti miao** A Chinese temple dedicated to the God of War (a general in the Han dynasty, 200 B.C.). Also called **wu miao** (martial temple).

kub, kubovatoye pokrytiye A type of roof structure on an early Russian wooden building which is square in plan; constructed of wood, it has four identical faces, with a profile similar to a squared-off **onion dome.**

kubba **1.** A dome in a **mosque.** **2.** A dome over a Muslim tomb.

kudarimune See **onigawara.**

Kufic Arabic writing originating in Kufa, Mesopotamia; its angular characters are used decoratively in early **Muslim architecture.**

kullpi A pre-Inca stone dwelling of the Peruvian highlands, constructed of boulders and resembling the **chullpa** burial towers.

鼓楼 **ku lou** In traditional Chinese architecture, a drum house; a structure that houses a large drum, either a pavilion or a tower located at the left side of an entrance court of temples and shrines, or at the left side of a city gate or palace entrance.

kumimono In traditional Japanese construction, a system of structural supports composed of weight-bearing blocks and bracket arms; also called **tokyō.**

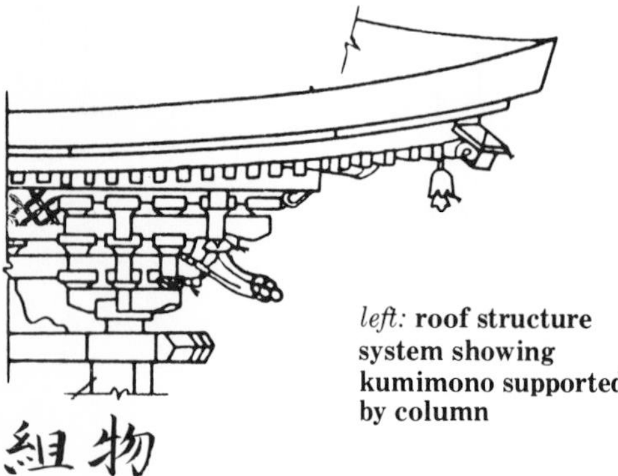

left: **roof structure system showing kumimono supported by column**

宮 **kung** In traditional Chinese architecture, buildings of no special importance which are within a compound, esp. for royalty and/or monasteries; often not constructed along the central axis of the site plan.

栱 **kung** A cantilever bracket in the **tou kung** system of construction.

孔廟 **k'ung miao** A Confucian temple having a palace of learning attached to it; since the Sung dynasty, all large cities had such a temple. Also called **wên-miao.**

廓 **k'uo** In Chinese architecture: **1.** A citadel. **2.** A fortified city wall. **3.** The battlements on a city wall.

kuo tzŭ chien See **k'ung miao.**

kurgan A **tumulus** or burial mound in the southern part of Russia and Siberia.

経蔵 **kyōzō** A small building within the precinct of a Japanese Buddhist temple, used as a repository for sutras, the sacred scriptures of Buddhism.

kyptikon The pew of an emperor; located at gallery level.

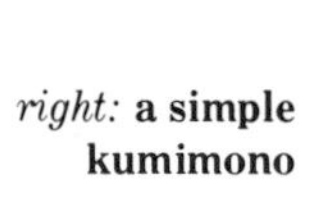

right: **a simple kumimono**

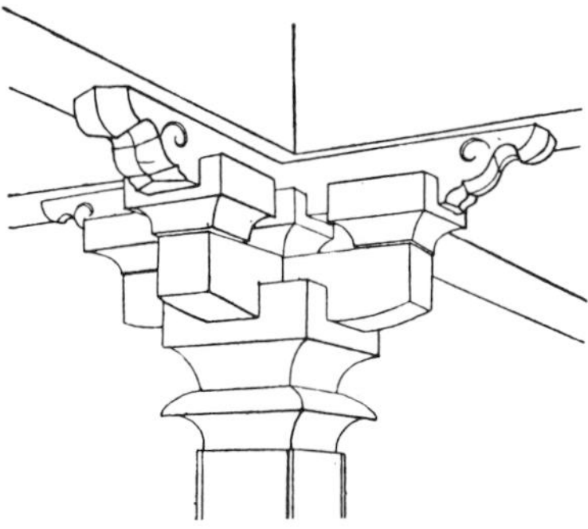

label, label molding A square-arched **dripstone** or **hoodmold;** extends horizontally across the top of an opening and returns vertically downward for a short distance.

label, St. Erasmus Church, Westminster

label molding See **label.**

label stop **1.** The termination of a hoodmold or arched dripstone in which the lower ends are turned away from the opening horizontally. **2.** Any decorative boss or other termination of a dripstone, hoodmold, sill, etc.; a **knee.**

label stop, 2: Merton College Chapel (1277), Oxford

labyrinth **1.** A maze of twisting passageways. **2.** In medieval cathedrals, the representation of such a maze inlaid in the floor. **3.** A garden feature of convoluted paths outlined by hedges, often with a garden house at the center.

labyrinth

labyrinth fret, key pattern, meander A fret with many involved turnings.

laceria In Islamic architecture, decorative geometric patterns formed by the intersection of straight lines; esp. used in molding in the **Mudejar style.**

lacework Architectural decorations resembling lace.

lacing course A course of brick or tile inserted in a rough stone or rubble course as a **bond course.**

laconicum The sweat room in a Roman bath; the semicircular end of the **caldarium.**

lacunar, laquear A **coffer** or **coffering.**

lacunaria The ceiling of the ambulatory around the cella of a temple, or of the portico.

Lady chapel A major chapel dedicated to the Virgin Mary, on the axis of a church at its east end.

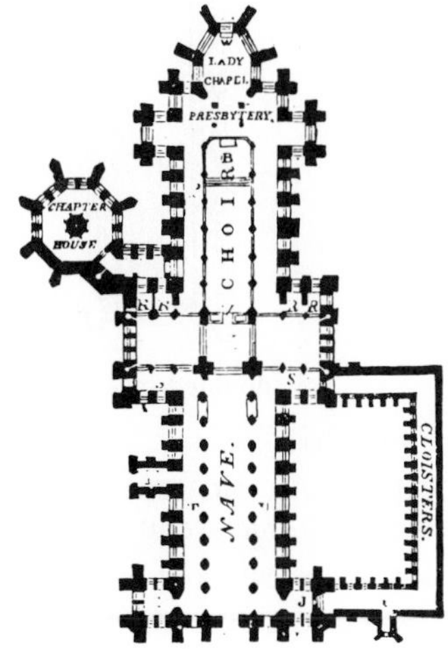

Lady chapel, shown at east end (top of illustration)

lageolum Same as **lectorium.**

Lamassu The monumental human-headed, winged bulls that guarded the entrances to Mesopotamian palaces and temples.

lama ssŭ See **ssŭ.**

lambruscatura The medieval equivalent of **wainscot.**

lamb's-tongue **1.** The end of a handrail which is turned out or down from the rail and curved so as to resemble a tongue. **2.** A cut molding, usually two ovolos separated by a fillet and set off by fillets at the other ends.

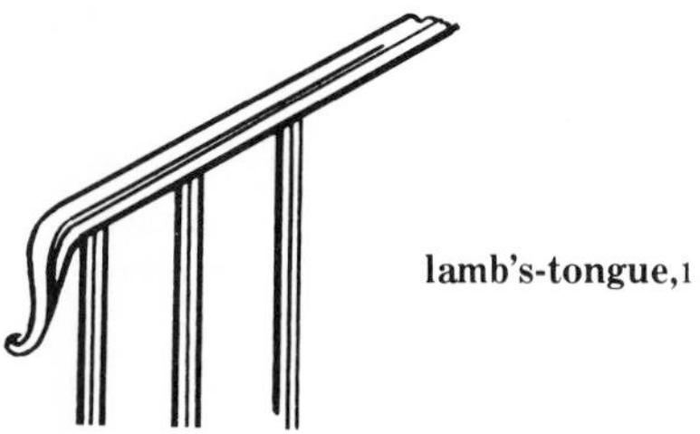

lamb's-tongue,1

lanai A living room or lounge area which is entirely, or in part, open to the outdoors.

lancet, lancet window **1.** A narrow window with a sharp pointed arch typical of English Gothic architecture from ca. 1150 to ca. 1250. **2.** One light shaped like a lancet window.

lancet window

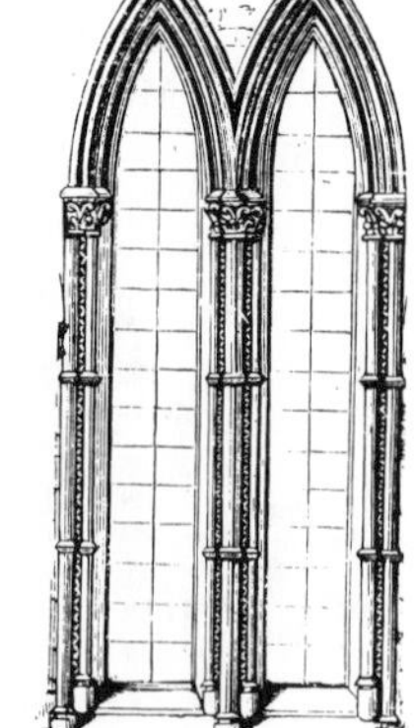

double lancet window

lancet arch An **acute arch.**

Lancet architecture An old term for the Early English phase of Gothic architecture.

lanceted Having a lancet window or arch.

lancet window See **lancet.**

lanciform Having a sharp point.

lancet arch, Westminster Abbey

landing, pace The horizontal platform at the end of a stair flight or between two flights of stairs.

landing newel, angle newel A **newel** which is located on a stair landing or at a point where stairs change direction.

landmark **1.** Any building, structure, or place which has a special character or special historical or aesthetic interest or value as part of the development, heritage, or cultural characteristics of a city, state, or nation. **2.** A monument, fixed object, or marker used to designate the location of a land boundary on the ground.

廊 **lang** In traditional Chinese architecture, a covered walkway which connects buildings; may be entirely enclosed or may be open; some are lean-tos against a building, as in a garden.

lang chu See **chu.**

廊院 **lang yüan** In traditional Chinese architecture, a courtyard which is surrounded by a covered walkway.

欄杆 **lan kan** In traditional Chinese architecture, a balustrade of wood, bamboo, stone, or brick; the designs in masonry were derived from wood construction.

lantern A windowed superstructure crowning a roof or dome; also called a *lantern light.*

lantern

lanterne des morts A graveyard lantern; a slender, tower-like structure, usually in the form of a hollow column, terminated by a pierced turret containing a light which shone through the openings; such towers (many erected in medieval times) were common in France.

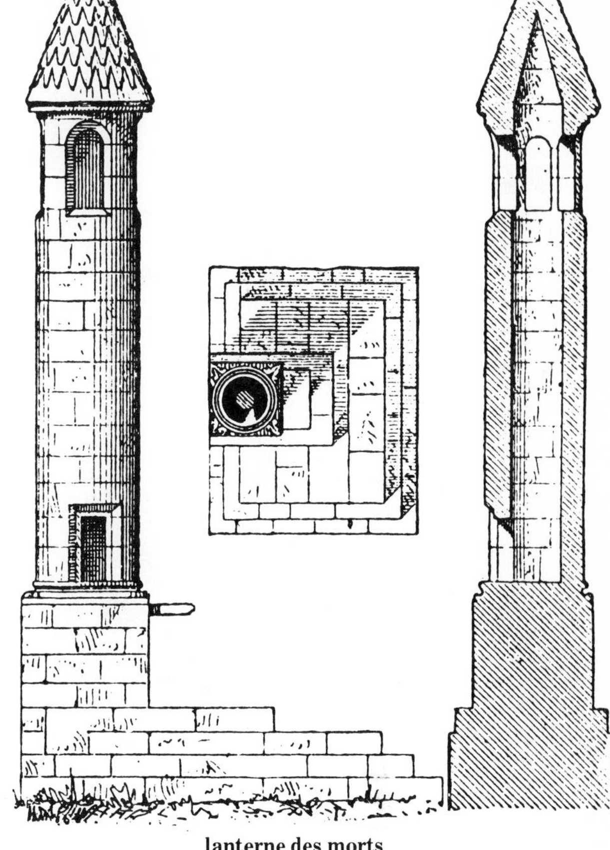
lanterne des morts

lapis Same as **milliarium.**

lap siding See **clapboard.**

laquear See **lacunar.**

lararium In Roman houses, a small shrine to the household gods (lares).

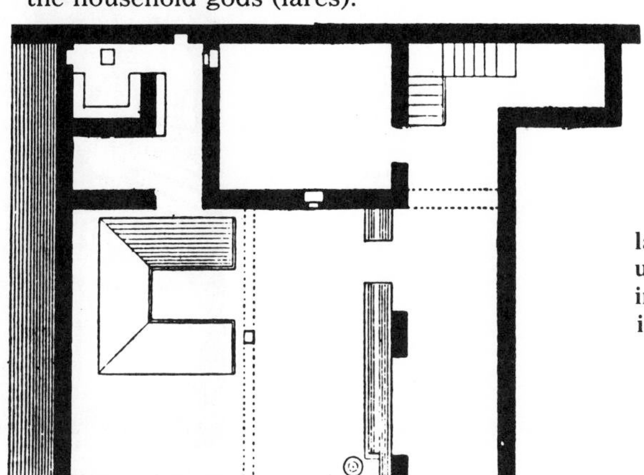
lararium (small room at upper left), house in Pompeii; an altar is surrounded by benches

larder A room where food is stored.

lardos, lardose A screen behind an altar, at the back of a seat, etc.

lares compitales Two shrines at the intersection of two ancient Roman roads (one for each road), honoring the lares as tutelary divinities.

altar of lares compitales, Pompeii

larmier, lorymer 1. A **corona.** 2. Any horizontal member or stringcourse similar in profile to a corona and projecting from a wall to throw off rain; a **roll molding, drip,** etc.

lat In Indian architecture, an isolated shaft or pillar serving various purposes, as for bearing inscriptions or religious emblems or for a statue or image.

latch A simple fastening device having a latch bolt, but not a **dead bolt;** contains no provisions for locking with a key; usually openable from both sides.

latch

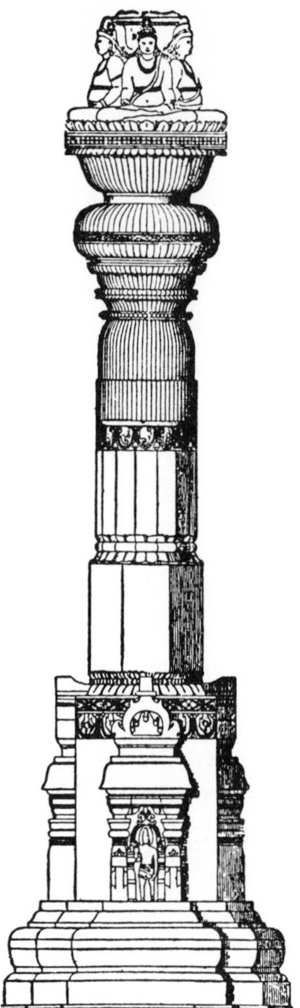

lat, court of Indra Sabba

lat at Elura

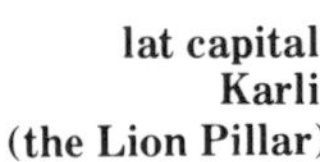

lat capital, Karli (the Lion Pillar)

later A brick, formed in a mold and dried in the sun or baked in a kiln by the early Greeks and Romans; much larger and much thinner than modern bricks; each brick was stamped with the name of the maker and the year in which it was made. Fancy bricks were made in molds of all shapes and sizes to imitate the designs produced with a chisel in stone or marble structures, but ordinary bricks usually were rectangular, square, or triangular in shape.

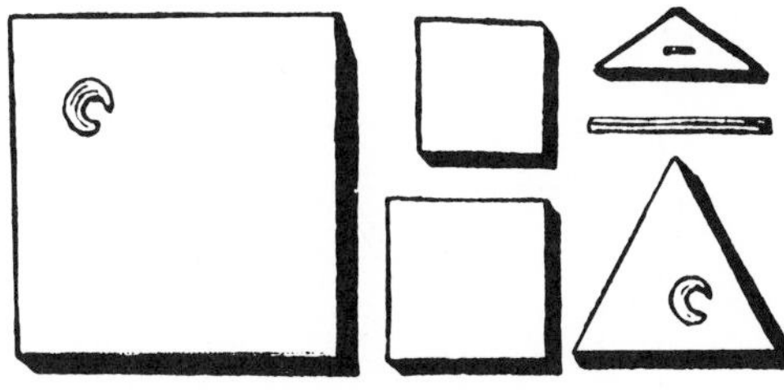

later of various types

later coctus, later coctilis Same as **coctilis.**

later crudus A brick baked in the sun rather than in an oven.

laterculus Diminutive of **later.**

latericius Built of brick.

lateritum opus Brickwork of the ancient Romans.

lath Same as **lat.**

latifundium In ancient Rome, a large estate.

Latin cross A cross which has an upright much longer than the crossarm; three arms are approx. equal in length and the fourth is much longer.

Latin cross

latrina An ancient Roman term for a bath or place to wash, or to designate a water closet in a private home.

latrobe A stove or heater set under a mantelpiece, heating the room by direct radiation and one or more rooms above by hot air.

lattice **1.** A network, often diagonal, of strips, rods, bars, laths, or straps of metal or wood, used as screening or for airy, ornamental constructions. **2.** A regular member triangularly braced.

lattice molding A wood molding, rectangular in section and broad in relation to its projection, resembling the wood strips used in latticework.

lattice window A window casement, fixed or hinged, with glazing bars set diagonally.

latticework Reticulated or net-like work formed by the crossing of laths or narrow, thin strips of wood or iron, usually in a diagonal pattern.

latrina, Pompeii

lavabo In monasteries of the Middle Ages, a large stone basin from which the water flowed through a number of small orifices around the edge, for the convenient performance of ablutions before religious exercises or meals.

lavabo, Abbey of Valmagne

lavacrum A place for washing.

lavatory A small stone basin with a hole at the bottom to carry off water through a drain beneath; usually placed near the altar in an ancient church; used by the priest for washing his hands.

lavatory

lavra An assemblage of cells for monks around a common center which contains a church and sometimes a refectory.

laylight A glazed opening in a ceiling to admit light (either natural or artificial) to a room below.

lazaret, lazarette, lazaretto, lazar house A segregated area for infectious medical patients, esp. for their quarantine.

leaded light A window having small diamond-shaped or rectangular panes of glass set in lead **cames.**

leaded light

leaf and dart, heart and dart In Greek architecture and derivatives, a pattern of alternating, conventionalized, deltoid and lanceolate leaves, usually applied to a **cyma reversa.**

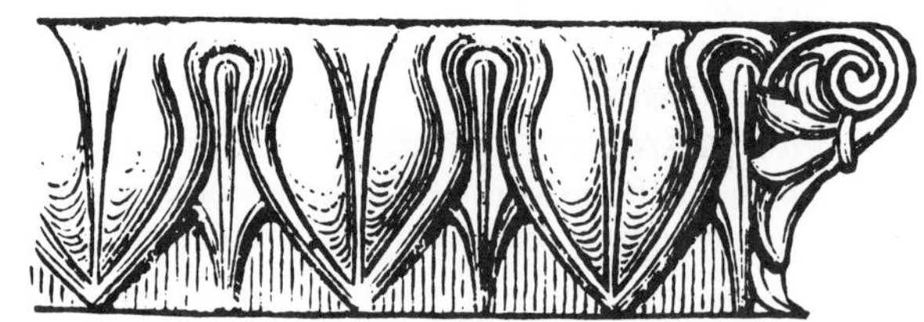

leaning tower A tower, usually detached and slender for its height, which overhangs its base; the most famous example of such a tower is at Pisa, Italy, where the 179 ft (54.6 m) tower is 16.5 ft (5 m) out of perpendicular.

Leaning Tower (Campanile) of Pisa (1174–1271)

lean-to A small extension to a building with a roof (having but one slope) whose supports lean against the building.

lean-to house Same as **saltbox.**

lean-to roof, half-span roof A roof having a single pitch, carried by a wall which is higher than the roof.

lectern In a church or lecture hall, a stand with a slanting top to hold a book, speech, or music at the proper height for reading.

lectorium, lectrinum, lectricium The place in a Christian church from which parts of the Scripture were read.

ledged door See **batten door.**

ledgement table, ledgment table A band course, stringcourse, or belt course, usually molded; esp. one carried along the lower portion of a building.

ledger A flat slab of stone, such as that laid horizontally over a grave.

ledgment, ledgement A horizontal, decorative **stringcourse** of brick or stone.

lemekh Same as **gont.**

leontarium A supply of water, not for ablution but for lustration, or as a symbol of purification; placed in the atrium or courtyard of a basilican church, sometimes surrounded with lions which spout water.

leper's squint See **low-side window.**

Lesbian cyma A **cyma reversa.**

Lesbian leaf Same as **water leaf, 2.**

lesche In ancient Greece, a public portico, clubhouse, or the like, frequented by the people for conversation or the hearing of news; such buildings were numerous in Greek cities, and their walls often were decorated by celebrated painters.

lesche at Delphi

lesene See **pilaster strip.**

leshchad A thin stone slab used in early Russian construction, as in flooring.

levecel An **appentice.**

lever board Same as **louver board.**

liang In traditional Chinese construction, a beam; usually a bearing member perpendicular to the purlins or a bearing member parallel to the purlins. Similar to the **hari** in Japanese architecture.

Liberty See **Neo-Liberty** and **Stile Liberty.**

lichaven A **dolmen** having only two supporting stones.

lich-gate See **lych-gate.**

lich-stone See **lych-stone.**

lierne rib In Gothic vaulting, any small subordinate rib which is inserted between the main ribs, more often as an ornament than for reasons of construction.

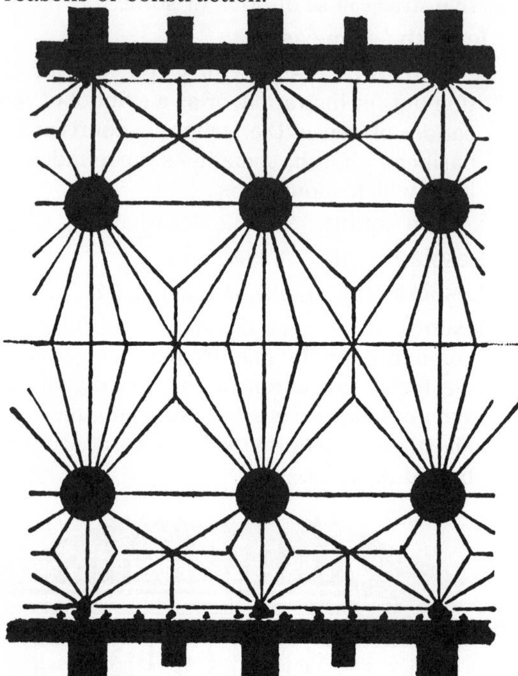

lierne ribs: plan of vaulting, nave of Lincoln Cathedral

lierne vaulting Vaulting in which lierne ribs are used.

ligger **1.** A **ledger.** **2.** A long stick (often of willow) used along the ridge of a thatched roof.

light **1.** An aperture through which daylight is admitted to the interior of a building. **2.** A pane of glass, a window, or a compartment of a window.

li kung In ancient China, a palatial resort complex serving as the administrative center for the emperor during the months when the capital was especially hot or cold or when he wished to hunt; sometimes had gardens in which foreign settings were reproduced.

limen equorum The threshold or doorway of the stalls in the circus from which the horses and chariots emerged when they were about to start a race.

limen inferior, limen inferum In ancient Roman construction, a door **sill.**

limen superior, limen superum The **lintel** of a door.

linenfold, linen pattern, linen scroll A form of carved paneling representing a symmetrical fold or scroll of linen.

linenfold

陵 **ling** A group of buildings at the cemetery of a Chinese emperor.

linga, lingam A phallus; a divine emblem of the god Siva in Hindu architecture.

櫺星門 **ling hsing mên** A Chinese gateway having two main posts; an inclined member is attached to each post, at an angle which tilts upward toward the centerline; constructed of wood or stone.

lining Material which covers any interior surface, such as framework around a door or window, or boarding which covers the interior surfaces of a building.

lintel A horizontal structural member (such as a beam) over an opening which carries the weight of the wall above it; often of stone or wood.

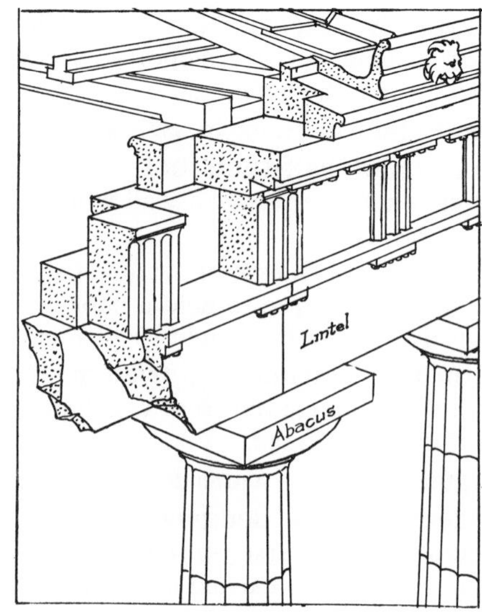

stone lintel

opening spanned by a lintel, Arch of the Goldsmiths, Rome.

Only a portion of the pier on the right is shown

lintel course In stone masonry, a course set at the level of a lintel, commonly differentiated from the wall by its greater projection, its finish, or its thickness, which often matches that of the lintel.

檩子 **lin tzŭ** In traditional Chinese construction, a purlin which is round in section; also see **fang.** Similar to **keta** in Japanese construction.

禮拜殿 **li pai tien** **1.** In China, a main hall used for worship and for performing ritual ceremonies. **2.** A Christian church in China.

lip molding A molding resembling an overhanging or pouting lip; common in buttress caps and base moldings carved during the Perpendicular period.

lis See **fleur-de-lys.**

lisena A Romanesque pilaster strip.

list, listel A **fillet, 1.**

listatum opus See **opus listatum.**

lithostrotum opus In ancient Greece and Rome, any ornamental pavement, such as mosaic.

litre A band upon which the coats of arms of the pious founders of a church were painted; the band encircled some churches of the Middle Ages and the Renaissance.

琉璃 **liu li** In traditional Chinese architecture, a decorative porcelain glaze on terra-cotta tile or brick; a means of weatherproofing.

lobe A segment of a circle in tracery; a **foil.**

lobed arch A **cusped arch.**

lock A device which fastens in position, as a door, gate, window, etc.; may be operated by a key or a **dead bolt.**

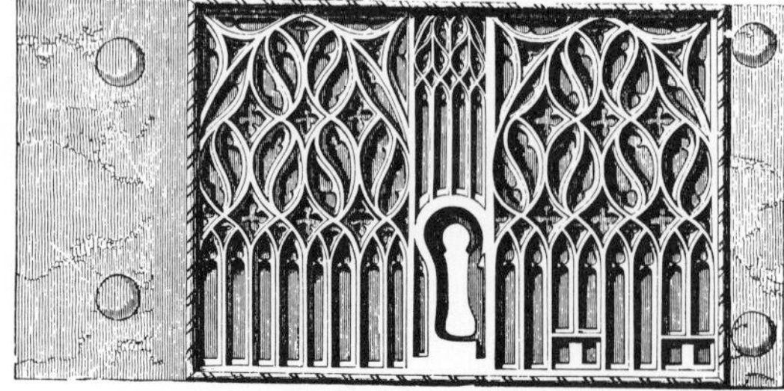

lock, Rouen Cathedral (1202–1230 and later)

lockband A course of **bondstones.**

loculus In ancient tombs, a recess for a sarcophagus or cinerary urn.

locutorium Same as **locutory.**

locutory A place for conversation; esp. the parlor of a monastic establishment.

loft **1.** Unceiled space beneath a roof, often used for storage. Also see **attic, garret.** **2.** Upper space in a church, e.g., choir loft, organ loft. Also see **rood loft.**

log cabin, log house A house built of logs which are horizontally laid and notched and fitted at the ends to prevent spreading.

log cabin

logeion, logeum, logeium The raised platform for the actors in the Classical theatre, corresponding to the modern stage.

loggia **1.** An arcaded or colonnaded structure, open on one or more sides, sometimes with an upper story. **2.** An arcaded or colonnaded porch or gallery attached to a larger structure. Also see **arcade, 2.**

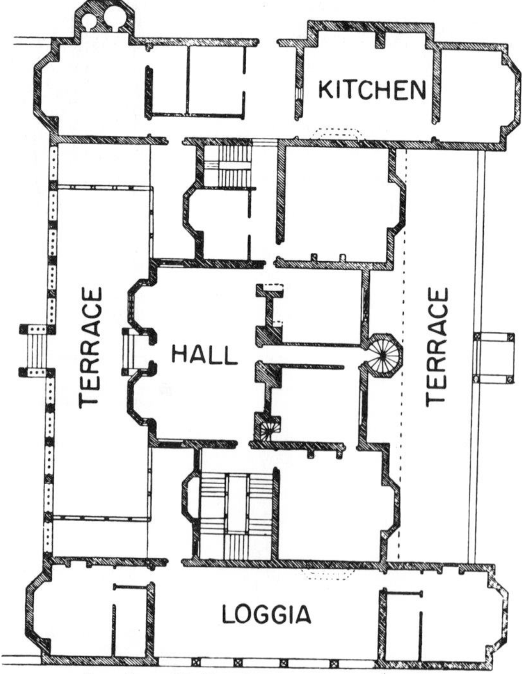

loggia,2: Holland House, Kensington, London: Early Renaissance

loggia,1

log house See **log cabin.**

Lombard architecture North Italian pre-Romanesque architecture in the 7th and 8th cent., during the rule of the Lombards, based on Early Christian and Roman forms.

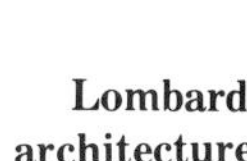

Lombard architecture

examples of Lombard architecture

London stock brick Originally, handmade bricks produced in the vicinity of London, made on a "stock," i.e., a block of wood that locates the mold on the mold table; now machine-made brick of a coarse-textured yellow.

long-and-short work In rubble masonry, quoins which are placed alternately horizontally and vertically.

long-and-short work

long gallery A **gallery** in the upper stories of an Elizabethan or Jacobean manor house; often used as a promenade or family room.

lookout, lookout rafter, tail, tail piece A rafter, bracket, or joist which projects beyond the side of a building and supports an overhanging portion of the roof.

lookout tower A **belvedere.**

loop A **loophole.**

loophole **1.** See **arrow loop.** **2.** Any opening in a parapet or wall to provide for vision, light, or air.

loop window A long, narrow, vertical opening, usually widening inward, cut in a medieval wall, parapet, or fortification for use by archers; an arrowloop.

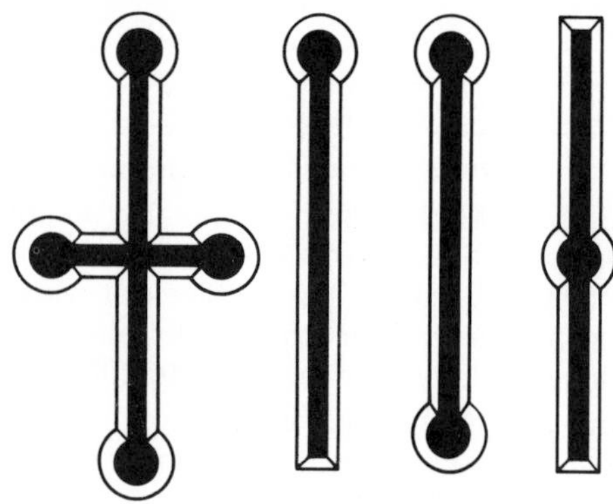

loop windows

lopatka In early Russian architecture, a pilaster without a capital.

loricula Same as **squint,** 1.

lorymer A **larmier.**

lotiform Having the shape of a lotus bud or flower, as used in some Egyptian column capitals.

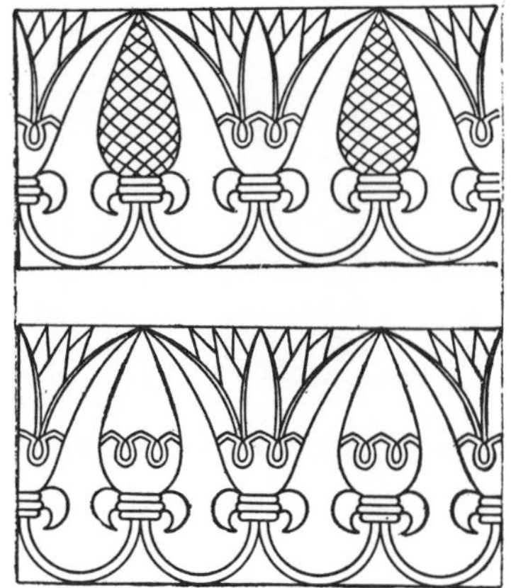

lotiform decorations

lotus capital In ancient Egyptian architecture, a capital having the shape of a lotus bud.

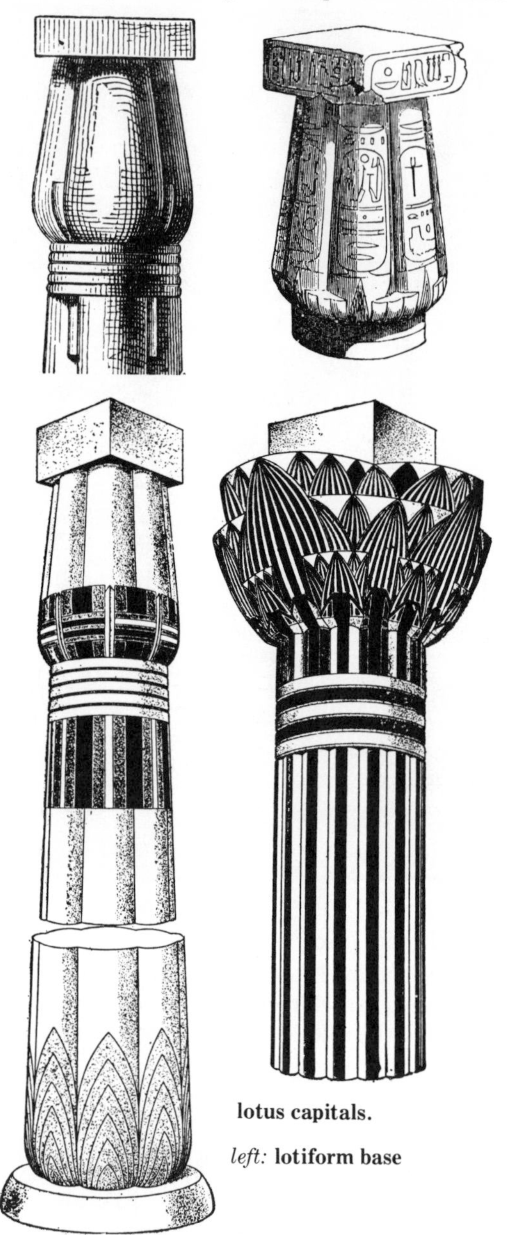

lotus capitals.

left: lotiform base

lou In traditional Chinese architecture: **1.** A multistoried building. **2.** Rooms that are not on the ground floor.

lou ch'uang See **hua chuan.**

Louis XIV, Louis Quatorze style The style of the high Classical period in France under the rule of Louis XIV (1643–1715) in architecture, decoration, and furniture, culminating in the building of Versailles.

section of the Great Gallery and part elevation of the central block, Palais de Versailles (1661—1756)

central compartment, northern façade, Louvre

details of door panel

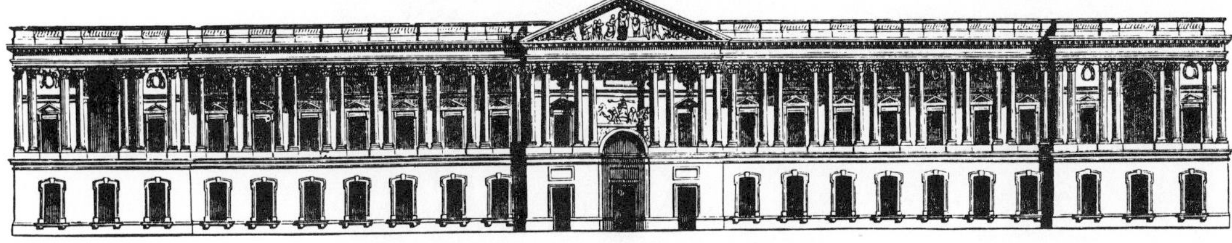

eastern façade, Louvre, Paris (1667–74)

Louis XIV (Quatorze) style

Versailles: Court of the Great Stable
(1679–82)

Versailles: panel over door in the
Salon de l'Abondance (1683)

ceiling decoration

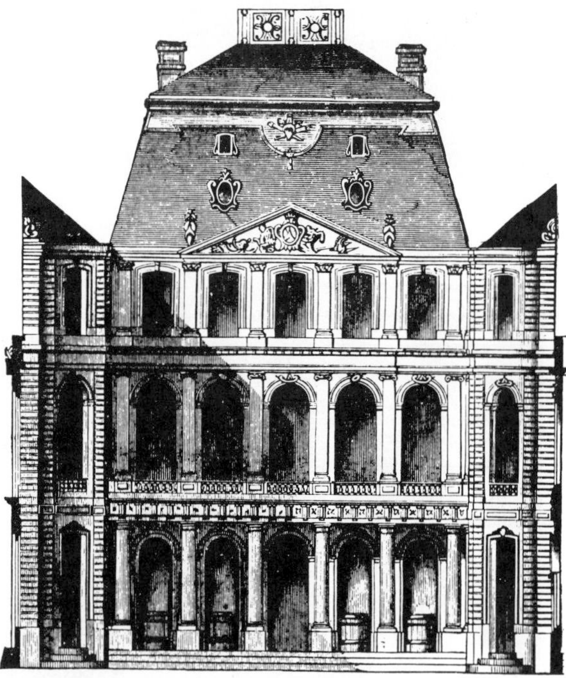

Hotel de Noailles

overdoor panel

Louis XV, Louis Quinze style The Classical and Rococo style in France under the rule of Louis XV (1715–1774) in architecture, decoration, and furniture.

façade, Louis XV style, Paris

doorway of Hotel de Clermont-Tonnerre, Paris

façade, St. Roch (1739)

Louis XV (Quinze) style

altar (c. 1730)

Pavilion, Hotel Soubise, Paris (c. 1730)

Louis XVI, Louis Seize style The later Rococo and classicist phase of the 18th cent. in France under the rule of Louis XVI (1774–1792), terminated by the French Revolution.

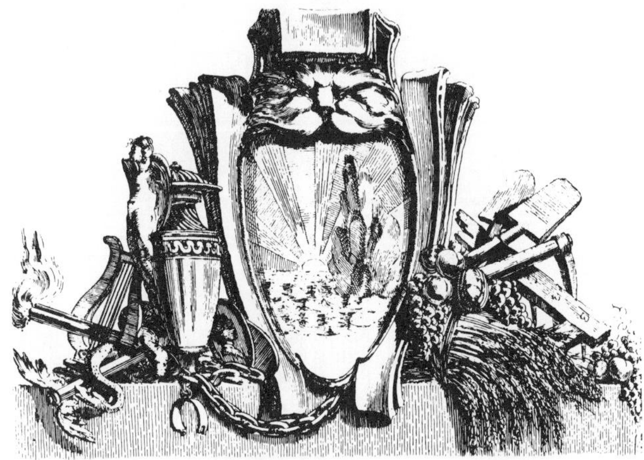

façade, St. Eustache, Paris (rebuilt 1772–78)

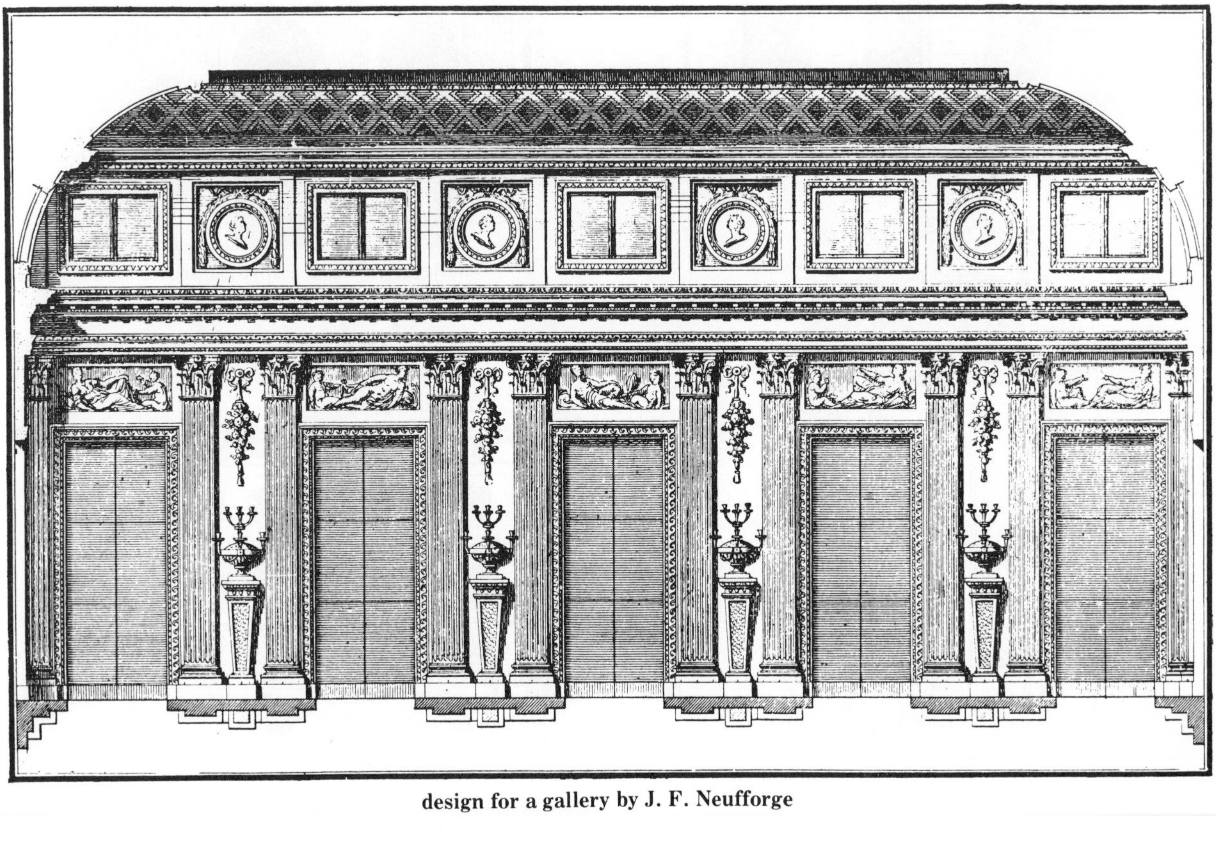

design for a gallery by J. F. Neufforge

Louis XVI (Seize) style

town house, Paris

Galleries of Palais-Royal, Paris (1781–86)

design for hotel by J. F. Neufforge

louver 1. An assembly of sloping, overlapping blades or slats; may be fixed or adjustable; designed to admit air and/or light in varying degrees and to exclude rain and snow. 2. A dome or turret rising from the roof of the hall of a medieval English residence, originally open at the sides to allow the escape of smoke from the open hearth below; also called a **lantern.**

louver board One of the narrow boards, placed at an angle, in a **louver** or **louver window;** also called a **luffer board.**

louver window 1. A window having louvers which fill all or part of the opening instead of glass. 2. An open window in the tower of a church.

louver window

louvre Same as **louver.**

low relief Same as **bas-relief.**

low-side window, leper's squint, offertory window, squint A small low window, usually on the right side of the chancel, through which the altar may be seen.

low-side window

louver,2

lozenge 1. A rhomb or, more rarely, a rhomboid; usually one of a series. 2. In a double lancet window, a small light which pierces the space between the heads of the two lancets.

lozenge,2 between heads of the two lancets

lozenge fret, lozenge molding A type of **diamond fret.**

lozenge fret

lucarne A small dormer window in a roof or spire.

lucullite A variety of black marble used in ancient Roman construction; first brought to Rome from Assan on the Nile River.

ludion An ancient Greek term for a tile used as a brick.

luffer board Same as **louver board.**

lukovitsa In early Russian architecture, an **onion dome.**

lune Anything in the shape of a crescent or half-moon.

lunette **1.** A crescent-shaped or semicircular area on a wall or vaulted ceiling, framed by an arch or vault. **2.** An opening or window in such an area. **3.** A painting or sculpture on such an area.

lunnitsa In early Russian architecture, a semicircular **pendant.**

luthern Same as **dormer window.**

Luxor See **Thebes.**

lyceum A building for general education by means of public discussions, lectures, concerts, etc.

lych-gate, lich-gate A roofed gateway at the entrance to a church or cemetery where a coffin may be placed temporarily before proceeding to the grave.

lychnoscope Same as **low-side window.**

lychnus A lamp suspended from the ceiling.

lych-stone A stone at the entrance to a churchyard, intended to receive a bier.

lymphaea A type of artificial grotto.

Lysicrates See **Monument of Lysicrates.**

lysis A plinth or step above the cornice of the podium of some Roman temples; when present in a columnar edifice, it constitutes the stylobate proper.

lunette,2

lych-gate

early Roman lychnus

macellum A Roman meat or produce market in a covered hall.

maceria In ancient Roman construction, a rough wall having no facing; constructed in a wide variety of materials.

maceria

machicolation An overhanging defensive structure at the top of a medieval fortification, with floor openings through which boiling oil, missiles, etc., could be dropped on attackers.

machicolation; floor opening at *B*

Machu Picchu The most celebrated Inca citadel, on a promontory 2,000 ft (610 m) above the Urubamba valley in the Andes of Peru. The site includes buildings which surround an oblong plaza. The houses were built around courts, with stairs, windows, interior niches, narrow doorways (capped with stone lintels), and thatch-covered gabled roofs; some houses were carved out of rock. Some chambers and connecting stairs are hewn out of the mountain. The site is dominated by the Sun Temple atop a huge pyramidal rock.

madar In Jain architecture (India), a large subsidiary shrine.

madina **1.** An Arabic word for city. **2.** In North Africa, the native quarter of a city.

窓 **mado** In Japanese architecture, a window; similar to **ch'uang** in Chinese architecture.

madrasah A theological school, generally arranged around a courtyard, from the 11th cent. A.D. on, in Anatolia, Persia, and Egypt.

maeander See **labyrinth fret.**

maenhir Same as **menhir.**

maenianum **1.** In ancient Rome, a balcony or gallery for spectators at a public show. **2.** Originally, the balcony in the Forum at Rome, for spectators of the gladiatorial combats. **3.** In the Roman theatre or amphitheatre or circus, an entire range of seats, rising in concentric circles between one crossover and another, but divided radially into a number of compartments (**cunei**) by the flights of steps (**scalae**). **4.** In an ancient Roman house, an upper story which projects beyond the ground floor.

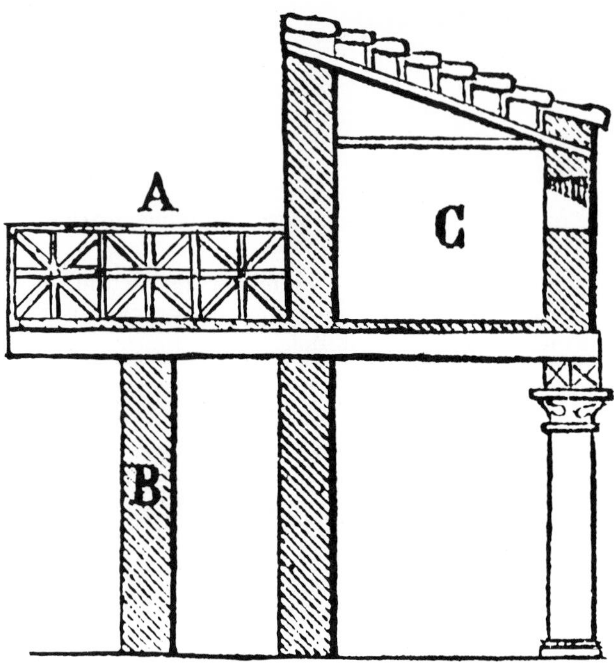

maenianum,4: *A*, balcony; *B*, pillar; *C*, upper story

magazine A storage place, particularly for explosives and projectiles.

mahal In **Mogul architecture,** a palace.

maiden tower The **keep** or principal tower of a castle.

main tie In a roof truss, a member which connects the feet of the rafters.

maira-do A sliding door composed of an outer frame which is filled with thin boards over which horizontal crosspieces are placed; used in the **Shoin style.**

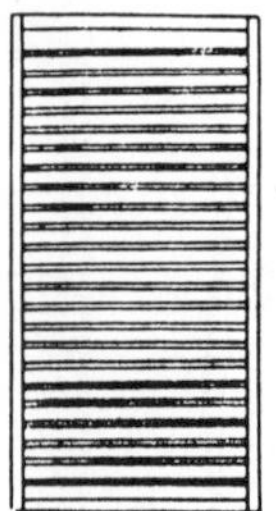

maira-do

舞良戸

majolica A type of pottery decorated with an opaque white glaze and a colored overglaze; a type of **faïence tile.**

example of majolica floor, Oratorio of St. Catherine, Siena (1405–1520)

makara A sea monster with the features of a crocodile or elephant seal (sea elephant) belonging to the sculptural repertory of Indonesian or Indo-Chinese architecture; an emblem of water.

makovitsa **1.** In early Russian architecture, a small cupola. **2.** In early Russian architecture, any type of **crowning.**

maksoorah In a mosque, an area which is enclosed by a screen or partition and which is reserved for prayer or surrounds a tomb.

Maltese cross A cross formed by four equal triangles or arrowheads joined at their points.

maltha **1.** In ancient Roman construction, a type of bitumen, various cements, stuccos, and the like, used for repairing cisterns, roofs, etc. **2.** A bituminous substance midway in consistency between asphalt and petroleum.

malus In ancient Roman theatres and amphitheatres, one of the poles over which the **velarium** was stretched.

mali on a Roman theatre

manara Same as **minaret.**

manastambha In Indian architecture, a freestanding pillar in front of a temple.

mandapa In Indian architecture, a large open hall, esp. of a temple.

mandira A Hindu temple, palace, or hall.

mandoral Same as **mandorla.**

mandorla, vesica piscis An aureole, almond-shaped, depicted around the full form of a sacred person.

mandorla

Mannerism Transitional style in architecture and the arts in the late 16th cent., particularly in Italy, characterized in architecture by unconventional use of classical elements.

manor house **1.** The house occupied by the lord of a manor. **2.** The most important house in a country or village neighborhood.

manor house (15th–16th cent.)

mansard roof, mansard **1.** *(U.S.A. and Brit.)* A roof having a double slope on all four sides, the lower slope being much steeper. **2.** *(Brit.)* Same as **gambrel roof** *(U.S.A.).*

mansard roof

Mansard style See **Second Empire style in the U.S.A.**

manse The dwelling of a clergyman.

mansion **1.** A large and imposing dwelling. **2.** An apartment in a large building or dwelling. **3.** A manor house.

mantapa Same as **mandapa.**

mantel **1.** The beam or arch which serves as a support for the masonry above a fireplace; also called a **manteltree.** **2.** All the work or facing around a fireplace. **3.** A **mantelshelf.**

mantelpiece **1.** The fittings and decorative elements of a mantel, including the cornice and shelf carried above the fireplace. **2.** A **mantelshelf.**

mantelshelf That part of a mantelpiece which constitutes a shelf.

manteltree See **mantel, 1.**

mantle **1.** Same as **mantel.** **2.** The outer covering of a wall which differs from the material of the inner surface.

Manueline architecture The last phase of Gothic architecture in Portugal, so named after King Manuel I (1495–1521).

maq'ad In the Near East, an arched veranda or loggia overlooking the courtyard of a palace or house.

maqbara A Muslim tomb monument.

maqsura An enclosure in a mosque which includes the praying niche, made usually of an openwork screen; originally meant for the sultan during public prayers.

margin draft In masonry, the plain-dressed border on the face of a hewn block; the middle part of the face may be dressed or left rough; also see **draft.**

margines Same as **semitae.**

margin light See **side light.**

marigold window A round window whose mullions of tracery radiate; a **rose window.**

marmoratum In ancient Roman construction, a cement formed of pounded marble and lime mortar which were well mixed; used in building walls, terraces, etc.

marmoratum opus In plastering, a finish coat made of calcined gypsum mixed with pulverized stone or, for the finest work, with pulverized marble; used by the ancient Romans.

marmoset, marmouset An antic figure, usually grotesque, introduced into architectural decoration in the 13th cent.

marouflage A technique for fastening canvas (or the like) to a wall by means of an adhesive.

mantelpiece: Hotel de Clare, Toulouse (c. 1575)

marmoset

marquee A permanent roof-like shelter over an entrance to a building.

marquee

marquetry Inlaid pieces of a material, such as wood or ivory, fitted together and glued to a common background. Also see **inlay.**

marquetry

martello tower A small circular tower, usually two stories high (the lower for stores, the upper for troops), erected in Ireland, Jersey, and elsewhere during the Napoleonic wars. Its name is derived from a similar fortification at Cape Mortella, Corsica.

martyrium A place where the relics of a martyr are deposited.

marugawara See **hongawara-buki.**

mascaron, mask The representation of a face, a human or partly human head, more or less caricatured, used as an architectural ornament.

masged See **masjid.**

mashhad A Muslim shrine.

mashrebeeyeh See **meshrebeeyeh.**

masjid, masged A Muslim house of worship; a mosque.

mask See **mascaron.**

mass bell Same as **sanctus bell.**

mascarons

mastaba A freestanding tomb used in ancient Egypt, consisting of a rectangular superstructure with inclined sides, from which a shaft leads to underground burial and offering chambers.

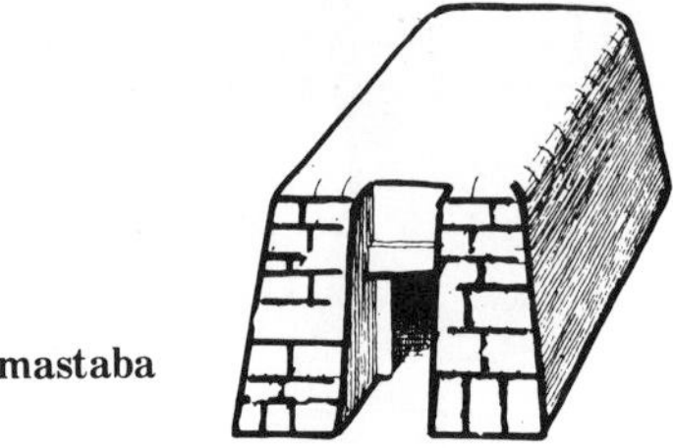

mastaba

materiato A collective term including all timberwork employed in ancient Roman roof construction.

matha In Indian architecture, a convent or monastery.

matroneum To the right of the sanctuary in an ancient basilican church, a place for matrons, separated by a balustrade with a door opening onto a lower section for unmarried females.

mausoleum **1.** A commemorative edifice for the reception of a monument; a **cenotaph.** **2.** A sepulchral chapel to contain tombs.

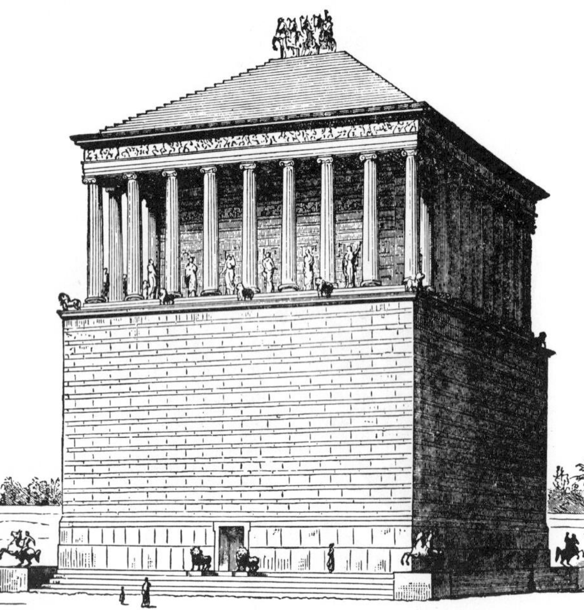

Mausoleum of Halicarnassos (355–350 B.C.); one of the Seven Wonders of the World

Maya arch A corbeled arch of triangular shape common in the buildings of the Maya Indians of Yucatan.

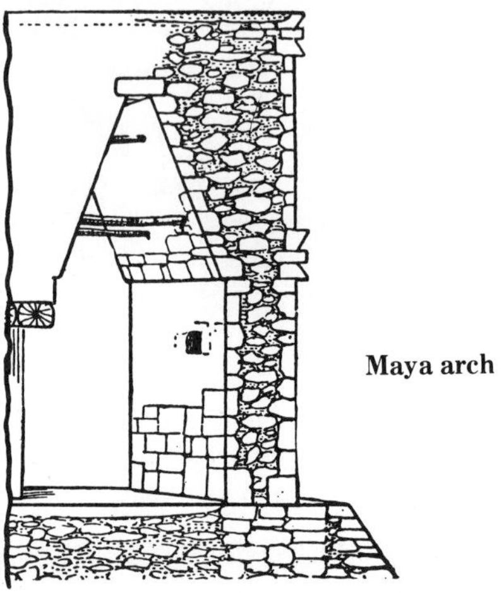

Maya arch

Maya architecture An architecture of Mesoamerica which reached its highest development ca. 600–900 A.D. at sites such as Tikal in the lowland jungles of Guatemala, Copán in western Honduras, and Palenque in the Usumacinta drainage basin of Mexico; characterized by monumental construction which included soaring temple pyramids, palaces with sculptured façades, ritual ball courts, plazas, and interconnecting quadrangles. There were some variations in style in the different regions. To achieve height and grandeur, all buildings were erected on platforms. Some styles made use of a *roof comb* which sometimes exceeded the height of the building; in other, the decorative elements on the roof merely formed an open parapet. The interior walls were massive to compensate for the weakness of the Maya arch. The lower section of exterior walls usually was plain; the upper section was a continuous frieze carrying intricate decoration of masks, human figures, and geometric forms. Exterior surfaces of structures, temple platforms, and stairways commonly were covered with lime-stucco and were painted in strong colors. The sites were rebuilt periodically, leaving previous structures covered and intact.

maze In a garden, a confusing and intricate plan of hedges, usually above eye level, forming a labyrinth.

meander A **labyrinth fret.**

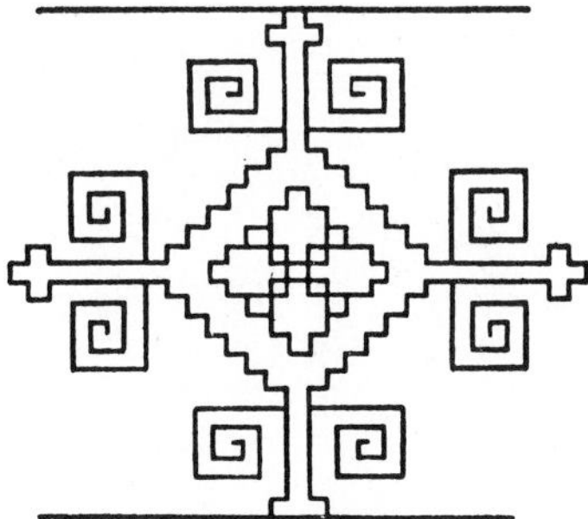

Early Russian meander

medallion 1. An ornamental plaque (usually oval or square, but may be of any other form) on which is represented an object in relief, such as a figure, head, flower, etc., applied to a wall frieze, or other architectural member. **2.** An ornamental motif, more or less centralized and isolated.

medallion

medallion molding A molding consisting of a series of medallions, found in the later and richer examples of Norman architecture.

medallion molding

medhi A square or round terrace which serves as a base for a Hindu temple or a **stupa.**

Medieval architecture The summary term for the architecture of the European Middle Ages from the 5th to the 15th cent., in particular the Byzantine, pre-Romanesque, Romanesque, and Gothic.

Medusa In Greek mythology, the one of the three Gorgons who was mortal and whose head was cut off by Perseus.

Medusa

Medusa head Same as **gorgoneion.**

meeting house A house of worship, esp. that of the Society of Friends (Quakers) and the Mormons.

megalithic Built of unusually large stones.

megalithic monument

megaron **1.** The principal hall of a Mycenaean palace, consisting of a squarish room with a hearth in the center and a porch of columns **in antis**. **2.** In many Greek temples, a space divided off and sometimes subterranean, which only the priest was allowed to enter. **3.** The great central hall of the Homeric house or palace.

mehrab Same as **mihrab.**

mellarium A place where the early Romans kept bees to make honey; an apiary.

melon dome A melon-like ribbed dome (either an exterior or interior dome), esp. found in Islamic architecture.

memorial An architectural or sculptural object or plaque commemorating a person or an event.

memorial arch An arch commemorating a person or event, popular during the Roman Empire, and again at the time of Napoleon and later. If the event is a military one, it is also called a **triumphal arch.**

memorial arch: Arch of Septimus Severus, Rome (203 A.D.)

memorial arch: Arch of Constantine, Rome (312 A.D.)

memorial stone, memorial tablet A stone or tablet set up, or placed on or in a wall, to commemorate some person or event.

memorial window In a church, a window of painted or colored glass to the memory of a person or family.

Memphis Situated near the apex of the Nile delta, 12 miles (19 km) south of Cairo; capital of Egypt during the Old Kingdom (2780 to 2558 B.C.), and northern capital at the time of the Empire (1580–1205 B.C.). Then a great port city, as well as an agricultural, trading, administrative, and religious center; included a residential quarter, many temples (e.g., Temple of Ptah), palaces, and large commercial and industrial districts. Today only a few ruins remain, mainly from the time of Ramses II. Nearby, at the western edge of the desert, extending for 20 miles (32 km) to **El Gizeh** in the north are the necropolises of the Memphite IIIrd to VIth dynasties, giving a clue to the size of the ancient capital.

門 **men** In Chinese architecture, a gate or door.

mêng ku pao Same as **yurt.** 蒙古包

menhir A prehistoric monument consisting of a single large standing stone, sometimes rudely sculptured.

menhir at Carnac, Brittany

menianum Same as **maenianum.**

mensa **1.** The stone slab or other piece forming the top of an altar. **2.** The upper surface of an altar.

mensao Same as **menhir.**

mensole Same as **keystone** of an arch.

merlon In an embattled parapet, one of the solid alternates between the embrasures. Also see **battlement.**

merlon (indicated by arrow)

meroes In the architecture of Bali, a pagoda.

meros The frontal area between two grooves of a triglyph.

Meru The 'world mountain' in Indian mythology; the vertical axis of the universe. Symbolized in multistoried Hindu temples, in the **chandis** of Java, and in the **puras** of Bali.

merus Same as **meros.**

mesalorium Same as **aspasticum.**

mesaulos In an ancient Greek house: **1.** A passageway connecting the **andron** with the **gynaeceum.** **2.** The door in this passageway. **3.** A door leading to the workroom of the female servants.

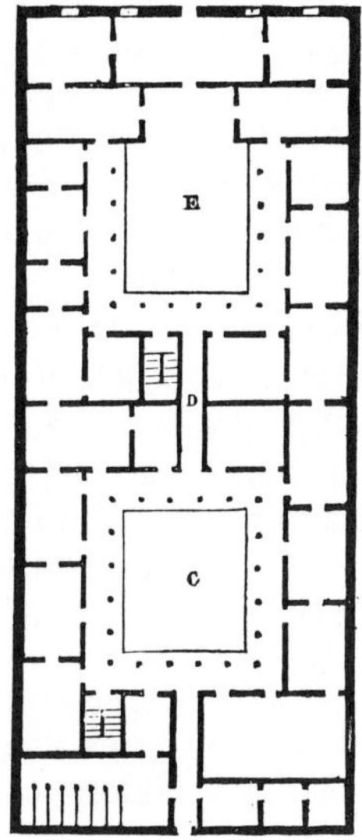

plan of Greek house: *D*, mesaulos connecting *C*, aula of the andron, with *E*, aula of the gynaeceum or gynaekonitis

meshrebeeyeh, mashrebeeyeh, mushrabiya **1.** In Islamic countries, an elaborately turned or carved wood screen or wood lattice which encloses a balcony window. **2.** Such a screen otherwise used. **3.** A balcony with a parapet and machicolations projected over a gate to defend the entrance; the parapet may be either embattled or plain.

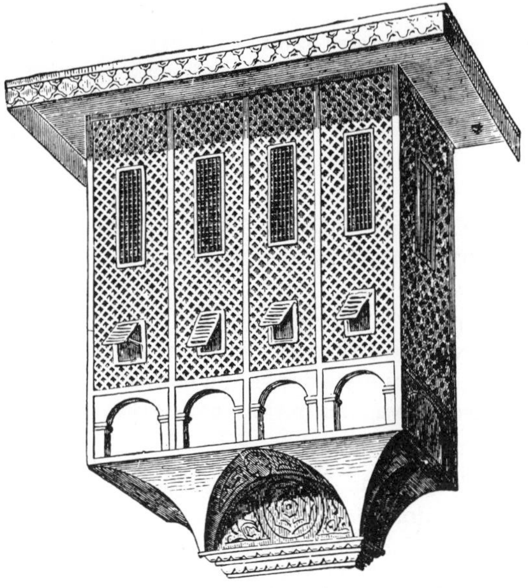

meshrebeeyeh,1

meshrebeeyeh,3

Mesoamerica The area of Mexico and Central America in which the presence of certain pre-Hispanic culture traits permits the classification of the cultures of the region as one civilization; includes central and southern Mexico, the Yucatán peninsula, Guatemala, El Salvador, and parts of Honduras, Nicaragua, and northern Costa Rica.

Mesopotamian architecture Architecture developed by the Euphrates and Tigris Valley civilizations, from the 3rd millennium to the 6th cent. B.C. Primarily a massive architecture of mud bricks set in clay mortar or bitumen. The heavy walls were articulated by pilasters and recesses; important public buildings were faced with baked or glazed brick. Rooms were narrow and long and generally covered by timber and mud roofs, but in certain cases also by tunnel vaults; columns were seldom used; openings usually were small.

messuage A dwelling with all attached and adjoining buildings and curtilage together with adjacent lands used by the household.

meta In a racetrack, a column or monument to mark a turn.

meta

metatome The space between two dentils.

metatorium Same as **aspasticum.**

metaulos See **Greek house.**

metoche Same as **metatome.**

metope The panel between the triglyphs in the Doric frieze, often carved. Also see **triglyph.**

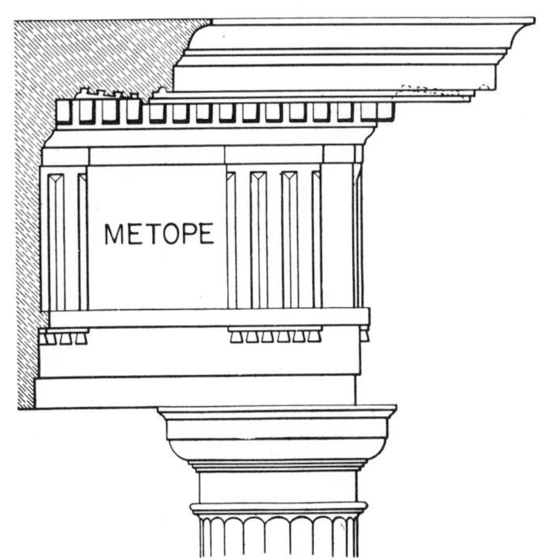

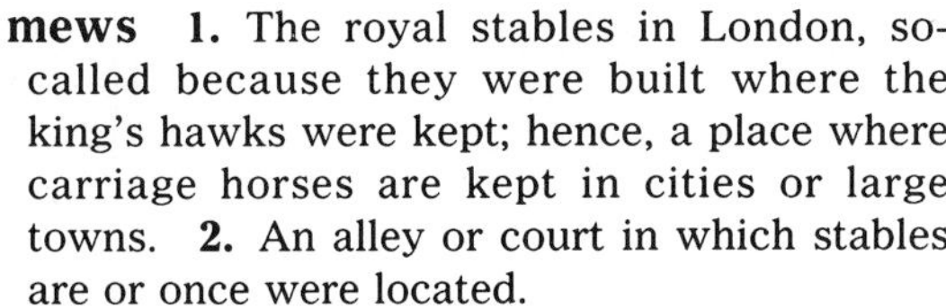

mews **1.** The royal stables in London, so-called because they were built where the king's hawks were kept; hence, a place where carriage horses are kept in cities or large towns. **2.** An alley or court in which stables are or once were located.

meydan See **midan.**

mezzanine, entresol A low-ceilinged story or extensive balcony, usually constructed next above the ground floor.

E-E, **mezzanine or entresol; house in Paris**

mezzo-rilievo, mezzo-relievo Casting, carving, or embossing in moderate relief, intermediate between **bas-relief** and **high relief.**

miao In traditional Chinese architecture, a temple.

mida'a, midha A place for ritual ablutions in a **mosque.**

midan, meydan An open square; originally a polo ground in **Muslim architecture.**

midha See **mida'a.**

migdol **1.** A watchtower or citadel in ancient Israel and Canaan. **2.** A fortress temple.

mid-wall column A column which carries a part of a wall much thicker than its own diameter.

mid-wall column

mihrab A niche in the mosque or any religious Muslim building indicating direction of prayer toward Mecca. Focal point of decoration with dome in front.

mihrab, Mosque El Moyed, Cairo. *right:* the minbar

mikdash A sanctuary; a temple in ancient Israel.

mille passus An ancient Roman measure of length equal to 1,000 **passus;** equivalent to 4852.4 ft (1,479 m).

milliarium A column placed at intervals of one Roman mile (equivalent to 0.92 mile or 1.48 km) along a Roman road to indicate distance.

milliarium aureum A golden column erected by Augustus in 29 B.C. at the point where the principal roads of the Roman empire terminated.

mimbar Same as **minbar.**

minah See **minar.**

minar, minah A tower, usually a memorial monument, found esp. in India.

minaret A tall tower in, or contiguous to, a mosque with stairs leading up to one or more balconies from which the faithful are called to prayer.

minarets flanking portal with dome

minbar The pulpit in a mosque.

minchery A nunnery.

minch house A roadside inn.

minka A traditional Japanese farmhouse; varies in style according to the region.

milliarium, Nic-sur-Aisne, France

Minoan architecture The architecture of Bronze Age Crete, which reached its apogee between the 19th and 14th cent. B.C. Most important were its palaces, in which a great number of rectangular rooms of various sizes, serving different functions and connected by long labyrinthine passages, were clustered around a large central courtyard. Gate buildings with columnar porches provided access to the otherwise unfortified compounds, which were generally constructed on sloping sites, utilizing terracing and split and multilevel organization of buildings with a great number of open and enclosed stairs; light wells, air shafts, elaborate drainage and sewage systems, and flushing toilets were the engineering features.

Foundation walls, piers, lintels, and thresholds were built in ashlar stone; upper walls and stories in timber framework with rubblestone masonry faced by stucco and decorated by wall paintings. Ceilings were of wood, as were the frequently used columns with their typical downward-tapering shape.

minster A monastic church; since many English cathedrals were originally associated with monasteries, the term applies to them by extension.

minstrel gallery A small balcony on the inside of a church or manor house hall, usually over the entrance.

mirador In Spanish architecture and derivatives, a lookout, whether an independent structure, a bay window, or a roof pavilion.

miserere, subsellium A ledge on the bottom of a hinged seat in a church; when the seat is raised, the ledge provides some support for a worshiper or choir singer who, in standing, leans against it.

misericord **1.** In monastic architecture, a room or separate building where monastic rule was relaxed. **2.** Same as **miserere.**

mission **1.** A church dependent for support on a larger church or on a monastic order. **2.** See **mission architecture.**

mission architecture Church and monastery architecture of the Spanish religious orders in Mexico and California, mainly in the 18th cent.

mission tile, Spanish tile A clay roofing tile, approximately semicylindrical in shape; laid in courses with the units having their convex side alternately up and down.

mission tile

mitatorium An emperor's dressing room, usually in a palace or church.

miter arch, mitre arch Two straight blocks of stone set diagonally over an opening, the upper ends resting against each other.

miter arch

miserere, All Souls College, Oxford (1715-40). The miserere seat is turned back, showing carving; at right, the seat is turned down

mithraeum An underground cave-like sanctuary devoted to the mystery cult of the Persian sun god Mithra. Such sanctuaries were constructed throughout the Roman Empire during the 2nd and 3rd cent. A.D.

mithuna A celestial couple, a pair of lovers, belonging to the sculptural vocabulary of Buddhist or Hindu architecture.

mixed arch A three- or four-centered arch; a **composite arch.**

mixed garden wall bond In brickwork, a bond similar to **English garden wall bond,** except that the course of **headers** is replaced by one consisting of alternate headers and **stretchers.**

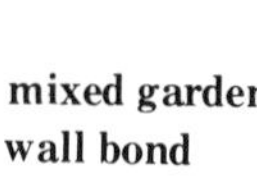

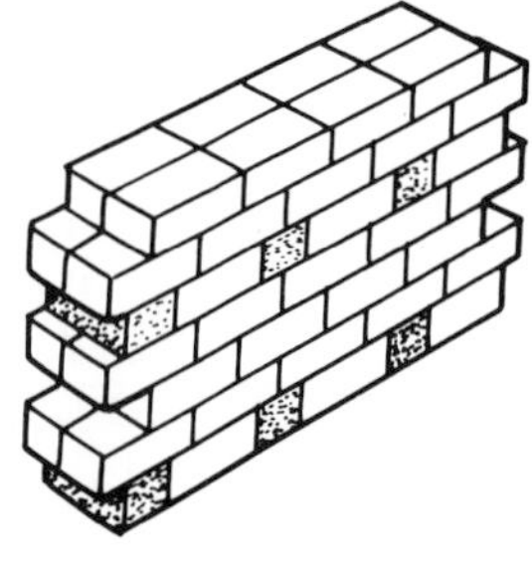

mixed garden wall bond

Mixtec architecture In the state of Oaxaca, Mexico, a type of Mesoamerican architecture, ca. 1000 A.D., characterized by great mass, use of interior stone columns, and emphasis on horizontal lines. The minutely detailed fretwork of the interior and exterior paneled friezes was produced by an assembly of thousands of small decorative elements set into clay, like a mosaic. The use of **scapulary tablets** on building facades and the presence of elaborate cruciform underground tombs are indicative of strong Zapotec influence. At Mitla, the free-standing buildings, around large courts, were oriented according to the cardinal points of the compass.

mixtilinear arch In Moorish and Spanish architecture, an arch composed of various geometric shapes.

mizuya, mizunoya In traditional Japanese architecture, the room in which preparations are made for the tea ceremony.

moat A broad, deep trench surrounding the ramparts of a town or fortress; usually filled with water.

mocarabe Same as **ajaraca.**

Moderne Style Same as **Style Moderne**; see **Art Deco.**

Modernismo The Spanish, particularly Catalan, version of Art Nouveau.

modillion A horizontal bracket or console, usually in the form of a scroll with acanthus, supporting the corona under a cornice. If in the form of a plain block, it is a **block modillion** or **uncut modillion.** Found in Corinthian, Composite, and, less frequently, Roman Ionic orders.

right: **modillion;** *below:* **location**

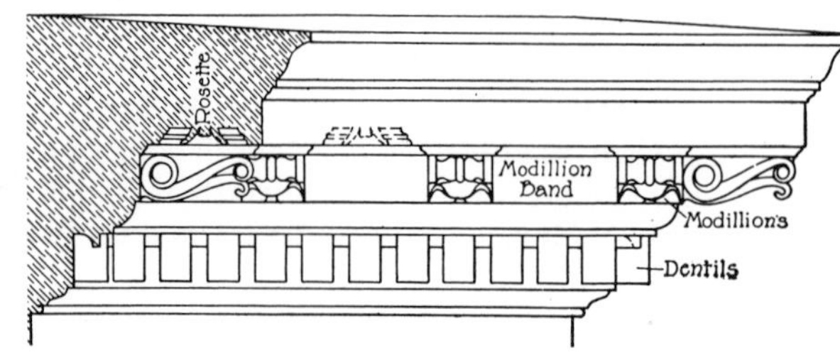

moellon Stone rubble used as filling between the facing walls of a structure.

moenianum Same as **maenianum.**

Mogen David See **Star of David.**

Moghul architecture See **Mogul architecture.**

Mogul architecture The later phase of Indian **Islamic architecture,** named after the Mogul dynasty (1526–1707), typified by monumental palaces and mosques and detailed decorative work. The Taj Mahal is the most famous example.

Mohammedan architecture Same as **Muslim architecture, Islamic architecture.**

molded brick **1.** A specially shaped brick, usually for decorative work. **2.** Ordinary brick which is neither cut with a wire nor pressed.

molding A member of construction or decoration so treated as to introduce varieties of outline or contour in edges or surfaces, whether on projections or cavities, as on cornices, capitals, bases, door and window jambs and heads, etc.; may be of any building material, but almost all derive at least in part from wood prototypes (as those in classical architecture) or stone prototypes (as those in Gothic architecture). Moldings are generally divided into three categories; rectilinear, curved, and composite-curved.

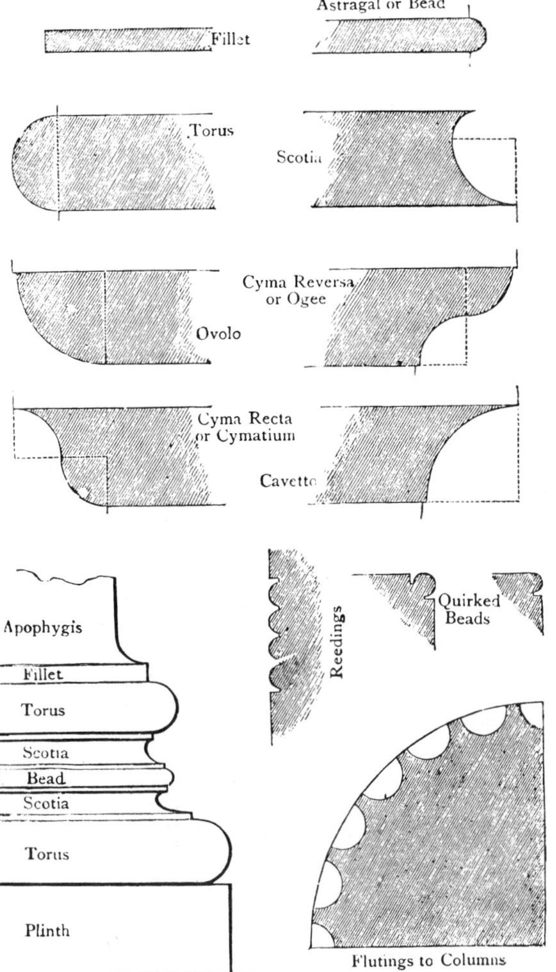

Roman modification of Greek moldings

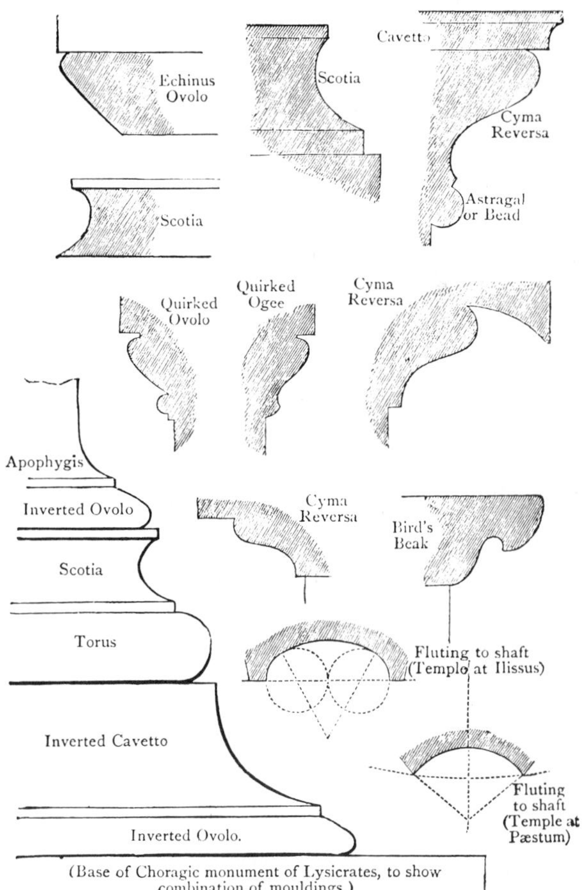

principal Greek moldings

For illustrations of other moldings, see specific types.

mold stone The **jambstone** of a door or window.

monastery A building complex of a monastic order.

monelle Same a **mullion.**

moneta In early Rome, a mint or place where money was coined.

monial Same as **mullion.**

monolith An architectural member (as an obelisk, the shaft of a column, etc.) consisting of a single stone.

monolithic **1.** Shaped from a single block of stone, as a monolithic column. **2.** Composed of monoliths. **3.** Characterized by massiveness and complete uniformity.

monopteron In Greek architecture, a circular peripteral building, as a temple, having only a single row of columns.

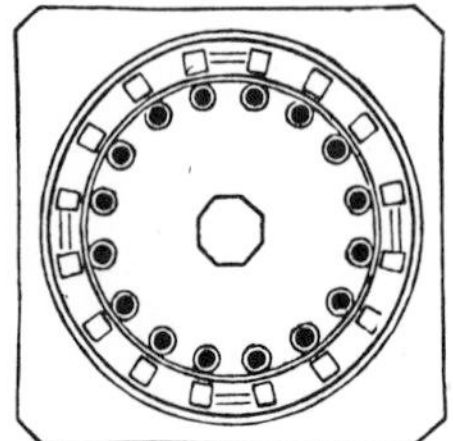

plan of monopteron temple

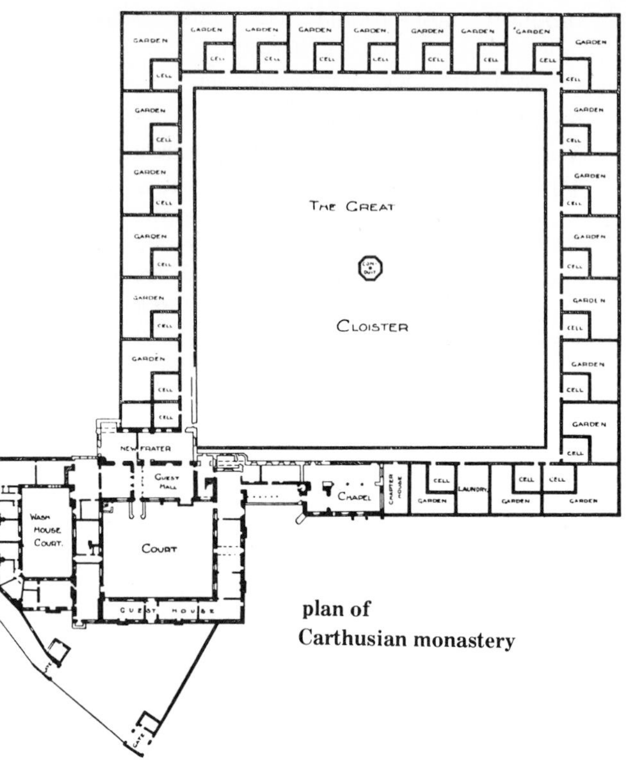

plan of Carthusian monastery

monostyle **1.** Having but a single shaft; applied to medieval pillars. **2.** Having the same style of architecture throughout.

monotriglyphic In the Doric order, having one **triglyph** over the space between two columns.

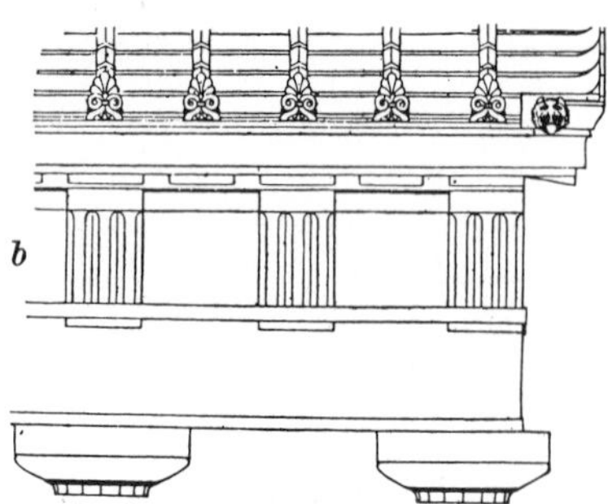

monotriglyphic

monstrance See **ostensory.**

Monte Albán See **Zapotec architecture.**

monument **1.** A permanent natural or artificial object marking the corners and boundaries of real property or establishing the location of a triangulation or other important survey station. **2.** A stone, pillar, megalith, structure, building, or the like, erected in memory of the dead, an event, or an action.

Druid monument, La Roche-aux-Fées

Neville Monument, East Ham Church; Early Renaissance

monument, Coleshill Church, Warwickshire (14th cent.)

monument, Meriden Church, Warwickshire (c. 1440)

monument in Sta. Maria del Popolo, Rome (15th cent.)

Monument of Lysicrates A **choragic monument** in Athens to the victory in the contests won by Lysicrates in 334 B.C. when he was leader of the chorus. From a slender square base rises a small round temple; six engaged Corinthian columns surround its circular wall and support the entablature, on the frieze of which there is a representation of a scene in the legend of Dionysus; over the entablature is a flat dome made of a single block of marble, and from the center of the roof rises a finial of acanthus leaves, formerly crowned by the tripod which was the prize of victory.

detail of dome of the Choragic Monument of Lysicrates; the entire structure is illustrated under *choragic monument*

monyal Same as **mullion.**

moon gate In traditional Chinese architecture, a circular opening in a wall.

Moorish arch Same as **horseshoe arch.**

Moorish architecture The **Islamic architecture** of North Africa and of the regions of Spain under Islamic domination. Also see **Hispano-Moresque architecture.**

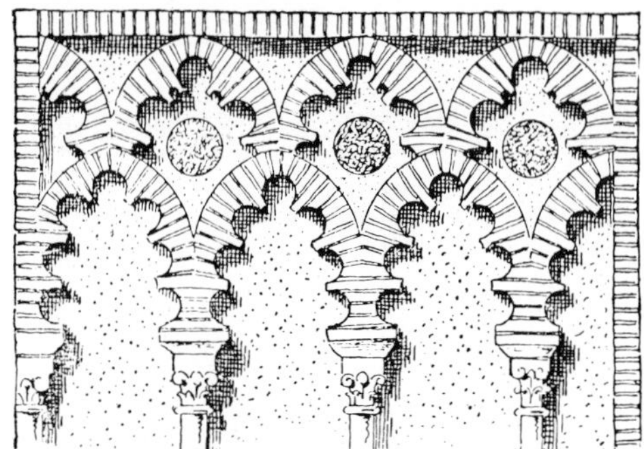

Moorish architecture: arcade in Seville

Moorish architecture: Great Mosque, Córdoba (785 A.D. and later)

Moorish architecture: *above and at left,* **decorations from the Alhambra (14th cent.)**

moot hall A place of public assembly; a hall for meeting, debate, or judgment; a town hall.

morning room A family, or private, sitting room, usually sunlit early in the day.

mortuary temple A temple for offerings and worship of a deceased person, usually a deified king, as distinguished from a **cult temple.**

mosaic 1. A pattern formed by inlaying small pieces of stone, tile, glass, or enamel into a cement, mortar, or plaster matrix. 2. A form of surface decoration, similar to marquetry, but usually employing small pieces or bits of wood to create an inlaid design.

portion of Pompeii mosaic of the Battle of Issus *(actual size)*

mosaic pavement, Pompeii

Italian Gothic marble floor mosaic, Lucca Cathedral, 1204

Byzantine mosaic from Hagia Sophia, Constantinople

Moslem architecture See **Muslim architecture.**

mosque A Muslim house of worship.

below: **section of Mosque of Sultan Hassan, Cairo (1462)**

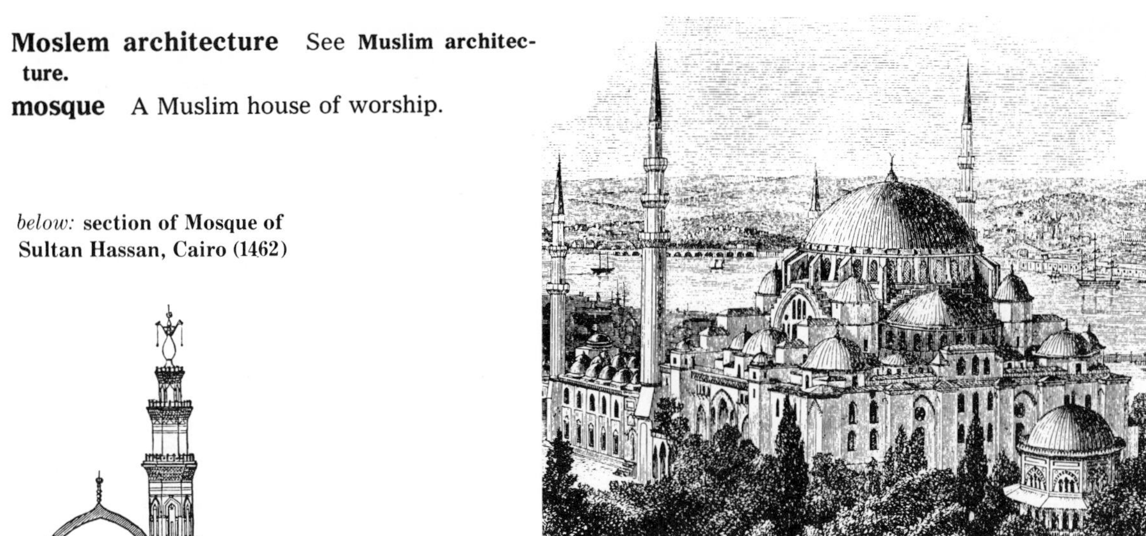

above: **view of Suleiman Mosque, Cairo**

section of Suleiman Mosque, Constantinople (1557)

Mosque of Córdoba See **Great Mosque of Córdoba.**

Mosque of Ibn Tulun One of the largest and most important extant early mosques, built in Cairo by Ahmed Ibn Tulun in 879 A.D. A large central court is surrounded by **riwaqs** five aisles deep on one side and two aisles deep on the other three sides, which are entered through broad outer courts. Brick piers with engaged columns, molded in brick, support stilted pointed arches. All surfaces are coated with fine, hard stucco in which ornamental bands, soffits, capitals, and bases are cut. The openwork windows are of alabaster. The minaret has an exterior open stair which winds around the two square lower floors and the circular upper floor to an octagonal kiosk, in a zigguratlike fashion. One of the earliest mosques, in which no Roman or Byzantine materials were used.

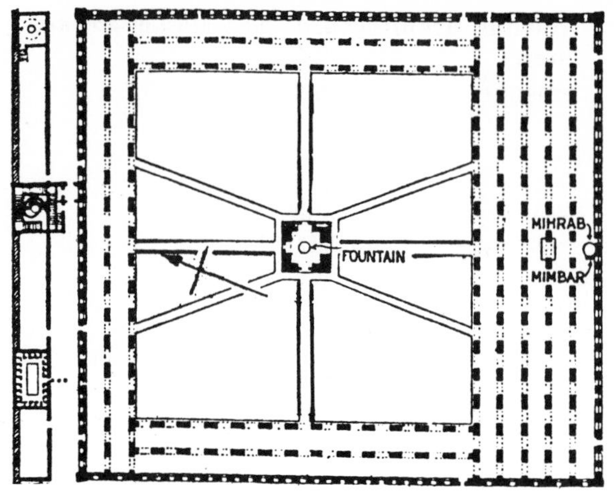

Mosque of Ibn Tulun, Cairo (876–79 A.D.): plan

Mosque of Omar A designation sometimes applied erroneously to the **Dome of the Rock.**

motif A principal repeated element in an ornamental design.

motte A steep mound of earth surrounded by a ditch and surmounted by a timber stockade and tower; the main feature of a Norman castle.

moucharaby See **meshrebeeyeh.**

mouchette In 14th cent. Gothic tracery and derivatives, a typical small motif, pointed, elongated, and bounded by elliptical and ogee curves; a dagger motif with a curved axis.

moulding British variant of **molding.**

mourners Same as **weepers.**

母屋 **moya** The central core of a traditional Japanese wooden structure, esp. in temple buildings; separated from adjacent areas by pillars, between which may be placed sliding doors or hanging screens.

moynall, moynel, moynialle Same as **mullion.**

Mozarabic style Northern Spanish architecture built after the 9th cent. by Christian refugees from Moorish domination, characterized by the horseshoe arch and other Moorish features.

mu In Chinese architecture, a tomb.

Mosque of Ibn Tulun: courtyard

mud brick In building construction in the Near East, any type of sun-dried clay brick; Near Eastern equivalent of **adobe brick.**

Mudejar style A Spanish style created by Moors under Christian domination in the 13th and 14th cent., but retaining Islamic elements such as the horseshoe arch.

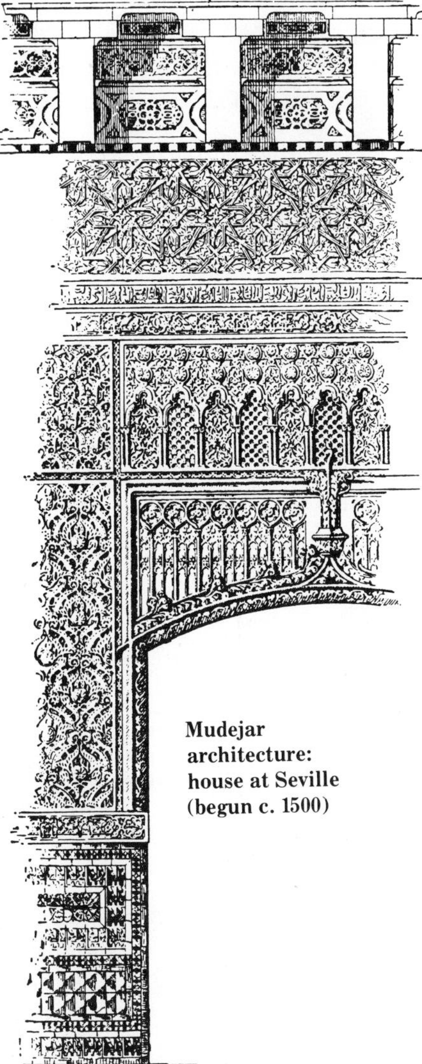

Mudejar architecture: house at Seville (begun c. 1500)

mud room In a farmhouse or country residence, a small entryway where muddy footwear may be removed.

mudsill A **groundsill,** usually laid directly in mud or in the soil.

mud wall See **cob wall.**

Mughal architecture See **Mogul architecture.**

mukhashala An assembly porch of a temple in northern India; also called a **jagamohan.**

mukuri-yane A roof on a traditional Japanese structure which has a convex curvature.

mukuri-yane 起屋根

mullion A vertical member separating (and often supporting) window, doors, or panels set in series. Also see **door mullion.**

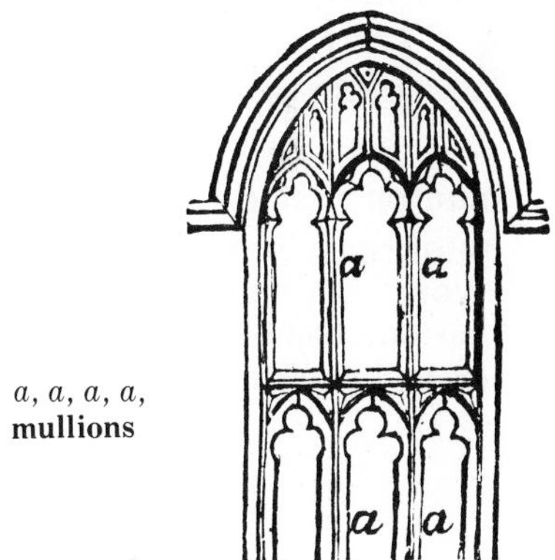

a, a, a, a, mullions

multicentered arch An arch having a shape composed of a series of circular arcs with different radii, giving an approximation to an ellipse. These arcs are symmetrically disposed about a vertical axis and occur in odd numbers.

multifoil Having more than five foils, lobes, or arcuate divisions.

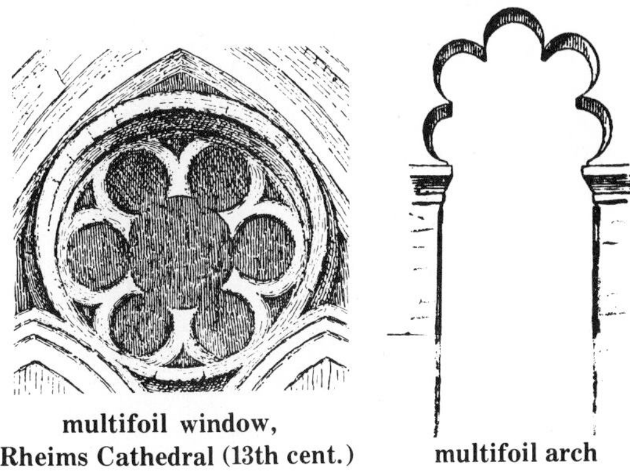

multifoil window, Rheims Cathedral (13th cent.)

multifoil arch

棟 **mune** In traditional Chinese architecture, the ridge of a roof.

muniment house, *Brit.* **muniment room** A secure structure or area for storing and displaying important documents, official seals, etc.

munnion 1. A **mullion.** 2. A **muntin.**

muntin 1. A secondary framing member to hold panes within a window, window wall, or glazed door. 2. An intermediate vertical member that divides the panels of a door.

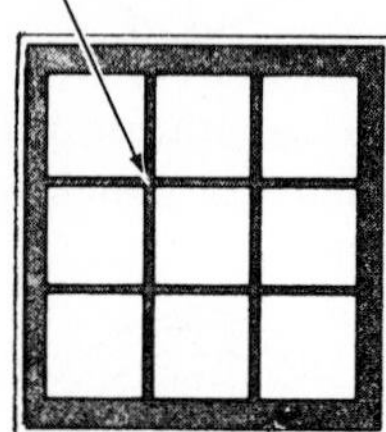

muntin

munton Same as **mullion.**

muqarnas, honeycomb work, stalactite work An original Islamic design involving various combinations of three-dimensional shapes, corbeling, etc.

muqarnas, Islamic design

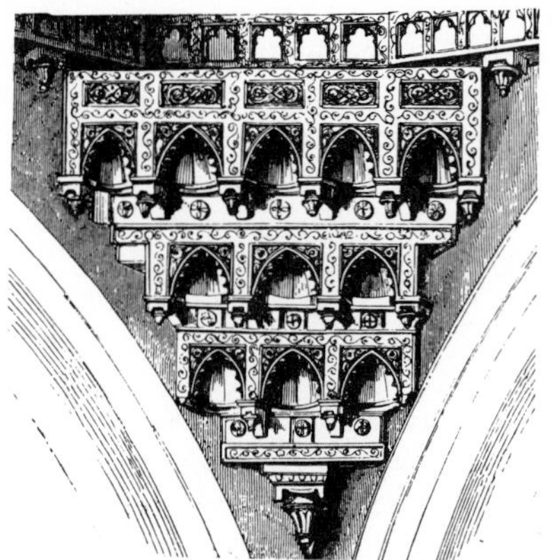

muqarnas from a mosque in Old Delhi

mural arch An arch in a wall which was constructed in the plane of the meridian; used for attachment of astronomical instruments in the Middle Ages.

muristan A medieval Muslim hospital.

murus A wall of stone or brick, built as a defense and fortification around an ancient Roman town. Also see **paries.**

murus: section of wall

murus coctilis A wall built of bricks hardened by fire.

musalla A place of Muslim worship; a prayer hall.

mushrabiya See **meshrebeeyeh.**

mushrebeeyeh Same as **meshrebeeyeh.**

musivum Same as **opus musivum.**

musiya In early Russian architecture, a mosaic.

Muslim architecture, Muhammadan architecture, Saracenic architecture Architecture developed from the 7th to the 16th cent. A.D., in the wake of the Muhammadan conquests of Syria and Egypt, Mesopotamia and Iran, North Africa and Spain, Central Asia and India, countries from which it absorbed in turn elements of art and architecture. A new building type was developed from the Christian basilica—the multi-aisled, arcaded, columnar, or pillared mosque; a new type of domed mosque, tomb, or madrasah from the vaulted, centrally organized Byzantine and Sassanian structures. Uses many variations of basic architectural elements; pointed, horseshoe, "Persian," multifoil, and interlacing arches; bulbous, ribbed, conical, and melon domes; tunnel, cross-rib, and stalactite vaults; a wide variety of crenelations. Surfaces are covered by abundant geometric, floral, and calligraphic decorations executed in stone, brick, stucco, wood, and glazed tile. Also called **Islamic architecture.** (See illustrations under **Islamic architecture.**)

mutule A sloping flat block on the soffit of the Doric cornice, usually decorated with rows of six **guttae** each; occurs over each triglyph and each metope of the frieze.

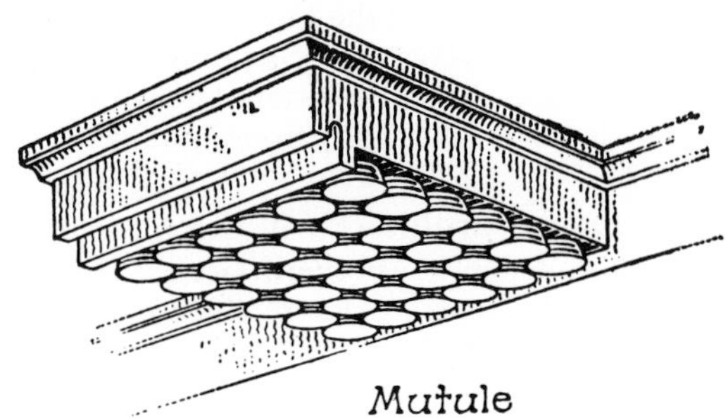

above: **mutule**

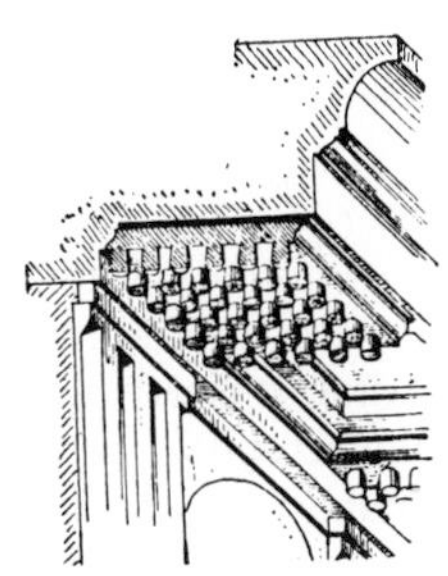

left: **cross section through cornice, showing location of mutule**

below: **cornice soffit viewed from below, showing mutules**

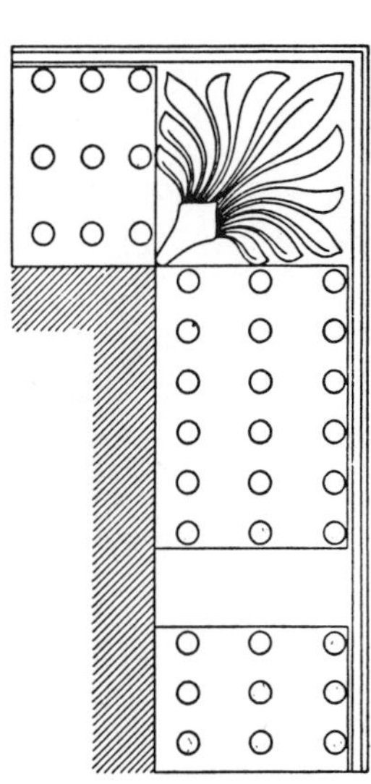

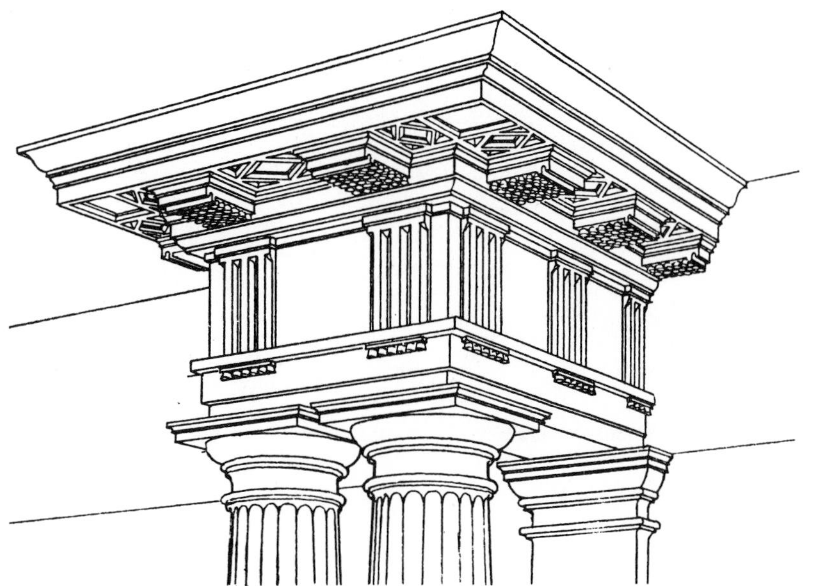

Mycenae

Mycenae One of the most ancient Greek cities, located in the southern part of Greece. Strategically located as a citadel, it was the center of Mycenaean civilization. The city was approached through the Lion Gate, of massive masonry construction, surmounted by affronted lions. Other important ancient remains include the Treasury of Atreus and the beehive tombs.

Mycenaean architecture Architecture of the heroic age in southern Greece from the 17th to 13th cent. B.C. Exemplified in the earliest phase by shaft graves cut into the sloping rock, with sidewalls of stone masonry and a timber roof; in the middle period by monumental beehive tombs constructed of superimposed layers of enormous stone blocks progressively projecting to create a parabolic corbeled vault, with a stone-faced, inclined access passage leading to the entrance composed of upward-slanting jambs and a heavy stone lintel supporting a characteristic Mycenaean relief triangle; in the late period by fortified palaces having Cyclopean walls, underground passages with corbeled vaults, postern gates, and cisterns, laid out on an irregular ground plan, with distinctive **propylaea,** one or more unconnected columnar halls with porches facing individual courts, and long corridors linking auxiliary and storage rooms.

Lion Gate, Mycenae (c. 1250 B.C.)

Cyclopean wall, Mycenae (c. 1250 B.C.)

detail of lions on Lion Gate

SECTION

R

DROMOS

PLAN

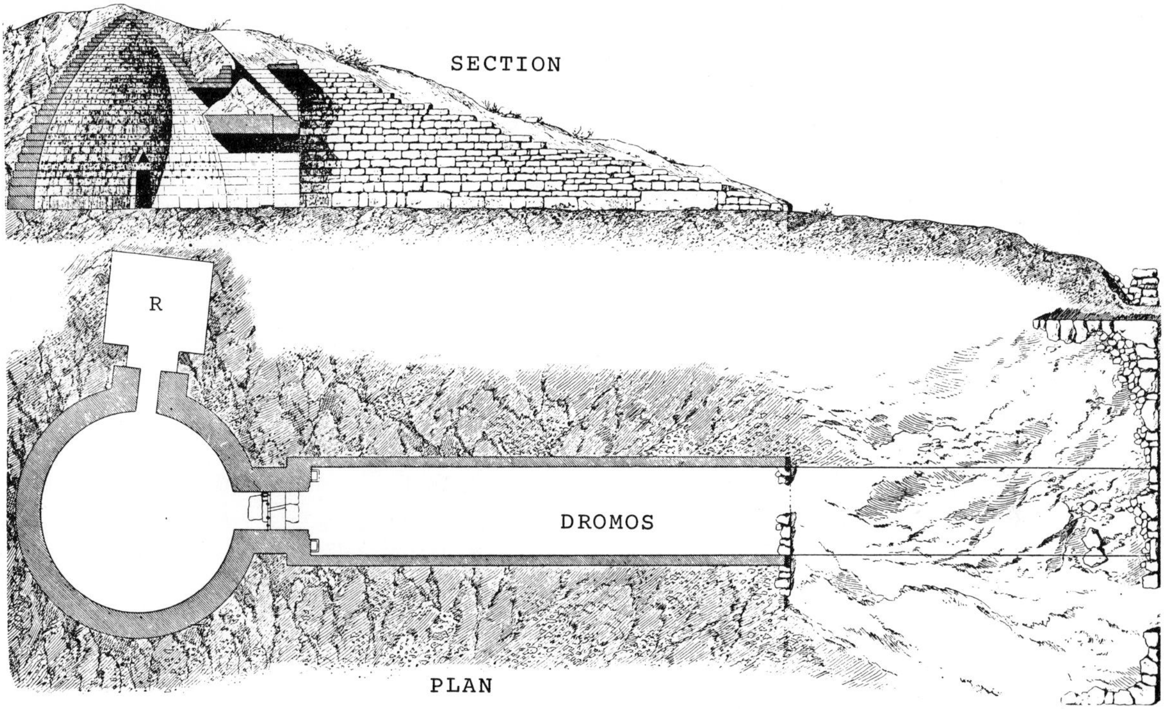

Treasury of Atreus, Mycenae, also known as the "Tomb of Agamemnon" (c. 1325 B.C.)
***R*, a rock-cut chamber, probably was the burial place of Agamemnon**

fragment of pillar in front of Treasury of Atreus

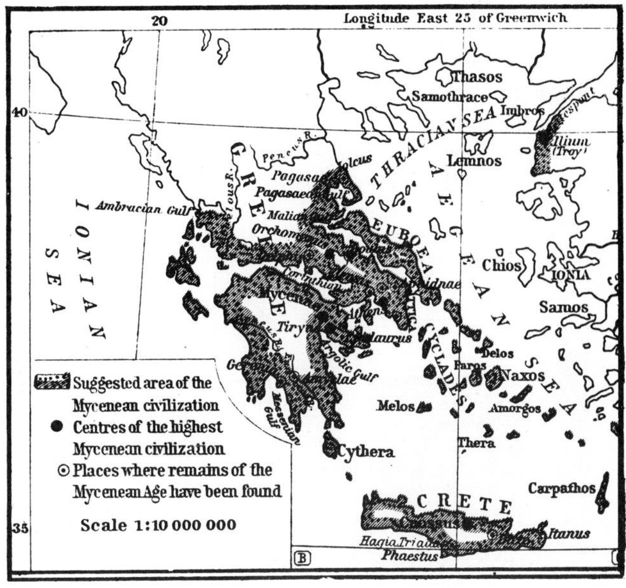

nagara A town or city laid out according to strict rules; an architectural style in northern India (literally "city-dweller style").

流造

Nagare style, Nagare-zukuri The most popular style of Japanese architecture for a shrine, characterized by its gabled roof with a concave profile. The front slope of the building is longer than the rear and extends beyond the steps to form a protective canopy for the worshipers. The roof (which has no **chigi** or **katsuogi**) has a thick cypress-bark covering in multiple layers.

Nagare style

nagaya In traditional Japanese architecture, a long house which is divided into many small apartments, each occupied by a family in the employ of a landowner or lord.

長押

nageshi In traditional Japanese architecture, a horizontal beam used to connect pillars. Later this term was used for a horizontal board secured to the inner and/or outer sides of columns.

arrow points to nageshi

nailhead **1.** An ornament, often highly decorated, resembling the head of a nail. **2.** The enlarged top of a nail.

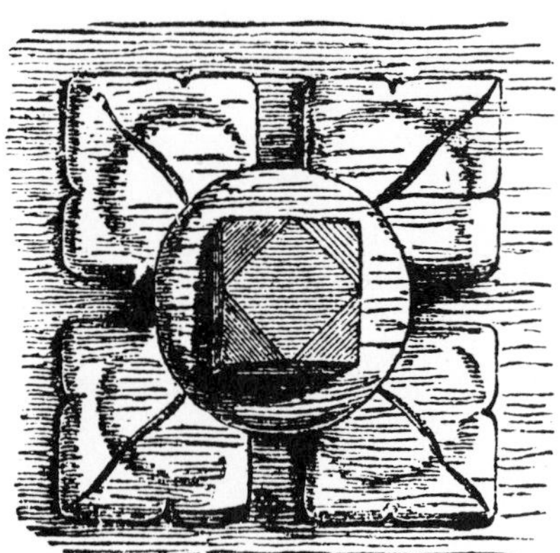

nailhead

nailhead molding A molding decorated with a series of quadrangular pyramidal projections resembling the heads of nails.

nailhead molding

naiskos A small shrine.

naka-nuri The second coat of plaster on a wall of a traditional Japanese building; applied before the finish coat.

nalichnik An encircling border or decorative frame around a window or door in early Russian architecture; often with columns and a pediment.

nana-jū-no-tō See **tō.**

nandaimon The gate at the entrance of a Japanese Buddhist monastic compound (literally "south great gate").

naos Greek term for **cella.**

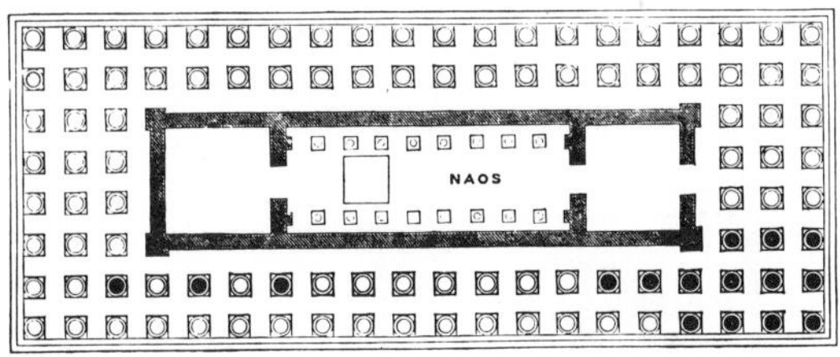

naos (inner sanctuary of a temple)

Nara See **Hōryūji.**

narthex An enclosed porch or vestibule at the entrance to some early Christian churches.

nashki Cursive writing used decoratively in Muslim architecture.

natte A basket weave, as a pattern carved or painted to imitate interlaced withes of matting.

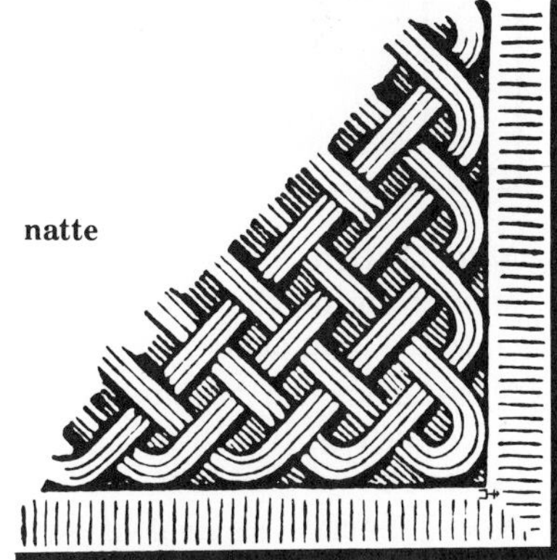

natte

naumachia, naumachy In ancient Rome, a place where mock sea fights were held. An artificial pond or lake holding sufficient water to float ships was surrounded by stands or seats for spectators. Some amphitheatres and circuses could be flooded for spectacles of this type.

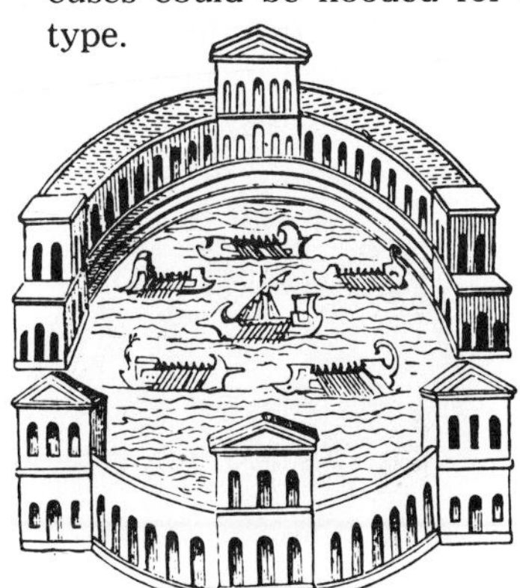

naumachia

navaranga In Indian architecture, the central hall of a temple.

nave **1.** The middle aisle of a church. **2.** By extension, both middle and side aisles of a church from the entrance to the crossing or chancel. **3.** That part of the church intended primarily for the laity.

nave arcade The open arcade between the central and side aisles.

neat work Brickwork set at the base of a wall above the footings.

nebulé molding, nebuly molding A characteristic Norman molding with an undulating lower edge.

nebulé molding

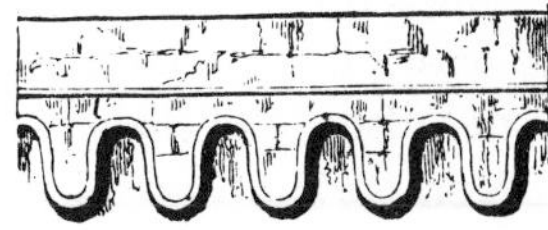

necessarium The privy of an ancient castle or of a monastery.

neck In the classical orders, the space between the bottom of the capital and the top of the shaft, which is marked by a sinkage or a ring of moldings.

necking **1.** Same as **neck.** **2.** A molding or group of moldings between a column and capital. **3.** Any ornamental band at the lower part of a capital; a **hypotrachelium.**

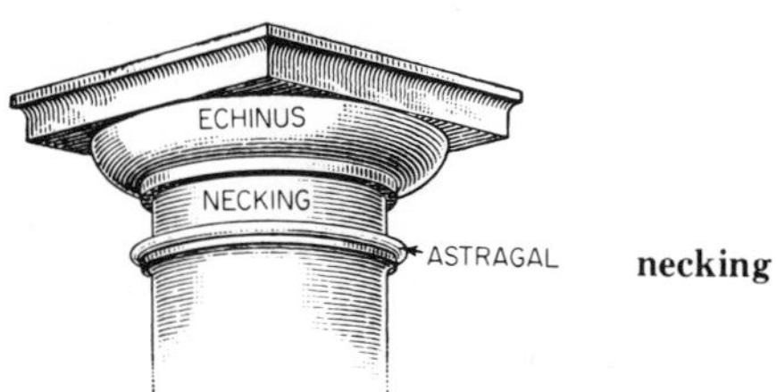

necking

neck molding A **necking** which takes the form of a molding of any type; same as **necking, 2.**

necropolis **1.** A city of the dead; a large cemetery in ancient Egypt, Greece, Phoenicia, Carthage, etc. **2.** An ancient or historic burial place.

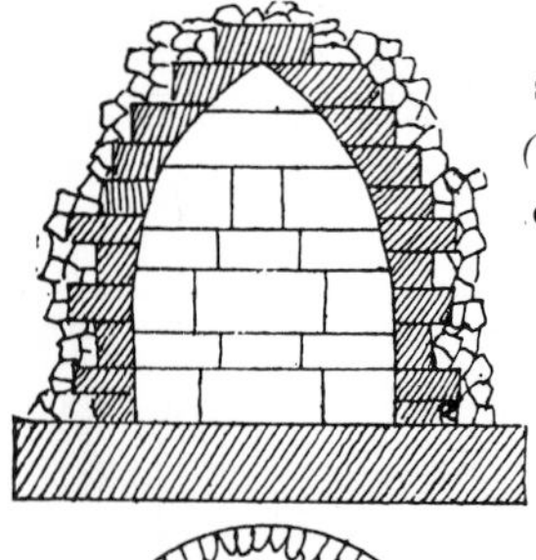

section *(above)* **and plan** *(below)* **of the necropolis of Tantalus, Sipylus**

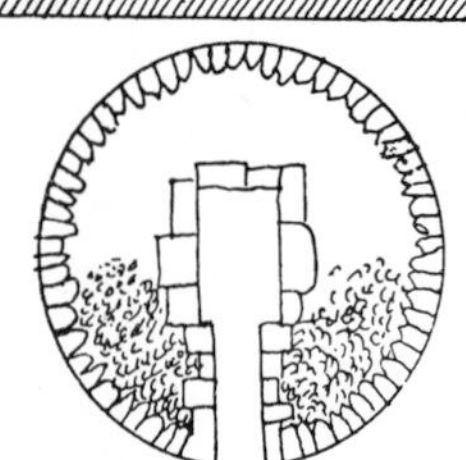

needle spire A slender **spire** surmounting the center of a tower roof.

needlework A form of construction combining a framework of timber and a plaster or masonry filling; common in medieval houses.

nei chu See **chu.**

Neo-Byzantine See **Byzantine Revival.**

Neoclassicism The last phase of European classicism, in the late 18th and 19th cent., characterized by monumentality, strict use of the orders, and sparing application of ornament. Also see **Classic Revival.**

Neoclassicism

Neo-Gothic Refers to the use of Gothic forms during the second half of the 19th and into the 20th cent.

Neo-Grec An architectural style developed in France in the 1840s, applying Greek forms to brick and cast iron.

Neo-Liberty Revival of Art Nouveau forms in Italy after 1945.

Neo-Romanesque See **Romanesque Revival.**

nerve Same as **nervure.**

nervure Any one of the ribs of a groined vault, but esp. a rib which forms one of the sides of a compartment of the groining.

net tracery Tracery with repetitive motifs or openings.

net tracery

New Brutalism See **Brutalism.**

newel **1.** The central post or column around which the steps of a circular staircase wind, and which provides support for the staircase. **2.** A **newel-post.**

newel,1

newel cap The terminal feature of a newel-post; often molded, turned, or carved in a decorative shape.

newel collar A turned wood collar used to lengthen the base of a newel.

newel drop An ornamental, terminal projection of a newel-post, often through a soffit.

newel joint The joint between a **newel-post** and the handrail or between the newel-post and the **string** of a stair.

newel-post A tall and more or less ornamental post at the head or foot of a stair, supporting the handrail.

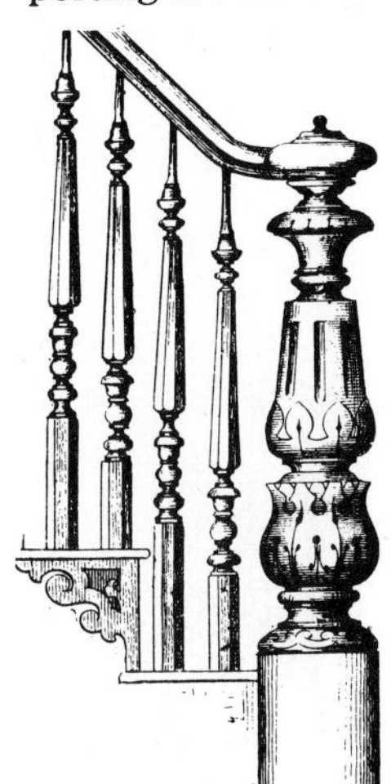

newel-post

newel stair **1.** A **screw stair.** **2.** Same as **solid newel stair.**

niche A recess in a wall, usually to contain sculpture or an urn; often semicircular in plan, surmounted by a half dome.

Norman niche, Norfolk (c. 1160)

Decorated style niche

Renaissance niche, Rome (1507)

nidged ashlar, nigged ashlar Stone dressed on the surface with a pick or sharp-pointed hammer.

躙口 **nijiriguchi** A guest entrance, miniature in size, to a Japanese tea-ceremony house; approx. 25½ in. (65 cm) high and 23½ in. (60 cm) wide; to enter, one must kneel.

Nijō-jō A superb example of the **Shoin style** of Japanese architecture, in Kyōto city, originally constructed for the use of Tokugawa Ieyasu when he visited Kyōto. Important structures include: the Karamon, erected at the beginning of the Edo period but reflecting the Momoyama style; the Ni-no-maru, a sprawling asymmetrical structure which housed officials, bodyguards, and the shōgun himself and which contained ceremonial and audience halls.

日光 **Nikkō** A religious center in the Tochigi prefecture of Japan, famous for its shrines and temples; the location of the Tōshōgū Shrine (the mausoleum of Tokugawa Ieyasu), completed between 1634 and 1636. The shrine is especially known for the Haiden (Oratory), Honden (Main Hall), Karamon (Chinese Gate), and Yōmeimon (Gate of Sunlight), all of the early Edo period (1600–1868).

nimbus A halo or disk of light surrounding the head in representations of divine and sacred personages.

Nimrud See **Assyrian architecture.**

Nineveh See **Assyrian architecture.**

nodus In ancient Roman construction, a **keystone,** or a **boss** in vaulting.

noel An old English term for **newel.**

nogging Brickwork carried up in panels between timber quarters; the filling of brickwork between members of a frame wall or partition.

nook An alcove opening off a room to provide additional or more intimate space, sometimes at a fireplace or adjoining a kitchen for dining.

nook shaft A column or colonnette set in a square break, as at the angle of a building, or where the jamb of a doorway meets the external face of a wall.

noraghe Same as **nuraghe.**

norma A square for measuring right angles; employed in ancient Roman construction by masons, carpenters, builders, etc.

Norman architecture The Romanesque architecture of England from the Norman Conquest (1066) until the rise of the Gothic around 1180.

Early Norman arch, Westminster Hall (1090)

Norman arch, Christ Church, Oxford (c. 1150; screen inserted c. 1528)

Norman arch, Great Malvern, Worcestershire (c. 1100)

Norman gateway, College Green, Bristol

Norman arch and pillars, Gloucester Cathedral

St. John's Chapel, Tower of London (1086–97)

Norman architecture

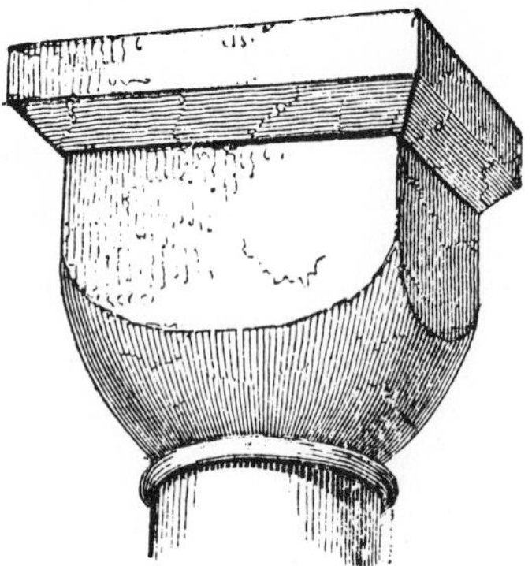

Worcester Cathedral (1084–89)

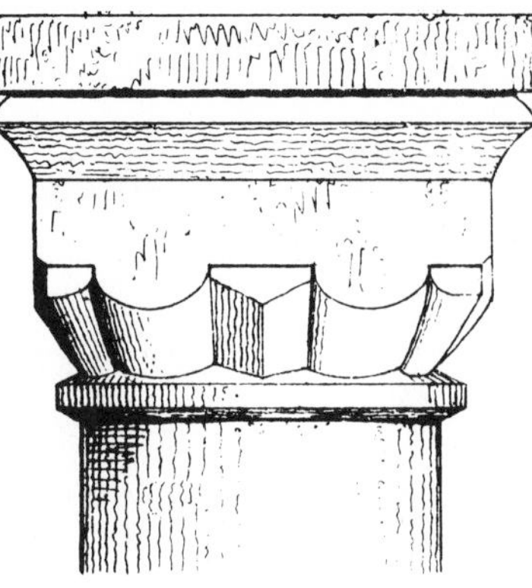

early Norman capital

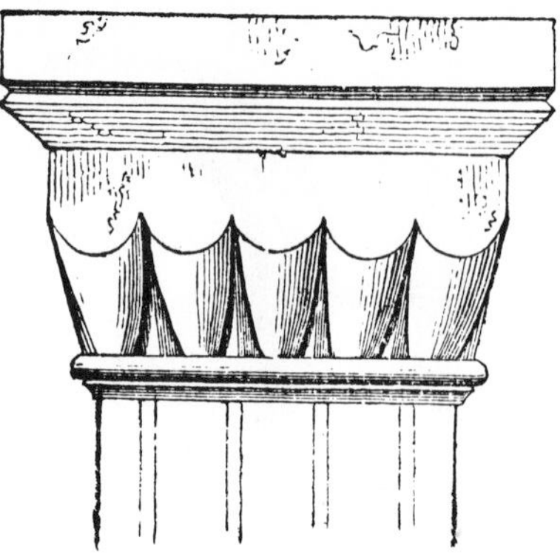

Winchester Cathedral (begun 1079)

crypt, Canterbury Cathedral (1070–89)

crypt, Canterbury Cathedral

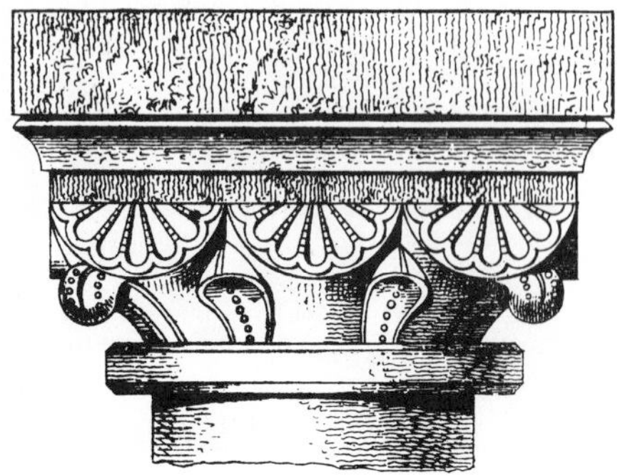

crypt, Canterbury Cathedral

St. Peter's, Northampton (c. 1160)

Norman architecture

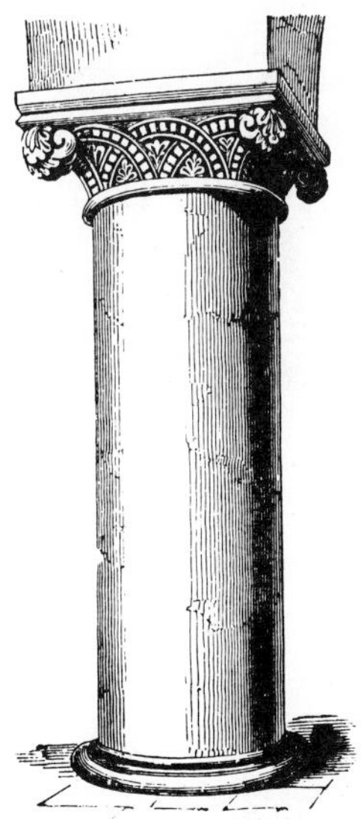

types of Norman piers

Winchester Cathedral
(begun 1079)

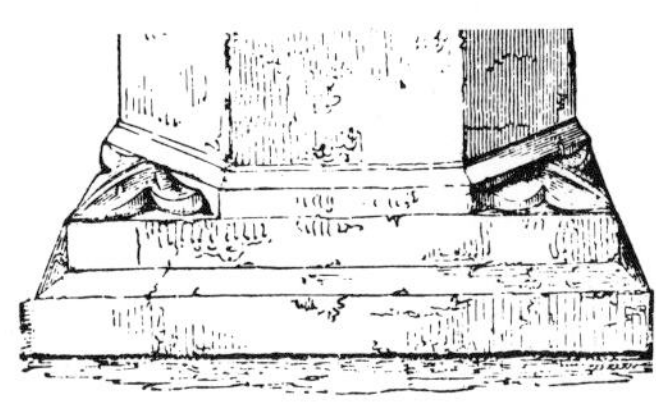

base, Rochester (c. 1150)

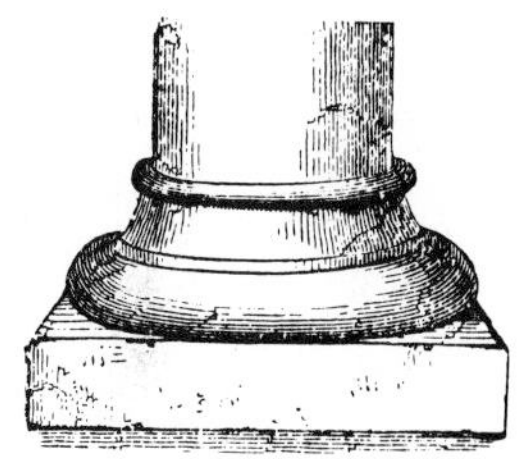

Norwich Cathedral
(1096–1145)

piscina, Romsey Church,
Hampshire (c. 1130)

arcade, St. Botoph's,
Colchester (c. 1120)

arcade, St. Augustine's,
Canterbury

Norman architecture (doors)

Iffley Church, Oxfordshire (c. 1120)

Essendine Chapel, Rutland (c. 1130)

Fritwell, Oxfordshire (c. 1150)

Kirkham Priory, Yorkshire (c. 1180)

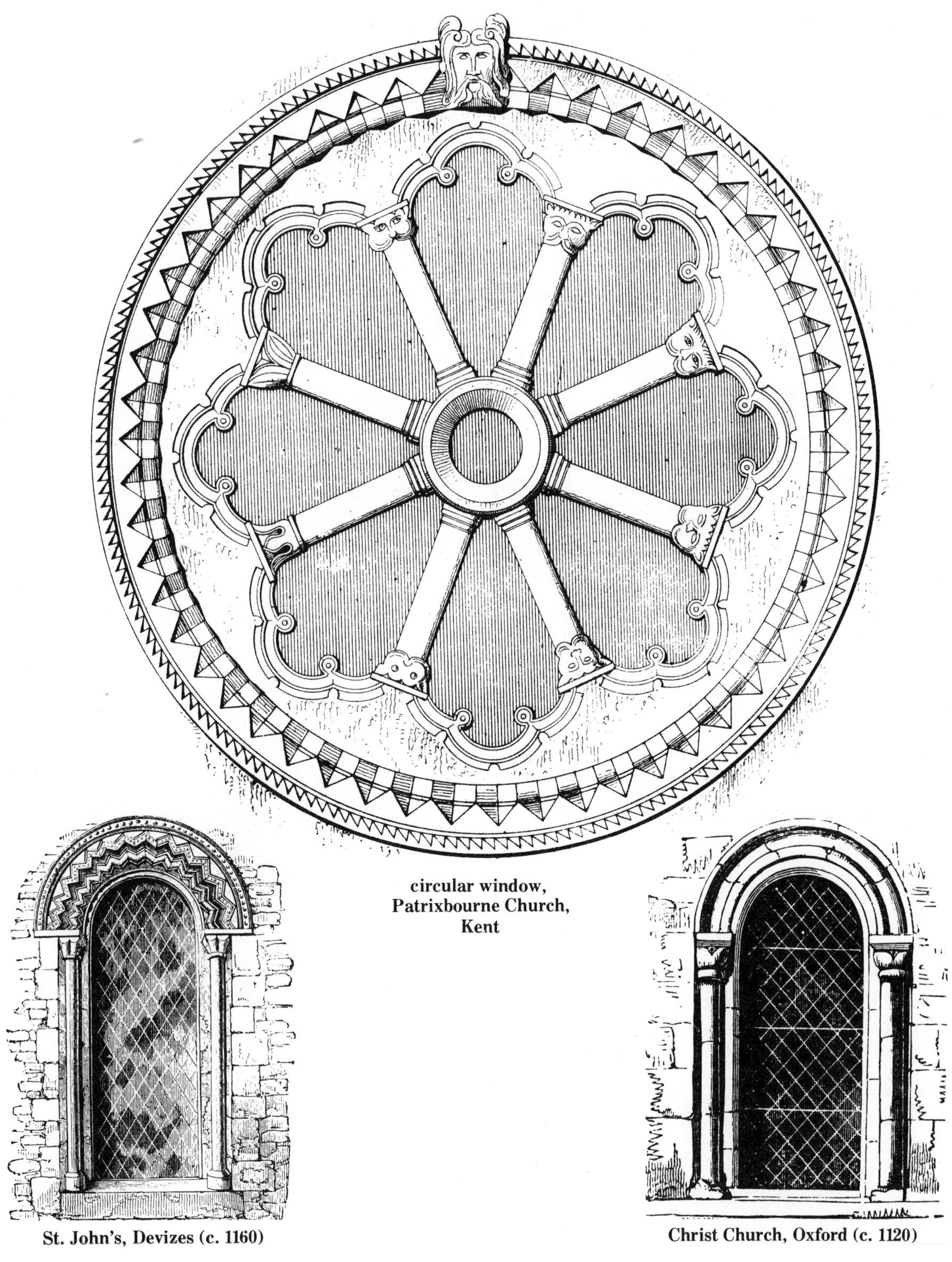

circular window,
Patrixbourne Church,
Kent

St. John's, Devizes (c. 1160)

Christ Church, Oxford (c. 1120)

Norman brick A brick whose nominal dimensions are 2⅔ in. by 4 in. by 12 in. (8.5 cm by 10.2 cm by 30.5 cm).

north aisle The aisle of a church on the left side of a church as one faces the altar; so called because medieval churches almost invariably had their sanctuaries at the east end and the main doors at the west end.

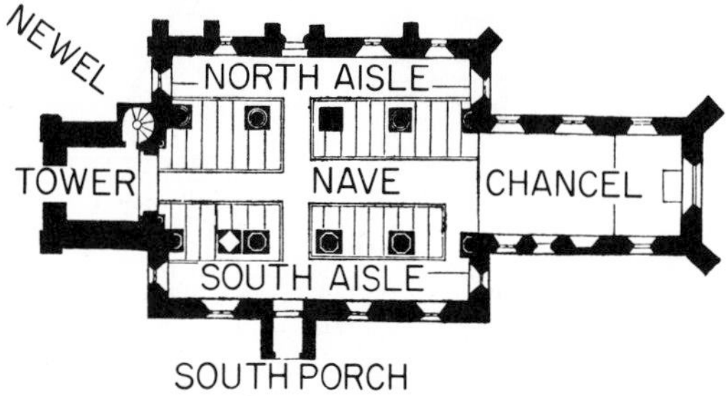

north porch A porch which shelters the entrance to a church; located on the left side of the church as one faces the altar.

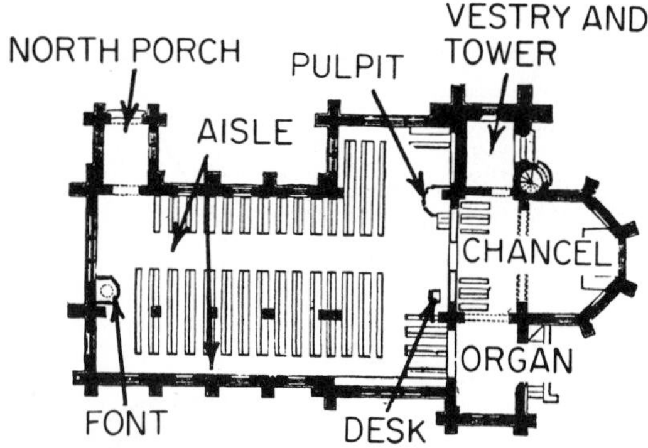

nosocomium, nosokomion A hospital or infirmary for the poor.

notchboard A stringer in a flight of stairs; a **face string.**

notched molding, notch ornament An ornament produced by notching the edges of a band or fillet.

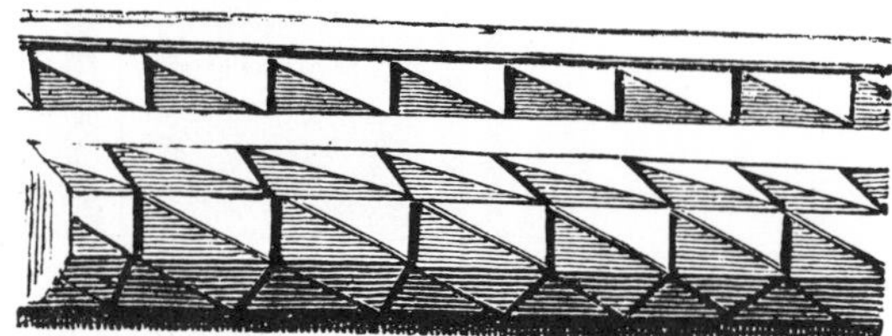

notched moldings

notch ornament See **notched molding.**

nubilarium On an ancient Roman farm, a large shed or barn, open on one side, situated close to the threshing floor (which was in the open air), used to store grain until it was threshed and to shelter it from sudden showers or to dry a crop of corn in unfavorable weather.

nucleus In ancient construction, the internal part of the flooring, consisting of a strong cement, over which the pavement was laid, bound with mortar.

nuki In traditional Japanese architecture, a penetrating tie; fits into a slot or penetrates a pillar.

nulling A quadrant-shaped detail on decorative moldings, esp. in Jacobean architecture.

nunnery A convent for females.

nuraghe, noraghe Prehistoric round towers and agglomerations of stone huts peculiar to Sardinia.

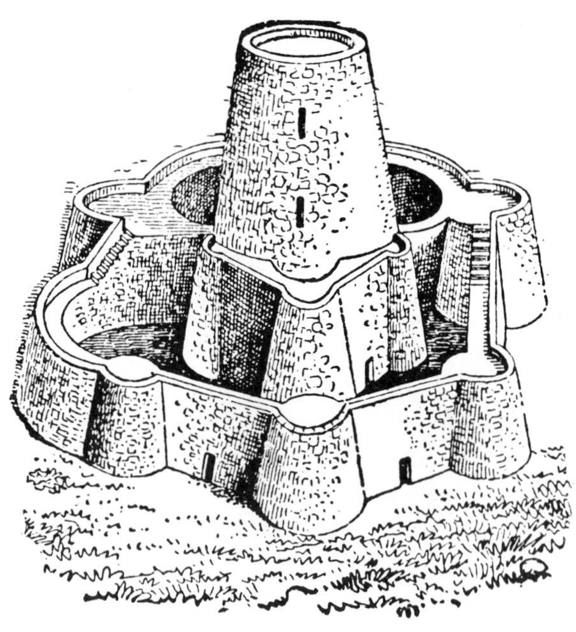

nuraghe

nure-yen In traditional Japanese architecture, a veranda unprotected by an **amado** or outside wall.

nutmeg ornament A common ornamental feature of Early English work in the north of England, resembling a half a nutmeg.

nymphaeum **1.** A room decorated with plants, sculpture, and fountains (often decorated with nymphs), and intended for relaxation. **2.** A building dedicated to the nymphs; a large chamber, decorated with columns, statues, and pictures and having a stream of spring water gushing from a fountain at its center, providing a cool and pleasant retreat.

nymphaeum at Nîmes, restored

nymphaeum; Nîmes, France (c. 2nd cent. A.D.)

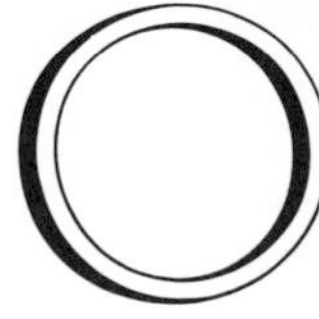

obelisk **1.** A monumental, four-sided stone shaft, usually monolithic and tapering to a pyramidal tip. **2.** In Egyptian art, such a shaft mostly covered with hieroglyphs; originally erected as cult symbol to the sun god.

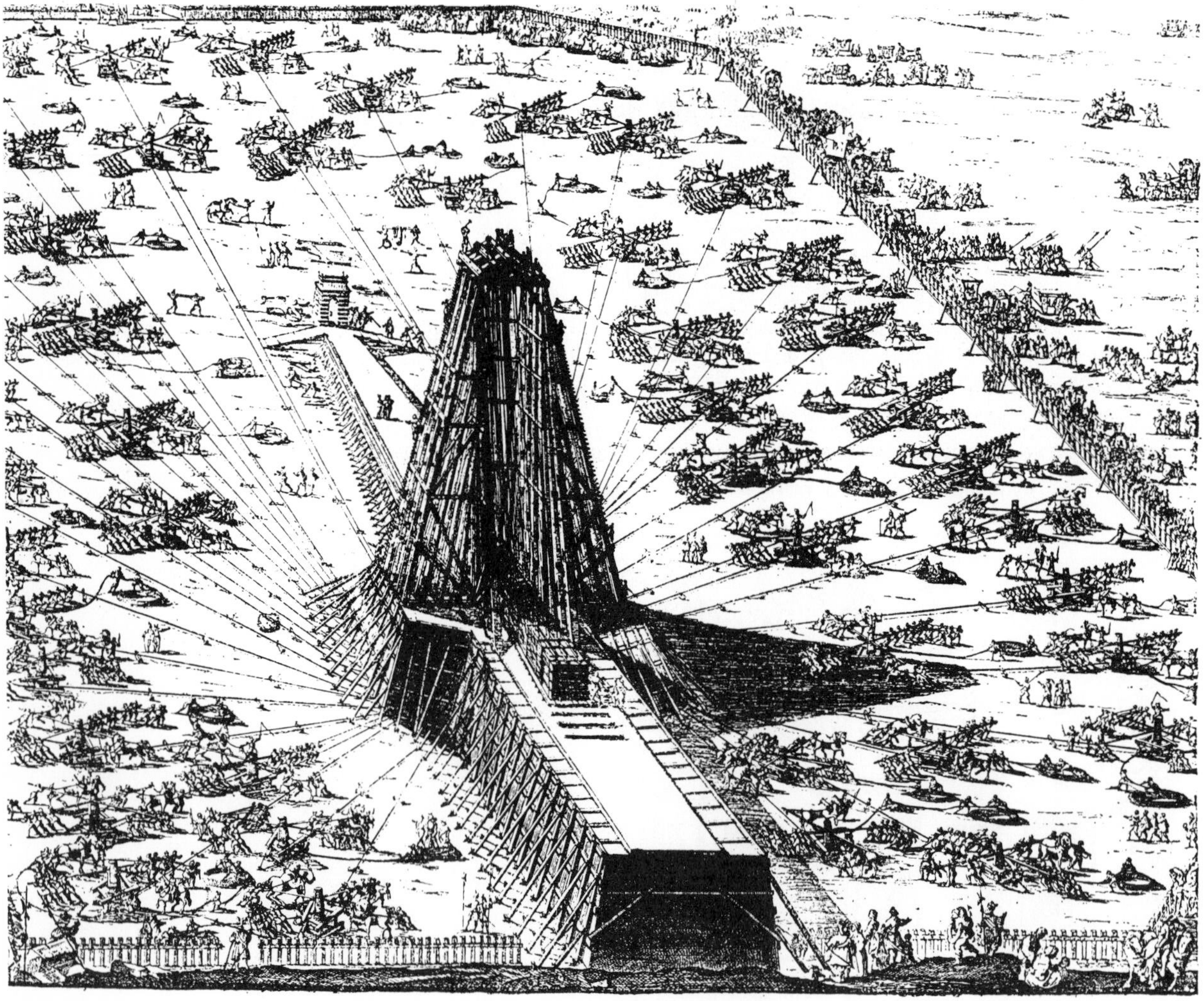

raising the obelisk in Piazza San Pietro, Rome (1586)

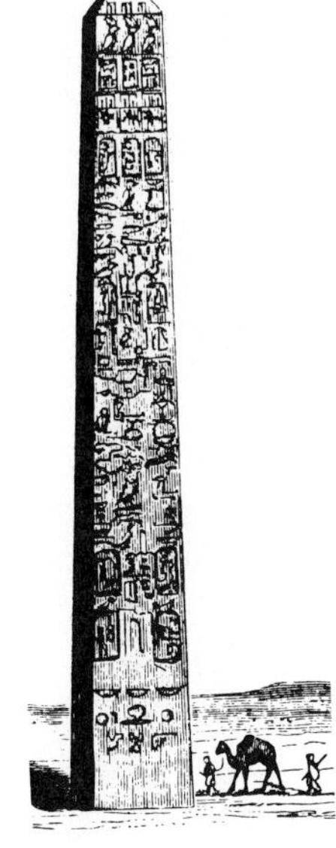

an Egyptian obelisk

obices See **repagula.**

oblique arch Same as **skew arch.**

obraznaya The room in which icons are kept in a Russian Orthodox church.

observatory **1.** A structure in which astronomical observations are carried out. **2.** A place, such as an upper room, which affords a wide view; a lookout.

obtuse angle arch A type of **pointed arch,** formed by arcs of circles which intersect at the apex; the centers of the circles are nearer together than the width of the arch.

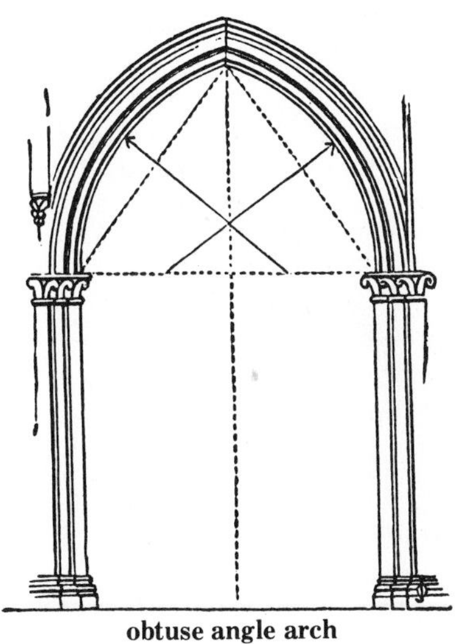

obtuse angle arch

octagon house A Victorian house having eight sides; esp. found in the Hudson Valley of New York.

octagon house

octastyle A temple façade or portico having eight columns in the front or end row.

octastyle: Temple of Diana, Ephesus (356 B.C.)

octopartite vault One of the vaults covering a square space, enclosed by walls, with eight oblique cells.

oculus **1.** See **roundel.** **2.** See **bull's-eye, 2.** **3.** An opening at the crown of a dome.

odeion Same as **odeum.**

odeum, odeon A small ancient Greek or Roman theatre, usually roofed, for musical performances.

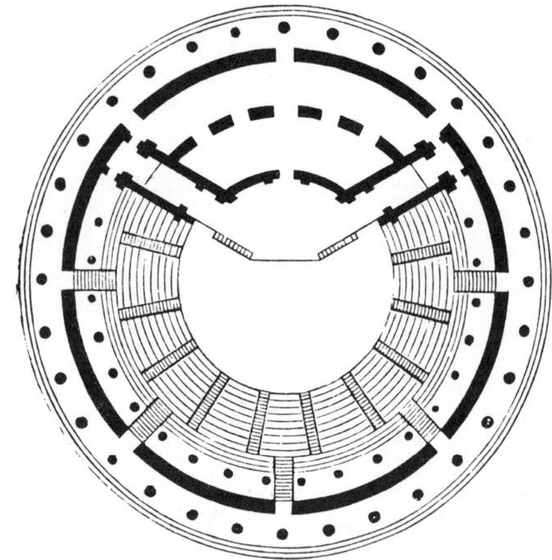

plan of the Odeon at Athens

oecus In a house in the ancient Roman empire, an apartment, hall, or large room.

oecus Aegyptus An **oecus** whose roof over the central portion was supported on a double row of columns so that the central portion was a story higher than the surrounding areas; the side areas were covered with a flat roof which was paved to serve as a promenade or gallery around the central (higher) portion of the building.

oecus Corinthius An oecus resembling an **atrium Corinthium,** except that it had a vaulted roof, supported on columns at a certain distance from the side walls, but without any opening in the center or impluvium below.

oecus Cyzicenus An oecus having glass doors or windows reaching down to the ground so as to provide a view of the surrounding country for those reclining at a table; this type of oecus was used frequently in Greece, but was somewhat of a novelty in Italy.

oecus tetrastylos A four-columned oecus resembling an **atrium tetrastylum,** but having no impluvium; the square within the four columns and the aisles around them were covered by a roof.

oeil-de-boeuf, oxeye See **bull's-eye, 2.**

offertory window See **low-side window.**

ogee **1.** A double curve, formed by the union of a convex and concave line, resembling an S-shape. **2.** A molding having such a shape, an **ogee molding.**

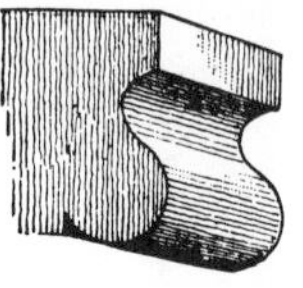

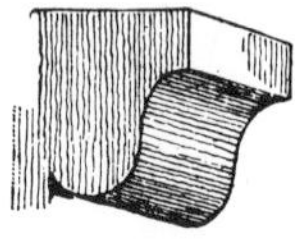

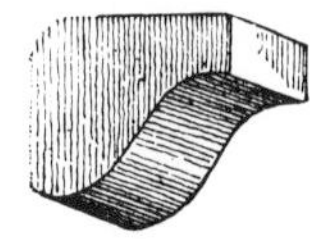

ogee, 2

ogee arch A pointed arch composed of reversed curves, the lower concave and the upper convex.

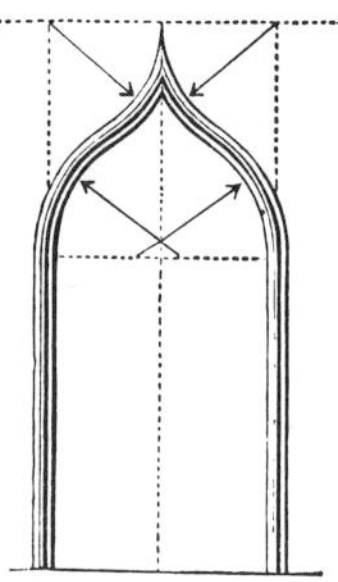

ogee arch

ogee molding See **ogee, 2.**

ogee roof A roof whose section is an **ogee, 1.**

ogee roof

ogive **1.** In general, a pointed arch. **2.** Strictly, the diagonal rib in Gothic vaults.

oillet, oillette A small opening, or circular loophole, in a fortification of the Middle Ages.

大壁 **o-kabe** In traditional Japanese architecture, a type of stud wall covered with plaster or boards which hide the structural components.

okala In Islamic countries, a hostelry.

okhlupen In early Russian architecture, a **ridge beam.**

okonchina In early Russian architecture, a framework of grooved bars for holding glass in a window.

ollarium A niche in an ancient Roman sepulchral vault, in which cinerary urns were deposited, usually in pairs.

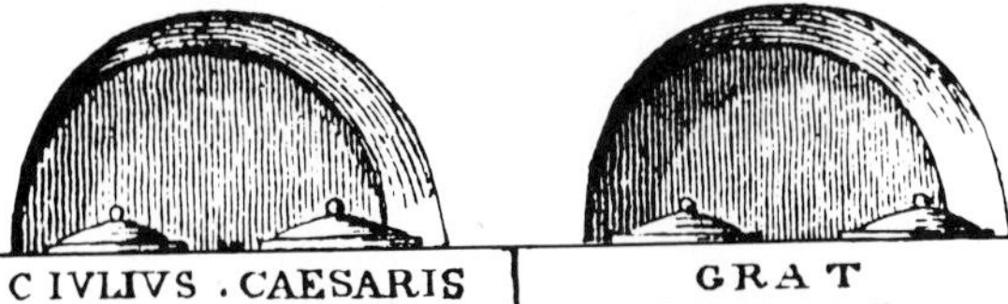

ollarium

Olmec architecture Architecture of the most ancient civilization of Mesoamerica (1500–400 B.C.), which influenced subsequent Mesoamerican architecture. The earliest architectural characteristics to appear were: the north-south orientation of the ceremonial center, the stepped pyramid, the **talud** or sloping wall, the use of platforms on which to construct buildings or temples, and the arrangement of structures around a ceremonial court or plaza. The most outstanding example of Olmec architecture and planning is La Venta in Tabasco state, Mexico.

omphalos A sacred stone in the temple of Apollo at Delphi, believed by the ancient Greeks to mark the exact center of the earth.

one-centered arch Any arch struck from a single center, such as a round, segmental, or horseshoe arch.

onigawara Ornamental tiles placed at the ends of the main ridge of the roof of a traditional Japanese structure, at the lower ends of the angle formed by two descending roof slopes (*kudarimune*) and/or at the corner ends (*sumimune*). The most common form of decoration is an ogre mask, from which the tile gets its name.

onigawara

鬼瓦

onion dome In Russian Orthodox church architecture, a bulbous dome which terminates in a point and serves as a roof structure over a cupola or tower.

church surmounted by an onion dome

opa In a classical temple, a cavity which receives a roof beam.

opaion **1.** In ancient Rome and Greece, an opening (as in a roof) for smoke to escape. **2.** In Greek architecture, a **lacunar.**

open cornice, open eaves Overhanging eaves where the rafters are exposed at the eaves and can be seen from below.

open eaves See **open cornice.**

open heart molding A common Norman molding consisting of a series of overlapping shapes resembling the outlines of a heart.

open heart molding

open-newel stair, hollow newel stair, open-well stair A stair built around a well, leaving an open space between the strings.

open pediment Same as **broken pediment, 1.**

open roof, open-timbered roof A roof construction in which the rafters and roof sheathing are visible from below; there is no ceiling.

open slating, spaced slating In roofing, a slating pattern in which spaces are left between adjacent slates in a course.

open stair, open-string stair A stair whose treads are visible on one or both sides.

open stair

open string, open stringer, cut string In a stair, a **string** which has its upper edge notched to fit the profile of treads and risers of the steps.

open-timbered Having timberwork exposed; having the wooden framework not concealed by sheathing, plaster, or other covering.

open-timbered roof Same as **open roof.**

open-timber floor A floor in which the floor joists and construction are exposed on the underside.

openwork **1.** Any work, esp. ornamental, characterized by perforations. **2.** In fortifications, any work not protected at a **gorge, 3** by a parapet or otherwise.

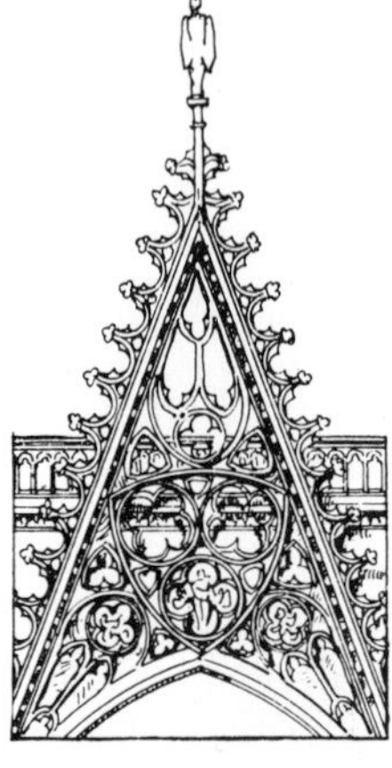

Gothic openwork gable

opisthodomos, epinaos, opisthodomus, posticum The inner portico at the rear of the cella of a classical temple, corresponding to the pronaos in front.

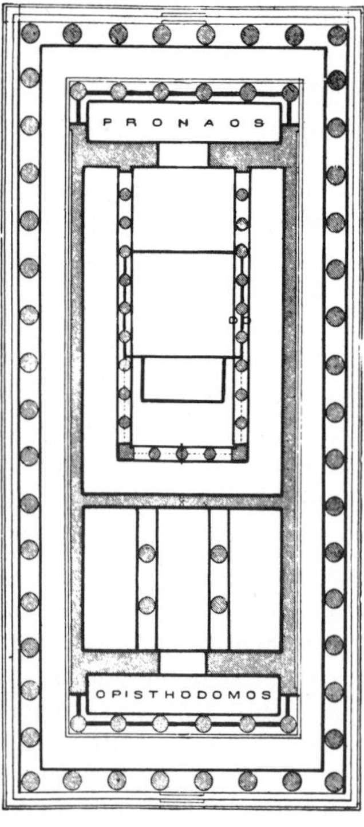

oppidum **1.** An ancient Roman town. **2.** The mass of buildings occupying the straight end of an ancient Roman circus; these included the stalls for the horses and chariots, the gates through which the Circensian procession entered the course, and the towers which flanked the whole on each side, all of which together presented the appearance of a town.

opus albarium Same as **albarium opus.**

opus Alexandrinum A mosaic of relatively large pieces of marble or stone, cut to shape and arranged in geometric patterns, usually a mosaic pavement consisting of geometrical figures in black and red tesserae on white ground.

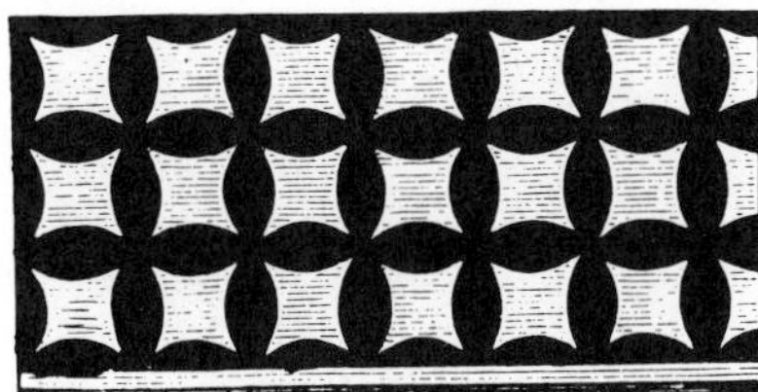

opus Alexandrinum

opus antiquum Same as **opus incertum.**

opus caementicium Ancient Roman masonry construction using undressed stones laid in a mortar composed of sand, lime, and pozzolan; in some Roman provinces, pozzolan was not used in the mortar.

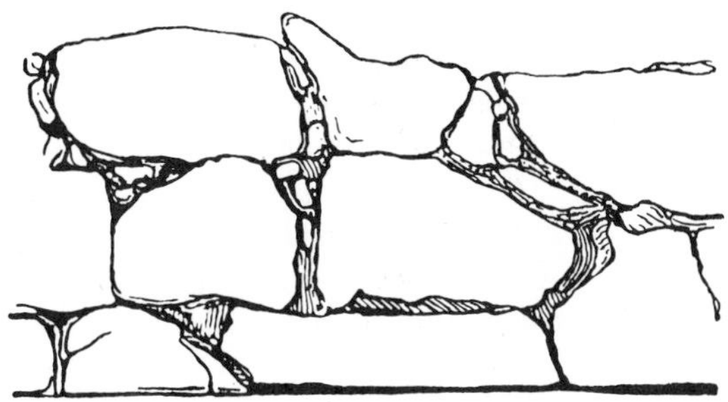

opus caementicium

opus incertum In ancient Rome, masonry formed of small rough stones set irregularly in mortar, sometimes traversed by beds of bricks or tiles.

opus incertum

opus interrasile Decoration produced either by cutting away the ground and leaving the pattern or by cutting out the pattern so that the openings form the design.

opus isodomum Same as **isodomum.**

opus latericium, opus lateritium Roman masonry of brick or tiles, or of a brick or tile facing on a concrete core.

opus lateritum See **lateritum opus.**

opus listatum Ancient Roman masonry formed by alternating courses of brick and small stone blocks.

opus lithostrotum Same as **lithostrotum opus.**

opus marmoratum See **marmoratum opus.**

opus mixtum A wall facing of alternate courses of brick and small blocks of tufa; used from the 4th to 6th cent. A.D. in Roman construction.

opus mixtum

opus musivum A Roman mosaic decoration employing small cubes of colored glass or enameled work.

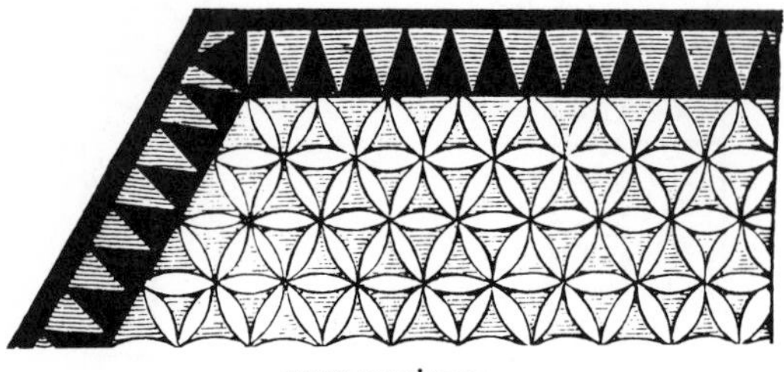

opus musivum

opus pseudisodomum In ancient Roman masonry, coursed ashlar having courses of unequal height.

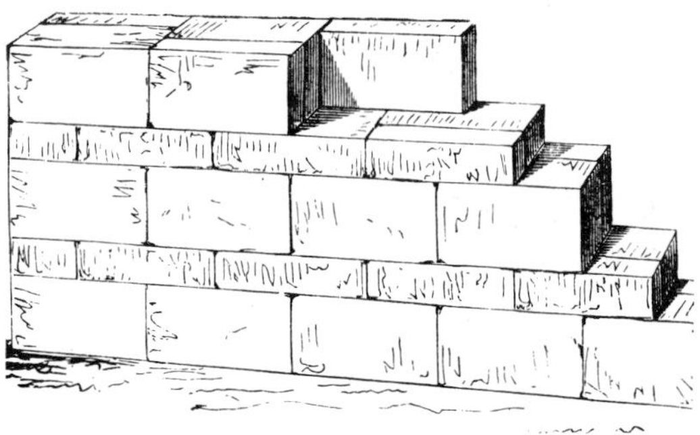

opus pseudisodomum

opus quadratum Masonry of squared stones in regular ashlar courses.

opus reticulatum A decorative Roman wall facing, backed by a concrete core, formed of small pyramidal stones with their points embedded in the wall, their exposed square bases, set diagonally, forming a net-like pattern.

opŭs reticulatum

opus scalpturatum See **scalpturatum.**

opus sectile See **sectile opus.**

opus signinum Same as **signinum opus.**

opus spicatum Same as **spicatum opus.**

opus tectorium A type of stucco used in ancient Rome; used to cover walls in three or four coats, the finishing coat being practically an artificial marble, usually polished to serve as a surface for paintings.

opus tessellatum A pavement with designs executed in pieces of different-colored **tesserae,** of larger size and more regular form than the pieces used in mosaic.

opus testaceum In ancient Roman masonry, a facing composed of fragments of broken tile.

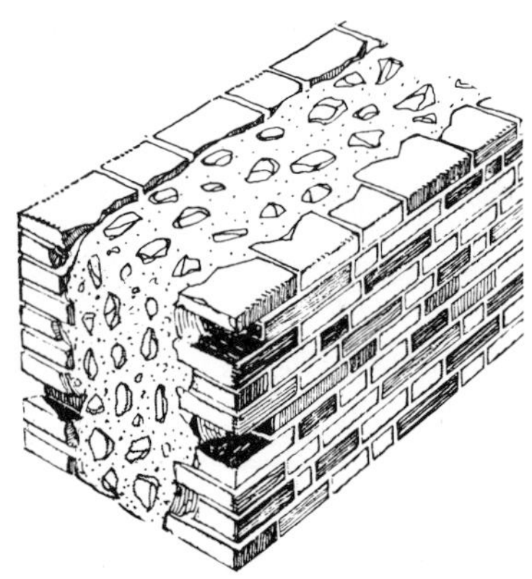

opus testaceum

opus topiarium See **topiarium opus.**

opus vermiculatum See **vermiculated mosaic.**

orangery A building or greenhouse for the cultivation of orange and other ornamental trees in cool climates; has large, tall windows along the southern exposure. Now often used for social and exhibition purposes.

oratory A small private chapel furnished with an altar and a crucifix.

orb **1.** A plain circular boss, as a decorative accent where two or more ribs (of a vault) cross. **2.** The medieval name for the tracery of blank windows or stone panels.

orchestra **1.** In the early Greek theatre, the place occupied by the dancers and chorus about the altar of Dionysus; later, the circular space reserved for the dancers and chorus, between the proscenium and auditorium. **2.** In the early Roman theatre, a semicircular level space between the stage and the first semicircular rows of seats, reserved for senators and other distinguished spectators.

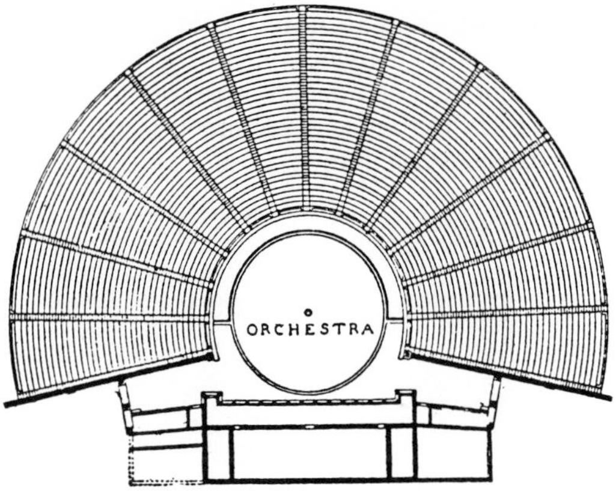

orchestra,1 Greek theatre

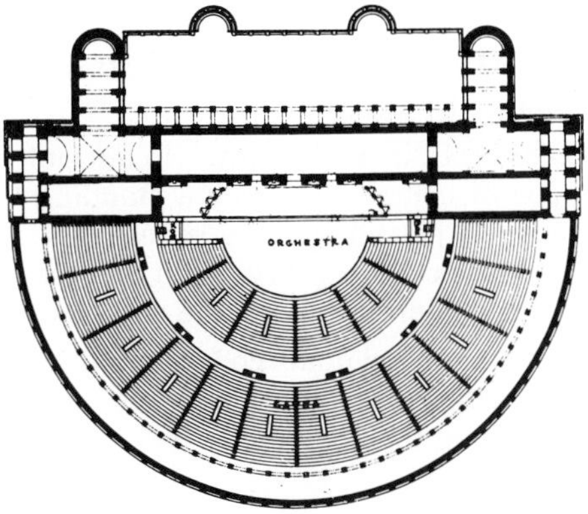

orchestra,2, Roman theatre

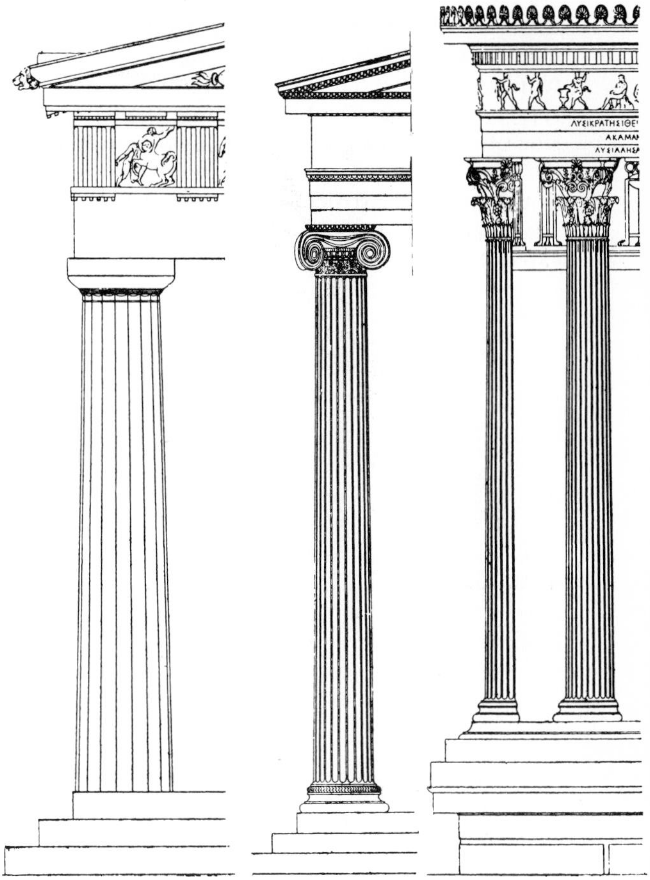

order **1.** An arrangement of columns with an entablature. **2.** In classical architecture, a particular style of column with its entablature, having standardized details. The Greek orders were the Doric, Ionic, and Corinthian; the Romans added the Tuscan and Composite. **3.** In masonry, one ring of several around an arch.

ordinary A village tavern in an early American community.

ordo Same as **chorus.**

Organic architecture A philosophy of architectural design, emerging in the early 20th cent., asserting that in structure and appearance a building should be based on organic forms and should harmonize with its natural environment.

organ loft In a church, the gallery or loft where the organ is located, usually high above the floor.

the three Greek orders:
left: **Doric (Parthenon)**; *center*: **Ionic (Erechtheion)**; *right*: **Corinthian (Monument of Lysicrates)**

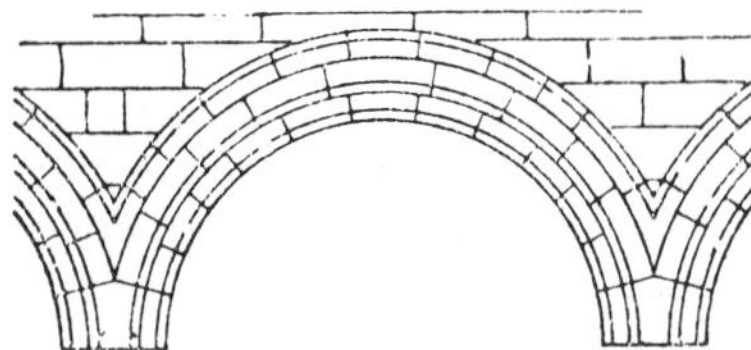

arch with two orders,3

organ screen **1.** An ornamental screen of stone or timber which closes off the organ chamber in a church. **2.** A **rood screen** which supports an organ.

oriel 1. In medieval English architecture, chiefly residential, and derivatives: *(a)* a bay window corbeled out from the wall of an upper story; *(b)* a projecting bay, forming the extension of a room; *(c)* a windowed bay or porch at the top of exterior stairs. 2. *(rare)* In medieval Continental structures and derivatives, a subsidiary bay, or a corbeled, enclosed feature, exterior or interior.

oriel, Vicar's Close, Wells (c. 1348)

orientation 1. The placement of a structure on a site with regard to local conditions of sunlight, wind, and drainage. 2. The siting of a Christian church so that the main altar is housed toward the east end of the building, a common ritual disposition.

orle, orlet A narrow band, or series of small members, taking the form of a border.

orlo 1. A plinth which supports the base of a column. 2. The smooth surface between parallel flutes or grooves. 3. An **orle.**

ormolu 1. Gold crushed with mercury to form a paste. 2. An article or ornamental appliqué of bronze, first coated with such paste, then heated to evaporate the mercury, leaving pure gold evenly and securely deposited. 3. Any metal or substitute finished to resemble mercury-gilded bronze.

ornament In architecture, every detail of shape, texture, and color that is deliberately exploited or added to attract an observer.

ornate Elaborately ornamented.

ornithon In ancient Rome, a house where poultry was kept; an aviary.

orthostat One of many large stone slabs, set vertically as a revetment at the lower part of the cella in a classical temple, or at the base of a wall in the ancient architecture of Anatolia, northern Syria, and Assyria.

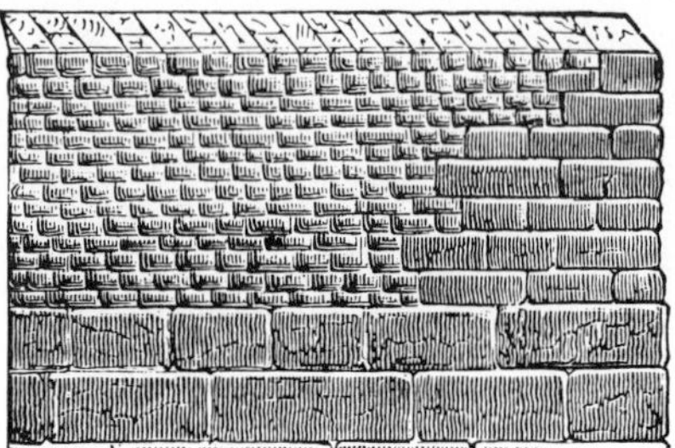

orthostata at base of a wall

orthostyle A colonnade in a straight line.

osier See **withe, 2.**

Osiride, Osirian column In ancient Egypt, a type of column in which a standing figure of Osiris is placed before a square pier; it differs from the classical caryatid in that the pier, and not the figure, supports the entablature.

Osiris An Egyptian god who, with his sister and wife Isis, enjoyed the most general worship of all the gods.

Osiride

Osiris

ossature The framework or skeleton of a building or part of a building, as the ribs of a groined vault or the frame of a roof.

ossuary, bone house, ossarium A storage place for the bones of the dead; either a structure or a vault lined with such bones ornamentally arranged.

ossuary

ostensory, monstrance A device in which the Eucharistic wafer may be displayed.

ostiole A small entrance.

ostiolum A small opening; a small door.

ostium **1.** In an ancient Roman house, a hallway which connected the door to the street with the atrium. **2.** A door within a house. **3.** A door, esp. one of the doors which closed the front of the stalls in which the chariots and horses were stationed at the circus.

otoshigake A beam, across the top front of a **toko-no-ma,** which supports the narrow overhanging wall.

Ottoman architecture The later phase of Turkish **Muslim architecture,** from the 14th cent. onward, much influenced by Byzantine forms.

Ottonian architecture The pre-Romanesque round-arched architecture of Germany during the rule of the Ottonian emperors in the second half of the 10th cent.

ostium,1

oubliette **1.** A secret dungeon in the deepest parts of a medieval stronghold, having as its only entry a trapdoor through which prisoners were dropped; used for persons condemned to perpetual imprisonment or to perish secretly. **2.** A secret pit, usually in the floor of a dungeon, into which an unsuspecting person could be dropped and thus destroyed.

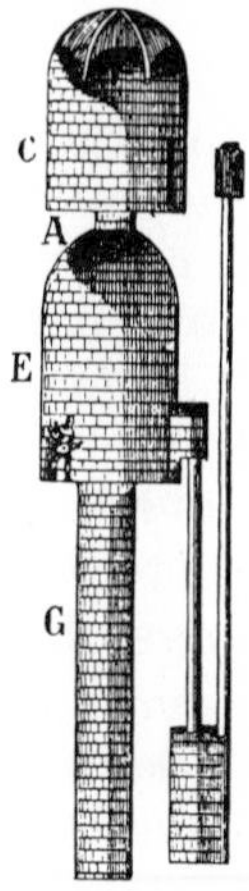

C, upper dungeon; *E*, lower dungeon, with access from *C* by the trapdoor *A*; *G*, oubliette, into which a victim could be dropped from *C* or *E* through the open trapdoors in the floors

oundy molding See **wave molding.**

outer hearth See **front hearth.**

outer string The **string** at the outer and exposed edge of a stair, away from the wall.

outlooker A member which projects and supports that part of a roof construction beyond the face of a gable.

outwindow A projecting **loggia** or the like.

overdoor, sopraporta A wall area, more or less ornamented, directly above a doorway.

overdoor

overglaze decoration A ceramic or metallic decoration applied and fired on the previously glazed surface of ceramic ware.

overhang **1.** The projection of an upper story or roof beyond a story immediately below. **2.** See **jetty.**

oversailing course A masonry course which projects beyond the general face of a wall.

overshot Same as **jetty.**

overstory **1.** An upper floor. **2.** Same as **clerestory.**

overthrow A panel of ornamental metalwork placed like a lintel above metal gates.

ovolo A convex molding, less than a semicircle in profile; usually a quarter of a circle or approximately a quarter-ellipse in profile.

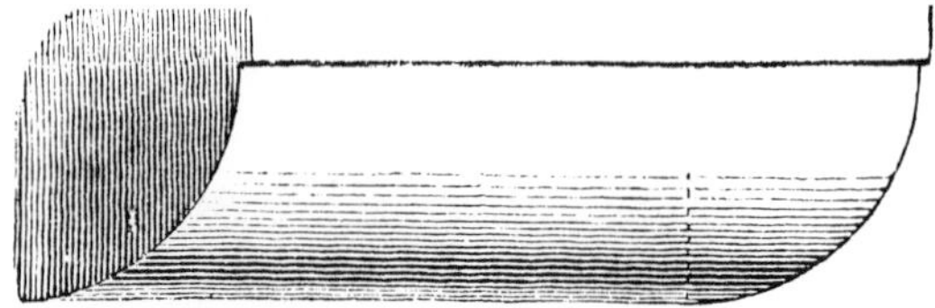

Roman ovolo,1: Theatre of Marcellus, Rome (23–13 B.C.)

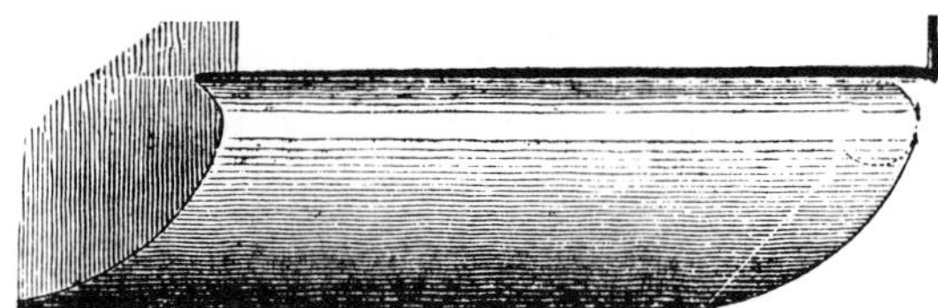

Grecian ovolo,1: Temple at Corinth

ovum In classical architecture and derivatives, an egg-shaped ornamental motif.

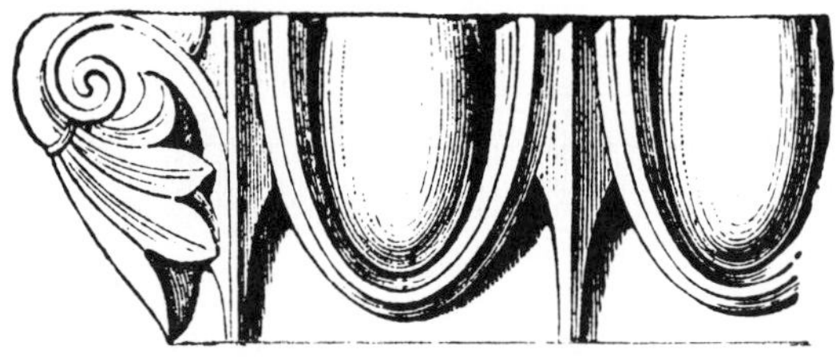

ovum

richly decorated Roman ovum

oxeye A **bull's-eye, 2.**

oxeye molding A concave molding less hollow than a **scotia** but deeper than a **cavetto.**

oyelet, oylet Same as **eyelet.**

P

pace **1.** See **landing.** **2.** A broad step, or slightly raised area around a tomb. **3.** A small area which is raised slightly above the general floor area.

padma In the architecture of India, a sculptured molding which is **lotiform** in section.

padmam In Indian architecture, a pedestal.

padstone, pad A strong block bedded in a wall to distribute a concentrated load; a **template, 2.**

pagoda A multistoried shrine-like tower, originally a Buddhist monument crowned by a **stupa.** Stories may be open pavilions of wood with balconies and pent roofs (prevalent in Japan) or built-in masonry, of diminishing size with corbeled cornices.

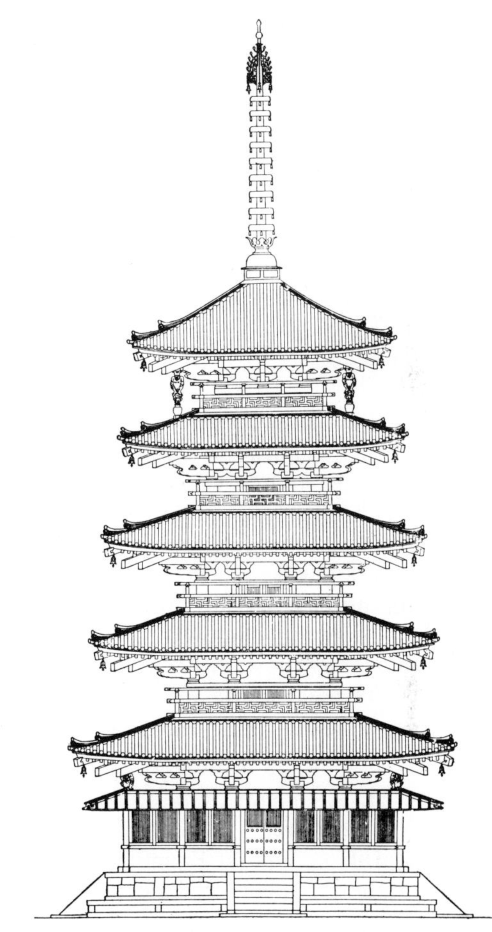

pagoda, Nara, Japan (originally 730 A.D.; rebuilt 1426)

paillasse Same as **palliase.**

paillette In decorative work, a bit of metal or colored foil used to obtain a jeweled effect.

pai-lou A monumental Chinese arch or gateway with one, three, or five openings; erected at the entrance to a palace, tomb, or processional way. Usually built of stone in imitation of wood construction.

pai-lou

牌樓

pai t'a A stupa in a Chinese lamasery; first appeared in 6th cent. and flourished in the Yuan dynasty (1279–1368); usually incorporated as a feature in Lamaist temples where bronze statues of the Mongolian khans were installed.

palaestra **1.** A Greek or Roman building for athletic training, smaller than a gymnasium, consisting of a large square court with colonnades, rooms for massage, baths, etc. **2.** A part of an ancient Roman villa which was specially fitted for the purpose of active games and exercises.

palazzo In Italy, a palace, but the term is applied to any public building or private residence which is impressive.

pale **1.** A flat strip (slat) or round stake, usually of wood; set in series to form a fence. **2.** An area enclosed by such stakes.

palestra Same as **palaestra.**

palisade A series of stout poles, pointed on top and driven into the earth, used as a fence or fortification. Also see **stockade.**

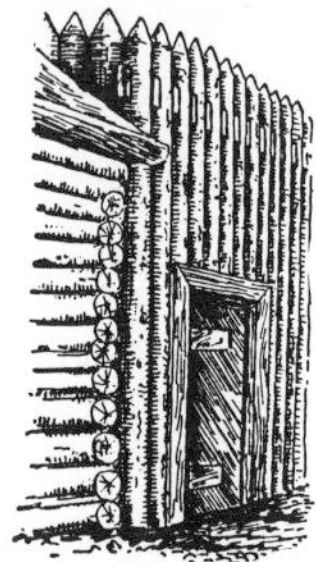

palisade

Palladianism A mode of building following the strict Roman forms, as set forth in the publications of the Italian Renaissance architect Andrea Palladio (1508–1580); particularly in England under the influence of Lord Burlington in the 18th cent.

Palladian motif, Serlian motif, Venetian motif A door or window opening in three parts, divided by posts, with a lintel flat over each side but arched over the center.

Palladian window See **Venetian window.**

palliase In masonry, a supporting bed.

palmate **1.** A column capital resembling the leaves of a palm tree. **2.** A **palmette.**

palm capital A type of Egyptian capital resembling the spreading crown of a palm tree.

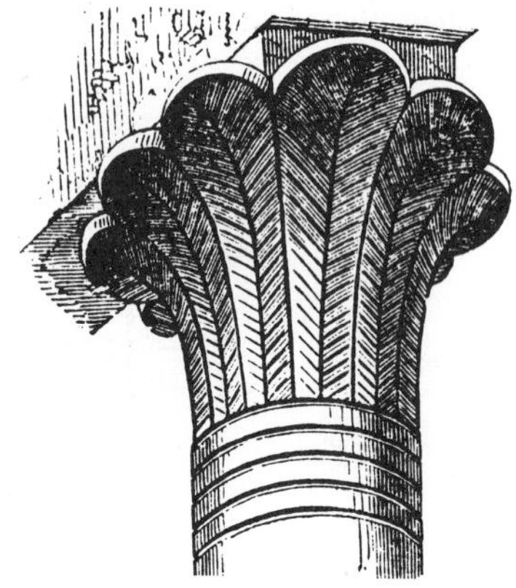

palm capital, Temple of Horus, Edfu (257-37 B.C.)

Palladian facade (c. 1570)

palmette An ornament derived from a palm leaf.

palmiform Having the form of a palm leaf or the crown of a palm tree.

palmettes

pampre An ornament consisting of vine leaves and grapes used to fill cavettos and other continuous hollows in a group of moldings.

panache The triangle-like surface of a **pendentive.**

pan-and-roll roofing tile Single-lap roofing tile of two types used in combination: a flat, tapered undertile having flanges, and a half-rounded tapered overtile.

pancarpi Garlands or festoons of flowers, fruits, etc.

pancharam One of a number of miniature shrines located on the roof, on the cornices, or on the lintels of a Hindu temple; used as a decorative feature.

pandokeion In ancient Greece, a type of private inn which accommodated and entertained travellers.

panel A portion of a flat surface recessed or sunk below the surrounding area, distinctly set off by molding or some other decorative device.

panel, Colchester (c. 1500)

left and right: **panels, Layer Marney, Essex (c. 1530)**

panel divider A molding which separates two wood panels along their common edge.

panel house A brothel in which the rooms are lined with sliding panels which facilitate robberies of house patrons.

panel molding A molding surrounding a panel. See also **bolection molding, drop molding.**

panel tracery Same as **perpendicular tracery.**

邦克楼 **pang k'o lou** In China, a pavilion in a Muslim temple (located in the middle or at one corner of a courtyard) which functions as a minaret. In Sinkiang province, similar to the minarets of the Middle East. Also called **kuang t'a.**

panier See **corbeil.**

panopticon A building (often a jail) planned with corridors which radiate from a single, central point. A person located at the central point can observe each of the converging halls.

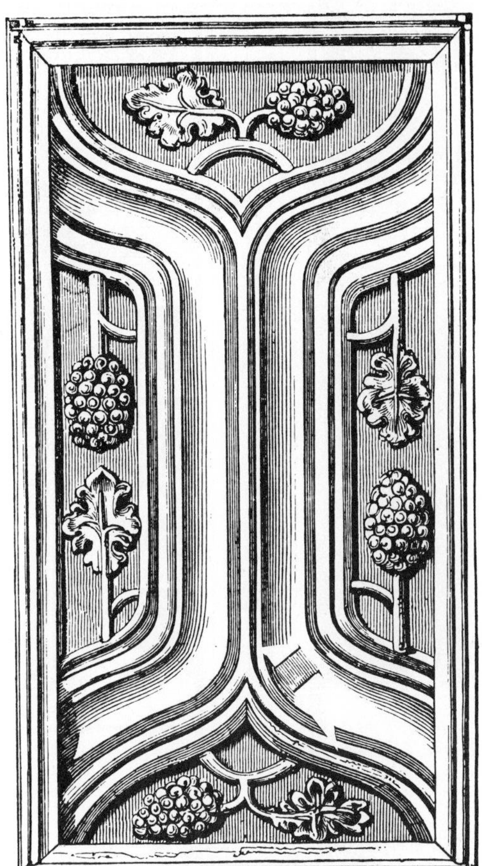

pantheon **1.** A temple dedicated to all the Gods. **2.** *(Cap.)* The Rotunda in Rome, formerly a temple to all the gods, now a church. **3.** The Pantheon in Paris, the former Church of Sainte-Geneviève, now a shrine to national heroes.

Pantheon, Rome: interior view (120–124 A.D.)

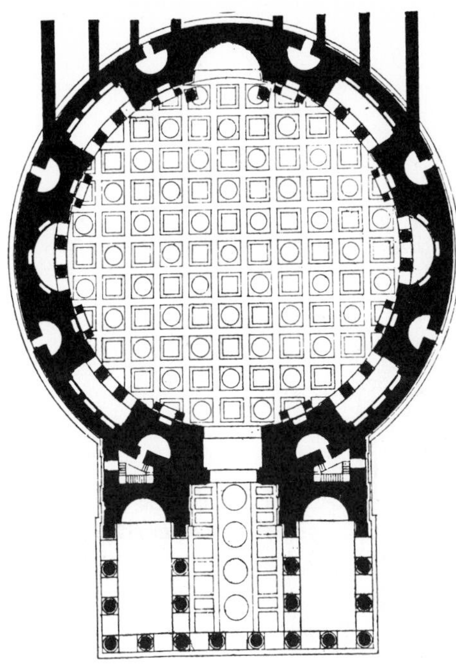

Pantheon: plan (120–124 A.D.)

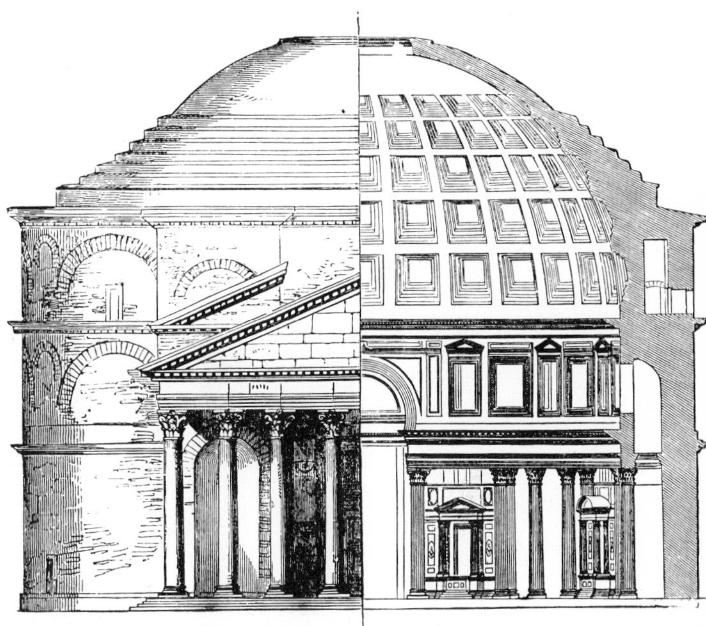

Pantheon: half elevation, half section

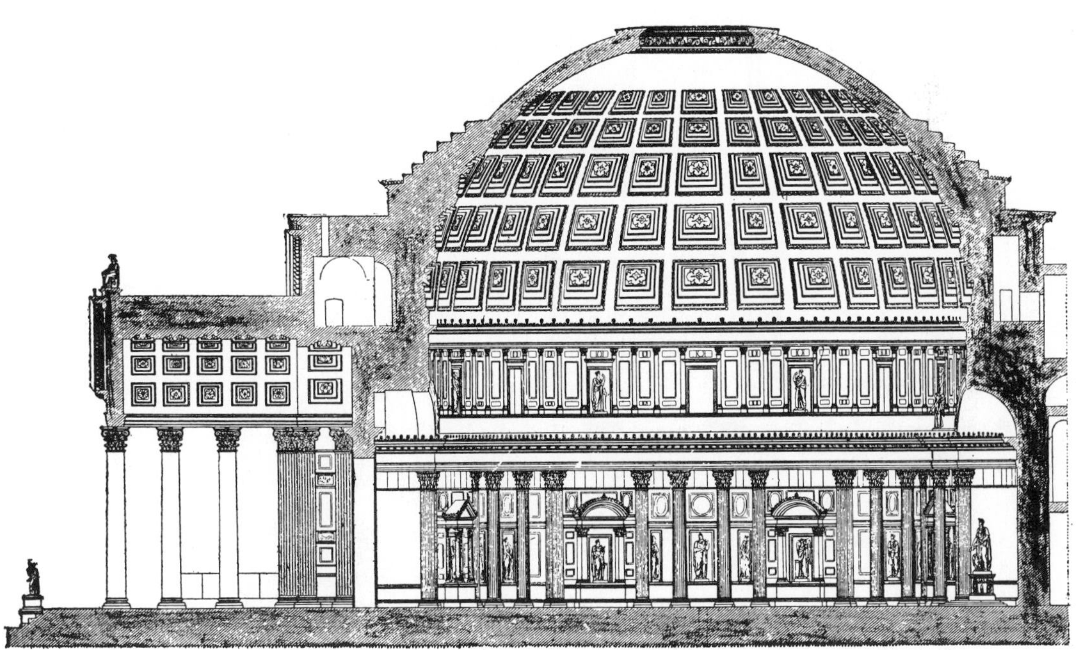

Pantheon: cross section

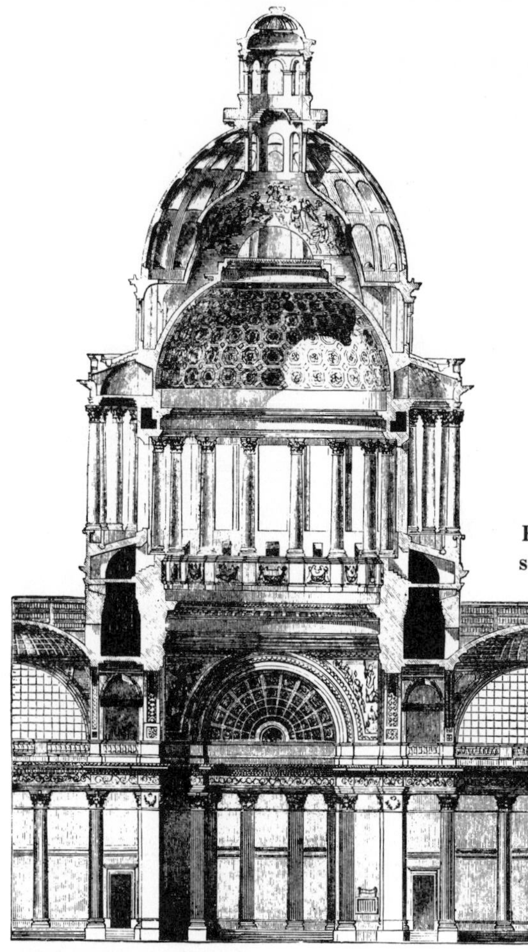

Pantheon, Paris: section of dome (1755–92)

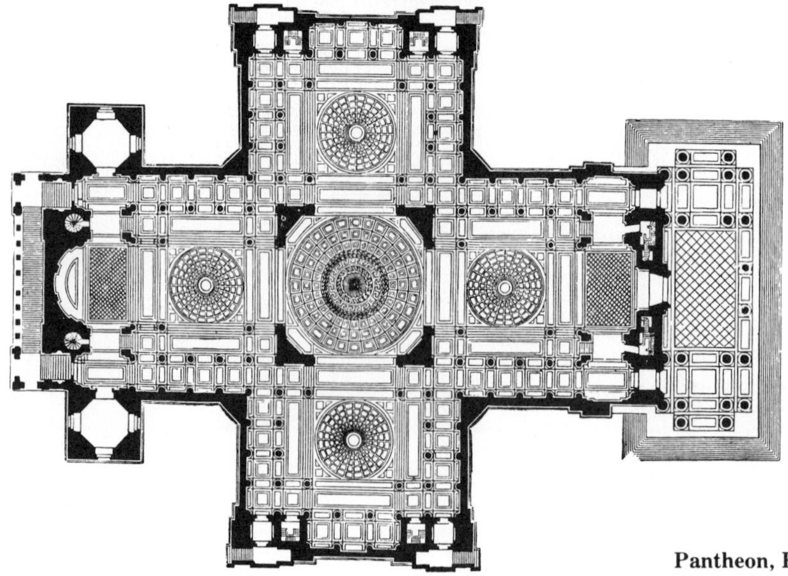

Pantheon, Paris: plan (1755–92)

pantile A roofing tile which has the shape of an S laid on its side.

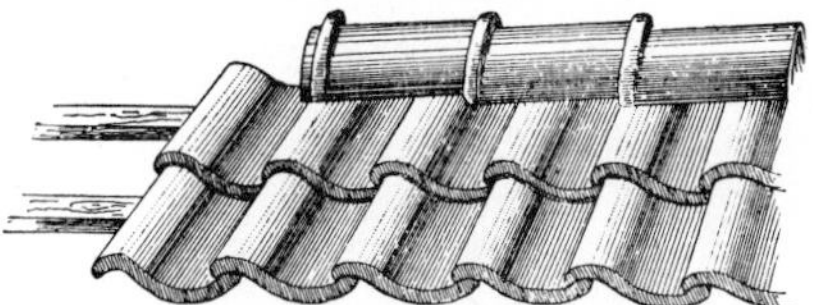

pantile

papert The **parvis** of a Russian Orthodox church.

papier-mâché A material composed principally of paper; usually prepared by pulping a mass of paper (sometimes glue is added) to a dough-like consistency and molding to a desired form.

papyriform Descriptive of a capital of an Egyptian column having the form of a cluster of papyrus flowers.

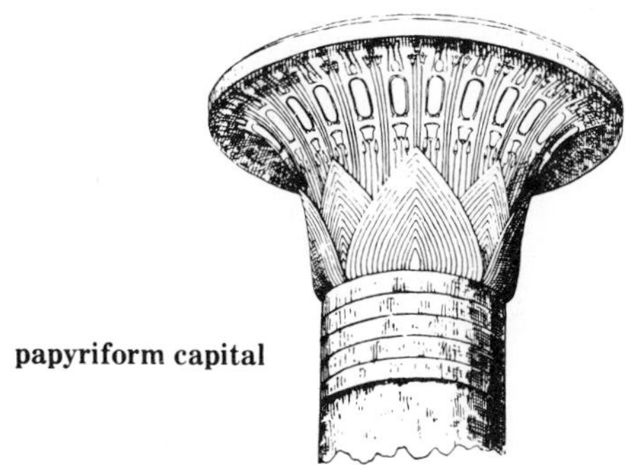

papyriform capital

parabema A chamber to the side of the bema or sanctuary in Greek churches.

parabolic arch An arch similar to a three-centered arch but whose intrados is parabolic, with a vertical axis.

paradise **1.** The court of the atrium in front of a church. **2.** The **garth** of a cloister. **3.** A Persian pleasure garden, usually elaborately planted.

paradisus Same as **paradise.**

parados Earthworks behind a fortified place.

parapet **1.** A low guarding wall at any point of sudden drop, as at the edge of a terrace, roof, battlement, balcony, etc. **2.** A defense wall. **3.** In an exterior wall, the part entirely above the roof.

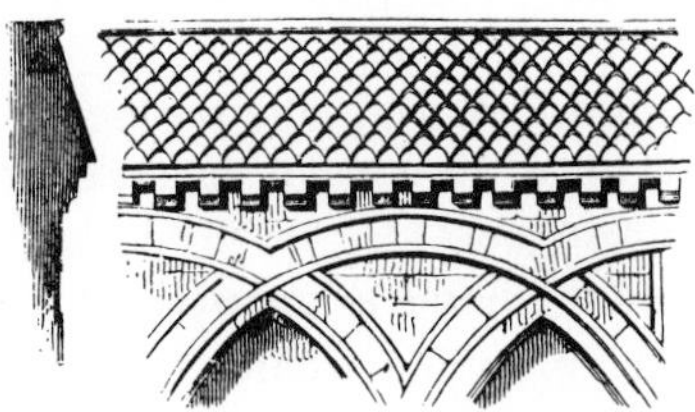

Norman parapet, St. Etienne, Caen (c. 1160)

Early English parapet, Salisbury Cathedral (c. 1250)

Decorated style parapet St. Mary Magdalene, Oxford (1337)

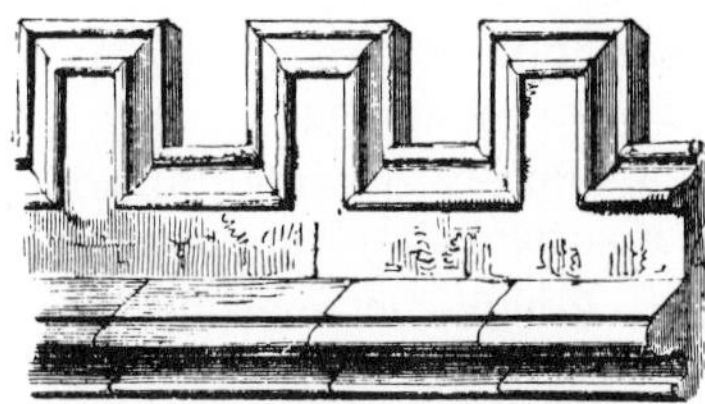

Perpendicular style parapet

Flamboyant style parapet

parapetasma In the **cella** of an ancient Greek temple, a solid enclosure, latticework, or curtain which screened the statue in the temple.

parapet gutter A gutter which is constructed behind a parapet wall.

parapet wall That part of a wall which is entirely above the roof.

parascenium A wing-like projection extending forward, at the ends of the **skene,** in ancient Greek theatres.

paraskenion Same as **parascenium.**

parastara In Indian architecture, an entablature.

parastas **1.** The end of a wall, terminating in an **anta,** such as that enclosing the pronaos of a temple. **2.** A pedestal-like wall, as the abutment of the end of a monumental stairway. **3.** A flat column or pilaster, used to decorate the angular terminations of a square building.

parastatica A pilaster attached to a Greek temple; a **parastas, 3.**

parathura The back door of an ancient Greek house.

paratorium The place at the east end of a basilican church, usually on the north side, for the offerings; in some Greek churches, located on the south side.

paratory In a church, a place where any preparation is made; a vestry or sacristy.

parclose, perclose **1.** In medieval churches and derivatives, a screen dividing a special space from general space. **2.** The parapet round a gallery.

parekklesion A Greek chapel; may be attached or free-standing.

parerga Purely ornamental additions to a work of ancient Greek architecture.

paretta Rough-cast masonry having a surface of protruding pebbles.

pargeting, pargetting, parget, pargework, parging **1.** Elaborate plasterwork; esp. an ornamental facing for plaster walls, sometimes decorated with figures in low relief or indented; often used on the exterior of houses in the Tudor period. **2.** An interior lining of a flue to provide a smooth surface and to aid in fire protection.

parclose, Fyfield, Berkshire (c. 1480)

pargeting, High Street, Oxford

pargeting, Bishop King's Palace, Oxford (16th cent.)

paries In ancient Roman construction, a wall of a house or other edifice. Also see **murus.**

paries communis A **party wall.**

paries craticius A wall made of canes and hurdles, covered with a coating of clay; similar to our lath and plaster walls; used in ancient times for an external wall, and subsequently for a partition in the interior of a house.

paries dealbatus An exterior wall which was treated with **albarium opus,** producing an appearance similar to white marble.

paries directus A wall or partition within a building, separating one room from another.

paries e lapide quadrato An **ashlar** wall, consisting of stones cut and squared by chisel.

paries formaceus A **pisé** wall made of rammed earth.

paries fornicatus A wall perforated with arched openings to save materials without diminishing its structural integrity.

paries intergerivus Same as **paries communis.**

paries lateritius A brick wall; the usual thickness of an ancient Roman exterior wall was 18 in. (45.7 cm).

paries solidus A blind wall or **blank wall.**

parietes The walls of private rooms of ancient Roman houses; frequently lined with marble; more often covered with paintings.

parlatory A room in a monastic establishment where visitors may be received.

parodos One of the two side entrances to an ancient theatre between the seats and the stage; used principally by the chorus, but also by the public.

parotides, parotis Same as **ancon.**

parpaing Same as **perpend.**

parpend stone See **perpend.**

parquet **1.** Inlaid wood flooring, usually set in simple geometric patterns. **2.** Same as **parquetry.**

parquetry A flat inlay pattern of closely fitted pieces, usually geometrical, often employing two or more colors or materials; used for ornamental parquet flooring or wainscoting, in stone or wood.

parrel, chimney breast A chimneypiece or the ornaments of a chimneypiece collectively.

Parthenon **1.** Originally, the room behind the cella in the great temple of Athena Parthenos on the Athenian Acropolis. **2.** More commonly, the name of the entire temple.

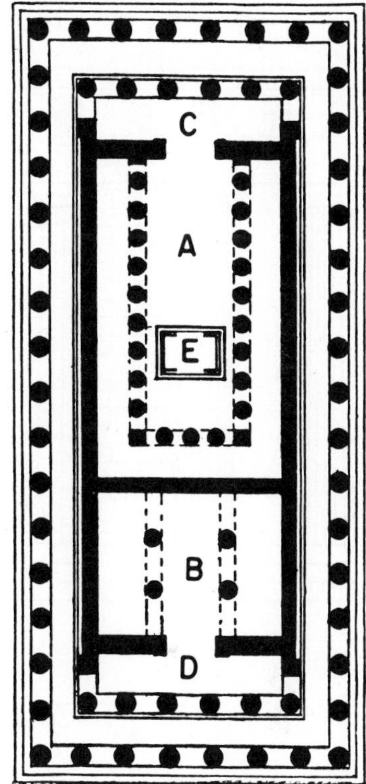

plan of the Parthenon (447-432 B.C.):
A, cella (naos); *B*, parthenon; *C*, pronaos; *D*, opisthodomos; *E*, statue of Athena Parthos

Parthenon: section

Parthenon

Parthenon: elevation

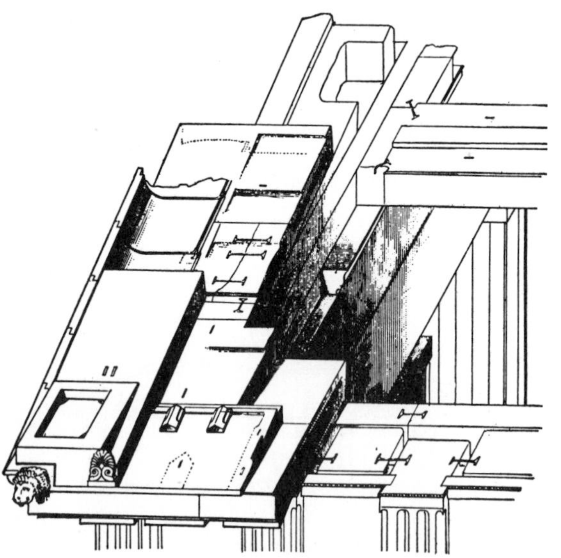

construction details of frieze and cornice blocks

detail of lion's head

Parthian architecture An architectural style developed under Parthian domination (3rd cent. B.C. to 3rd cent. A.D.) in western Iran and Mesopotamia, combining classical with autochthonous features. Its major achievement is the monumental **iwan** covered by a barrel vault in stone or brick.

Parthian architecture: part of the Palace of Al Hadbr

party arch An arch on the line separating the property of two owners.

party wall A wall used jointly by two parties under easement agreement, erected upon a line dividing two parcels of land, each of which is a separate real estate entity; a common wall.

parus In early Russian architecture, a **pendentive.**

parvis **1.** The open square in front of a large church. **2.** An enclosed court or room in front of a church.

parvis,2: Northamptonshire (1440)

pas-de-souris In a castle, the steps leading from the moat to the entrance.

passage grave, chamber tomb In prehistoric Europe, a chamber approached by a long passage, of megalithic construction, covered and protected by an artificial mound.

passion cross Same as **Calvary cross.**

passus An ancient Roman measure of length; equal to 5 **pedes;** equivalent to 58.2 in. (1.48 m).

pastas In ancient Greek architecture, a term for **vestibule.**

pastophoria The apartments occupied by a class of Egyptian priest called *pastophori;* they carried the statues of gods in processions.

pastophorium, pastophorion In the early church, one of the two apartments at the sides of the bema or sanctuary; this arrangement has been retained in the modern Greek Orthodox church.

pata In Indian architecture, a beam or lintel.

patand See **patten.**

patera A representation of a flat round or oval disk or medallion in bas-relief; used as an ornament in friezes.

paterae

paternoster A small round molding cut in the form of beads like a rosary; a **bead molding.**

patience Same as **miserere.**

patin See **patten.**

patina, patination **1.** A greenish brown crust which forms on bronze. **2.** Any thin oxide film which forms on a metal; often multicolored. **3.** A film, similar in color, which forms on a material other than metal. **4.** Such effects artificially induced, or imitated.

patio An outdoor area adjoining or enclosed by the walls or arcades of a house; often paved and shaded. Also see **terrace.**

patten, patand, patin 1. The base of a column or pillar. 2. A base or a **groundsill** which supports a column, post, or pillar.

pavilion 1. A detached or semidetached structure used for entertainment or (as at a hospital) for specialized activities. 2. On a façade, a prominent portion usually central or terminal, identified by projection, height, and special roof forms. 3. In a garden or fairground, a temporary structure or tent, usually ornamented.

pavilion roof 1. A roof hipped equally on all sides, so as to have a pyramidal form; a pyramidal hipped roof. 2. A similar roof having more than four sides; a polygonal roof.

pavimentum In ancient Roman construction, a pavement formed by pieces of crushed stone, flint, tile, and other materials set in a bed of ashes or cement and consolidated by beating down with a rammer.

pavimentum sectile See **sectile opus.**

pavimentum tessellatum See **opus tessellatum.**

pavimentum testaceum See **opus testaceum.**

pavimentum vermiculatum See **vermiculated mosaic.**

pavior, paviour A brick used for paving.

pavonaceum A method of laying tiles that are rounded at one end, so that in overlapping each other they present a scalloped appearance.

pavonazzo, pavonazzeto A marble, used by the ancient Romans, characterized by very irregular veins of dark red with bluish and yellowish tints.

pawn A covered passageway or **gallery.**

peak arch A **pointed arch.**

pear drop 1. A pear-shaped **pendant,** often used as a handle or support. 2. In 18th cent. architecture, a support for a small arch.

pearl molding A molding decorated with a continuous series of pearl-like shapes.

pebble wall 1. A wall built of pebbles in mortar. 2. A wall faced with pebbles embedded, at random or in pattern, in a mortar coating on the exposed surface.

pechura In early Russian architecture, a niche in a masonry wall.

pectinated Having teeth like a comb.

pedes See **pes.**

pedestal A support for a column, statue, urn, etc., consisting in classical architecture of a base, dado, or die and a cornice, surbase, or cap.

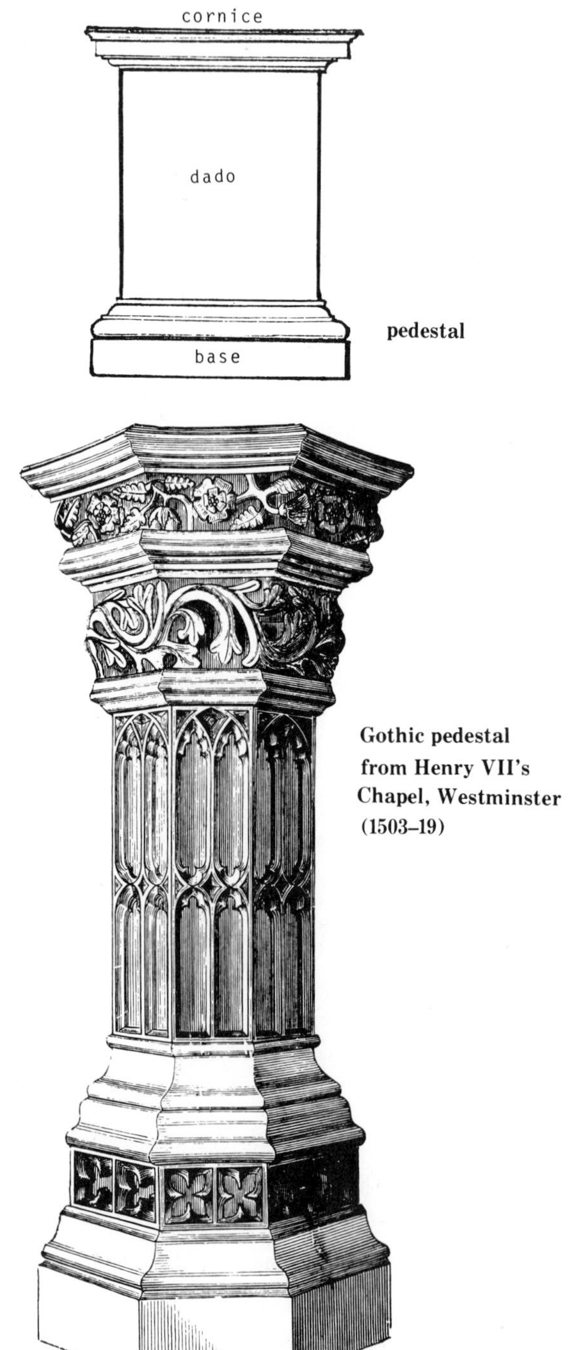

pedestal

Gothic pedestal from Henry VII's Chapel, Westminster (1503–19)

pede window In a church, a window oriented with respect to a larger one so as to symbolize one of the feet of Christ.

pediment **1.** In classical architecture, the triangular gable end of the roof above the horizontal cornice, often filled with sculpture. Also called a **fronton** when used to crown a subordinate feature, as a window. **2.** In later work, a surface used ornamentally over doors or windows; usually triangular but may be curved.

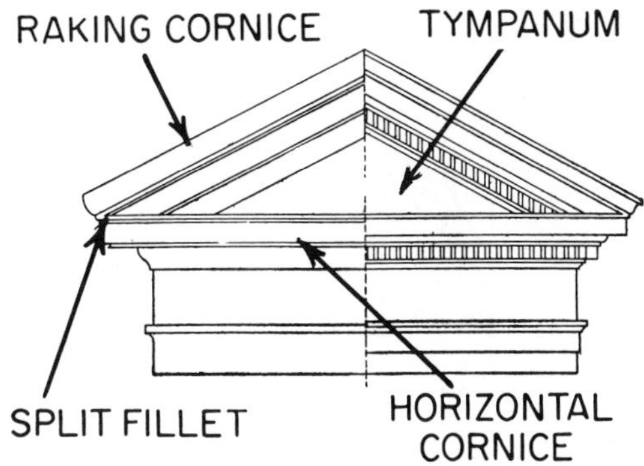

pediment terminology

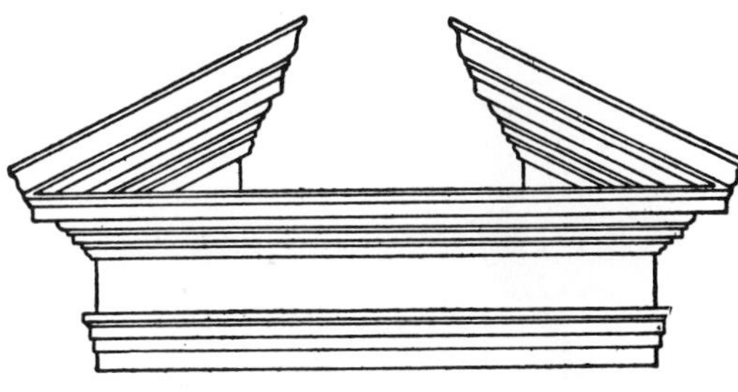
broken pediment

broken scroll pediment

pediment arch A **miter arch.**

peel, pele In northern England and Scotland in the Middle Ages, a small, emergency defense structure, generally a low, fortified tower, usable as a dwelling place.

peel tower Same as **peel.**

peel

pegma **1.** In ancient construction, anything made of boards joined together. **2.** A machine used in ancient amphitheatres to produce a sudden change of scene. **3.** A lift by which cages for wild animals could be raised from the substructure of an arena (where they were housed) to the grade level of the arena.

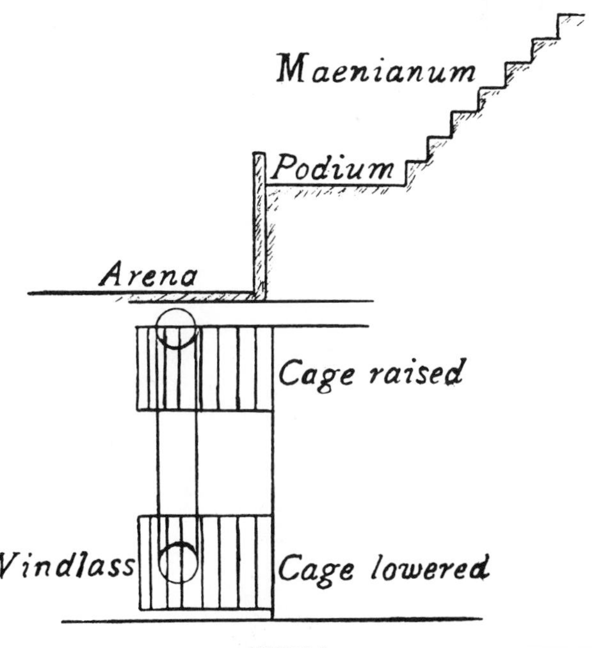

pegma,3

碑 **pei** A pylon or upright tablet (usually of stone), the height of which is double that of a **chieh;** carries a carved inscription, usually historical, poetic, or religious in character; usually 9 to 30 ft (approx. 3 to 10 m) in height; the upper part may be carved in various shapes.

pele See **peel.**

pellet Any small, round, decorative projection; usually one of many.

pellet molding A molding decorated with a series of small, flat disks or hemispherical projections.

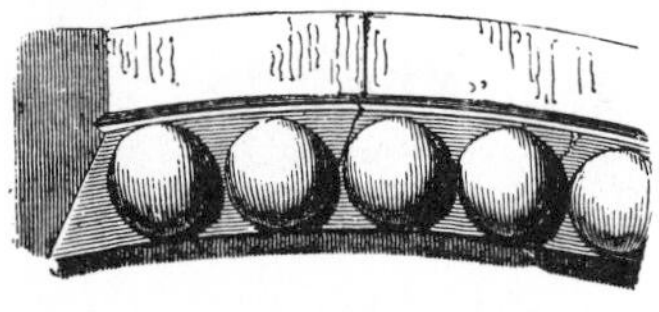

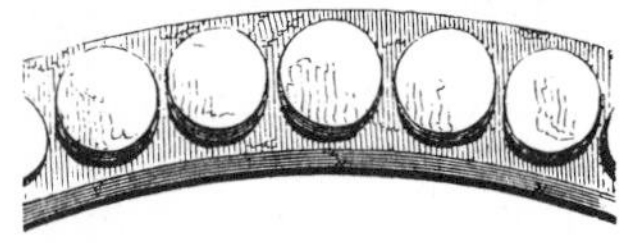

pellet moldings, two types

pelmet A valance or cornice, sometimes decorative, built into the head of a window to conceal the drapery track or blind brackets or fittings.

pelmet board A board, at the head of the interior side of a window, which acts as a pelmet.

pend A vaulted roof without groining.

pendant A suspended feature or hanging ornament used in the vaults and timber roofs of Gothic architecture. Also called a **pendent.**

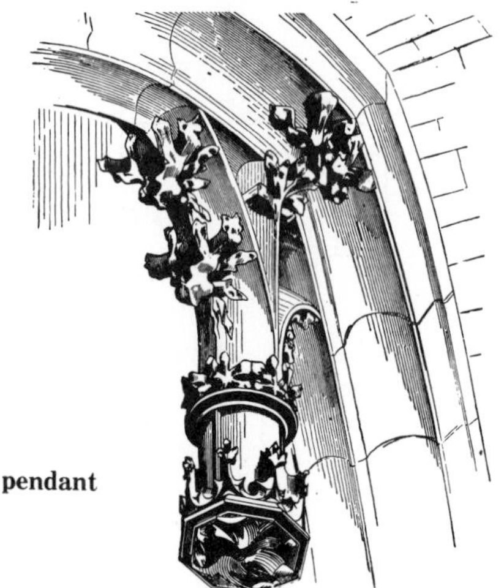

pendant

above: construction showing pendant at *A* in Henry VII's Chapel, Westminster (1500)

left: detail showing the pendant

below: types of pendants

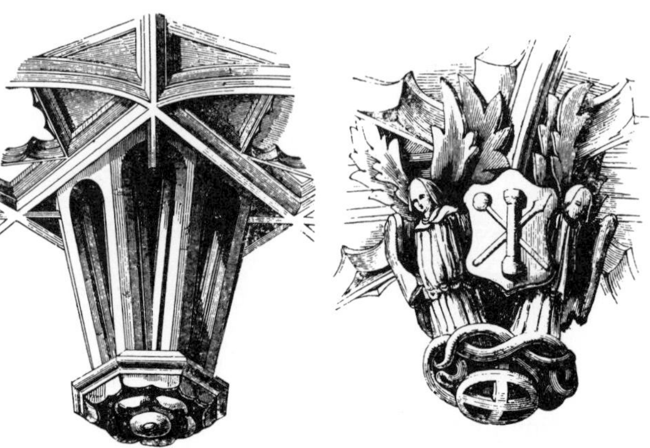

pendant post In a **hammer-beam roof,** the lower post at the foot of the truss.

pendent Same as **pendant.**

pendentive **1.** One of a set of curved wall surfaces which form a transition between a dome (or its drum) and the supporting masonry. **2.** In medieval architecture and derivatives, one of a set of surfaces vaulted outward from a pier, corbel, or the like.

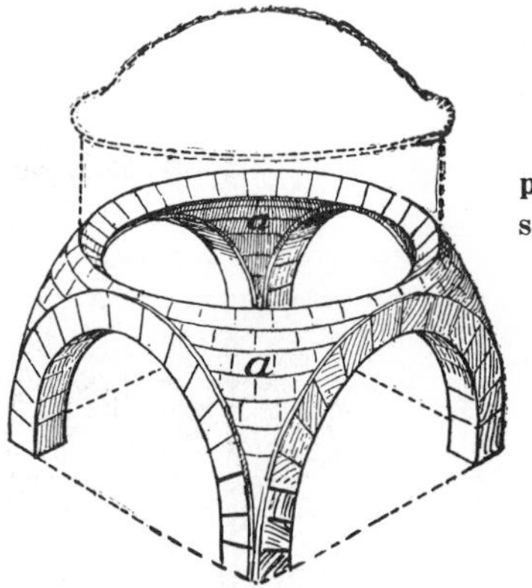

pendentive,1 shown at *a*

example of pendentives,1 supporting the drum of a cupola

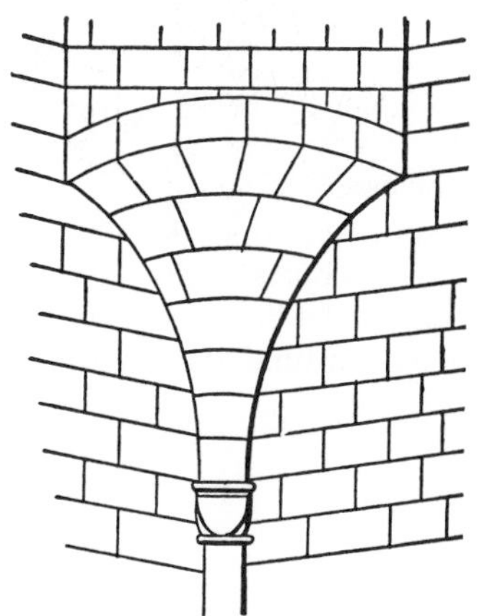

pendentive,2

pendentive bracketing Corbeling in the general form of a pendentive; common in Moorish and Muslim architecture.

pendentive cradling The curved ribs in arched and vaulted ceilings, used to carry or support the plasterwork.

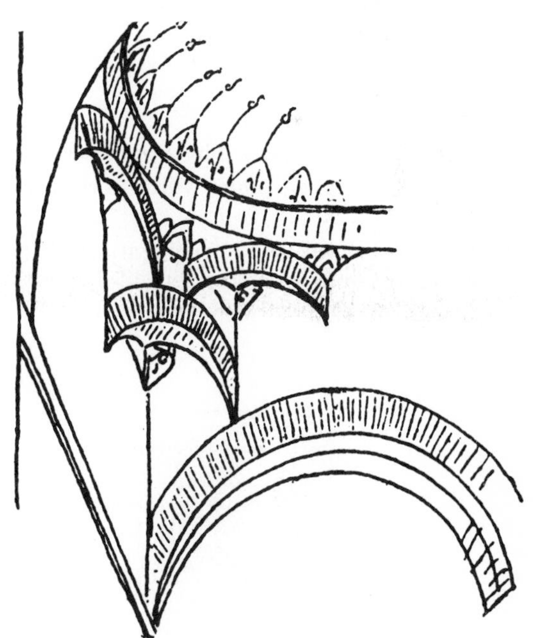

pendentive bracketing

pendent post, pendant post **1.** In a medieval principal roof truss, a short post placed against the wall, its lower end supported on a corbel or capital, and its upper end carrying the tie beam or hammer beam. **2.** The support of an arch across the angles of a square.

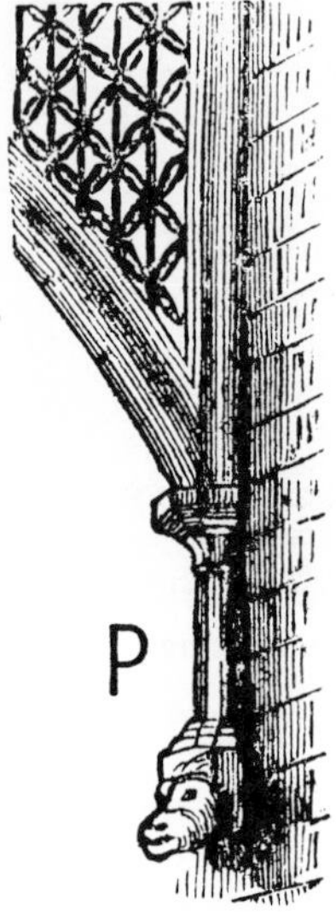

p, **pendent post**

pendice See **penthouse.**

pendiculated Supported by a **pendicule.**

pendicule A small pillar which serves as a support.

pendill A carved wood ornament which terminates the bottom end of second-floor posts in **framed overhang** construction.

pendill

penetralia **1.** The interior part of a building, as a sanctuary. **2.** An inner apartment.

pentacle In Gothic tracery a five-pointed star motif with a pentagon in the center.

pentastyle A portico or temple front having five columns.

penthouse, pendice, pentice **1.** A structure occupying usually less than half the roof area of a flat-roofed building. **2.** An **appentice.**

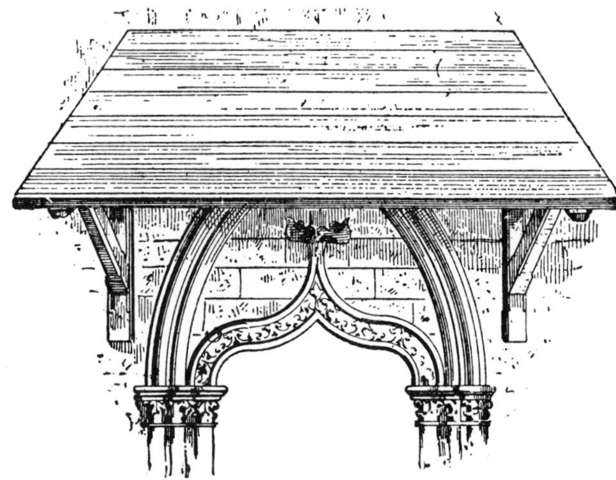

penthouse,2

pentice See **penthouse.**

pent roof, shed roof A small, sloping roof, the upper end of which butts against a wall of a house, usually above the first-floor windows; if carried completely around the house, it is called a **skirt-roof.**

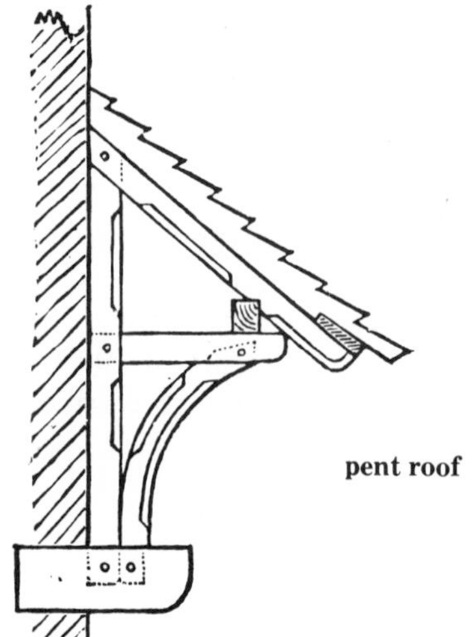

pent roof

pepperbox turret A turret circular in plan and with some form of conical or domical roof.

perch A **bracket** or **corbel.**

perclose See **parclose.**

perforated tracery Same as **net tracery.**

perforated wall See **pierced wall.**

pergenyng Same as **parget.**

perget Same as **parget.**

pergola **1.** A garden structure with an open wooden-framed roof, often latticed, supported by regularly spaced posts or columns. The structure, often covered by climbing plants such as vines or roses, shades a walk or passageway. **2.** A colonnade which has such a structure. **3.** Any building added to the side of a house or building, beyond the original ground plan, as a lean-to. **4.** A stall or balcony constructed over the colonnades of an ancient forum and abutting the buildings adjacent; chiefly intended as an office for bankers and moneychangers.

pergula Same as **pergola.**

periaktos In an ancient Greek theatre, one of the two pieces of machinery placed on both sides of the stage for shifting scenes. Consisted of three painted scenes on the faces of a revolving frame in the form of a triangular prism. The scene was changed by turning one periaktos or both, so as to exhibit a new face to the audience.

peribolos, peribolus A wall enclosing a sacred area such as a temple or church grounds.

peridrome In an ancient peripteral temple, the open space or passage between the walls of the cella and the surrounding columns.

peridromos Same as **peridrome.**

periform Pear-shaped; said of a roof in the form of a pear (as some baptisteries and Eastern churches) or said of a molding having a pear shape.

peripteral Surrounded by a single row of columns.

peripteros, periptery A building having a peristyle of a single row of columns.

peristalith A series of standing stones or stone slabs which surround an object such as a burial mound or barrow.

peristasis The ring of columns which encircles a peripteral building.

peristele One of the upright stones in a **peristalith.**

peristerium The inner or second ciborium.

peristyle **1.** A colonnade surrounding either the exterior of a building or an open space, e.g., a courtyard. **2.** The space so enclosed.

peristylium See **Roman house.**

peristylon See **Greek house.**

perpend, parpend stone, perpend stone, perpent stone, perpin stone, through stone A **bondstone** which extends completely through the entire thickness of a masonry wall and is exposed on both wall faces.

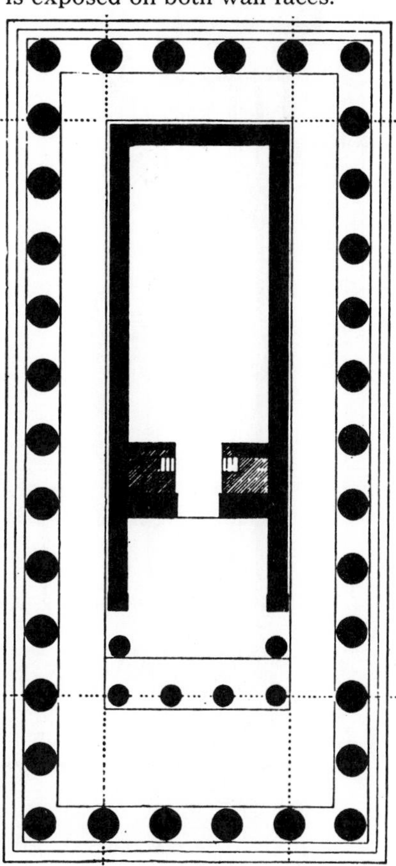

peripteral Temple of Ceres (Demeter) at Paestum, Italy (c. 510 B.C.)

Perpendicular style

Perpendicular style, Rectilinear style The last and longest phase of Gothic architecture in England, ca. 1350–1550, following upon the Decorated style and eventually succeeded by Elizabethan architecture. Characterized by vertical emphasis in structure and frequently elaborate fan vaults. Its final development (1485–1547) is often referred to as Tudor architecture.

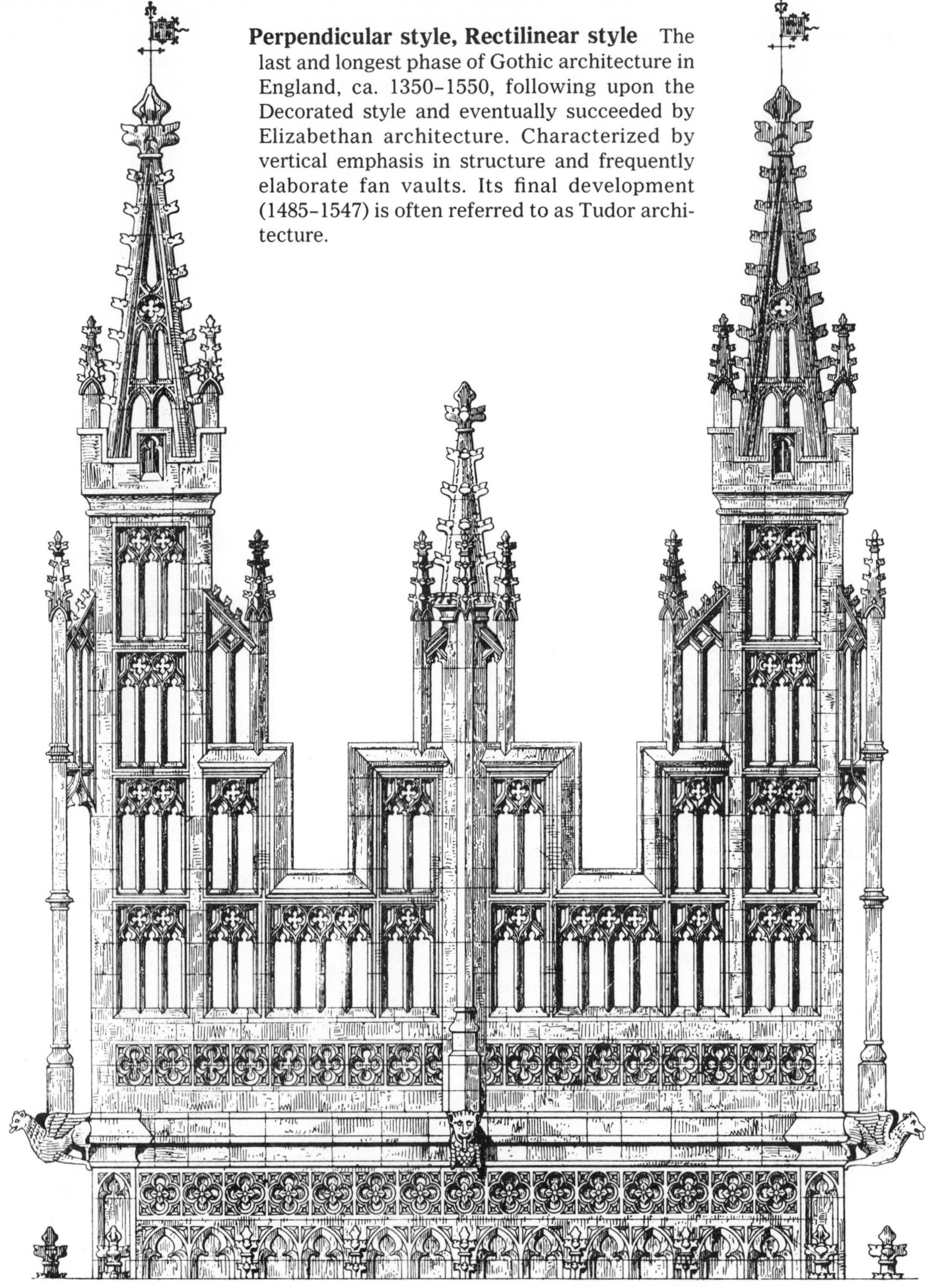

St. Mary Magdalen's Church, Taunton, Somerset: battlements of tower

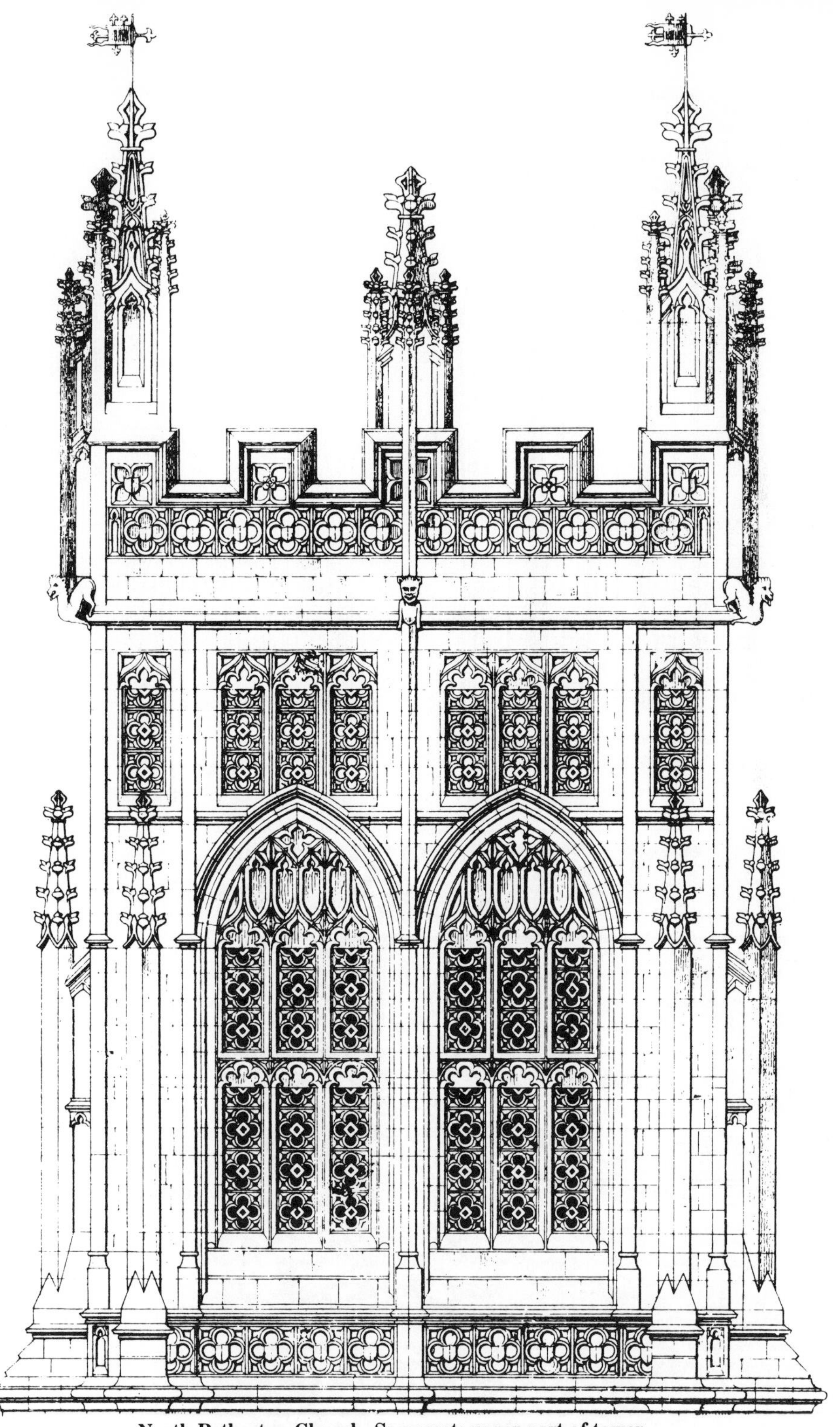

North Petherton Church, Somerset: upper part of tower

Perpendicular style

Perpendicular style window, St. Mary's, Oxford (1488)

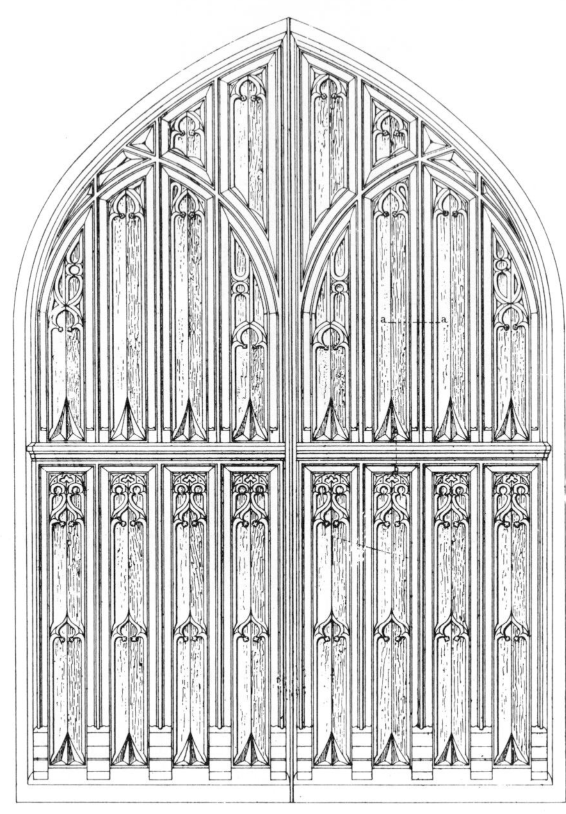

Perpendicular style door, Holy Trinity Church, Stratford-on-Avon

cornice of rood screen: Trull Church, Somerset (16th cent.)

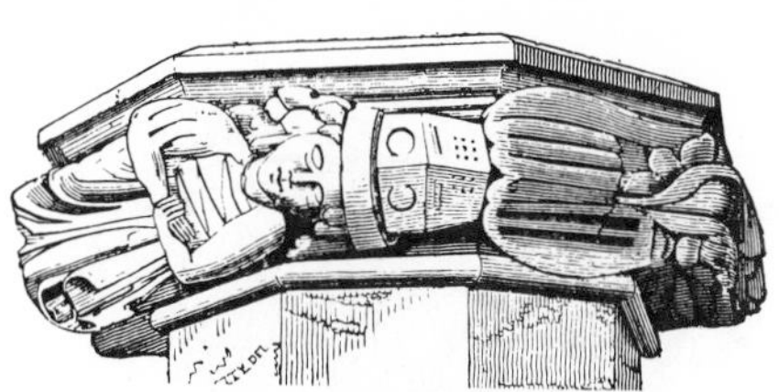

capital, Cottingham Church, Northamptonshire (14th cent.)

capital, Piddleton, Dorset (1505)

capital, Upwey, Dorset (c. 1500)

arch, Newbold-on-Avon, Warwicks

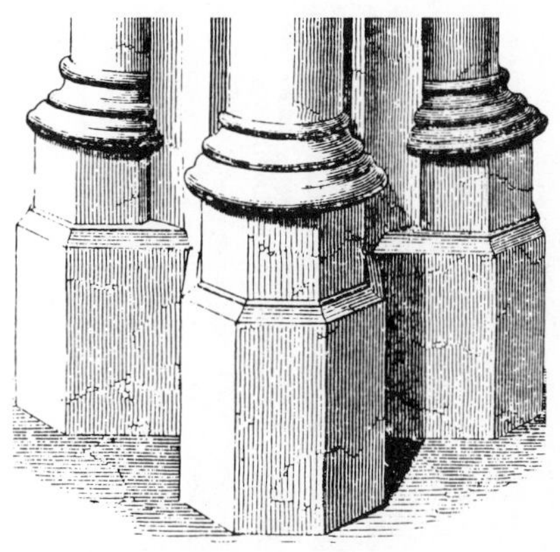

base, Croyden, Surrey (c. 1450)

bench ends, Trull Church, Somerset

fireplace, Coulston House, Bristol

perpendicular tracery, rectilinear tracery Tracery of the Perpendicular style with repeated perpendicular mullions often rising to the curve of the arch, the mullions crossed at intervals by horizontal transoms producing repeated vertical rectangles.

perpendicular tracery, King's College Chapel, Cambridge (1446–1515)

perpend wall

perpendiculum A plumb line, employed by ancient masons, bricklayers, etc.

perpend wall, perpeyn wall **1.** A wall built of **perpends** or of ashlar stones, all of which reach from one side to the other. **2.** A buttress or pier, projecting from a wall.

perpeyn Same as **perpend.**

perron **1.** A formal terrace or platform, esp. one centered on a gate or doorway. **2.** An outdoor flight of steps, usually symmetrical, leading to a terrace, platform, or doorway of a large building.

perron

Persepolis The ceremonial center of the Persian empire, built by Darius I and Xerxes on an enormous fortified terace; located in the heartland of the Fars region, northeast of present-day Shiraz, Iran. A monumental gateway preceded by a grand double staircase provided access to the complex, which included reception halls (e.g., the **apadana** and the throne room), residence halls, harem, treasury, and garrison quarters. The entire complex was largely destroyed by Alexander the Great.

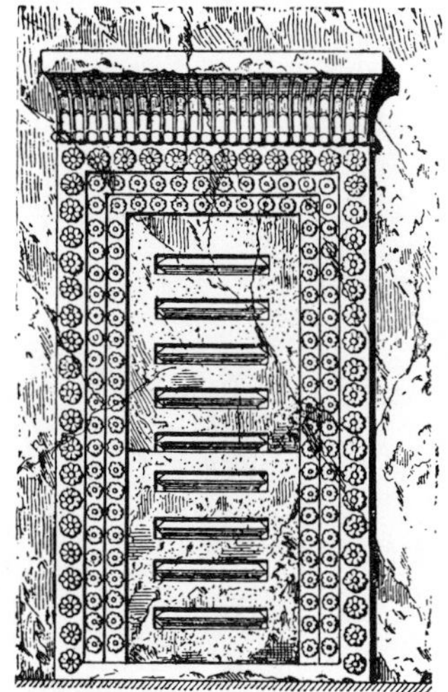

door architrave and cornice, Persepolis (518–416 B.C.)

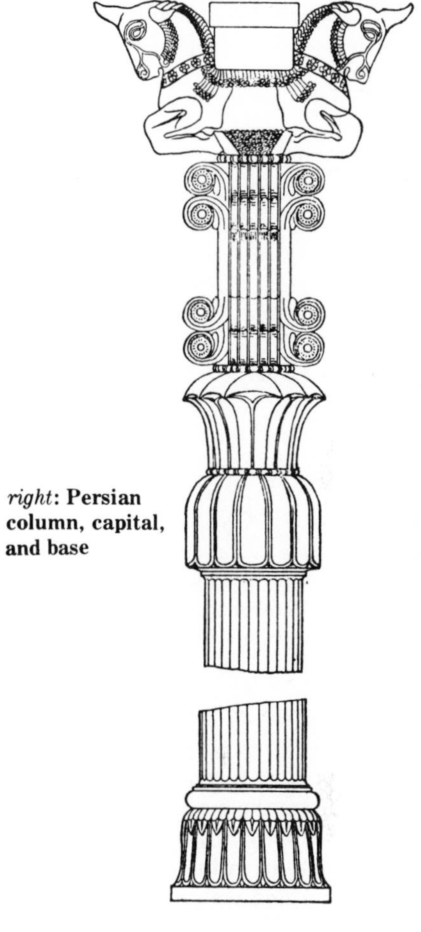

right: **Persian column, capital, and base**

relief from Persepolis

parapet wall of staircase

Persian A **telamon,** esp. one portrayed in Persian dress.

Persian

persienne An exterior **louver window** having adjustable slats.

persona A mask of terra-cotta, marble, etc., designed to imitate the human face or the head of an animal, usually in grotesque form, employed as an antefix in buildings, as an ornament for discharging water, or as a gargoyle.

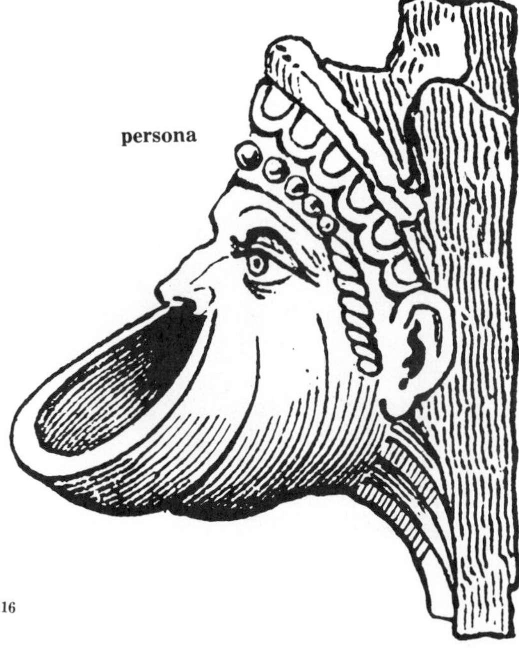

persona

pertica In medieval churches, a beam behind the altar from which relics were suspended on festival days.

pes (*pl.* **pedes**) An ancient Roman measure of length; a Roman foot; equal to 11.65 in. (29.6 cm).

pessulus A bolt for fastening a leaf of an ancient Roman door. Their doors, usually having two leafs, had two (sometimes four) bolts fixed to them, one at the top and one at the bottom of each leaf.

pew In a church, a bench with a back and ends. Also see **box pew.**

pews, Montreal, Burgundy; Early Renaissance (c. 1520)

pew chair A hinged seat, attached to the end of a church pew.

phane Old term for **vane.**

pharos, pharus In ancient Greek and Roman architecture, a lighthouse.

Phoenix Hall See **Byōdō-in.**

photisterium Same as **baptistery.**

phra-chedi See **prachedi.**

Phrygian marble Same as **pavonazzo.**

phylaca An ancient prison or place of custody.

phyrctorion In ancient Greece, a watchtower from which a sentinel could warn of the approach of a hostile force, by means of fire.

piache A covered arched walk, or portico.

piano nobile In Renaissance architecture and derivatives, a floor with formal reception and dining rooms; the principal story in a house, usually one flight above the ground.

piazza A public open space or square surrounded by buildings.

picnostyle, pycnostyle See **intercolumniation.**

Picts' house A house, circular in plan, of conical shape, with an opening at the top; large stones, without cement, were employed in its construction. The internal area was often considerably less in diameter than the thickness of the wall, within which were sometimes staircases and small cell-like rooms. Constructed by the Picts who formerly inhabited the highlands of Scotland and some of the islands of Scotland.

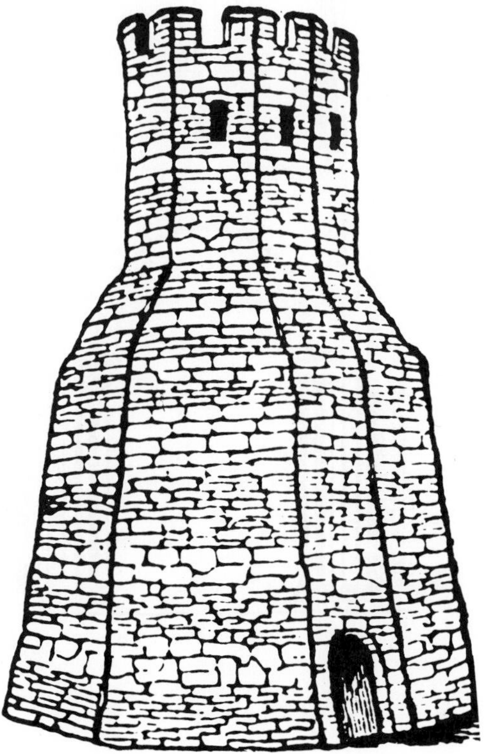

pharos: ancient Roman lighthouse in Britain

pida In the architecture of India, a receding terraced roof, terminating the **mukhashala** or **jagamohan.**

pieh kuan A structure in an elaborate Chinese garden which by its design attracts special attention; usually served as the studio for the emperor or a famous scholar.

pien, piend **1.** The ridge of a roof. **2.** An **arris;** a salient angle.

pien check, piend check In a stair constructed with hanging steps of stone, a rabbet cut along the lower front edge of a step which fits into the back of the step next below it.

pien joint In a stone stair, the joint between two steps which are secured by a **pien check.**

pier **1.** A column designed to support concentrated load. **2.** A member, usually in the form of a thickened section, which forms an integral part of a wall; usually placed at intervals along the wall to provide lateral support or to take concentrated vertical loads.

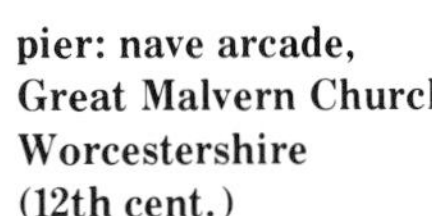

pier: nave arcade, Great Malvern Church, Worcestershire (12th cent.)

base of clustered pier, Salisbury Cathedral (c. 1250)

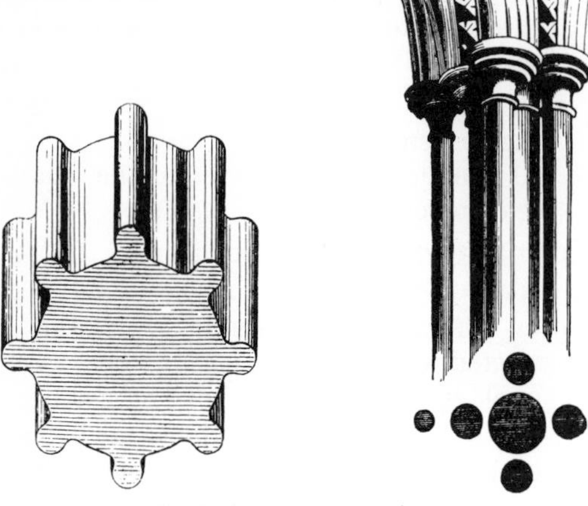
Early English style piers

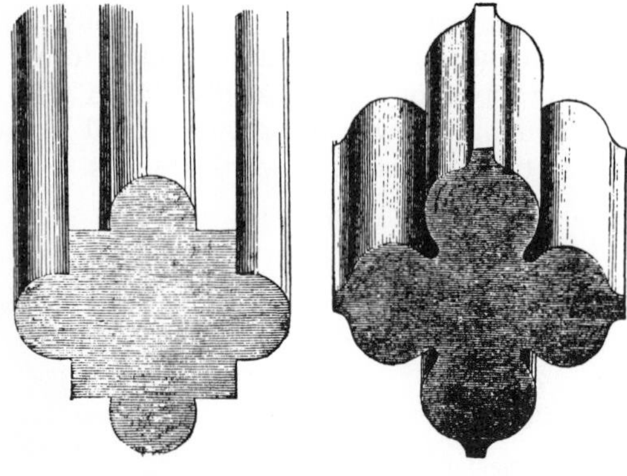
cross sections of piers:
left: Norman; *right*: Decorated style

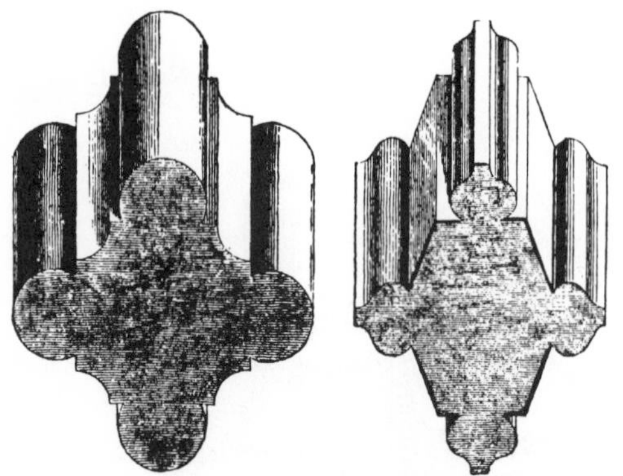
cross sections of Perpendicular style piers

pier arch An arch resting on piers, esp. one along a **nave arcade.**

pier arch: nave arcade, Fountains Abbey, Yorkshire (c. 1180)

pier buttress A **pier,** 1 which receives the thrust of a flying buttress.

pierced wall, perforated wall, screen wall A nonbearing masonry wall in which an ornamental pierced effect is achieved by alternating rectangular or shaped blocks with open spaces.

pierced work Decoration which consists mainly or partially of perforations.

pierced work: window slabs, Central Syria

pierrotage In Southern Colonial architecture in U.S.A., small stones mixed with mortar; used as a filler between framing members.

pila **1.** In churches in Italy, a holy-water font, consisting of a bowl mounted on a shaft, as distinguished from a font hanging from or secured to a wall or pier. **2.** A square block or epistyle, just over the columns, to support a rooftimber. **3.** A mortar which is valuable or curious on account of its antiquity or design.

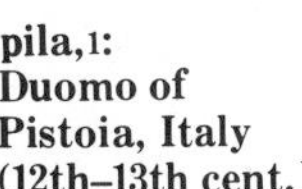

pila,1: Duomo of Pistoia, Italy (12th–13th cent.)

pilaster **1.** An engaged pier or pillar, often with capital and base. **2.** Decorative features that imitate engaged piers but are not supporting structures, as a rectangular or semicircular member used as a simulated pillar in entrances and other door openings and fireplace mantels; often contains a base, shaft, and capital; may be constructed as a projection of the wall itself.

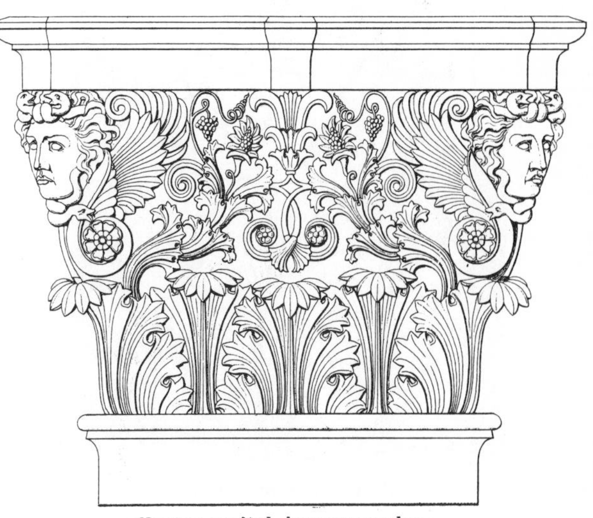

pilaster capital, inner propylaea at Eleusis

pilaster base Same as **base block.**

pilaster face The form for the front surface of a pilaster, parallel to the wall.

pilaster face, ancient Rome

pilaster mass An engaged pier built up with the wall, usually without the capital and base of a pilaster.

pilaster side The form for the side surface of a pilaster, perpendicular to the wall.

pilaster strip, lesene Same as **pilaster mass** but usually applied to slender piers of slight projection; in medieval architecture and derivatives, often joining an arched corbel table.

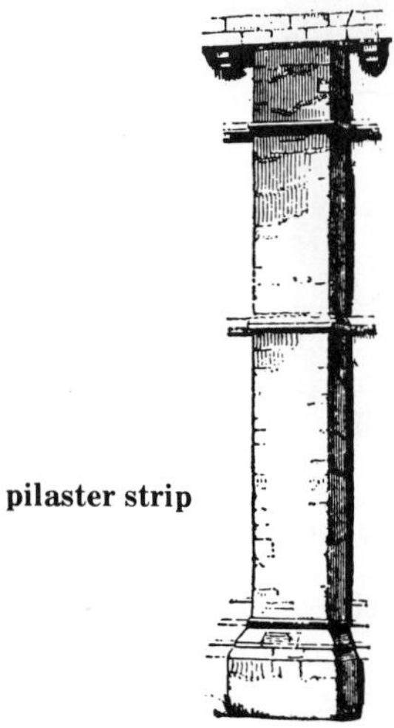

pilaster strip

pilastrade A line of pilasters.

pile tower Same as **peel.**

pilier cantonné High Gothic form of the **compound pier,** with a massive central core to which are attached at 90° intervals four colonnettes supporting the arcade, the aisle vaultings, and the responds of the nave vaults.

pillar A **pier;** a post or column.

pillar-stone **1.** Same as **cornerstone.** **2.** A stone memorial, usually pillar-shaped.

pillow capital See **cushion capital.**

pillowed See **pulvinated.**

pillowwork The decorative treatment of any surface with pillow-like projections.

pilotis The free-standing columns, posts, or piles which support a building, raising it above ground level.

pinacotheca A picture gallery.

pinaculum In ancient Greek or Roman architecture, a roof terminating in a ridge (the ordinary covering for a temple; in contrast, private houses had flat roofs).

pinax A decorative panel which fills the intercolumniations of the **proskenion** or the thyromata (pl. of **thyroma**) at the back of the stage of an ancient Greek or Roman theatre.

pineapple **1.** An ovoid, imbricated finial. **2.** A decorative molding.

pineapple,2

p'ing chu See **chu.**

ping ch'üan In Chinese architecture, a **multicentered arch.** 拼券

屏風 **ping fêng** A movable screen having a wood or bamboo frame, used in traditional Chinese homes to supply privacy or to provide a setting for pieces of furniture. The panels, set into the frame, may be paintings on paper, fabric or lacquered boards, or carved wood, carved ivory, or precious stone. Both sides of the screen may be painted or carved. One large panel may be used or a number of smaller, equally sized panels connected by hinges.

pinnacle **1.** An apex. **2.** In Gothic architecture and derivatives, a small, largely ornamental body or shaft terminated by a pyramid or spire. **3.** A turret, or part of a building elevated above the main building.

right: **pinnacle, St. Peter's, Oxford (c. 1100)**

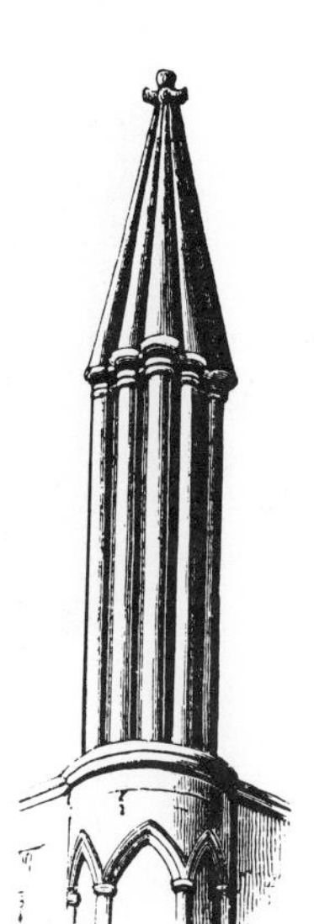

Christ Church, Oxford (c.1180)

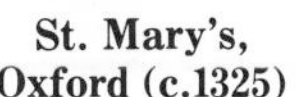

St. Mary's, Oxford (c.1325)

St. Stephen's, Bristol (c. 1500)

pirca A type of crude wall construction using dry-laid unshaped stones; found in the Andes.

pisay Same as **pisé.**

piscina **1.** A shallow basin or sink, supplied with a drain pipe, generally recessed in a niche. **2.** In ancient Roman construction, any type of reservoir or pond. **3.** A large swimming pool in the open air, either with tepid water warmed by the heat of the sun or water from naturally warm springs, but sometimes reduced in temperature by the admixture of snow; differs from a **baptisterium** in not being under cover and usually cooler. **4.** A pool or basin of water in Roman bathrooms.

Norman piscina,1: Kirkland Abbey, Yorkshire (1160)

left: **Norman piscina,1**

Early English style piscina, 1

Decorated style piscina, 1

Perpendicular style piscina, 1

piscina limaria In ancient Rome, a tank constructed at the beginning or the end of an aqueduct to permit sediment to be deposited before the water was transmitted to the city.

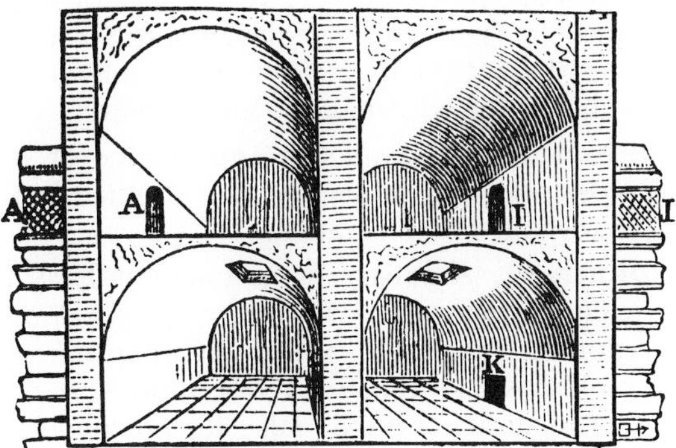

piscina limaria: *A-A*, inlet; *I-I*, outlet; *K*, sluice gate through which sediment is discharged

pisé **1.** A building whose walls are made of compressed earth, usually stiff clay formed and rammed in a movable frame or formwork. **2.** The building material itself, i.e., stiff earth or clay, rammed until it becomes firm; used to form walls and floors. **3.** **Cob** used as a wall material.

pishtaq In Muslim or Persian architecture, a monumental gateway marking the entrance to a mosque, càravanserai, madrasah, or mausoleum.

pistrinum A mill associated with an ancient Roman bakery.

pitched stone A rough-faced stone having each edge of the exposed face pitched at a slight bevel, nearly in the plane of the face.

pitcher house A wine cellar.

pitch-faced In masonry, having all arrises cut true and in the same plane, but with the face beyond the arris edges left comparatively rough, being simply dressed with a pitching chisel.

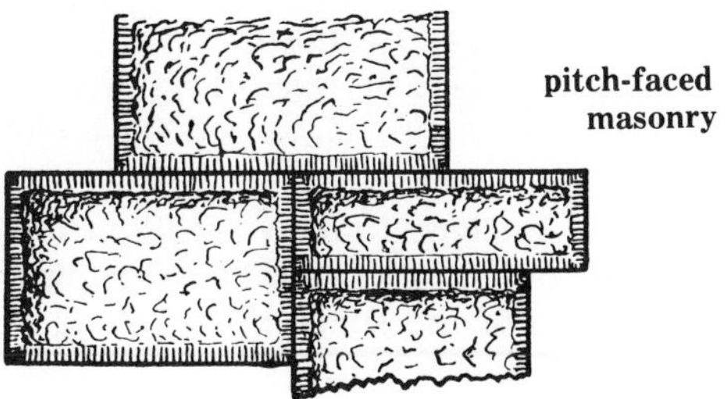

pitch-faced masonry

pitching piece See **apron piece.**

pitha In the architecture of India, a pedestal or plinth.

pixis, pix A shrine to contain the host or consecrated wafer.

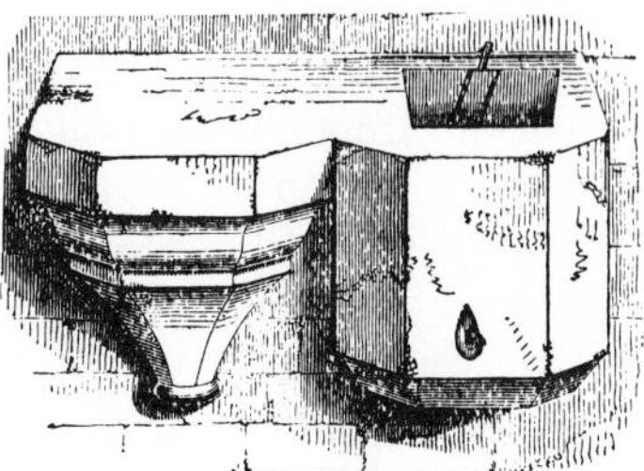

pix, Bridlington Priory Church, Yorkshire

placage An ornamental thin masonry facing (revetment) of a building.

placard Same as **parget.**

plafond A **ceiling,** esp. one of decorative character; flat or arched.

planceer Same as **plancier.**

planch *(Brit.)* **1.** A floorboard. **2.** A plank floor.

planching Same as **flooring.**

plancier, planceer, plancer, plancher **1.** The soffit or underside of any projecting member, as a cornice. **2.** A **planch,** 1.

plancier piece A board which forms a **plancier.**

plank house A large house, generally rectangular, constructed of vertical planks without studs; the interior may be plastered; often the exterior was covered with shingles or clapboards.

plano-convex A shape of sun-dried brick, flat on one side, convex on the other, typical of early Mesopotamian construction.

planted molding, applied molding A molding which is nailed, laid on, or otherwise fastened to the work rather than cut into the solid material.

plaque A tablet, often inscribed, added to or set into a surface.

plasta Same as **antefix.**

plaster cornice A plaster molding where the wall and ceiling meet, crowning the top of the wall.

platband **1.** Any flat, rectangular, horizontal molding, the projection of which is much less than its height; a **fascia,** 1. **2.** A decorative lintel or false flat arch over a doorway, etc. **3.** The fillets between the flutes of a column; **stria.**

plate **1.** In wood frame construction, a horizontal board or timber connecting and terminating posts, joists, rafters, etc. **2.** A timber laid horizontally (and on its widest side) in a wall or on top of a wall or on the ground to receive other timbers or joists.

platea In ancient Rome, a wide passageway or a wide street.

plated parquet Parquetry having inlaid hardwood pieces applied to a framed backing.

plate rail, plaque rail A narrow shelf or rail along the upper part of the walls of a room, grooved to hold chinaware plates or decorations.

Plateresque architecture "Silversmith-like"; the richly decorative style of the Spanish Renaissance in the 16th cent. Its early phase is also referred to as **Isabelline architecture,** after Queen Isabella I (1474-1504).

plate tracery Tracery whose openings are or seem to be pierced through thin slabs of stone.

plate tracery, St. Andrea, Mantua (1472–94)

platfond Same as **plafond.**

platted molding Same as **reticulated molding.**

pleasance chamber A room of state in a royal palace.

plethron, plethrum **1.** A measure of length of the ancient Greeks; equivalent to 100 Greek feet, i.e., 101¼ ft (30.86). **2.** A unit of area equal to the square of the above length.

plexiform Having the appearance of network, weaving, or plaiting, as in Celtic and Romanesque ornamentation.

plinth **1.** A square or rectangular base for column, pilaster, or door framing. **2.** A solid monumental base, often ornamented with moldings, bas reliefs, or inscriptions, to support a statue or memorial. **3.** A recognizable base of an external wall, or the base courses of a building collectively, if so treated as to give the appearance of a platform.

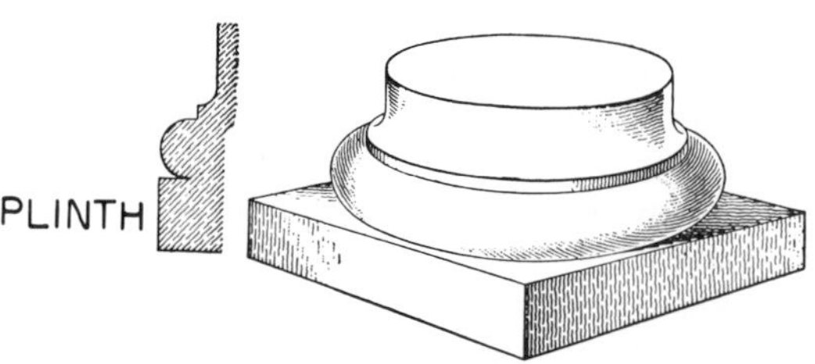

plinth course **1.** A masonry course which forms a continuous **plinth.** **2.** The top course in a brick plinth.

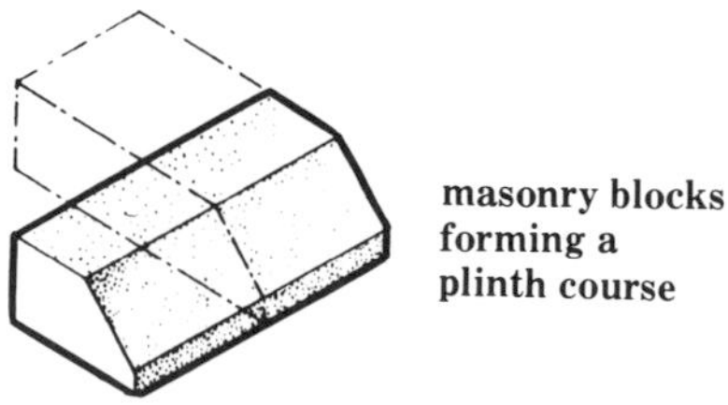

masonry blocks forming a plinth course

plowshare twist, plowshare vault A vault in which the surface between the stilted wall rib and the diagonal rib is warped like a plowshare.

pluteus In ancient Roman architecture, a dwarf wall or parapet; esp. one closing the lower portion of the space between the columns of a colonnade.

Pnyx A public place of assembly in ancient Athens near the Acropolis; an open, paved, semicircular area surrounded by a wall; speakers addressed the people from a platform.

podium **1.** In general, an elevated platform, such as one for a speaker's stand. **2.** The high platform on which Roman temples were generally placed. **3.** In a **circus,** the lowest row of seats running immediately above the racecourse and protected from the wild animals by a railing and a trench **(euripus)** 10 ft (3.05 m) in width and depth; occupied by the emperor, the curule magistrates, and the Vestal virgins. **4.** A low step-like projection from the wall of a room or building, intended to form a raised platform for placing objects on it. **5.** A **socle;** a projecting base of a building.

podium, 4

podzor **1.** In early Russian architecture, a carved bargeboard. **2.** A decorative band of ironwork on a masonry building.

poecile A stoa or porch on the agora of ancient Athens having walls adorned with paintings of historical and religious subjects.

poikile Same as **poecile.**

pointed arch Any arch with a point at its apex, characteristic of, but not confined to, Gothic architecture.

pointed arch

Pointed architecture Old term for Gothic architecture.

pointed ashlar Stonework having face markings produced with a pointed tool.

Pointed style See **Pointed architecture.**

pointed work In masonry, the rough finish which is produced by a pointed tool on the face of a stone.

Norman pointed arch molding

pointel, pointelle **1.** A pattern in a pavement, formed by small squares or lozenges laid diagonally. **2.** Any similar pattern.

pointing **1.** In masonry, the final treatment of joints by the troweling of mortar or a putty-like filler into the joints. **2.** The material with which the joints are filled. **3.** In stone carving, creating points from a model and establishing their position on the stone that is to be carved.

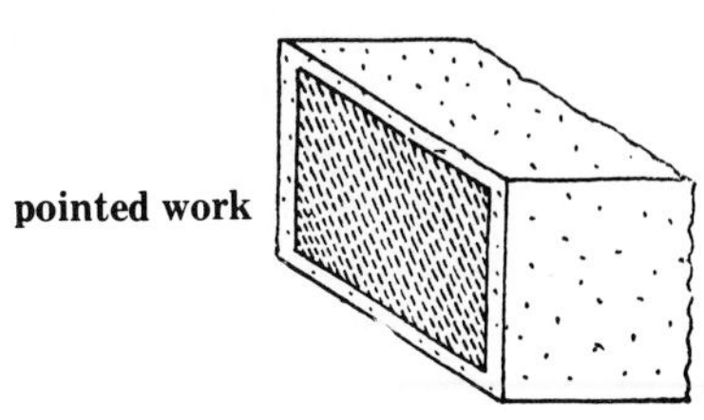

pointed work

pole piece A **ridgeboard.**

pole plate A horizontal timber resting on the ends of the tie beams of a roof; supports the lower ends of the common rafters, directly above the wall; raises the rafters above the top plate of the wall.

polyandrion In ancient Greece, a monument or a burial enclosure provided by the state for a number of men, usually for those of its citizens who had fallen in battle.

polychromy The practice of decorating architectural elements, sculpture, etc., in a variety of colors.

polychromy, Sweden (17th cent.)

polyfoil Same as **multifoil.**

polygonal masonry Masonry which is constructed of stones having smooth polygonal faces.

polygonal masonry

polygonium opus Same as **polygonal masonry.**

pomerium **1.** The space, originally along an ancient Roman city wall within and without, which was left vacant and considered holy; marked off by stone pillars and consecrated by a religious ceremony. **2.** A peripheral ring road around a fortress or fortified city.

pommel, pomel A rounded finial.

pomoerium Same as **pomerium.**

Pompeii A city near Naples in southern Italy partly destroyed by an earthquake in 63 A.D., and by another which occurred later; the city was then entombed by cinders, stones, and ash from a series of volcanic eruptions of Mount Vesuvius in 79 A.D.; excavations began in 1755.

Pompeii: Street of Tombs

Pompeian house, wall decoration

right: **Pompeian ceiling decoration**

above, right and left: **Pompeian wall decoration**

pontifical altar An isolated altar, such as under the dome of St. Peter's at Rome, covered by a **baldachin;** usually placed in the great Roman basilicas.

popina An ancient Roman restaurant or tavern frequented by the lower classes.

poppyhead, poppy An ornament generally used for the finials of pew ends and similar pieces of church furniture.

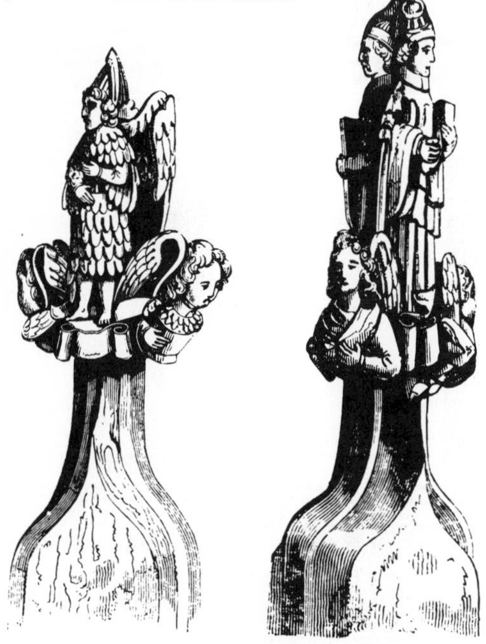

All Souls Chapel, Oxford (c. 1450)

pew ends with carved poppyheads

Christ Church, Oxford (c. 1400)

porch **1.** A structure attached to a building to shelter an entrance or to serve as a semi-enclosed space; usually roofed and generally open-sided. **2.** A **portico.**

west porch, church in Woodstock, Oxfordshire

Norman porch,1: Kelso Abbey, Scotland (c. 1160)

porebrik In early Russian architecture, a frieze constructed of bricks which are set at an angle of 45° to the surface of a wall.

porta The gate of an ancient Roman city or citadel, or of any open space enclosed by a wall. Also see **janua.**

porta of an ancient Roman city

portal An impressive or monumental entrance, gate, or door to a building or courtyard, often decorated.

north porch, Sta. Maria Maggiore, Bergamo (1353)

portal of the Ducal Palace, Nancy

porta pompae The gate through which the Circensian procession entered the circus; situated in the center of the straight end of the circus, with the stalls for the horses arranged on each side of it.

portcullis A defensive grating, of massive iron or timber, movable vertically in retaining grooves cut in the jambs of a fortified gateway.

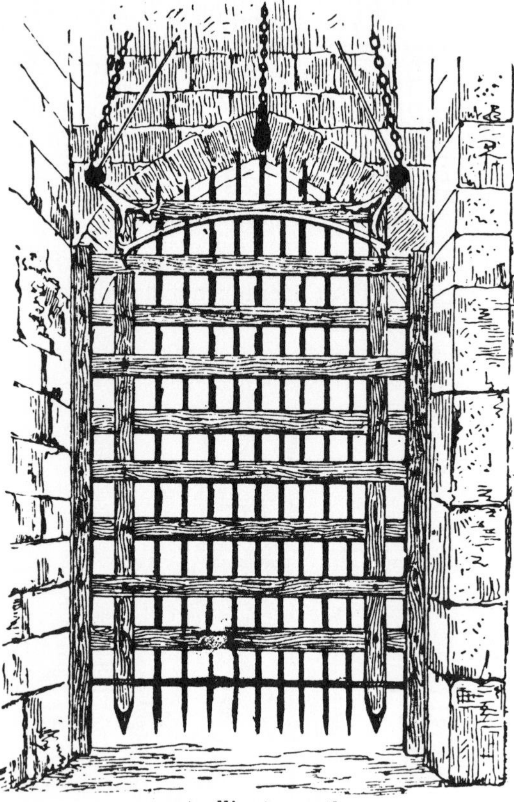

portcullis at a castle

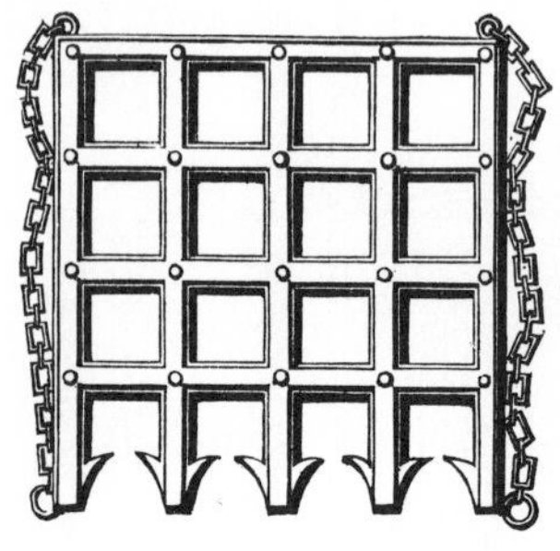

portcullis: Henry VII's Chapel, Westminster (1503–19)

porte cochère 1. A carriage porch. 2. A doorway large enough to let a vehicle pass from street to parking area.

porte cochère, rue Ménars, Paris (19th cent.)

portico 1. A porch or covered walk consisting of a roof supported by columns; a colonnaded (continuous row of columns) porch. 2. A freestanding roofed colonnade; a **stoa.**

portico of a Greek temple

porticus Same as **portico.**

posada In Spanish-speaking countries, an inn.

post-and-beam framing A type of framing in which horizontal members rest on a post as distinguished from a wall.

post-and-lintel construction A type of construction characterized by the use of vertical columns (posts) and a horizontal beam (lintel) to carry a load over an opening—in contrast to systems employing arches or vaults.

post and pane, post and petrail A system of construction consisting of timber framings filled in with brickwork or lath and plaster; half-timbered construction.

postern 1. A minor, often inconspicuous, entry. 2. A small door near a larger one. 3. Any small door or gate, esp. one far from the main gate in a fortified place. 4. Under a city rampart, a stone tunnel of **corbel vault** construction leading to an inconspicuous rear gate; used for sorties in war and as a shortcut during peacetime.

postern,2

postiche Superadded; done after the work is finished, esp. when superfluous, inappropriate, or in poor taste.

posticum 1. The open vestibule of an ancient temple in the rear of the cella, corresponding to the **pronaos** at the front of the temple; in Greek architecture, an **opisthodomos.** 2. The back door of an ancient Roman house.

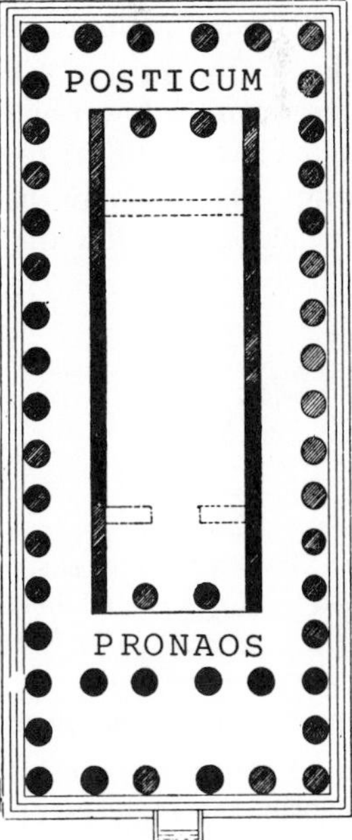

Temple of Apollo at Syracuse, Sicily (c. 565 B.C.)

postique Same as **postiche.**

postis In ancient Roman construction, the jamb of a door, supporting the lintel.

postscenium, postscaenium **1.** In the ancient theatre, the rooms behind the stage where the actors dressed and where machines were stored. **2.** The back part of the stage of a theatre, behind the scenes.

pounced Decorated with indentations or perforations.

poyntel Same as **pointel.**

pozzolan, pozzolona, pozzuolana A siliceous or siliceous and aluminous material, which in itself possesses little or no cementitious value but will, in finely divided form and in the presence of moisture, chemically react with calcium hydroxide at ordinary temperatures to form compounds possessing cementitious properties.

pozzolan cement Pozzolan interground with lime; a natural cement used in ancient times.

prachedi, phra-chedi A Siamese **stupa** having a tapering, slender finial; literally "sacred shrine."

pradakshina-patha A circumambulatory path around a **stupa** or Hindu sanctuary.

praecinctio In the ancient Roman theatre, a walkway between the lower and upper tiers of seats, running parallel to the rows of seats.

praefurnium The mouth of the furnace in an ancient Roman bath or of a kiln.

praefurnium: the arched mouth of a kiln shown in the foreground

praetorium Same as **pretorium.**

prakaram **1.** In Hindu architecture a wall which encloses a temple compound. **2.** The courtyard enclosed by such a wall.

prang In Thai architecture of the 13th to 18th cent. A.D., a sanctuary consisting of a tower-like main temple with a porch structure.

prasada **1.** A Buddhist assembly hall. **2.** A Dravidian Hindu temple.

prasat A Cambodian sanctuary or temple.

prastara In Indian architecture, an entablature.

preaching cross A cross erected in the immediate vicinity of a small chapel (on a highway or in an open place) to mark a place where monks or others could assemble for religious purposes. Also see **weeping cross.**

preaching cross at Inverary, Argyllshire, Scotland

precinctio Same as **praecinctio.**

pre-Columbian architecture Architecture of the indigenous peoples of the Americas prior to contact with European civilization.

predella **1.** The bottom tier of an altarpiece, between the principal panel or bas-relief and the altar itself. **2.** The broad platform on which the altar rests. **3.** An altar ledge.

pre-Romanesque architecture The several regional and transitional styles between the fall of the Roman Empire and the emergence of Romanesque architecture in the 11th cent., including **Lombard, Carolingian,** and **Ottonian.**

presbytery, presbyterium The actual sanctuary of a church beyond the choir and occupied only by the officiating clergy.

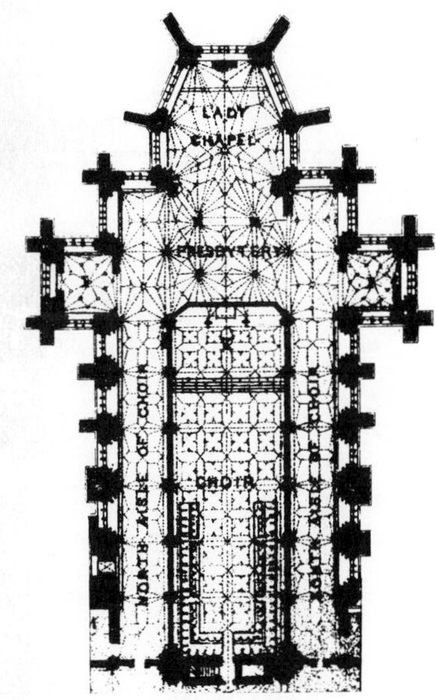

detail of the east end of a cathedral, showing the relation between the choir and presbytery

presence chamber, presence room The room in which a great personage receives his guests or those entitled to come before him; a hall of state.

presidio In Spanish America, a frontier outpost or fort.

prestol In the Russian Orthodox church, an altar or sanctuary table.

pritvor The **narthex** of a Russian Orthodox church.

pretorium In the ancient Roman Empire, the official residence of a provincial governor; a hall of justice; a palace.

prick post In a framed structure, any secondary post or side post, as a **queen post.**

prie-dieu A small desk before which a person may kneel when praying.

priest's door The door by which the priest enters the chancel from the side.

princess post In a truss, a vertical post between the **queen post** and the wall to supplement the support of the queen post.

principal In a framed structure, a most important member, such as a truss which supports the roof.

principal beam The largest or main beam in a framework.

principal post A corner post in a **timber-framed building.**

principal rafter One of the diagonal members of a **roof truss** which support the purlins on which the common rafters rest.

print room In English 18th cent. interiors and derivatives, a room decorated by affixing prints to the walls.

priory A religious house governed by a prior or prioress.

prismatic billet molding A common Norman molding consisting of a series of prisms, with alternate rows staggered.

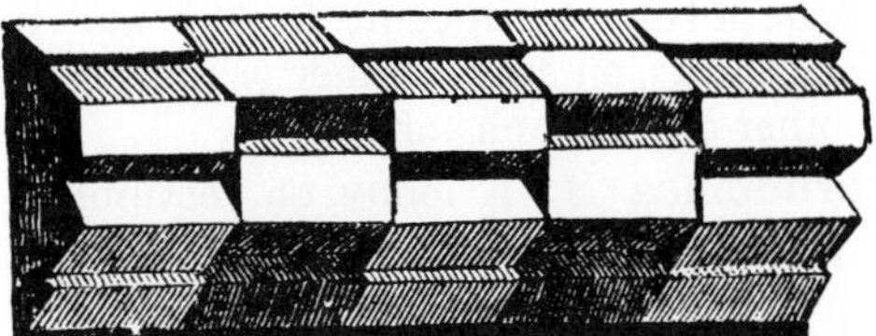

Norman prismatic billet molding

ruins of the Pretorium at Musmiyeh, Syria (c. 170 A.D.)

prismatic rustication In Elizabethan architecture, rusticated masonry with diamond-shaped projections worked on the face of every stone.

privy chamber Same as **presence chamber.**

proaulion In the early Church, and in the modern Greek Church, the porch or vestibule of the church; an outer porch before the narthex.

procathedral A church used as the cathedral church of a diocese while the proper church remains unfinished or under repair.

processional way A monumental roadway for ritual processions in ancient cities, e.g., Babylon.

procession path A continuation of the choir aisles behind the high altar in an apsidal (and sometimes in a square-ended) church.

procoeton In ancient Greece and Roman dwellings, an antechamber or room preceding other rooms or chambers.

prodomos **1.** A lobby or vestibule. **2.** A **pronaos.**

projection **1.** In masonry, stones which are set forward of the general wall surface to provide a rugged or rustic appearance. **2.** Any component, member, or part which juts out from a building.

projection of bricks beyond face of a wall

promenade A suitable place for walking for pleasure, as a mall.

promptuarium A storeroom.

pronaos The inner portico in front of the naos, or cella, of a classical temple.

pronaus Same as **pronaos.**

propnigeum The furnace serving the sweating room in a Greek gymnasium.

ancient Egyptian processional way

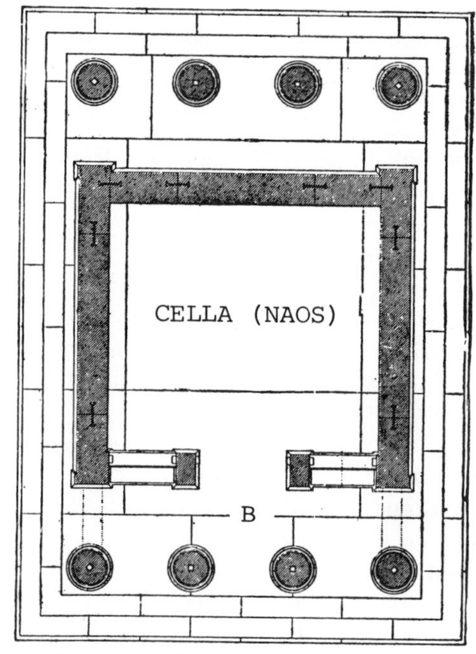

B, pronaos: Temple of Nike Apteros (Wingless Victory), Athens (427 B.C.)

propylaeum 1. The monumental gateway to a sacred enclosure. 2. *(pl., cap.* Propylaea) Particularly, the elaborate gateway to the Acropolis in Athens.

Propylaea, Athens (437–432 B.C.): conjectural restoration

above: reflected ceiling plan of outer porch

right: perspective section showing northern half (restored)

below: plan of Propylaea; the dotted portions outline buildings that were projected but not actually constructed

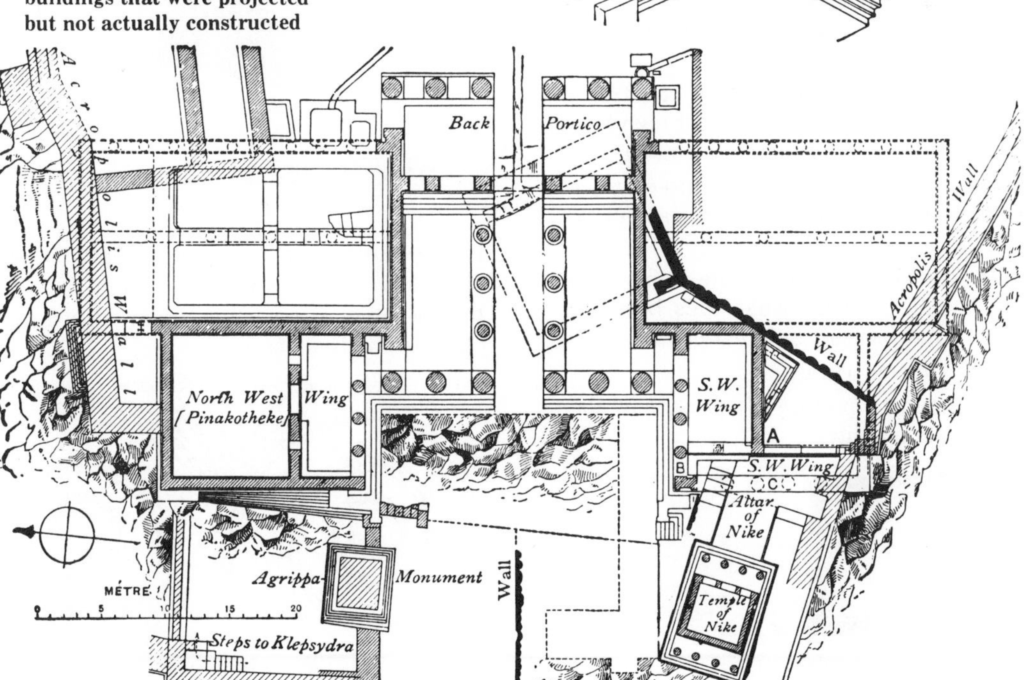

propylon In ancient Egyptian architecture, a monumental gateway, usually between two towers in outline like truncated pyramids, of which one or a series stood before the actual entrance or pylon of most temples or other important buildings.

propylon at Karnak

proscenium In the ancient theatre, the stage before the scene or back wall.

proskenion In the ancient Greek theatre, a building before the **skene;** the earliest high Hellenistic stage; later, the front of the stage.

prostas **1.** In ancient Greek architecture, a vestibule or antechamber. **2.** Same as **prostasis, 1.**

prostasis **1.** The portion of the front of a classical temple in antis which lies between the **antae.** **2.** A pronaos before a cella.

prostoon Same as **portico.**

prostyle Having a portico of columns at the front of a building only.

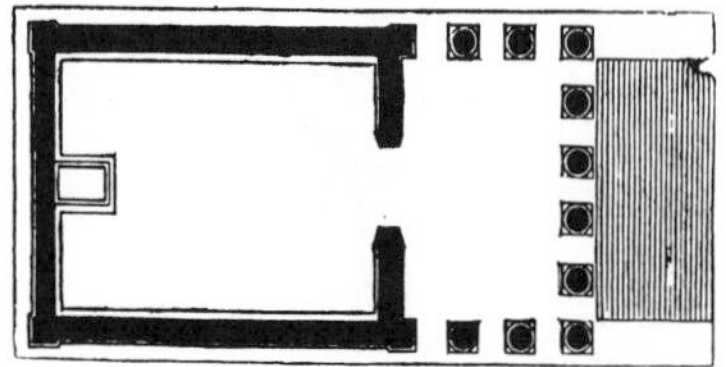

plan of a prostyle temple

prothesis In a Greek church, a chapel beside the sanctuary, usually on the north side of the bema.

prothyris In ancient Greek architecture, a **crossbeam.**

prothyron In an ancient Greek house, an entrance vestibule.

prothyron

proto-Doric Of a style apparently introductory to the Doric style.

proto-Ionic Of a style apparently introductory to the Ionic style.

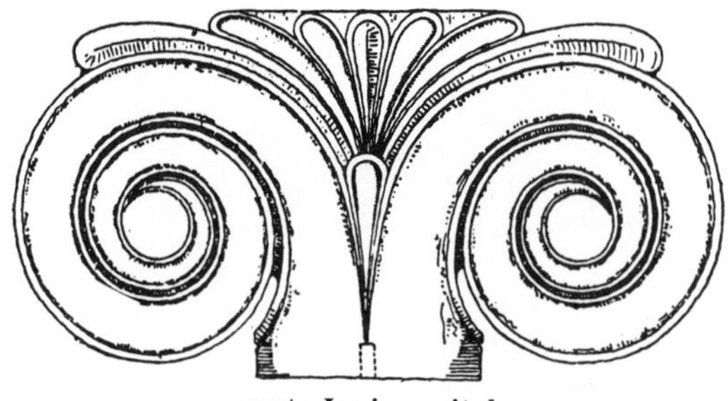

proto-Ionic capital

protome, protoma In classical architecture and derivatives, a projecting half figure, animal or human, used in a decorative scheme.

prutaneion See **prytaneum.**

prytaneum **1.** A public hall in ancient Greek states and cities where public officials received and entertained distinguished guests, honored citizens of high public merit, etc. **2.** In many ancient Greek towns, a public building consecrated to Hestia and containing the State hearth.

pseudisodomum In Greek or Roman masonry, ashlar of regular cut stone in which the heights of the courses are not uniform.

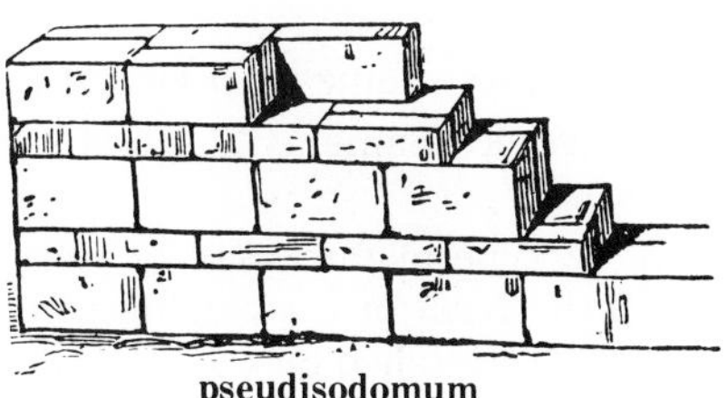

pseudisodomum

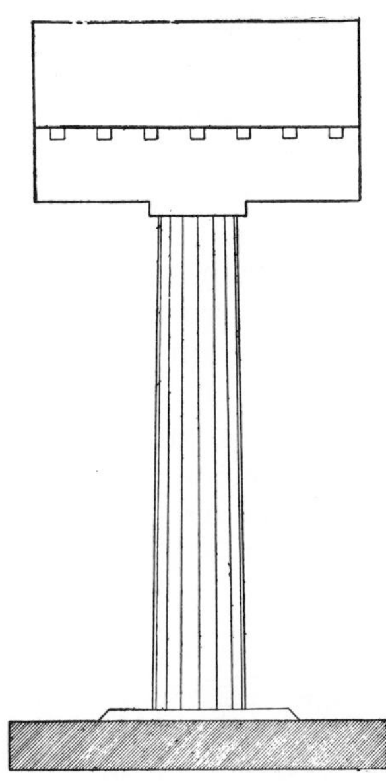

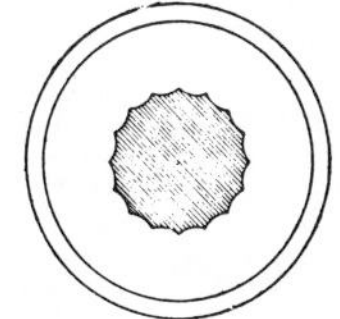

proto-Doric column, Beni Hasan, Egypt (2130–1785 B.C.)

pseudodipteral In classical architecture, having an arrangement of columns similar to the dipteral, but with the essential difference of the omission of the inner row, thus leaving a wide passage around the cella.

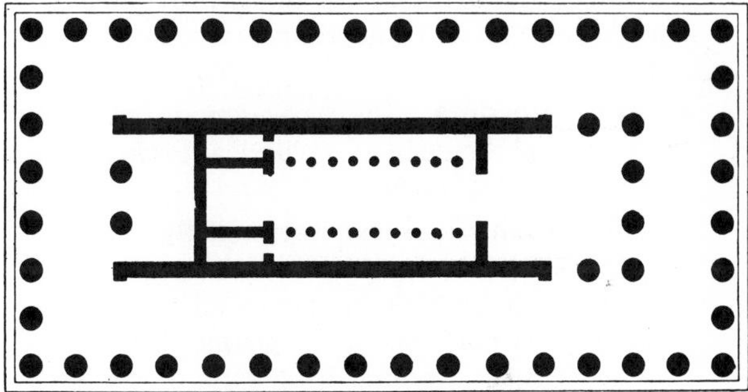

pseudodipteral temple, Selinus

pseudoperipteral Describing a classical temple or other building having columns all the way around, those on the flanks and rear being engaged, not freestanding.

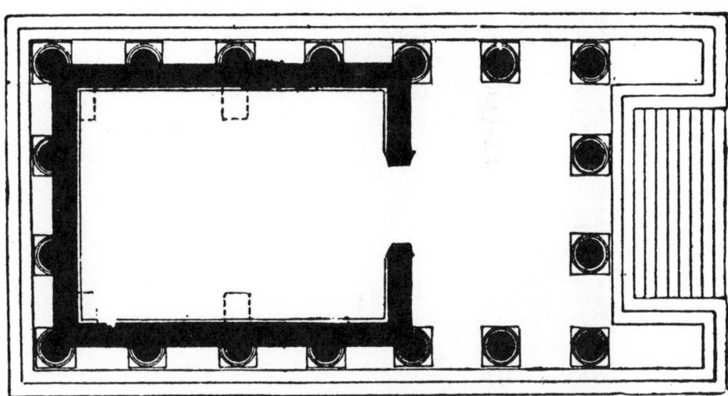

pseudoperipteral Temple of Fortuna Virilis, Rome (c. 40 B.C.)

pseudoperipteral Choragic Monument of Lysicrates, Athens (334 B.C.)

pseudoprostyle In Classical architecture, same as **prostyle** but without a **pronaos,** the columns of the portico being set less than the width of an intercolumniation from the front wall, or being actually engaged in it.

pseudothyrum A secret door, providing ingress and egress to a premise without being observed.

pteron, pteroma The passageway between the walls of the cella of a classical temple and the columns of the peristyle.

pueblo Communal dwelling, usually of stone or adobe, built by the Pueblo Indians of southwestern U.S.A.; built in excavated hollows in the faces of cliffs or on the plains, valleys, or mesas. Usually entered by means of ladders.

pulpit An elevated enclosed stand in a church in which the preacher stands.

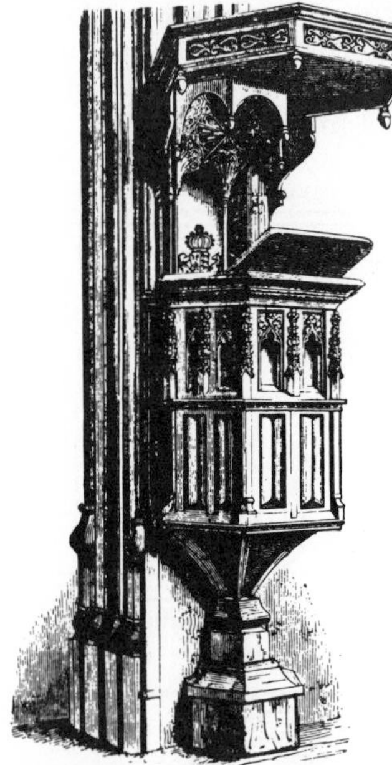

pulpit, Fotheringhay, Northamptonshire (1440)

pulpitum **1.** In a Roman theatre, the part of the stage adjacent to the orchestra; corresponds to the **logeion** of a Greek theatre. **2.** The **tribune,** 1 of an orator. **3.** A lectern in a church. **4.** In a large church, a screen which provides structural support for the gallery between the nave and the ritual choir.

pulvinarium A room in an ancient Roman temple in which was set out the couch *(pulivar)* for the gods at a special religious feast (the feast of the lectisternium).

pulvinated, pillowed Cushion-shaped, bulging out, as in the convex profile of the frieze in some Ionic orders.

pulvinus **1.** The baluster at the side of an Ionic capital. **2.** An **impost block,** a **dosseret.**

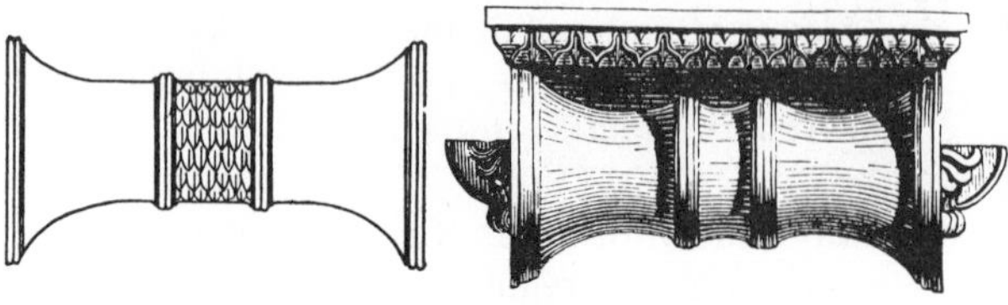

pulvinus,1 examples

pumpkin dome Same as **melon dome.**

punched work Same as **broached work.** Also see **broach,** 1.

punkah A type of fan (used in Asia, esp. in India) in the form of a swinging screen; consists of cloth stretched on a rectangular frame, hung from the ceiling and kept in motion by a cord pulled by a servant.

pura **1.** In Bali, a terraced sanctuary consisting of three courts enclosed by walls, connected by richly decorated gates; symbolizes **meru,** the "world mountain." **2.** A house, village, or town in Bali.

purlin, purline A piece of timber laid horizontally on the **principal rafters** of a roof to support the common rafters on which the roof covering is laid.

puteal **1.** A circular stone enclosure, usually surrounding the mouth of a well to prevent people from falling into it. **2.** More rarely, a similar wall constructed around a spot struck by lightning.

puteal,2

puteus **1.** In ancient Roman construction, an opening or manhole in an aqueduct. **2.** A well dug in the ground and supplied from its own spring of water. **3.** A fountain in an ancient Roman house.

puteus,1

舗地 **pu ti** Stone or tile paving, in various patterns, in traditional Chinese architecture.

putti (pl. of *putto*) In Renaissance architecture and derivatives, a decorative sculpture or painting representing chubby, usually naked infants.

putti

Puuc style A style of **Maya architecture** centered in the Puuc hills of western Yucatán (Mexico), ca. 600–950 A.D. The free-standing buildings had façades which were separated into an upper section and a lower section by moldings; the lower section usually was faced with a plain limestone veneer; the upper section was highly decorative, with a mosaic of latticework, frets, undulating sky serpents, stylized rain-god masks, and occasionally stylized replicas of native huts. Among the Puuc innovations were entrance columns with a square capital, stepped pyramids (often with an interior chamber), and monumental arches.

puzzolano Same as **pozzolan.**

pycnostyle See **intercolumniation.**

pylon Monumental gateway to an Egyptian temple, consisting of a pair of tower structures with slanting walls flanking the entrance portal.

pylon: Temple of Edfu, Upper Egypt; a pair of obelisks stand in front of the pylon (257–37 B.C.)

pyramid A massive funerary structure of stone or brick with a square base and four sloping triangular sides meeting at the apex; used mainly in ancient Egypt. In Central America stepped pyramids formed the bases of temples; in India some temples had the shape of truncated pyramids. Also see **Great Pyramid** and **step pyramid.**

pyramidal hipped roof Same as **pavilion roof, 1.**

pyramid city A city built near a pyramid to house its workers, servants, and priests.

pyramidion A small pyramid, such as the cap of an obelisk.

pyramid roof A roof which has four slopes terminating at a peak.

pyriform Same as **periform.**

pyxis, pyx Same as **pixis.**

qa'a Same as **ka'a.**

qala'a See **kal'a.**

qasr See **kasr.**

qibla See **kiblah.**

quadra **1.** A square frame or border enclosing a bas-relief. **2.** The **plinth** of a podium. **3.** Any small molding of plain or square section, as one of the fillets above or below the scotia of an Ionic base.

quadrangle, quad **1.** A rectangular courtyard or grassy area enclosed by buildings or a building. Most often used in connection with academic or civic building groupings. **2.** Buildings forming a quadrangle.

quadratura In Baroque interiors and derivatives, painted architecture, often continuing the three-dimensional trim, executed by specialists in calculated perspective.

quadrel A square tile or the like; a **quarrel.**

quadrifores ianuae Ancient Roman doors with leaves hinged like shutters.

quadrifrons **1.** Having four fronts or faces looking in four directions. **2.** Same as **tetrapylon, 2.**

quadriga In classical ornamentation and derivatives, the representation of a chariot drawn by four horses, i.e., a royal or divine accouterment. Also see **triga, biga.**

quadripartite Divided by the system of construction employed into four compartments, as a vault.

quadripartite vault A groined vault over a rectangular area, the area defined by ribs on each side and divided into four parts by intersecting diagonals.

quadriporticus An **atrium** which is nearly square and surrounded by colonnaded porticoes.

quadrivium An open space where streets or roads intersect; a place where streets go in four directions.

quadrifrons: base of a pillar in Cambodia

ancient Roman quadrifrons

quadripartite vault

quarrel A small piece of glass or tile, usually square- or diamond-shaped; often set diagonally.

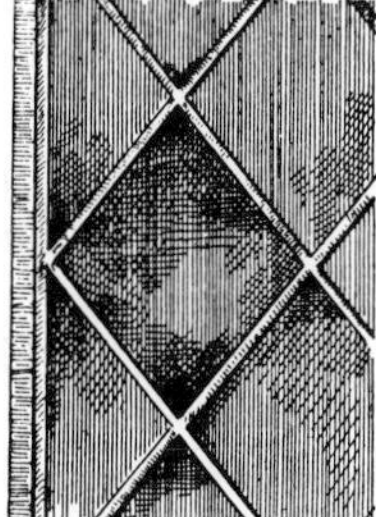

quarrel

quarry-faced Descriptive of the freshly split face of ashlar, as it comes from the quarry, squared off only for the joints; usually used in massive masonry work.

quarry-faced masonry

quarterpace, quarterpace landing, quarter-space landing A stair landing, often square in plan, between two flights which make a right-angle (90°) turn.

quarter round A convex molding the profile of which is exactly or nearly a quarter of a circle.

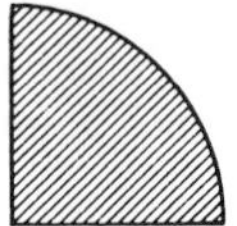

quarter round

quatrefoil A four-lobed pattern divided by **cusps;** also see **foil.**

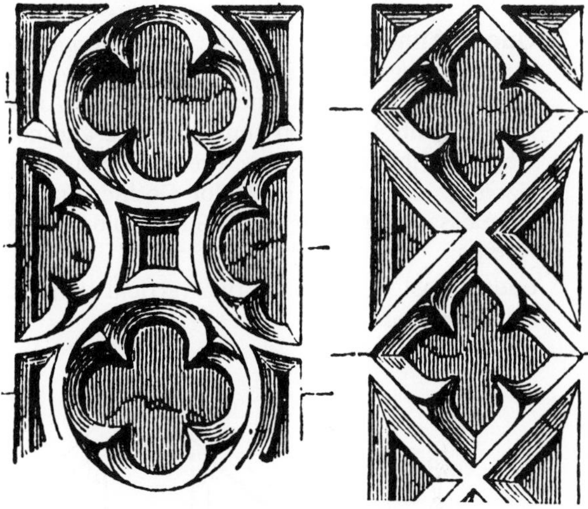

quatrefoils, King's College Chapel, Cambridge (1446–1515)

quatrefoils from the portal of Amiens Cathedral, France (13th cent.)

Quattrocento architecture Renaissance architecture of the 15th cent. in Italy.

qubba Same as **kubba.**

Queen Anne arch An arch over the triple opening of the so-called Venetian or Palladian window, flat over the narrow side lights, round over the larger central opening.

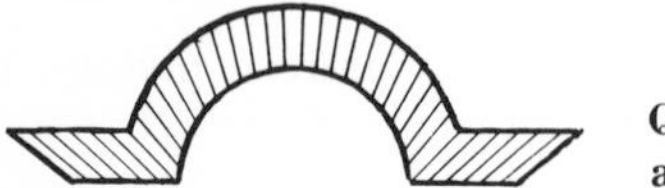

Queen Anne arch

Queen Anne style Eclectic style of domestic architecture of the 1870s and 1880s in England and the U.S.A.; misnamed after Queen Anne, but actually based on country-house and cottage Elizabethan architecture. It is characterized by a blending of Tudor Gothic, English Renaissance and, in the U.S.A., Colonial elements.

queen post One of the two vertical supports in a **queen-post truss.**

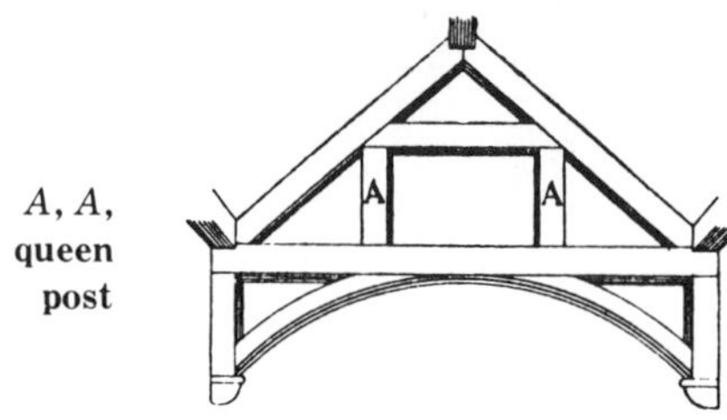

A, A, queen post

queen-post roof A roof supported by two queen posts.

queen-post truss, queen truss A roof truss having two vertical posts between the rafters and the tie beam; the upper ends of the vertical posts are connected by a **straining piece,** 1 (such as a tie rod or cable).

queen rod, queen bolt A metal rod which serves as a **queen post.**

queen truss See **queen-post truss.**

quincunx An arrangement of elements so that four are symmetrically placed around a central one.

quine Same as **quoin.**

quinquefoil, quintefoil See **cinquefoil.**

quire, quier Same as **choir.**

Queen Anne house in the U.S.A.

quirk An indentation separating one element from another, as between moldings, or between the abacus and echinus of a Doric capital.

quirk bead, bead and quirk, quirked bead **1.** A bead with a quirk on one side only, as on the edge of a board. **2.** A recessed **bead** which is flush with the adjoining surface and separated from it by a quirk on each side. Also called **flush bead.** **3.** A **return bead,** in which the bead is at a corner with quirks at either side at right angles to each other. **4.** A bead with a quirk on its face.

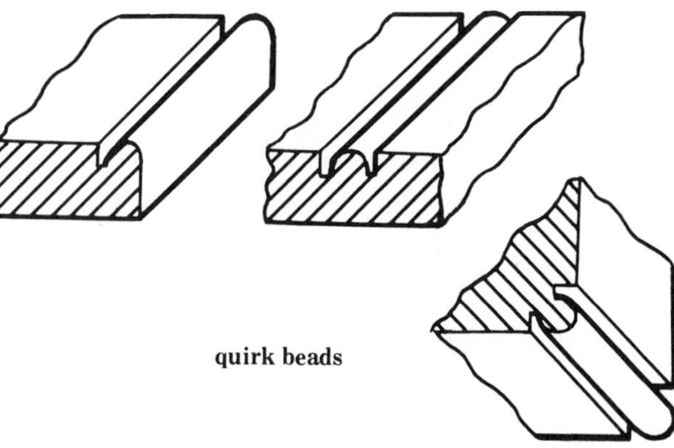

quirk beads

quirk molding, quirked molding A molding characterized by a sudden and sharp return from its extreme projection or set-off and made prominent by a quirk running parallel to it.

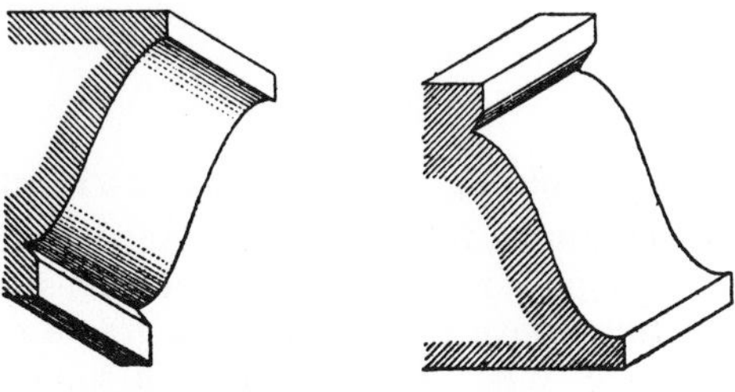
quirked cyma recta

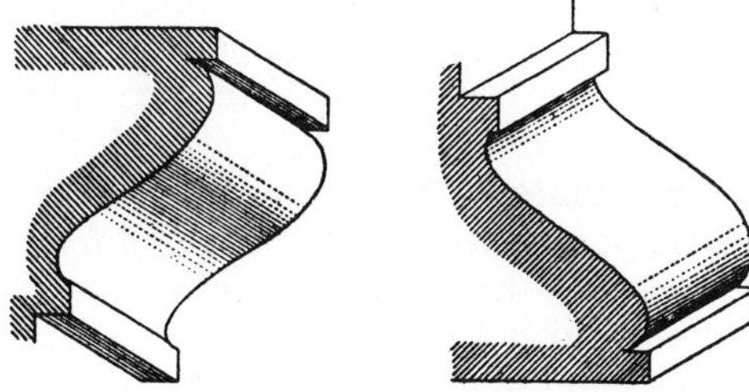
quirked cyma reversa

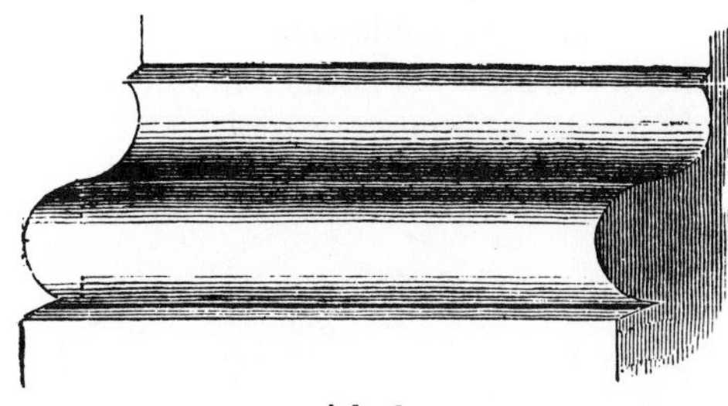
quirked ogee

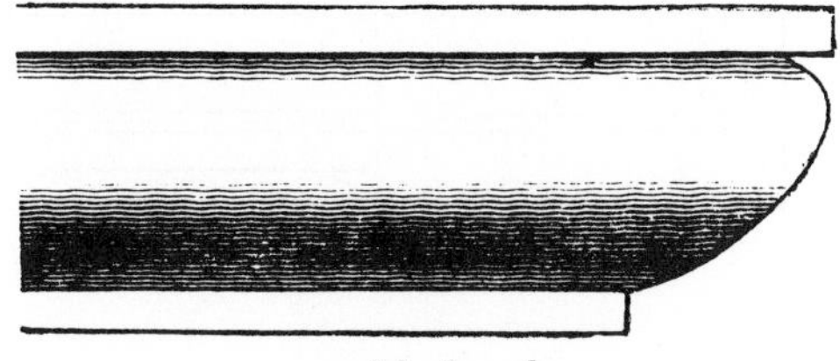
quirked ovolo

quoin, coign, coin In masonry, a hard stone or brick used, with similar ones, to reinforce an external corner or edge of a wall or the like; often distinguished decoratively from adjacent masonry; may be imitated in non-load-bearing materials.

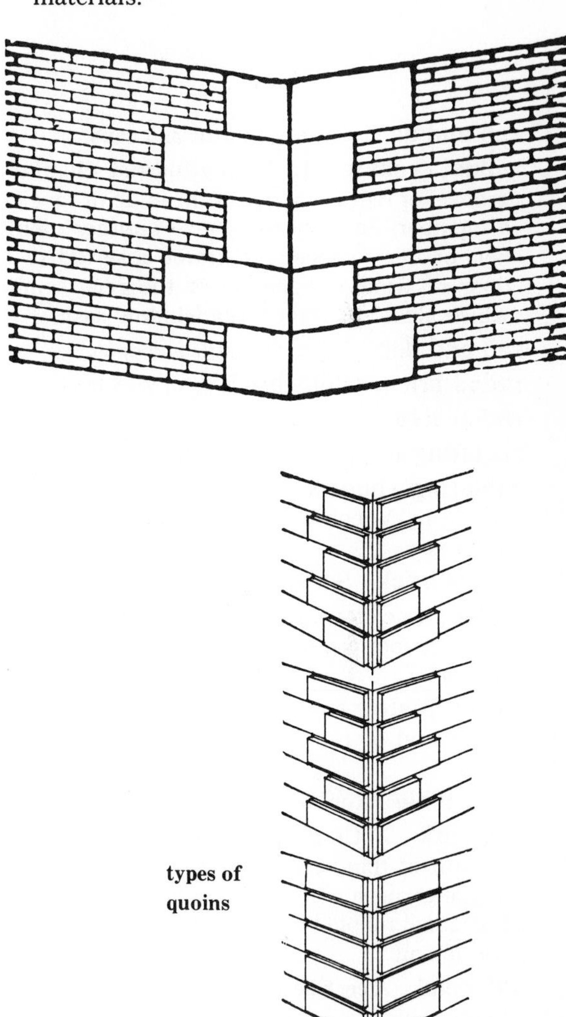
types of quoins

quoin header A quoin which is a header in the face of a wall and a stretcher in the face of the return wall.

quoining Any architectural members which form a **quoin.**

quoin post Same as **heelpost, 2.**

quoin stone A **quoin.**

rab and dab Same as **wattle and daub.**

rabbet, rebate 1. A longitudinal channel, groove, or recess cut out of the edge or face of a member; esp. one to receive another member, or one to receive a frame inserted in a door or window opening, or the recess into which glass is installed in a window sash.

rad and dab Same as **wattle and daub.**

radial brick, radius brick An **arch brick.**

radial step Same as **winder.**

radiating brick An **arch brick.**

radiating chapels Chapels projecting radially from the curve of an ambulatory or rarely of an apse.

radius brick See **arch brick.**

rafter One of a series of inclined members to which a roof covering is fixed. Also see **common rafter.**

rafter plate A **plate,** 1, which supports the lower end of rafters and to which they are fixed.

rag rubble Rubblework of thin small stones.

ragwork 1. Crude masonry, laid in a random pattern of thin-bedded, undressed stone (like flagging); most commonly set horizontally. 2. Polygonal rubble which is set on edge as exterior facing.

rail bead A **cock bead** when on a uniform continuous surface, and not at an angle, reveal, or the like.

rail fence A fence in which the rails are set into the posts; adjoining rails either butt against each other or overlap.

rainbow roof, whaleback roof A pitched roof whose slope on each side of the ridge is slightly convex.

rain leader See **downspout.**

rainwater head See **leader head.**

rainwater pipe A **downspout.**

raised molding Same as **bolection molding.**

raised panel, fielded panel A panel with the center portion thicker than the edges or projecting above the surrounding frame or wall surface. When exposed on both sides (as on both sides of a door), it is called a **double raised panel.**

raising piece A piece of timber laid on a brick wall, or on the top of posts or puncheons of a timber-framed house, to carry a beam or beams; a template.

raising plate A horizontal timber resting on a wall, or upon vertical timbers of a frame, and supporting the heels of rafters or other framework; also called a **wall plate.**

raked molding Same as **raking molding.**

raking Inclining; having a rake or inclination.

raking arch Same as **rampant arch.**

raking coping A coping set on an inclined surface, as at a gable end.

raking cornice A cornice following the slope of a gable, pediment, or roof.

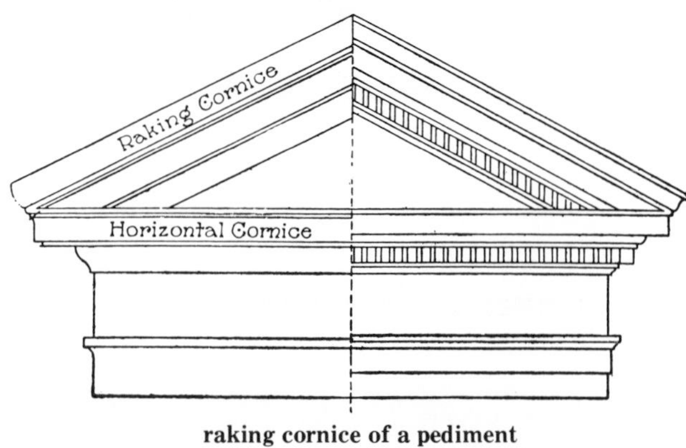

raking cornice of a pediment

raking course A course of bricks laid diagonally between face courses of a thick wall to strengthen it.

raking molding, raked molding **1.** Any molding adjusted at a slant, rake, or ramp. **2.** Any overhanging molding which has a rake or slope downward and outward.

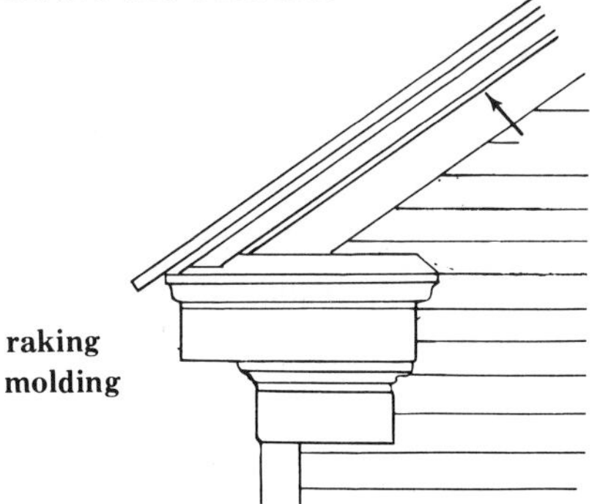

ramada **1.** In Spanish architecture and derivatives, a rustic arbor or similar structure. **2.** An open porch.

ramma In traditional Japanese architecture, a type of pierced decorative transom, varying from intricately carved to plain lattice, placed between the top of a sliding-door track and the ceiling. 欄間

rampart Earthen or masonry defense wall of a fortified site.

rampart with crenellated parapets

carved-wood ramma

rammed earth A material usually consisting of clay, sand, or other aggregate (such as sea shells) and water, which has been compressed and dried; used in building construction.

rampant arch, raking arch An arch in which the impost on one side is higher than that on the other.

rampant vault A continuous wagon vault, or a cradle vault, whose two abutments are located on an inclined plane, such as a vault supporting or forming the ceiling of a stairway.

rampant arch

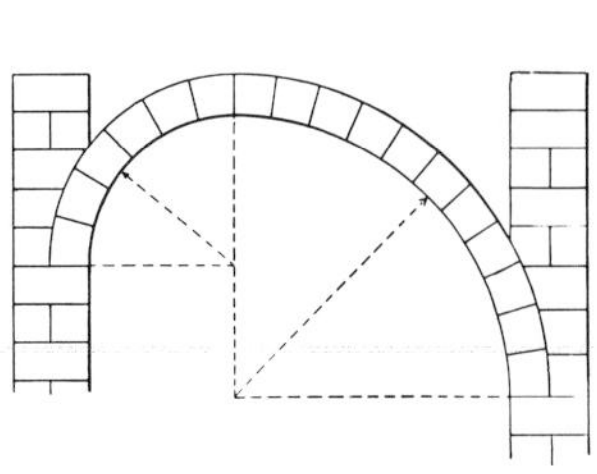

rampant vault

rand *(Brit.)* A border, or a fillet cut from a border in the process of straightening it.

random ashlar, random bond Ashlar masonry in which rectangular stones are set without continuous joints and appear to be laid without a drawn pattern, although the pattern actually may be repeated.

random ashlar

random bond See **random ashlar.**

random course One of a number of horizontal stone masonry courses which are of unequal height.

random range ashlar Same as **random work.**

random rubble Same as **rubblework.**

random work, broken ashlar, random range ashlar, random range work **1.** Random stonework. **2.** Masonry of rectangular stone not laid in regular courses, but broken up by the use of stones of different heights and widths, fitted closely.

random work, 1

range **1.** In masonry, a row or course, as of stone. **2.** A line of objects in direct succession, as a range of columns.

ranged rubble Same as **rubblework.**

range masonry, rangework See **coursed ashlar.**

rangework Same as **coursed ashlar.**

ranzumi See **kidan.**

ratha **1.** A shrine; a Hindu temple built to resemble a chariot. **2.** The vertical salient or recess of a **nagara** temple wall.

rauza In Mogul architecture, a mausoleum.

ravelin, demilune In fortifications, a projecting outwork forming a salient angle.

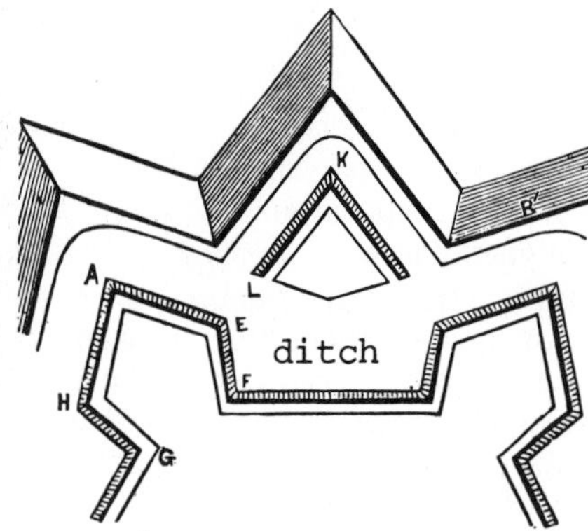

fortification system: *LKL'*, ravelin; *GHAEF*, bastion

Rayonnant style The middle phase of French Gothic architecture in the 13th and 14th cent., characterized by radiating lines of tracery.

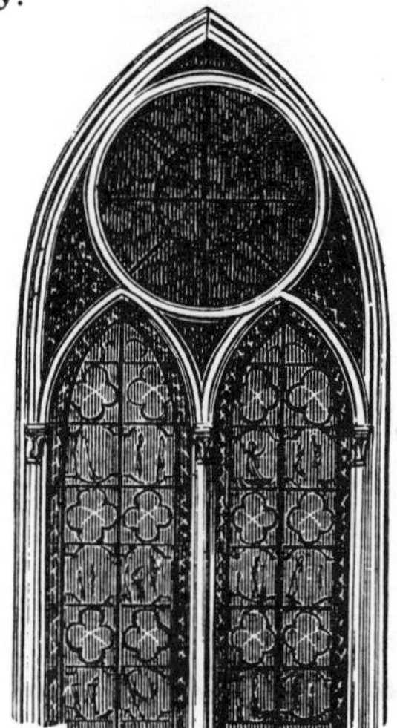

Rayonnant style

Rayonnant style

rear arch 1. An inner arch of an opening which is smaller in size than the external arch of the opening and may be different in shape. 2. See **arrière-voussure.**

rear vault 1. A small vault over the space between the tracery or glass of a window and the inner face of the wall. 2. An **arrière-voussure.**

rear vault,1

receptorium Same as **aspasticum.**

recessed arch An arch with a shorter radius set within another of the same shape.

recessed bead See **quirk bead, 2.**

Rectilinear style See **Perpendicular style.**

rectilinear tracery See **perpendicular tracery.**

rectory The residence of a rector.

redan A diminutive **ravelin.**

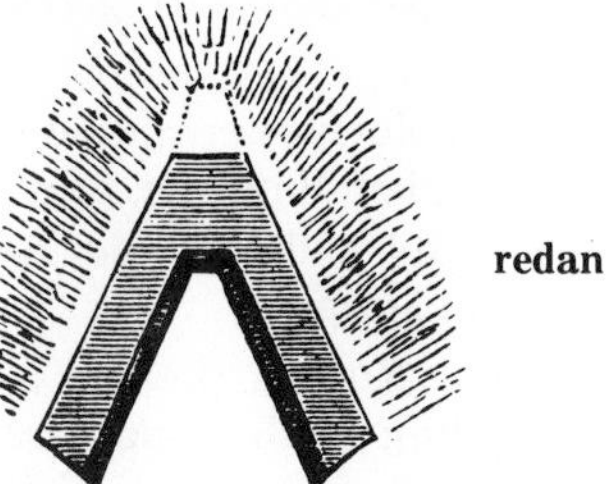
redan

redoubt A small fortification detached from the principal site.

reed 1. A small convex molding, usually one of several set close together to decorate a surface. 2. *(pl.)* Same as **reeding.** 3. A strawlike material prepared for thatching a roof.

reeding An ornament of adjacent, parallel, protruding, half-round moldings (reeds); the reverse of **fluting.** Also see **cabling.**

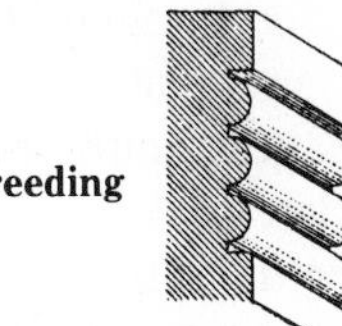
reeding

reel and bead See **bead and reel.**

refectory A hall in a convent, monastery, or public secular institution where meals are eaten.

refectory, Christ Church, Oxford

Régence style The decorative and elegant Rococo style flourishing under the regency of Philip of Orleans (1715–1723) during the minority of Louis XV.

Regency style The colorful neoclassic style, often combined with oriental motifs, prevalent in England between 1811 and 1830, during the Regency and reign of George IV.

regia On the ancient Roman theatre stage, the central door, leading to the palace of the main hero; the royal door.

reglet A fillet or small flat-faced projection, as used in a fret molding or to cover a joint between two boards.

regula **1.** In the Doric entablature, one of a series of short fillets beneath the taenia, each corresponding to a triglyph above. **2.** Any long straight piece of lath (either wood or metal) used in ancient Roman construction. **3.** A rule used by ancient carpenters and masons for drawing straight lines and making measurements.

regular coursed rubble Same as **coursed ashlar.**

reja A bronze or iron grill to guard a chapel or tomb in a Spanish church.

rekha The curved portion of a **sikhara.**

rekha-deul A square **sikhara** in a **nagara**-style temple.

relief **1.** Carving, chasing, or embossing raised above a background plane. Also see **bas-relief, high relief.** **2.** In general, the elevation or projection of part of a surface above some ground or datum plane.

relieve To lighten a color in order to reduce its intensity.

relieved work Ornamentation done in relief.

relieving arch A **discharging arch;** a **safety arch.**

relieving arch, wall of Pantheon, Rome

relievo Same as **relief,** 1.

relief from Pergamon: Hecate, Ares, and Giants

marble relief from Pharsalos, Greece

relief from Nimrud (ancient capital of Assyria)

Renaissance architecture The architectural style developed in early 15th cent. Italy during the rebirth *(rinascimento)* of classical art and learning. It succeeded the Gothic as the style dominant in all of Europe after the mid-16th cent., and evolved through the Mannerist phase into Baroque and in the early 17th cent. into classicism. Initially characterized by the use of the classical orders, round arches, and symmetrical composition.

Italian Renaissance pilaster capital

Santa Maria dei Miracoli, Venice (1481–1489)

Old Library of St. Mark, Venice (1536–1553)

Renaissance architecture

right: **part of the façade of the Tiene Palace, Vicenza (1556)**

below: **interior view of St. Peter's Cathedral, Rome, looking toward the high altar (1506–1629)**

Pavillon Richelieu, Louvre, Paris (1546–1654)

right: **part of the Tuileries, Paris (begun 1564)**

below: **frieze in Louvre, Paris (mid-16th cent.)**

rendering 1. A coat of plaster directly on an interior wall or stucco on an exterior wall. 2. A perspective or elevation drawing of a project or portion thereof with artistic delineation of materials, shades, and shadows.

rendu An architectural rendering of a design problem.

repagula, claustra, obices The fastenings of an ancient Roman door; commonly consisted of bars or bolts which could be slid or rotated into position to secure the door.

replum An upright rail (from lintel to sill) which divides a doorframe in two parts; used with a door having two leaves, which close against it.

repoussé Raised in relief by embossing or by beating on the underside with a hammer.

reprise In masonry, the return of a molding in an internal angle.

rere-arch Same as **rear arch.**

reredorter A privy behind a monastery or convent.

reredos An ornamental screen or wall at the back of an altar.

reredos, St. Thomas's Church, Salisbury (c. 1450)

reredosse In an ancient hall, the open hearth upon which a fire was lit, immediately under the **louver, 2**.

resaunt Same as **ressant.**

resonators See **golosniki.**

respond A support, usually a corbel or pilaster, affixed to a wall to receive one end of an arch, a groin, or a vault rib.

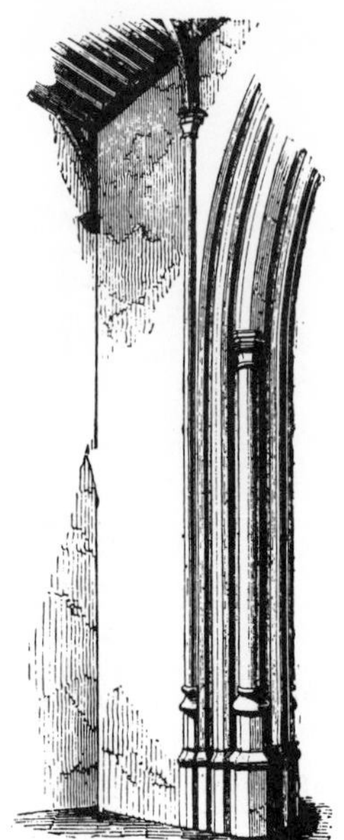

respond

ressant, ressaut 1. Medieval name for **ogee, 2.** 2. A projection of any member or part from another, such as a projecting portion of a molding. 3. A **roll molding.**

ressault See **ressant.**

restoration 1. The process of returning an object, material, or building as nearly as possible to its original form and condition. 2. A replica of a building, or portion thereof, designed to indicate the original appearance.

retable A decorative screen set up above and behind an altar, generally forming an architectural frame to a picture, bas-relief, or mosaic.

retaining wall A wall, either freestanding or laterally braced, that bears against an earth or other fill surface and resists lateral and other forces from the material in contact with the side of the wall.

retaining wall supported by buttresses at *a*

reticulata fenestra A lattice window; one protected by small bars of wood or metal, crossing each other in a reticulated pattern.

reticulated Covered with netted lines; netted; having distinct lines crossing in a network.

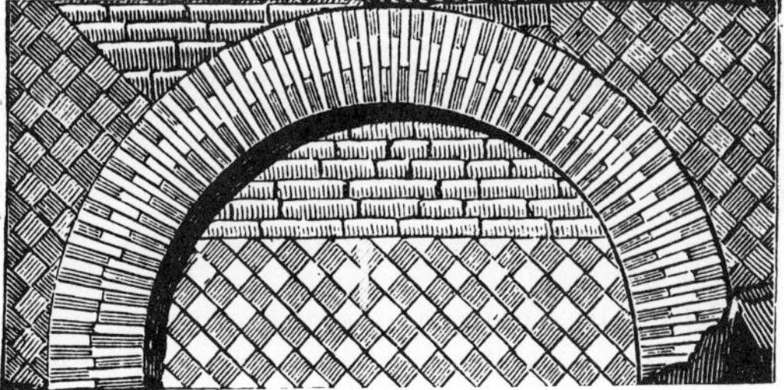

reticulated brickwork

reticulated molding A molding decorated with fillets interlaced to form a network or mesh-like appearance.

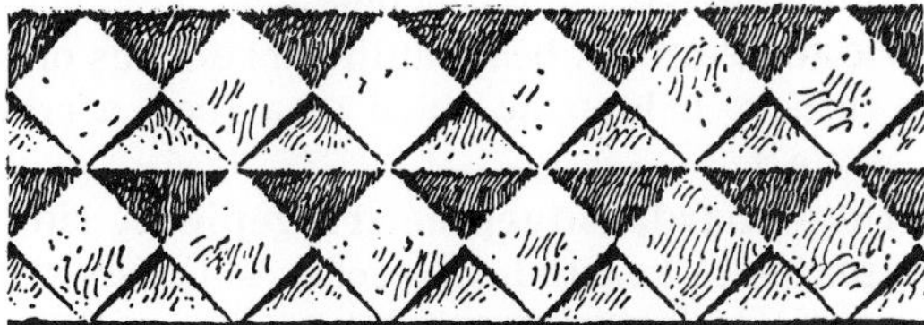

reticulated molding: wall in Old Sarum, Wiltshire

Norman reticulated molding

reticulated tracery Tracery whose openings are repetitive like the meshes of a net.

reticulated work Same as **opus reticulatum.**

reticulatum opus Same as **opus reticulatum.**

retrochoir A chapel behind the high altar of a church but in front of the Lady chapel if there is one.

return The continuation of a molding, projection, member, or cornice, or the like, in a different direction, usually at a right angle.

return bead The continuation of a bead in a different direction, usually at a right angle.

returned end The end of a molding having a shape which is the same as the profile of the molding.

returned molding A molding continued in a different direction from its main direction.

returned molding, St. Martin's, Canterbury

returned stalls Stalls in a church which run along the long axis of a cruciform church and which are returned transversely at the western end of the choir.

revalé A stone molding, carved in place.

reveal The side of an opening for a door or window, doorway, or the like, between the doorframe or window frame and the outer surface of the wall; where the opening is not filled with the door or window, the whole thickness of the wall.

reveal lining Moldings or any other finish applied over a reveal.

revel Same as **reveal.**

reversed zigzag molding A common Norman molding consisting of a series of zigzags.

reversed zigzag molding

revestry Old form of **vestry.**

revetment **1.** Any facing of stone, metal, or wood over a less attractive or less durable substance or construction. **2.** A retaining wall or breast wall; a facing on an embankment to prevent erosion.

Revival architecture The use of older styles in new architectural movements, most often referring to the **Gothic Revival** and the **Classic Revival,** but also applicable to the Romanesque, Egyptian, Etruscan, Colonial, and other revivals of the late 18th and 19th cent.

rez-de-chaussée The ground floor of a building.

rib 1. A curved structural member supporting any curved shape or panel. 2. Moldings which project from the surface and separate the various roof or ceiling panels.

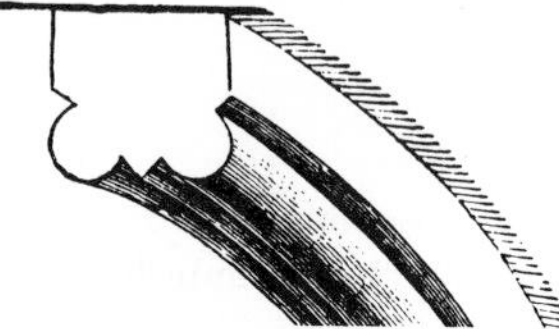

rib,1 of an arch

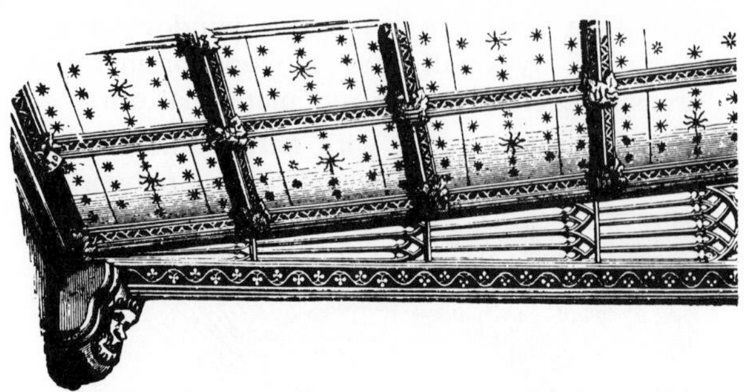

ribs,2 dividing a ceiling into panels

riband, ribband Same as **ribbon strip.**

ribat In **Muslim architecture,** a frontier garrison or fortified barracks.

ribbed arch An arch composed of individual curved members or ribs.

ribbed fluting 1. *(Brit.)* Flutes alternating with fillets. 2. See **cabled fluting.**

ribbed vault A vault in which the ribs support, or seem to support, the web of the vault.

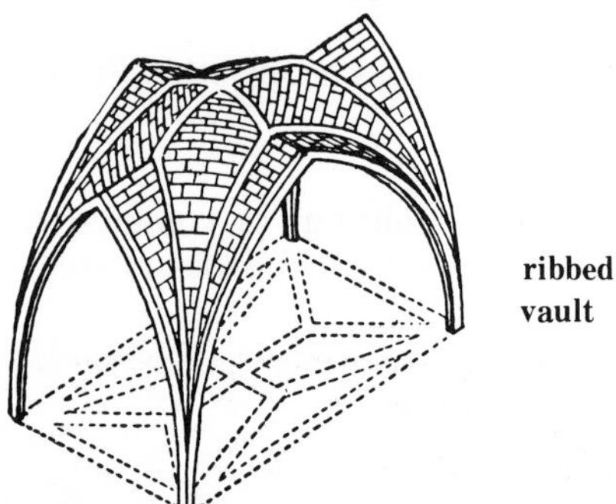

ribbed vault

ribbing An assemblage or arrangement of ribs, as timberwork sustaining a vaulted ceiling.

ribbon 1. A **ribbon strip.** 2. In stained glass work or the like, a strip or bar of lead to hold the edge of the glass. Also called a **came.**

ribbon strip, girt strip, ledger board, riband, ribband A wood strip or board let into the studs to add support for the ends of the joists.

Richardsonian Romanesque The massive style of Romanesque Revival in the U.S.A. as practiced by Henry Hobson Richardson (1838–1886) and his followers, characterized by heavy arches, rusticated masonry walls, and dramatic asymmetrical effects, esp. in public architecture.

riddle In a church, one of the pair of curtains enclosing an altar on the north and south; often hung from rods driven into the wall.

ridel Same as **riddle.**

ridge 1. The horizontal line at the junction of the upper edges of two sloping roof surfaces. 2. The internal angle or nook of a vault.

ridge batten Same as **ridge roll.**

ridge beam A beam at the upper ends of the rafters, below the ridge of a roof; a **crown plate, 2.**

ridgeboard, ridgepole, ridgepiece, ridgeplate A longitudinal member at the apex of a roof which supports the upper ends of the rafters.

ridgecap, ridge capping, ridge covering Any covering (such as metal, wood, shingle, etc.) used to cover the ridge of a roof.

ridge course The last or top course of roofing tiles, roll roofing, or shingles.

ridge covering See **ridgecap.**

ridge crest The ornamentation of the ridge of a roof.

ridge fillet A fillet between two depressions, as between two flutes of a column.

ridgepole See **ridgeboard.**

ridge rib 1. A horizontal rib marking the crown of a compartment of vaulting, characteristic of English Gothic architecture from the early 13th cent. on, but occasionally found on the Continent. 2. A **rib** which follows the ridge of a vault.

ridge roll 1. A wood strip, rounded on top, which is used to finish the ridge of a roof; often covered with lead sheeting. 2. A metal or tile covering which caps the ridge of a roof; also called a **hip roll.**

ridge roof A pitched roof; the rafters meet at the apex of a ridge; the end view is that of a **gable roof.**

ridge tile, crown tile A tile which is curved in section, often decorative, used to cover the ridge of a roof.

ridging The covering of the ridge of a roof.

riding house, riding school A structure specifically designed for teaching the skill of horse riding.

rinceau In classical architecture and derivatives, an ornamental band of undulant and recurving plant motifs.

rinceau

ring course In an arch, an outer course of stone or brick.

ringed column See **banded column.**

ringhiera In Italian Medieval architecture, a balcony, on the front of the town hall, from which speeches and decrees were read.

ring stone One of the stones of an arch which show on the face of the wall, or the end of the arch; one of the voussoirs of the face forming the archivolt.

Rio Bec style A style of **Maya architecture,** ca. 550–900, transitional between that of Tikal and Uxmal; characterized by lavishly decorated structures flanked by soaring nonfunctional temple pyramids with steeply raked steps; typical sites are Rio Bec and Xpuhil in southeast Campeche, Mexico.

riprap **1.** Irregularly broken and random-sized large pieces of quarry rock; used for foundations and revetments. **2.** A foundation or parapet of stones thrown together without any attempt at regular structural arrangement.

risen molding Same as **bolection molding.**

rising arch An arch having a **springing line** which is not horizontal.

riding house

riwaq A colonnaded or arcaded hall of a mosque.

riznitsa A **sacristy** in a Russian Orthodox church.

robur The lower chamber in an underground dungeon of the ancient Romans, where capital punishment was carried out.

robur in ancient Rome

rocaille A scroll ornament of the 18th cent., esp. during the reign of Louis XV, combining forms apparently based on those of water-worn rocks, plants, and shells; characteristic of the Rococo period.

rock-cut Said of a temple or tomb excavated in native rock without the aid of masonry, or with but little masonry; usually presents an architectural front with dark interior chambers, of which sections are supported by masses of stone left in the form of solid pillars.

rock-faced Said of the natural face of a stone used in building, or one dressed to resemble a natural face.

rock rash A patchwork appliqué of oddly shaped stone slabs; used on edge as a veneer; often further embellished with cobbles or geodes.

rockwork 1. **Quarry-faced** masonry. 2. Stonework in which the surface is left irregular and rough.

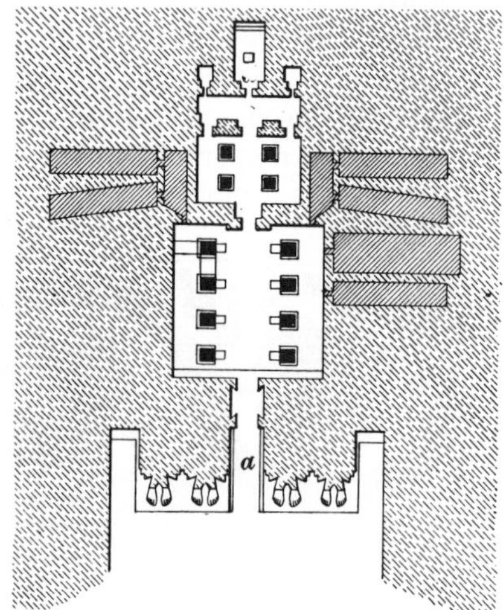

rock-cut temple at Ipsamboul (Abu Simbel), Egypt (c. 1301 B.C.); *left*: section; *right*: plan

rock-cut tomb at Antiphellus, Lycia

rock-cut Lycian tomb

Rococo A style of architecture and decoration, primarily French in origin, which represents the final phase of the Baroque around the middle of the 18th cent.; characterized by profuse, often semiabstract ornamentation and lightness of color and weight.

right: **Rococo decoration**

salon in the Palace of the Archbishop of Speyer, Bruchsal, Germany (c. 1760)

rode Middle English form of **rood.**

Rokuonji See **Kinkakuji.**

roll-and-fillet molding A molding of nearly circular cross section with a narrow band or fillet on its face.

roll-and-fillet molding

Roman arch in Castor, Northamptonshire (now destroyed)

roll billet molding A common Norman molding consisting of a series of **billets,** 1 which are cylindrical in cross section, usually staggered in alternate rows.

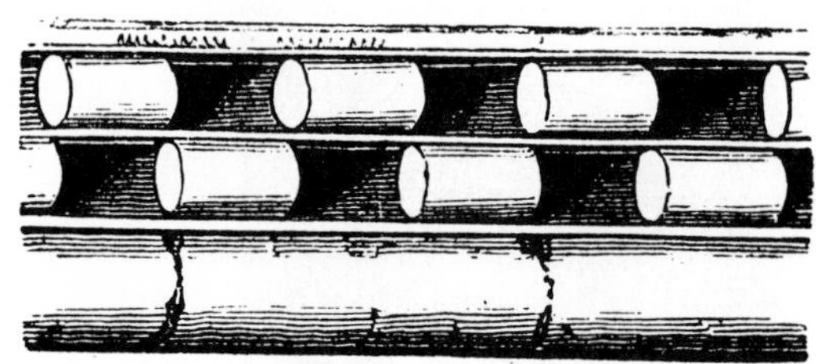

roll billet molding

roll molding Any convex, rounded molding, which has (wholly or in part) a cylindrical form.

rollock Same as **rowlock.**

rolock See **rowlock.**

rolok See **rowlock.**

Roman arch A semicircular arch. If built of stone, all units are wedge-shaped; the usual arch in Roman architecture.

Roman brick See **later.**

Roman bronze A copper-zinc alloy to which a small quantity of tin has been added to give it greater corrosion resistance and hardness.

Roman cement A quick-setting natural cement; a hydraulic cement or hydraulic lime; unknown to the early Romans.

Roman arch construction

Romanesque architecture The style emerging in Western Europe in the early 11th cent., based on Roman and Byzantine elements, characterized by massive articulated wall structures, round arches, and powerful vaults, and lasting until the advent of Gothic architecture in the middle of the 12th cent.

Cathedral of Speyer, Germany: interior (1165–1190)

"La Trinité" Abbaye aux Dames, Caens (1062–c. 1110)

Great doorway of the Abbey Church of Vézelay, France (12th cent.)

Romanesque capital, Collegiate Church, Aschaffenburg

Romanesque tympanum border, Worms Cathedral (1110)

Romanesque Revival The reuse in the second half of the 19th cent. of massive Romanesque forms, characterized by the round arch.

Roman foot See **pes.**

Roman house The ancient Roman dwelling consisted of a quadrangular court (**atrium**) which was entered by the door of the house and which served as the common meeting place for the family. An opening (**compluvium**) to the sky provided light and served as a chimney and as an inlet for rain which fell into the **impluvium,** a tank sunk in the floor beneath. The **tablinum** served as the master's office. In some homes a garden surrounded by side buildings and covered colonnades was added at the back of the house; it was called the *peristylium* and usually was entered through corridors (**fauces**) located near the tablinum. Great houses had a kind of entrance hall (**vestibulum**) raised above the street and approached by stairs. In the ordinary house, there was only an indication of one; the door led directly into the **ostium,** which opened directly into the atrium. In later Roman houses, a second story became usual. As the dining room was generally in the upper story, all the rooms in the upper story were called **coenacula.** There were three-story houses in Rome as early as the end of the republic.

Roman mosaic A pavement that is **tessellated.**

Roman Revival See **Classic Revival.**

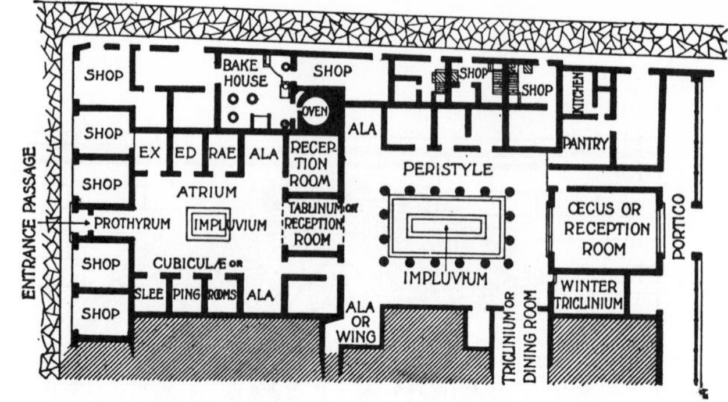

plan of Roman house in Pompeii

House of Sallust, Pompeii

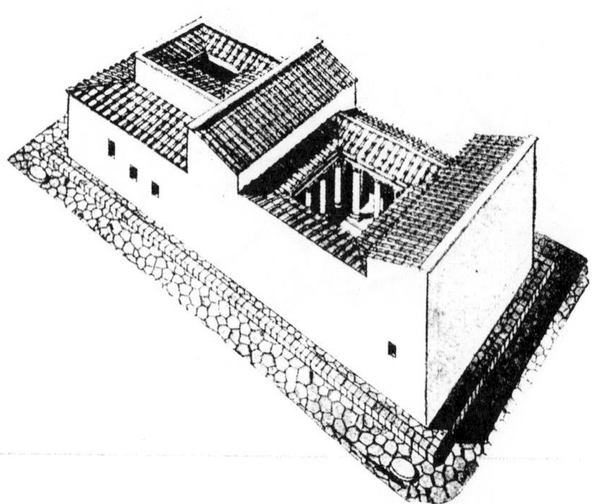

perspective view, Roman house in Pompeii

section through Roman house in Pompeii

Roman theatre An open-air theatre constructed by the ancient Romans; sometimes built on a hillside, but more often on level ground—usually with a richly decorated outer façade, with a colonnade gallery and vaulted entrances for the public. The **orchestra, 2** usually was a half-circle; behind it was a stage having a richly decorated proscenium and stage background. Also see **Greek theatre.**

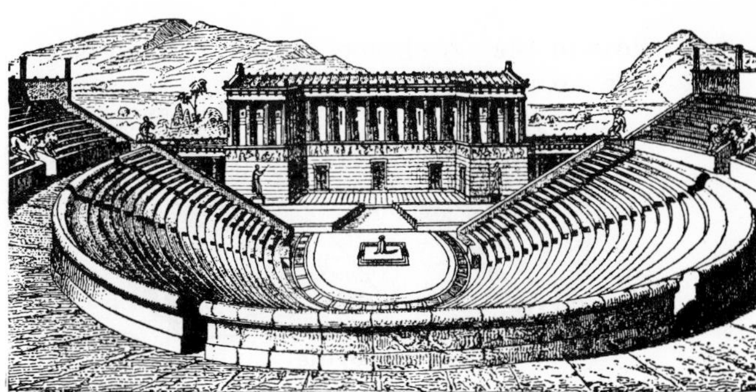

theatre at Segresta, restored view (100 B.C.)

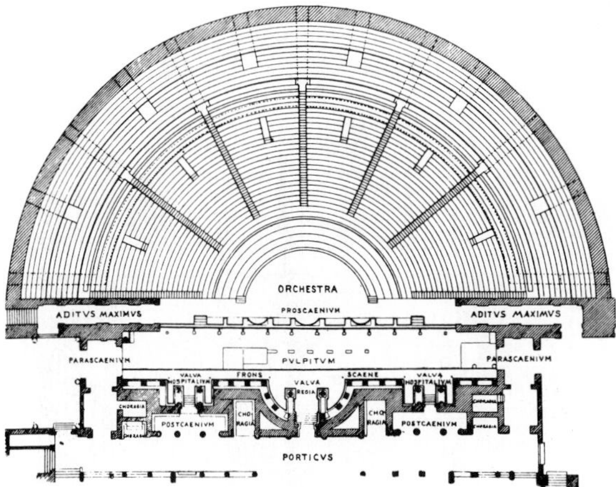

Roman theatre, Merida, Spain
(rebuilt by Hadrian c. 135 A.D.)

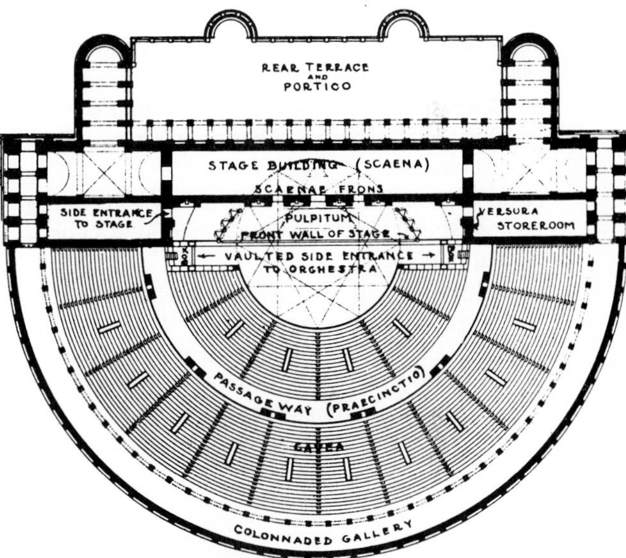

Theatre of Marcellus, reconstructed plan (c. 11 B.C.)

scaene of Roman theatre at Aspendos, Pamphylia, Asia Minor (c. 161-180 A.D.)

Roman tile A channel-shaped, tapered, single lap, roofing tile.

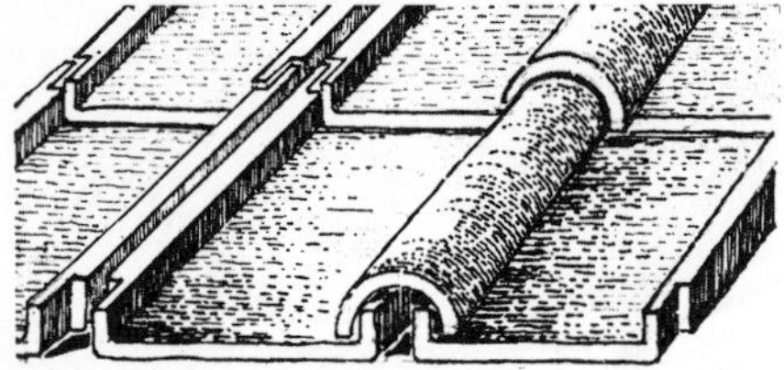

Roman tile

rondel A circular piece of window glass.

rood A large crucifix, esp. one set above the chancel entrance.

rood altar An altar standing against the nave side of a rood screen.

rood arch The central arch in a rood screen; rarely, the arch between nave and chancel over the rood.

rood beam A horizontal beam extending across the entrance to the chancel of a church to support the rood.

rood loft A gallery of a church where the crucifix (rood) and images of the Holy Trinity were placed; above the rood screen, it was reached by a staircase. From this location sermons were sometimes preached and the scripture read to the people assembled in the nave.

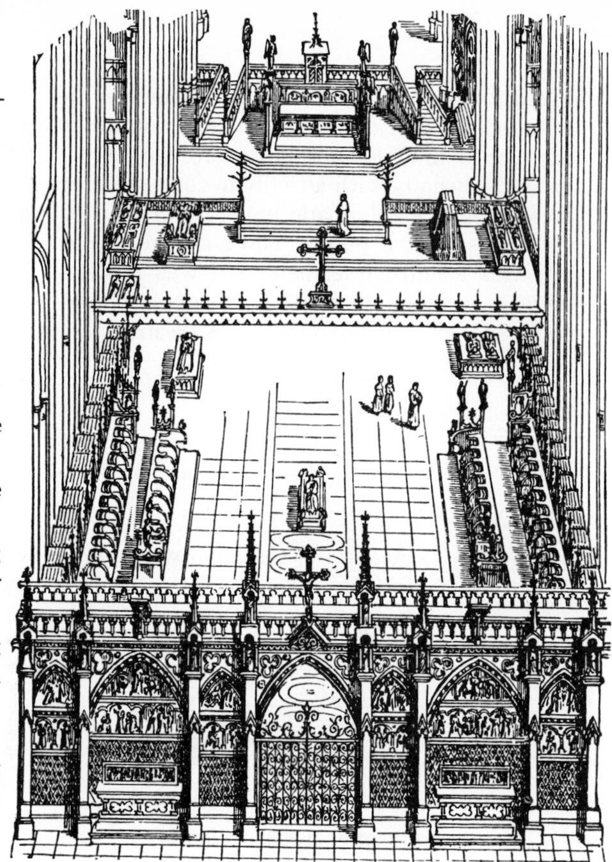

rood loft (now destroyed), Abbey of St. Denis (13th cent.)

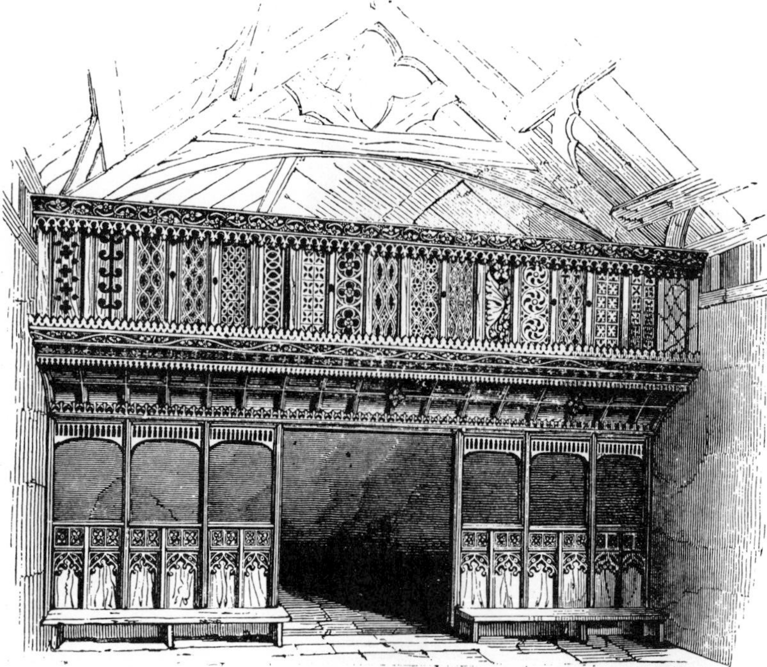

rood loft, Llanegrynn, Meriontshire (c. 1500)

rood screen A screen, open or partly closed, usually of carved wood or stone, separating the nave and chancel and intended to carry the large crucifix, or rood. Also see **jube.**

rood spire A spire over the crossing of the nave and transepts. Also see **flèche.**

rood stairs Stairs by which the rood loft is approached.

rood tower A tower built over the crossing and hence approximately above the rood.

rood spire

rood screen, Church of S. Madeleine, Troyes, France

roof The cover of a building, including the roofing and all other material and construction (such as supporting members) necessary to carry and maintain it on the walls or uprights.

typical basilican roof, Church of S. Miniato, Florence (1018 onward); a wooden gallery rests on tie beams, a detail of which is illustrated under tie beam

roof comb, roof crest A wall along the ridge of a roof; used to give an appearance of additional height.

roof crest See **roof comb.**

roof dormer Same as **dormer.**

roofed ingle A **chimney corner.**

roof gallery See **widow's walk.**

roof gutter See **gutter.**

roof plate A **wall plate** which receives the lower ends of the rafters of a roof.

roof principal A **roof truss.**

roof purlin Same as **purlin.**

roof tie **1.** A **collar beam.** **2.** A **tie beam.**

rooftree The **ridgeboard** of a roof.

roof truss A structural support for a roof.

hammer-beam roof, Trunch Church, Norfolk

roof with cambered cross beams carrying a system of braces and struts: hall of Malvern Abbey, Worcestershire (c. 1350)

collar-braced roof

tie beam roof, St. Mary's Church, Leicester

rope molding A bead or torus molding carved in imitation of a rope; also see **cabling.**

rosace See **rosette, 1.**

rose molding An ornament used esp. in Norman architecture, chiefly during its later and richer period.

rose nail A nail with a conical head which is hand-hammered into triangular facets.

rosette **1.** A round pattern with a carved or painted conventionalized floral motif; a **rosace.** **2.** A circular or oval decorative wood plaque used in joinery, such as one applied to a wall to receive the end of a stair rail. **3.** An ornamental nailhead or screwhead.

rosette, Temple of Jupiter Tonans, Rome

rosette, Forum of Nerva, Rome

rose molding

rose window, Catherine-wheel window, marigold window, wheel window A large, circular medieval window, containing tracery disposed in a radial manner.

rose window, Barfreston, Kent (c. 1180)

rostra The stage in the Roman Forum from which the orators addressed the people.

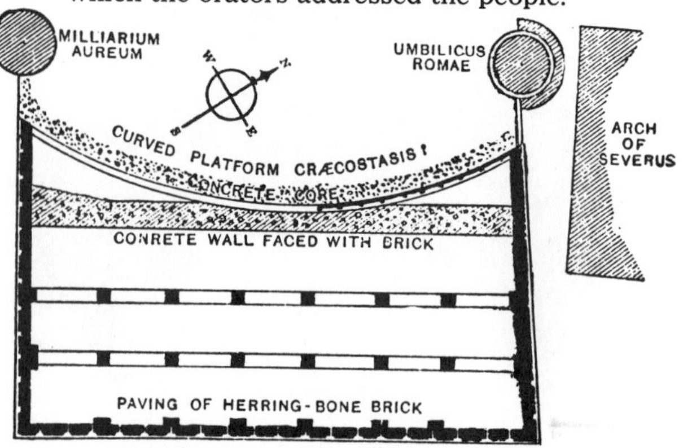

plan of rostra in the Roman Forum

rostral column A column, in honor of a naval triumph, ornamented with the rostra or prows of ships.

rostral column

rostrum A platform, elevated area, pulpit, or the like for addressing an audience.

rotonda Same as **rotunda.**

rotunda **1.** A building round both inside and outside, usually domed. **2.** A circular hall in a large building, esp. one covered by a cupola.

rough arch Same as **discharging arch;** built with rectangular bricks and wedge-shaped mortar joints.

rough-axed brick An **axed brick.**

rough bracket A bracket under stair steps, fastened to the supporting carriage.

rough carriage A **carriage** which is unplaned, usually concealed from view.

round arch A **semicircular arch.**

Round Arch style See **Rundbogenstil.**

round billet molding Same as **roll billet molding.**

round church One whose plan is a circle; by extension, a church designed around a central vertical axis such as those of polygonal or Greek-cross form, though these are more accurately described as churches of the central type.

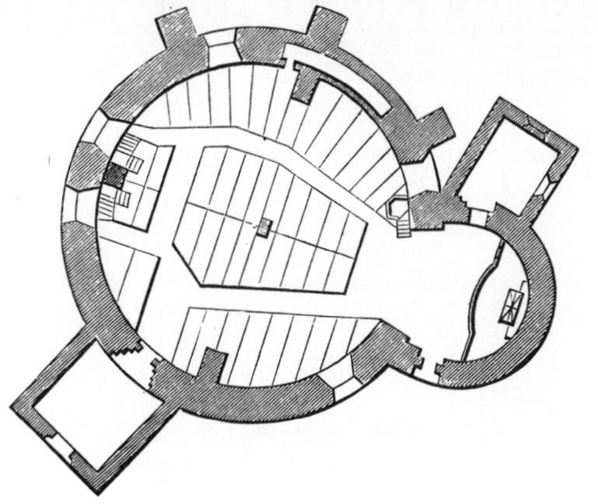
round church, Hagby, Sweden

roundel 1. A small circular panel or window; an **oculus.** 2. In glazing, a bull's-eye or circular light like the bottom of a bottle. 3. A small **bead molding** or **astragal.**

round molding, round A fairly large molding, the section of which is circular (or nearly circular) and convex.

round pediment A rounded **pediment, 2** used ornamentally over a door or window.

round pediment

round ridge The ridge of a roof, finished with a rounded surface.

round step, rounded step, round-end step A step having a bullnose.

round tower In early Christian architecture, esp. in Ireland, a conically capped circular tower of stone construction; used for defense.

round tower and chancel arch, Fineens Church, Clonmacnoise, Ireland

round window A **wheel window, Catherine-wheel window,** or **rose window.**

rover Any member, as a molding, that follows the line of a curve.

row house, row dwelling 1. One of an unbroken line of houses sharing one or more sidewalls with its neighbors. A **group house.** 2. One of a number of similarly constructed houses in a row; usually in a housing development.

row houses, Queen Anne style

rowlock, rolok, rollock **1.** A brick laid on its edge so that its end is visible. **2.** One ring of a **rowlock arch.**

rowlock arch An arch wherein the bricks or small voussoirs are arranged in separate concentric rings.

rowlock arch

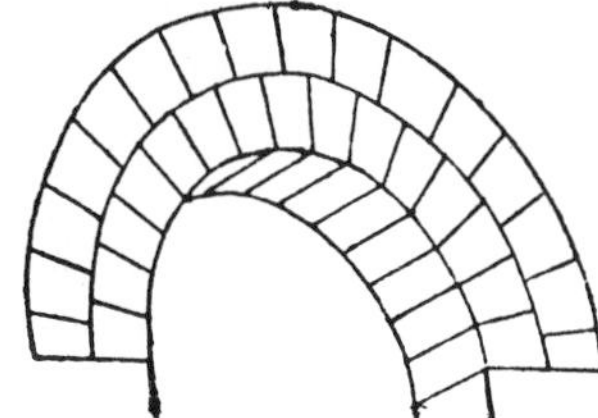

rubbed finish A finish obtained by using an abrasive to remove surface irregularities from stone or brick.

rubble Rough stones of irregular shapes and sizes; used in rough, uncoursed work in the construction of walls, foundations, and paving.

rubble arch See **rustic arch.**

rubble ashlar wall A **rubble wall** which has an ashlar facing.

rubble masonry Same as **rubblework.**

rubble wall A wall, either coursed or uncoursed, of rubble.

rubblework Stone masonry built of **rubble.**

rubblework

rudenture Same as **cabling, 2.**

ruderatio A type of pavement in ancient Rome used for common floors; composed of pieces of brick, tiles, stones, etc.

ruderation The process of paving with pebbles or small stones and mortar.

Rundbogenstil German eclectic mid-19th cent. style, combining Romanesque and Renaissance elements and characterized by arcaded round arches.

runic cross See **Celtic cross.**

runic knot An interlaced or twisted ornament common in Anglo-Saxon architecture.

run molding A molding of plaster, and occasionally of other such material, formed by passing a metal or wood template over the material while wet.

running Linked in a smooth progression, inclining to the right or the left, within a band; applied to various ornamental motifs.

running dog See **Vitruvian scroll.**

running ornament, running mold Any molding ornament in which the design is continuous, in intertwined or flowing lines as in foliage, meanders, etc.

Egyptian running ornament

floriated running ornament

running ornament on casing of the "Tomb of Agamemnon"

Russo-Byzantine architecture The first phase of Russian architecture (11th to 16th cent.) derived from the Byzantine architecture of Greece; mainly stone churches characterized by cruciform plans and multiple bulbous domes.

rustic Descriptive of rough, hand-dressed building stone, intentionally laid with high relief; used in modest structures of rural character.

rustic arch, rubble arch An arch laid up with rough or irregular stones, the spaces between them being filled with mortar.

rusticated Said of cut stone having strongly emphasized recessed joints and smooth or roughly textured block faces; used to create an appearance of impregnability in banks, palaces, courthouses, etc. The border of each block may be rebated, chamfered, or beveled on all four sides, at top and bottom only, or on two adjacent sides; the face of the brick may be flat, pitched, or diamond-point, and if smooth may be hand- or machine-tooled.

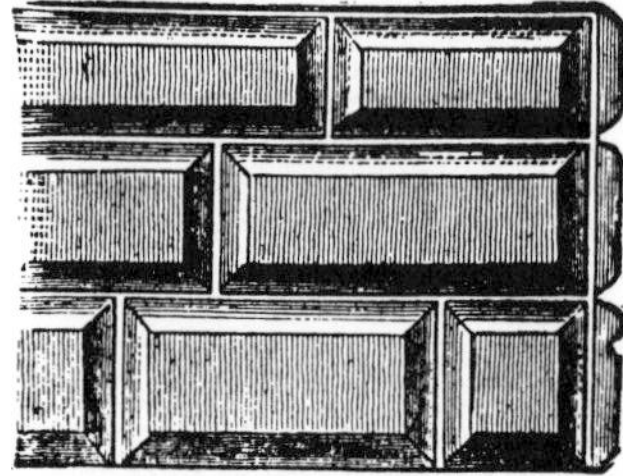

rusticated stone

rusticated column See **banded column.**

rusticating Applying a coarse texture on the face of clay bricks or stone.

rustication Same as **rustic work.**

rustic brick A fired-clay brick having a rough-textured surface; used for facing work; often multicolored.

rustic joint In stone masonry, a deeply sunk mortar joint that has been emphasized by having the edges of the adjacent stones chamfered or recessed below the surface of the stone facing.

rustic quoin A quoin treated with sunken joints, the face of the quoins being generally roughened and raised above the general surface of the masonry.

rustic slate One of a number of slate shingles of varying thickness, yielding an irregular surface when installed.

rustic stone Any rough, broken stone suitable for rustic masonry, most commonly limestone or sandstone; usually set with the elongate dimension exposed horizontally.

rustic woodwork Decorative or structural work constructed of unpeeled logs or poles.

rustic work Stonework of which the face is roughly hacked or picked; the separate blocks are marked by deep chamfers.

rustic work, façade of a palazzo in Venice (end of 16th cent.)

S

sabha mandapa In Indian architecture, an assembly hall.

sacellum A small Roman sanctuary, usually an unroofed enclosure with a small altar. Sometimes, a roofed funerary chapel.

sackering bell Same as **sanctus bell.**

sacrarium **1.** Any consecrated place, in Roman or medieval architecture; a shrine, a chapel, or a sacristy for keeping liturgical objects. **2.** In ancient Rome, a sort of family chapel in a private house, in which the images of the penates were kept.

sacrarium in a Pompeian house

sacringe, sacring bell Same as **sanctus bell.**

sacristy A room in a church, near the chancel, where the robes and altar vessels are stored, where the clergy vest themselves for services, and where some business of the church may be done; usually a single room, but sometimes a very large one.

saddle **1.** Same as **threshold.** **2.** Any hollow-backed structure suggesting a saddle, as a ridge connected to two higher elevations or a **saddle roof.**

saddleback A coping stone having its top surface sloped with its high point along the center ridge, so that rainwater spills on either side; also called **saddle-backed coping.**

saddle-backed coping See **saddleback**.

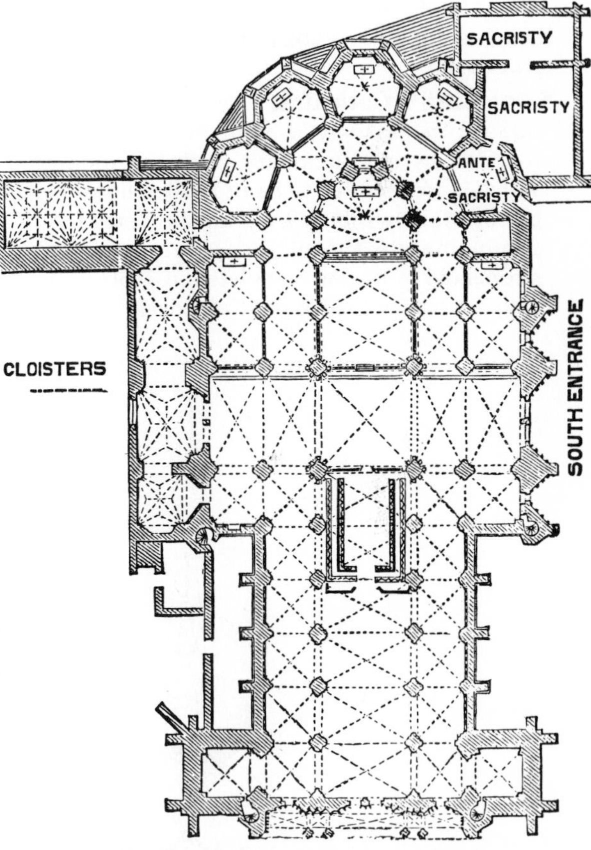

plan of Leon Cathedral, Spain (1255–1303) showing the location of the sacristies and the antesacristy

saddleback roof Same as **saddle roof.**

saddle board A board at the ridge of a pitched roof which covers the joint at the ridge. Also see **comb board, ridgeboard.**

saddle coping A **saddle-backed coping;** see **saddleback.**

saddle roof, saddleback roof A roof having two gables and one ridge, suggesting a saddle.

saddle stone **1.** An **apex stone.** **2.** Obsolete term for a stone containing saddle-shaped depressions.

safety arch A **discharging arch.**

sagitta The **keystone** of an arch.

sahn Central court of a mosque.

sail-over Any projection or jutting beyond the general wall surface.

Saint Andrew's cross bond See **English cross bond.**

Saint Basil's Cathedral At one end of Red Square in Moscow, a central church surrounded by nine auxiliary churches (one of which is consecrated to Saint Basil, a holy beggar of Moscow); built by Ivan the Terrible to commemorate the victory over the Tatar stronghold of Kazan; completed in 1560; originally known as Pokrovsky Cathedral.

saddle roof

Saint Basil's

Saint Peter's Church, Basilica of St. Peter The largest church in the Christian world; located in the Vatican, Rome, over the grave of Peter the Apostle; has 29 altars in addition to the high altar. Interior length, 615 ft (187 m); width at front, 87 ft (26.5 m); length of transept 450 ft (137 m). First consecrated in 326 A.D.; rebuilt with many changes in plans, among which was Bramante's, which was later changed from a Greek cross to a Latin cross ground plan. After 1547, construction was under the direction of Michelangelo, who designed the dome, which has a diameter of 138 ft (42 m) and a height of 404 ft (123 m) to the top of the lantern; consecrated in 1626.

above: **elevation of the dome**

left: **section of the interior**

below: **ground plan**

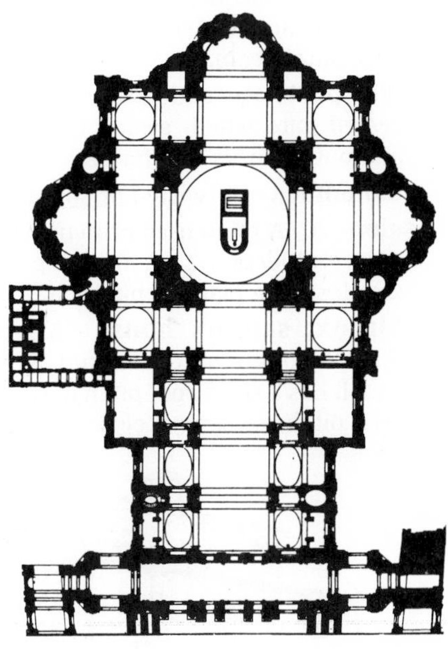

saint's bell Same as **sanctus bell.**

Saint Sophia Same as **Hagia Sophia.**

sakbe In Maya construction, a raised causeway built of huge stone blocks, leveled with gravel and paved with lime plaster; used to link sections of a city or to connect them with secondary centers.

sakha In the architecture of India, a doorjamb or doorframe.

saliens An artificial fountain in which the water shoots up under its own pressure, as a result of passing through a constricting tube.

salient Describing any projecting part or member, as a salient corner.

salient corner A corner which projects outward; the opposite of a reentrant corner.

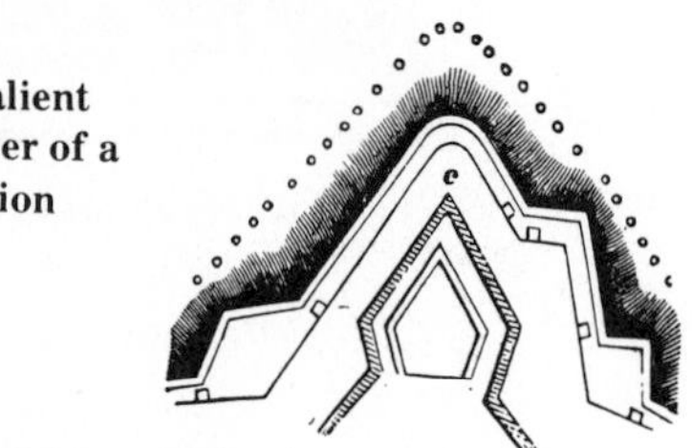

c, salient corner of a bastion

sally A projection, as the end of a rafter beyond the notch which has been cut to fit over a horizontal beam.

sally port An underground passage or concealed gate which serves to link the central and outer works of a fortress.

salomónica A twisted or spiral column.

salon **1.** A room used primarily for exhibition of art objects. **2.** A drawing room. **3.** A small, stylish place of business.

saltbox, saltbox house A wood-framed house, common to colonial New England, which has a short roof pitch in front and a long roof pitch, sweeping close to the ground, in back.

saltbox

salunkha In Indian architecture, an altar.

salutatorium In medieval churches, a porch or a portion of the sacristy where the clergy and the people could meet and confer.

sancte bell Same as **sanctus bell.**

sanctuary **1.** In a church, the immediate area around the principal altar. **2.** The sacred shrine of a divinity.

sanctum sanctorum, sancta sanctorum **1.** The innermost or holiest place of a tabernacle or temple, the "holy of holies." **2.** Any especially private place or retreat which may not be entered except by special permission.

sanctus bell A bell hung in an exterior turret or a bell cot over or near the chancel arch, which was rung to fix the attention of those not in the church to the service of the mass.

sanctus bell

sandrik In early Russian architecture, a door or window **pediment.**

sangarama In Indian architecture, a monastery.

sangawara-buki A **pantile** developed in Japan in the latter half of the 17th cent.; the original function of the *marugawara* and the *hiragawara* are combined into one tile; see **hongawara-buki.**

san-jū-no-tō See **tō.**

sankha In Indian architecture, a shell which is the emblem of the god Vishnu.

山門 **sanmon** A type of large (usually 5 **ken** wide by 2 ken deep) gate at a Zen temple; has two roofs, the upper one of which usually is of the hip and gable type (see **irimoya-yane**). This type of gate has a second story containing a room for Buddhist images.

Santa Sophia Same as **Hagia Sophia.**

santorin A lightweight, gray, volcanic tuff; used as **pozzolan.**

sapheta Same as **soffit.**

Saracenic architecture Same as **Muslim architecture.**

sarasin A **portcullis.**

sarcophagus An elaborate coffin for an important personage, of terra-cotta, wood, stone, metal, or other material, decorated with painting, carving, etc., and large enough to contain only the body. If larger, it becomes a **tomb.**

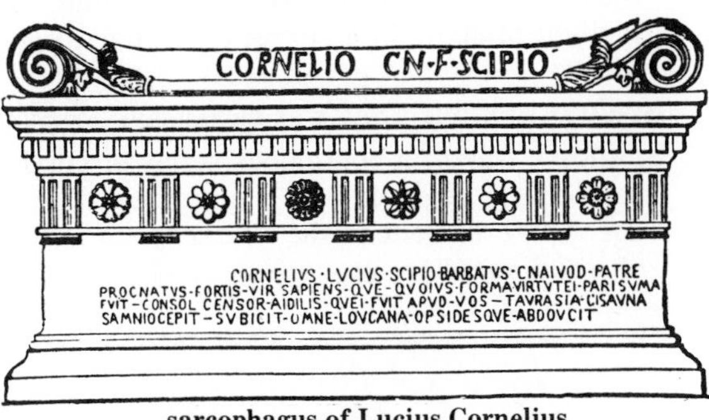

sarcophagus of Lucius Cornelius Scipio Barbatus

sarrasine A **portcullis.**

sash, window sash Any framework of a window; may be movable or fixed; may slide in a vertical plane (as in a double-hung window) or may be pivoted (as in a casement window).

Sassanian architecture Architecture prevalent in Persia under the Sassanian dynasty (3rd to 7th cent. A.D.); excelled in large palace complexes with open **iwans** and the extensive use of barrel vaults and parabolic domes on squinches of brick or rubblestone, set in plaster mortar and constructed without centering. The massive walls were covered with stucco decor or articulated by pilasters and cornices.

elevation of the Great Arch, Sassanian Palace at Ctesiphon on the Mesopotamian plain (531–579 A.D.)

sarcophagus of Roman Imperial time from Tomb of Cecilia Metella near Rome

säteri roof In Swedish architecture of the 17th and 18th cent., a type of hipped roof with vertical breaks which were often provided with windows.

saucer dome A dome whose rise is much less than its radius.

sawtooth molding Same as **notched molding.**

Saxon architecture See **Anglo-Saxon architecture.**

scabellum In Roman architecture and derivates, a high, freestanding pedestal.

scabellum with decorative vase: modern French

scaena A temporary building or booth for players behind the acting area in the ancient theatre; later the permanent back building of the theatre.

scaena ductilis In the ancient theatre, a movable screen which served as a background.

scaena frons The richly decorated front of the scaena, facing the audience.

scaffold **1.** A temporary platform to support workers and materials on the face of a structure and to provide access to work areas above the ground. **2.** Any elevated platform.

scagliola Plaster work imitating stone, in which mixtures of marble dust, sizing, and various pigments are laid in decorative figures; designs may be routed into a surface.

scalae **1.** A staircase in an ancient private house or other edifice; usually against a wall in the interior or on the exterior of a building. **2.** A flight of stairs in a circus, amphitheatre, or theatre.

scale ornament Same as **imbrication.**

scallop One of a continuous series of curves resembling segments of a circle, used as a decorative element on the outer edge of a strip of wood, molding, etc.

Norman molding with scallops

scalloped capital The term applied to a medieval block (cushion) capital when each lunette is developed into several truncated cones.

scalloped capital

scalpturatum A type of pavement in ancient Roman construction, resembling inlaid work; a pattern was chiseled out and filled with colored marble.

scamillus **1.** In Classical and Neoclassical architecture, a plain block placed under the **plinth** of a column, thus forming a double plinth. **2.** A slight bevel at the outer edge of a block of stone, as occurs between the necking of a Doric capital and the upper drum of the shaft.

s, scamillus,1

Scamozzi order An order similar to the Ionic but having volutes of the capital which radiate at 45°.

scandula A shingle, used by the ancient Romans as a roof covering for houses.

scandularis Descriptive of an ancient roof covered with shingles.

scansorium, scansoria machina In early Roman construction; scaffolding.

scape **1.** Same as **apophyge.** **2.** Same as **scapus.**

scapulary tablet In Zapotec style architecture, a regional variation of the **tablero.** The Zapotecs modified the original tablero, heightening the chiaroscuro effect of the wall below.

scapus The shaft of a column.

scarcement In building, a setback in the face of a wall, or in an earthen embankment; a footing or ledge formed by the setting back of a wall.

scarp A steep slope constructed as a defensive measure in a fortification.

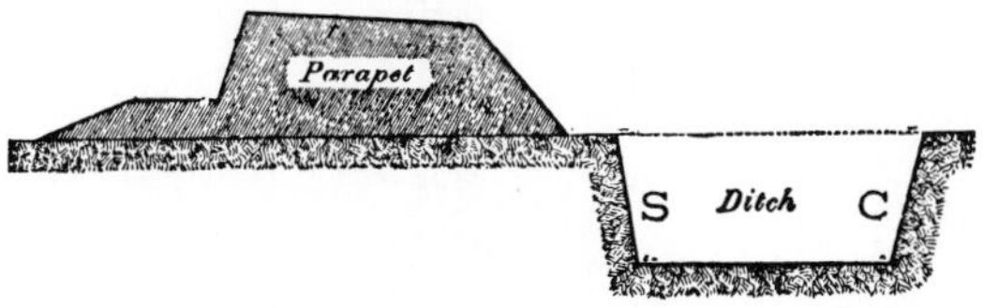

s, scarp; *c*, counterscarp

scena Same as **scaena.**

sceuophylacium Same as **diaconicon, 1.**

schabellum Same as **scabellum.**

scheme arch An arch which forms part of a circle which is less than a semicircle.

schola **1.** The apse or alcove containing a tub in Roman baths. **2.** A platform or ambulatory around an ancient Roman (warm) bath. **3.** An exedra or alcove in a palaestra for relaxation or conversation.

schola alvei The vacant space on the floor of a **caldarium** which surrounds the warm water bath (**alveus**).

sciagraph The geometrical representation of a building, showing its interior structure or arrangement.

scialbo Same as **intonaco.**

scima Same as **cyma.**

scimatium Same as **cymatium.**

scintled brickwork Same as **skintled brickwork.**

scoinson arch Same as **sconcheon arch.**

scollop Same as **scallop.**

sconce **1.** An electric lamp, resembling a candlestick or a group of candlesticks, which is designed and fabricated for mounting on a wall. **2.** Same as **squinch, 2.**

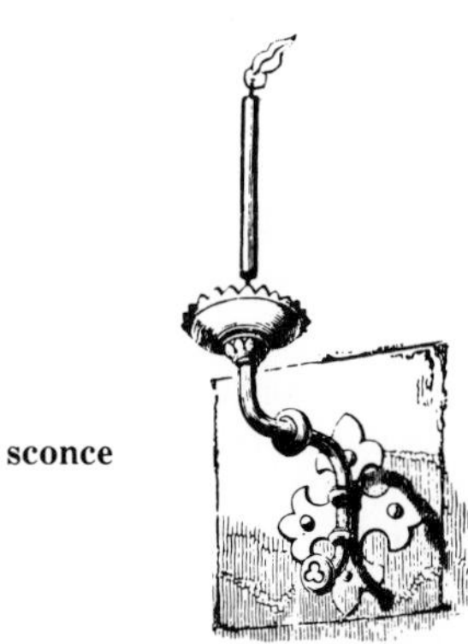

sconce

sconcheon, esconson, scuncheon **1.** The **reveal** of an aperture (such as a door or window) from the frame to the inner face of the wall. **2.** See **squinch, 2.**

sconcheon arch, scoinson arch An arch which includes the sconcheons of a door or window.

scotia A deep concave molding, esp. one at the base of a column in Classical architecture. Also called a **gorge, trochilus.**

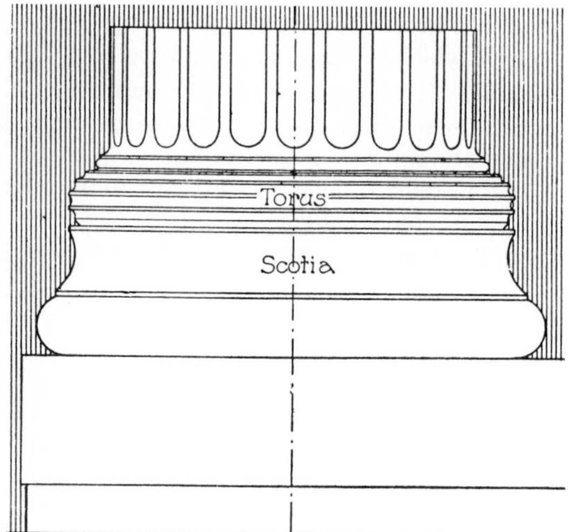

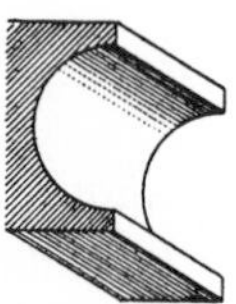
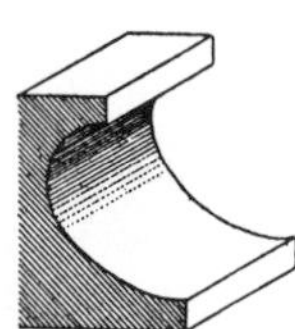
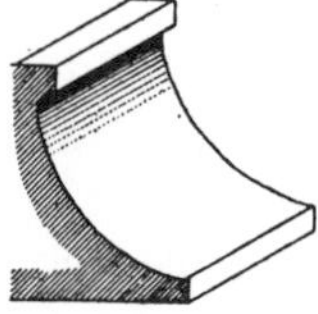

scotias

scrabbled rubble Same as **rubblework.**

scraped finish A European style of plaster finish which is obtained by scraping the stucco finish coat with a steel tool (sometimes serrated) as the stucco is setting.

scratchwork Same as **sgraffito.**

screen 1. Any construction whose essential function is merely to separate, protect, seclude, or conceal, but not to support. 2. The partition that divides one part of a church from another.

Early English style screen

Decorated style screen

Perpendicular style screen

screen façade A nonstructural facing assembly used to disguise the form or dimensions of a building.

screens passage In a medieval hall, the space between the screen (which acts as a visual barrier) and the doors to the service rooms (buttery, kitchen, pantry).

screwed work In wood turning, work in which the cutting is done in a spiral direction, so as to leave a spiral fillet or other ornamental spiral pattern.

screw stair, winding stair A circular stair whose steps wind around a central post. Also called a **newel stair** or **vice stair.**

screw stair

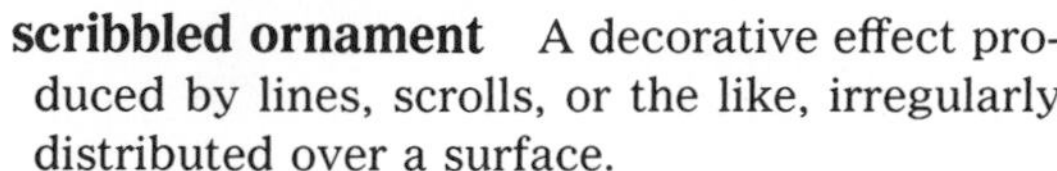

scribbled ornament A decorative effect produced by lines, scrolls, or the like, irregularly distributed over a surface.

scriptorium A writing room; specifically, the room assigned in a monastery for the copying of manuscripts.

scroll An ornament consisting of a spirally wound band, either as a running ornament or as a terminal, like the volutes of the Ionic capital or the scrolls on consoles and modillions.

scroll molding A form of **roll molding;** a large projecting molding, resembling a scroll with the free end hanging down, found in stringcourses and similar locations requiring a drip. Also see **torsade, 1.**

scroll step See **curtail step.**

scrollwork **1.** Ornamental work of any kind in which scrolls, or lines of scroll-like character, are an element. **2.** Decorative woodwork cut with a scroll saw.

scroll, Monument of Lysicrates (c. 334 B.C.)

ancient Roman acanthus scroll

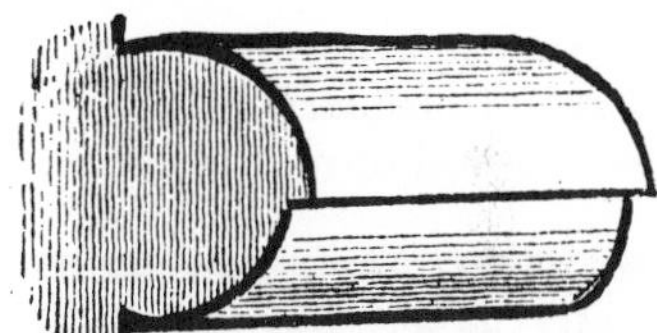

scroll molding

wrought iron scrollwork

scullery A room, generally annexed to a kitchen, used to prepare food for cooking, and/or as a pantry.

scuncheon Same as **sconcheon.**

scupper An opening in a wall or parapet that allows water to drain from a roof.

scutcheon Same as **escutcheon.**

scutilagium A small **close** or enclosure, as a garden.

scutula A segment of marble or other material, cut in the shape of a diamond or rhombus and used for inlaying floors or pavements.

secco See **fresco secco.**

seclusorium In ancient Roman aviaries, the place where birds were confined.

Second Empire architecture The eclectic style of the French Second Empire (1852–1870).

Second Empire style in the U.S.A. A stylistic designation named after the French Second Empire of Napoleon III (1852-1870), but referring to grand eclectic architecture in the U.S.A., not only in the 1860s, but also the 1870s, primarily public buildings. Its characteristic feature is the high mansard roof, for which it is also called **Mansard style.**

secos Same as **sekos.**

secretarium A **sacristy.**

sectile opus A kind of pavement formed of slabs or tiles of glass or other material, the pieces having a uniform size (far larger than the tesserae of ordinary mosaic) and being either plain-colored or mottled and veined.

two types of sectile opus

sectroid A twisted surface which is between the groins of a vault.

sedge A plant which grows in dense tufts in marshy places; used to form a ridge on a thatched roof.

sedile A seat (usually one of three) for the clergy to the right of an altar, often set in a canopied niche in the chancel wall.

Norman sedile

Early English style sedile

Decorated style sedile

seel Old English for **canopy.**

seggio A council chamber.

segmental arch A circular arch in which the intrados is less than a semicircle.

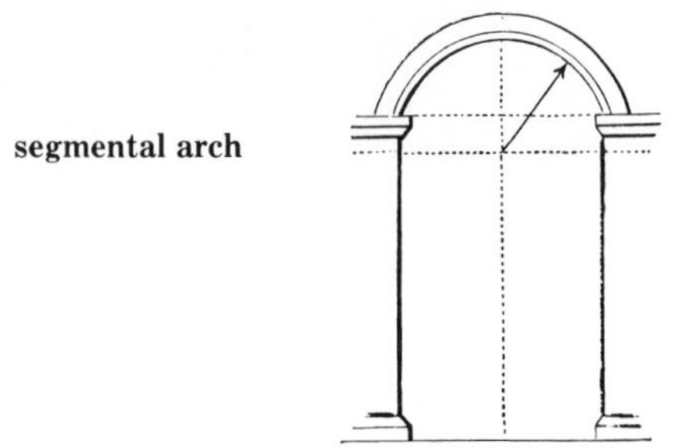

segmental arch

segmental billet A **billet,** a molding formed by a series of segments of cylinders.

segmental billet

segmented pediment A **pediment** in the form of a segmental arch.

segment head The **head** of a door in the shape of the arc of a circle.

sekos In ancient Greece: **1.** A shrine or sanctuary. **2.** The cella of a temple. **3.** A building which only the specially privileged might enter. **4.** An assembly hall for ordinary citizens, serving a religious purpose.

Seljuk architecture The earlier phase of Turkish **Muslim architecture** (11th to 13th cent.), much influenced by Persian architecture, predominantly mosques and minarets.

sell Same as **sill.**

sellary, sellaria A large sitting-room, drawing room, or reception room that is furnished with chairs or benches.

semiarch An arch having only one half of its sweep developed, as in a flying buttress.

semicircular arch A round arch whose intrados is a full semicircle.

semicircular dome A dome in the shape of a half sphere.

semicircular vault A **barrel vault.**

semi-column Same as **half column.**

semidome A dome equivalent to one-quarter of a hollow sphere, covering a semicircular area, such as an apse.

semidome, Villa Madama, Rome; (1516–) designed by Raphael

semielliptical arch Strictly, an arch whose intrados is half an ellipse; in practice the term usually denotes a three- or five-centered arch.

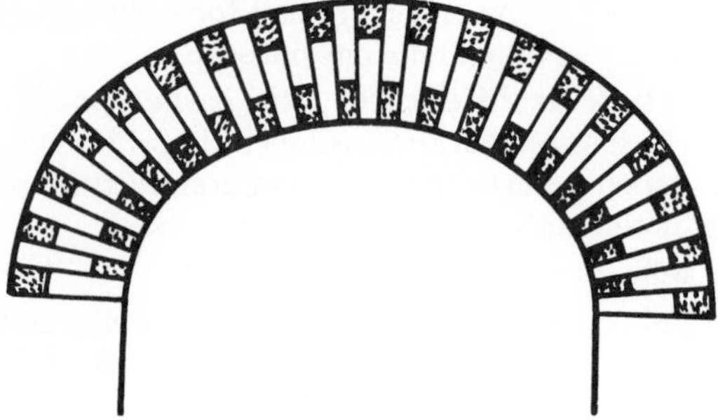
semielliptical arch

section of the Altun-Oba sepulcher, Crimea

seminary A place of education; a school, academy, college, or university; esp. a school for the education of men for the priesthood.

semitae In an ancient Greek gymnasium, a barrier which separated the wrestlers from the public.

senaculum An ancient Roman council chamber.

senatorium The left side of the sanctuary in the basilica of the Latin church, opposite the **matroneum,** and separated from the sanctuary by a balustrade.

sepimentum A fence.

septizonium A special type of edifice of great magnificence, consisting of seven stories of columns, one above the other, supporting seven distinct entablatures or zones.

septum **1.** A low marble wall or balustrade which divided the nave of the ancient basilican church into a middle section (for the clergy) and two side sections (for the laity). **2.** A low wall around a tomb. **3.** The enclosure of the Holy Table made by the altar rails in a church.

sepulcher **1.** A tomb. **2.** A receptacle for relics, esp. in a Christian altar. **3.** A shallow arched niche in the chancel to hold the elements of the Eucharist between their consecration on Maundy Thursday and the Easter High Mass.

sepulchral Of, or pertaining to, a tomb.

sera A bar used to secure an ancient Roman door.

seraglio **1.** An enclosed or protected place. **2.** A palace.

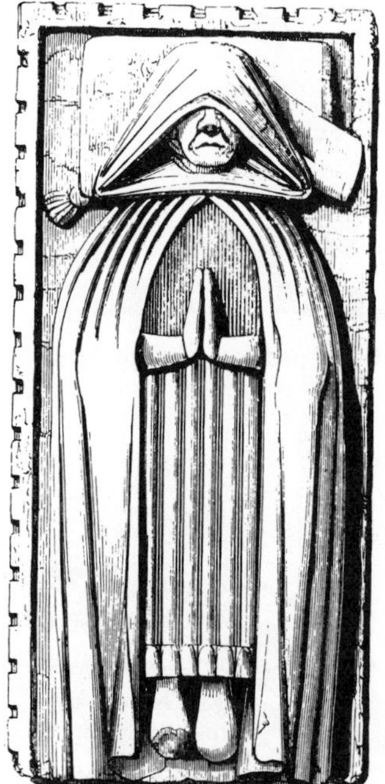
sepulchral effigy, Priory Church, Northumberland (15th cent.)

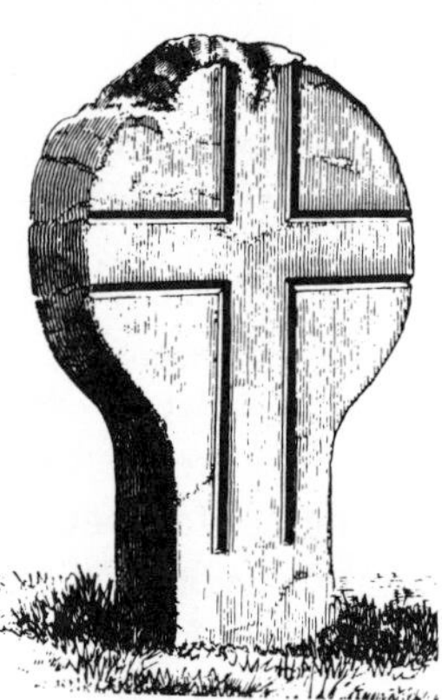
sepulchral headstone cross, Goodnestone, Kent

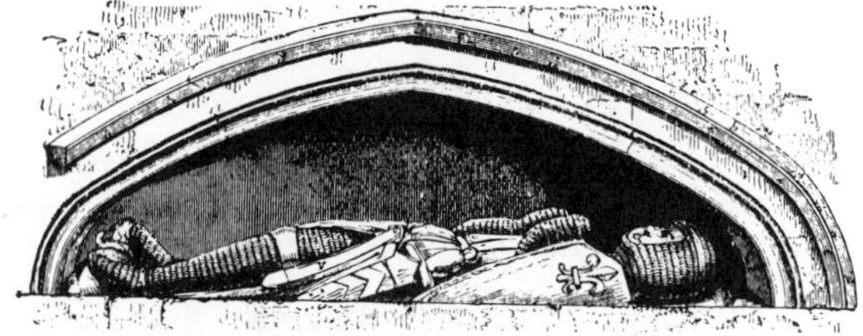
sepulchral arch and effigy, Coleshill Church, Warwickshire (14th cent.)

serai **1.** A Turkish palace, **harem,** or **seraglio.** **2.** A **caravanserai.**

serdab **1.** In ancient Egyptian architecture, a closed statue chamber. **2.** In Mesopotamian town houses, a cellar under the courtyard, ventilated and lighted by skylights, serving as a living room during the summer months.

Serlian motif See **Palladian motif.**

serpent column A type of column used in **Toltec architecture;** features a feathered serpent (Quetzalcoatl) whose open-fanged head serves as the base and whose tail rattlers are the roof support, as at Chichén Itzá and Tula.

serpentine A group of minerals consisting of hydrous magnesium silicate, or rock largely composed of these minerals; commonly occurs in greenish shades; used for decorative stone; the prominent constituent in some commercial marbles.

serrated Notched on the edges, like a saw.

setback buttress A buttress near but not at the corner of a building.

Seven Wonders of the World The seven most remarkable structures of ancient times: the pyramids at **El Gizeh,** the Mausoleum at Halicarnassus, the Temple of Artemis at Ephesus, the walls and **Hanging Gardens** of Babylon, the Colossus at Rhodes, the statue of Zeus by Phidias in the great temple at Olympia, and the Pharos or lighthouse at Alexandria; of these, only the pyramids at El Gizeh remain.

severy, civery **1.** A **baldachin.** **2.** One bay or compartment in a vaulted ceiling or structure.

sexfoil A **foil** having six points.

sexpartite vault A ribbed vault whose lateral triangles are bisected by an intermediate transverse rib producing six triangles within a bay.

sextry The **sacristy** of a church.

Sezession The Austrian variant of Art Nouveau, so named because its adherents seceded from the official Academy of Art in Vienna.

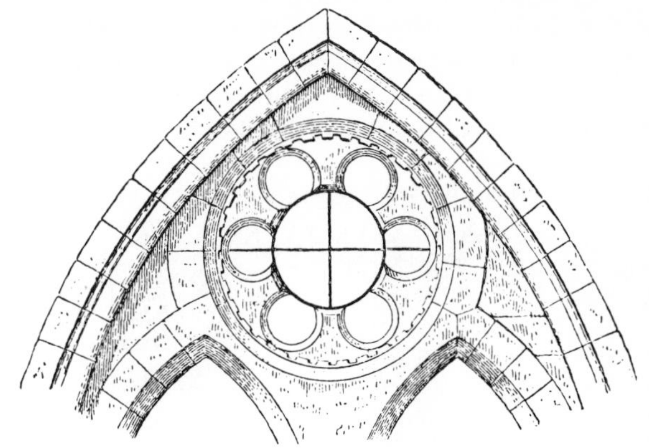

sexfoil

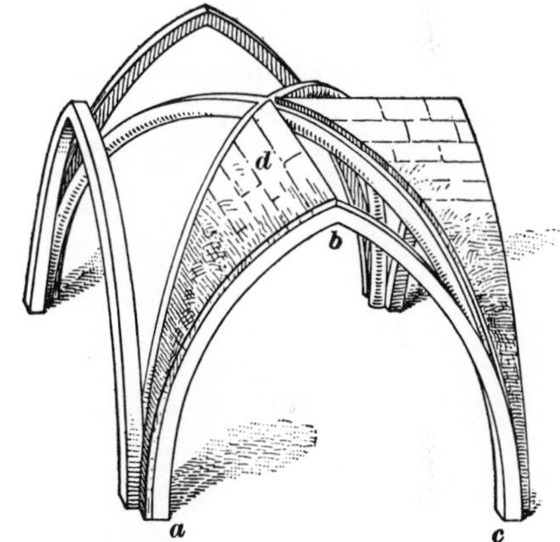

a, *b*, *c*, *d*: **severy,2**

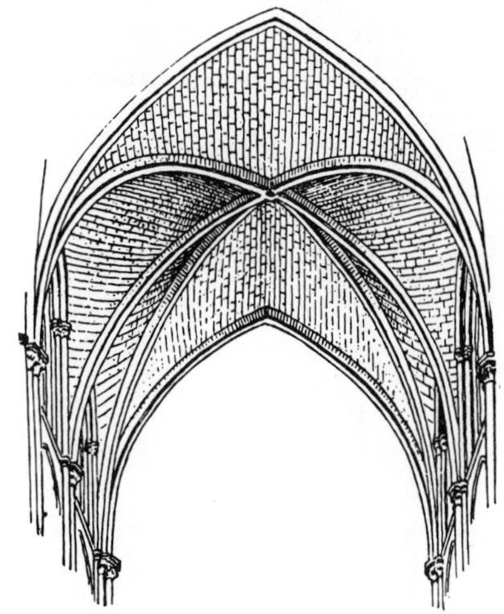

sexpartite vault

sgraffito A type of decoration executed by covering a surface, as of plaster or enamel, of one color, with a thin coat of a similar material of another color, and then scratching or scoring through the outer coat to show the color beneath.

part of façade painted in sgraffito

shaft The portion of a column, colonette, or pilaster between the base and the capital.

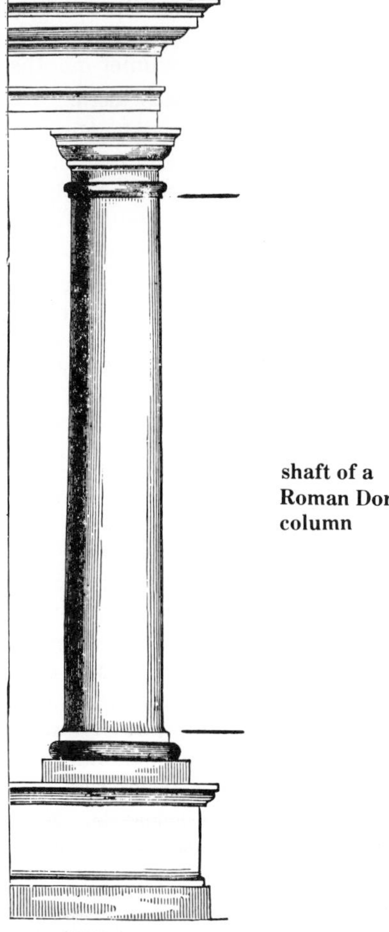
shaft of a Roman Doric column

shafted impost In medieval architecture, an **impost** with horizontal moldings, the section of the moldings of the arch above the impost being different from that of the shaft below it.

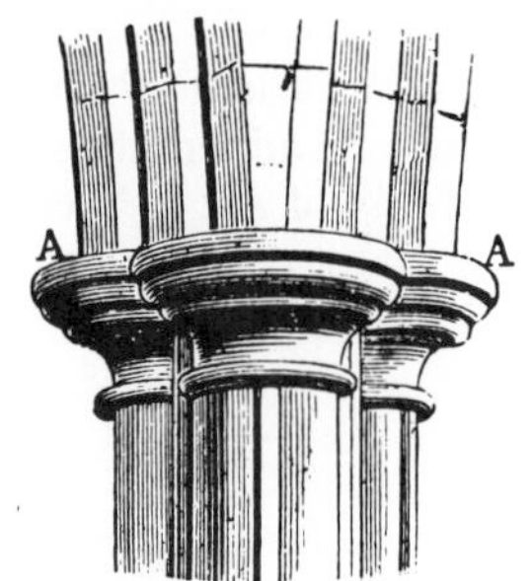

A, *A*, shafted impost

shafting In medieval architecture, an arrangement of shafts, wrought in the mass of a pier or jamb, so that corresponding groupings of archivolt moldings may start from their caps at the impost line.

shaft ring See **annulet.**

shaft tomb A tomb consisting of a vertical shaft leading to one or more underground chambers; esp. found in Colombia, Ecuador, western Mexico, Panama, and Peru; dating from the early Christian era, the most spectacular such tomb has been found in Jalisco, Mexico, 52 ft (15.8 m) deep, with three chambers radiating from a central core.

shake Any thick hand-split shingle or clapboard, usually edge-grained; formed by splitting a short log into tapered radial sections.

尺 **shaku** A linear unit of measurement in traditional Japanese construction; equal to 0.994 ft (0.303 m).

山墻 **shan ch'iang** In traditional Chinese architecture, a gable.

上林苑 **shang lin yüan** A royal garden within the capital of an ancient Chinese state; opened to the public once a year.

shank One of the plain spaces between the channels of a triglyph in a Doric frieze.

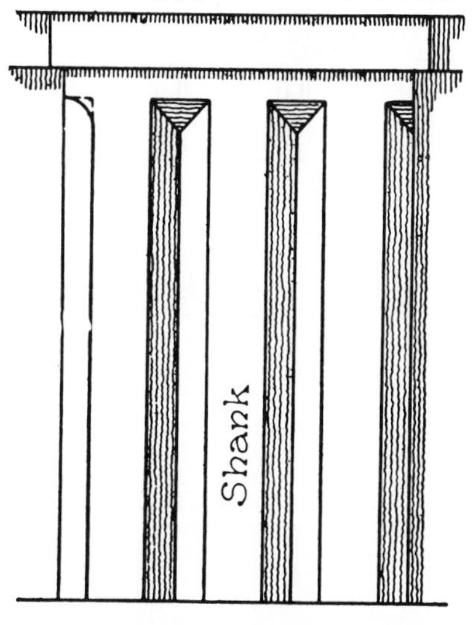

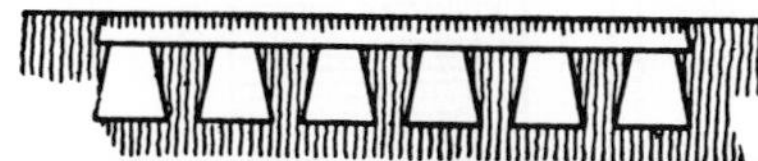

shank of a triglyph

shaped gable A **gable, 2,** each side of which is multicurved.

shaped work Curved carpentry or joinery.

shater, shatrovoye pokrytiye In early Russian architecture, a roof which is steeply pyramidal in shape, having four or more sides.

shchipets In early Russian architecture, a **gable.**

sheathing The covering placed over exterior studding or rafters of a building; provides a base for the application of wall or roof cladding.

shed dormer A **dormer** window whose eave line is parallel to the eave line of the main roof instead of being gabled; provides more attic space than a gabled dormer.

shed roof, pent roof A roof shape having only one sloping plane.

sheiya In early Russian architecture, a **drum, 2** having no windows, which supports a dome.

舍利塔 **shê li t'a** A Chinese stupa or pagoda, usually of masonry, used as a shrine to house the relics of a prominent Buddhist monk or sage.

shell ornament Any decoration of which a shell form is a characteristic part. Also see **coquillage.**

shell ornament frieze

神廚 **shen ch'u** A sacred kitchen, used to prepare offerings; located at the rear left side of a traditional Chinese temple, tomb, or shrine.

神庖 **shen pao** A sacred slaughterhouse used to prepare live sacrifices; located at the rear right side of a traditional Chinese temple, tomb, or shrine.

神道 **shen tao** A sacred path leading to a traditional Chinese temple, tombs, or shrines; located along the central axis of approach.

仕上げ壁

shiage-kabe The finish coat of plaster on a wall in traditional Japanese construction.

shibi A type of **acroterion** in the shape of a dolphin's tail; placed at each end of the roof ridge in traditional Japanese architecture. In ancient times it was believed to be a protection against fire.

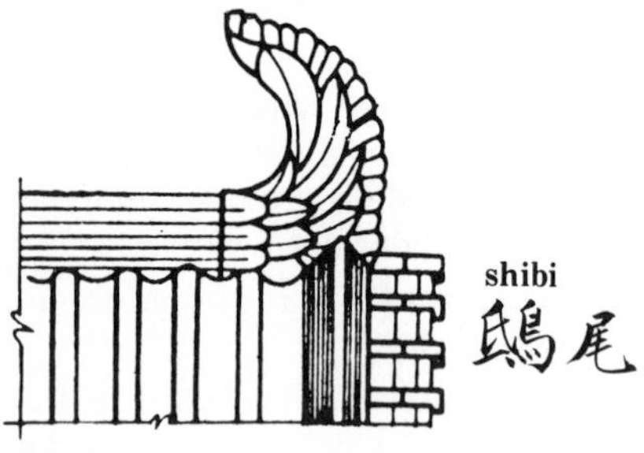

shichū-yane Same as **yosemune-yane.**

shikii In traditional Japanese architecture, the lower grooved beam which holds a sliding partition or screen. Also see **kamoi.**

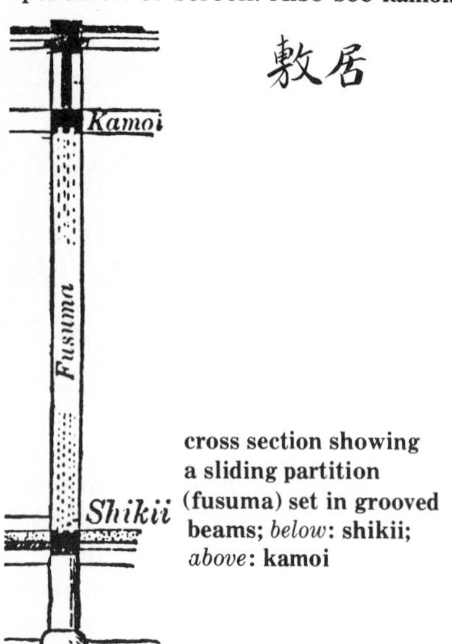

cross section showing a sliding partition (fusuma) set in grooved beams; *below*: shikii; *above*: kamoi

shikkui A plaster, mortar, stucco, or whitewash, made from a mixture of lime and clay and having the consistency of glue; used in traditional Japanese construction.

神明造

Shimmei style, Shimmei-zukuri A style of shrine architecture embodying the original style of Japanese building before the continental influences which came with the introduction of Buddhism. It is characterized by a small unpainted rectangular structure raised well above ground level, whose supporting columns are inserted directly into the ground and have no stone bases; there is a free-standing column at each end of the gable which supports the ridge. A railed veranda surrounds the entire structure at floor level. The bargeboards extend outward from the roof, forming crossed finials (**chigi**) at each end. The roof is thickly thatched with zebra grass, across which are placed **katsuogi.**

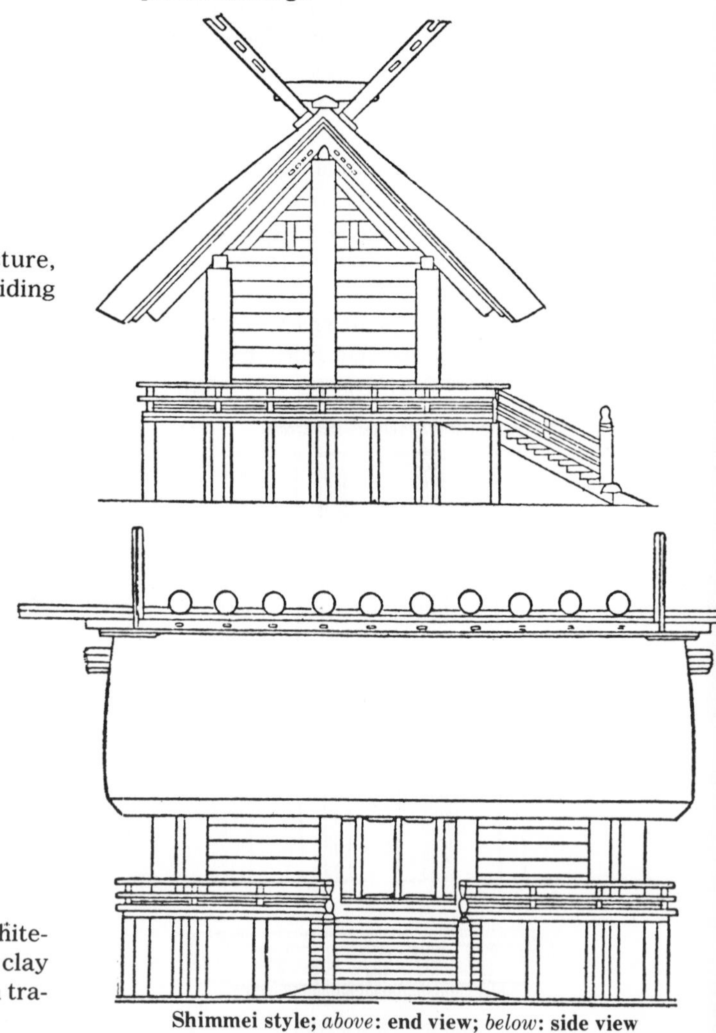

Shimmei style; *above*: end view; *below*: side view

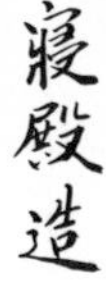

Shinden style, Shinden-zukuri The palace style during the Heian period in Japan, esp. during the Fujiwara era (9th to 12 cent.), consisting of a complex of one-story rectangular buildings interconnected by long covered open corridors. The main building, the *shinden*, faced south toward a ceremonial court, beyond which was a pond with islands connected with each other and with the shore by bridges.

shingle A roofing unit of wood, asphaltic material, slate, tile, concrete, asbestos cement, or other material cut to stock lengths, widths, and thickness; used as an exterior covering on sloping roofs and side walls; applied in an overlapping fashion.

Shingle style An American eclectic style, primarily in domestic architecture during the second half of the 18th cent.; characterized by extensive use of unpainted wood-shingle covering for roofs as well as for walls, in frequently asymmetrical and fluid arrangements.

Shingle style

真壁 **shin-kabe** In traditional Japanese architecture, a type of plastered wall in which the structural members are exposed.

shiplap, shiplap boards, shiplap siding Wood sheathing whose edges are rabbeted to make an overlapping joint.

shirinka An ornamental insert in early Russian architecture; a framed rectangular or square recess in a masonry wall; may have an ornamental stone or brick at its center.

下塗 **shita-nuri** In traditional Japanese architecture, the first or ground coat of plaster applied to a wall.

蔀戸 **shitomi-do** A type of latticed door first associated with the Shinden style in Japan; it is divided horizontally at the center, enabling the upper half to be raised outwardly to hook on to a specially placed bar beneath the eaves; the lower half can be removed and stored.

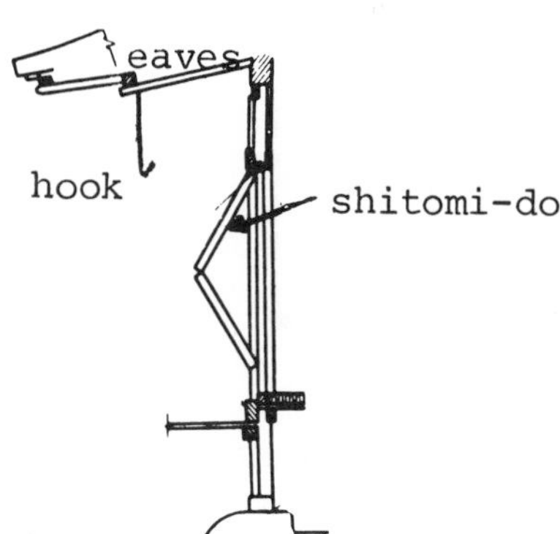

shoe **1.** A piece of timber, stone, or metal, shaped to receive the lower end of any member; also called a **soleplate**. **2.** A metal base plate for an arch or truss which resists lateral thrust.

Shoin style, Shoin-zukuri A style of Japanese residential architecture deriving its name from the main room which was equipped with a built-in, shelf-like table or writing desk (*tsuke-shoin*) which was used for writing or reading; adjacent to the desk were shelves (**chigai-dana**) and alcove (**toko-no-ma**); originally a bay extending out on the garden side of the house, later it merely faced the garden. The style developed from that of the temple abbot's private study.

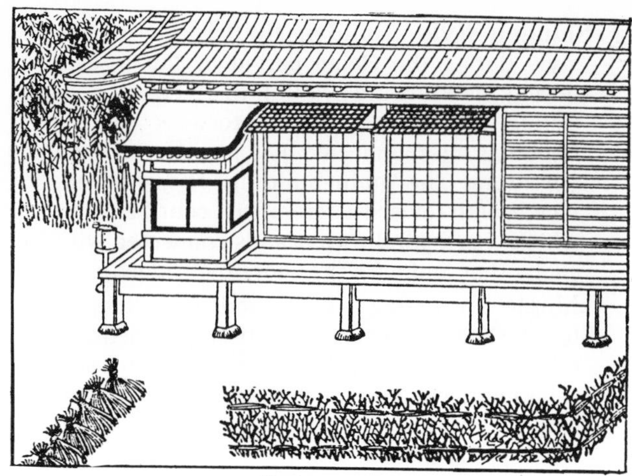

Shoin style

書院造

shōji A very lightweight sliding partition used in Japanese architecture; consists of a wooden lattice covered on one side with translucent white rice paper. The lattice is most often composed of small horizontal rectangles, but narrow vertical rectangles or asymmetrical shapes also are used. The lower section is occasionally filled by a thin wooden panel.

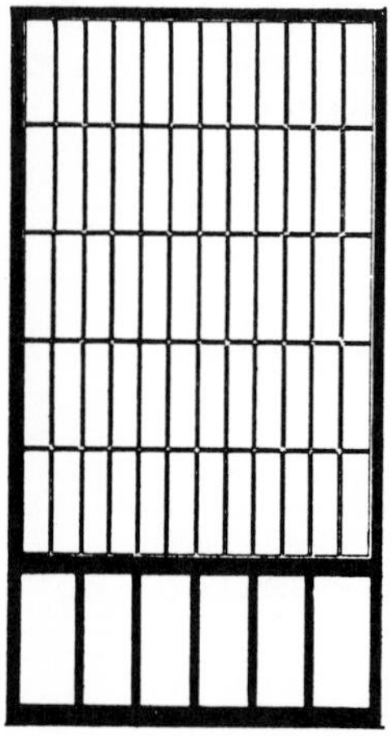

shōji

障子

shōrō A small structure from which a bell is hung in a Japanese temple compound.

shot hole Same as **loophole.**

shot tower A high tower, usually round, in which shot are made by dropping molten lead from an upper story into a cistern of water.

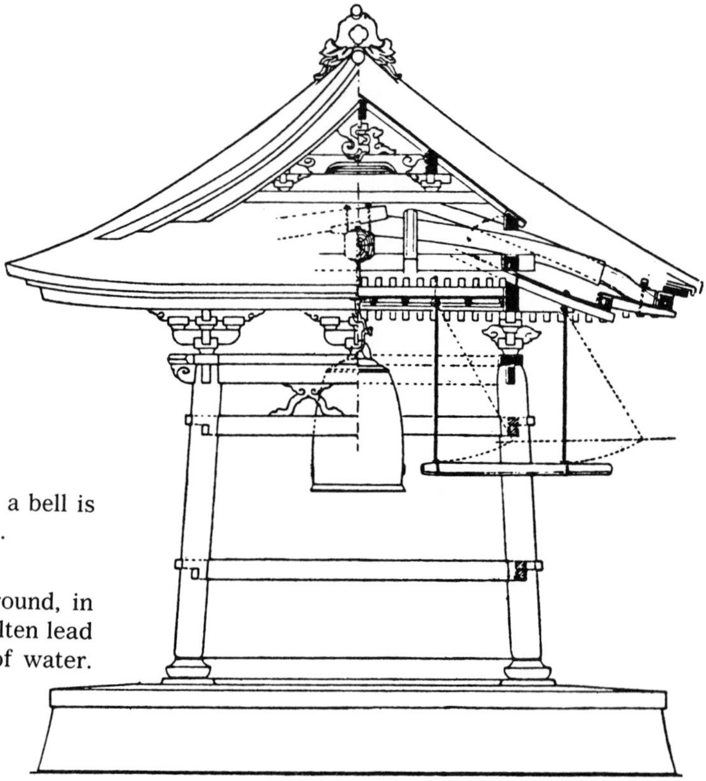

shōrō

鐘楼

shoulder **1.** A projection or break made on a piece of shaped wood, metal, or stone, where its width or thickness is suddenly changed. Also called **ear, elbow.** **2.** The angle of a bastion included between the face and the flank of a fortification. Also called **shoulder angle.**

shoulder angle See **shoulder, 2.**

shouldered arch A lintel carried on corbels at either end; a squareheaded trefoil arch.

shoulder piece Same as **crossette, 2**; a bracket.

show rafter A rafter exposed below a cornice; often ornamental.

shreadhead Same as **jerkinhead.**

shrine A receptacle to contain sacred relics; by extension, a building for that purpose.

shrine chapel A small enclosed structure containing the tomb of a sainted person.

shriving pew Same as **confessional.**

shroud A place under ground, as a crypt of a church.

shrowd Same as **shroud.**

shutting post The post at the side of a gate against which it shuts.

shutting shoe A device of iron or stone with a shoulder, sunk in the middle of a gateway, against which the gate is shut and secured.

side chapel A chapel to the side of the choir.

side light A framed area of fixed glass alongside a door or window opening; also called **winglight, margin light, flanking window.**

siding, weatherboarding The finish covering of an exterior wall of a frame building.

siel Old English for **canopy.**

sigma A semicircular **portico.**

signinum An ancient Roman construction material employed for making flooring; consisted of tiles broken into minute pieces and mixed with mortar.

signinum opus A type of ancient Roman surfacing material consisting of tiles beaten to powder and mixed with mortar; esp. used to coat the interior of aqueducts and as a floor surface to keep out moisture.

sikhara, sikra A tower or spire, usually having a convex taper, of an Indian temple; esp. one crowned by an **amalaka.**

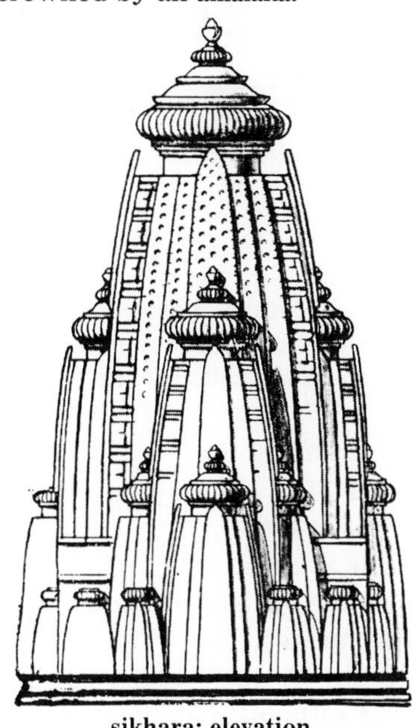

sikhara: elevation

sikhara: partial plan

silex **1.** Flint or flintstone. **2.** By extension, any kind of hard stone cut into polygonal blocks.

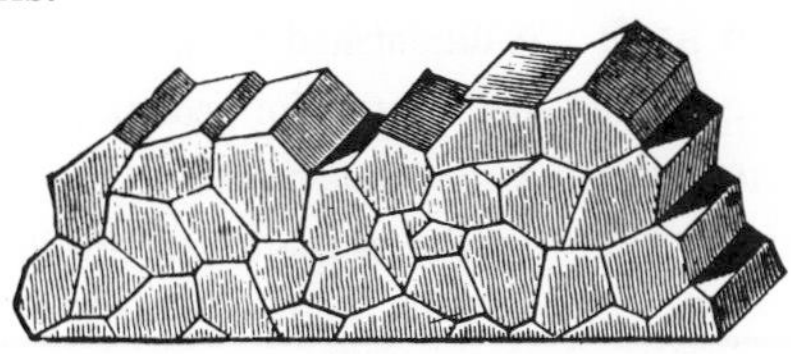

silex,2

sill 1. A horizontal timber, at the bottom of the frame of a wood structure, which rests on the foundation. 2. A **doorsill.** 3. The horizontal bottom member of a window frame or other frame.

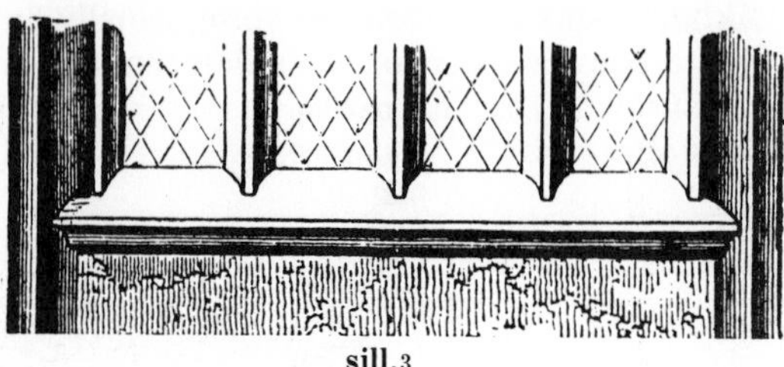
sill,3

sill course In stone masonry, a **stringcourse** set at windowsill level; commonly differentiated from the wall by its greater projection, its finish, or its thickness.

sill plate Same as **sill,** 1.

silpa-sastra The science of architecture and cognate arts in India.

sima Same as **cyma.**

simple cornice A cornice consisting of only a frieze and molding.

simple vault A vault which has a smooth, continuous intrados; has no cross arches or ribs.

sine postico A temple which is peripteral on the front and sides, but not in back.

singing gallery A gallery for singing, usually in churches of the Italian Renaissance, richly decorated with carving; a rood loft.

siparium 1. In an ancient Roman theatre, a piece of tapestry, stretched on a frame, which served as a drop scene; it was depressed below the level of the stage when the play began and raised when the play ended. 2. A folding screen serving a similar function.

siras In Indian architecture, the capital of a column or pillar.

skeen arch A **diminished arch.**

skene The Greek term for **scaena** (Latin).

skene arch A **diminished arch.**

skenotheke In the **skene** of an ancient Greek theatre, a storeroom for the properties.

skew A **kneeler,** 1.

skew arch An arch having jambs not at right angles to its face.

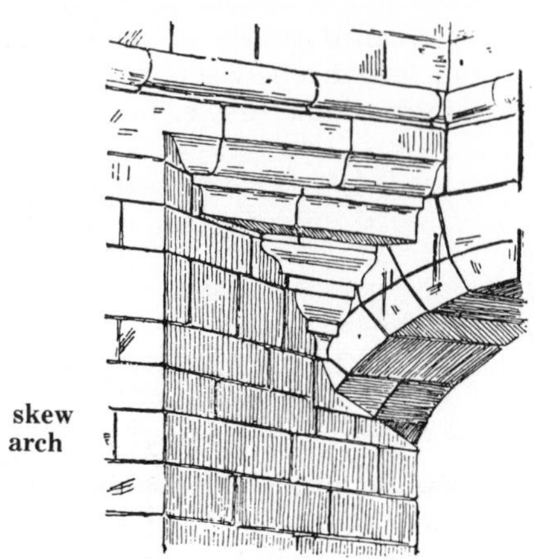
skew arch

skewback 1. The sloping surface of an abutment which receives the thrust of an arch. 2. The stone, or course of stones, providing such a sloping surface.

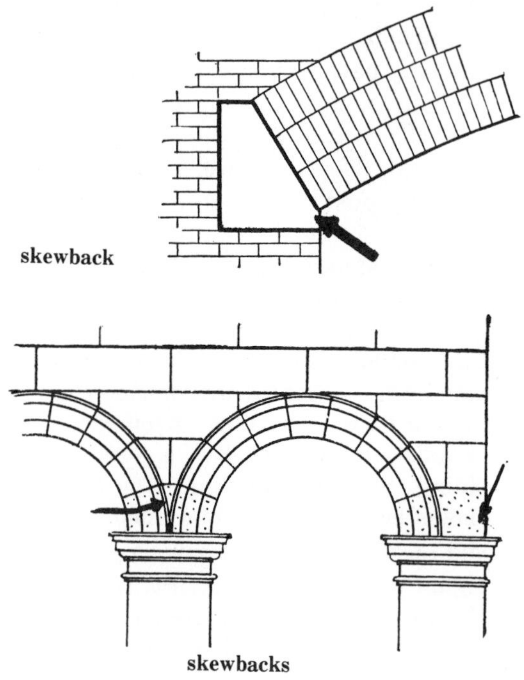
skewback

skewbacks

skew block See **gable springer.**

skew butt See **gable springer.**

skew corbel, skew putt A stone built into the bottom of a gable to form an abutment for the coping, eave gutters, or wall cornices.

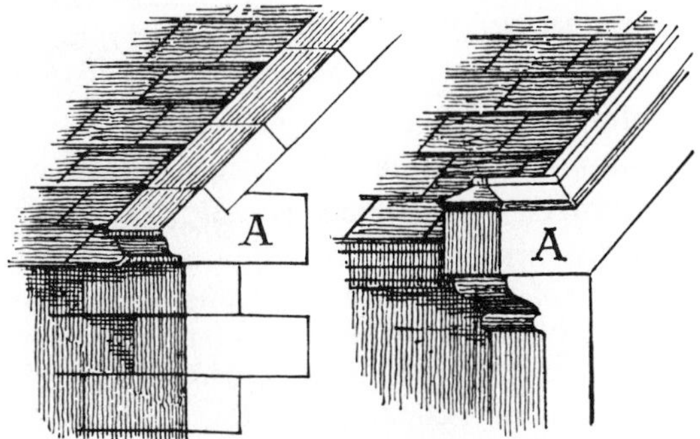

A, A, skew corbels

skew fillet A fillet nailed on a roof along the gable coping to raise the slates there and divert the water from the joining.

skew table A variety of **kneeler,** cut integrally with the lowest section of a gable coping; serves as a lower stop for sloping sections of coping above.

skintled brickwork Brickwork which has been laid so as to form a wall with an irregular face.

skirt-roof A false roof between stories of a building.

skirt-roof

slab house A house built of rough-hewn planks.

slate hanging See **weather slating.**

sleeper **1.** One of a number of horizontal timbers that are laid on a slab or on the ground and to which the flooring is nailed. **2.** Any long horizontal beam, at or near the ground, which distributes the load from posts or framing.

slip **1.** A long seat or narrow pew in a church. **2.** A narrow passage between two buildings.

sluing arch A **splayed arch.**

slype **1.** A narrow passage as between two buildings; a **slip, 2.** **2.** In some English cathedrals, a passage leading from the transept to the chapter house or to the deanery.

smalto Colored glass or other pieces of vitreous material, esp. in minute regular squares, used in mosaic work.

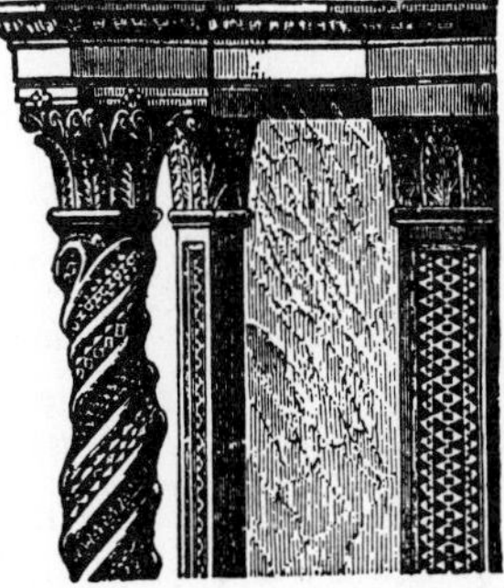

smalto work, Church of Aracoeli, Rome (rebuilt 1250)

snecked rubble, snecked masonry Masonry laid up with rough irregular stones, fitted so as to produce a strong bond.

snecking Same as **rubblework.**

sōbō The living quarters for priests in Japan during the Asuka, Nara, and Heian periods.

socket The piece that receives and holds a **malus** (a pole supporting a velarium).

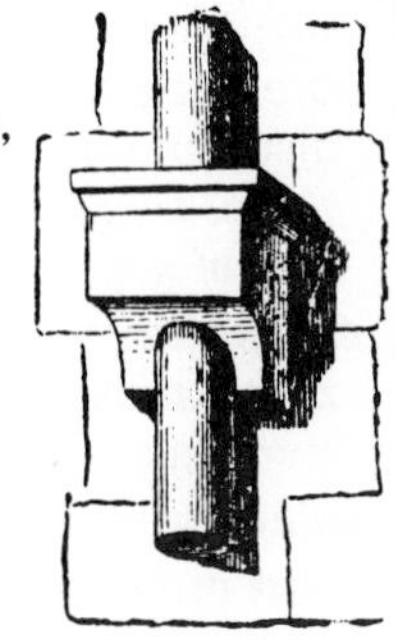

socket, the Colosseum, Rome

socle A low, plain base course for a pedestal, column, or wall; a plain **plinth.**

sod house A house having walls constructed of sod, usually in layers; the roof usually is of logs covered with earth and sod.

soffit The exposed undersurface of any overhead component of a building, such as an arch, balcony, beam, cornice, lintel, or vault.

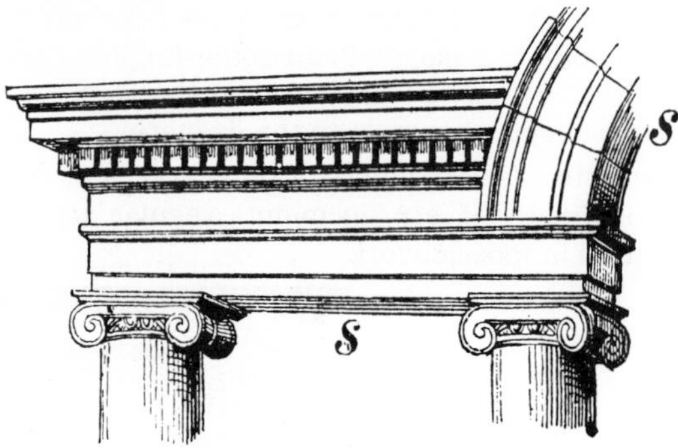

S, *S*, soffits

soffit board A **plancier piece.**

solar A room or apartment on an upper floor, as in an early English dwelling house.

solarium In ancient architecture, a terrace on the top of a house built with a flat roof, or over a porch, surrounded by a parapet wall but open to the sky.

soldier arch A flat arch in brick, having the stretchers (long sides) of the uncut bricks set vertically.

sole 1. Same as **solepiece.** 2. Same as **soleplate.**

solea A raised walkway between the ambo and bema in an Early Christian or Byzantine church.

soleiya A dais or altar steps in front of (and the full width of) an **iconostasis.**

solepiece 1. A horizontal member used to distribute the thrust of one or more uprights, posts, or struts. 2. A member on which the foot of a raking shore rests.

soleplate 1. Same as **solepiece.** 2. A horizontal timber which serves as a base for the studs in a stud partition.

soler Middle English term for **solar.**

solid molding See **struck molding.**

solid newel A **newel** into which the ends of a winding stair are built, as distinguished from a **hollow newel.**

solid newel stair A stair whose tapered treads wind around, and engage in, a central newel. Also called **spiral stair, vis.**

solium 1. The seat at the bottom of an ancient circular warm-water bath, on which the bather sat and washed himself. 2. A **sarcophagus** of imposing character, usually made of valuable marbles and enriched by sculpture; esp. used as a receptacle for the body of a king or great personage.

sollar, soller Same as **solar.**

Solomonic order See **spiral column.**

Solomon's Temple See **Temple of Solomon.**

sommer Same as **summer.**

sophronisterium Among the ancients, a house of correction or workhouse where slaves were confined by their masters and kept at hard labor for offences.

sopraporta See **overdoor.**

sōrin The crowning spire on a Japanese pagoda; usually made of bronze.

sōrin

sounding board A canopy over a pulpit to direct the sound of a speaker's voice toward the audience; see **abat-voix.**

souse, souste Same as **corbel.**

south aisle The aisle of a church on the right side as one faces the altar; so called because medieval churches almost invariably had their sanctuaries at the east end and the main doors at the west end.

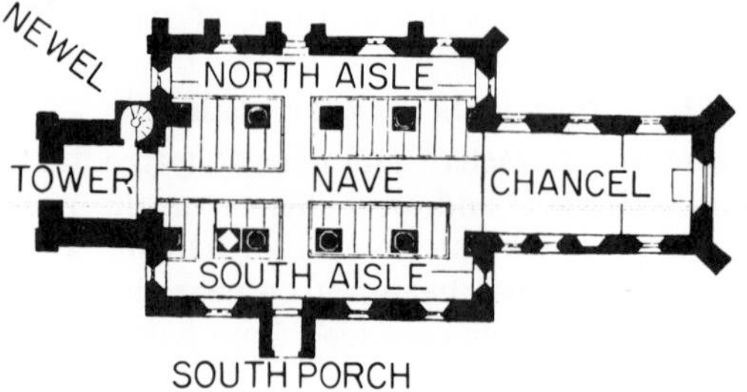

south door A small door into the chancel (for the priest), usually on the south side as it led to his residence, which was on that side of the church.

south porch A porch which shelters the entrance to a church; located on the right side of the church as one faces the altar.

spall A small fragment or chip removed from the face of a stone or masonry unit by a blow or by action of the elements.

span **1.** The interval between two terminals of a construction. **2.** The distance apart of any two consecutive supports, esp. as applied to the opening of an arch. **3.** A structural member (or part of a member) between two supports.

spandrel, spandril **1.** An area, roughly triangular in shape, included between the extradoses of two adjoining arches and a line approximately connecting their crowns (or a space approximately equal to half this in the case of a single arch); in medieval architecture, often ornamented with tracery, etc. **2.** In a multistory building, a wall panel filling the space between the top of the window in one story and the sill of the window in the story above. **3.** A surface, roughly triangular in shape, as below a stair string.

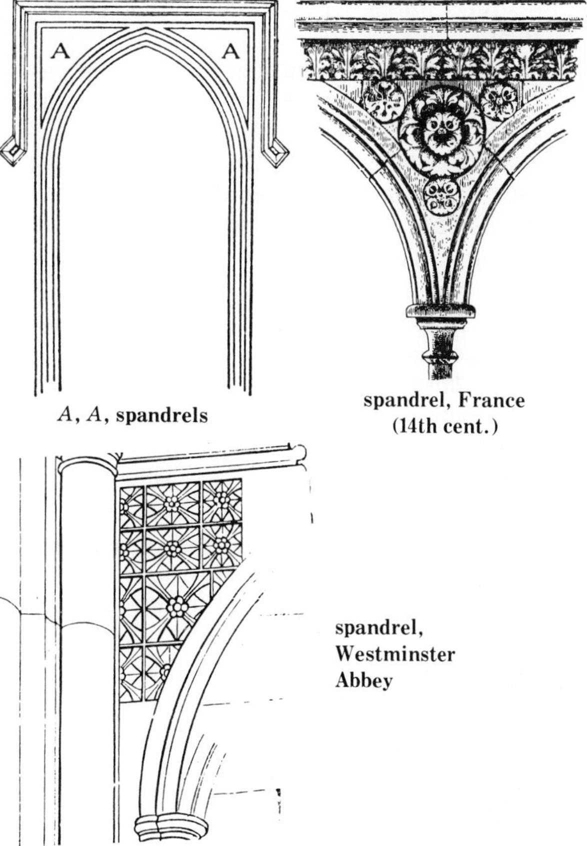

A, A, **spandrels**

spandrel, France (14th cent.)

spandrel, Westminster Abbey

Gothic spandrel, Stone Church, Kent

spandrel panel A panel covering a **spandrel** area.

spandrel step A solid step, triangular in section, whose hypotenuse forms part of the sloping soffit of the stair flight.

spandrel wall A wall built on the extrados of an arch, filling in the spandrels.

Spanish tile See **mission tile.**

spanner, span piece A horizontal cross brace or **collar beam.**

spar **1.** A **common rafter.** **2.** A bar for fastening a gate or door. **3.** A heavy round timber. **4.** See **brotch.**

sparpiece See **collar beam.**

speaking tube A tube, usually of metal, used to transmit the voice from one part of a building to another, before the days of electronics.

specula A watchtower of the ancient Romans, on which guards were regularly stationed to keep a lookout and to transmit signals.

specularia Windowpanes of the ancients; made of thin sheets of mica (lapis specularis).

speculatorium A peephole with a grating in a door for inspecting visitors.

specus In early Roman architecture, the covered channel of an aqueduct in which water flows.

speer See **spere.**

speos In ancient Egypt, a temple or part of a temple, or a tomb of some architectural importance, excavated in solid rock; a grotto temple or tomb.

spere, speer, spier, spur In medieval English residences and derivatives, a fixed screen projecting from the side of a great hall, near a door, to mitigate drafts.

spere-truss In a medieval hall of timber construction, a roof-supporting wooden arch, rising from trusses attached to the sidewalls, marking the division between the principal area of the hall and the **screens passage.**

sperone A **buttress.**

sphaeristerium In ancient Rome, an enclosed place or structure for ball playing, usually attached to a gymnasium or a set of baths.

spherical vault A dome shaped like a half globe.

sphinx **1.** In Greek mythology, a female monster (represented with the body of a lion or dog, winged, and the head and often the breasts of a woman), said to have proposed a riddle to the Thebans who passed her as she sat on a rock by the roadside, and to have killed all who were unable to guess the answer. **2.** In Egyptian antiquity, a figure somewhat similar to that of the Greek, having the body of a lion (never winged) and a male human head or an animal head. Also see **Great Sphinx.**

sphynx Same as **sphinx.**

sphinx at Thebes

Greek sphinx

spicae testaceae Oblong bricks for pavements, used in **spicatum opus.**

spica testacea Oblong tiles set in a **herringbone pattern** in ancient Roman floors.

spicatum opus Ancient Roman masonry laid in a **herringbone pattern.**

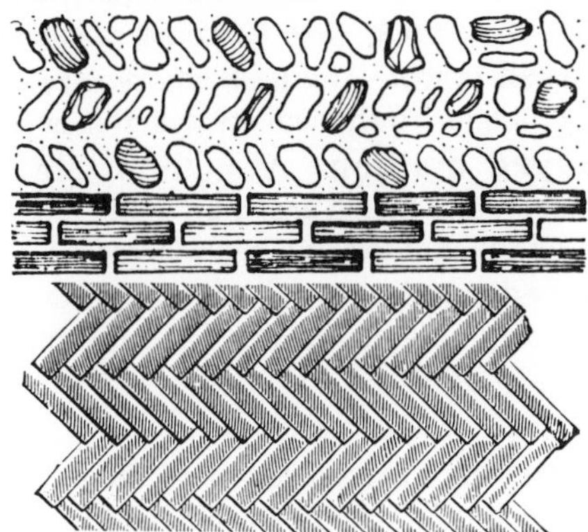

examples of spicatum opus

spier See **spere.**

spina A barrier dividing an ancient Roman circus lengthwise, about which the racers turned.

spira The molding at the base of a column; a **torus.**

spiral column A **barley-sugar column, salomónica, torso,** or **twisted column.**

spiral stair, caracole, circular stair, cockle stair, corkscrew stair, spiral staircase A flight of stairs, circular in plan, whose treads wind around a central newel. Also called a **helical stair, solid newel stair.**

spire Any slender pointed construction surmounting a building; generally a narrow octagonal pyramid set above a square tower.

spire: Church of St. Mary-le-Bow, London (1670-73)

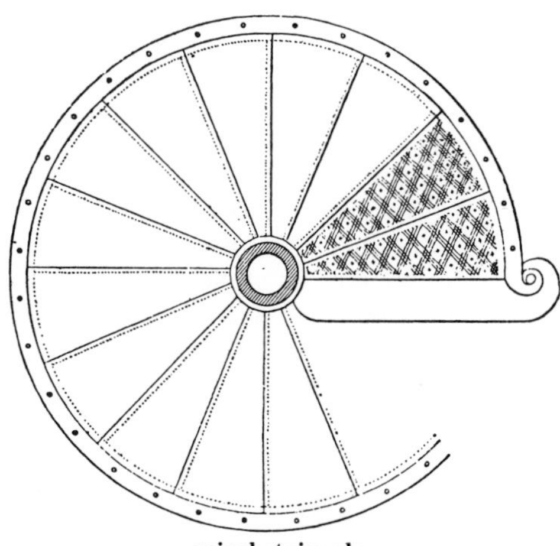

spiral stair: plan

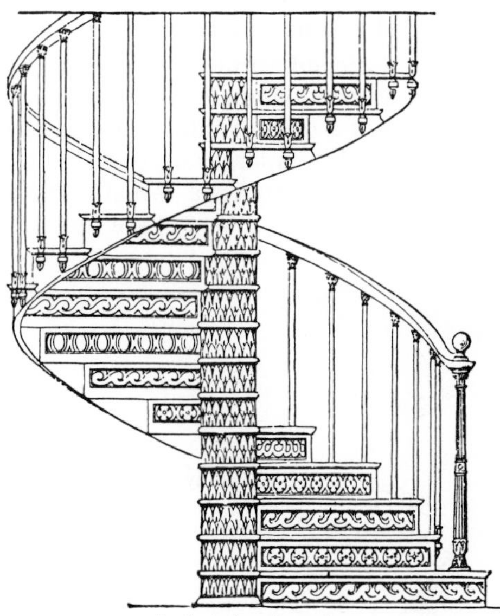

spiral stair: elevation

spirelet A small spire as of a pinnacle or turret.

spire light A window in a spire; frequent in the Early English period, common during the Decorated, and occasional in the Perpendicular.

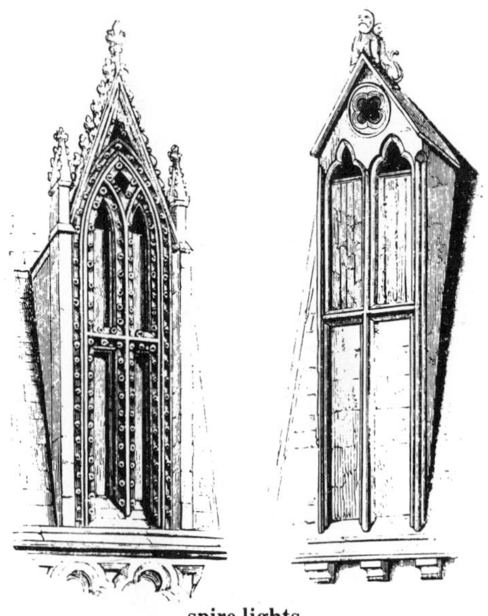
spire lights

spire-steeple A **spire** atop a steeple.

spital A hospital.

splandrel Same as **spandrel.**

splay A sloped surface, or a surface which makes an oblique angle with another, esp. at the sides of a door, window, proscenium, etc., so the opening is larger on one side than the other; a large chamfer; a reveal at an oblique angle to the exterior face of the wall.

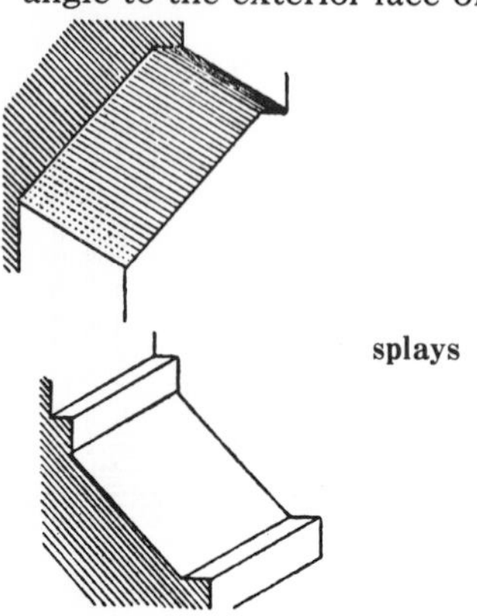
splays

splayed arch An arch opening which has a larger radius in front than at the back.

splayed coping See **featheredged coping.**

splayed jamb Any **jamb** whose face is not at right angles to the wall in which it is set.

splayed mullion A mullion joining two glazed units which are at an angle to each other, as the mullion of a **bay window.**

splayed window A window whose frame is set at an angle with respect to the face of the wall.

splocket Same as **sprocket.**

spoliarium The place where the dead bodies of combatants were dragged after their appearance in an ancient Roman amphitheatre; the bodies were dragged through the arches at the two ends of the arena (through which they previously had entered as combatants), into a room where they were stripped of clothing and the arms they bore.

spoliatorium A place for the clothing of the bathers in an ancient bathing establishment.

spout A short channel or tube used to spill storm water from gutters, balconies, exterior galleries, etc., so that the water will fall clear of the building. Also see **gargoyle.**

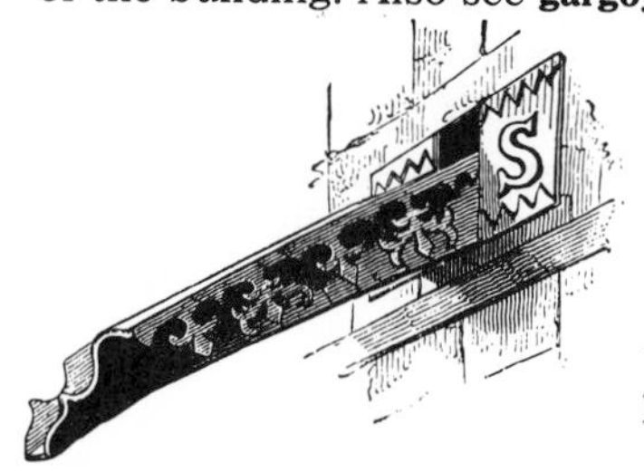

lead spout, Woodland Church, Northamptonshire

springer, skewback, summer **1.** The impost or place where the vertical support for an arch terminates and the curve of the arch begins. **2.** The lower voussoir, or bottom stone of an arch, which lies immediately on an impost. **3.** The bottom stone of the coping of a gable. **4.** The rib of a groined roof or vault; also see **cross springer.**

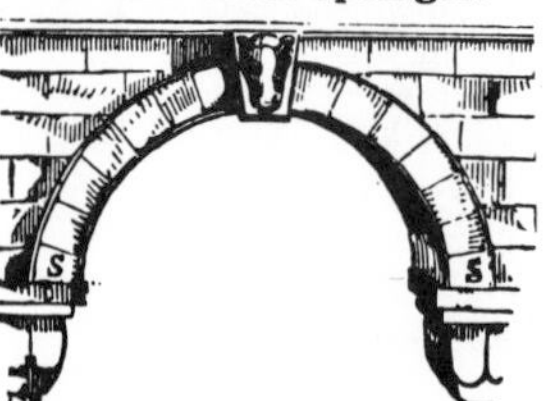

S, *S*, springers,2

springhouse A building enclosing a natural spring; sufficiently cool for use as a storehouse of milk and other dairy products.

springing, spring **1.** The point where an arch rises from its supports. **2.** The angle of rise of an arch.

springing course In masonry, the stones upon which the first stones of an arch rest.

springing line The imaginary horizontal line at which an arch or vault begins to curve; the line in which the springers rest on the imposts.

springing wall Same as a **buttress.**

sprocked eaves The eaves of a roof which have been raised by **sprockets.**

sprocket, cocking piece, sprocket piece In roofing, a strip of wood, fixed to the upper side of rafters at the eaves; raises the edge of the eaves and forms a break in the roof line.

sprung molding A curved molding.

spur **1.** An appendage to a supporting structure, as a shore, prop, or buttress; a decorative appendage of the base of a round column resting on a square or polygonal plinth, set at the corners, and taking the form of a grotesque, a tongue, or leafwork. Also called a **griffe.** **2.** A **spere.**

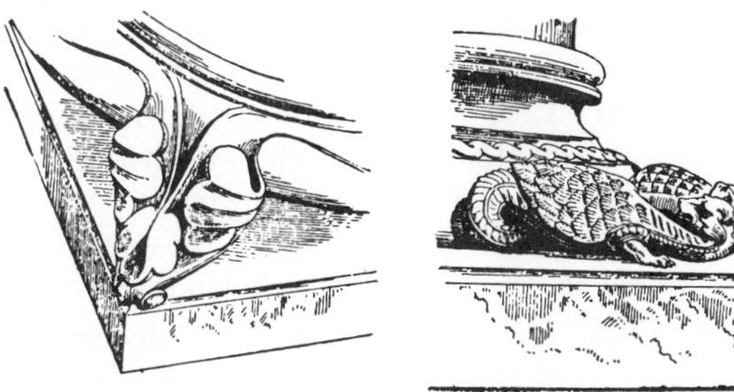

spurs,1: France (end of 12th cent.)

spur beam A horizontal timber, across the thickness of a wall, which is fixed to a wall plate, rafter, and ashlaring.

square and rabbet Same as **annulet.**

square billet A Norman molding consisting of a series of projecting cubes, with spaces between the cubes.

square billet

squared log A **balk.**

square dome Same as **cloistered arch.**

squared rubble Wall construction in which squared stones of various sizes are combined in patterns that make up courses as high as or higher than the tallest stones.

square-headed Cut off at right angles above, as an opening with upright parallel sides and a straight horizontal lintel, as distinguished from an opening that is arched.

square-headed window

square-rigger house A colonial New England **hip roof** house with chimneys at both gable ends, or on both sides of a central hall, or centered between the front and back rooms. Many such houses had a widow's walk and/or cupola on the roof.

square shoot A wood **downspout.**

square-turned Said of ornamental balusters or the like which are molded or decorated on all four sides; not turned on a lathe.

squinch **1.** Corbeling, often arcuate, built at the upper corners of a structural bay to support its tangent, smaller dome or drum. **2.** A small arch across the corner of a square room which supports a superimposed mass; also called a **sconce.**

squinch arch See **squinch, 2.**

squinch,1: Salisbury Cathedral (c. 1300)

squinch,2: Oxford Cathedral (c. 1240)

squint **1.** A small opening, often obliquely cut, in the wall of a church, generally so placed as to afford a view of the high altar from the transept or aisles. **2.** A **squint brick.**

squint,1: Crawley Church, Hampshire

squint brick, squint quoin A building stone or brick of special shape; used at an oblique corner.

squint quoin See **squint brick.**

squint window See **squint, 1.**

sringa The dome of a Hindu temple in southern India.

寺 **ssŭ** A Chinese temple in a monastery; special types include: **fo ssŭ** (Buddhist temple), **ch'ing chên ssŭ** (Islamic temple), and **lama ssŭ** (Lamaist temple).

stabulum An inn or public house for the accommodation of travelers.

staddle **1.** A rack or supporting framework placed beneath a stack, such as a haystack. **2.** Any similar supporting framework.

staddle stone One of the stones which supports a **staddle, 1**; usually mushroom-shaped.

stadium **1.** A sports arena, usually oval or horseshoe-shaped **2.** An ancient Roman measure of length equal to 607 ft (185 m).

staff Ornamental plastering, made in molds and reinforced with fiber; usually nailed or wired into place.

Staffordshire blue A **blue brick.**

stained glass Glass given a desired color in its molten state, or by firing a stain into the surface of the glass after forming; used in decorative windows or transparent mosaics.

stained-glass window A window whose glass is colored.

stair A series of steps, or flights of steps connected by landings, which permit passage between two or more levels or floors.

staircase **1.** A flight of stairs, or a series of such flights, including supports, handrails, and framework. **2.** The structure containing a flight of stairs.

stair dormer A **dormer** built sufficiently wide to accommodate the upper part of a staircase leading to an upper half-floor or attic.

stair tower **1.** A **staircase.** **2.** A **stair turret.**

stair turret **1.** A building containing a winding stair which usually fills it entirely. **2.** A stair enclosure which projects beyond the building roof.

stair turret, Church of S. Vulfran, Abbeville, France (1488-1534)

stained-glass window, Chartres Cathedral (13th cent.)

stalactite work See **muqarnas.**

stalk See **cauliculus.**

stall **1.** One of a number of seats, enclosed either wholly or in part, at the back of the seats in a chancel or choir, for use of the clergy. **2.** A theatre seat, usually one in the front division of the parquet or orchestra stalls; application of the term is variable.

stall,1: Church of Notre Dame, Paris (17th cent.)

stamba, stambha Same as **lat.**

stanchion **1.** A prop, upright bar, or piece of timber giving support to a roof, a window, or the like. **2.** An upright bar, beam, or post, as of a window, screen, railing, etc.

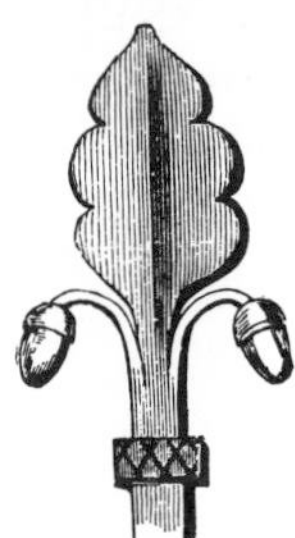

stanchion,2

stanza A room or chamber within a building, as the stanza of Raphael in the Vatican.

star molding A common Norman molding whose surface is a succession of projecting starlike shapes.

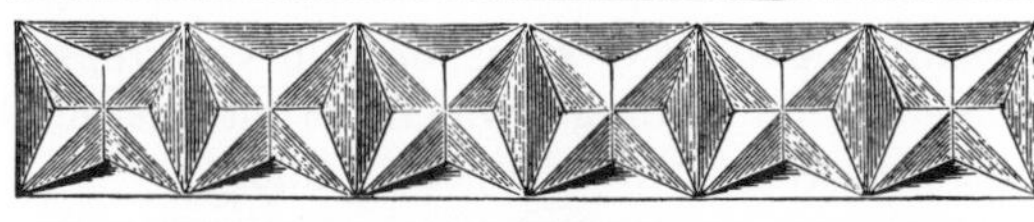

star molding

Star of David, Mogen David A six-pointed star composed of two equilateral triangles, one superimposed upside down on the other; a symbol of Judaism.

star-ribbed vault Same as **star vault.**

starting newel The newel-post at the foot of a stair.

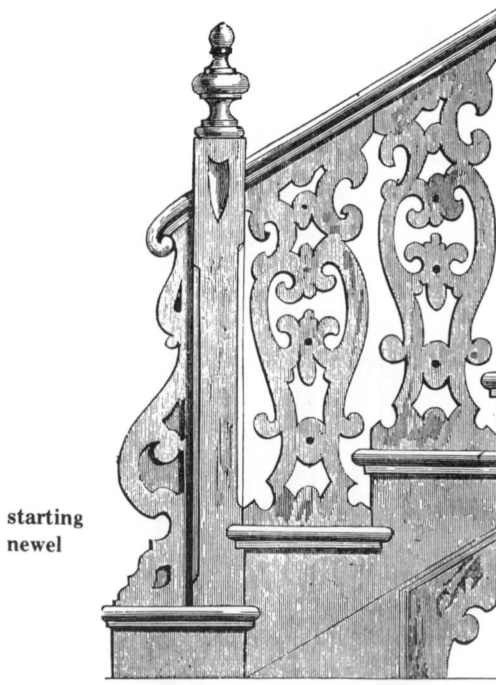

starting newel

star vault, stellar vault A vault whose rib pattern suggests a star.

statio The Latin name for a castle, citadel, or fort.

staunchion Same as **stanchion.**

stave One of a number of narrow boards used to build up a curved surface.

stave church A Norwegian mast-framed steep-roofed church of the 12th and 13th cent., constructed entirely of wood, highly original in structure and with fantastic semipagan decorative features.

stave church, Borgund, Norway

St. Basil's Cathedral See **Saint Basil's cathedral.**

Steamboat Gothic A richly ornamental mode of **Gothic Revival** building in the Ohio and Mississippi river valley during the 19th cent., based on steamboat decoration.

steening The brick or stone lining, often laid dry, of a cesspool, cistern, or well.

steeple A tall ornamental structure; a tower, composed of a series of stories diminishing in size, and topped by a small pyramid, spire, or cupola.

steining Same as **steening.**

stele, stela **1.** In classical architecture and derivatives, an upright stone, usually a slab, marking a grave. **2.** A wall area set aside as a memorial.

stellar vault See **star vault.**

step A stair unit which consists of one tread and one riser.

step gable See **corbie gable.**

stepped arch An arch in which some or all of the voussoirs have their outer ends cut square to fit into the horizontal courses of the wall to the sides of the arch.

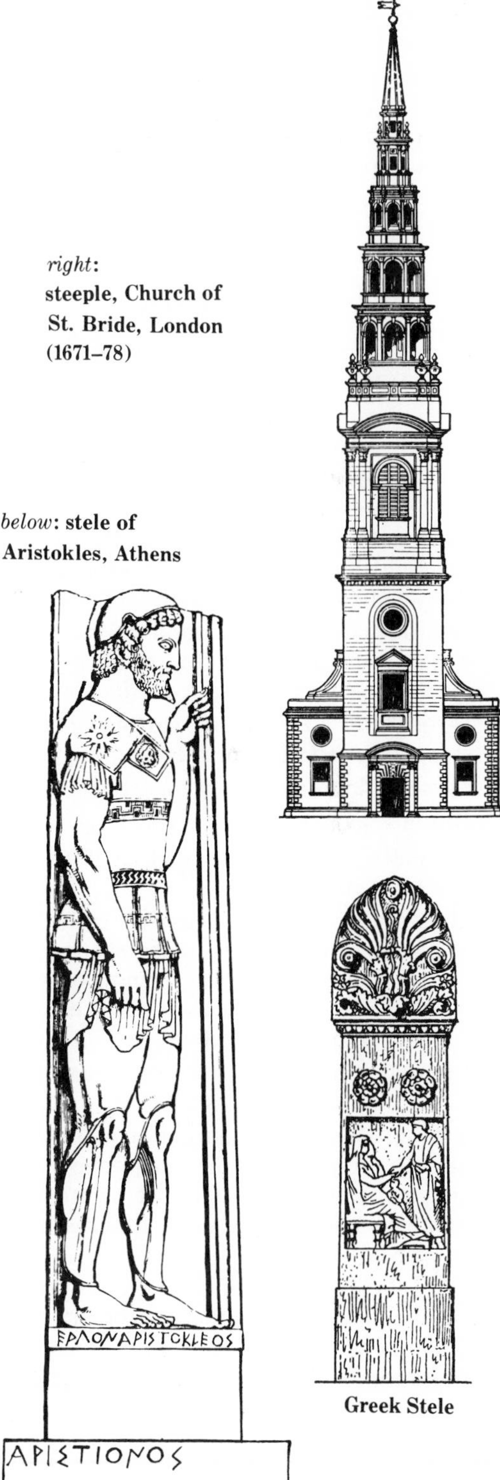

right: **steeple, Church of St. Bride, London (1671–78)**

below: **stele of Aristokles, Athens**

Greek Stele

stepped gable Same as **corbie gable.**

stepped voussoir A **voussoir** which is squared along its upper surfaces so that it fits horizontal courses of masonry units.

step pyramid An early type of **pyramid** having a stepped superstructure.

step pyramid

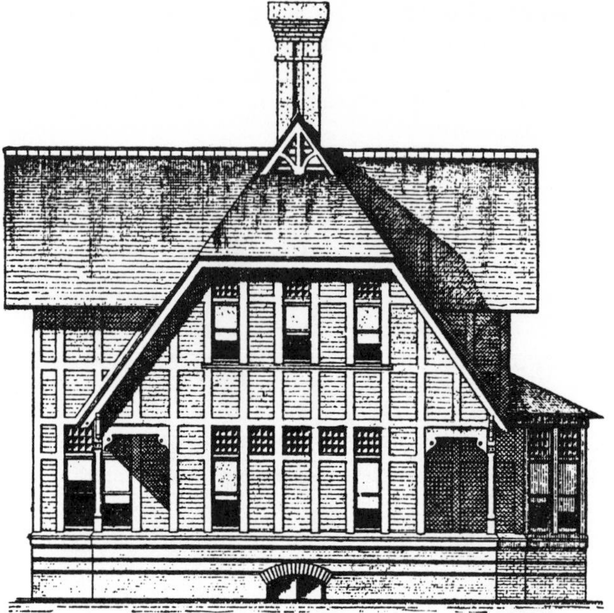

Stick style

stereobate The substructure, foundation, or solid platform upon which a building is erected. In a columnar building, it includes the **stylobate** (the uppermost step or platform of the foundation upon which the columns stand).

stereochromy A method of painting in which water glass serves as the connecting medium between the color and its substratum.

stereotomy The art of cutting solids, e.g. stone, into certain figures or shapes.

steyre Old English term for **grees.**

sthupa Same as **stupa.**

stiacciato In very low relief, as if a **bas-relief** had been pressed flatter.

Stick style Eclectic American style, mainly of cottage architecture, in the second half of the 19th cent., predominantly in wood, characterized by jagged, angular elements expressing exposed frame construction.

stiff leaf In medieval ornament and derivatives, a formalized leaf shape.

stile **1.** One of the upright structural members of a frame, as at the outer edge of a door or a window sash. **2.** A set of steps, or a framework of bars and steps, for crossing over a fence or wall.

Stile Liberty The Italian version of Art Nouveau, so named after the firm of Liberty and Co. in London.

stillicidium In Doric buildings, **dripping eaves** in which the roof terminates.

stilted arch An arch whose curve begins above the impost line.

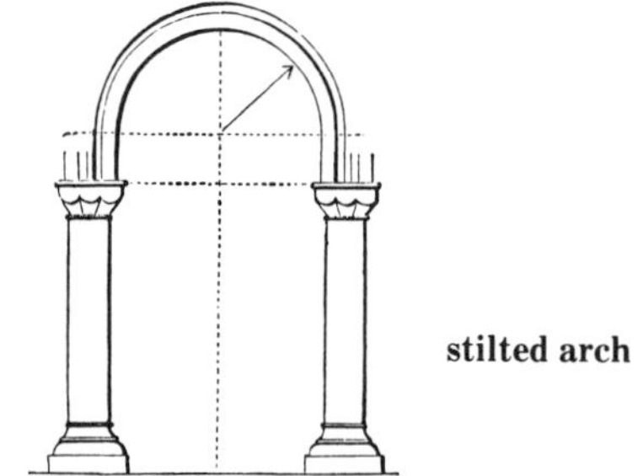

stilted arch

stilted arch, Church of S. Fosca, Torcello (1108)

stoa A portico, usually detached, often of considerable extent, providing a sheltered promenade or meeting place.

Greek stoa

stob A small post, as one of the uprights in fencing.

stockade A defensive barrier; logs or timbers driven into the ground to form an enclosure.

Stonehenge A megalithic, prehistoric monument near Salisbury, England, in Wiltshire; the most imposing megalithic monument in existence; probably constructed between 1800 and 1400 B.C.

Stonehenge; *above*: remains; *below*: reconstructed view

stone lantern An outdoor lantern, usually Japanese, used as a permanent garden ornament.

Japanese stone lanterns

stoneware, earthenware A hard, vitrified, ceramic ware, usually salt-glazed.

stonework 1. Masonry construction in stone. 2. Preparation or setting of stone for building or paving.

stoop A platform or small porch, usually up several steps, at the entrance to a house.

stoop

stop 1. The molding or trim on the inside face of a door or window frame against which the door or window closes; a **bead, 2.** 2. The projecting boss or other ornament against which the termination of a molding abuts.

stop bead See **bead, 2.**

stop chamfer, stopped chamfer A chamfer which curves or angles, becoming narrower until it meets the arris.

stop molding A solid or struck molding which is terminated short of the end of the member into which it is cut.

stopped chamfer See **stop chamfer.**

stopped flute In classical architecture and derivatives, a flute terminated, usually about two-thirds of the way down a column or pilaster. Below this, the shaft may be smooth or faceted, or the fluting may be incised partway, leaving a flat surface sunk between fillets. A cabled flute is sometimes called "stopped."

storey See **story.**

story, *Brit.* **storey** **1.** The space in a building between floor levels, or between a floor and a roof above. In some codes and ordinances a basement is considered as a story; generally a cellar is not. **2.** A major architectural division even where no floor exists, as a tier or a row of windows.

stoup A basin for holy water, sometimes free-standing but more often affixed to or carved out of a wall or pillar near the entrance of a church.

stoups; ***left*****: Crowmarsh (c. 1150);** ***right*****, Warmington (c. 1220)**

stoup: Decorated style

stoup: Romsey Church, Hampshire (c. 1130)

marble stoup: Orvieto Cathedral, Italy (early 16th cent.)

stove A warming or cooking apparatus, often of iron, and portable. In cold countries the stove may be a more important and permanent structure, built of glazed tiles, more or less decorative in character, and generally so situated as to warm contiguous rooms.

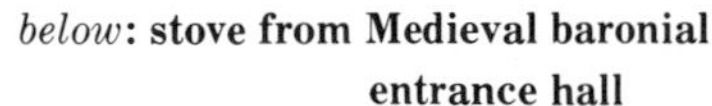

below: **stove from Medieval baronial entrance hall**

elevation

side view

section through stove

straight arch A **flat arch.**

straining arch An arch used as a strut, as in a flying buttress.

straining beam, straining piece, strutting piece In a truss, a horizontal strut above the tie beam or above a line joining the feet of the rafters, commonly between the joists at midspan; esp. in a queen post truss, the strut between the upper ends of the two queen posts.

straining piece **1.** Same as **straining beam.** **2.** Any member which is fixed between opposing struts to take their thrusts.

straining sill In a timber roof, a **straining beam** which is placed on the upper surface of the tie beam of a roof truss, between posts, to resist the inward thrust from struts.

strapped wall See **battened wall.**

strapwork A type of ornament consisting of a narrow fillet or band which is folded, crossed, and interlaced.

stretcher A masonry unit laid horizontally with its length in the direction of the face of the wall.

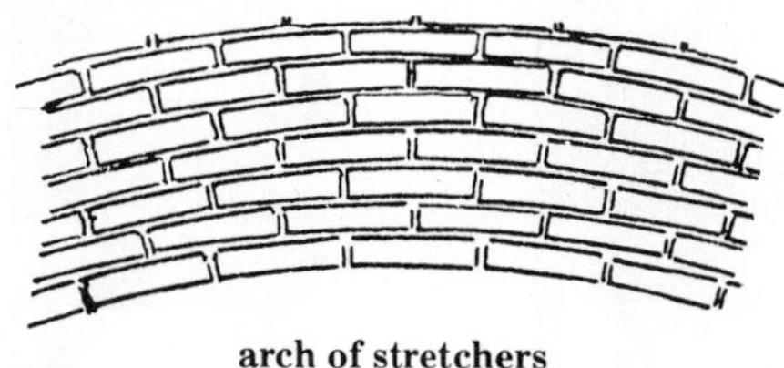

arch of stretchers

stria **1.** A **fillet.** **2.** A rib, esp. one repeated to give texture.

striated Fluted, as a column.

striatura The **fluting** on columns.

striga A fluting of a column.

strigil ornament In Roman architecture, a decoration of a flat member, as a fascia, with a repetition of slightly curved vertical flutings or reedings.

string **1.** In a stair, an inclined board which supports the end of the steps; also called a **stringer.** **2.** In a lattice roof truss, a horizontal tie. **3.** A **stringcourse.**

stringboard Same as **face string.**

stringcourse, belt course A horizontal band of masonry, generally narrower than other courses, extending across the façade of a structure and in some instances encircling such decorative features as pillars or engaged columns; may be flush or projecting, and flat-surfaced, molded, or richly carved.

stringer **1.** A **string, 1.** **2.** A long, heavy horizontal timber which connects the posts in a frame which supports a floor.

strix A **flute,** or concave **canalis;** a fluting of a column.

stroked work Stone which has been tooled so as to produce a finely fluted surface.

c, c, **stringcourses, Old State House, Boston, Mass.**

stroll garden A garden designed to be viewed from a footpath, which usually proceeds from one of a series of vantage points to another.

stronghold See **fortress, 1.**

struck molding, solid molding, stuck molding A molding cut into rather than added to or planted on a member.

structura A general term for masonry of the ancient Greeks and Romans; see various types under **opus.**

structura antiqua Same as **opus incertum.**

structura caementicia Same as **opus caementicium.**

structura reticulata Same as **opus reticulatum.**

strutbeam Same as **collar beam.**

strutting beam Same as **collar beam.**

strutting piece Same as **straining beam.**

St. Sophia, Sta. Sophia Same as **Hagia Sophia.**

Stuart architecture Architecture of the English Late Renaissance (1603–88).

stuc Plaster applied to form an imitation stone.

stucco **1.** An exterior finish, usually textured; composed of portland cement, lime, and sand, which are mixed with water. **2.** A fine plaster used for decorative work or moldings.

stuck molding See **struck molding.**

stump tracery Tracery, late German Gothic, whose interpenetrating bars are cut off like stumps.

stupa, tope A Buddhist memorial mound, erected to enshrine a relic or to commemorate a sacred site; consists of an artificial mound, raised on a platform and surrounded by an outer ambulatory with a stone railing and four gateways, crowned by a multiple sunshade.

representation of stupa at Amaravati, Madras (3rd cent. A.D.)

stupa, Anuradhapura, Ceylon (c. 246 B.C.)

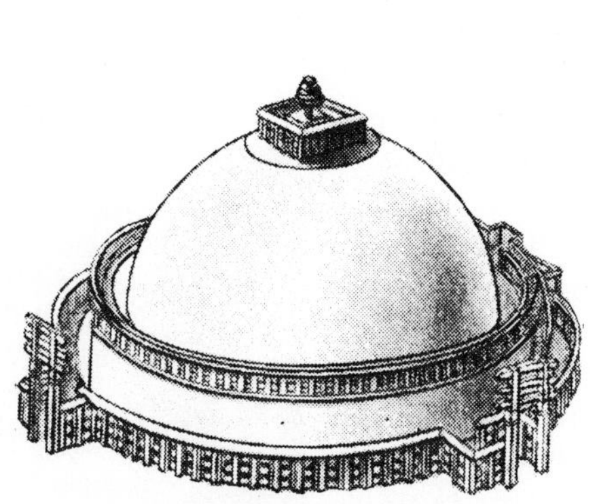

stupa, Sanchi, India (1st cent. B.C.)

stupa, Cha Heng, Nan, Siam (c. 14th cent.)

Style Moderne See **Art Deco.**

Style Rayonnant See **Rayonnant Style.**

stylobate **1.** Strictly, the single top course of the three steps of the **crepidoma** upon which the columns rest directly. **2.** Any continuous base, plinth, or pedestal, upon which a row of columns is set. Also see **stereobate.**

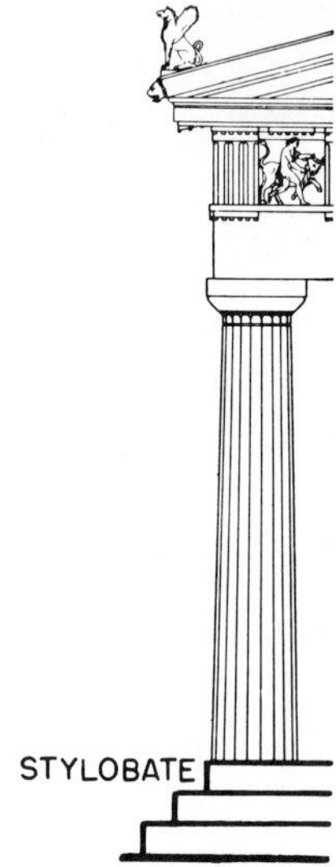

subarch One of two or more minor arches beneath and enclosed by an outer arch.

subbase The lowest projection of a base molding or baseboard with more than one horizontal subdivision.

sublica In ancient construction, a pile driven into the earth, or into ground covered by water, to support a structure.

suborder A secondary architectural **order,** introduced chiefly for decoration, as distinguished from a main order of a structure.

subplinth A secondary plinth sometimes placed under the usual one in column and pedestal bases.

subsellium Same as **miserere.**

sudatorium In an ancient Roman bath, a hot room for inducing sweat, used by athletes.

suggestus **1.** The stage in the Roman Forum. **2.** In the Flavian Amphitheatre in Rome, the elevated location of the emperor's box.

sugido Wood-paneled sliding doors in traditional Japanese architecture; they may or may not be decorated.

sudatorium

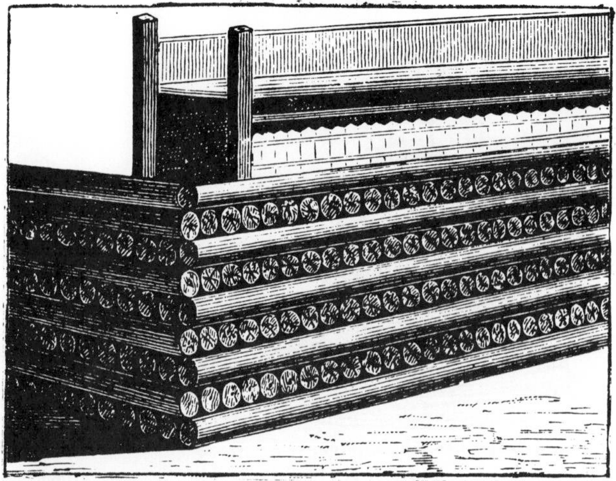

suggestus,1

sukiya **1.** A Japanese teahouse or tearoom. **2.** A style of Japanese domestic architecture, greatly influenced by the teahouse, used for mansions and villas during the Momoyama and Edo periods.

数寄屋 **sukiya, Nan-en-ji Temple, Kyoto**

Sumerian architecture A monumental architecture developed by the Sumerians, who dominated southern Mesopotamia from the end of the 4th to the end of the 3rd millennium B.C. Made use of locally available building materials: tall rushes and clay; tied bundles of reeds (used as structural framing for variously shaped huts, houses, and halls); reed mats and **wattle and daub** (used for walls and roofing); and clay (used as sun-dried bricks laid in mud or bitumen-mortar). To give character and structural strength to the mud-brick walls, the walls were articulated by buttresses or built with alternating pilasters and recesses. Rooms were narrow, mostly covered by timber and mud roofs; sometimes walls were faced with burnt brick or tile. Large cities were protected by strong ramparts. There were monumental temples and palaces, built around a series of courtyards, with well-developed drainage and sanitation systems. The **ziggurat** of Ur is the most famous of many which were constructed.

sumimune See **onigawara.**

summer **1.** A horizontal beam supporting the ends of floor joists or resting on posts and supporting the wall above; also called a **summertree.** **2.** Any large timber or beam which serves as a bearing surface. **3.** The **lintel** of a door or window; a **breastsummer.** **4.** A stone laid on a column and serving as a support for construction above, as in the construction of an arch.

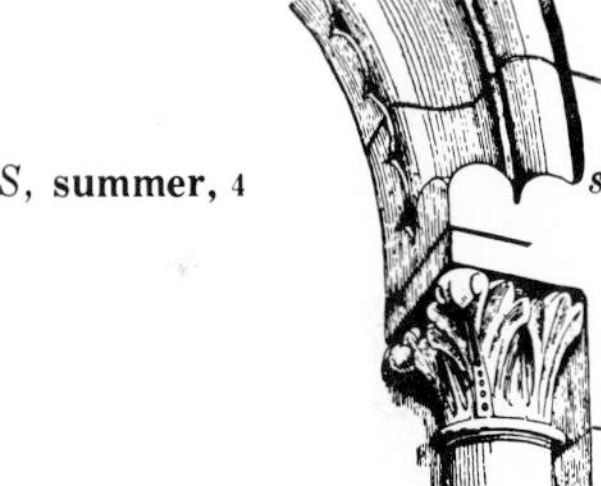

S, **summer, 4**

summertree See **summer, 1.**

sunburst light A **fanlight.**

sun disk A disk (representing the sun) with wings; esp. used in Egyptian antiquity as emblematic of the sun god.

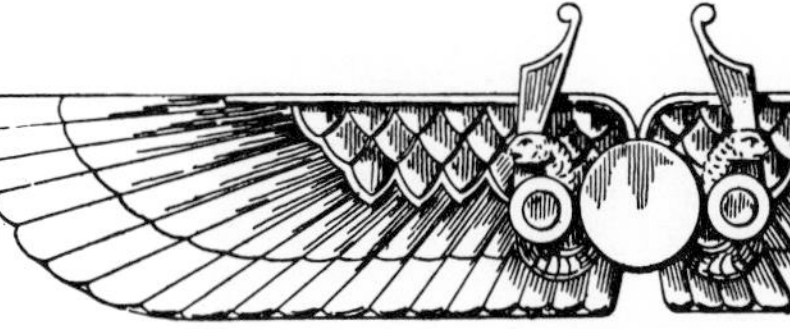

sun disk

sunk draft A margin around a building stone which is sunk below the face of the stone to give it a raised appearance.

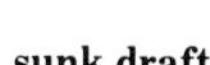

sunk draft

sunken garden A garden, sometimes geometrically planned, at a level below prevailing grade, or surrounded by raised terraces.

sunk face A building stone having a face from which material has been removed to give the stone the appearance of a sunken panel.

sunk fence A **ha-ha.**

sunk fillet A **fillet** formed by a groove in a plane surface.

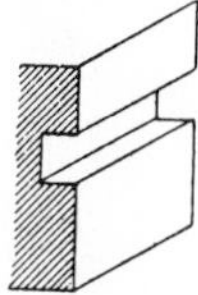

sunk fillet

sunk molding A molding slightly recessed behind the surface on which it is located.

sunk panel A panel recessed below the surface of its surrounding framing or carved into solid masonry or timber.

sunk relief, cavo-relievo, cavo-rilievo, intaglio rilevato Relief which does not project above the general surface upon which it is wrought.

sunk relief, Court of Edfu, Egypt (2nd cent. B.C.)

sun room Same as **solarium.**

superabacus An **impost block.**

supercapital An **impost block.**

supercilium **1.** The fillet above the uppermost molding or cyma of a cornice. **2.** The small fillet on either side of the scotia of an Ionic base. **3.** The lintel of a doorcase; so-called because it stretches from the top of one doorpost to the other, like an eyebrow over the eye.

supercolumniation The placing of one **order** above another.

supercolumniation: Theatre of Marcellus, Rome (23–13 B.C.)

superposition Same as **supercolumniation.**

surbase **1.** The crowning moldings or cornice of a pedestal. **2.** A border or molding above a base or dado. **3.** The molding at the top of a baseboard.

a, surbase, 1

surbased arch An arch whose rise is less than half the span.

surface arcade Same as **blind arcade.**

surface rib A decorative rib on the soffit of a vault.

surmounted arch A semicircular **stilted arch.**

surround **1.** An encircling border or decorative frame. **2.** See **chimneypiece.**

suspensura Any building or flooring raised from the ground and supported on arches, piles, or pillars; esp. applied to the flooring of an ancient Roman bath suspended over the flues of a furnace on low pillars so that steam may circulate freely under it.

Sussex bond, Sussex garden wall bond Same as **Flemish garden wall bond.**

swag A **festoon.**

swan-neck **1.** The curved portion of a handrail of stairs which joins the newel-post. The member's upper part is convex on the top; the lower part is concave on the top. **2.** A downspout connector between a gutter and the downpipe, where the eaves overhang.

sway In thatched roof construction, one of the small willow or hazelwood rods laid at right angles to the thatching to hold it down.

sweathouse, sweat lodge **1.** A structure used for sweating of tobacco. **2.** An American Indian structure heated by steam produced by pouring water on hot stones, and used for therapeutic sweating or ritual.

swelled chamfer See **wave molding.**

swinging post See **hanging post.**

Synadicum marble Same as **pavonazzo.**

synagogue A place of assembly for Jewish worship.

synodal hall A hall in which the clergy of a whole diocese meet.

synoecia In ancient Greece, a residence shared by several families.

synthronon A bench, in an Early Christian or Byzantine church, reserved for the clergy.

Syrian arch On a classical façade, an arched entablature carried over the central intercolumniation.

syrinx In ancient Egypt, a narrow and deep rock-cut channel or tunnel forming a characteristic feature of Egyptian tombs of the New Empire.

systyle See **intercolumniation.**

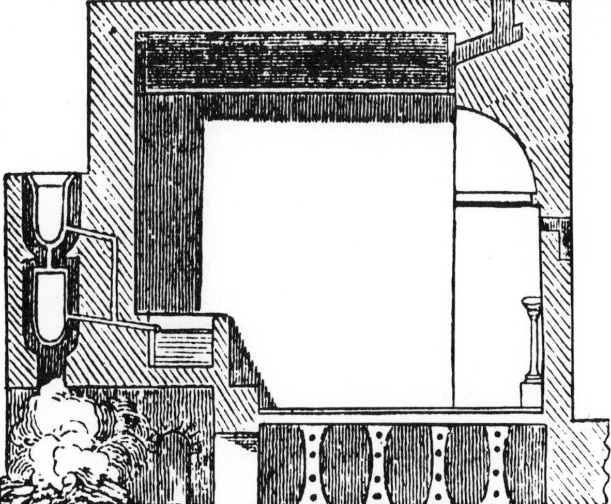

suspensura: the flooring of the room is supported on hollow tubular tiles, perforated down the sides to admit the steam vapor. A warm-water bath is shown to the right of the boilers

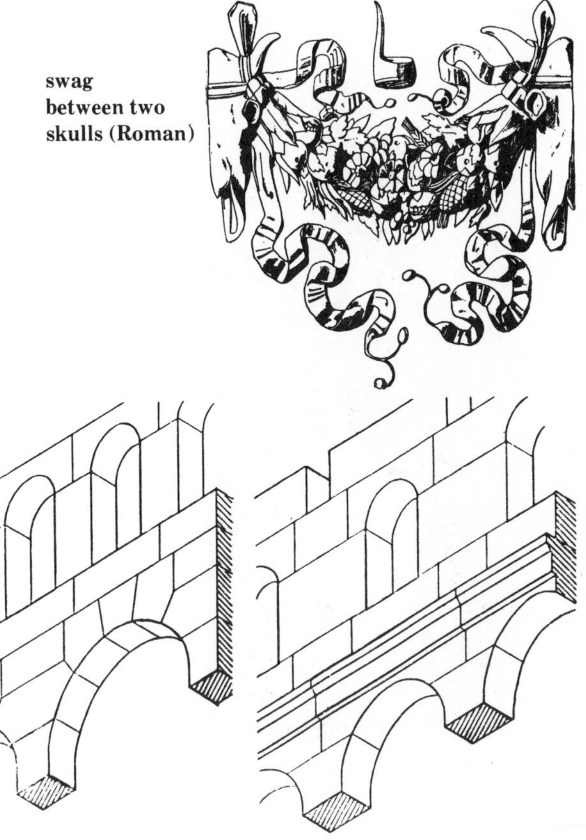

swag between two skulls (Roman)

right: Syrian arches

塔 **ta** In Chinese architecture, a pagoda, esp.: **1.** A high tower used for observing scenery or for military purposes. **2.** A tower, of religious origin, used as a memorial; built of timber with a masonry core, or built completely of masonry.

tabby A mixture of lime and water with shells, gravel, or stones; when dry, forms a mass as hard as rock; used as a building material.

taberna In ancient Rome, a booth, shop, or stall.

tabernacle **1.** A decorative niche often topped with a canopy and housing a statue. **2.** A church for a large Protestant congregation.

tabernacle, 1: Hàddiscol Church, Norfolkshire (c. 1160)

tabernacle,1: Lady Chapel, Exeter Cathedral (c. 1280)

tabernacle,1: Queen Eleanor's Cross, Northampton (1294)

tabernacle finial to a buttress

tabernacle work A highly decorated arcade or screen with canopies and sculpture.

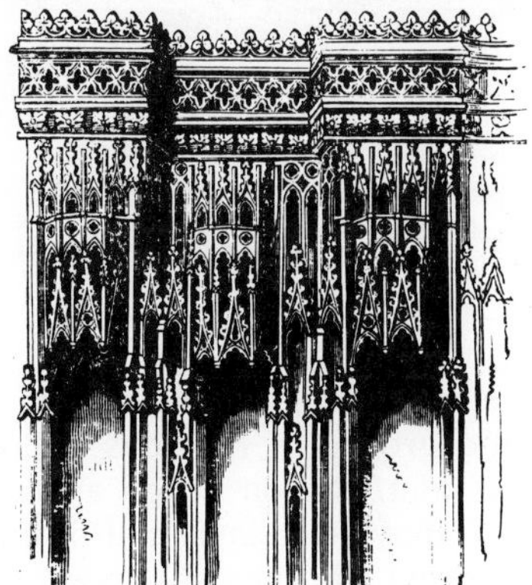

tabernacle work: part of altar screen, Winchester Cathedral (c. 1480)

taberna diversoria See **diversorium.**

tabia A **rammed earth** mixed with lime and pebbles.

tablature **1.** A tabular surface or structure. **2.** A painting or design on a part of an extended surface, as a ceiling.

table **1.** In medieval architecture, the frontal on the face of the altar. **2.** A slab set horizontally and carried on supports.

table,1

table,2 over a door: Palace of St. Cloud, France

table-base Same as **base molding, 2.**

tablero In the architecture of **Mesoamerica,** a rectangular framed panel which is cantilevered over an outward sloping apron **(talud)**, with which it is always used; characteristic of the Teotihuacán style of architecture, constituting their most prominent architectural contribution; introduced ca. 150 A.D.; widely copied throughout Mesoamerica, with regional variations.

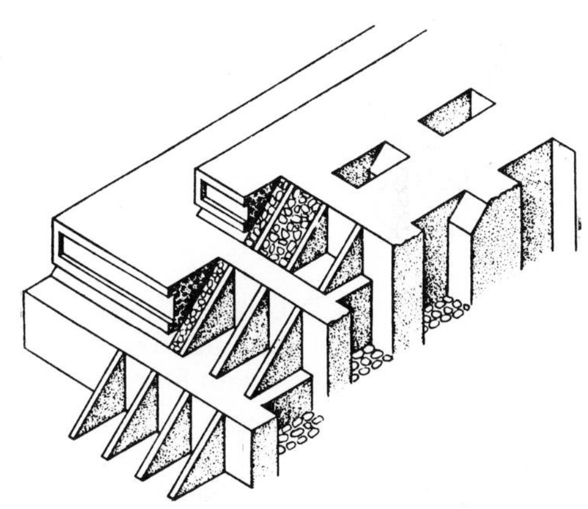

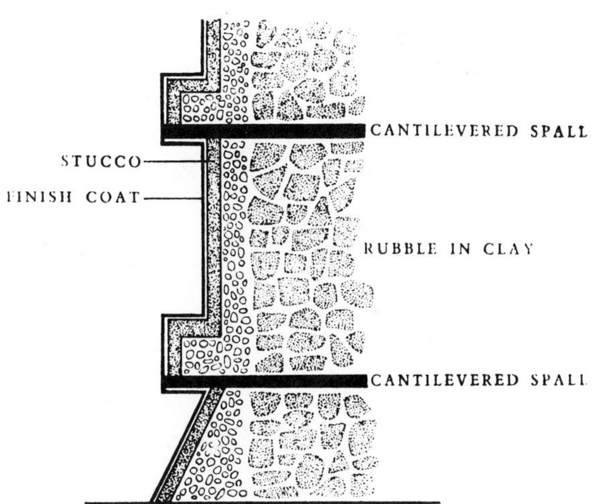

diagram of assembly *(above)* and section *(below)* of a tablero: inner core of central platform, Teotihuacán, Ciudadela (before 500 A.D.)

table stone Same as **dolmen.**

tablet **1.** A regularly shaped, separate panel, or a representation thereof, often bearing an inscription or image. **2.** A **coping stone,** set flat; also called **tabling.**

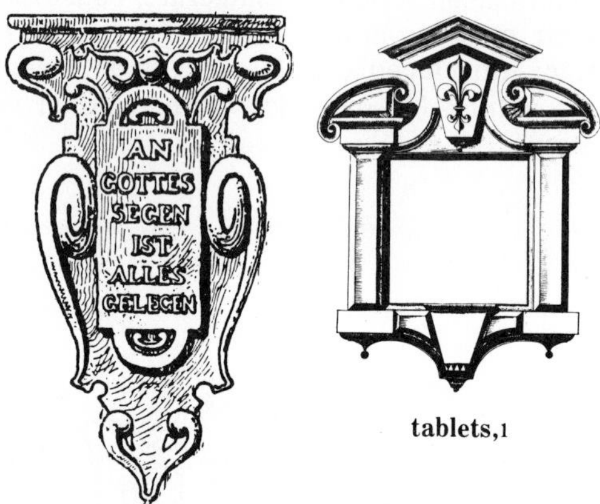

tablets,1

tablet flower In Decorated Gothic architecture, a variation of the **ballflower,** having the form of an open flower with four petals.

tablet tomb In the Roman catacombs, a rectangular recess in a gallery, parallel with the passageway, containing a burial chest of stone or masonry with a flat cover.

tabling Same as **tablet, 2.**

tablinum In ancient Roman architecture, a large open room or apartment for family records and hereditary statues; situated at the end of the **atrium** farthest from the main entrance.

tabularium See **archivium.**

tachara The residence hall at Persepolis, built by Darius.

taenia, tenia A narrow raised band or fillet, particularly the topmost member of the Doric architrave. Also see **order.**

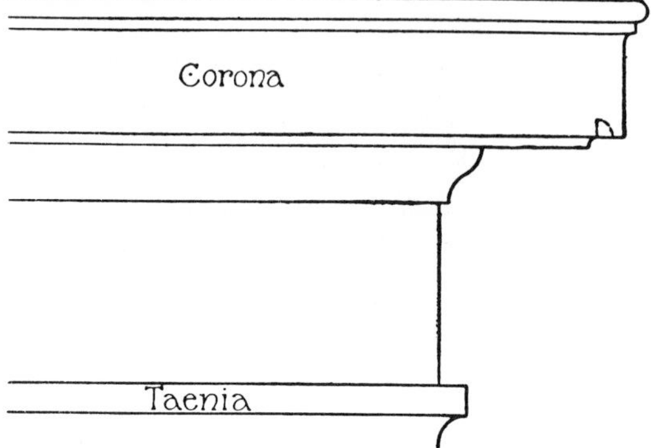

tablet,1

台 **t'ai** In the traditional Chinese architecture of palaces and groups of religious buildings, a pedestal or platform on which a building is constructed; may be a single platform or a series of platforms, the number of platforms designating the importance of the building. Some were rectangular in plan with several receding stories.

tail See **lookout.**

tailpiece A **lookout.**

t'ai miao An official shrine for royal Chinese ancestors; usually located on the east side of a royal palace.

tai-no-ya Literally "confronting houses." In the **Shinden style** of Japanese architecture, one of the residence annex buildings which were erected to the east and west of the main building, and sometimes to the north; these were connected to the main building by open corridors.

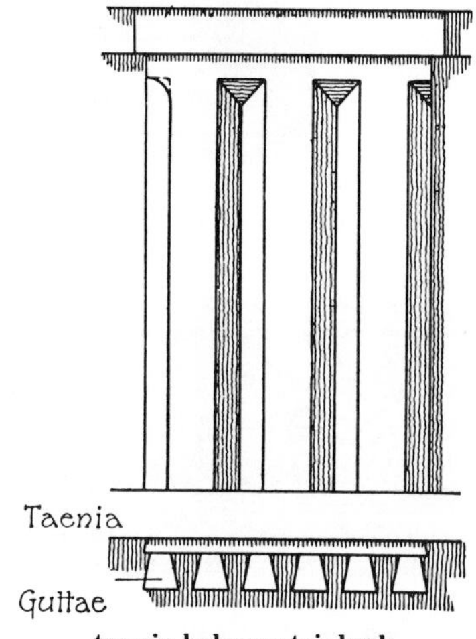

taenia below a triglyph

Taisha style The oldest style of Shinto shrines in existence. The Grand Shrine of Izumo on the coast of the Sea of Japan is the outstanding example, consisting of four compartments surrounded by a verandah with a balustrade.

Tajin Site of the outstanding example of architecture of the Totonacs (c. 200–900 A.D.), in the State of Vera Cruz, Mexico. The Pyramid of the Niches has six tiers which are deeply niched, in an adaptation of the **tablero;** a stairway flanked by balusters rises on its eastern slope; characteristic of the **El Tajin style** of Mesoamerican architecture of the Totonacs.

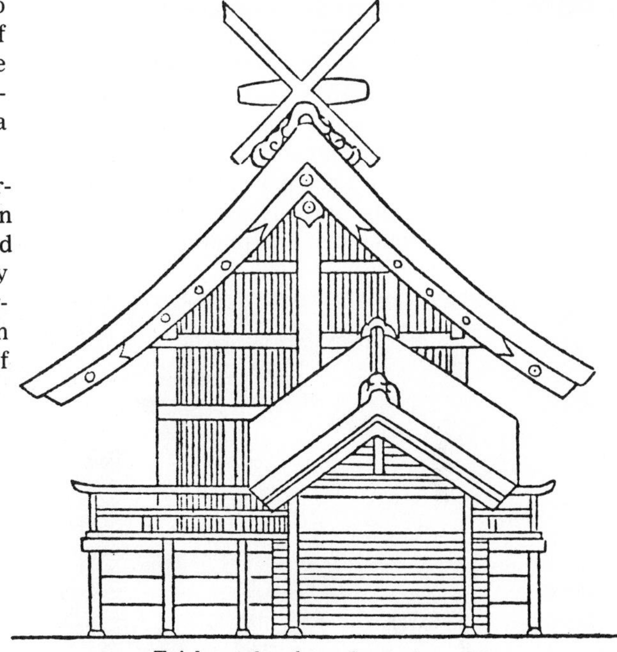

Taisha style; *above*: front view of the Grand Shrine of Izumo, Japan; *below*: side view

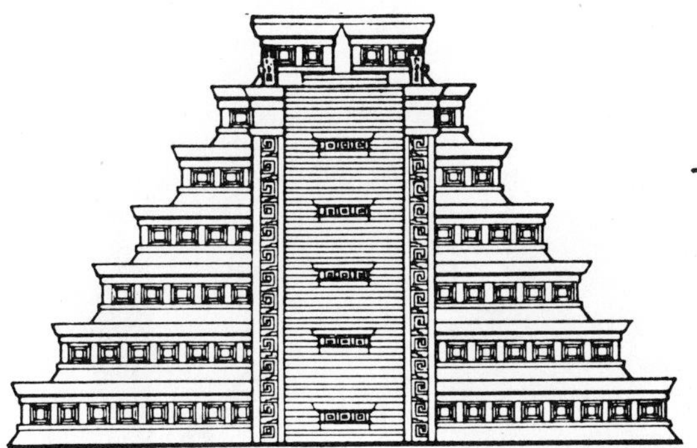

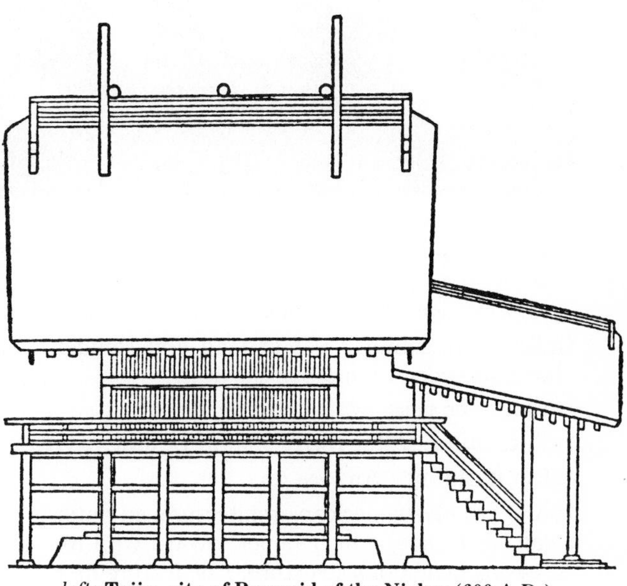

left: Tajin, site of Pyramid of the Niches (600 A.D.)

Taj Mahal An outstanding example of Indian **Muslim architecture,** a tomb erected at Agra by Shah Jehan after the death of his favorite wife, Mumtaza Mahal, in 1629, to contain her remains; also contains his remains. The outer court is surrounded by arcades and adorned by four gateways. The principal gateway leads from the court to the gardens containing marble canals and fountains. The building, which is reflected in an oblong pool of water, is on a raised, marble-faced platform 313 ft (95.4 m) square with a minaret at each corner. At the center of the raised platform stands the mausoleum, which has a principal dome 80 ft (24.4 m) high. Under this dome is an enclosure formed by a screen of trelliswork of white marble enclosing two tombs (the actual bodies rest in plainer tombs in a vault, directly below).

Taj Mahal, Agra, India

takayuka jūtaku A type of Japanese structure with an elevated floor, perhaps used as a grain storage house during the Yayoi period.

tallboy A chimney pot of long and slender form, intended to improve the draft.

tallus See **talus.**

tallut, tallet, tallot *(Brit.)* A loft or attic.

talon molding An **ogee, 2.**

talud In Mesoamerican architecture, an outer wall (or façade) which slopes inward with increasing height of a structure. This feature first appeared at the Olmec site of La Venta, Tabasco (Mexico), ca. 800 B.C.

talud-tablero An architectural feature combining a **tablero** with a sloping **talud,** over which it is cantilevered. This combination is repeated over the façade of stepped temple pyramids; an original contribution of Teotihuacán architecture, widely copied throughout Mesoamerica. *(See illustration under* ***tablero.****)*

talus, tallus The slope or inclination of any work, as a **talus wall.**

talus wall A wall having an inclined face; a **battered wall.**

tambour **1.** A column drum. **2.** Any generally drum-shaped member.

大木作 **ta mu tso** A traditional Chinese method of timber construction above the columns of the building and below the roof, used with the **tou kung** system, usually used in elaborate buildings, such as for royalty, temples, and large monasteries.

壇 **tan** In traditional Chinese architecture, a series of raised platforms used as a podium or altar.

堂 **t'ang** In a traditional Chinese house, a living room or a room for receiving guests. Sometimes there was a separate building for this function, always on the central axis of the site plan.

taper A gradual diminution of thickness in an elongated object, as in a **spire.**

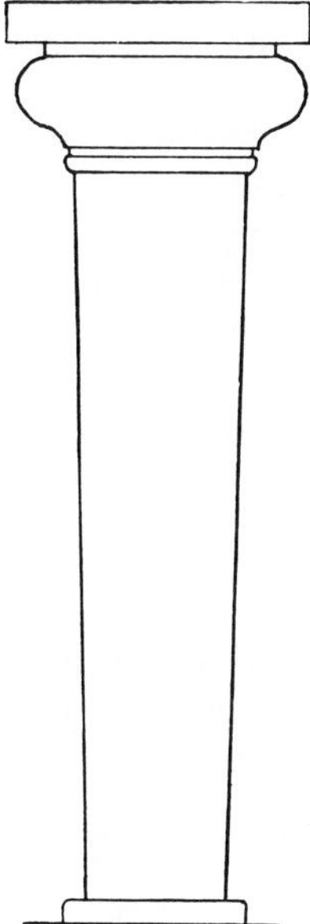

a column that tapers toward its base (restored); Cnossus, Crete

tapestry A fabric, worked on a warp by hand, the designs employed usually being pictorial; used for wall hangings or the like.

taphos A barrow or mound of earth or stones, as an ancient Greek tomb or memorial.

tapia An adobe-like building material, consisting mainly of earth or clay.

tarras Same as **trass.**

tarsia Same as **inlay.**

棰 **taruki** In traditional Japanese construction, a rafter.

tas-de-charge **1.** The lowest voussoir or voussoirs of an arch or vault with the joints horizontal instead of radial. **2.** In vaulting, that section of a group of vault ribs between the line where they spring and the line where they separate.

tatami A thick straw floor mat, covered with smooth, finely woven reeds and bound with plain or decorated bands of silk, cotton, or hemp; serves as a floor covering in a Japanese house; has a standard size of approx. 6 ft by 3 ft (approx. 2 m by 1 m); used as a standard unit of area in the measurement of room size.

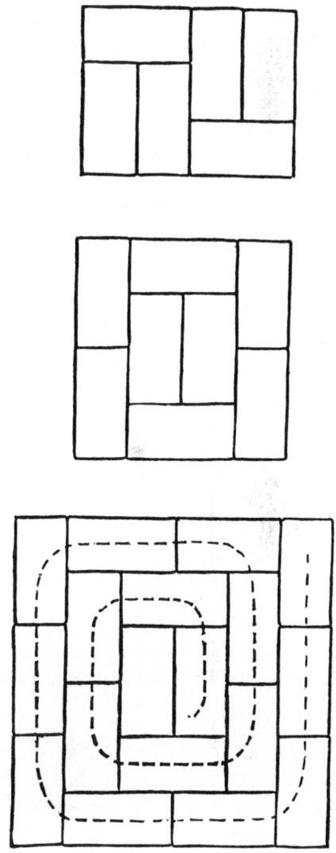

tatami arrangements for different-sized rooms

tauriform See **bull's head.**

tchahar taq Square open pavilion in Sassanian architecture (A.D. 224–651), composed of four columns with four arches supporting a dome, mostly over an altar.

tea garden **1.** A Japanese garden next to a teahouse, usually small and serene. **2.** An outdoor tearoom in a public garden, serving refreshments, including tea.

teagle post In timber framing, a post supporting one end of a tie beam.

teahouse A Japanese garden house used for the tea ceremony. See **sukiya.**

tease tenon See **teaze tenon.**

teaze tenon, tease tenon A tenon, having a stepped outline, on the top of a post; esp. cut to receive two horizontal pieces of timber that cross each other (at right angles) at the post.

tebam The reader's platform in a synagogue.

tectiform Like a roof in form or use.

tectonic Of or pertaining to building or construction; architectural.

tectorial Covering, forming a roof-like structure.

tectorium opus See **opus tectorium.**

tee A **finial** in the form of a conventionalized umbrella, or the like, used on stupas, topes, and pagodas.

tegimen Same as **baldachin.**

tegula A tile, esp. one of unusual shape or material.

tegurium A roof over a sarcophagus, usually double-sloped and supported by narrow columns.

tekkiya A communal dwelling of dervishes or Sufi monks; smaller than a **khangah.**

telamon, *pl.* **telamones** A sculptured male human figure used in place of a column to support an entablature; also called an **atlas.**

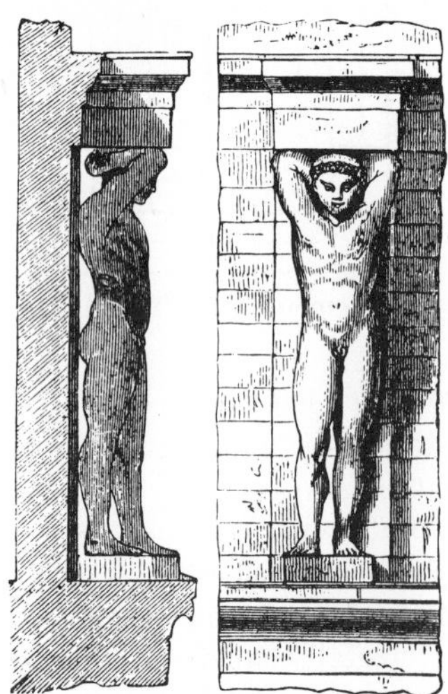

telamon: Temple of Zeus Olympius, Agrigentum (510–409 B.C.)

tell The Arabic name, in the Near East, for an artificial mound created by the accumulation of the debris of ancient cities.

left: **a tee as the finial of a pagoda;**
right: **a tee cut in rock; Temple of Ajanta, India (c. 250 A.D.)**

telonium A customhouse of the ancient Romans.

temenos A sacred enclosure surrounding a temple or other holy spot.

tempera A rapidly drying paint consisting of egg white (or egg yolk, or a mixture of egg white and yolk), gum, pigment, and water; esp. used in painting murals.

tempietto A small temple, esp. one of ornamental character, during the Renaissance or later; many such structures are found in the gardens of imposing country houses.

template, templet **1.** A pattern, usually of sheet material, used as a guide for setting out work and in repeating dimensions. **2.** A piece of stone, metal, or timber placed in a wall to receive the impost of a beam, girders, etc., and to distribute its load. **3.** A beam or plate spanning a door or window space to sustain joists and transfer their load to piers.

telamon: Roman

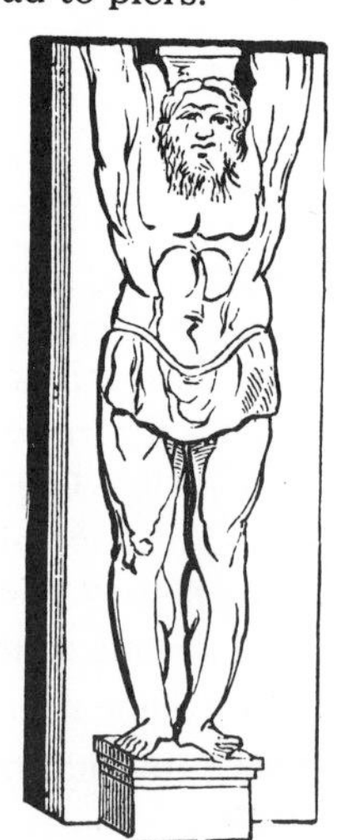

telamon, Pompeii

temple 1. An edifice dedicated to the service of a deity or deities, and connected with a system of worship. 2. A synagogue. 3. An edifice erected as a place of public worship, esp. a Protestant church. 4. A pretentious edifice for some special public use.

a restored view of the Temple of Aphaia, Aegina (c. 490 B.C.): *A*, stereobate; *B*, stylobate; *C*, *C*, columns of peristyle; *D*, inferior columns of cella; *E*, capital of column; *h*, abacus; *i*, echinus; *j*, hypotrachelium; F, entablature; *a*, architrave; *b*, frieze; *c*, cornice; *d*, triglyph; *e*, metope; *f*, *f*, mutules; *g*, regula with guttae; *G*, acroterium; *H*, *H*, portions of pediment; *I*, *I*, walls of cella; *K*, *K*, hypothetical apertures in roof to admit light to the cella

below: a temple having a peripteral, octastyle plan; the Parthenon, Athens (447–432 B.C.)

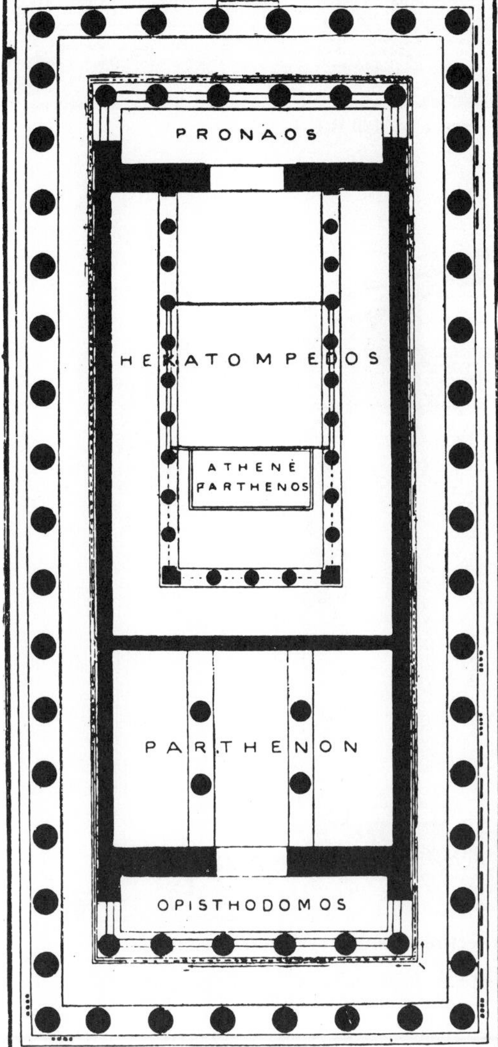

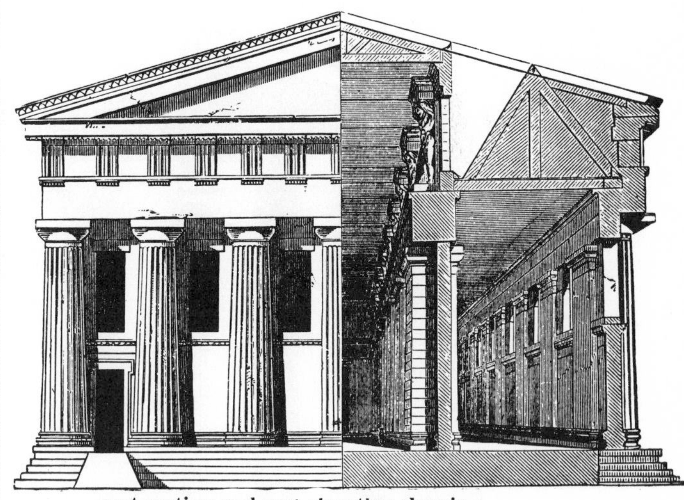

part section and part elevation showing construction of the Temple of Zeus Olympius (510–409 B.C.)

Temple of Poseidon, Paestum, Greece (c. 460 B.C.)

restored view of Temple of Apollo Epicurius: cross section through cella and peristyle; Bassae, Greece (450–425 B.C.)

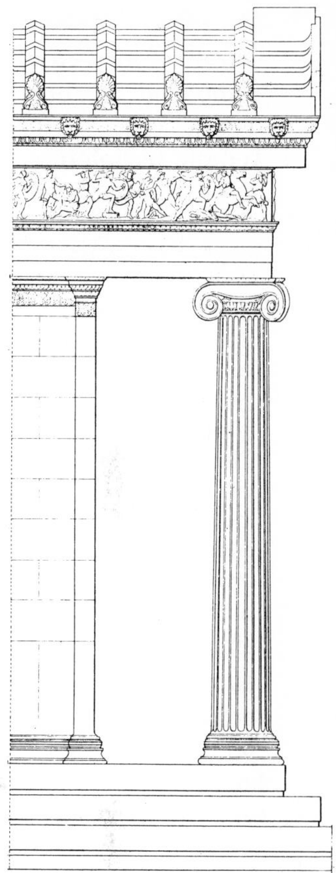

above: **Temple of Nike Apteros, Athens (437–432 B.C.)**

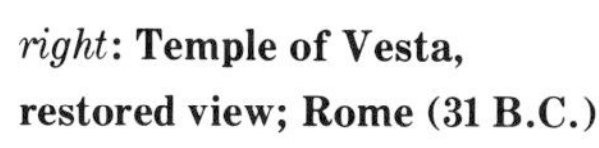

right: **Temple of Vesta, restored view; Rome (31 B.C.)**

Temple of Artemis See **artemision, 2.**

temple of heaven See **t'ien tan.**

Temple of Marduk See **Babylonian architecture.**

Temple of Solomon A temple built in Jerusalem by King Solomon ca. 950 B.C., destroyed by Nebuchadnezzar in 586 B.C. Constructed by Phoenician artisans, it was oblong in shape, and consisted of three main parts: an outer hall (*ulam*), the main sanctuary (*hekhal*), and the holy of holies (*debir*). The sanctuary was surrounded by a three-storied storage building (*yatzia*); two free-standing bronze pillars (Yachin and Boaz) stood in front of the vestibule. The temple, located in the middle of a courtyard, was of modest size [about 150 ft (46 m) in length], but exquisitely built in stone and cedarwood and decorated with gold leaf. Its layout followed Phoenician and Canaanite prototypes, known from excavations.

templet Same as **template.**

temple tower A **ziggurat.**

templon A trabeated colonnade which closes off the bema of a Byzantine church.

tenia See **taenia.**

天井 **tenjō** In traditional Japanese construction, a ceiling.

tenshu-kaku The keep or donjon of a Japanese castle. 天守閣

tent ceiling Same as **camp ceiling.**

Teotihuacán The largest and most influential ritual center of Mesoamerica, located near Mexico City. Its outstanding contribution to Mesoamerican architecture was the introduction of the **tablero** and **talud** for the façades of stepped pyramids and altar platforms. Site planning included large rectangular structures in a spatial arrangement along the north-south axis. Teotihuacán's influence reached north to El Tajin, Vera Cruz; south to Monte Albán, Oaxaca; and east into the Maya zone at Kaminaljuyu, Guatemala. In contrast to the Maya pattern of ceremonial centers, which were surrounded by widely scattered hamlets, Teotihuacán was a true city with satellite dwelling suburbs that housed its artisans.

tepe In Anatolia (Turkey) and Persia, the equivalent of a **tell.**

Temple of Antonius and Faustina, Rome (141 A.D.)

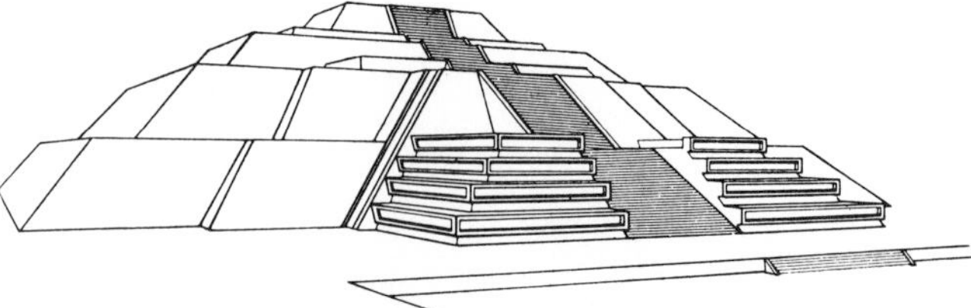

Teotihuacán, Pyramid of the Moon (c. 300 A.D.)

tepidarium In ancient Roman baths, a room of moderately warm temperature.

right: **tepidarium from thermae at Pompeii (c. 100 B.C.)**

below: **restored view of one bay of the tepidarium of the Thermae of Diocletian, Rome (302 A.D.)**

term 1. Same as **terminal figure.** 2. See **terminus.**

terminal figure, terminal statue A decorative figure in which a head, or a head and bust, or the human figure to the waist and including the arms, is incorporated with (as if it were springing out of) a pillar which serves as its pedestal.

terminal pedestal A pedestal prepared for a bust, so that the two together comprise a **terminal figure.**

terminal pedestal

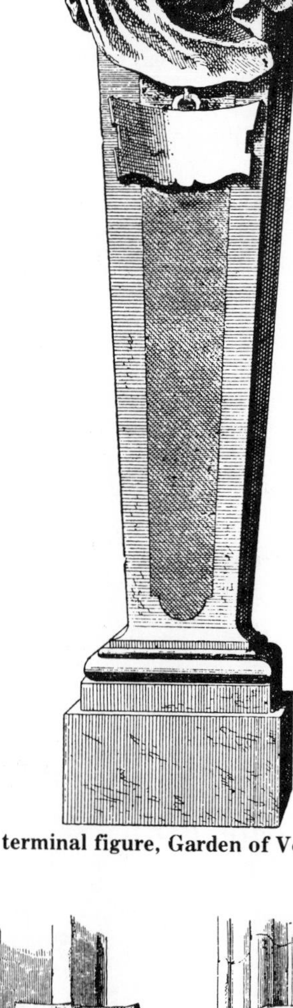

terminal figure, Garden of Versailles

termination An ornamental element which finishes off an architectural feature such as a **dripstone.**

below: various dripstone terminations

Norman

Early English style

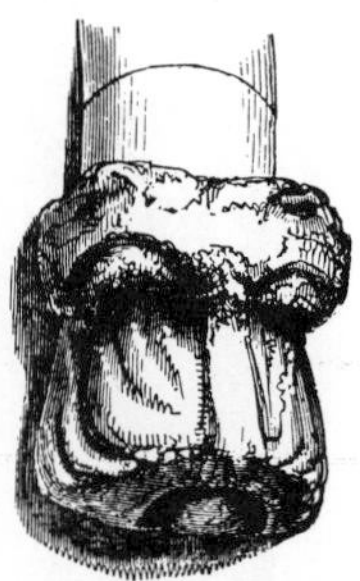

Early English style

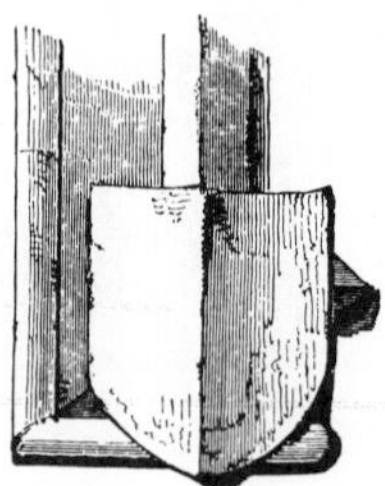

Perpendicular style

Perpendicular style

terminus **1.** A bust or figure of the upper part of the human body springing out of a plain block of rectangular form, pilaster, or the lower part of a console, bracket, or the like; a terminal figure. **2.** A stone used by the ancients to mark a territorial boundary; frequently a short inverted obelisk, surmounted by busts of human beings or fauns.

terrace **1.** An embankment with level top, often paved, planted, and adorned for leisure use. **2.** A flat roof or a raised space or platform adjoining a building, paved or planted, esp. one used for leisure enjoyment.

terrace house One of a row of houses situated on a **terrace,** or similar site.

terra-cotta Hard, unglazed fired clay; used for ornamental work and roof and floor tile.

terreplein An earth embankment, flattened at the top.

tessellated Formed of small square pieces of marble, stone, glass, or the like, in the manner of an ornamental mosaic.

tessellated work Inlay work composed of **tesserae.**

tessellatum opus See **opus tessellatum.**

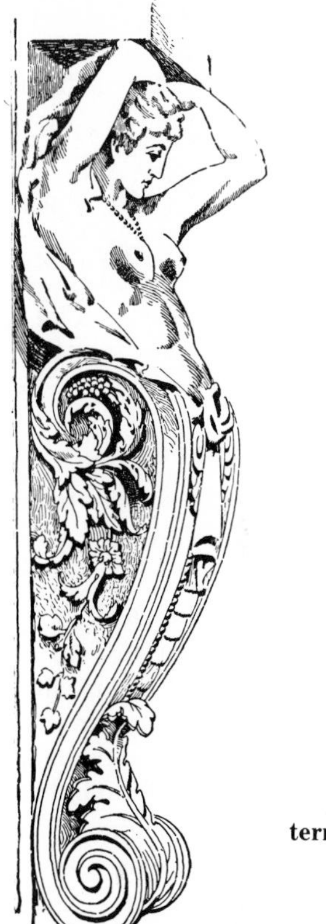

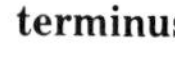

terminus

below: **Roman terra-cottas**

tessera A small squarish piece of colored marble, glass, or tile, used to make mosaic patterns, either geometric or figurative.

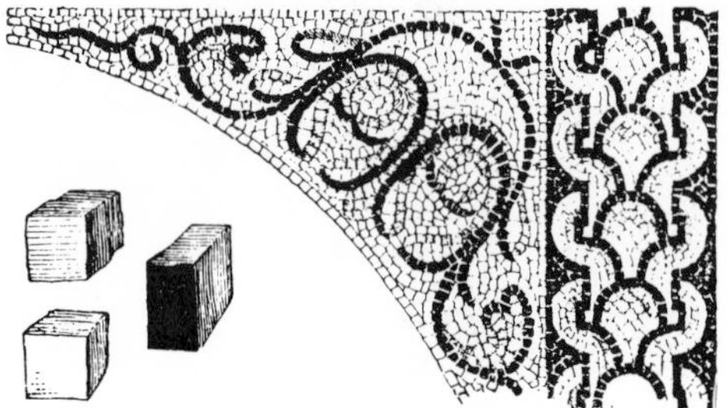

tesseris structum Same as **opus tessellatum.**

testaceum Same as **opus testaceum.**

tester A flat canopy, as over a bed, throne, pulpit, or tomb.

testudinate Having a ridge roof.

testudo In ancient Roman construction, an arched or vaulted roof (usually a light vault of wood covered with mortar or cement); used in large houses having no opening (compluvium) in the center and in Roman baths.

tetrakionion An aedicula or pavilion supported by four columns.

tetraprostyle Said of a classical temple having a portico of four columns in front of the cella or naos.

tetrapylon **1.** A structure characterized by having four gateways as an architectural feature. **2.** An archway having four equal façades, at the intersection of two streets.

tetrastoon A courtyard with porticoes or open colonnades on each of its four sides.

tetrastyle Having four columns in the front or end row; consisting of a row or rows of four columns.

texture The tactile and visual quality of a surface or substance other than its color.

thabha The post of a **stupa** railing.

thalamos, thalamium In early Greek architecture, an inner room or chamber, esp. the women's apartment or the master bedroom.

that A Siamese **stupa.**

thatch The covering of a roof, or the like, usually made of straw, reed, or similar materials fastened together to shed water and sometimes to provide thermal insulation; in tropical countries palm leaves are widely used.

tetrastyle Temple on the Ilissus, Athens (449 B.C.)

theatre A building or outdoor structure providing a stage (and associated equipment) for the presentation of dramatic performances and seating for spectators. Also see **Greek theatre, Roman theatre.**

theatre (Shakespearian): Fortune Theatre, Golden Lane, London (mid-17th cent.)

Thebes A ruined city, a former capital of the Egyptian empire, located on the Nile; a wide fertile plain is to the south. Only a rudimentary architectural skeleton survives, mainly in the enormous temple compounds of Karnak and Luxor [1½ miles (2.4 km) to the south] on the eastern bank of the river, and in the string of great **mortuary temples** beneath the towering cliffs of the western desert where the pharaohs of the New Kingdom dug their rock tombs. These include: Hatshepsut's mortuary temple at Deir El-Bahri, the Rameseum of Ramses II, and the mortuary temple of Ramses III at Medinet Habu. Nothing remains of the actual city which surrounded the great temples on the east bank and occupied the space between the Nile and the necropolis on the west bank. The Great Temple at Karnak devoted to Amen as the universal god of Egypt embodies the history of the Empire. Each king, chiefly during the 18th and 19th dynasties, took pride in adding obelisks, pylons, courtyards, temple annexes, and chapels to the Great Temple; its main glory is the colossal **hypostyle hall, 1** started by Amenhotep III. This temple was linked with the Temple of Mut and the large Temple of Amum at Luxor by **processional ways** flanked by sphinxes.

theologeion, theologium A small upper stage or balcony in the stage structure of the ancient theatre, on which persons representing divinities sometimes appeared and spoke.

thermae See **baths, 3.**

therm window Same as **Venetian window.**

thesaurus In ancient Greece, a treasury house.

Theseum, Theseion **1.** A temple built in Athens ca. 460 B.C. to receive the bones of the hero-king Theseus. **2.** A hexastyle peripteral Doric temple of Pentelic marble, dating from the second half of the 5th cent. B.C., standing in Athens at the foot of the Acropolis and Areopagus; the most perfect surviving example of a Greek temple. Although called the Temple of Theseum, it is probably that of Hephaestus (Vulcan).

thole **1.** Same as **tholos.** **2.** A niche or recess in which votive offerings were made. **3.** A knot or escutcheon at the apex of a timber vault.

tholobate The circular substructure of a dome.

tholos **1.** In Greek architecture, any round building. **2.** The corbeled, domed tombs of the Mycenaean period. **3.** A domed rotunda.

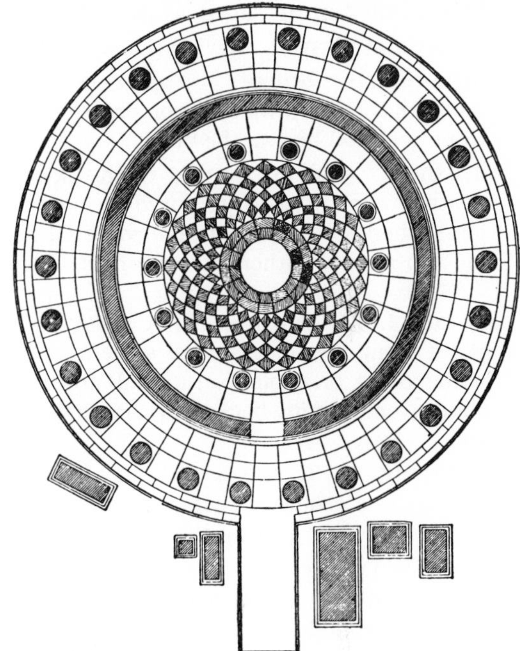

plan of the Tholos,1: Epidaurus (350 B.C.)

tholos tomb See **beehive tomb.**

tholus Same as **tholos.**

three-centered arch An arch struck from three centers; two, on the sides, have short radii; the central one has a longer radius; the resultant curve of the intrados approximates an ellipse.

three-decker A pulpit for a meetinghouse with the clerk's desk at the bottom, the reader's desk above it, and the pulpit on top.

three-hinged arch An arch with hinges at the two supports and at the crown.

three-light window **1.** A window with three panes. **2.** A window which is three panes high or three panes wide.

three-pinned arch Same as **three-hinged arch.**

three-pointed arch See **equilateral arch.**

three-quarter house A **Cape Cod house** or **saltbox** having two windows on one side of the front door and one on the other.

threshold A strip fastened to the floor beneath a door, usually required to cover the joint where two types of floor material meet; may provide weather protection at exterior doors.

throat **1.** See **throating.** **2.** A groove which is cut along the underside of a member (as a stringcourse or coping on a wall) to prevent water from running back across it (toward the wall).

throating **1.** A **drip** or **drip mold.** **2.** See **throat.** **3.** A **chimney throat.**

through arch Any arch which is set in a thick, heavy wall.

through stone A **bondstone** which extends the full thickness of the wall.

thymele In the orchestra of an ancient Greek theatre, a small altar dedicated to Bacchus; usually at the center of the orchestra circle and marked by a white stone.

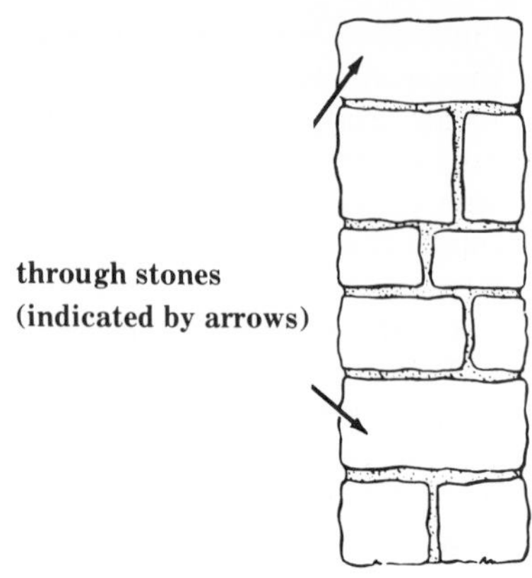

through stones (indicated by arrows)

thyroma **1.** Of an ancient house, a door which opens on the street. **2.** A large doorway in the second story at the rear of the stage of the ancient Roman theatre.

thyrorion, thyroreum Of an ancient Greek house, a passageway leading from the entrance to the peristyle.

tie beam In roof framing, a horizontal timber connecting two opposite rafters at their lower ends to prevent them from spreading; also see **collar beam.**

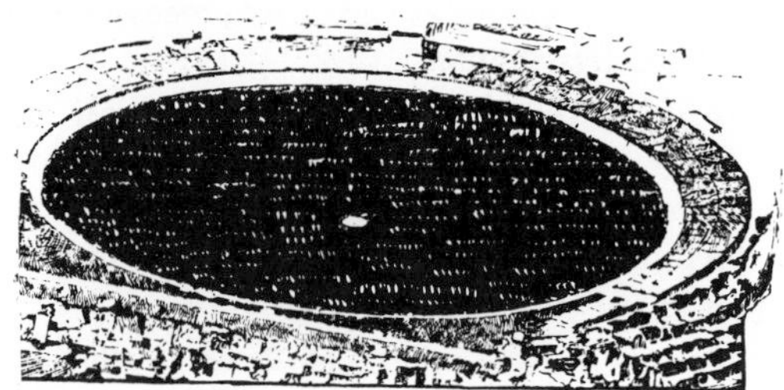

right: thymele in the orchestra of the Theatre at Epidaurus, Greece (350 B.C.)

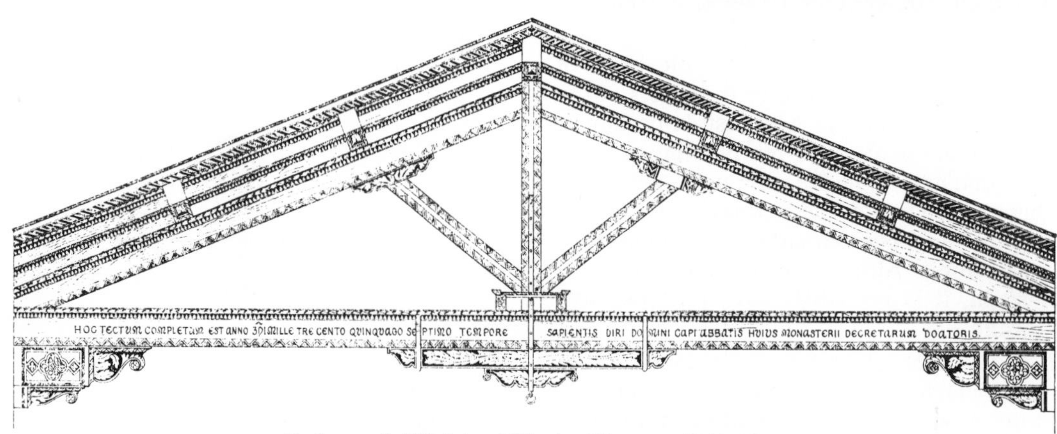

tie beam, S. Miniato al Monte, Florence (1018–62)

鉄塔 **t'ieh t'a** In ancient Chinese architecture, a masonry pagoda which is clad with bronze-colored glazed terra-cotta panels in relief; usually of Buddhist origin. Because of the color of the glaze, the Chinese characters mean literally "iron tower."

殿 **tien** In traditional Chinese architecture, an important building within a compound especially for royalty and/or monasteries. Such buildings were on raised platforms with steps and were always constructed along a central axis of the site plan.

天井 **t'ien ching** In Chinese architecture, a courtyard which is surrounded by buildings.

田庄 **t'ien chuang** A Chinese farm with wells, ponds, forest, housing for men and animals, storage houses, walls which encircle the area, and watchtowers for defense.

天花 **t'ien hua** **1.** In Chinese architecture, a suspended ceiling in a temple, palace, or prosperous home; a wood ceiling to which two layers of paper are glued; the paper often carries a design which is decorated in color. **2.** A general term for a ceiling.

天壇 **t'ien tan** A "temple of heaven," the building (one of a group) which contained an altar at which the Chinese emperor paid tribute to heaven at the beginning of each year; each dynasty had one such temple at its capital.

Hall of Prayer for Good Harvest

天文台 **t'ien wen tai** A Chinese term for an observatory.

tie piece Same as **tie beam.**

tierceron In medieval vaulting, a secondary rib springing from an intersection of two other ribs; an intermediate rib that rises between the main diagonal and transverse ribs from the impost of the pier to the ridge rib.

tige The shaft of a column, from the base moldings to the capital.

tignum In ancient Roman construction, a beam or timber for a building; generally applied to the **tie beam** of a roof.

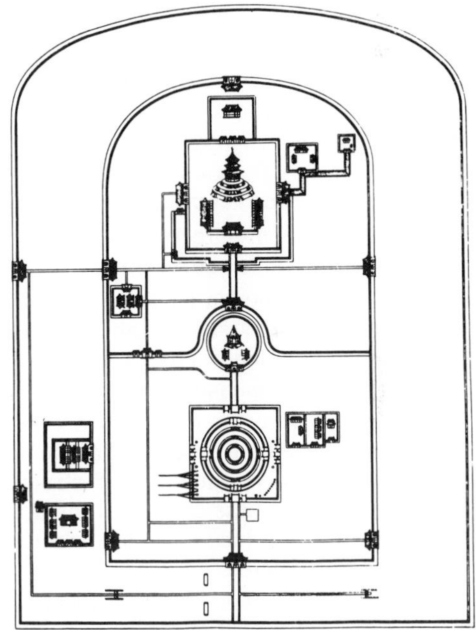

t'ien tan (Temple of Heaven), Peking (15th cent.)

above: plan showing the entire complex within two walled enclosures, the outer about 4 miles (6.4 km) long; the inner surrounds the three principal elements aligned along a north-south axis: to the north, the *Hall of Prayer for Good Harvest* atop three concentric marble terraces, all within a square courtyard. This is joined to the *Imperial Heavenly Vault* surrounded by a cylindrical wall, noted for an acoustical phenomenon—a person whispering near the wall on one side of the courtyard can be heard clearly on the opposite side. This leads to the *Altar of Heaven (Round Mound)* consisting of three concentric circular terraces which step upward toward the center (representing the heavens); surrounding the terraces is a huge square enclosure (representing the world)

tile creasing A weather-protective barrier at the top of a brick wall; consists of two courses of tiles which project beyond both faces of the wall, so as to throw off rainwater. Also see **creasing.**

tile hanging See **weather tiling.**

timber-framed building A building having timbers as its structural elements, except for the foundation.

timber framing **1.** See **framing, 1** and **2.** **2.** See **half-timbered.**

timber house A type of house, usually lofty, found in secular Gothic architecture, esp. in Central Europe; characterized by a lower story of masonry which supports the timber construction above, usually with richly carved gables.

timber house, Market Place in Hildesheim, Lower Saxony, Germany

廳 **t'ing** A living room or reception room, more formal than a **t'ang;** sometimes a separate building for this function, in which case it is always on the central axis of the site plan.

 **t'ing** In Chinese architecture, a yard which is surrounded by walls and/or structures.

t'ing An open wooden pavilion or a group of pavilions of various shapes; an essential feature of a Chinese landscape garden.

tjandi A Hindu sepulchral monument, prevalent in Java from the 8th to 14th cent. A.D., consisting of a square base, a cella-like temple, and a prominent pyramidal roof structure; a small room in the base contained the urn with the ashes of the prince in whose memory the structure was erected.

tlatchtli In ceremonial centers in **Mesoamerica,** an I-shaped ritual ball court.

塔 **tō** A type of Japanese pagoda of two (*tahō-tō*), three (*sanjū-no-tō*), five (*gojū-no-tō*), or seven (*nana-jū-no-tō*) stories which enshrines Buddhist holy relics. In Japan these are usually square, but the tahō-tō differs in that it has a stupa-like round protuberance above the lower square roof which, in turn, carries a cylindrical railed section crowned by a square roof bearing a sōrin (as do all other multistoried pagodas).

tobi Same as **tapia.**

Tōdaiji An ancient, very extensive monastic complex, begun in the middle of the 8th cent., located in Nara city, Japan. Important buildings include: Shōsōin, an 8th cent. storehouse of the **azekura** style; Tegaimon, 8th cent., but greatly repaired during the Kamakura period; Hokkedō, also known as Sangatsudō, of the early 8th cent.; Kaisandō, founder's hall, of the Kamakura period; Nandaimon, the great south gate, of the Kamakura period; Shōrō, the belfry, of the Kamakura period; and Daibutsuden, of the Kamakura period.

tōhō-tō See **tō.**

tokobashira The visible nonstructural post which marks one of the front sides of a **toko-no-ma.**

床の間

toko-no-ma An alcove having a raised floor, located in the most formal room of a traditional Japanese-style residence; used to display a hanging, scroll, small objects, a flower arrangement, etc.

tokyō See **kumimono.**

tolbooth Same as **tollbooth.**

tollbooth **1.** A booth, office, or stall, where tolls, duties, or taxes are collected. **2.** A town jail; so-called because the temporary hut in which duties were collected often was used as a place of confinement or detention for those who did not pay or were charged with some breach of the law in buying or selling. **3.** A town hall. **4.** A guild hall.

tollhouse **1.** A house near a tollgate of a highway or bridge, serving as the residence of the keeper. **2.** A tollbooth.

Toltec architecture An austere, geometric, Mesoamerican architecture, ca. 1000 A.D.; which formed the basis for Aztec architecture and other architecture in Mesoamerica; characterized by the use of colonnades several ranks deep, atlantes, square-carved roof supports, monumental serpent columns, balustrades, **coatepantli,** and narrative relief panels set in plain wall surfaces. Important examples of Toltec architecture are at Tula and Chichén Itzá.

interior of a Japanese house: on the extreme left is a shoji; the toko-no-ma is shown with a flower arrangement; to its right is the tokobashira; on the extreme right is the chigai-dana; tatami (floor mats) are shown in the foreground

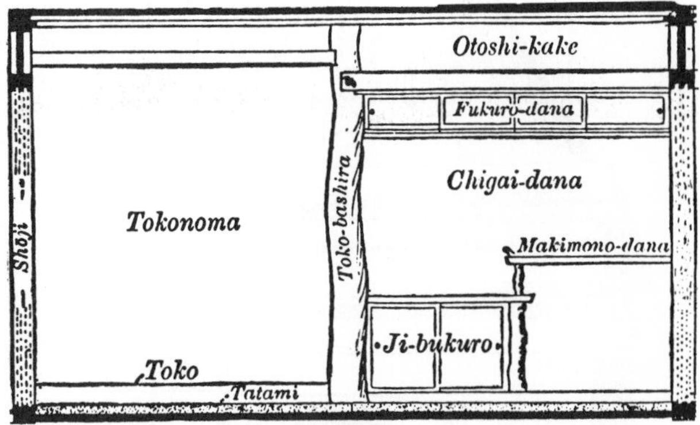

a cross section through a Japanese house indicating many of its essential features

tomb In architecture, a memorial structure over or beside a grave.

interior of the Tomb of the Two Seats, Cervanti, Italy (500 B.C.)

right: tomb, Khurbet-Hass, Syria (4th cent. A.D.)

Etruscan tomb at Castel d'Asso

Lion Tomb, Cnidos, Greece (c. 350 B.C.)

Tomb of Iamblichus, Palmyra (83 A.D.)

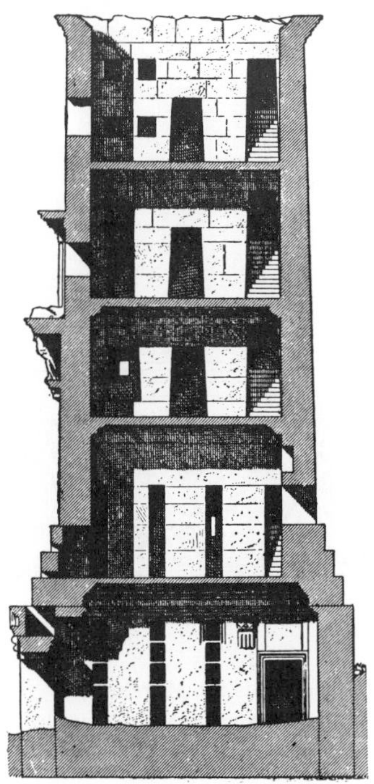

section of Tomb of Iamblichus

Tomb of Edward II, Gloucester Cathedral

tomb chest A stone coffin-like box.

tomb chest of the sons of Charles VIII, Tours, France

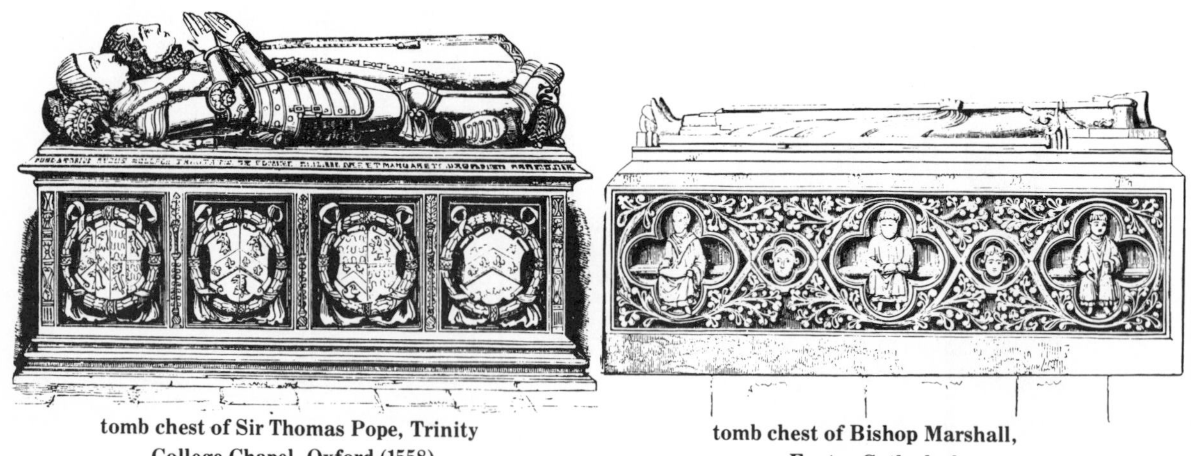

tomb chest of Sir Thomas Pope, Trinity College Chapel, Oxford (1558)

tomb chest of Bishop Marshall, Exeter Cathedral

tombstone A stone or slab placed over a grave to preserve the memory of the deceased; a sepulchral monument.

top right: **slab over the tomb of Duke Henry IV, Bresslau, Prussia**

bottom center: **tombstone, Church of St. Martin, Laon, France (13th cent.)**

bottom right: **slab over the tomb of Rudolph of Swabia, Meresburg, Prussia**

slab over the grave of Archbishop Peter von Aspelt, Cathedral of Mainz

tombstone light A small window with lights in the shape of an arched tombstone; usually in the transom above a doorway.

tondino **1.** A small **tondo.** **2.** A circular molding.

tondo A circular plaque or medallion.

toother Same as **dogtooth, 2.**

tooth ornament, dogtooth A decoration, generally in the hollow of a Gothic molding, consisting of four-leaved flowers, the centers of which project in a point.

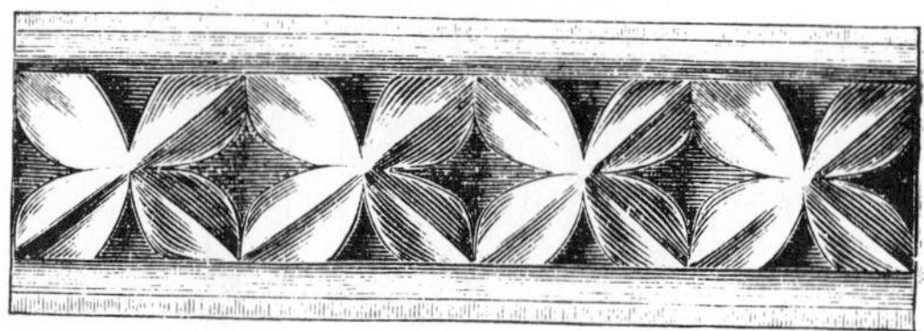

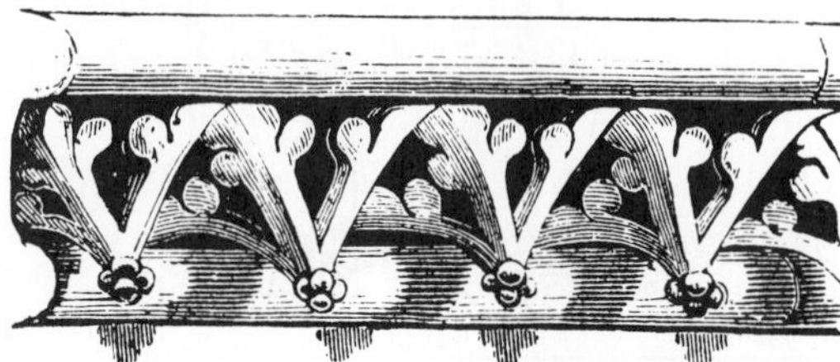

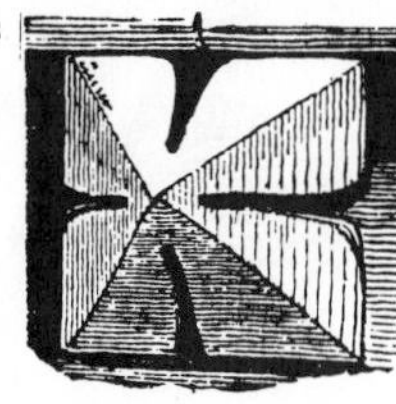

tooth ornaments

top beam A **collar beam.**

tope See **stupa.**

topha, taph stone Same as **tufa.**

topiarium opus A wall painting representing trees, shrubs, and trelliswork, as at Pompeii.

topiary work The clipping or trimming of plants, trees, and shrubs, usually evergreens, into ornamental and fantastic shapes.

torana, toran A monumental and richly decorated gateway in the enclosure of a Buddhist stupa in Indian architecture.

torchère An ornamental support for a **flambeau** or other source of light.

tore Same as **torus.**

鳥居 **torii** A monumental, freestanding gateway to a Shintō shrine, consisting of two pillars with a straight crosspiece at the top and lintel above it, usually curving upward.

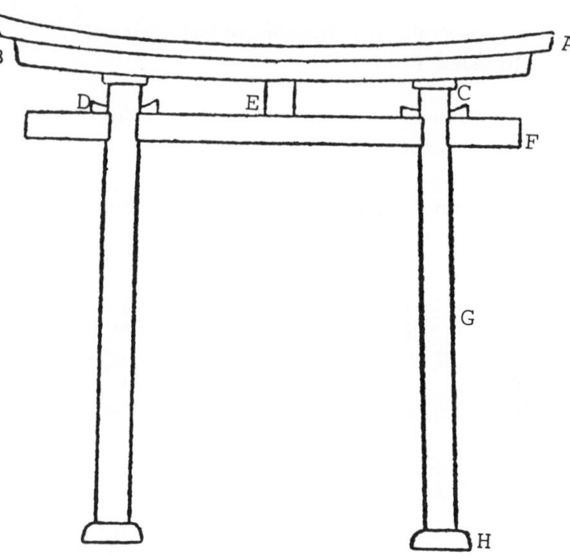

a torii, showing its components:

A, kasagi
B, shimagi
C, daiwa
D, kusabi
E, gakuzuka
F, nuki
G, hashira
H, kamebara

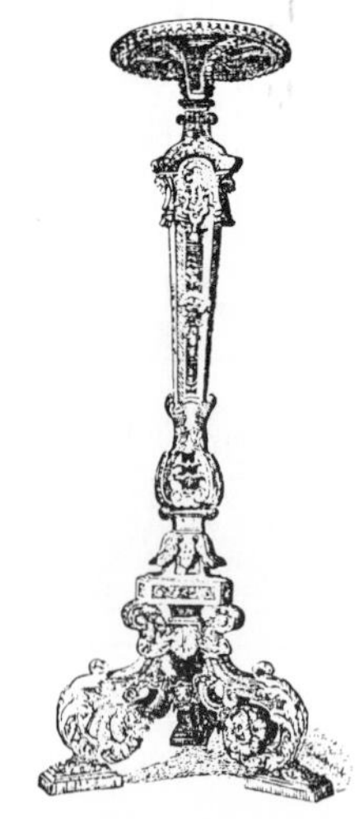

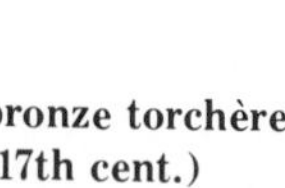

bronze torchère (17th cent.)

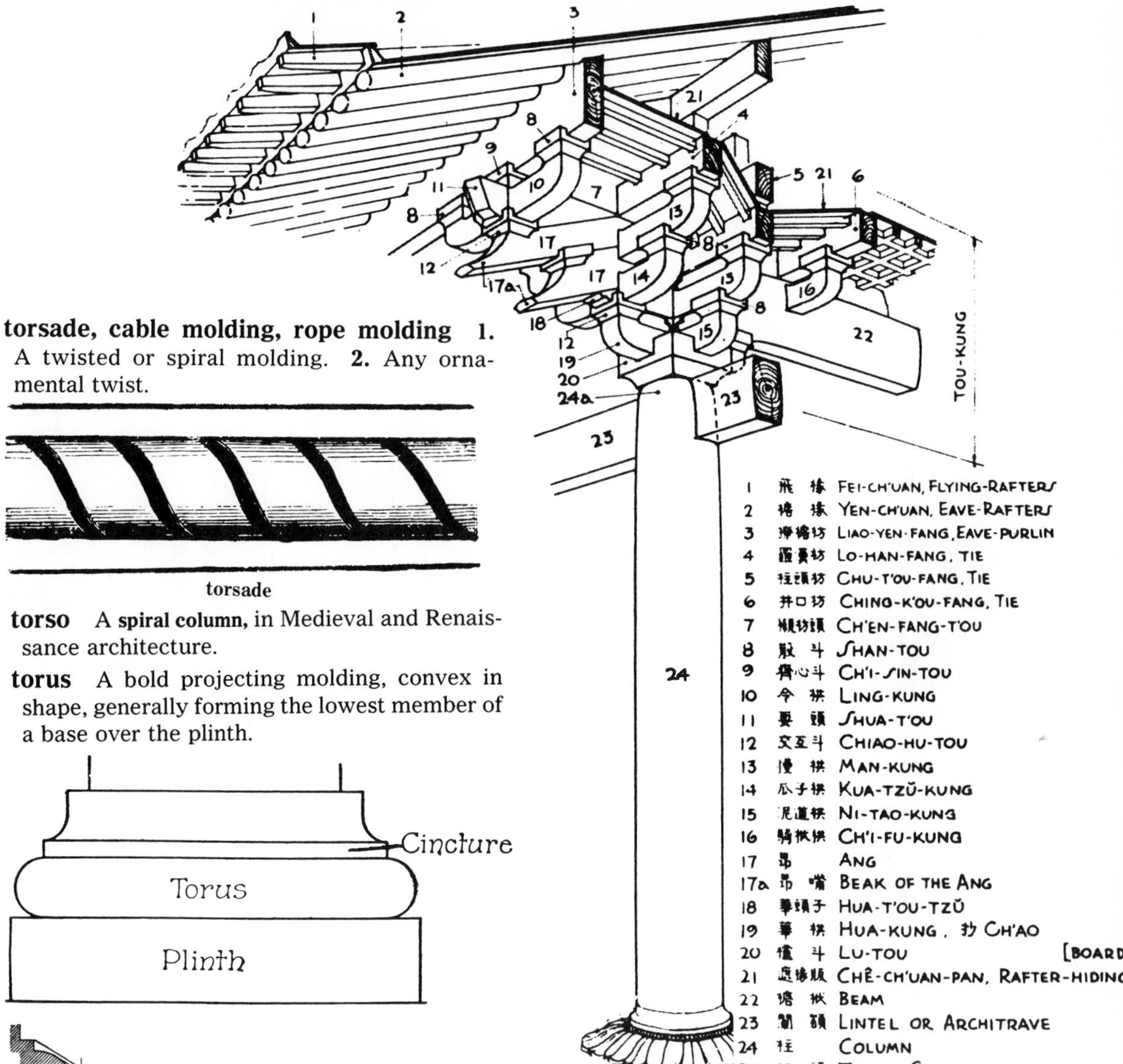

tou kung system of construction

torsade, cable molding, rope molding **1.** A twisted or spiral molding. **2.** Any ornamental twist.

torsade

torso A **spiral column,** in Medieval and Renaissance architecture.

torus A bold projecting molding, convex in shape, generally forming the lowest member of a base over the plinth.

torus

唐招提寺 **Tōshōdaiji** In Nara city, Japan, a temple established in 729 by the Chinese priest Chien Chen. Important buildings include: the Kondō, of the Nara period (8th cent.); Kōdō, a palace of the Nara period (ca. 710 A.D.); and Korō, now a drum house but first used as a **kyōzō,** for the storage of sutras, built in the Kamakura period (1240).

Tōshōgū shrine See **Nikkô.**

斗 **tou** A bearing block, used for support in the **tou kung** system of construction.

斗栱 **tou kung** A cantilevered bracket in traditional Chinese construction; tiers or clusters of brackets are used to carry rafters which support purlins far beyond the outermost columns of a building.

tourelle A **turret.**

tower A building characterized by its relatively great height.

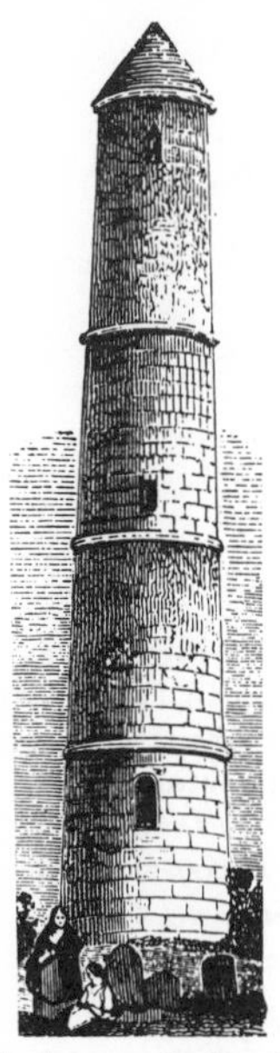

Ardmore, Ireland

Anglo-Saxon; Sompting, Sussex

Middleton Stoney, Oxfordshire (c. 1220)

Oddington, Oxfordshire (c. 1300)

Coggs, Oxfordshire (c. 1350)

Islip, Oxfordshire (c. 1450)

Torrazzo (tower), Cremona (1261-81):
highest in Italy—122 m (c. 400 ft)

Wollaton Hall,
England (1590)

Town Church,
Graz, Austria
(c. 1780)

tower bolt Same as **barrel bolt.**

Tower of Babel See **Babylonian architecture.**

tower of silence A tower, usually about 25 ft (7.6 m) high, on which the Parsees expose the bodies of their dead to be stripped of flesh by vultures; usually arranged so that the denuded bones fall through a grating into a pit, from which they are removed for burial.

tower of silence near Teheran

town hall A public hall or building, belonging to a town, where public offices are established, the town council meets, the people assemble in town meetings, etc.

trabeated **1.** Descriptive of construction using beams or lintels, following the principle of post and lintel construction, as distinguished from construction using arches and vaults. **2.** Furnished with an entablature.

trabeation Construction using beams and posts; lintel construction.

trabes, trabs In ancient Rome, a beam, esp. a long beam supporting the joists of a ceiling.

tracery The curvilinear openwork shapes of stone or wood creating a pattern within the upper part of a Gothic window, or an opening of similar character, in the form of mullions which are usually so treated as to be ornamental. By extension, similar patterns applied to walls or panels. See **bar tracery, branch tracery, fan tracery,** etc.

trachelium In classical architecture, any member (usually part of the necking) which comes between the hypotrachelium and the capital.

trabeated construction: cloister of Sta. Maria della Pace (c. 1495)

Trajan's Column A cylindrical column composed of large blocks of marble erected by the Roman senate in honor of the emperor to celebrate his victories; approx. 125 ft (38 m) high from the base of the pedestal to the statue which surmounts the column; originally the statue was of Trajan but this was replaced by that of St. Peter. A spiral flight of stairs goes to the top. Reliefs about 1 m wide, winding around the column, commemorate the wars and triumphs of Trajan.

transenna **1.** Latticework of marble or metal enclosing a shrine. **2.** In ancient Roman construction, a **crossbeam.**

transept The transverse portion of a church crossing the main axis at a right angle and producing a cruciform plan.

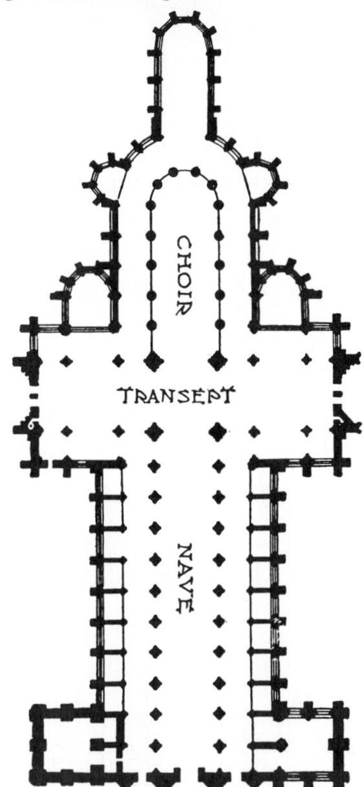

plan of Rouen Cathedral (1202–30 and later)

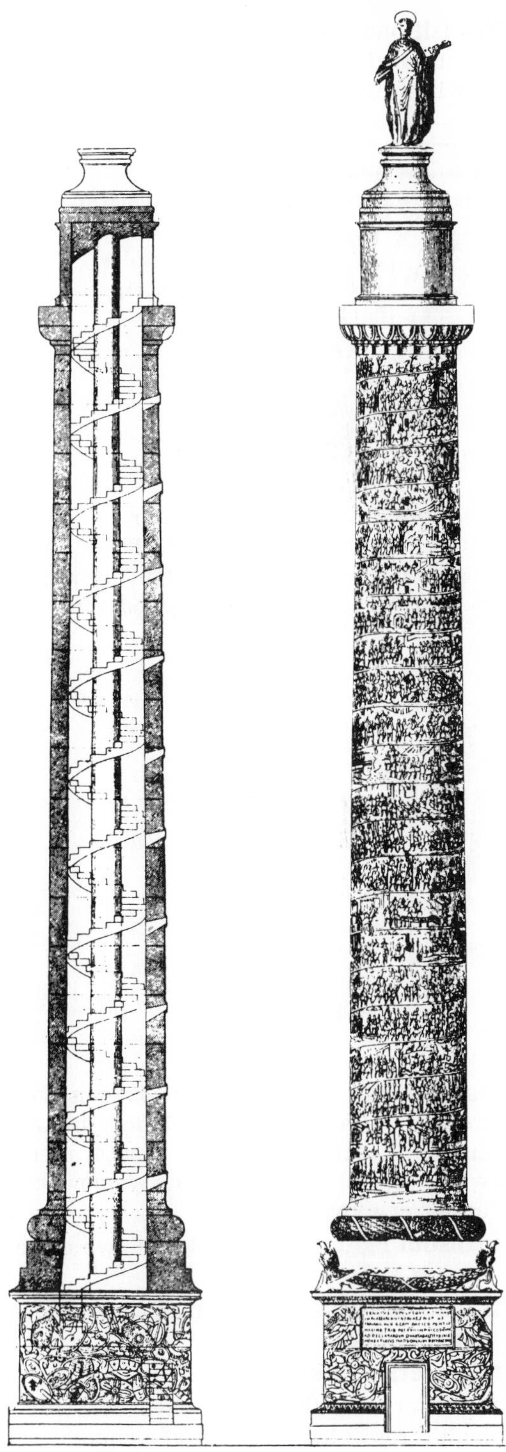
Trajan's Column, Rome (113 A.D.)

transept aisle An aisle on the side of a transept.

transept chapel A chapel entered from a transept, usually on its east side.

Transitional style A term used to describe the transition from Romanesque to Gothic in the 12th cent.

Transitional style capital, Church of St. Sebaldus, Nuremberg

transom **1.** A horizontal bar of wood or stone across a window. **2.** The cross-bar separating a door from the fanlight above it. **3.** A window divided by a **transom bar.**

transom,3

transom bar **1.** An intermediate horizontal member of a doorframe, window frame, or similar structure. **2.** A horizontal member which separates a door from a window, panel, or louver above.

transom light A glazed **light** above the **transom bar, 2** of a door.

transtrum In ancient Roman construction, a horizontal beam.

transverse See **chambranle.**

transverse arch The arched construction built across a hall, the nave of a church, or the like, either as part of the vaulting or to support or stiffen the roof.

transverse rib A rib in vaulting spanning the nave, aisle, or transept at right angles to its longitudinal axis and dividing its length into bays or compartments.

transverse rib indicated by arrow

transverse arch, south aisle of the abbey church, Vézelay (12th cent.)

transyte See **tresaunce.**

trapeznaya A **refectory** in the monastery of a Russian Orthodox church.

trascoro In Spanish church architecture, a part of the choir separated from the main choir by an open passage at the crossing.

trass A natural **pozzolan** of volcanic origin.

travated Divided into traves.

trave **1.** A crossbeam; a beam or a timber crossing a building. **2.** One of the divisions or bays, as in a ceiling, made by crossbeams.

travertine A variety of limestone deposited by springs; usually banded; commonly coarsely cellular; used as building stone, esp. for interior facing and flooring.

traviated Having a series of transverse divisions or bays, as in a ceiling.

travis See **trave, 2.**

tray ceiling Under a gabled roof, a horizontal ceiling constructed part of the way up toward the ridge.

trayle See **vinette.**

tredyl Old English term for **grees.**

treenail, trenail, trunnel **1.** A long pin of hardwood; used for fastening planks or timbers in early post-and-beam construction. **2.** See **gutta.**

trefoil A three-lobed, cloverleaf pattern; also see **foil.**

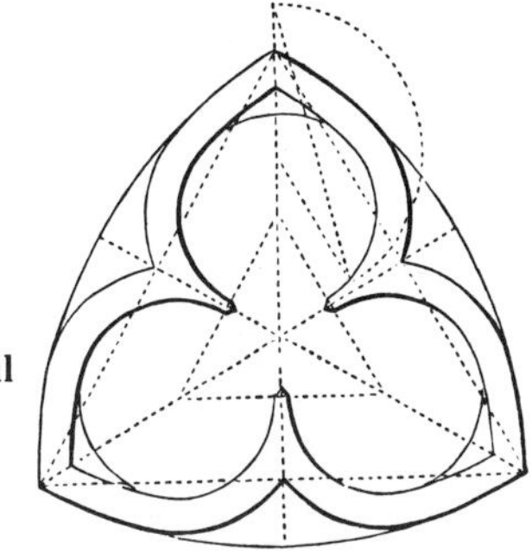

development of trefoil

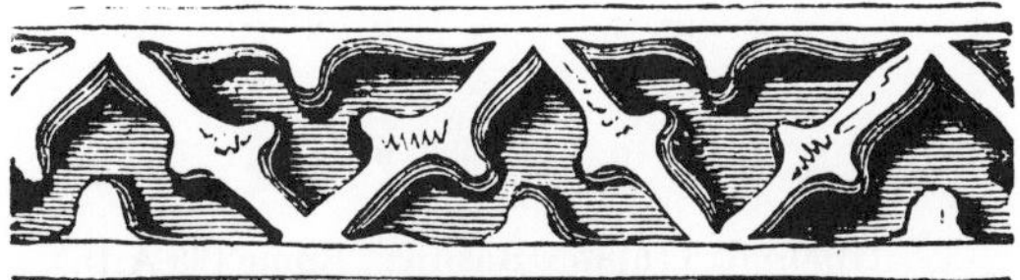

trefoil molding

trefoil arch An arch whose intrados has three lobes or foils.

trefoil arch, Beverley Minster (c. 1300)

treillage A **trellis** support for vines or espaliers.

trellage Same as **treillage.**

trellis **1.** An open grating or latticework, of either metal or wood. **2.** An arbor or framework for the support of vines; a **treillage.**

trellis,1

trellis molding, trellice molding An ornament, used in buildings of the Norman style, consisting of a series of overlapping zigzag lines which produce a trellis-like appearance.

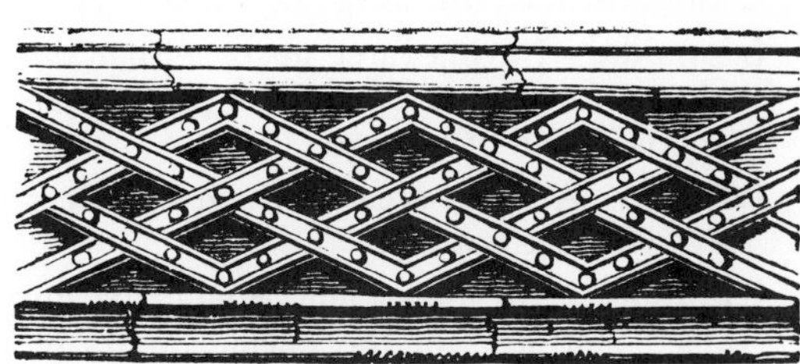

a studded trellis molding

trellis window Same as **lattice window.**

trenail Same as **treenail.**

tresaunce, transyte, trisantia In medieval architecture and derivatives, a narrow vestibule or passageway.

tresse Flat or convex **bandelets** which are intertwined; esp. such interlacing ornamentation used to adorn moldings.

tresse

trevis See **trave, 2.**

triangular arch 1. A structure composed of two stones laid diagonally and mutually supporting each other to span an opening. 2. A **Maya arch.**

Norman triangular arches

triangular fret molding See **dovetail molding.**

triapsidal Having three apses, either side by side or forming a cloverleaf pattern at the sanctuary end of a church.

tribelon A triple arcade which connects the nave with the narthex.

tribunal 1. In an ancient Roman basilica, a raised platform for the curule chairs of the magistrates. 2. A place of honor, immediately to the right and to the left of the stage in a Roman theatre, one for the magistrate who provided for the play and for the emperor, and the other for the Vestal Virgins and the empress.

tribune 1. A slightly elevated platform or dais for a speaker. 2. The apse of a church. 3. The raised platform at one end of a Roman basilica, frequently in a small addition of semicircular plan, which constituted the official station of the pretor; the tribunal; hence, in Christian churches of basilican plan, the throne of the bishop (which originally occupied the place of the pretor's seat) and that part of the church containing it.

tribune,3: Torcello Cathedral, Italy (rebuilt 1008)

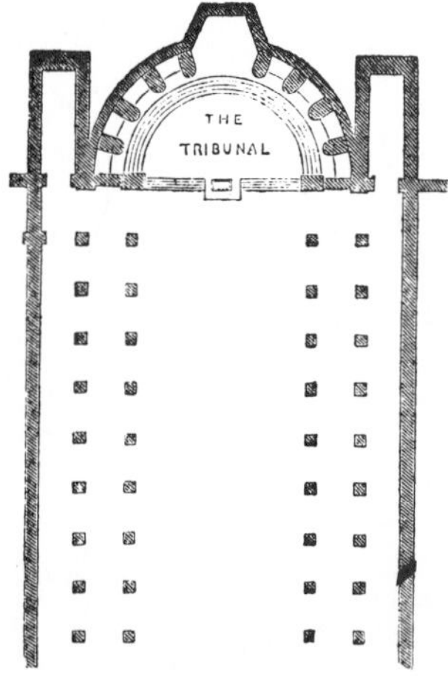

tribunal: Trajan's Basilica, Rome (98 A.D.)

trichila, trichilum A bower constructed on the pleasure grounds of an ancient Roman villa (or any other location) to provide a shady retreat for dining during pleasant weather; frequently constructed of wood and trellis work, over which vines, gourds, and other plants were trained.

tricla, triclia Same as **trichila.**

triclinium A dining room in an ancient Roman house, furnished with a low table, surrounded on three sides by couches.

triconch Having apses with semidomes on three sides of a square chamber; some churches, chapels, and tombs are built on this plan.

triforium In medieval church architecture, a shallow passage above the arches of the nave and choir and below the clerestory; characteristically opened into the nave.

trichila

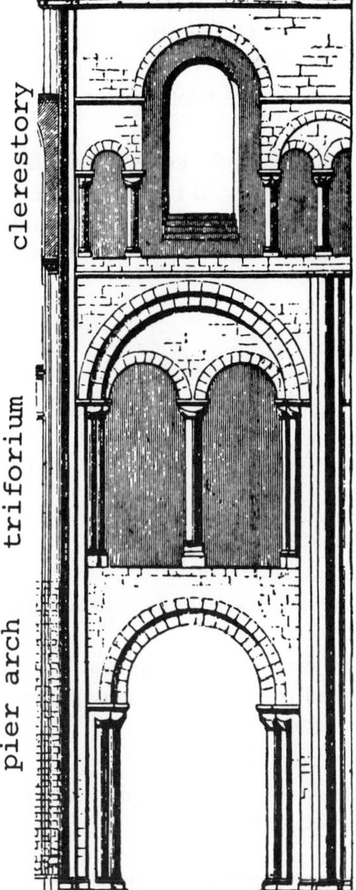

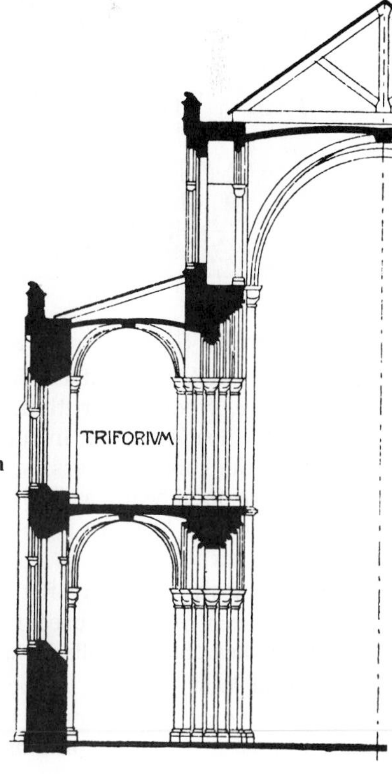

right: **half-section of a cathedral, showing the triforium**

triga A chariot similar to a **quadriga** but drawn by three horses.

triglyph The characteristic ornament of the Doric frieze, consisting of slightly raised blocks of three vertical bands separated by V-shaped grooves. The triglyphs alternate with plain or sculptured panels called **metopes.** Also see **order.**

trigonum A mosaic of triangular pieces of marble, terra-cotta, glass, or other material.

trigonum mosaic

trilith, trilithon A monument, or part of a monument, consisting of three large stones; esp. one in prehistoric antiquity consisting of two upright stones with a lintel stone resting upon them as at Stonehenge.

trilith

trilobe arch Same as **trefoil arch.**

trimmer **1.** A piece of timber inserted in a roof, floor, wooden partition, or the like, to support a header which in turn supports the ends of the joists, rafters, studs, etc. **2.** A small horizontal beam, as in a floor, into which the ends of one or more joists are framed. **3.** A **trimmer arch.**

trimmer arch A nearly flat arch, usually a low-rise arch of brick; used for supporting a fireplace hearth; also called **trimmer.**

trimming joist A joist, supporting a **trimmer,** of larger cross section but of the same length as, and parallel to, the common **joists.**

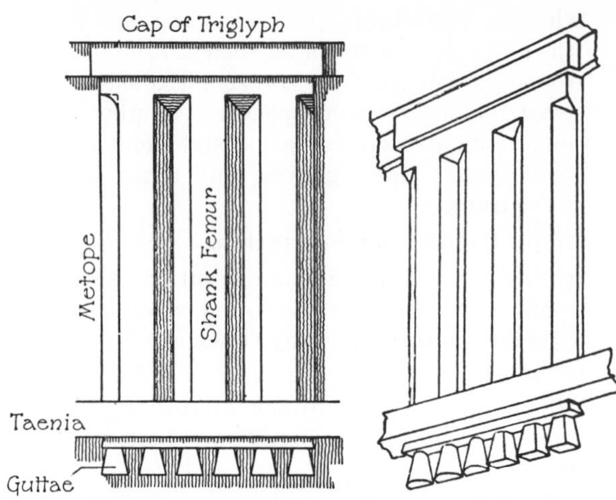

triglyph; *left*: front elevation; *right*: as seen from an angle

trimstone, trim In masonry, the stone used as decorative members on a structure built or faced largely with other masonry material, as brick, tile, block, or terra-cotta; includes sills, jambs, lintels, coping, cornices, and quoins.

tringle A small square **fillet** molding or ornament.

tripartite vault A vault, covering a triangular space, which is formed by the intersection of three barrel vaults or three expanding vaults; esp. common in Romanesque buildings.

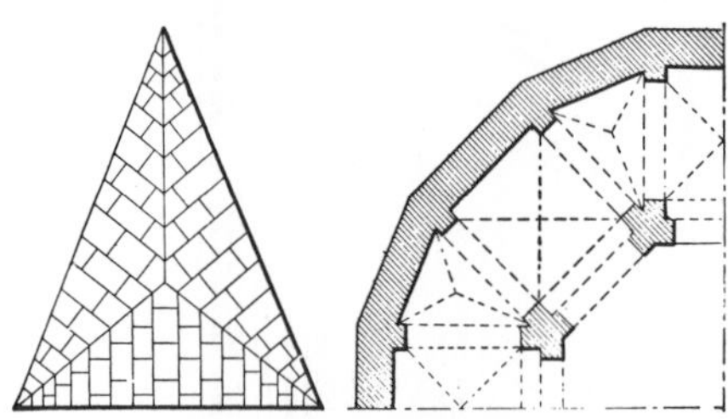
plan of tripartite vault

tripteral Having three wings or three rows of columns.

triquetra An ornament composed of three half circles or ellipses crossed and joined together at their ends.

trisantia See **tresaunce.**

tristyle in antis A portico which has three columns between antae.

trisula A three-pointed ornament or emblem, esp. one associated with the god Siva.

Triton A sea monster, half man and half fish; often used in classical and Renaissance ornamentation.

triumphal arch An arch commemorating the return of a victorious army, usually in the line of march during its triumphal procession. Also see **memorial arch.**

trivium The place where three ancient Roman streets or roads met.

trochilus A **cavetto** or **scotia.**

trompe A piece of vaulting of conical or partly spherical shape, or resembling one corner of a cloistered vault.

trompe

tropaeum A monument erected on the spot where there had been a military victory or, in the case of naval warfare, on the nearest point of land to the place where the action had taken place.

trophy A sculptured composition of arms and armor as an emblem of, or a memorial to, victorious battles or triumphant military figures.

triumphal arch: Arch of Titus, Rome (82 A.D.)

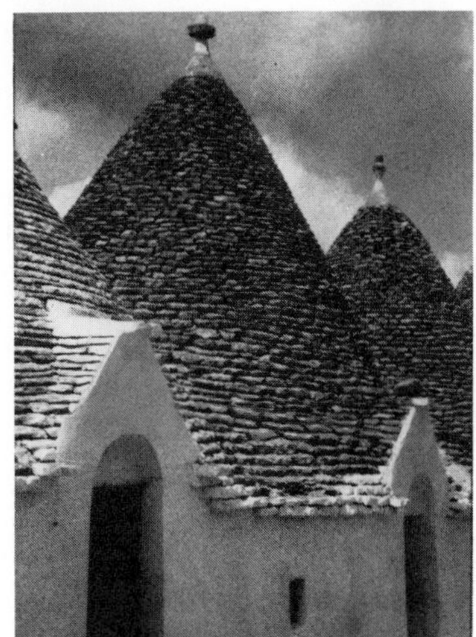

trulli, Alberobello, Italy

trulli In the Apulia region of southern Italy, cone-shaped constructions over 1,000 years old; constructed without mortar or cement by piling stones in a cylindrical shape (about 2 m high) and then tapering into a characteristic cone at the top; the tip of the cone usually is whitewashed and painted with figures or symbols; usually located among vineyards to serve as storage structures or as temporary living quarters during the harvest.

trullo A dry-walled rough stone shelter, circular in plan, with a corbeled domical roof, resembling ancient structures and still used in southern Italy.

trumeau The central support of a medieval doorway.

trumpet arch A conically shaped **squinch, 2.**

trunnel See **treenail.**

truss A structure composed of a combination of members, usually in some triangular arrangement so as to constitute a rigid framework.

彩畫 **ts'ai hua** In Chinese architecture, decorative color patterns on ceilings, structural members, and panels in buildings; different dynasties and different building types used different designs.

tsarskiya vrata In the **iconostasis** of a Russian Orthodox church, the middle of three pairs of doors which lead to the main altar.

坪 **tsubo** A traditional Japanese unit of area; equal to 1 square **ken** or 3.95 sq ft (3.305 sq m)

tsuke-shoin See **Shoin style.**

村落 **ts'un lo** A Chinese village or group of farmhouses.

Tudor arch A four-centered pointed arch, common in the architecture of the Tudor style in England.

trumeau: central support of the north door of the west front, Cathedral of Notre Dame (c. 1210)

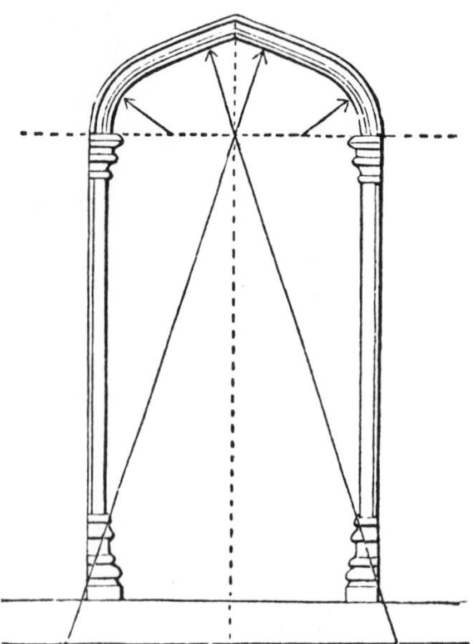

Tudor arch, showing the four centers from which the arch is struck

Tudor arch: gateway (end of 15th cent.)

Tudor architecture The final development of English Perpendicular Gothic architecture, during the reigns of Henry VII and Henry VIII (1485–1547), preceding Elizabethan architecture and characterized by four-centered arches.

Tudor flower An ornament of English Perpendicular Gothic buildings; a trefoil flower developed from the upright points of the crossing or the cusps of a foliated arch.

Tudor flower

Tudor rose A conventionalized rose pattern, usually with five petals, a superposition of white and red roses, the heraldic emblem of the Tudor dynasty.

Tudor rose

tufa A building stone, of consolidated volcanic material, having a cellular texture, easily cut by bronze tools; used by the ancient Romans, esp. for **opus quadratum.** Volcanic tufa forms the various hills on which Rome stands.

tullianum An underground dungeon belonging to the state prisons at Rome; so-called after Servius Tullius, by whose orders it was made.

tumbling course A sloping course of brickwork which intersects a horizontal course.

Tudor architecture

Henry VII Chapel, Westminster Abbey (1503–19); panels of bronze gates.

tumulus A mound of earth or stone protecting a tomb chamber or simple grave; a **barrow.**

t'ung ch'üan In Chinese architecture, a **semicircular arch.**

tunnel vault See **barrel vault.**

turned work In stone and wood cutting, pieces having a circular outline, such as columns, balusters, etc.; usually cut on a lathe, although some shapes are cut by hand.

turning bar See **chimney bar.**

turnpike stair A spiral staircase.

turrellum A low Latin term for **turret.**

turret, tourelle A diminutive tower, characteristically corbeled from a corner.

turret

turret step A stone step, triangular in section, which forms, with other turret steps, a spiral or solid newel stair. Turret steps are tapered and have shaped ends which, laid upon each other, constitute the central column or solid newel.

turriculated Describing a building in which the characteristic feature is a row of turrets.

turris A tower of a fortification, placed at intervals in the walls of an ancient city or any other fortified enclosure.

Etruscan tumulus at Assio

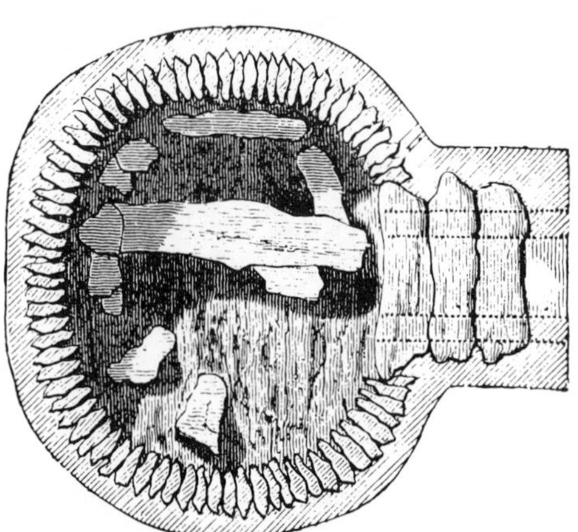

Gallic Tumulus, Fontenay le Marmion: *above*: section; *below*: plan

Tuscan order A simplified version of the Roman Doric order, having a plain frieze and no mutules in the cornice.

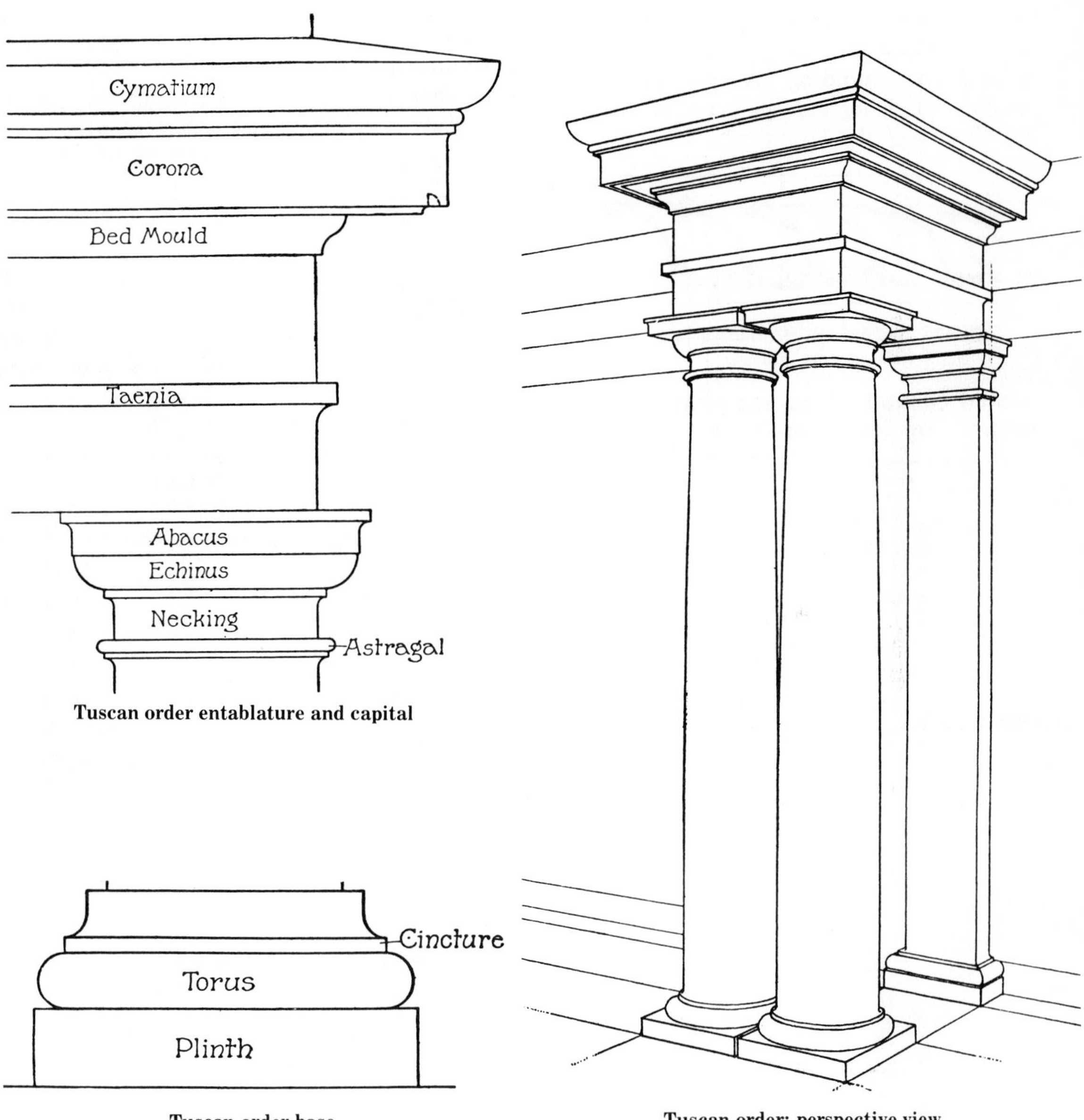

Tuscan order entablature and capital

Tuscan order base

Tuscan order: perspective view

土地廟 **tu ti miao** A Chinese temple or enclosure dedicated to a local deity, sometimes combined with the image of a *ch'êng huang miao* deity.

twin archway An opening having two archways side by side.

twining stem molding A common Norman molding consisting of a **half round** entwined by a stylized tendril.

twisted stem molding

twisted column A column so shaped as to present a twisted or spiral form.

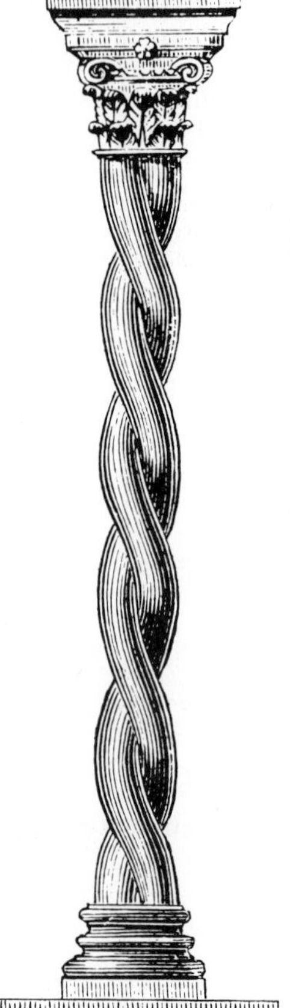

twisted column

two-centered arch An arch struck from two centers, resulting in a pointed arch. Also see **equilateral arch.**

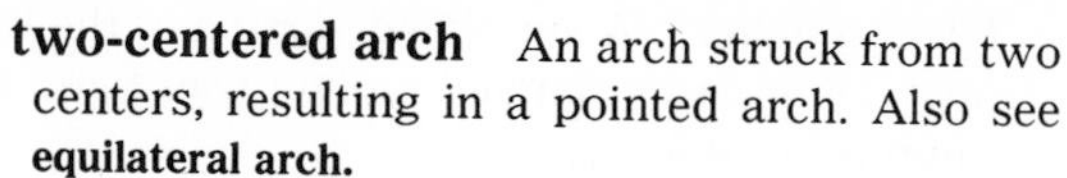

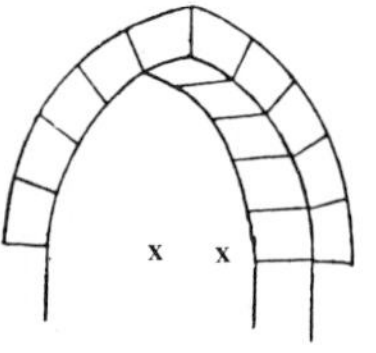

two-centered arch: the x-marks indicate the centers from which the curves are struck

two-hinged arch An arch with hinges at the supports at both ends.

two-light window **1.** A window with two panes. **2.** A window which is two panes high or two panes wide. **3.** A **gemel window.**

tympanum, tympan **1.** The triangular or segmental space enclosed by a pediment or arch. **2.** Any space similarly marked off or bounded, as above a window, or between the lintel of a door and the arch above.

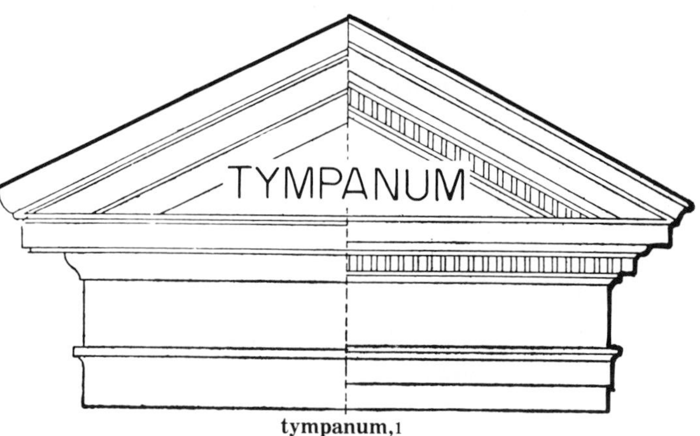

tympanum,1

tzompantli **1.** At **Chichén Itzá,** Yucatán, a Toltec stone altar platform decorated with carved skulls. **2.** In **Mesoamerica,** a rack to which the heads of sacrificial victims were skewered; usually located in a sacred precinct.

tympanum of door, Tomb of Pancrati, Rome (2nd cent. A.D.)

tympanum of window, El Barah, Syria (5th–6th cent.)

tympanum of doorway, Essendine, England (1130)

Tympanum, Naumburg Cathedral (12th cent.)

ualuryng Same as **alure.**

ubapitam In Indian architecture, a pedestal.

ulam The outer hall of the **Temple of Solomon,** which served as an anteroom.

umbo **1.** Anything rising or projecting from another surface, esp. when such projection has a round or conical shape. **2.** A curbstone which forms a raised margin on each side of a street.

umbo, 2: Pompeii

umbraculum Same as **baldachin.**

umbrella See **chattra.**

umbrella dome Same as **melon dome.**

uncoursed Said of masonry which is not in layers with continuous horizontal joints, but is laid irregularly.

unctuarium Same as **alipterium.**

uncut modillion See **modillion.**

undé, undée See **wave molding.**

undercroft **1.** A vaulted basement of a church or secret passage, often wholly or partly below ground level. **2.** A **crypt.**

underpitch groin A groin formed by an **underpitch vault.**

underpitch vault, Welsh vault A construction formed by the penetration of two vaults of unequal size, springing from the same level.

underthroating The cove of an outside cornice when treated so as to serve as a **drip.**

undulating molding See **wave molding.**

undulating tracery See **flowing tracery.**

undy molding See **wave molding.**

unframed door A door not in a frame, as a **batten door.**

upana In Indian architecture, the pedestal of a column.

upapitha In Indian architecture, a pedestal.

ushnisha In Indian architecture, a coping.

ustrinum In ancient Rome, the place where a corpse was burned, if the ashes were to be deposited in a different location. Also see **bustum.**

uttira In Indian architecture, an entablature.

上塗 **uwa-nuri** The finish coat of plaster on a wall in a traditional Japanese structure.

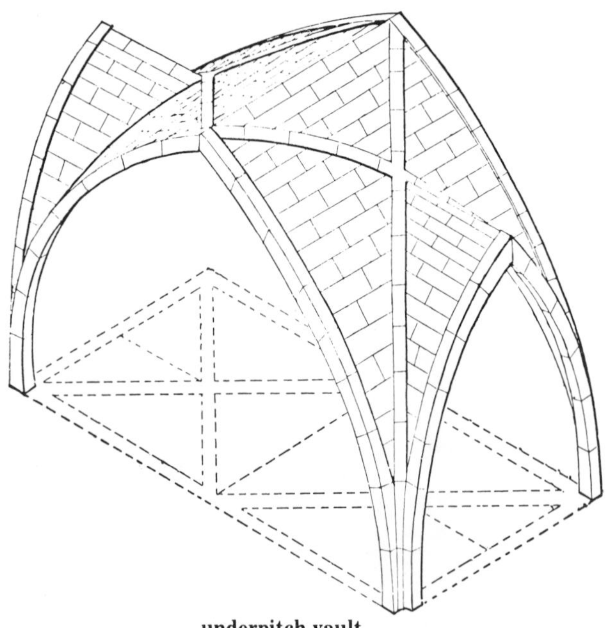

underpitch vault

Uxmal The site, in the Puuc hills in western Yucatán (Mexico), of the finest example of late classic **Maya architecture.** Many of the buildings are in groups (constructed on raised platforms) which form quadrangles. The imposing 324 ft (99 m) long Palace of the Governors is the most refined and highly developed building in the **Puuc style.** The Nunnery is composed of four free-standing palaces around a court. Other prominent structures include the dominant Pyramid of the Magician, the Great Pyramid, Turtle House, and the House of the Pigeons.

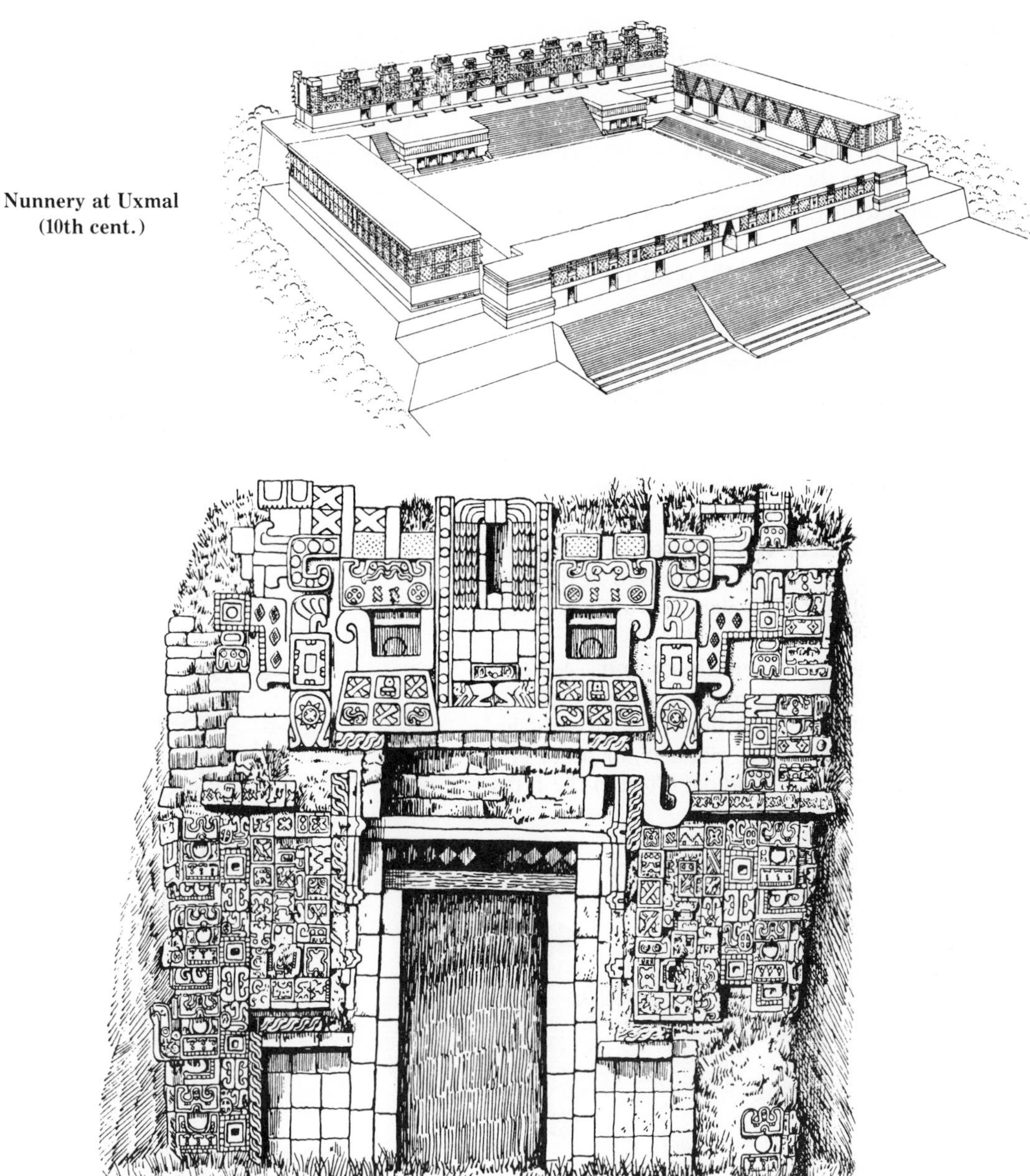

Nunnery at Uxmal (10th cent.)

Uxmal: northeast pyramid, House of the Magician, serpent-mask façade (7th-9th cent.)

vagina The upper part of the pedestal of a **terminus, 1** from which the bust or figure seems to arise.

valance **1.** A frame at the top of a window to conceal the tops of decorative draperies. **2.** The draperies themselves.

valetudinarium In Roman antiquity, an infirmary or hospital.

vallatorium A late Latin term for a projection of a building.

valley The trough or gutter formed by the intersection of two inclined planes of a roof.

vallum A rampart, esp. a palisaded rampart; the ramparts with which the Romans enclosed their camps.

valva A leaf of a folding door; usually used in the plural.

vamure, vaimure, vauntmure **1.** In fortifications, a false wall; a work raised in front of the main wall. **2.** The **alure** or walkway along ramparts behind the parapet.

vane, weathercock, weather vane A metal plate fixed on a freely rotating vertical spindle so as to indicate wind direction; usually located on top of a spire, pinnacle, or other elevated position on a building; often in the form of a cock.

variegated Said of material or a surface which is irregularly marked with different colors; dappled.

vas Same as **ahenum.**

vase See **bell.**

vat See **wat.**

vaulsura A Latin term for **vault.**

vane, U.S.A. (19th cent.)

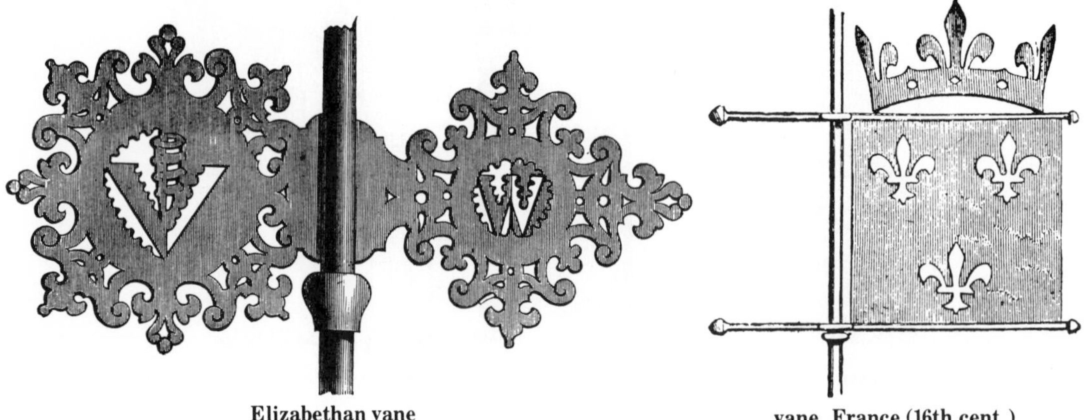
Elizabethan vane

vane, France (16th cent.)

vault A masonry covering over an area which uses the principle of the arch.

section of nave of St. Stephen, Caen; *right*: before vaulting *left*: after vaulting

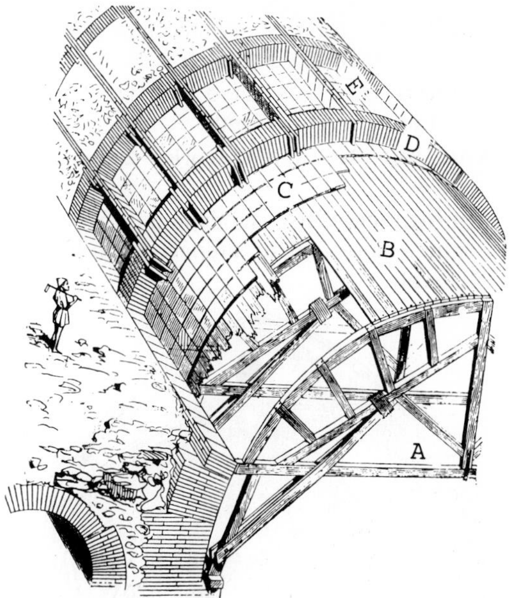

barrel-vault construction, according to Viollet-le-Duc: *A*, light framing; *B*, planks laid across; *C*, double layer of Roman bricks; *D*, rings of bricks on edge; *E*, horizontal brick ties

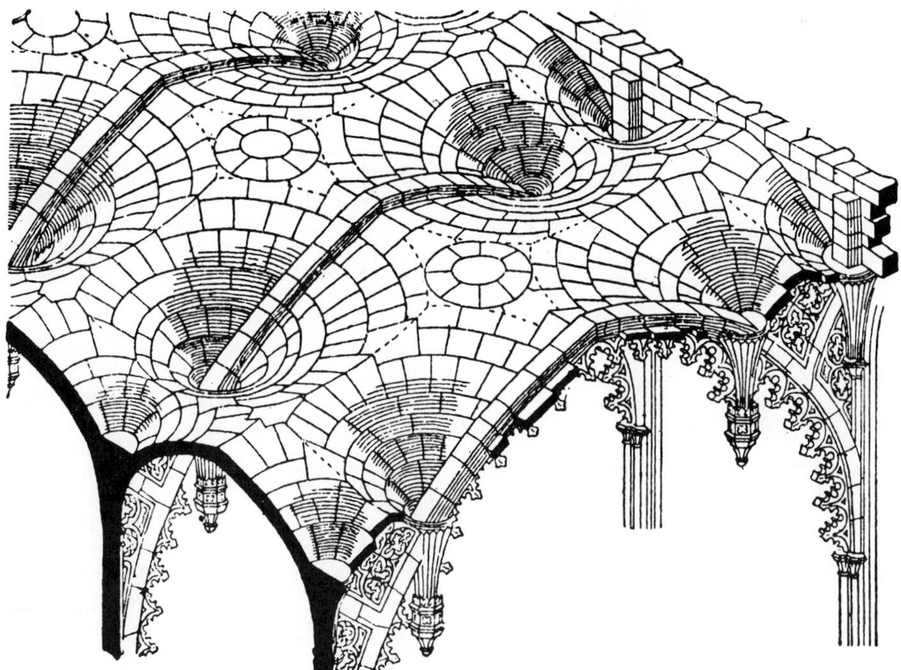

vault construction, Chapel of Henry VII, Westminster Abbey (1503–19)

vault bay An area of vaulting limited by two transverse ribs; a **severy.**

vaulted **1.** Constructed as a vault. **2.** Covered or closed by a vault.

vaulting **1.** Vaulted work. **2.** Vaults, collectively.

vaulting capital The capital of a pier or colonnette intended to support a vault or a rib thereof.

vaulting course A horizontal course made up of the abutments or springers of a vaulted roof.

vaulting shaft A colonette in a membered pier that appears to support a rib in a vault.

vault rib An arch under the soffit of a vault that seems to support it.

vaulting: Decorated style

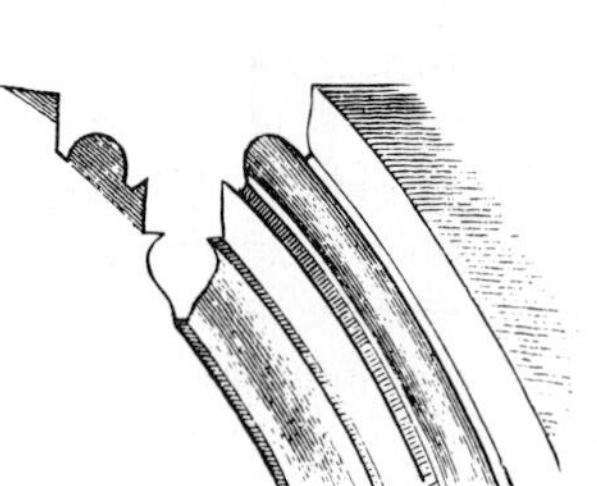

vault rib: Flamboyant style

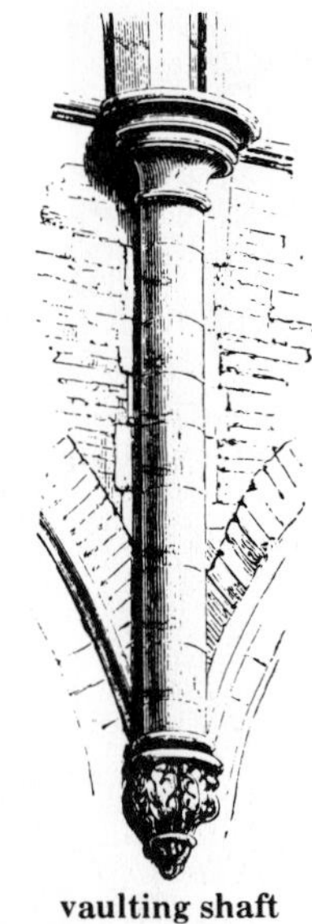

vaulting shaft

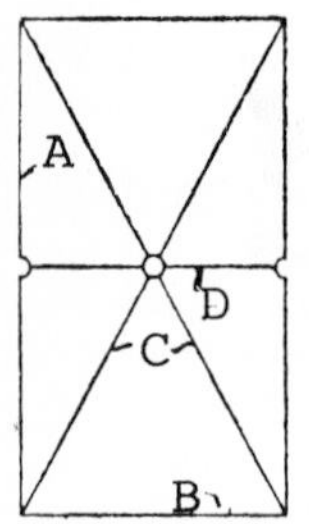

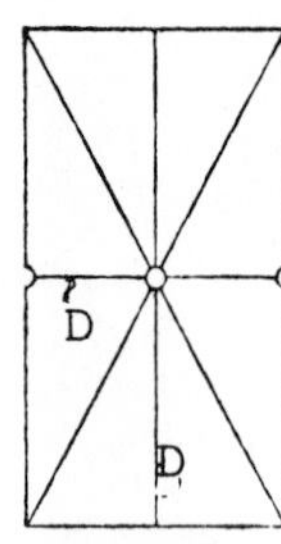

VAULTS WITH RIDGE RIBS

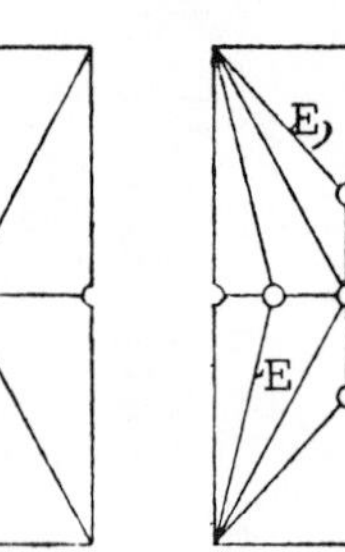

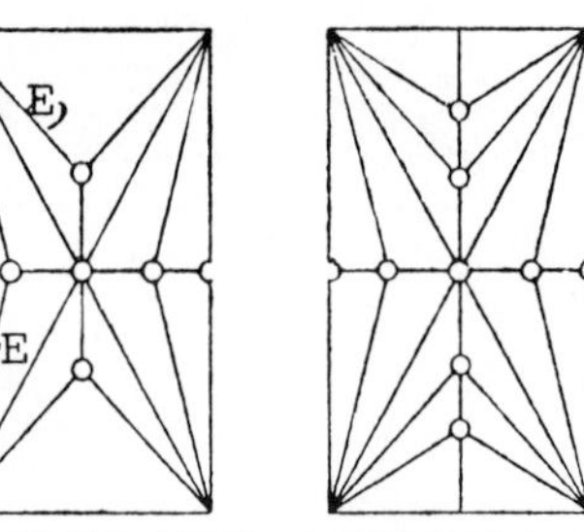

VAULTS WITH TIERCERONS

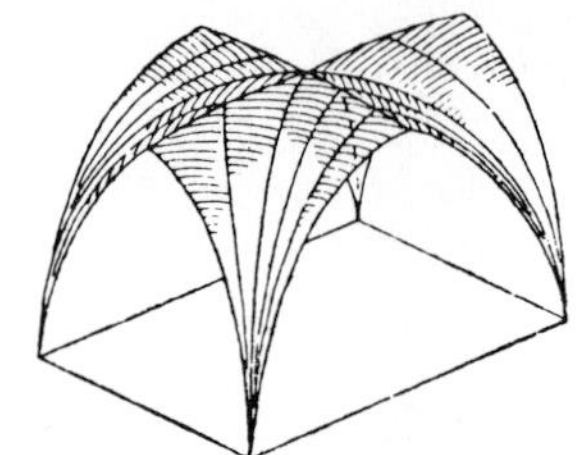

diagrams of vault rib development

A, **transverse ribs**
B, **wall ribs**
C, **diagonal ribs**
D, **ridge ribs**
E, **tiercerons**
F, **lierne ribs**
○, **bosses**

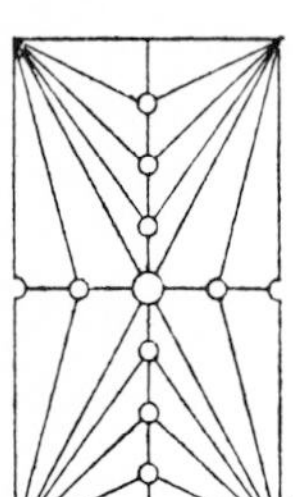

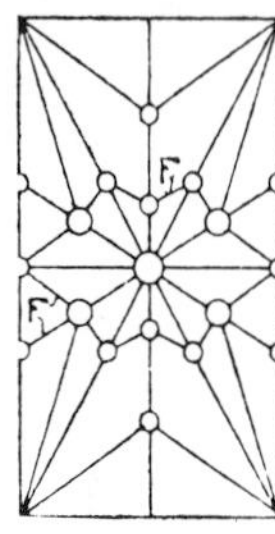

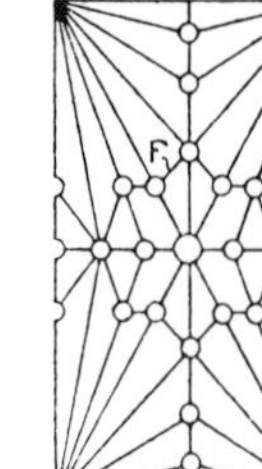

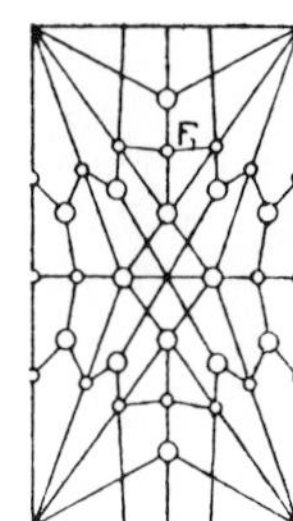

V A U L T S W I T H L I E R N E R I B S

vawcer Same as **voussior.**

vedika **1.** Originally, a hall for reading the vedas (sacred Hindu writings). **2.** A railing which encloses a sacred area, such as a **stupa.**

velarium The awning sheltering the seats in an ancient Roman theatre or amphitheatre from sun and rain.

velum Same as **velarium.**

Venetian, Venetian mosaic A type of terrazzo topping containing large chips.

Venetian arch A **pointed arch** in which the intrados and extrados are farther apart at the peak than at the springing line.

Venetian dentil A type of **dentil;** a notched ornamentation consisting of a series of cubical projections alternating with sloped surfaces.

Venetian door A door having a long narrow window at each side which is similar in form to that of a **Venetian window.**

Venetian mosaic See **Venetian.**

Venetian motif See **Palladian motif.**

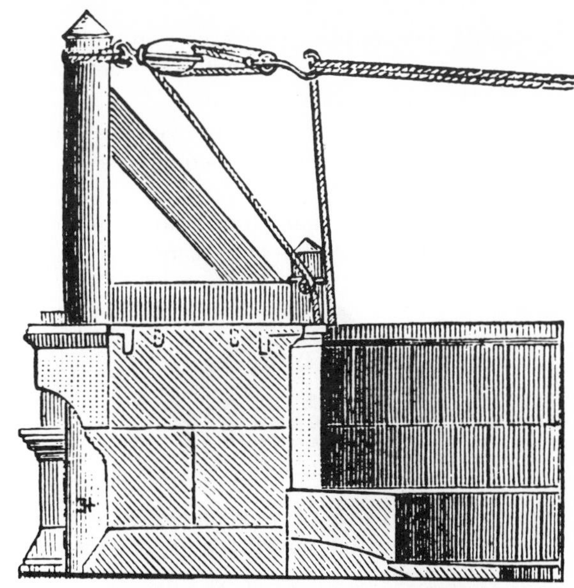

above: **mechanism for holding a velarium**

below: **velarium covering a Roman theatre**

Venetian window, Palladian window, Diocletian window A window of large size, characteristic of neoclassic styles, divided by columns or piers resembling pilasters, into three lights, the middle one of which is usually wider than the others, and is sometimes arched.

ventilating eyebrow Same as **eyebrow.**

Venetian window

veranda, verandah A covered porch or balcony, extending along the outside of a building, planned for summer leisure.

verge **1.** The edge projecting over the gable of a roof. **2.** The shaft of a column; a small ornamental shaft.

vergeboard An ornamental board hanging from a projecting roof; a **bargeboard.**

vergeboard

verge fillet A strip of wood nailed to the roof battens over a gable; covers the upper edges of the gable walls.

vermiculated Ornamented by irregular winding, wandering, and wavy lines, as if caused by the movement of worms.

vermiculated mosaic An ancient Roman mosaic of the most delicate and elaborate character; the Roman **opus vermiculatum;** the **tesserae** are arranged in curved, waving lines, as required by the shading of the design.

vermiculated work **1.** A form of masonry surface, incised with wandering, discontinuous grooves resembling worm tracks. **2.** A type of ornamental work consisting of winding frets or knots in mosaic pavements, resembling the tracks of worms.

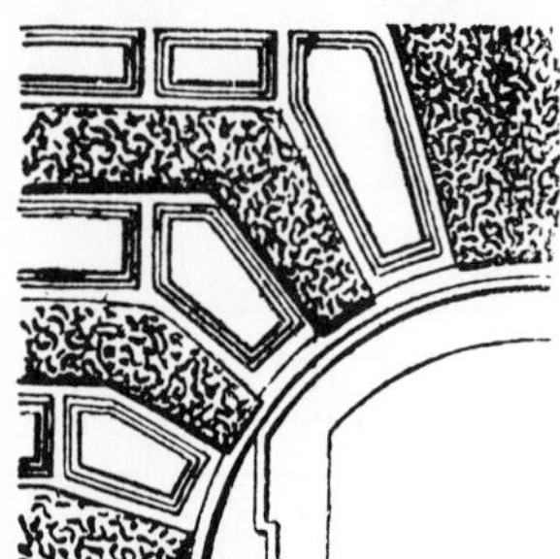

vermiculated work

vermiculatum opus See **vermiculated mosaic.**

Vernacular architecture A mode of building based on regional forms and materials.

versurae The side wings of the stagehouse of an ancient Roman theatre.

vesara An architectural style which blends elements of northern and southern India.

vesica piscis A long and sometimes pointed oval form; a **mandorla.**

vesica piscis

vestiary A room for the keeping of vestments, garments, or clothes; a wardrobe.

vestibule An **anteroom** or small foyer leading into a larger space.

vestibulum A space before the door of an ancient Roman house, forming a court which was surrounded on three sides by the house and was open on the fourth to the street.

vestry, revestry A chamber in a church, near the sanctuary, for the storage of the utensils used in a service and for the robes of the clergy and choir.

veusura Same as **voussoir.**

via A paved Roman road (said to be an invention of the Carthaginians) for horses, carriages, and foot passengers, both in town and country; esp. such roads as formed a main channel of communication from one district to another. Roman roads were constructed with the greatest regard for durability and convenience; they consisted of a carriageway paved with polygonal blocks of lava, imbedded in a substratum formed by three layers of different materials (the lowest of small stones or gravel, the next of rubble, and the upper one a bed of fragments of brick and pottery mixed with cement); there was a raised footway on each side flanked with curbstones.

Via Appia The first Roman highway, named for the censor Appius Claudius Caecus who constructed it; built in 312 B.C. to join Rome to Capua, and later continued to Brundisium; a stone causeway, constructed with embankments, and of such width that two broad wagons could pass each other easily; paved with closely fitted polygonal blocks of hard stone.

Via Appia

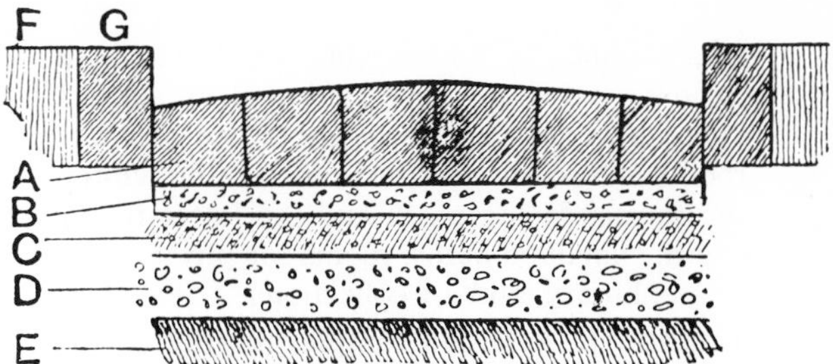

via munita: *A*, dorsum or agger via, the crown of the road made of polygonal blocks of silex or rectangular blocks of saxum quadratum; *B*, nucleus, a bedding of fine cement; *C*, rudus, broken stones and lime; *D*, statumen, large stones; *E*, earth, level and rammed; *F*, crepido, raised sidewalk; *G*, gomphi or curbstones

via munita A Roman road paved with a top layer of polygonal blocks of stone or lava.

via terrena Any plain Roman road of leveled earth.

vicarage In England, the home or residence of a vicar.

vice See **vis.**

vice stair A **screw stair.**

Victorian architecture The Revival and Eclectic architecture in 19th cent. Great Britain, named after the reign of Queen Victoria (1837–1901); also used for its American counterpart.

vicus In ancient Rome, originally a term meaning a house, but later applied to a collection of houses.

vignette **1.** Same as **vinette.** **2.** A portion of a French design for an iron balconet, used as a protection at window openings.

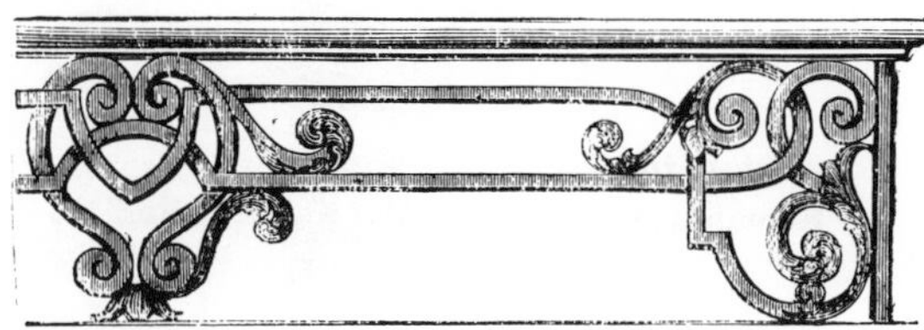
vignette,2

vihara A Buddhist or Jain monastery in Indian architecture.

section through a vihara of four stories

villa **1.** In the Roman and Renaissance periods, a country seat with its dwelling, outbuildings, and gardens, often quite elaborate. **2.** In modern times, a detached suburban or country house of some pretension.

villa rustica A Roman villa which served agricultural purposes; included apartments for the *vilicus* or steward who superintended money matters, the bookkeeper, and slaves; contained stalls and storerooms.

villa urbana A Roman villa which was built for purposes of pleasure; designed to take advantage of the landscape; contained separate rooms and colonnades for summer and winter, the former facing north and the latter facing south; contained baths, rooms for physical exercise, library, and art collections.

vimana **1.** A Hindu temple, mainly of the Deccan and southern India. **2.** The sanctuary in such a temple containing a cella in which a deity is enshrined.

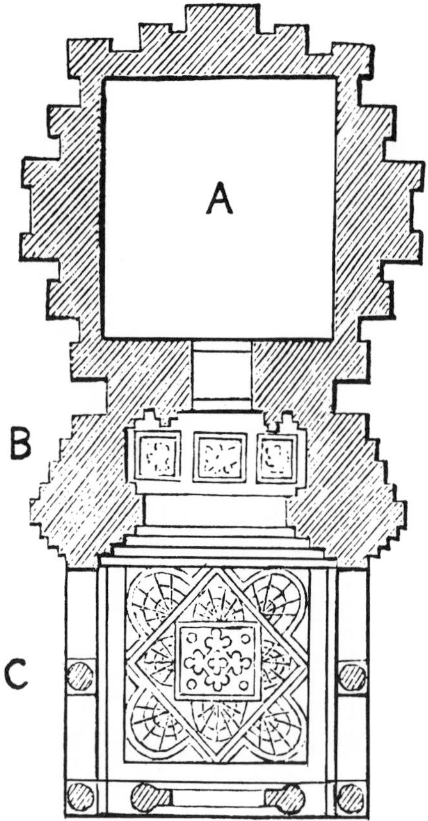

A, vimana,2 of temple; *B*, inner vestibule; *C*, porch

vinette, trayle, vignette An ornament of running vine scrolls with grape clusters and leafwork.

vinette

vis, vice, vise A spiral staircase generally of stone, whose steps wind around a central shaft or newel; a **screw stair.**

vitrum Glass, in ancient Roman construction, used in mosaic pavements, in sheets as a wall or ceiling lining, in thick sheets as flooring, and in thin sheets for windows.

Vitruvian scroll, Vitruvian wave A common motif in classical ornament: a series of scrolls connected by a wave-like band; also called a **wave scroll** or **running dog.**

Vitruvian scroll

vivarium An enclosure for raising animals and keeping them under observation.

volsura Same as **voussoir.**

volute **1.** A spiral scroll, as on Ionic, Corinthian, or Composite capitals, or on consoles, etc. **2.** A stair crook having an easement with a spiral section of stair rail.

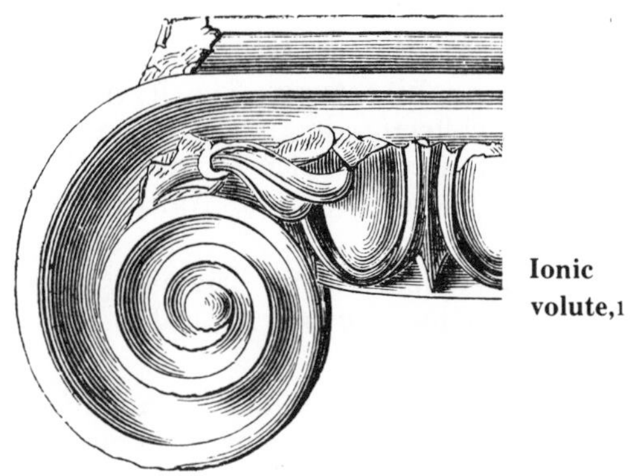

Ionic volute,1

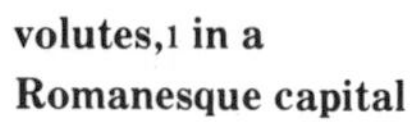

volutes,1 in a Romanesque capital

vomitorius A **vomitory** in an ancient Roman theatre or amphitheatre.

vomitorius, Colosseum, Rome

vomitory An entrance or opening, usually one of a series, which pierces a bank of seats in a theatre, stadium, or the like.

voussoir A wedge-shaped masonry unit in an arch or vault whose converging sides are cut as radii of one of the centers of the arch or vault.

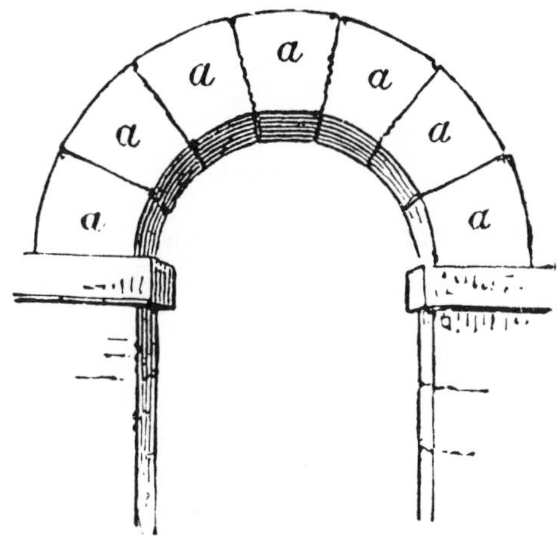

a, *a*, voussoirs

voussoir brick Same as **arch brick.**

vulne window Same as **low-side window.**

vys See **vis.**

vyse See **vis.**

瓦 **wa** A tile roof in traditional Chinese architecture.

wagon ceiling A ceiling of semicylindrical shape, as a **barrel vault.**

wagon-headed Having a continuous round arched vault or ceiling, as in barrel vaulting.

wagonhead vault A **barrel vault.**

wagon roof See **barrel roof, 1.**

wagon vault A semicylindrical vault; a **barrel vault.**

wagon vault

wa-goya In a traditional Japanese structure, a roof-truss system, distinct from European truss systems; consists only of a combination of horizontal and vertical members. 和小屋

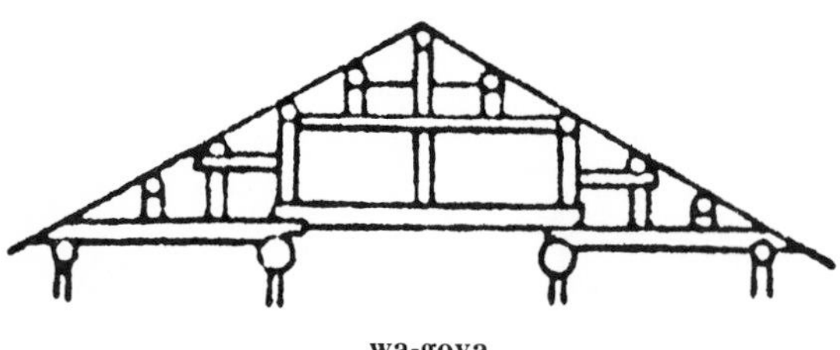

wa-goya

wainscot A decorative or protective facing applied to the lower portion of an interior partition or wall, such as wood paneling or other facing material.

wainscot

wall anchor See **beam anchor.**

wall arcade A **blind arcade** used as an ornamental dressing to a wall.

wall base See **base, 2.**

wall column A column which is embedded, or partially embedded, in a wall.

wall garden A garden of plants set in the joints of a stone wall, where soil pockets have previously been arranged.

wall piece See **wall plate, 2.**

wall plate **1.** A horizontal member to carry the end of a beam and distribute its load or to serve as a means of attachment for other structural elements. **2.** A board which is placed vertically against a wall and to which the shoring for the wall is fitted; also called a **wall piece.**

wall rib In medieval vaulting, a longitudinal rib against an exterior wall of a vaulting compartment.

wall shaft A colonette supported on a corbel or bracket which appears to support a rib of vaulting.

wall tower A tower built in connection with or forming an essential part of a wall, esp. one of a series of towers to provide a strengthening of the fortification.

wall tower

ward The outer defenses of a castle. Also see **bailey.**

wardrobe, garderobe A room for the storage of garments.

wat, vat Buddhist monastery in Cambodia.

watching loft **1.** Same as **excubitorium,** 1. **2.** A lookout in a tower, steeple, or other high building.

watch turret Same as **bartizan.**

water leaf **1.** In early Roman and Greek ornamentation, a type of lotus leaf or an ivy motif. **2.** Similar to **water leaf,** 1 but divided symmetrically by a prominent rib; also called a **Lesbian leaf.** **3.** Late 12th cent. capital with a large leaf at each angle, broad, smooth, curving up toward the abacus corner and then curling inward.

water ramp A series of pools, arranged so that water flows from one to another.

wattle A framework of interwoven rods, poles, or branches.

wattle and daub, wattle and dab A very common form of primitive construction, consisting of a sort of coarse basketwork of twigs woven between upright poles, then plastered with mud; a substitute for brick **nogging** in partitions.

wave molding, oundy molding, swelled chamfer, undulating molding, undy molding A molding decorated with a series of stylized representations of breaking waves.

wave molding

wave scroll See **Vitruvian scroll.**

weatherboarding **1.** A type of wood siding commonly used in the early U.S.A. as an exterior covering on a building of frame construction; consists of boards, each of which has parallel faces and a rabbeted upper edge which fits under an overlapping board above. **2.** Same as **clapboard** or **siding.**

weathercock See **vane.**

weathered **1.** Descriptive of a material or surface which has been exposed to the elements for a long period of time. **2.** Having an upper surface which is splayed so as to throw off water.

weather slating, slate hanging Slate which is hung vertically on the face of a wall; provides protection against moisture.

weather tiling, tile hanging Tile which is hung vertically on the face of a wall; usually attached by nailing; provides protection against moisture.

weather vane See **vane.**

simple water leaf,1;

enriched water leaf,1

wedge coping See **featheredge coping.**

weepers Statues of mourners sometimes incorporated into tombs.

weeping cross A type of **preaching cross** esp. used for public penance.

well curb The enclosure around and above the top of a well.

well curb

Welsh arch A small flat arch consisting only of a keystone supported on each side by two projecting stretchers that are shaped to fit the keystone.

Welsh groin A groin formed by an **underpitch vault.**

Welsh vault See **underpitch vault.**

wên miao See **k'ung miao.**

west end The end of a church that is opposite the sanctuary; usually where the main doors are located; so called because medieval churches almost invariably had their sanctuaries at the east end.

west end doorway, Lichfield Cathedral: Early English style

wheeler Same as **winder.**

wheeling step Same as **winder.**

wheel step, wheeling step A **winder.**

wheel tracery Tracery radiating from a center, as the spokes of a wheel.

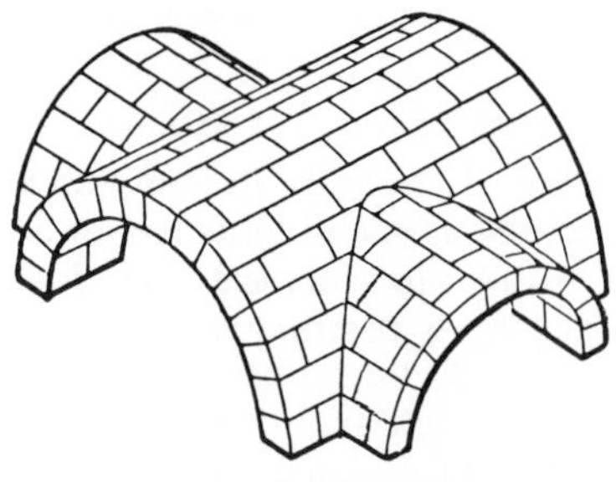

Welsh groins, formed by the intersection of two vaults of unequal size

wheel window A large circular window on which the radiation of tracery from the center is suggested; a variety of **rose window**; a **Catherine wheel window**.

wheel window, western façade, Chartres Cathedral (end of 12th cent.)

whispering gallery, whispering dome A large dome or vault that reflects sounds (esp. high frequencies) along a large concave surface so that even whispers may be heard some distance away.

wicket A small door or gate, esp. one forming part of a larger one.

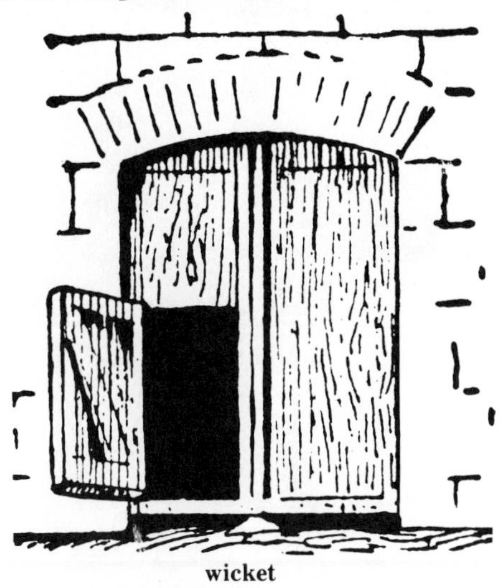

wicket

widow's walk A walkway or narrow platform on a roof, esp. on early New England homes with a view of the sea.

wigwam American eastern Indian dwelling; round or oval in plan, with a rounded roof structure consisting of a bent pole framework covered by pressed bark or skins.

wind beam A **collar beam.**

wind-brace **1.** Any brace, such as a strut, which strengthens a structure or framework against the wind. **2.** A diagonal brace to tie rafters of a roof together and prevent racking; in medieval roofs the wind-braces usually are arched and run from the principal rafters to the purlins.

winder, wheel step A step, more or less wedge-shaped, with its tread wider at one end than the other, as in a **spiral stair.**

winding stair **1.** Any stair constructed chiefly or entirely of **winders.** **2.** See **screw stair.**

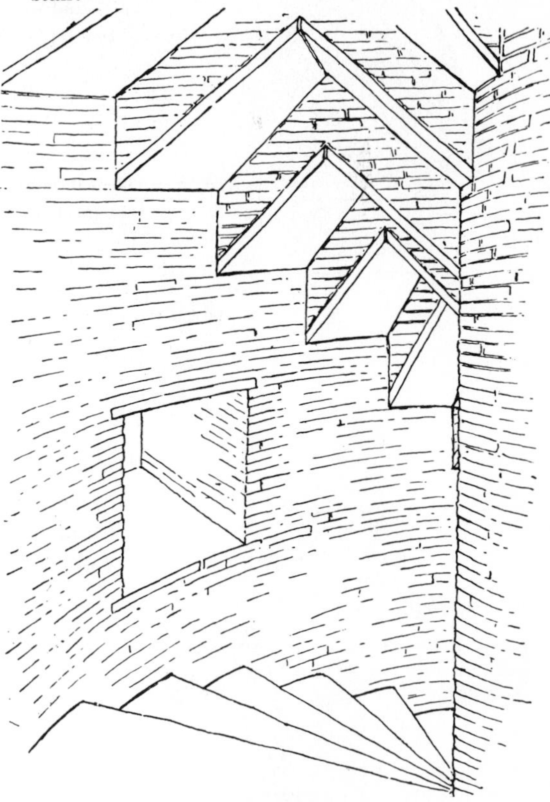

winding stair of brick, Basilica of Constantine, Rome (310–313 A.D.)

window An opening in an external wall of a building to admit light and (usually) air; usually glazed.

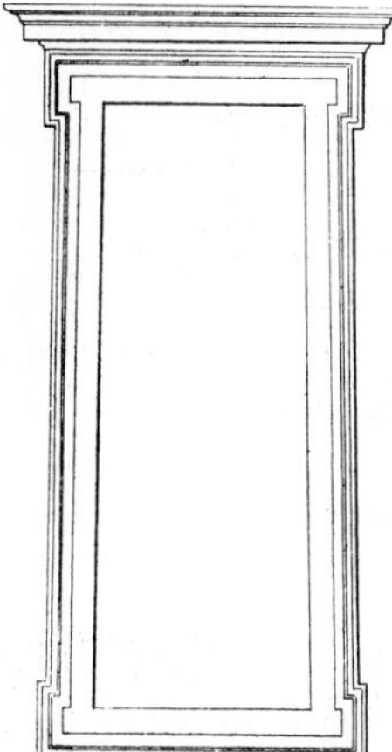

left: **internal view of window in Temple of Vesta, Tivoli, Italy (80 B.C.)**

right: **early Greco-Roman window, Palace at Shakka (c. 3rd cent. A.D.)**

left: **window, Mosque of Ibn Tulun (c. 879 A.D.)**

right: **Islamic lattice window (see meshrebeeyeh,1)**

right **and** *left*: **Byzantine windows, Ish Khan Church, Tortoom**

Anglo-Saxon windows

Brixworth, Northants. (c. 670 A.D.)

Monkswearmouth Church (c. 671 A.D.)

Barton upon Humber, Lincolnshire (c. 800 A.D.)

Norman windows

below: Lambourne, Berkshire (c. 1160)

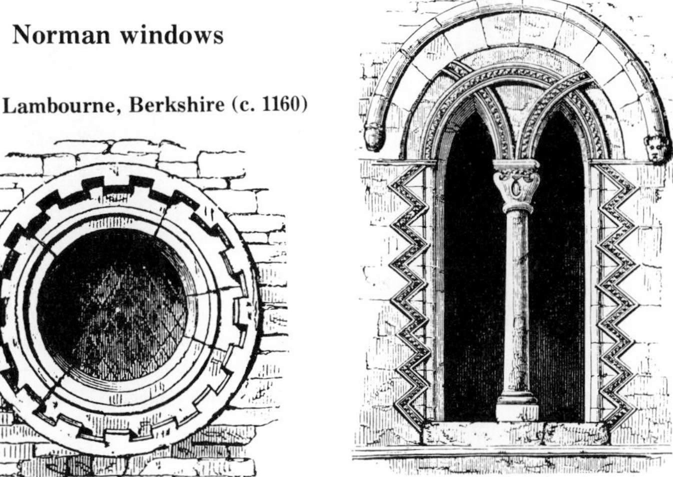

Early English style windows

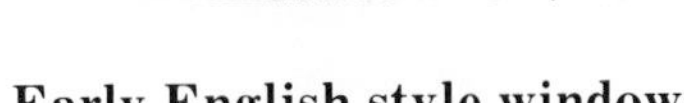

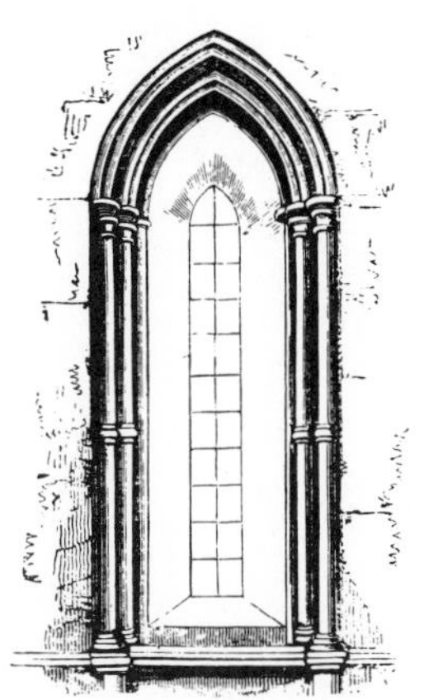

Jesus College Chapel, Cambridge (c. 1250)

Shipton Olliffe, Gloucestershire (c. 1250)

Salisbury Cathedral (1220-58)

Decorated Style Windows

St. Mary Magdalene, Oxford (1320)

Farington, Berkshire (1320)

Little St. Mary, Cambridge (1350)

Perpendicular Style Windows

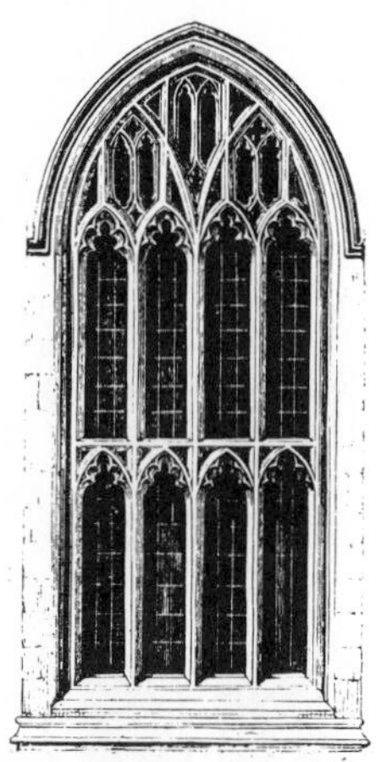

New College Chapel, Oxford (1386)

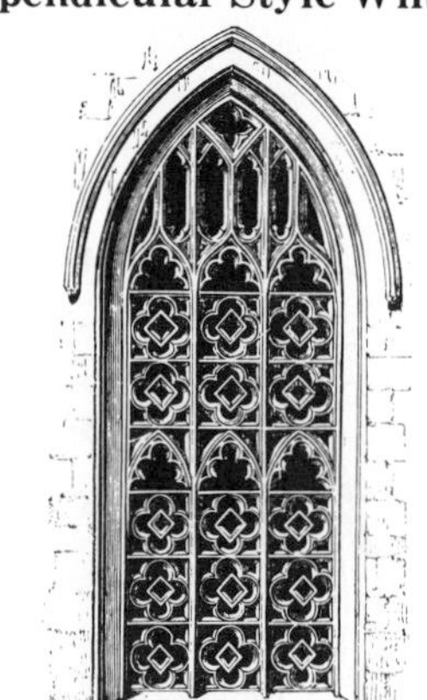

Huish Episcopi, Somerset (1450)

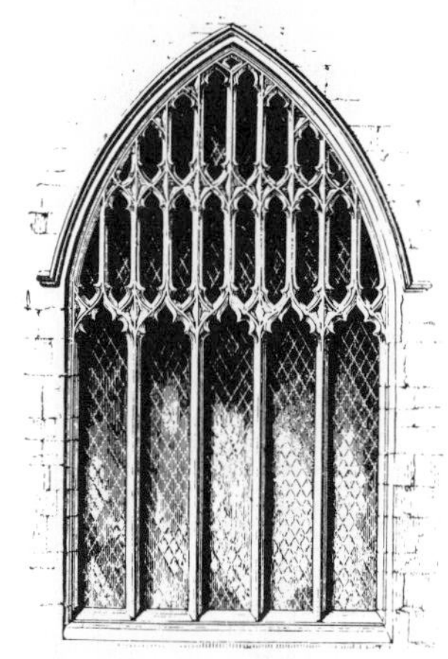

Swinbrook, Oxford (1500)

Italian Renaissance Style Windows

Venetian (14th–16th cent.)

(mid-15th to early 16th cent.)

Palazzo Bartolomei, Florence (17th cent.)

window head The upper horizontal cross member or decorative element of a window frame.

window head, Hotel Vogue, Dijon

window seat **1.** A seat built into the bottom inside of a window. **2.** A seat located at a window.

window seat, Alnwick Castle, Northumberlandshire (c. 1310)

wine cellar, wine vault A storage room for wine, usually underground so as to be cool and dark.

wing A subsidiary part of a building extending out from the main portion.

winged bull An Assyrian symbol of force and domination, of frequent occurrence in ancient Assyrian architectural sculpture; pairs of winged human-headed bulls and lions of colossal size usually guarded the portals of palaces.

winged bull

winged disk, winged globe Same as **sun disk.**

winged disk

winglight See **side light.**

withe, wythe **1.** A partition dividing two flues in the same chimney stack. **2.** A flexible, slender twig or branch; an **osier;** esp. used to tie down thatching on roofs.

wivern A monster with the forelegs and wings of a dragon and the hind part of a serpent with a barbed tail.

wivern

wood mosaic **1.** See **mosaic, 2.** **2.** See **parquetry.**

woodwork Work produced by the carpenter's and joiner's art, generally applied to parts of objects or structures in wood rather than the complete structure.

wreath **1.** The curved portion of the string or handrail which follows a turn in a geometrical stair, usually a quarter circle, and therefore corresponds to a portion of the surface of a vertical cylinder; also called a **wreath piece.** **2.** A twisted band, garland, or chaplet, representing flowers, fruits, leaves, etc.; often used in decoration.

wreathed column **1.** A column entwined by a band which presents a twisted or spiral appearance. **2.** A **twisted column.**

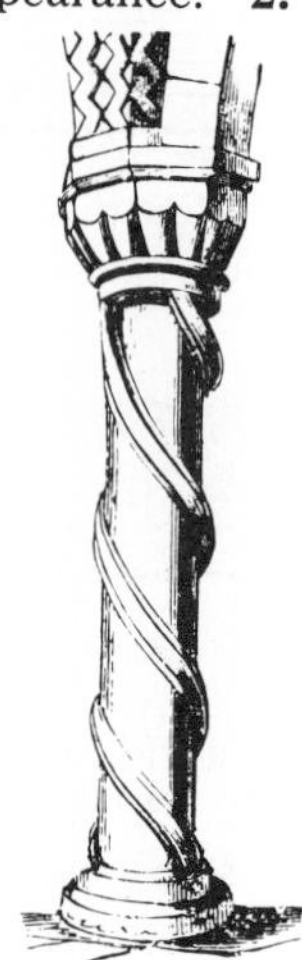
wreathed column

wrought-iron garden gate, Belvedere Palace, Vienna (early 18th cent.)

wreathed stair Same as **geometrical stair.**

wreathed string See **wreath, 1.**

wreath piece A curved section of a stair string; a **wreath, 1.**

wrought-iron work Iron that is hammered or forged into shape, usually decorative, either when the metal is hot or cold.

wrought nail A nail individually wrought by hand, often with a head forged into a decorative pattern.

wu miao See **kuan ti miao.**

wu pao A fortification used by ancient Chinese landlords or small warlords. 塢堡

wu ting In traditional Chinese architecture, a roof. 屋頂

wye tracery See **Y-tracery.**

wyvern Same as **wivern.**

xenodocheum In classical architecture, a room or building devoted to the reception and accommodation of strangers or guests.

xenones Plural of **xenodocheum.**

xyst **1.** In classical architecture, a roofed colonnade for exercise in bad weather. **2.** In ancient Rome, a long, tree-shaded promenade. **3.** A tree-lined walk.

xyst,1

yácata A circular Tarascan mound used as a base for a temple, ca. 1500 A.D., such as that at Tzintzuntzan, Michoacán, Mexico.

Yachin and Boas The two free-standing columns in front of the **Temple of Solomon.**

櫓 **yagura** **1.** In Japanese architecture, any turret or tower. **2.** In Japanese castle architecture, any tower except the donjon.

yane In traditional Japanese architecture, a roof.

窰 **yao** A cave dwelling in the clay regions of northwest China, of three common types: **1.** A simple hole dug into a cliff. **2.** A simple hole dug into a cliff, covered by a lean-to. **3.** A vaulted chamber in a cliff; has rounded arch-shaped sections; some arches and walls are reinforced with bricks or stones.

yasti The central shaft of a **stupa,** which supports the **chattravali.**

yatzia The three-storied structure which surrounded the **Temple of Solomon** on three sides.

yen chu See **chu.**

ying pi A free-standing wall, either inside or outside the main entrance of a Chinese building courtyard; usually constructed of masonry, but may be of wood or clay; used to block vision, providing greater privacy and a windbreak; the middle section of these walls carried decorative reliefs. Also called **chao ch'iang** or **chao pi.**

yosemune-yane In traditional Japanese architecture, a hipped ridge roof having a sloping rectangular shape on each long side and a sloping triangular shape on each short side.

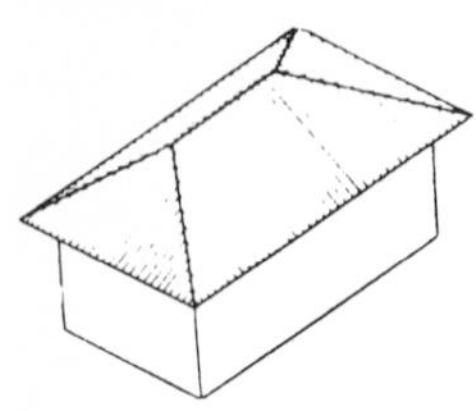

yosemune-yane
寄棟屋根

Y-tracery A type of **tracery** in which the mullions split in the shape of the letter Y.

院子 **yüan tzǔ** In Chinese architecture, a courtyard which is surrounded by walls and buildings. Also **t'ien ching.**

床 **yuka** In traditional Japanese architecture, a floor.

yukimi-shōji A small removable panel within a **shōji.**

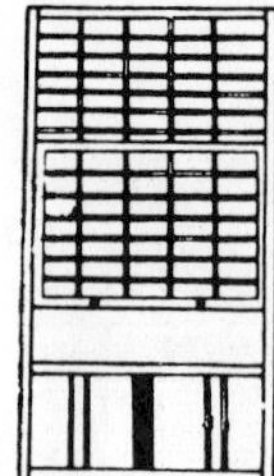

yukimi-shōji
雪見障子

yurt A circular tent-like dwelling, usually movable, used by natives of northern and central Asia; constructed of skins, felt, etc., stretched over a framework.

yurt

Z

Zapotec architecture An eclectic architecture of Mesoamerica, in Oaxaca, Mexico. The Zapotecs assimilated influences from the Olmecs (700–300 B.C.), from Chiapas or Guatemala (300–100 B.C.), and esp. from Teotihuacán during the classic period (300–900 A.D.) culminating in a recognizable regional style, characterized by: (*a*) pyramids having several terraces, ascended by broad stairways decreasing in width at higher levels and accented by wide balustrades whose tops were decorated with **scapulary tablets;** (*b*) the use of circular supporting columns; and (*c*) free-standing structures placed around a large plaza which was oriented in a north-south direction. Monte Albán, a carefully planned Zapotec ceremonial complex, is situated on a leveled mountain above Oaxaca, Mexico; noted for its funerary architecture; large underground tombs, entered by stairs, were decorated with paneled friezes and wall paintings.

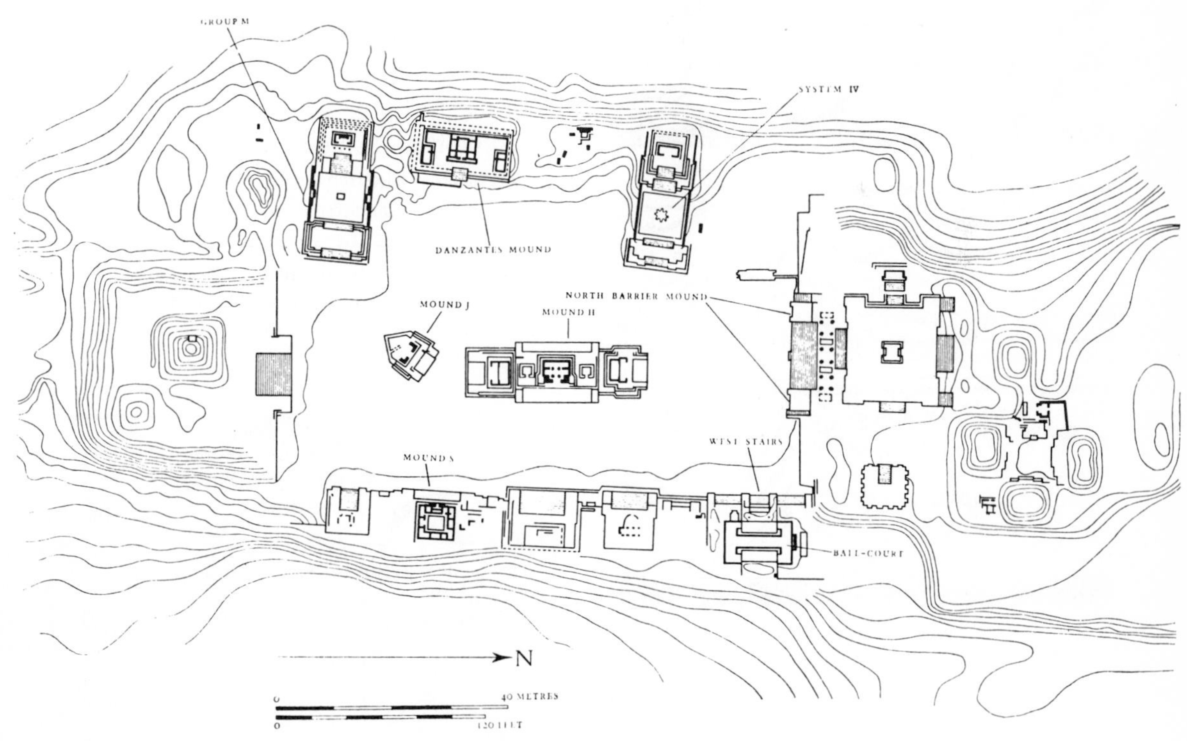

plan of Monte Albán (c. 700 A.D.)

zashiki In a Japanese-style house, the main room used for entertaining guests; its floor is covered with **tatami;** usually has a **toko-no-ma.**

zeta **1.** A closed or small chamber. **2.** A room over a porch of an early Christian church, where the porter or sexton lived and where documents were kept.

ziarat The tomb of a saint in Muslim India.

ziggurat A Mesopotamian temple tower; from the end of the 3rd millennium B.C. on, ziggurats rose in three to seven stages, diminishing in area and often in height, square (Sumer) or rectangular (Assyria), built of mud brick and faced with baked brick laid in bitumen; had outside staircase and a shrine at the top.

zigzag molding, dancette An ornamental molding of continued **chevrons.**

Norman zigzag moldings

zikkurat Same as **ziggurat.**

ziyada A court or series of courts around a mosque which serves to shelter it from immediate contact with secular buildings.

zocco; zoccolo, zocle Same as **socle.**

zoophoric column A column bearing a figure or figures of one or more men or animals.

zoophorus A horizontal band bearing carved figures of animals or persons, esp. the Ionic frieze when sculptured.

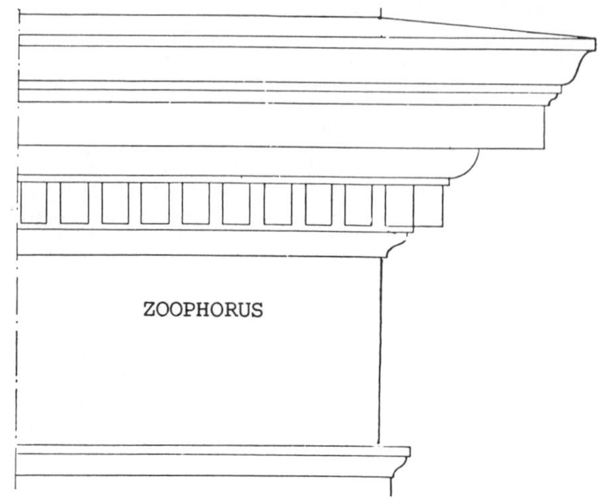

entablature showing location of zoophorus

zophorus Same as **zoophorus.**

造作 **zōsaku** Fixtures and fittings of a traditional Japanese structure; includes the floor, ceiling, etc., but not the structural members.

zotheca **1.** In Near Eastern architecture and derivatives, an alcove off a living room. **2.** A niche for a statue or other object, as in a sepulchral chamber.

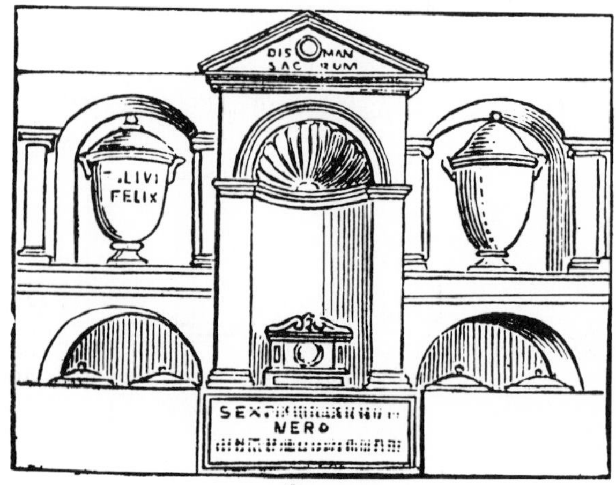

zotheca,2

zulla A covered colonnade in a mosque.

zvonnitsa In early Russian architecture, a **bell gable.**

zwinger **1.** The protective fortress of a city. **2.** By extension, the modern name of several German palaces, or parts of palaces.

part of the Zwinger Palace, Dresden, Germany

zystos Among the ancients, a portico or aisle of unusual length, commonly used for gymnastic exercises.